HONG KONG
BUSINESS

**World Trade Press
Country Business Guides**

CHINA Business
HONG KONG Business
JAPAN Business
KOREA Business
MEXICO Business
SINGAPORE Business
TAIWAN Business

HONG KONG
BUSINESS

The Portable Encyclopedia
For Doing Business With Hong Kong

Christine A. Genzberger   Edward G. Hinkelman
David E. Horovitz   William T. LeGro
Jonathan W. Libbey   Charles Smithson Mills
James L. Nolan   Stacey S. Padrick
Karla C. Shippey, J.D.   Kelly X. Wang
Chansonette Buck Wedemeyer Alexandra Woznick

Auerbach International • CIGNA Property and Casualty
Ernst & Young • Far Eastern Economic Review
Foreign Trade • Hong Kong Trade Development Council
Reed Publishing (USA) Inc.

Series Editor: Edward G. Hinkelman

WORLD
TRADE
PRESS ®

Resources for International Trade

1505 Fifth Avenue
San Rafael, California 94901
USA

Published by World Trade Press
1505 Fifth Avenue
San Rafael, CA 94901
USA

Cover and book design: Brad Greene
Illustrations: Eli Africa
Color Maps: Gracie Artemis
B&W maps: David Baker
Desktop Publishing: Kelly R. Krill and Gail R. Weisman
Charts and Graphs: David Baker and Kelly R. Krill
Prepublication Review: Aanel Victoria

Library of Congress Cataloging-in-Publication Data
Hong Kong business : the portable encyclopedia for doing business with
   Hong Kong / Christine Genzberger . . . [et al.].
      p.   cm. – (World Trade Press country business guides)
   Includes bibliographical references and index.
   ISBN 0-9631864-7-7 : $24.95
      1. Hong Kong—Economic conditions.   2. Hong Kong—Economic policy.
   3. Investments, Foreign—Government policy—Hong Kong.
   4. International business enterprises—Hong Kong.   I. Genzberger,
   Christine.   II. Series.
   HC470.3.H6655   1994   93-44197
   658.8'48'095125–dc20   CIP

Printed in the United States of America

ACKNOWLEDGMENTS

Contributions of hundreds of trade and reference experts have made possible the extensive coverage of this book.

We are indebted to numerous international business consultants, reference librarians, travel advisors, consulate, embassy, and trade mission officers, bank officers, attorneys, global shippers and insurers, and multinational investment brokers who answered our incessant inquiries and volunteered facts, figures, and expert opinions.

A special note of gratitude is due to those at the U.S. Department of Commerce, the Hong Kong Trade Development Council, and the Singapore Trade Development Board.

We relied heavily on the reference librarians and resources available at the Marin County Civic Center Library, Marin County Law Library, San Rafael Public Library, San Francisco Public Library, University of California at Berkeley libraries, and U.S. Department of Commerce Library in San Francisco.

Thank you to attorneys Robert T. Yahng and Anne M. Kelleher, with Baker & McKenzie, San Francisco, and John Lo and Frankie Leung, with Lewis, D'Amato, Brisbois & Bisgaard, San Francisco, who spent precious time in assisting us with the law section. We also extend our sincere appreciation to Barry Tarnef, with CIGNA Property and Casualty Co., who graciously supplied information on world ports.

We also acknowledge the valuable contributions of Philip B. Auerbach of Auerbach International, San Francisco, for translations; all the patient folks at Desktop Publishing of Larkspur, California; and Theresa Wong, Leslie Endicott, and Susan August for reviewing, proofing, and correcting down to the smallest details.

Thanks go to Elizabeth Karolczak for establishing the World Trade Press Intern Program, and to the Monterey Institute of International Studies for its assistance.

To Jerry and Kathleen Fletcher, we express our deep appreciation for their immeasurable support during this project.

Very special thanks to Mela Hinkelman, whose patience, understanding, generosity, and support made this project possible.

DISCLAIMER

We have diligently tried to ensure the accuracy of all of the information in this publication and to present as comprehensive a reference work as space would permit. In determining the contents, we were guided by many experts in the field, extensive hours of research, and our own experience. We did have to make choices in coverage, however, because the inclusion of everything one could ever want to know about international trade would be impossible. The fluidity and fast pace of today's business world makes the task of keeping data current and accurate an extremely difficult one. This publication is intended to give you the information that you need in order to discover the information that is most useful for your particular business. As you contact the resources within this book, you will no doubt learn of new and exciting business opportunities and of additional international trading requirements that have arisen even within the short time since we published this edition. If errors are found, we will strive to correct them in preparing future editions. The publishers take no responsibility for inaccurate or incomplete information that may have been submitted to them in the course of research for this publication. The facts published indicate the result of those inquiries and no warranty as to their accuracy is given.

Contents

Chapter 1   Introduction 1

Chapter 2   Economy 3

Chapter 3   Current Issues 21

Chapter 4   Opportunities 29

Chapter 5   Foreign Investment 45

Chapter 6   Foreign Trade 51

Chapter 7   Import Policy & Procedures 59

Chapter 8   Export Policy & Procedures 63

Chapter 9   Industry Reviews 67

Chapter 10   Trade Fairs 83

Chapter 11   Business Travel 113

Chapter 12   Business Culture 127

Chapter 13   Demographics 141

Chapter 14   Marketing 145

Chapter 15   Business Entities & Formation 155

Chapter 16   Labor 167

Chapter 17   Business Law 175

Chapter 18   Financial Institutions 201

Chapter 19   Currency & Foreign Exchange 215

Chapter 20   International Payments 219

Chapter 21   Corporate Taxation 233

Chapter 22   Personal Taxation 235

Chapter 23   Ports & Airports 239

Chapter 24   Business Dictionary 243

Chapter 25   Important Addresses 261

Index 295

Introduction

Hong Kong is one of the world's most dynamic economies. A tiny entity with no resources other than a fine harbor and favorable geographic location on China's southeast coast, Hong Kong is not only a thriving commercial and industrial center in its own right, it is also the gateway to mainland China's rapidly growing economy.

Since the 1950s Hong Kong has built a modern, internationally-oriented economy largely from scratch. This vibrant economy is based on low-cost, high-quality export production and state-of-the-art business and financial services. It grew at an average rate of more than 12.2 percent per year between 1982 and 1992. Hong Kong, a free port, is also the tenth largest trading economy in the world. Its trade has grown at an annual rate of about 20 percent since 1982.

Although concerns remain over the return of Hong Kong to Chinese sovereignty in 1997, China and Hong Kong are mutually dependent and the structure for Hong Kong's continued fast-track business operations is firmly in place. In fact, local business interests speak confidently of their annexation of China.

Ranked second in the world among newly industrialized countries in the 1993 *World Competitiveness Report*, Hong Kong is a market well worth investigating from a number of perspectives. For buyers Hong Kong can provide a wide range of competitive goods at virtually any level of sophistication. It is a leading producer and reexporter of apparel and textiles; electrical machinery and components; telecommunications equipment; toys, games, and sporting goods; computers and office machines; watches and clocks; footwear and luggage; and various types of machinery; among other items. Its businesses can handle anything from the smallest to the largest orders and it is the primary broker for trade with China.

From the seller's standpoint Hong Kong needs a wide range of agricultural and industrial raw materials, intermediate components, and specialty items to feed its own active industries and those of China. Both the upgrading of its industrial base and its large public-sector development projects require

materials, capital goods, and services. And the rapidly rising demands of Hong Kong's affluent, cosmopolitan, and sophisticated consumers offer opportunities to place goods in the colony's avid consumer market. Hong Kong has relied on Japan for many of its goods, but the strength of the yen has made Japanese products less competitive, opening up opportunities for new suppliers.

For manufacturers Hong Kong has a pool of well-educated semi-skilled to highly skilled labor experienced in the areas already noted as well as in many others. Hong Kong has up-to-date plant and its business infrastructure is second to none. These conditions provide a competitive base for a variety of outsourcing needs. Hong Kong also manages production for many of China's factories, enabling foreigners to gain access to mainland capabilities through intermediaries who know how to deal with both Chinese and Western businesspeople.

For investors Hong Kong is perhaps the world's most wide open business venue. Restrictions are few, regulations are minimal, and procedures are well established in a stable system presided over by a pro-business government. Hong Kong's industrial, trade, service, and financial markets are all well developed and highly active, providing a variety of investment opportunities.

A sophisticated, world-class business center, Hong Kong moves at a frenetic pace. And the overall tempo and level of change is expected to accelerate with the approach of 1997, but Hong Kong is and will remain one of the most compelling and user-friendly—as well as one of the most complex and challenging—places on the globe to do business.

HONG KONG Business was designed by businesspeople experienced in international markets to give you an overview of how things actually work and what current conditions are in Hong Kong. It will give you the head start you need as a buyer, seller, manufacturer, or investor to be able to evaluate and operate in Hong Kong's. Further, it tells you where to go to get more specific information in greater depth.

The first chapter discusses the main elements of the country's **Economy,** including its development, present situation, and the forces determining its future prospects. **Current Issues** explains the major concerns affecting Hong Kong now and during its next stage of development. The **Opportunities** chapter presents nine major areas of interest to importers plus 10 additional hot prospects, 12 major areas for exporters plus 12 more hot opportunities, and discussions of eight major sectoral growth areas. The chapter also clarifies the nature of the government procurement process that drives Hong Kong's US$14 billion development plan with its focus on construction; airport and seaport facilities; transportation, including highways, railways, and rail-based mass transit; water supply; and waste-management projects. **Foreign Investment** details policies, regulations, procedures, and restrictions, with particular reference to Hong Kong's developing high technology and service sectors.

Although Hong Kong is banking on services and high technology as the wave of the future, it remains a diversified export-oriented economy with many thriving low- and medium-technology operations. The **Foreign Trade, Import Policy & Procedures**, and **Export Policy & Procedures** chapters delineate the nature of Hong Kong's trade: what and with whom it trades, trade policy, and the practical information, including nuts-and-bolts procedural requirements, necessary to trade with it. The **Industry Reviews** chapter outlines Hong Kong's 11 most prominent industries and their competitive position from the standpoint of a businessperson interested in taking advantage of these industries' strengths or in exploiting their competitive weaknesses. **Trade Fairs** provides a comprehensive listing of trade fairs in Hong Kong, complete with contact information, and spells out the best ways to maximize the benefits offered by these chances to see and be seen.

Business Travel offers practical information on how to travel in Hong Kong, including travel requirements, resources, getting around, local customs, and ambience, as well as comparative information on accommodations and dining in the colony. **Business Culture** provides a user-friendly primer on local business style, mind-set, negotiating practices, and numerous other tips designed to improve your effectiveness, avoid inadvertent gaffes, and generally smooth the way in doing business in Hong Kong. **Demographics** presents the basic statistical data needed to assess the Hong Kong market, while **Marketing** outlines resources, approaches, and specific markets in the colony, including seven rules for selling your product and five ways to help your local agent.

Business Entities & Formation discusses recognized business entities and registration procedures for setting up operations in Hong Kong. **Labor** assembles information on the availability, capabilities, and costs of labor in Hong Kong, as well as terms of employment and business-labor relations. **Business Law** interprets the structure of the Hong Kong legal system, giving a digest of substantive points of commercial law prepared from Martindale-Hubbell with additional material from the international law firm of Baker & McKenzie. **Financial Institutions** outlines the workings of the financial system, including banking and financial markets, and the availability of financing and services needed by foreign businesses. **Currency & Foreign Exchange** explains the workings of Hong Kong's complex foreign exchange operations. **International Payments** is an illustrated step-by-step guide to using documentary collections and letters of credit in trade with Hong Kong. Ernst & Young's **Corporate Taxation** and **Personal Taxation** provide the information on tax rates, provisions, and status of foreign operations and individuals needed to evaluate a venture in the country.

Ports & Airports, prepared with the help of CIGNA Property and Casualty Company, gives current information on how to physically access the country. The **Business Dictionary,** a unique resource prepared especially for this volume in conjunction with Auerbach International, consists of more than 425 entries focusing specifically on Hong Kong business and idiomatic usage to provide the business-person with the basic means for conducting business in Hong Kong. **Important Addresses** lists more than 600 Hong Kong government agencies and international and foreign official representatives; local and international business associations; trade and industry associations; financial, professional, and service firms; transportation and shipping agencies; media outlets; and sources of additional information to enable businesspeople to locate the offices and the help they need to operate in Hong Kong. Full-color, detailed, up-to-date **Maps** aid the business traveler in getting around the major business venues in Hong Kong.

HONG KONG Business gives you the information you need both to evaluate the prospect of doing business in Hong Kong and to actually begin doing it. It is your invitation to this fascinating society and market. Welcome.

Economy

During the last 45 years, Hong Kong, once a merely exotic colonial outpost, has been transformed into a world-class trade, business, and financial center—one of the richest, most free wheeling markets in Asia and the world. This colonial dependency, which is scheduled to revert to Chinese sovereignty as a Special Administrative Region in July 1997, consists of 236 islands of varying size, and Kowloon and the New Territories on the adjacent mainland.

Located on the southeast coast of China, east of the mouth of the Pearl River which leads to Gunagzhou, Hong Kong, which has a total area of 1,074 square km (about 413 square miles), is about one third the size of Rhode Island, the smallest of the 50 United States. In contrast to other places in the world, Hong Kong's total area keeps growing incrementally due to reclamation, usable land being the colony's scarcest resource.

Hong Kong has an official population of about 5.9 million. However, its actual population is probably closer to 6.1 million, giving it an average population density of more than 14,750 inhabitants per square mile. Because less than half of the territory is developed and habitable, actual population densities in selected areas rise into the tens of thousands. Some 98 percent of Hong Kong's people are ethnic southern Chinese, and 60 percent are native born.

The subtropical maritime area is 70 percent hilly to mountainous, and 30 percent of the total land area is urban. Some 7 percent is considered arable, although less than 1 percent is actually cultivated. Forested areas represent 12 percent of the total and grasslands 1 percent. Despite Hong Kong's dense urban buildup, 40 percent of its total area has been designated as park land. Hong Kong has no natural resources other than its sheltered deepwater harbor; its strategic location which gives it access to the Chinese mainland; and some minor deposits of quarriable stone. Hong Kong has depended on trade since its founding, and it has parlayed its role as a business broker into its current dominant position.

Hong Kong always seems to be in a hurry, probably due to its chronic historic concern about tomorrow's uncertainties.

HISTORY OF THE ECONOMY

Premodern Hong Kong

Premodern Hong Kong was home to small, scattered settlements of farmers, fisher folk, pirates, and smugglers who were essentially hangers-on of the nearby port of Canton, now known as Guangzhou, China's main trading port with the outside world. The Portuguese were the first Europeans to enter the area. They founded the enclave of Macao, 64 km (40 miles) west of Hong Kong, in 1557. Canton was partially opened to other European traders in 1685.

The Chinese kept tight control over this trade, accepting only silver for their goods. In the late 18th century, the British East India Company turned the tables by importing opium from India into China and taking out large quantities of silver in return. The Chinese, disturbed by this loss of specie, the growing corruption, and the impact of Western influence in Canton, unsuccessfully tried to restrict access. The authorities in Beijing finally instituted a crackdown in 1839, and local officials seized and destroyed European opium shipments. The British retaliated in the First Opium War (1841-1842), taking Hong Kong as a base and retaining it through permanent cession after soundly defeating the Chinese.

The British expanded their holdings by annexing the adjacent Kowloon Peninsula in 1856, a cession ratified by treaty after the Second Opium War in 1860. In 1898 Britain completed its colony by dictating a 99-year lease on the New Territories, which extend to the Shenzhen River on the mainland.

The Colonial Era

Hong Kong's population, which had been negligible in 1841, was 33,000 in 1851, 500,000 in 1914, and nearly 1.5 million in 1941. From the turn of the century until the beginning of World War II, the sharp rise in population was due primarily to the flight of Chinese seeking a safe haven from unrest in China. However, during the harsh Japanese occupation between 1941 and 1945 Hong Kong's population fell by 60 percent to 600,000. The civil war between the Chinese Communists and the Nationalist Kuomintang in the late 1940s sent additional waves of refugees to Hong Kong, and by 1949, following the Communist victory and the flight of the Kuomintang, Hong Kong's population stood at 2.5 million. Between 1949 and 1962, Hong Kong absorbed at least one million refugees.

Despite perennial fears that the Communists would seize Hong Kong, China has remained content to hover on the other side of the border, often ominously but never making serious incursions. In 1967, during the Cultural Revolution, there were Red Guard inspired riots in Hong Kong, and Chinese militiamen crossed the border, killing five Hong Kong police before withdrawing. However, Hong Kong's many benefits to China have kept Beijing from forcibly seizing the enclave.

Looking Forward to 1997

Following China's pragmatic opening in the late 1970s and prolonged negotiations during the early 1980s, Britain agreed in 1984 to relinquish all of Hong Kong, including the portions that had been permanently ceded to it, when its lease rights expire in 1997. The Chinese, under the slogan of One Country, Two Systems, promised to allow Hong Kong to become a separate Special Administrative Region within China, retaining its customary political and economic arrangements as a quasi-independent entity for 50 years.

A great deal of uncertainty surrounds how this will work out in practice, and the two sides continue to jockey for position over implementation of the accords. However, business continues to boom, and observers cannot believe that China, despite its penchant for command and control, would kill the goose that lays such golden eggs. Today, Hong Kong is the source of between 30 and 40 percent of China's total foreign exchange, and almost 70 percent of all foreign investment in China is channeled through the colony. China could expect to have these flows sharply curtailed—something it could ill afford—if it were to renege on its promise to turn a blind eye to the colony's unfettered practice of capitalism.

Economic Development: Trade Plus

For its first 70 years as a British colony, Hong Kong existed strictly to serve the China trade, but as unrest in China during the 1920s and 1930s caused Chinese capitalists to flock to the British controlled area, its economy began to broaden, expanding into small-scale entrepreneurial manufacturing. The Japa-

nese dismantling of the colony was a setback, but recovery was strong and rapid following the war. The Communist takeover of China proved to be a boon to Hong Kong, because it made Hong Kong the de facto exclusive foreign access point to China.

This happy situation was derailed by the UN embargo on trade with China imposed in 1951 as part of sanctions for China's participation in the Korean War. Hong Kong, which suddenly had to find a new way of generating the foreign exchange that it needed for its continued survival, turned almost overnight from a primary focus on trade to manufacturing. Manufacturing grew throughout the 1950s, 1960s, and 1970s. During the 1970s and 1980s growth was primarily in ancillary services, especially business and financial services.

In the 1970s, as China began to reestablish relations with the outside world, Hong Kong again became the broker for China's trade. By 1990 at least one-quarter of Hong Kong's economy depended on China, up from a total of 5 percent in 1980. As it faces the 1990s, Hong Kong has moved much of its low-level manufacturing activity offshore to China, and it is concentrating on high-value-added manufactures and services.

SIZE OF THE ECONOMY

Although Hong Kong is one of the smallest formal entities in Asia, both geographically and demographically, its gross domestic product (GDP) lags only slightly behind that of some of its much larger neighbors. Hong Kong's GDP is about one-half the size of Taiwan's and one-third the size of South Korea's, both nations that are much larger and much more heavily industrialized than the colony. Hong Kong's GDP is almost one-fourth that of China, making it the economic tail that wags the much larger Chinese dog.

Hong Kong's GDP was US$97.9 billion in 1992, up 5.2 percent in real terms from the US$82.8 billion registered in 1991. Between the 1950s and the mid-1980s, Hong Kong's economy regularly grew at double-digit rates. Between 1980 and 1990, growth of GDP slipped to an average annual real rate of 7.8 percent, and that rate was muted by a slowdown in growth at the end of the decade. Real growth in GDP fell from 14 percent in 1987 to 7 percent in 1988 and 2.3 percent in 1989, as China instituted austerity measures, Chinese domestic political unrest cut worldwide trade with China, and the global recession set in.

Hong Kong's GDP grew by an anemic 2.4 percent in 1990, recovering to 3.8 percent growth in 1991 and 5.2 percent in 1992. Nevertheless, the economy grew at a respectable average real rate of 4.7 percent between 1987 and 1992, faster than Japan's 4.2 percent growth for the same period, twice the rate of increase in the European Community, and three times that in

Hong Kong's Gross National Product (GNP)

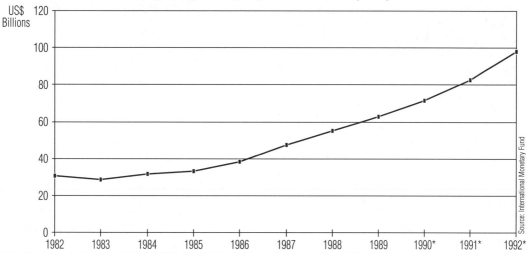

Source: International Monetary Fund

* Hong Kong has reported Gross Domestic Product (GDP) since 1990; historic differences between Hong Kong's GDP and GNP have generally been less than 1 percent.

the United States. Midyear figures for 1993 show an annualized 5.3 percent real rate of increase for 1993, a rate that would put Hong Kong's GDP at around US$106 billion if trends continue.

Standard of Living

Hong Kong's per capita GDP was US$16,288 in 1992, up 14 percent from the US$14,276 recorded in 1991. Over the last five years, per capita GDP has risen by almost 50 percent, with an average annual growth rate of 9.7 percent. Current per capita income places Hong Kong third among nations along the eastern Pacific Rim behind Japan and Australia. In 1990 per capita income in Hong Kong, as adjusted to take purchasing power into account, put the colony in 10th place among the nations of the world, behind Finland and Australia but ahead of Belgium and France. As an auxiliary index of living standard, Hong Kong has the highest per capita concentration of Rolls Royces in the world, and its inhabitants bet US$6 billion a year—more than 6 percent of GDP—at the Happy Valley racetrack.

CONTEXT OF THE ECONOMY

Hong Kong is something of a special case in that, like Singapore, it had no real economy before it became a British colonial port. Its rapid rise has placed it among the top nations of the world in income, services, and trade, leaving it in some respects stronger that its colonial master, Great Britain, and its soon-to-be sovereign, China. Britain generally has maintained a hands-off attitude, allowing Hong Kong to function as the most extreme example of a free market capitalist economy in the world with a minimum of interference, even during periods when an

unsympathetic, socialist-oriented Labor government ruled at home. And China, although huffing and puffing on the doorstep, also has left Hong Kong alone to develop as the antithesis of the professed Communist economic and social ideal.

The Importance of China

Hong Kong's economy has always been tightly linked with that of China as well as with such major trading partners as the United States. The only drop from double-digit economic growth between 1960 and 1990 coincided with austerity programs in China in the late 1980s. Observers note that a change in quotas set in the international Multifabric Arrangement (MFA) could decimate Hong Kong's dominant textile and apparel industry, while a decision by the United States to revoke China's most favored nation (MFN) trade status would affect 70 percent of Hong Kong's essential trade with China. In general, a slowdown in China is currently good for a loss of 1 percent to 2 percent in Hong Kong's GDP.

Governmental Controls or the Lack Thereof

The business of Hong Kong is truly business, and its overseers seem to believe that the government that governs best is the government that governs least. Hong Kong is driven by the engine of free enterprise and free trade; enabled by a modern business and logistical infrastructure that includes superb communication and transport links; and administered by a laissez-faire government that sees its only function as providing infrastructure, stability, and a legal framework to facilitate commerce. Even most municipal services, such as utilities, are already in private hands, and the government is considering the privatization of remaining areas in which it has an interest before 1997.

As a colony, Hong Kong has been run with a minimum of official local consultation by an appointed governor who has answered only to authorities in London. Although the British have been involved in a process of creeping democratization, which they have accelerated in an attempt to leave China with a fait accompli in the form of a popularly elected legislative council, referred to locally as LEGCO, they have generally ruled autocratically, giving local representation a low priority.

For decades the governor's unstated instructions from London have included the maintenance of order without undue impositions on business in the form of regulations such as foreign exchange controls and investment restrictions or taxes and tariffs. There are relatively few of either, and despite its low tax rates, Hong Kong's government usually manages to show a surplus, due to the fact that it owns essentially all land in the colony. With land the scarcest resource and rents the highest in the world outside Japan, the government has been able to rely on leasehold revenues for the bulk of its operating budget.

Nor does the government spend much on conventional social services, although basic public education is either free or subsidized. Standards are kept high and costs are kept low. Some 45 percent of Hong Kong's population lives in government high-rise housing, although 6 percent continues to live in illegal squatter settlements. There is no social security system, but Hong Kong does have fairly strict workplace safety rules. And although Hong Kong has large military bases, the government spends virtually nothing

on defense because Britain assumes that responsibility; China will take it over in 1997.

Small Business

The colony has a highly urbanized, consumer society, and its competitive, money-oriented, generally savvy and well-educated people are grounded in the Confucian ethos of hard work and hierarchical obedience. The vast majority of economic activity is carried out by entrepreneurial small businesses, most of which are informal family-owned, -run, and -staffed operations employing fewer than 10 persons. Entrepreneurs are mercurial and opportunistic niche players, shifting rapidly to take advantage of a range of situations. They are involved primarily in bidding as subcontractors for portions of larger operations, mostly in manufacture or assembly. Most specialize in the production of small, high-value-added consumer items or intermediate services that require some skill and experience but little capital investment.

As a rule, these operators have a minimal investment in capital and capital equipment, and they do not make commitments in research and development, product development, or marketing support and distribution. They focus instead on short-term, low-risk, quick-turnaround situations. English is the language of business, and businesspeople, even at the most rudimentary level, are functional in it.

Big Business

Although Hong Kong's economy centers on much smaller entities typified by the 80 percent of firms that have fewer than 10 employees, Hong Kong has a parallel tradition of large trading companies that

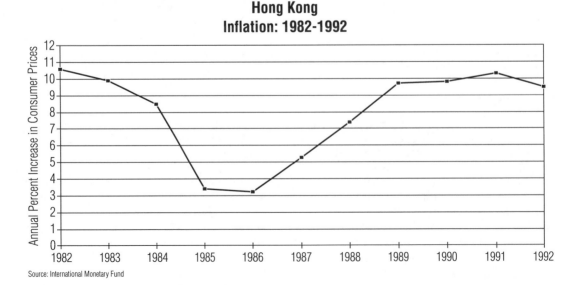

Hong Kong
Inflation: 1982-1992

Annual Percent Increase in Consumer Prices

Source: International Monetary Fund

dates back to the mid-19th century. The original entities were founded by *gwailo* (foreign entrepreneurs), known as *taipans* (big bosses) who built their operations into *hongs* (big trading firms). The majority of these firms have become true multinational corporations, and although management may consist mostly of European expatriates, it is now much more eclectically international than it was in the past. Although some companies retain their dominant British flavor, others have been bought out and transformed by local Hong Kong Chinese businessmen.

The biggest names among the *hongs* are Jardine Matheson, Hutchinson Whampoa, Wheelock Marden, and the Swire Group, which operate in trade, utilities, shipping, and manufacturing. Hongkong and Shanghai Banking Corporation comes from similar origins and plays a similar role in the area of finance. Many of the *hongs* have diversified their holdings and shifted their official headquarters offshore as a hedge against the pending Communist takeover in 1997. However, the majority have continued to invest in Hong Kong and China as well, and some of their managements are rather outspokenly pro-Chinese.

The *hongs* lack the influence that the analogous *zaibatsu* wield in Japan and the *chaebol* in Korea, primarily because the domestic market base is much smaller, but they still exercise substantial influence over the doings of local and regional markets, and they can sometimes have an impact in international markets as well. And like the Japanese *keiretsu*, or holding companies, which represent communities of shared interest, the *hongs*, which have interlocking directorates and social ties, have learned to cooperate even when they compete the most.

THE UNDERGROUND ECONOMY

Hong Kong's economic ambience is cutthroat but basically honest. Hong Kong is always in a hurry and cutting corners to get the deal done. Many foreign businesspeople complain about the curtness and even rudeness that they encounter in Hong Kong. With few regulations beyond the formal registration of businesses and the shifting and informal nature of many business entities that helps them evade the few regulations that do exist, caveat emptor is the order of the day. As a rich international port, Hong Kong has become a center for large-scale illegal activity, such as narcotics trafficking and money laundering. It is also noted for lower-level street crime, vice, and rip-offs, run mostly by the *triads*, local Mafia-like criminal societies.

Although Hong Kong is steeped in the traditions of Western business, it is still an Asian venue, and influence is a significant element in operations there. The civil service, which in 1991 had 186,000 employees—some 6.5 percent of the work force—used to be notorious for graft, especially in the days when virtually all its 3,500 supervisors were expatriates serving their tour abroad and expecting to come home set for life. The situation became so bad that the Independent Commission Against Corruption (ICAC) was formed in 1974 to root out irregularities in the civil service and the business community. With its broad powers, the ICAC has come to be feared, and although it has been accused of using authoritarian means, it has largely stopped official corruption, although cynics would say that the ICAC has merely driven those on the take deeper underground.

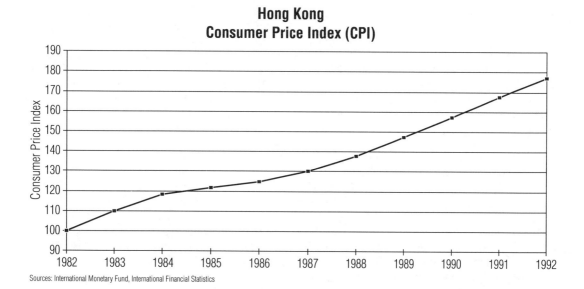

Hong Kong
Consumer Price Index (CPI)

Sources: International Monetary Fund, International Financial Statistics

Higher-level business irregularities occur less often than they do elsewhere in Asia, and perhaps not much more often than they do in Western countries. However, deals that hinge on the doing of favors are both relatively common and blatant by Western standards. Examples include the use of inside information and manipulation of the sales of stock and companies in less than arm's-length transactions. In 1993 investigated cases of corruption in the private sector rose by 52 percent. Official corruption rose as well. Authorities attribute the vast bulk of this activity to businesses paying bribes to officials and companies in China, where bribery is illegal but endemic. A recent survey found that 70 percent of Hong Kong-based companies routinely gave "gifts" to Chinese officials to facilitate business.

Intellectual Property Rights

Hong Kong operates under the British system of intellectual property. That system officially recognizes only copyrights, trademarks, and patents that have been registered in the United Kingdom. Although registration is relatively easy and enforcement relatively conscientious, Hong Kong, the small entrepreneurial capital of the world, is still known as a world center for counterfeit goods, and the authorities seem to be unable to wipe these goods out even with fairly zealous enforcement. The cutthroat climate makes the protection of business secrets another cause for concern.

INFLATION

Because Hong Kong's hands-off government has made relatively little effort to rein it in, inflation has often been as robust as the growth of Hong Kong's economy. Because most commodities and consumer goods are imported into the colony at world market prices, the government has had no way of controlling prices short of deficit-inducing subsidies. Nor have officials tried to soften or manage the numbers, as they have in some other countries.

Consumer prices rose at an annual rate of 9.5 percent in 1992, down from the 10.3 percent increase recorded in 1991. Inflation was 12 percent in 1979, and it surged to a high of 16 percent in 1980. Between 1980 and 1990, inflation averaged 8 percent, although it fluctuated between a low of 3.2 percent and a high of 10.6 percent during that period. In the second quarter of 1993, inflation rose at an annual rate of 8 percent.

LABOR

As with much else, Hong Kong's government basically keeps out of labor relations. Hong Kong has a well-educated, hard-working, and motivated labor force. School attendance is free and mandatory for nine years, and additional attendance is encouraged. Schooling beyond the secondary level is subsidized, but a lack of slots makes admissions at higher levels highly competitive. The government moved recently to expand opportunities in higher education. However, in keeping with its hands-off policy, it does not invest in worker training. The fact that most firms are very small militates against formal worker training in the private sector.

The Labor Shortage

Despite Hong Kong's historic ability to absorb immigrant workers, it currently has a labor shortage. High sustained growth and the opening of new ventures, primarily with China, have increased demand, while the departure of skilled middle- and upper-level personnel in anticipation of the Chinese takeover in 1997 and a slowing flow of immigrants have reduced the labor pool on the supply side. The government has instituted a labor importation scheme allowing employers to bring in foreign labor under two-year contracts, which can be renewed for a total of six years. Quotas restrict the manpower acquired under this arrangement to roughly 15 percent of the labor that had been requested by the private sector. Foreign workers are not to exceed 0.1 percent of the total work force, which is currently three million.

Emigration

The so-called brain drain, motivated by fears of the impending takeover by China, means that the colony has lost a number of highly skilled, highly educated, and affluent persons. However, after increasing their options by obtaining passports abroad, many emigrés subsequently return to Hong Kong as expatriate staff, so the disruption may be more temporary than permanent. The situation may change as 1997 draws nearer and if residents have second thoughts about the new regime.

Emigration has been growing at a steady pace since the early 1980s, when annual out migration was around 20,000. It reached 70,000 in 1991, but was expected to drop to 60,000 in 1992. The cumulative number of emigrants between 1982 and 1992 is estimated at close to 425,000.

In 1991 Canada received 41 percent of Hong Kong's emigrants, Australia 21 percent, and the United States 19 percent. Vietnam accounted for a surprising 11 percent, although some of these may represent the forced repatriation of boat people, New Zealand for 4 percent, and the United Kingdom for only 2 percent, with other countries together taking the remaining 2 percent. The UK has adamantly refused to accept substantial numbers of Hong Kong citizens even in the pending takeover.

Unemployment

Unemployment in Hong Kong has been so low, particularly during the past decade, that the colony can be said to have virtually no structural unemployment. Over the past ten years, unemployment has averaged 2 percent, peaking at 3 percent during the downturn in 1985 and dropping as low as 1.3 percent in 1990. Unemployment held at 2 percent in 1992, rising slightly to 2.1 percent in early 1993.

Unionization

Hong Kong guarantees unions the right to organize workers, and it guarantees workers the right to join unions, but the government also maintains a right-to-work environment. Relatively few workers belong to unions, although union membership is on the increase. In 1992 about 18 percent of the work force was unionized, up from 17.5 percent in 1991 and 15.2 percent in 1990. Hong Kong unions are not generally militant, and there have been virtually no strikes or serious labor disputes in recent years. Unions focus primarily on establishing trade association standards and self-help such as mutual benefit functions. They have not been heavily involved in the vigorous negotiation of wages and benefits or the taking of political positions.

Labor Costs

Hong Kong's high standard of living and its labor shortage mean that wage costs are relatively high, although Hong Kong has not priced itself out of the market to the extent that many other Asian countries already have. Wages have increased steadily but not sharply, rising by 40 percent in real terms between 1970 and 1990.

In 1991 the average weekly wage of manufacturing workers was an estimated US$248.69; mandated and customary benefits estimated at a liberal 20 percent of wages (US$49.74) brought the average weekly total to US$298.43. In comparison, the nominal average weekly wage for the same period was US$245 in Taiwan, US$295 in South Korea, US$261 in Singapore, US$705 in Japan, and US$7.37 in China.

Most employers provide subsidized meals and an annual bonus equal to one or two months' salary. Larger employers often provide subsidies for transportation and health care, and award attendance bonuses. Although there is no legal minimum wage in Hong Kong, it is difficult to find workers below prevailing wage levels. Less-skilled workers are paid on a piecework or daily basis, while more skilled personnel are paid a monthly salary.

There is no social security system in Hong Kong. Some larger firms are beginning to offer supplemental health and retirement benefits. The government does require employers to provide workmen's compensation insurance, sick leave and maternity leave, severance payments, paid holidays—there are 11 annual official paid holidays—and seven to 14 days of paid vacation for permanent employees. The government also prohibits child labor; sets standards regarding hours and working conditions and for industrial health and safety; and protects union activity.

Executive compensation is comparable to that in other world-class cities, with large salaries, bonuses, and benefit packages that for expatriate staff usually include free or subsidized housing, an allowance for children's education, home leave and transportation, and club memberships. It is at least as expensive to maintain professional and executive

Structure of the Hong Kong Economy - 1991

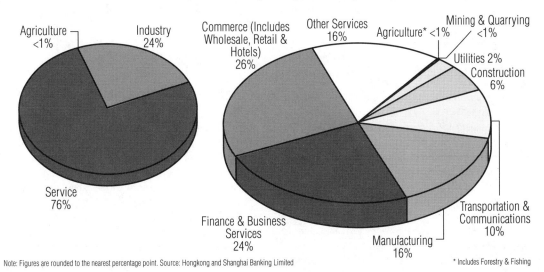

Agriculture <1%
Industry 24%
Service 76%

Commerce (Includes Wholesale, Retail & Hotels) 26%
Other Services 16%
Agriculture* <1%
Mining & Quarrying <1%
Utilities 2%
Construction 6%
Transportation & Communications 10%
Manufacturing 16%
Finance & Business Services 24%

Note: Figures are rounded to the nearest percentage point. Source: Hongkong and Shanghai Banking Limited

* Includes Forestry & Fishing

staff in Hong Kong as it is in major cities in developed countries around the world.

Workweek

Hong Kong's official workweek is 48 hours long. Some workers put in even longer hours. Government workers and service personnel customarily work a five-and-a-half-day 44 hour week. However, some multinational firms have instituted a five-day 40 hour workweek. Because there are few controls on hours worked, official statistics on actual time worked are lacking.

Hong Kong's estimated average workweek of about 46 hours compares with 47.9 hours in South Korea, 46.7 hours in Singapore, 46.1 hours in Japan, and 45.5 hours in Taiwan. In comparison, the average workweek is 43.6 hours in the United Kingdom, 39.9 hours in Germany, 39 hours in France, and 34.3 hours in the United States.

SECTORS OF THE ECONOMY

Hong Kong still relies heavily on its manufacturing sector, which in 1991 accounted for 16 percent of GDP, although this subsector has been shrinking since the mid-1980s, as high overhead led lower-skill jobs to be exported to cheaper locations, primarily in neighboring China. In 1991 manufacturing and industry together produced 23.8 percent of GDP, far less than the dominant service sector, which accounted for 76 percent of GDP. Agriculture and fisheries contributed an insignificant 0.2 percent, a share that continues to fall. Some 38 percent of the work force is employed in manufacturing, 59.3 percent in services, and 2.7 percent in agriculture and fishing.

Hong Kong's average annual fixed investment was about 25 percent of GDP between 1988 and 1992. Comparative figures for the same period were 33 percent in Japan and 15 percent in the United States. Savings and investment rates in Hong Kong are not as impressive as they are elsewhere in Asia due mainly to Hong Kong's high cost of living and its orientation toward consumption. Nevertheless, savings and investment are still substantially higher than they are in most Western economies.

The government sector accounts for expenditures equal to about one-fifth of GDP. As a colony, Hong Kong lacks independent international borrowing authority, and thus it has no official external debt, although the government began issuing short-term bills in 1990. Intelligence sources estimate actual foreign obligations to be a manageable US$9.5 billion, less than 10 percent of GDP.

The government, which usually has budget surpluses, is preparing to run up a deficit in order to fund large infrastructure projects between now and 1997. Officials have hiked business tax rates by 1 percent to 17.5 percent; they reportedly do not plan to raise personal taxes or institute any new revenue programs. A weakening in the real estate market due to uncertainty about the transition to Chinese control could force the issue, because the government funds more than one-third of its activity from rents received. The prospect of burgeoning debt has caused tension with China, which does not want to inherit it in 1997.

AGRICULTURE

Hong Kong's agricultural and fishing tradition is colorful and strong, and a disproportionate percentage of the work force is still employed in these pursuits. However, they do not exercise undue political influence. Although agriculture and fisheries, to which can be added the negligible pursuits of mining, quarrying, and forestry, employ 2.7 percent of the work force, they produce only 0.2 percent of GDP. Hong Kong's dependence on imported foodstuffs is far too great for it to chase the ideal of self-sufficiency. Moreover, the colony's leaders are far too pragmatic to preserve agriculture when the property could be put to better use. In most cases it cannot be, because agricultural plots tend to be in less accessible areas of the New Territories.

Overall Hong Kong is only 20 percent self-sufficient in food production. It produces a larger share of its needs in certain specific areas of production, such as fresh vegetables (34 percent), poultry (37 percent), pigs (18 percent), freshwater fish (15 percent), and marine fish (74 percent). Hong Kong's main crops include root crops, such as sweet potatoes, yams, and taro; sugar cane; greens, such as cabbage, lettuce, kale, and watercress; vegetables, such as radishes; and some rice. Fruits, nuts, and flowers are also grown. Most agriculture is of the market garden variety, carried out on small family plots.

Hong Kong imports the majority of its food needs, including such staples as rice and wheat. It must also import water, 50 percent of which is purchased from China. Agriculture and fisheries contribute very little to Hong Kong's export economy.

MANUFACTURING AND INDUSTRY

The manufacturing and industry sector, which includes utilities and construction, was the primary focus of Hong Kong's economy from the 1950s until the mid-1980s. Before the 1950's Hong Kong depended mostly on trade. Since 1986, trade—with a boost from financial and business services—has regained the lead. However, because 90 percent of Hong Kong's manufacturing output is exported, the two areas remain tightly linked. The shift to a trade focus underlines the weakening of Hong Kong's competitive position as a manufacturing entity due to high labor and other overhead costs. Manufacturers have had to accept increasingly lower profit margins in order to retain market share.

Manufacturing: The Numbers Game

Between 1973 and 1990 net output in the manufacturing sector increased at an average annual rate of 16 percent, while employment in the sector rose by only 1 percent. Manufacturing, which accounted for 24 percent of GDP in 1980, was down to 16 percent in 1991, although it was expected to maintain roughly the same share in 1992 and 1993.

In 1988 Hong Kong had more than 50,600 factories, which employed 845,000 workers, more than 31 percent of its total labor force. In 1991 the number of factories had slipped to 49,000 and manufacturing jobs had shrunk to 735,000. In mid-1993 manufacturing employment had fallen to 522,000. There are now more than three times as many manufacturing workers in adjacent Guangdong Province as there are in Hong Kong, and overall manufacturing employment in Hong Kong has dropped by at least one-third over the last five years.

Labor costs are not the only factor in this out migration: Hong Kong's high rents and high overhead associated with the colony's high standard of living are other reasons why owners have moved operations that did not have a compelling reason to be located in the colony itself. Most manufacturing is run out of small facilities located in multistoried urban buildings. Although industrial parks in the New Territories have been designed to accommodate some larger, specialized operations, Hong Kong factory spaces usually can be duplicated more cheaply elsewhere.

Areas of Specialization

Hong Kong, which specializes in light manufactures, remains one of the world's largest producers of toys and games, textiles, apparel, watches and clocks, metal watchbands, radios, hair dryers, flashlights, electric lamps, furs, and costume jewelry. Hong Kong's dominance in many of these products was established during the 1960s, when investment flowed into textiles, plastics, and metal fabrication. During the 1970s investment shifted to more complicated electronic products.

About 65 percent of the industrial work force is employed in apparel, textiles, electronics, plastics, and watch and clock manufacture. Together, these categories account for 61.5 percent of Hong Kong's domestic exports. But with between 60 and 70 percent of the colony's manufacturing capacity expected to move to China before 1997, the portion of the manufacturing sector that is not simply fading away is shifting from labor-intensive to capital-intensive pursuits.

Apparel and Textiles

Apparel and textiles are the largest category of manufactures in Hong Kong, accounting for 47 percent of manufacturing employment and nearly 12 percent of Hong Kong's total work force. Apparel alone employs 32 percent of the manufacturing work force, while textile operations employ an additional 15 percent, down from 27 percent in 1973. The labor shortage has left some of Hong Kong's spinning mills idle, while cheaper labor elsewhere now performs some of the low-skill labor-intensive garment operations that used to constitute Hong Kong's primary competitive advantage.

Clothing is still the colony's largest earner of foreign exchange, and Hong Kong, with 10 percent of the world market, is second only to Italy as an exporter of apparel. The apparel sector's strategy has been to go upmarket, concentrating on high fashion and better-quality products, while investing in computer-aided design and computer-aided manufacture (CAD/CAM) to hold costs down. Hong Kong's textile and apparel industries remain vulnerable to foreign protectionism, generally through quotas limiting the amount of its goods that Hong Kong can get into world markets. Nevertheless, Hong Kong holds large quotas for the important United States and European markets.

Electronics

Hong Kong's electronics industry focuses on the assembly of mostly low- and mid-range consumer items from imported components. Electronics is the second-largest manufacturing earner of foreign exchange and employs 12 percent of the manufacturing work force. The electronics subsector currently produces consumer products, such as radios, audio and videocassette recorders, audio components, and television sets; business equipment, such as computers, calculators, telephones, and facsimile machines; and other components. This subsector has been undermined not only by cheaper offshore assembly labor but also by recession, which has weakened demand in the West, where most of the goods are sold. Hong Kong is redirecting some of its output to less developed markets.

Electronics manufacturers are also attempting to go after higher-value-added new markets involving more sophisticated technology and relying on tighter quality control. This strategy entails a shift to more sophisticated consumer and business electronics, such as computer peripherals, modems, compact disc players, and telecommunications equipment, and to onshore production of more sophisticated components, such as semiconductors, printed circuit boards, and liquid crystal displays.

Other Light Industry

Plastics account for 7 percent of Hong Kong's domestic exports and 9 percent of its manufacturing employment. The major item in this category is injection-molded toys. This subsector has more than 1,000 factories employing nearly 23,000 workers. Watches and clocks and associated components are also imported, with an 8.5 percent share of exports and a 4.5 percent share of the labor force, followed by specialty printing, with 4 percent of the work force. Additional products include electrical and nonelectrical machinery, metal products, jewelry, and optical and photographic goods.

Medium and Heavy Industry

Hong Kong produces machine tool and die equipment, such as molding and extrusion equipment, presses, lathes, shapers, drilling machines, polishing machines, printing presses, spinning and knitting machines, and looms, and electroplating equipment.

Although not generally known for heavy industry, Hong Kong has a significant shipbuilding and repair industry, an aircraft maintenance and repair industry, and an oil exploration and rig outfitting industry. Although Hong Kong does not smelt iron and steel, it does roll and fabricate intermediate steel products, and it has a respectable presence in basic chemical and cement plants that service regional demand for these products.

Construction

In 1991 the construction industry employed 2.6 percent of Hong Kong's work force and accounted for 5.5 percent of its GDP. Building activity tends to be cyclical, and it is driven by public works construction. Because the government owns all land, private construction can only be accomplished via long-term ground leases, a fact that has tended to brake private development as has concern over the status of private real estate improvements after 1997. Construction lost 11 percent of its jobs between June 1992 and June 1993, due to the hiatus between the completion of the last public and private construction boom and the anticipated beginning of new public works projects.

Although the public sector continues to account for the vast bulk of construction activity, its projects are increasingly varied. The government has completed a round of housing construction, and it is buckling down to focus on some massive infrastructure projects, which are set to include a new airport; container ship docks and facilities; bridge, highway, and other transportation projects; and redevelopment and telecommunications projects designed to leave Hong Kong in a state-of-the-art position in 1997.

SERVICES

In 1991 Hong Kong's service sector, which includes trade and commerce (wholesale and retail commerce, international trade, and domestic and tourist services, such as lodging and restaurants), finance and business services (including real estate and insurance), and other services (transport and communications, health care, and personal and government services) accounted for 76 percent of Hong Kong's GDP and employed 59.3 percent of its work force, up from 67 percent of GDP and 53 percent of the work force as recently as 1988. The sector should account for 80 percent of GDP within the next few years, and could reach 85 percent share by decade's end.

Trade and Commerce

The huge trade and commerce subsector, which produces 26.2 percent of GDP, is the largest single service category, but it can be broken down further into import-export trade, domestic wholesale and retail commerce, and domestic and tourist services. Between June 1992 and June 1993, employment in this subsector grew by 3.2 percent to almost 933,000.

Foreign trade is the core focus of Hong Kong's economy, and 90 percent of its manufacturing output is funneled into export markets. Most of the rest of the export market consists of reexported products, while the majority of the colony's imports consist of the raw or intermediate materials needed to fuel the export industry. Many larger import-export deals are handled by the giant trading firms, the *hongs*, although there is plenty of room for operators of all sizes.

This frenetic activity masks a relatively small domestic market, albeit one rich in possibilities because of its high level of consumption. Overall domestic retail sales grew by 18 percent in 1992.

Although there are significant practical entry barriers to domestic wholesale distribution, retail is as wide open as the rest of the economy. The difficulties in establishing supplier relationships that vertical integration and exclusionary practices create in other Asian markets do not exist in Hong Kong. However, the high turnover that facilitates entry is a two-edged sword, because it also means that there are few long-term relationships and little loyalty among either suppliers or customers, although consumers are highly brand conscious. Niche markets abound, especially in such diverse segments as boutique operations dealing in upscale hard goods, soft goods, and perishables, particularly luxury, branded items, and convenience and fast food outlets. On a larger scale, Japanese retailers have taken the lead in opening successful department and large specialty stores. And discounters are also beginning to make inroads in the Hong Kong market.

Tourism

Tourism-related businesses are particularly interesting. In contrast to most other Asian nations, where tourism is at best only ancillary, tourism is Hong Kong's second-largest source of foreign exchange. It has more visitors every year than it has inhabitants, and the influx of tourists is still growing. The colony serves as the travel gateway for the vast majority of business and recreational travel to China and as the primary hub for travel to Southeast Asia. For Chinese, Taiwanese, and Southeast Asian tourists, Hong Kong is major destination point in and of itself. Japanese tourism has started to slow recently due to the economic downturn in Japan.

Hong Kong's restaurant and lodging industry is geared to the tourist trade, especially at the upper end. As an index, the number of rooms in Hong Kong's accommodations market expanded at an average annual rate of 9.5 percent between 1986 and 1991, and occupancy levels have hovered around an industry-beating 79 percent except for dips during the Tiananmen crisis in 1989 and the Gulf War in 1991.

Financial and Business Services

Hong Kong is one of the top world financial markets as well as the foremost access point for business in Asia. And one of the fastest growing: between June 1992 and June 1993, employment in the financial services subsector grew by 7.2 percent to over 327,000. In 1991 the business and financial services sector accounted for 23.8 percent of GDP, second only to trade and commerce and surpassing the contribution of manufacturing.

For the last ten years it has been the world's third or fourth most important financial center every year, just behind or just ahead of Tokyo. Moreover, many observers rank Hong Kong well ahead of Tokyo and just behind New York and London as a financial and business center, because of its ease of access and relative lack of restrictive rules. The more developed Asian markets are already competing for Hong Kong's place in financial affairs after 1997. Although Hong Kong intends to retain its position, there are serious questions as to whether China will allow the same level of openness and freedom from restrictions that has enabled the colony to reach its current level of dominance.

Hong Kong has no central bank and allows its major local banks to manage finances in conjunction with the government. The largest banks even issue currency under contract to the government, but all notes are backed by hard currency reserves. Since 1983 the Hong Kong dollar (HK$) has been pegged to the US dollar at roughly HK$7.8, with the exchange rate allowed to fluctuate within a narrow range. As a result of this linkage, interest rates in Hong Kong closely track those in the United States.

Banking

Banking is prominent in Hong Kong because Hong Kong places few restrictions on deposits, lending, and other types of business. It is relatively easy to set up any of the several categories of licensed banks and like financial institutions. To date there has been plenty of business and a large pool of talent to support a multiplicity of financial institutions. In 1992 164 licensed banks were operating in Hong Kong. Of these, 12 were domestic and 152 were foreign. Total deposits rose to US$189 billion, and loans rose 24 percent. As of mid-1993 Hong Kong's prime rate was 6.5 percent. However, analysts predict that it will rise to 7.5 percent over the next twelve months as government borrowing, business, and inflation pick up.

In 1991 Hong Kong had 375 licensed financial institutions—a category broader than fully licensed banks—but this number was down 7.4 percent from the 405 recorded in 1990, due primarily to consolidation. The Hong Kong financial scene is finally experiencing a shakeout after years of unbridled growth.

Insurance companies also are relatively easy to set up under Hong Kong law, and there is a growing market for their products and many attractive investment opportunities for the premiums collected. Although the government owns title to all land in the colony, long-term building leases and improvements constitute real estate proxies, and there is a thriving property management industry. This market is difficult to enter directly, and observers warn that overvalued real estate constitutes a financial landmine in Hong Kong, much as it has been in the United States and Japan.

Securities Markets

With the market value of its listed shares at US$133 billion and rising in mid-1993, Hong Kong's stock exchange, the sixth largest in the world, is one of the world's most dynamic and best performing bourses. Although the Chinese takeover in 1997 casts some doubts on its future, the Hong Kong market is less volatile and more stable than it used to be. However, most businesses in Hong Kong are closely held, and the fact that local firms are required to make only 25 percent of their shares available in order to be listed on the exchange leaves only a small float which increases market volatility and opens up possibilities for manipulation.

Nevertheless, since 1979 Hong Kong's stock market has been the best-performing equities market in the world five times, and between 1982 and 1992 produced the highest average returns in the world in US dollar terms. However, it was also the only major exchange to cease trading during the crash in 1987. Hong Kong has active commodity, futures, and gold exchanges, and it is the second largest Asian dollar market after Singapore. Foreign and local brokerage outfits are well established in Hong Kong.

Transportation and Communications

Hong Kong has a world-class, deepwater harbor, and it is strategically located to manage trade with China. Its port facilities are among the best in the world, and the government is preparing to expand and upgrade them as part of its legacy to the colony. Hong Kong surpassed Singapore as the world's busiest container port in mid-1992. Hong Kong is home to 10 percent of the world's shipping, and tonnage handled in the port was up by 20 percent in 1992, while most of the rest of the world's ports experienced a flat or declining year. Private dock owners and operators have made attempts to set up pricing cartels. So far these efforts have resulted only in a boom for smaller competing lightering firms, whose business rose 63 percent in 1992.

Air cargo and passenger services are good, although capacity has been unable to keep up with demand resulting in bottlenecks. Hong Kong plans to supplement air transport facilities by building a new airport with three times the capacity of the existing Kai Tak airport. The colony's telecommunications links are among the best in the world. The government has advanced the idea of privatizing its interests in transportation and communications before 1997. The development projects, their cost, and their ownership have become a bone of contention with the Chinese, and the outcome is somewhat cloudy.

Personal, Professional, and Government Services

Because of its free market hands-off orientation, Hong Kong officially provides relatively few services.

Nevertheless, the civil service numbered 186,000 in the early 1990s, about 6.5 percent of the work force. The public service sector has been growing at about 3 percent a year, although the government has frozen civil service salaries and positions in an attempt to control inflation and hold down budgets.

The government manages necessary services, including education, utilities, and, to some extent, health care. While there are relatively few regulations, those that do exist are rather strictly enforced, providing employment for government workers. The accords with China are supposed to protect civil servants after 1997, but their future is somewhat in doubt, especially that of supervisory personnel, who consist largely of expatriate appointees.

Meanwhile, the private personal service sector continues to grow at double-digit rates, as entrepreneurs find niches associated with the growing affluence of Hong Kong's population. There are few legal restrictions on entry into health care, legal, accounting, engineering, management consulting, marketing, advertising, and public relations services. However, Hong Kong is highly competitive and although there are few legal entry barriers, there are some very real practical and cultural barriers to successful penetration of the market.

TRADE

Trade is Hong Kong's reason for being. Despite its small size, it is the world's 10th largest trading entity, and in 1992 its total trade was US$241.1 billion, two-and-one-half times as large as its GDP, US$241.1 billion. This represented a 21.7 percent increase over the US$198.1 billion recorded in 1991. Mid-year 1993 trade figures show trade at US$126.4

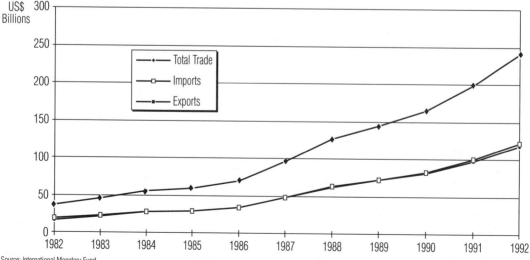

Hong Kong's Foreign Trade

US$ Billions. Legend: Total Trade, Imports, Exports. Years 1982 through 1992.

Source: International Monetary Fund

billion, which suggests that total trade for the year should reach at least US$275 billion, a 14 percent increase, if current trends hold.

Growth in Trade

Hong Kong's trade has hit new highs virtually every year since the early 1950s, having risen by more than 200 percent in real terms between 1979 and 1990. Between 1977 and 1987 trade grew at an average annual rate of 9 percent, better than double the pace of trade worldwide. Between 1987 and 1992 trade increased annually by an average of 16.4 percent in nominal terms and by more than two-and-a-half times in total volume. Despite turmoil in China and the worldwide economic slump, which have helped to hold down the growth of Hong Kong's GDP, trade never failed to increase by less than 13 percent in nominal terms between 1987 and 1992, with the increase rising as high as 31 percent in 1988 during China's boom period.

The Importance of China

About one-third of Hong Kong's total trade represents visible or merchandise trade with China, and the majority of growth in trade, especially since the late 1970s, has come from the colony's role as an entrepôt and reexport center for China. Nearly 75 percent of Hong Kong's total 1992 exports represents reexports, up from 55 percent in 1988 and 65 percent in 1990.

Besides serving as a gateway to China for the world at large, Hong Kong also fills a special role in trade between Taiwan and China, because Taiwan makes direct trade with China illegal. Nevertheless, perhaps 10 percent of Taiwan's total trade is with China, and most of it passes through Hong Kong middlemen.

Exporting, Importing, and Reexporting

Hong Kong's total exports, which have risen by 144 percent in nominal terms since 1987, reached an all-time high in 1992 of US$118.6 billion, up 20.8 percent from the year before, for an average annual increase of 16.1 percent. Imports, which have risen by 153 percent since 1987, also peaked in 1992, at US$122.5 billion; the average annual increase has been 16.7 percent. Exports grew faster than imports only in 1989. Otherwise, the two have been fairly evenly matched, with exports averaging a fairly consistent 49.8 percent and imports 50.2 percent of total trade during that period.

In 1990 64.7 percent of Hong Kong's total exports consisted of reexports, while only 35.3 percent of its exports were produced domestically. By 1992 reexports had soared to 74.7 percent of total exports, and in the first quarter of 1993, they moved up to 78.1 percent, with domestic exports representing only 21.9 percent of the total. On the import side, 64.4 percent of Hong Kong's imports in 1990 were reexported, while 35.6 percent were consumed locally. By 1992 domestic consumption had slipped to 27.7 percent of total imports, and in the first quarter of 1993 it slipped to 25.3 percent, which meant that Hong Kong reexported 74.7 percent of its imports, largely without adding significant value to them.

Local consumption of imports increased in absolute terms from US$29.3 billion in 1990 to US$33.9 billion in 1992, a total rise of 15.7 percent, for an average annual rate of 5 percent. During those same years, local production of export products rose in absolute terms from US$29 billion to US$30 billion, an extremely modest total increase of 3.4 percent and an average annual rise of only 1.1 percent. These numbers underline the ongoing shrinkage in Hong Kong's manufacturing sector.

Balance of Trade

During much of its history Hong Kong's balance of trade has been no better than break-even. During the last six years the balance has been positive or favorable in only two years, and it was unfavorable or negative in four. In only two of those six years did the absolute dollar value of the difference exceed US$1 billion, and in only one year was the imbalance greater than 1 percent of total trade.

Nevertheless, between 1987 and 1992 the overall trend has been negative. Hong Kong had a slightly positive balance of US$10 million in 1987. In 1992 it had a negative balance of US$3.9 billion, 1.6 percent of its total trade for that year. Figures for the first quarter of 1993 place Hong Kong's current trade balance at negative US$1.3 billion, 2.2 percent of total trade.

The factors explaining this ominous trend reflect Hong Kong's changing situation. First and foremost, as the colony moves manufacturing offshore, it produces fewer tangible exports. And as Hong Kong puts fewer of its direct imports into its exports, a larger share of those imports are consumed in Hong Kong, which is to be expected as its economy matures. Second, the negative balance echoes the general deficit position of Hong Kong's economy as the government undertakes expensive infrastructural improvements that cannot pay off in the near term.

However, the negative trade balance fails to take Hong Kong's burgeoning service sector into account. Its intangible exports are generating returns that are more than adequate to counteract the merchandise trade deficit. International reserves were estimated at US$28.9 billion in May 1993, and Hong Kong is well able to in effect subsidize its merchandise trade deficit with its intangible trade surplus.

Hong Kong's Leading Exports By Commodity - 1992

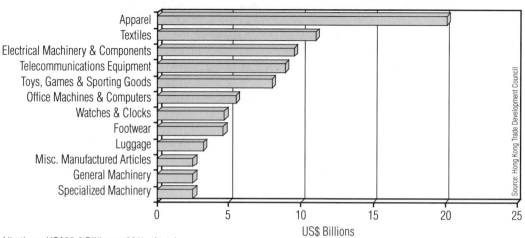

All others: US$35.6 Billion or 30% of total
Total 1992 Exports: US$118.6 Billion

EXPORTS

Domestic Exports

Hong Kong's main domestic exports are clothing (33 percent); textiles (7.4 percent); watches and clocks (6.6 percent); computers, office machinery, and parts (6.5 percent); telecommunications equipment and parts (4.7 percent); and semiconductors and other electronic parts (3.3 percent). Together these six categories account for 61.5 percent of Hong Kong's 1992 domestic exports. Jewelry, printed matter, finished plastic items, electrical apparatus, electrical machinery and parts, and intermediate plastic products account for another 10.1 percent. Other miscellaneous categories each account for less than 1.4 percent and make up the remaining 28.4 percent of Hong Kong's domestic exports.

During the first quarter of 1993 Hong Kong's exports of domestically produced consumer goods—things such as clothing, watches and clocks, jewelry, and printed matter—were off, while intermediate products, such as textiles, parts and accessories for office machines and computers, telecommunications equipment and parts, semiconductors and related parts, electrical apparatus, and electrical machinery and parts, were up substantially.

Total Exports

When total exports, including reexports, are examined, the picture is substantially different. Clothing is still the major item, with 16.8 percent of total exports. Textiles follow, at a 9.2 percent share; then toys, games, and sporting goods (6.3 percent); watches and clocks (4 percent); footwear (3.8 percent); telecommunications equipment and parts (3.6 percent); office equipment, computers, and parts (2.9 percent); semiconductors and related items (2.6 percent); luggage and related items (2.6 percent); and radios (2.1 percent). These ten categories account for 57.7 percent of Hong Kong's total exports. The next eight categories—intermediate plastic products, miscellaneous manufactures, cars, jewelry, printed matter, finished plastic items, electrical apparatus, and electrical machinery and parts—account for another 6.5 percent. Each of the categories in the remaining 39.7 percent accounts individually for less than 0.4 percent of the total.

The difference between the picture for domestic exports and total exports can be accounted for largely by China's highly diversified export economy, which is rapidly absorbing Hong Kong's independent manufacturing industries and fueling Hong Kong's export machine. High labor and overhead costs are rapidly eroding Hong Kong's traditional manufacturing base, which is 90 percent export oriented, and the colony is shifting to more value-added, sophisticated export items as well as to trade and service exports, such as financial and business services, including the management of offshore production.

IMPORTS

In 1992 Hong Kong's main imports were textiles (10.6 percent); electrical machinery (10 percent); clothing (8.4 percent); telecommunications, audio, and video equipment (7.9 percent); foodstuffs (4.6 percent); computers and office machines (3.6 percent); watches and clocks (3.4 percent); footwear (3.3 percent); toys, games, and sporting goods (3.3 percent); and automobiles (1.7 percent). Together, these categories account for 56.8 percent of Hong Kong's total imports. Each individual category in the remain-

Hong Kong's Leading Imports By Commodity - 1992

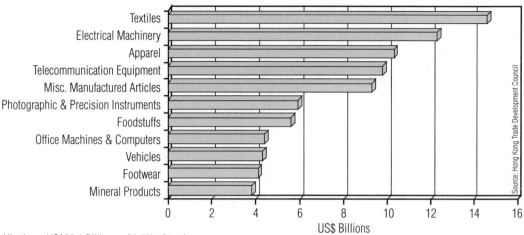

All others: US$38.1 Billion or 31.1% of total
Total 1992 Imports: US$122.5 Billion

ing miscellaneous 43.2 percent represents less than 1.7 percent of the total. Import were up in all categories during the first quarter of 1993.

These grand totals include items brought in for reexport that skew the picture. Traditionally, Hong Kong's imports have consisted of roughly 40 percent raw and intermediate materials used in its manufacturing industry, 35 percent consumer goods for the domestic market, 15 percent capital goods, 6 percent foodstuffs, and 2 percent fuels, an important category that does not make it out of the miscellaneous group when reexports are allowed to dominate the accounts.

TRADING PARTNERS

Export Partners

Hong Kong's reexport role, which is played out primarily with China, tends to blur the picture of its export and import trade relationships. In 1992 the largest share of Hong Kong's exports went to China, which received 29.6 percent. The United States was second with 23 percent, followed by Germany (5.3 percent), Japan (5.2 percent), the United Kingdom (3.6 percent), Taiwan (3.5 percent), Singapore (2.6 percent), Canada (1.7 percent), the Netherlands (1.6 percent), and South Korea (1.6 percent). Together, these seven countries received 77.7 percent of Hong Kong's export trade. Each of its with remaining export partners accounted for 1.5 percent or less of its total exports.

If reexports are excluded, Hong Kong's domestic exports show a definite trend. Between 1989 and the first quarter of 1993 the share of exports destined for Asia—primarily China—rose from 34.9 percent to 49.2 percent, while the share headed for North America—

primarily the United States—fell from 35 percent to 26 percent, and Europe's share declined from 23.8 percent to 19.4 percent. During this period, these three regions accounted for between 93.7 percent and 94.9 percent of Hong Kong's total export trade, which suggests that, despite Hong Kong's stated desire to diversify its products and partners, it has continued to market to essentially the same customers.

Import Partners

In 1992 Hong Kong's major import trade partners were China (37.1 percent), Japan (17.4 percent), Taiwan (9.1 percent), the United States (7.4 percent), South Korea (4.6 percent), Singapore (4.1 percent), Germany (2.3 percent), the United Kingdom (2 percent), and Italy (1.6 percent). Together, these countries accounted for 85.6 percent of Hong Kong's imports. The remaining 14.4 percent came from countries that each accounted for less than 1.5 percent of Hong Kong's total imports.

During the first quarter of 1993 Hong Kong bought slightly less from China and Taiwan and somewhat more from Singapore and the Western European countries than it had in the preceding year, but the same nine countries still accounted for 84.7 percent of total imports, and the short-term changes are not significant. Hong Kong's purchasing patterns have remained relatively stable since the late 1980s.

FOREIGN PARTICIPATION IN THE ECONOMY

Hong Kong's development has been built on a foundation of foreign trade and international investment. The colony has tried to make itself as user-friendly as possible to foreign investors and businesspeople without catering to any particular segment or favoring either domestic or overseas interests. Hong Kong's policy has been to make the business climate as attractive as possible by offering low taxes, a minimum of rules and restrictions, good services and infrastructure, a solid legal framework, and political and social stability—in hopes of capitalizing on its strategic location. The government does not protect its domestic firms or industries, nor does it offer incentives to outsiders. Hong Kong's Industry Department has created a One-Stop Unit, with offices both in Hong Kong and in several overseas locations, to link the 27 separate departments that have jurisdiction over business matters and provide potential investors with information.

Restrictions on Foreign Investment

Only two areas are not open to direct, unrestricted foreign ownership at the present time: the media and utilities. The government is currently considering schemes to open up areas, such as power and water utilities, communications, and transportation, that are now dominated by firms operating with government monopoly franchises. It has even toyed with the idea of privatizing many of the remaining public works.

Foreign investment requires no official approval. However, each company must register its Hong Kong interests with the appropriate government agencies. There are no specific organizational or structural requirements for foreign firms, although firms must comply with Hong Kong law, which generally follows British common law. There are no local ownership, personnel, or local content requirements, and no controls on foreign exchange or repatriation of funds. The only capital requirements are for financial institutions that require licenses to operate.

Hong Kong is a free port, and it generally does not levy tariffs or duties on imports or exports, although it does require import licenses and sets import quotas for certain items, and it levies excise taxes on others. Rice imports are controlled by quota, and licenses are required for imports of commodities that have been designated as strategic, such as computers, peripherals, integrated circuits, disk drives, arms and ammunition, meat, radioactive substances, pharmaceuticals, and pesticides, and of certain products from South Africa, although this last item is liable to change now that South Africa is regaining its international status.

Excise taxes are due on imports of alcoholic beverages, tobacco, soft drinks, cosmetics, methyl alcohol, and some hydrocarbon products. To discourage automobile usage in the crowded colony, Hong Kong slaps a hefty duty on imported vehicles. Hong Kong is particularly careful with the licensing of imports and exports of textiles and garments, because it is subject to strict quotas in importing countries that constrain production in Hong Kong of its most important exports.

Size and Nature of Foreign Participation

The scope of direct foreign investment in Hong Kong is unknown because the colony has no approval process. Because foreign investors do not need to establish eligibility for incentives or repatriation of funds, the government does not keep records on them. In 1988 cumulative direct foreign investment was estimated at US$3.4 billion, with the United States providing 34 percent of the total, Japan 26.6 percent, China 11.3 percent, and the United Kingdom 9 percent. No single country accounted for more than 3.5 percent of the remaining 19.1 percent. In 1988 there were 680 fully or partially owned and acknowledged foreign firms; 605 were manufacturing firms, which together employed 12 percent of the industrial work force. New foreign investment in industry was US$457 million in 1989, dwindling to US$154.1 million in 1990, as cost factors caused Hong Kong to move manufacturing capacity to China and political uncertainty further stemmed the tide.

By 1992 cumulative foreign investment had grown to an estimated US$60 billion, a staggering 1,665 percent increase during just five years. While the statistics are not very reliable, the trend is clear. The main investors are: China, which accounted for roughly US$20 billion or 33 percent of the total; Japan, with US$11.2 billion, or 18.7 percent; and the United States with US$7.1 billion, or 11.8 percent. In 1992 some 15 percent of the work force was estimated to be employed by foreign firms. However, 75 percent of the foreign investments were concentrated in the service sector, primarily trade and finance, and only 25 percent was in the traditional manufacturing sector.

A variety of national, provincial, local, and private Chinese entities have poured funds into Hong Kong, usually into its real estate or financial markets. The Bank of China built its distinctive, 70-story Hong Kong headquarters building, and Chinese municipalities have become major investors in offices and other structures. In 1991 China was the source of perhaps the majority of the estimated US$1.5 billion in venture capital money available in Hong Kong, and the colony has also become a magnet for private capital fleeing from China.

Hong Kong's outward foreign investment returns the favor by focusing on China: some 69 percent of the cumulative foreign investment in China is estimated to have come through Hong Kong and, to a lesser extent, Macao. This figure is artificially high because most of the investment funds coming from Hong Kong originated elsewhere, with investors using Hong Kong middlemen to facilitate their move into China.

GOVERNMENT ECONOMIC DEVELOPMENT STRATEGY

In contrast to virtually every other government in Asia and the world, Hong Kong's government has no formal development strategy. Its policy now, as in the past, is to keep hands off and rely on the generally favorable business climate that it maintains to attract investment.

Hong Kong's government has instituted a series of massive public works projects designed to position the colony as the state-of-the-art business center in Asia by 1997, when the colony is scheduled to pass to Chinese control. These projects include the construction of a new airport on landfill on Lantau island; substantial port projects, including additional capacity, improvements, and upgrades, especially in the Western Harbor area; construction of a fourth tunnel linking Hong Kong and Kowloon; and construction of a new highway between Hong Kong and Guangzhou, as well as various other infrastructure improvements. For the first time in Hong Kong's postwar history, the government is relying on deficit financing to support these projects. As of early 1994 the total cost of the improvements was estimated at US$20.5 billion, and this is only a base estimate before final bids and inevitable overruns.

POLITICAL OUTLOOK FOR THE ECONOMY

The crucial question for Hong Kong is the transfer of sovereignty from Britain to China in mid-1997. The two governments negotiated an agreement—the Sino-British Joint Declaration—in 1984, which calls for Hong Kong to become a quasi-independent Special Administrative Region of China, retaining its special character and separate administrative and economic structure for 50 years. This broad agreement left many specific issues and procedures to be negotiated between 1984 and 1997. The inevtable result has been uncertainty and considerable jockeying for position between the British and Chinese.

During the popular unrest in China in 1989, many factions in Hong Kong were outspoken in their support for the dissidents, and the harsh Chinese government crackdown led to considerable concern for the future of the colony. In 1990 in an attempt to reassure the local and international community of the position of the colony before 1997, the Chinese announced the Basic Law. This document asserts that the existing legal system; the rights of private property and ownership; existing financial arrangements; rights to existing leases; and the rights of free travel, association, employment, assembly, and free speech must all be maintained as defined by Britain. It reiterates Hong Kong's status as a free port and a separate international entity, and it calls both for a more direct way of electing Hong Kong's Legislative Council and for giving that body greater powers.

China has taken the position that this document goes far beyond the previously negotiated provisions, especially in matters of the democratic election of representatives, which Hong Kong never had under British rule. The Chinese see British actions as challenging their sovereignty and altering the agreement, and they have promised to disband the Legislative Council if they decide that it does not conform to their ideas of appropriateness. They also have threatened to nullify any contracts to which they are not explicitly a party, which has cast a pall over business activity. And although the Chinese had given approval to most of the proposed public works projects, they have subsequently raised issues over the deficit financing to be used to fund them. This increases the likelihood that the projects will be scaled back, delayed, or both.

All this leaves the British in a damage control mode, attempting to placate the belligerent Chinese while still working to get as many guarantees as they can for the future operation of Hong Kong. Negotiations have not broken down, although specific sessions have been cancelled or ended abruptly. And the talks have become less diplomatic and increasingly petulant in tone.

Despite the brouhaha, emigration has slowed, and business continues to boom, with most international observers and locals taking the position that China will eventually come around, because, while it is important for China to save face by being seen as firmly in control, it cannot afford to lose Hong Kong as Hong Kong is currently constituted. The Chinese speak of their sovereign rights over Hong Kong, but people in Hong Kong speak just as confidently about their pending annexation of China.

HONG KONG'S INTERNATIONAL ROLE

As a British crown colony, Hong Kong has no independent diplomatic relations, a situation that will continue after sovereignty is transferred to China in 1997. It does not have independent representation before any world bodies, such as the United Nations or the Association of Southeast Asian Nations (ASEAN), although the Joint Declaration gives it the right to associate or observer status in international trade bodies. Hong Kong is already a special contracting party to the General Agreement on Tariffs and Trade (GATT) and the Multi-Fiber Arrangement (MFA) governing trade in textiles. Because Hong Kong is a world trade and financial center, many entities located in it have a great variety of ties with international private and public entities, but these ties lack any official framework.

Current Issues

TIME FOR A CHANGE: THE TRANSITION FROM BRITISH TO CHINESE RULE

In the first major 19th century incursion by Western powers into China, Great Britain in 1842 forced the cession of Hong Kong under the terms of the Treaty of Nanjing following China's humiliating defeat in the First Opium War. This was followed up by the outright cession of Kowloon in 1856, confirmed by treaty after the Second Opium War ended in 1860. In 1898 China grudgingly leased the New Territories to the British for 99 years, the result of a renewed push by foreign interests for concessions in China, a push that led to the Boxer Rebellion in 1900, the last attempt by the Chinese under the old imperial system to expel foreigners. This lease, dictated according to European terms under European threats of force, rounded out Britain's possessions in Hong Kong.

Now 99 years are almost up, 1997 is just around the corner, and Hong Kong is scheduled to revert to mainland Chinese sovereignty and control. The Chinese and British governments have agreed in principle on the terms by which the British are to return Hong Kong to the Chinese, and both sides are actively—and sometimes not so actively—hammering out the details of this transition. China has already begun maneuvering to gain effective control on its own terms before midnight on June 30, 1997. Meanwhile, the UK government is doing its best to push programs that will present the Chinese with a fait accompli, including a functioning infrastructure, business structure, and democratic political structure, that will make it more difficult for them to dismantle the British system after the sun finally sets on this part of the British empire.

Integration or Hegemony?

The looming question is how can a booming, cosmopolitan, free-thinking, laissez-faire open city-state be integrated with a rapidly growing and economically unstable, ideologically opposed and control-oriented, gigantic nation in a way that works for both of them? Hong Kong is a dynamic city that welcomes and thrives on international trade, commerce, and contact. China was, until recently, a closed, ponderous, and stagnant nation, that repelled outside influences and all too often attracted international censure for its heavy-handed methods of control. How can China realistically lead Hong Kong when Hong Kong is the paradigm of openness and capitalistic economic success in Asia? And more importantly for both China and Hong Kong, how can China do so while keeping Hong Kong viable as its lifeline to the outside and maintaining the level of Hong Kong's much-needed contribution to China's economic health?

The Rules

In October 1982 Chinese and British representatives began their talks about Hong Kong's post-1997 future. After two years of negotiations, both sides agreed to a "Joint Declaration," signed in December 1984, which outlined the terms under which Hong Kong would return to Chinese control. The agreement stipulated that Hong Kong will become a Special Administrative Region (SAR) of the People's Republic of China (PRC) in 1997; will retain its current political, economic, and judicial systems; will continue to serve as a free port and independent customs zone, with a basically autonomous financial system; and will continue to participate as a quasi-independent entity in international agreements and organizations for a period of 50 years before coming under the total administrative control of China as a regular administrative unit subject to the standard laws of the PRC prevailing at that time. A Joint Liaison Group was established to work out the details of the general agreement and oversee their implementation during the transition.

In 1990 the Chinese presented the "Basic Law" which is intended to serve as Hong Kong's miniconstitution, establishing the political and legal structure after 1997. In this document, China committed to maintain a hands-off policy in running Hong Kong as an SAR. Basically the UK agreed to surrender Hong Kong without a fight, while China agreed not to interfere unduly with Hong Kong's capitalist system.

A Bumpy Road to Transition

Having surprised the world community by agreeing to cede Hong Kong to China, the British government appeared rather complacent and unconcerned about the matter. In fact, Britain considered various ways and means of hanging onto Hong Kong, but was unable to figure out any feasible strategy for doing so. China was not going to renew any leases or other such agreements. Although Britain could insist on its rights to Hong Kong and Kowloon under right of cession, even if it was successful, it would be left with a tiny enclave that couldn't be defended or supported (the new international boundary would even cut Britain off from Hong Kong's downtown airport). Discretion being the better part of valor, Britain decided to enter into negotiations to magnanimously return the whole packet to the Chinese.

However, against the backdrop of China's heavy-handed behavior in the face of popular protests in 1989, the once smooth road of transition began to exhibit its share of bumps and potholes. This situation has heightened since the appointment of Chris Patten as governor in 1992. Slated to serve as Britain's last colonial administrator, Patten arrived with a brief to push for additional guarantees that the status quo would be maintained after the Union Jack comes down at Government House for the last time. Under the British system, the governor is appointed by and owes allegiance and accountability only to the prime minister and ultimately parliament. Although this individual is given guidelines by the central authorities, he or she has wide discretionary powers to implement and alter policy. In this day of instant global communications, it is unlikely that Chris Patten speaks only for himself rather than for the British government, but he is still the one doing the speaking, and as such has drawn the fire of the Chinese as well as those who are made nervous by his rhetoric.

The Chinese government has also been throwing its share of political punches and bombshells. For instance, China became concerned that keeping in place Hong Kong civil servants steeped in the British system would result in the inability of the PRC to exercise effective control during and most particularly following the transfer. Although China had promised that it would allow Hong Kong natives to lead post-1997 Hong Kong, it changed its mind, blandly stating its intention to replace fully half of the existing civil service with its own appointees from the mainland. The implication is that such transplants will be there to give the PRC the upper hand and to monitor political orthodoxy.

Caught in the Middle

Hong Kong is like a child caught between two sets of parents. Although deeply indebted to its adoptive parents who for the last 150 years trained and guided it and made it for better or worse what it is today—a highly successful economic powerhouse—Hong Kong has undeniable ties to its natural parents who will soon regain legal custody. In the interim Hong Kong has matured as a separate entity with traits of both parental entities, but with a separate identity. It is a cocky adolescent, an international financial hub centered in the fastest-growing region of the world, ready to take on that world as an equal on its own terms.

Yet Hong Kong has not been treated like an adult by either of the putative parents. During its years of rule, local representation and self-determination were low priority items on the list of British administrators, who looked to London rather than to Hong Kong for instructions and legitimacy. The much disputed Legislative Council, or LEGCO, is a relatively recent invention and has only been authorized by the British to deal with the most mundane matters of local governance. It has now become a bone of contention between Britain and China as the British have sought to expand its representative nature and legislative powers prior to 1997 and in the face of Chinese resistance. And in a recent incident regarding the Final Court of Appeal, London and Beijing haggled over the structure of Hong Kong's future judicial branch while omitting any consultation with the locals, including Hong Kong's highly developed legal community, which knows more about practical application of the disparate Chinese and British legal codes than either party.

Hong Kong would like to maintain good relations with both its natural and adoptive parents. However, what it would really like to do is set its own course, something that neither side seems to be interested in allowing in the least. And Hong Kong, all too aware of China's past abusive tendencies, fears provoking the ire of its soon-to-be direct sovereign while at the same time wanting to be able to stand up for itself.

Fleeing for their Lives, or just for their Bank Accounts?

These fears have led many in Hong Kong to seek refuge abroad. During the heady days of the protests in China in 1989, Hong Kong citizens turned out in record numbers in supporting demonstrations, shocking the British, the Chinese, and to some extent themselves with their temerity. After the Chinese sent in the tanks, Hong Kong's sobered residents queued up for days at the British and other Western consulates attempting to obtain visas.

Between 1982 and 1992 an estimated 425,000 Hong Kong residents (about 7.5 percent of the population) emigrated to other countries. This flow—the *brain drain*, so-called because most emigrants consisted of the educated, the skilled, and the affluent—was a modest 20,000 a year during the early 1980s, swelling to 70,000 in 1991, and easing to around 60,000 in 1992. They have left Hong Kong to start new lives in Vancouver, Sydney, Los Angeles, and Wellington as well as other cities throughout the world. A surprising number have ended up in Ho Chi Minh City, although many of these represent involuntarily repatriated boat people.

Few have ended up in London. Britain has kept the floodgates closed by ruling that despite Hong Kong's status as a British crown colony and dependency, citizenship there does not entitle anyone to a UK passport. Britain has refused to grant citizenship to all but a handful of Hong Kong residents, mostly those of European extraction. This policy is at least partially cynically designed to stem the expected tide of potential refugees that could be a financial and social burden on England. It is also partially designed to placate the Chinese who realize that Hong Kong's people—and their moveable wealth—are one of its primary assets and have warned Britain not to allow wholesale repatriation of those human and financial assets. Now that China has said that it doesn't want a lot of Hong Kong's civil servants because it wants to replace them with its own people, observers expect a renewal of the fight over this issue, with various constituencies in both the UK and Hong Kong clamoring for Britain to offer a safe haven for these loyal, displaced persons.

As they move themselves and their families to safer ground, these Hong Kong economic refugees also move money, skills, and business ventures, creating a huge flight of intellectual and financial capital. In fact, many of the places offering a haven to such Hong Kong refugees have done so explicitly in return for substantial sums to be invested in the host country as a condition of granting them their papers. Those who remain in Hong Kong are skittish, with the ones at the bottom of the socioeconomic ladder having little choice in the matter and those at the top having mostly already secured their escape routes. Those in the middle are faced with an anguished decision of whether to risk all and go or risk all and stay. Despite all this turmoil, there is evidence that the rate of emigration is slowing substantially.

There is also a large contingent who, having obtained papers elsewhere, are choosing to return to Hong Kong, wait and see how things turn out, and make some more money in the interim. At least some Hong Kong businesspeople refer to such individuals as "passport" or "documentary" expatriates to distinguish them from the more usual "cultural" or "ethnic" expatriates from the West.

Some in Hong Kong have made the choice to bow to the inevitable and align themselves not with the powers-that-be but with the powers-to-be. Some are more ideologically attuned to Beijing than to the outgoing regime; some are simply opportunistic, blatantly hoping to advance themselves by catering to the new regime; and some are patriots or pragmatists, hoping to be able to work within the system, cooperating with the PRC for mutual benefit. This situation is creating additional tensions and areas of competition and distrust within the body politic in Hong Kong. For instance, there are now three separate labor confederations operating within Hong Kong: the pro-Beijing Hong Kong Federation of Trade Unions (FTU), the pro-Taiwan Hong Kong and Kowloon Trade Union Council (TUC), and the independent Hong Kong Confederation of Trade Unions (CFU).

PATTEN'S PUSH
FOR DEMOCRACY

As the time before the transfer grows shorter, tensions between the British and Chinese are rising. Christopher Patten emerged on the scene as Hong Kong's abrasive new governor with more on his mind than kowtowing to the Chinese leadership. Patten's instructions are to see that Britain's ambitious infrastructure program gets put into place along with a considerable dollop of democracy that ensures greater freedoms for Hong Kong by 1997, as part of Britain's legacy to its former colonial possession. Yet some in Hong Kong believe Patten's moves toward democracy are doing more harm than good by stirring up China and endangering Hong Kong's working relationship with its future sovereign.

Patten's Proposals

In October 1992 Patten, without any prior consultation with the Chinese, unilaterally announced a series of reform proposals. These proposals were designed to fortify the power and influence of Hong Kong's partly elected Legislative Council (LEGCO), endowing it with a new and unaccustomed authority that would allow it to act as a check and balance on the power of the dominant executive branch. According to the schedule given LEGCO's powers are expected to grow, especially after 1997. The scheme was designed to go into effect upon LEGCO's ratification of the proposals affecting itself without further approval being required from any other authority. However, the majority of LEGCO's members have been unenthusiastic because they fear having to choose one sovereign over another, especially as the one offering the favors is scheduled to fade away shortly after getting them to go on record. On March 12, 1993, ignoring the virulent protests and threats from the Chinese government, Patten officially published his proposals, which would, among other measures, increase the number of democratically elected seats with respect to the number of appointive seats in LEGCO.

China's Response

As might have been expected, China's leaders reacted with outrage. Hardliners fiercely opposed Patten's reforms and accused him of violating the agreement and purposely trying to defy China. The leaders argued that the British had broken the terms and intent of the Joint Declaration and the Basic Law. China's chief official dealing with Hong Kong threatened to establish a shadow government to serve as an alternative authority for Hong Kong. This "government" would be in position to replace the existing administration after 1997, thereby undermining any reforms that Patten would gain from an invigorated and empowered LEGCO. China also shocked the business community by threatening to declare null and void upon reversion all contracts negotiated with and under the auspices of the British Hong Kong government, including those in the private sector, unless they were also simultaneously approved by PRC authorities.

As part of its pressure game, China also rejected a government plan to add capacity to Hong Kong's container port and threatened to cancel its approval for the building of the new airport. In fact, Chinese protests over the anticipated overhang of long term debt that they foresee ensuing from the massive construction projects caused the Hong Kong government to release its figures on foreign reserves, which had been considered an official secret, in an attempt to placate the Chinese by showing them that the outlays could be supported. Needless to say, the climate has soured and negotiations with the British over transition particulars have deteriorated.

No Tea Party for the British

Clearly, retorted the British government, China aimed to challenge the agreed upon interim authority of the existing Hong Kong government and, in particular, of LEGCO, whose roots they were suddenly able to trace back to the Magna Carta. Yet the British were playing a subtle game. On the one hand, they knew that the Chinese would react, and according to many outside observers, with reason as the British tried to unilaterally alter the terms of the agreement. They were also counting that the Chinese would not want to fly into a snit and hamstring the agreement so as to leave Hong Kong as damaged goods. Familiar with China's internal maneuverings, they questioned what really was happening beneath the surface of the outraged unified front exhibited by the Chinese. Their sense of internal unrest apparently proved to be right in the late spring of 1993 when responsibility for negotiations over Hong Kong were taken out of the hands of hardliner Li Peng and transferred to the more liberal Zhu Rongji who announced the resumption of talks.

Not even all leaders of the British government agree with the more activist tack. Former chief secretary of Hong Kong and one-time acting governor Sir David Akers-Jones has publicly criticized Patten's proposals. He believes the new proposals do a disservice to Hong Kong and that the authorities should leave well enough alone instead of seeking to expand the charter of LEGCO. Akers-Jones has argued that it would be better to shore up the Executive Council as an effective arm of government rather than waste time on a legislative branch that has had no real role under the British in Hong Kong and, based on the trivial rubber stamp role the analogous body plays in China, the National People's Congress, has virtually no chance of exercising any real power within the new regime.

The View From Hong Kong

Hong Kong natives are caught between a rock and a hard place, often compelled to take sides with one sovereign against another. Some Hong Kong natives have argued that the British are setting the stage for increased oversight by China after 1997 as a result of Patten's pushy proposals which are a blatant challenge to PRC authority. They believe that any lasting benefits of a lightly augmented democracy will be more than offset by the cost in mistrust that would be created, not only toward the British government in the near term, but also toward Hong Kong civil servants who are trying to hang on and be in a position to ameliorate the administration of regulations in the post-1997 era, as well as to Hong Kong as a whole.

Cynics have argued that, under a facade of establishing autonomy for the people of Hong Kong, the British are merely staging a rather self-serving grand finale before leaving the stage. Rather than focus on the short-run changes in largely cosmetic electoral procedures designed to make them look more like democrats than they are, argue the critics, the British should focus their efforts on working behind the scenes to enhance guarantees for Hong Kong's autonomy.

Hong Kong businesspeople have also voiced concern, fearing the effects of the proposals on the Hong Kong stock market and future business deals. Certainly almost everyone in Hong Kong would like to ensure future democracy and even more important future freedom to pursue deals, but the means to attain it and the degree to which it is necessary are debatable. After all, Hong Kong got along without democracy for years under the British and did just fine. Business leaders don't want to cause a political storm that will encourage the Chinese government to send in an administrative SWAT team-or tanks-to fix the changes the British have made.

However, the dominant response to all this posturing has been a yawn. Most locals have become inured to the continuous noise generated by the issue and figure that most of it is just rhetoric. On a more pragmatically philosophical level, they see the crunch as still being some distance off. China could liberalize its own government and position before 1997. It could also crack down and ease up, perhaps more than once. In the meantime, there is money to be made, and most people in Hong Kong won't worry inordinately unless something occurs to interfere with that.

Keeping Their Fingers Crossed

After all the bluster, China's leaders began to budge from their adamant refusal even to discuss this or any other issue while the offending proposals remained on the table. In late spring 1993 they agreed to return to the bargaining table. On the British side, Patten agreed to tone down his initial proposal somewhat in an attempt to make it less offensive. However, after six months of fruitless negotiations marked by intransigence on both sides, talks broke off in late 1993, with the Chinese summarily announcing that they intended to disband LEGCO and impose their own local governmental structure following their assumption of power in 1997. China, which had unilaterally set up a committee headed by prominent pro-Chinese Hong Kong businesspeople to draw up recommendations for post-1997 regulations, announced that the committee would become active without British participation.

Observers, both insiders and outsiders, hope that economics will win out over egos as both sides realize that intransigence is neither a viable long term option nor a useful negotiating position. Britain would lose face if it allowed Hong Kong to be effectively dismantled and its people left to the mercy of an incensed autocratic China due to Britain's insistence on tweaking China's nose and unworkable programs. China, now the biggest investor in Hong Kong, would be the most affected by a tumultuous changeover in Hong Kong. With its own economy still unstable, China realizes that to heighten international anxiety over Hong Kong's future will hurt it in the long run more than a loss of face over giving in to the British.

There are hopeful signs. In mid-February 1994 there were indications that progress was being made on subsidiary issues, such as aspects of infrastructure debt financing and military hand-offs. Both sides seems to be nervous about pushing the issue of constitutional reforms and willing to push it to the side at least for now. Nevertheless, the end of the story has yet to be written.

MOST FAVORED NATION STATUS FOR CHINA—THE PERSPECTIVE FROM HONG KONG

The United States accords Most Favored Nation (MFN) status to virtually all of its trading partners throughout the world in an effort to promote world trade through minimizing restrictions and the levying of comparatively low duty rates. In fact, MFN status is the norm and the US withholds MFN from only about 10 nations worldwide, nations such as Iraq, Iran, Vietnam, and North Korea that it has singled out as essentially renegade nations worthy of punitive exclusion. The US has granted MFN status to both Hong Kong and China, but with one major difference. Hong Kong's status is secured indefinitely, whereas China's MFN status must be renewed by the president every June. And if this situation continues long enough, Hong Kong could be tarred with the broader China brush. And because the economies of China and Hong Kong are inextricably linked, any change in China's MFN status would have almost as shattering an effect on Hong Kong's economy as it would on China's. In fact, some argue that the effect would be even greater because China, with a larger economy would have more options both internal and external, whereas Hong Kong's options would be more severely limited.

Every spring the US Congress debates the renewal of China's MFN status, and a steady stream of lobbyists make their way to Capitol Hill with their lists of reasons why MFN status should or should not be renewed. In 1993, as President Clinton considered his response to the congressional debate, he had one special visitor from neither the United States nor China, but from a place no less affected by China's pending MFN status—Hong Kong. The Right Honourable Christopher Patten (as Hong Kong's governor is formally known) made a special trip to the White House to convince Clinton just how important China's MFN renewal was . . . to Hong Kong.

The Hong Kong Government's Arguments

MFN—Not a Political Lever As the memories of Tiananmen Square linger, many have strongly urged that the US must revoke or attach conditions to China's MFN status until China makes significant improvements in a number of areas, particularly human rights. Patten's argument to US legislative and executive leaders was not that human rights, political pluralization, religious freedom, forced convict labor, and the like are unimportant issues; indeed, he is an outspoken advocate of extending democracy in Hong Kong and elsewhere. However, he argued, these issues are political, not economic, and should be dealt with by other, more specific mechanisms, such as human rights treaties, lest the parties allow things to get out of hand. Patten believes that US concerns about China should be resolved through negotiated policy changes and bilateral agreements with China not through the bludgeoning of backdoor economic sanctions.

Punitive economic measures such as revocation of MFN status would disproportionately hurt the younger, more progressive, technocratic leaders who are in the forefront of China's reform efforts, while leaving the autocratic hardliners relatively unscathed, and perhaps even reinforced. And in all likelihood, the ultimate burden would fall on China's growing number of private enterprises—the key players in extending China's open market.

MFN—In the US's Interest China's market offers incredible opportunities for sales of US goods and services. In 1992 the US exported nearly US$7.5 billion worth of goods to China. Combined with US exports to Hong Kong, the total export figure exceeds US$16.5 billion. In order to preserve and further develop this potential relationship, where the US has an edge over many other countries, the US needs to make the maintenance of good economic relations with China a priority. And to cut off this flow, even for altruistic reasons, would lessen US influence over the situation in China.

Beijing has no qualms about retaliating against a US trade blow. In fact, Beijing has already lined up potential European replacements for US firms currently doing business in China should the US revoke China's MFN status. This is part bluster, but also partly true that a trade war would likely hurt the US more than it would hurt China. In addition to the harm that would be done to US firms operating in China, the pain would be felt by firms in the US exporting to China (particularly in the agricultural and equipment industries), US workers (who could end up in unemployment lines), and US consumers (who would experience major price hikes on many low-cost goods produced in the dominant Chinese market).

Diplomacy not Dogmatism The US is finding it more critical to maintain a positive diplomatic relationship with China as China becomes an increasingly important player on the world scene. China's unaccustomed support or at the very least neutrality in forums such as the United Nations has provided essential leverage in recent crises such as the Persian Gulf war, and, currently, in resolving conflicts as wide-ranging as those in Cambodia, Bosnia, Somalia, and North Korea. China is a political heavyweight, a nuclear and conventional military power to be reckoned with, and the world's fastest-growing major economic power. It also just happens to have the world's largest market. In sum China has become a nation that the US can no longer pressure unduly with impunity, and the US must pick its battles extremely carefully.

The Effects on Hong Kong

On his visit to Washington, Governor Patten noted all these arguments against revoking or placing conditions on China's MFN status. He also made a specific plea based on the effect unfavorable changes would have on Hong Kong. The message was blunt: should the US ignite a trade war by the revoking China's MFN status, Hong Kong's economy would be devastated. But surely such a booming economy wouldn't be that profoundly affected? Or would it?

Economic Interdependency Consider Hong Kong's growing economic interdependency with southern China, the region that would be most severely affected should MFN status be revoked. Hong Kong has experienced a steady decline in its domestic manufacturing base as many of its labor-intensive industries take advantage of southern China's cheaper labor and land costs. Hong Kong companies

provide employment to at least three million residents in Guangdong Province alone, and although most of these jobs are newly created, many represent transfers of Hong Kong jobs. Through these companies, Hong Kong is able to maintain price-competitive products on the international market. If these companies suffer, Hong Kong will suffer.

Two Losses Don't Equal a Profit Hong Kong is the largest investor in China. Approximately 40 percent of China's external trade is carried out through Hong Kong, and two-way trade between the two reached US$60 billion in 1991. Hong Kong companies are the principal investors in South China's electronics industry. Some observers estimate that revoking or limiting MFN status would result in losses for Hong Kong of up to US$21 billion of its trade, US$2.9 billion in income, and 69,000 jobs. Hong Kong's current growth rate could be seriously damaged, and no sector in its economy would be left untouched.

Governor Patten asserts "If China loses her MFN status, Hong Kong suffers . . . MFN is of very, very great importance to the people of Hong Kong, to the well-being of Hong Kong, to the future prosperity and stability of Hong Kong."

Hong Kong Founded on Free Trade

Hong Kong, an economic miracle of East Asia and a fighting dragon with a great deal of spunk, is a leading advocate of free trade. For Hong Kong, which makes its living off its booming trading relationships with other nations around the world, free trade is the lifeblood of its continued economic success. The Hong Kong government, eager to do away with any form of trade restriction, has argued that MFN status, especially as it has been constituted and come to be used, is a fundamental mechanism to facilitate

global economic growth, not a special privilege to be given only to those that mirror the interests and viewpoints of the US. In 1993, at least partially due to the eloquence and arguments advanced during Governor Patten's special visit, Hong Kong was able to breathe easier for another year and enjoy the benefits of free trade and a prospering economic relationship with China. However, observers worry that 1994 may be another story.

HONG KONG AND SOUTH CHINA—THE SUM THAT'S GREATER THAN ITS PARTS

Given all the current squabbling between the Chinese and British governments over the future state of Hong Kong, those interested in assessing what is really going on should look to the economic numbers, which reveal more than all the political rhetoric can serve to obscure. The economies of Hong Kong and China are deeply enmeshed with each other and probably well beyond the ability of any mere government edict or interference to disentangle. Since 1978 China has made strides toward economic reform and dramatically increased economic links with Hong Kong, resulting in a profound impact on the growth and development of the economy of both Hong Kong and on that of the fastest growing section—southeast China—of the fastest growing economy in the world.

"You Scratch My Back and I'll Scratch Yours"

Trade In 1978, the year China began the opening of its economy, its share of Hong Kong's total trade was 9.3 percent. By 1991 its share had grown to 32.4 percent (US$64.2 billion). In 1985 China overtook the US to become Hong Kong's largest trading partner. In 1987 Hong Kong overtook Japan to become China's largest trading partner.

Markets Hong Kong is China's largest export market, receiving 44.7 percent (US$32.1 billion) of China's total exports in 1991, particularly in items such as textile yarn, clothing, telecommunications equipment, electrical machinery, and footwear. Since 1982 China has served as Hong Kong's largest supplier of raw materials and semimanufactures, consumer goods, and foodstuffs. Likewise, Hong Kong is the principal supplier to China, and China is Hong Kong's second largest export market following the US.

A Reexport Market In addition to an extensive export market and trade relationship, the reexport market figures also highlight the interdependence of Hong Kong and China. Between 1978 and 1991 goods of Chinese origin reexported through Hong Kong to other parts of the world increased eighty-seven times from $US460 million to US$40.5 billion. Reexports to China through Hong Kong rose by nearly 71,800 percent from US$27.4 million to US$19.7 billion during the same period.

The Greater Hong Kong/ Guangdong Region (HKG)

Hong Kong businesspeople refer to Guangdong (the southeastern Chinese Province bordering Hong Kong) as their "economic hinterland." With its improved investment environment, infrastructure, and proximity to Hong Kong, Guangdong has emerged as a processing base for Hong Kong's manufacturers. Altogether, around three million workers—more than four times the number of Hong Kong's manufacturing workforce—are now employed in Guangdong by or on behalf of Hong Kong firms. Of the foreign-funded enterprises in Guangdong, an estimated 80 percent receive Hong Kong investment.

A Pair with a Punch Some call Guangdong the up and coming fifth Asian little dragon, following on the heels of the other four, Taiwan, Singapore, South Korea, and Hong Kong. Together, the economies of Hong Kong and Guangdong (which includes three of China's Special Economic Zones), deliver a powerful economic one-two punch. With Hong Kong's "brains" in financing, trading, and general management, and Guangdong's "brawn" in labor, land, and resources, they are a dynamic economic duo to be envied. Some observers already speak of the HKG region as China's outside unit, serving as the focus for external trade, finance, and business, while they expect Shanghai to develop into its inside unit, serving as the focus for its national, internal business economy.

Opportunities

OPPORTUNITIES FOR IMPORTING FROM HONG KONG

Hong Kong is well known for its policy of encouraging trade and foreign investment. Firms and individuals from many countries send their products and services to Hong Kong, and Hong Kong exports to all regions of the world.

Of particular importance to Hong Kong's continued export development is its role as a major transit and shipping point for goods partially manufactured or consumed in China (especially the southern coastal region). Goods made in China, which officially enter Hong Kong's customs territory for processing and shipment onward to other countries, are classified as reexports. These reexports comprise more than 75 percent of Hong Kong's total exports. Leading exports and reexports include textiles and clothing, electronics and telecommunications equipment, timepieces, and machinery products. The following section describes Hong Kong's most important industries and the opportunities they offer to foreign importers seeking sources in Hong Kong.

OPPORTUNITIES TABLE OF CONTENTS

Opportunities for Importing from
   Hong Kong 29
Opportunities for Exporting to
   Hong Kong 33
Opportunities for Growth 37
Public Procurement Opportunities .. 39
Public Procurement Process 42
Special Trade Zones 43

APPAREL AND TEXTILES

Apparel and textiles are Hong Kong's most important industries, employing more than 40 percent of the manufacturing work force. In recent years, labor shortages and escalating costs have prompted many manufacturers to move their factories to China's nearby Guangdong Province, especially to Shenzhen. Yet Hong Kong still receives many semifinished and finished products, which are processed and stored for eventual export.

Clothing and Accessories

Apparel is the largest manufacturing industry in Hong Kong, accounting for 33 percent of domestic exports. Hong Kong's garment makers have an excellent reputation for quality manufacturing and the ability to consistently meet demanding delivery schedules. The two primary exports are finished garments and ready-made clothing, including coats, jackets, shirts, pants, sportswear, and sweaters. Accessories include briefcases, travel bags, belts, hosiery, and neckties.

Textiles

Although rising wages have begun to erode the competitiveness of Hong Kong's textile industry, manufacturers continue to reach the yearly quotas for exports set by the United States and European countries. The industry remains healthy, but quota restrictions and unilateral protective measures tend to preclude rapid growth in exports.

The textile industry includes spinning, weaving, knitting, bleaching, dyeing, printing, and finishing. Cotton is the primary fiber, though production of synthetic fibers and yarns continues to rise.

Some of the HOT items:
- blouses
- coats and jackets
- cotton fabrics

- fashion accessories
- fur coats
- jeans
- knitted and crocheted fabrics
- knitwear
- leather garments
- textile fabrics
- textile yarns
- woolen and worsted yarns

- electricity distribution equipment
- electrostatic photocopiers
- high-fidelity systems
- liquid crystal displays
- parts and accessories for calculators
- parts and accessories for computers
- quartz crystals
- radios
- semiconductors
- transistors, resistors, and switches

ELECTRONICS

Exports of electronic products are second only to apparel and textiles in terms of total value. Hong Kong's electronics industry comprises more than 1,500 establishments employing more than 60,000 people. Production of electronic goods is growing rapidly, but many electronic assembly plants are relocating to southern China, where labor costs are lower and plant space is more affordable. The finished and semifinished products arrive in Hong Kong for final assembly before being reexported. Such reexports are growing more rapidly than domestic electronic exports. Primary products for export include consumer electronics, electrical machinery, and electronic components. As more assembly plants move to China, local Hong Kong manufacturers are focusing increasingly on higher-end products that make use of more advanced technologies.

Consumer Electronics and Electrical Machinery

The local consumer electronics industry consists mainly of product manufacturing and assembly, with product design taking place in other countries. Electrical machinery and appliances are also an important sector of the electronics industry, accounting for more than 25 percent of total exports. Some of the most important export products are audio systems, digital data processing machines, television sets, photocopying machines, facsimile machines, microcomputers and computer peripherals, and computer-aided design and testing equipment.

Parts and Components

The world market for electronic parts and components is expected to grow at an annual rate of 20 percent for the next few years. In response, Hong Kong manufacturers intend to step up production of computer components and electrical machine parts.

Some of the HOT items:
- cassette players
- digital automatic data processing machines
- digital data processing machines
- electric household appliances
- electrical machinery and parts

TELECOMMUNICATIONS EQUIPMENT AND PARTS

Hong Kong is one of East Asia's leading producers of telecommunications equipment and parts. The healthy growth of the information and electronics industries has spurred rapid expansion in Hong Kong's telecommunications industry. While the Hong Kong government has typically purchased many of the higher-end items, the increased manufacture and assembly of basic parts and equipment offers numerous opportunities for foreign importers.

Some of the HOT items:
- audio and video apparatus
- modems
- radio telecommunications parts and accessories
- telecommunications parts and accessories
- telephones
- television receivers

TIMEPIECES

Timepieces have traditionally been the third-largest export commodity in Hong Kong. Primary output focuses on production of both mechanical and electronic watches and clocks, cases, dials, metal bands, straps, and movements.

Although Switzerland rules the high-end market for timepieces, Hong Kong dominates the low-end export market. However, more and more of these timepieces are reexports orginated in China. LCD watches and electronic clocks are among the fastest-growing reexports.

Manufacturers of timepieces in Hong Kong are now targeting the low end of the high-price range by placing more emphasis on quality, design, and styling. An upgrading of technology is expected as manufacturers seek out more upscale markets.

Some of the HOT items:
- clocks
- watch cases and parts
- watch movements
- watch straps, bands, and bracelets
- wristwatches

TOYS AND GAMES

Hong Kong is one of the world's major toy exporters. The bulk of the industry's production consists of plastic toys and dolls, although electronic toys and games are growing export commodities. To remain competitive on the international market, Hong Kong's toy manufacturers have been subcontracting across the border to China.

Some of the HOT items:
- airplanes
- cars
- dolls
- electronic toys and games
- gimmicks
- miniature utility sets
- robots
- toy guns

PLASTICS AND MISCELLANEOUS MANUFACTURES

Hong Kong is a leading producer and exporter of a diversified range of plastic products. The plastics industry alone accounts for 7 percent of total domestic exports and 9 percent of total industrial employment. This industry serves as a primary link to most local light manufacturing industries.

Because product styles and durability tend to be important determinants of demand among North American and European buyers, Hong Kong manufacturers are beginning to produce higher-quality upmarket items.

Some of the HOT items:
- baby carriages
- cameras
- handbags
- housewares
- optical goods
- primary plastics
- sporting goods
- travel goods

JEWELRY

Jewelry is one of the oldest industries in Hong Kong, and it is also one of its top 10 export commodities. Over the past 30 years, the jewelry industry has had more than 1,500 establishments and more than 16,000 employees. Flexibility in manufacturing and the ability to follow the latest market trends and styles are this industry's key strengths.

Hong Kong's jewelers produce pieces made of precious metals and stones as well as imitation pieces. Crafted items include rings, earrings, necklaces, bracelets, pendants, bangles, brooches, beads, chokers, cufflinks, and tie clips.

Major markets include the United States, Japan, Germany, and the United Kingdom. High quality and reasonable prices are the factors most responsible for continued export growth in Hong Kong's jewelry industry.

Some of the HOT items:
- gem-set jewelry, especially diamonds
- imitation jewelry
- jade jewelry
- pearl and small-stones jewelry
- 24-carat gold jewelry

PRINTED MATERIALS

Hong Kong's printing industry has grown at an average annual rate of 7 percent for the past 15 years. More than 4,000 printing businesses are in operation, 80 percent of which have fewer than 20 employees. Printers and their related service factories form a close working network, which enables the industry to achieve high efficiency and quick delivery to customers.

The three basic sectors in the printing industry are small job printers, medium to large job printers, and pre- and post-press services. Small job printers are primarily engaged in printing small quantities of relatively simple items: business cards, greeting cards, pamphlets, and office stationery. Medium to large job printers usually specialize in printing books, journals, and periodicals. Such internationally known magazines as *Time, Readers' Digest, Newsweek, Far Eastern Economic Review, Asia Week,* and *Asia Business* are published and printed in Hong Kong. Pre-press services include typesetting, page imposition, and color-separation work. Post-press services include die cutting, foil stamping, embossing, and book binding.

Some of the HOT items:
- books
- calendars
- color separations
- 4-color printing
- greeting cards
- journals
- periodicals
- stationery
- telephone directories
- typesetting

FOOTWEAR

Labor shortages and escalating costs have led many of Hong Kong's footwear manufacturers to relocate their plants to nearby Guangdong and Fujian Provinces in China. Thus, sports shoes and plastic shoes are being manufactured in China, while Hong Kong is shifting to the manufacture of high-priced women's leather shoes.

One unique feature of the footwear industry is that almost all footwear producers have manufacturing plants in China but maintain their administrative offices in Hong Kong. These offices conduct the procurement of equipment and raw materials, and the marketing of products at home and abroad.

Some of the HOT items:

* athletic shoes
* leather shoes
* plastic shoes
* women's fashion footwear

TEN EXTRA PROSPECTS FOR IMPORTING FROM HONG KONG

* artificial flowers
* cameras and photography equipment
* hardware
* home appliances
* housewares
* lighting fixtures
* luggage
* machinery
* novelty items and souvenirs
* office supplies

OPPORTUNITIES FOR EXPORTING TO HONG KONG

Hong Kong is highly dependent on imported resources to satisfy both consumer and industrial needs. Demand is particularly strong for agricultural products, fuels, plastic raw materials, and capital-intensive and high-technology goods, such as avionics equipment, computer hardware and software, medical equipment, industrial packing equipment, and electronic parts and components. Consumer imports include cosmetics, stereo equipment, sporting goods, and household products. The following section describes the best prospects for foreign exporters to Hong Kong.

AIR CONDITIONING EQUIPMENT

There is significant demand in Hong Kong for air conditioning equipment, both for the domestic market and for reexport to China. While the market is predicted to grow annually by 6 percent through 1995, growth between 1995 and 1997 may be even higher due to private and public construction projects planned for Hong Kong and southern China.

Many private developers have switched to high quality central air conditioning equipment to meet the demands of Hong Kong's more affluent consumers, but government regulations ensure that room air conditioners will continue to dominate the residential market. Light equipment for small commercial establishments is also one of the fastest-growing market segments. The strongest demand within infrastructure projects is for reciprocating chillers of up to 1,000 tons.

In China domestic demand for air conditioning equipment for both light commercial and heavy equipment has been strong in the past few years. Hong Kong's reexports to China include compressors, coil units, and replacement parts.

Some of the HOT items:

- air supply equipment
- centrifugal chillers (1,000-2,000 tons)
- chilled water return units
- controls
- fan units
- light commercial package units (10hp-100hp)
- reciprocating chillers
- window and split-unit air conditioners

AIRBORNE AVIONICS EQUIPMENT

According to research conducted by Boeing and Airbus Industries, Asia's share of the world passenger airline industry will grow from just under 30 percent to approximately 45 percent by the beginning of the next century. Hong Kong is embarking on an ambitious project to build a major international airport that will handle 35 million passengers a year (50 percent more than the current volume) upon completion in mid-1997. Among the best prospects for foreign exporters are radar, radios, and flight instrumentation systems. Demand for helicopter parts is also expected to be particularly strong in the coming years.

Some of the HOT items:

- autopilot systems
- black boxes
- communications systems
- electronic flight instruments systems
- flight management systems
- helicopter parts
- inertial reference and navigation systems
- in-flight entertainment systems
- on-board radar
- radios
- voice recorders
- weather radar

COMPUTERS AND PERIPHERALS

Hong Kong's demand for the newest computer technologies and products continues to grow. Industrial, financial, and public sector applications present local sales opportunities for a wide range of suppliers. There is demand for large-, medium-, and small-scale systems.

Besides the financial community, public utilities, telecommunications companies, universities, and government represent a solid base of users of large-scale systems. The principal area of potential growth in sales, however, lies in medium-scale systems for computers that support 15 to 100 users in commercial environments. Networking via local area networks (LANs) also offers potential applications in Hong Kong. And there will continue to be an active market for smaller-scale systems. Both IBM PCs and IBM compatibles are being used increasingly in smaller professional settings. Portable items such as laptop, notebook, and handheld PCs are also growing in popularity.

Some of the HOT items:

- general-purpose computers
- high-speed scientific computers, especially in manufacturing
- IBM-compatible PCs
- information storage and retrieval equipment
- large- and medium-scale systems
- laser printers

- local area networks (LANs)
- multi-user UNIX-based systems
- portable computers
- thermal printers

CAD/CAM/CAE

Computer-aided design (CAD), computer-aided manufacturing (CAM), and computer-aided engineering (CAE) comprise one of the most successful specialized markets for foreign computer suppliers. In the last two years, CAD/CAM sales in Hong Kong grew by about 80 percent in value. The CAE market, still in its early stages of development in Hong Kong, is growing rapidly and will probably take about three years to reach maturity—the time it took for the CAD/CAM markets to reach maturity. Because the local market for technology is several years behind that in the United States, Japan, and Europe, future demand will be centered on upgrades of technology and equipment.

Sales of CAD/CAM/CAE equipment is divided among several sectors: graphic design (40 percent), textiles (30 percent), electronics (20 percent), and tooling, architecture, and other areas (10 percent). CAD/CAM/CAE is also starting to be used by consulting services and plotters, among others.

Of special note is the demand for workstations that support CAD/CAM/CAE and other precision graphics applications. This trend has created a market for versatile high-performance graphics adapters, which should prove to be a good opportunity for foreign suppliers. Personal computers with 80486DX processors, scanning software, mice, and high-resolution graphics monitors, as well as computers specialized for CAD/CAM applications offer significant opportunities for potential sales.

Some of the HOT items:
- CAD/CAM software for PCs (with applications for civil engineering, architecture, mold-making, textile, and consumer goods design)
- high-resolution graphics monitors
- personal computers
- scanning software
- specialized mice for CAD/CAM applications

ELECTRONIC PARTS AND COMPONENTS

As one of the world's top exporters of finished electric goods, Hong Kong is a major consumer of electronic parts and components produced by original equipment manufacturers (OEMs). Because local supplies of electronic parts and components tend to be at the lower end of price and technology, the electronics industry relies on imports of high-end parts

and components such as watch movements and personal computer chipsets. Thus, rather than compete with local lower-end producers, foreign exporters will find better opportunities by focusing on more sophisticated parts and components. Cellular telephone chipsets, microprocessor chips, and specialty integrated circuits (ICs) for color televisions are among the high-technology parts and components most needed by the electronics industry in Hong Kong.

Some of the HOT items:
personal computers and peripherals
- ink-jet print heads
- PC chipsets
- ROM chips

telecommunications
- cellular telephone chipsets
- telephone chips

industrial electronics
- 80x86 microprocessor chips
- power supplies
- sensors and transducers
- smart power devices

consumer electronics
- complete and assembled watch movements
- lenses, precision electronic motors, and noise suppression chips for VCRs and video cameras
- microcontrollers, sensors, solenoids, and activators for air conditioners
- specialty ICs for color televisions

INDUSTRIAL PROCESS CONTROLS

Hong Kong has a significant market for industrial process control (IPC) instruments and equipment. Total annual sales exceed US$100 million, in 1991 and volume could easily double in the next five years. In addition, the nearby China market has estimated import sales of at least US$800 million.

The principal consumers of IPC equipment in Hong Kong are the energy and pollution control industries and the textiles and dyeing industries. The rapid growth of production capacity in these industries heightens demand for more and better process control instrumentation and equipment. Prospects for sales to China are equally strong in the energy and pollution control industries and also in the iron, steel, and chemical industries.

Among the best prospects are individual instruments and sensors (as opposed to integrated control systems), including measurement, display, and process control instruments, counting devices, and radiation detection and monitoring instruments.

Some of the HOT items:
- electrical and mechanical regulators
- radiation detectors
- revolution and production counters
- surveying, hydrological, and geological controls for liquids and gases

MEDICAL DIAGNOSTIC EQUIPMENT

Hong Kong medical and health standards have risen considerably in recent years and are now among the highest in the world. Nearly 90 percent of Hong Kong's hospitals are either government controlled or government assisted, which means that companies intending to enter this market must understand the procedures for selling to the Hong Kong government. For now, the most economical means of market entry is to have an agent or distributor in Hong Kong. Companies that wish to enter China's markets through Hong Kong often establish a regional office.

Committed to improving medical services, the Hong Kong government is expected to increase its capital expenditure budget in the next few years. Demand for diagnostic equipment, in particular, is on the rise, and there is currently no domestic production of diagnostic equipment. Exporting opportunities range from cardiac output analyzers and computer tomography scanners to optical microscopes, photocolposcopes, and ultrasound scanners.

Some of the HOT items:
- compound optical microscopes
- electromedical and x-ray apparatus parts
- electromedical instruments and apparatus
- hydrometers, thermometers, and pyrometers
- instruments for physical chemical analysis
- optical appliances and instruments
- x-ray apparatus

PAPER AND PAPERBOARD

In Hong Kong imported paper and paperboard are primarily consumed by the printing and packaging industries. The food and beverage industry, the clothing industry, the electronics industry, and the toy industry are also key end users. Hong Kong does not produce any paper raw materials and relies on imports of newsprint, machine-made, and decorated printing paper, as well as kraft, coated, and corrugated paper. Because both printers and packagers like to use new materials, the average annual growth rate for these types of products is estimated at 10 to 15 percent for next three years. Local users of recycled paper and paperboard represent additional sales opportunities, particularly for recycled corrugated medium paper and kraft liner board.

Some of the HOT items:
- impregnated coated surface-decorated printing paper
- kraft paper
- machine-made printing paper
- newsprint
- recycled cardboard boxes
- recycled paper for consumer packaging
- wooden fiberboard

GRAPHIC ARTS EQUIPMENT

For the past 15 years, Hong Kong's printing industry has grown at an annual rate of 7 percent. To maintain the industry's reputation for high quality and service, printers are willing to invest in the most modern equipment available. Among the best opportunities for foreign exporters are desktop publishing systems, color and high-resolution monitors, and color separation, pagination, and platemaking systems.

Some of the HOT items:
- color separation systems
- high-resolution monitors
- pagination systems
- parts and components
- platemaking systems
- true color-capability monitors (24–32 bit)
- workstation-based systems

PLASTIC MATERIALS AND RESINS

Hong Kong has a very limited capacity to produce plastic raw materials. Thus, Hong Kong imports more than 80 percent of its raw materials. Except for Dow Chemical, which is the sole producer of polystyrene polymer resins from monomers, local manufacturers perform only processing functions. Key imports include polystyrene, polyethylene, polyvinyl chloride, and polypropylene. High-quality resins like acrylonitailebutadiene styrene, polycarbonate, linear low-density polyethylene, and nylon are also imported. The total import market for plastics is expected to grow at an average annual rate of 8 to 10 percent for the next three years.

Some of the HOT items:
- acrylonitailebutadiene styrene
- high-density polyethylene
- low-density polyethylene
- polypropylene
- polystyrene and high-impact polystyrene
- polyvinyl chloride

CARGO HANDLING EQUIPMENT

Hong Kong has of the best natural harbors in the world and was founded because its location made it an ideal place from which to conduct trade with China. Aside from being an entrepôt for China, the port has become the center of a booming inter-Asian trade.

Since its first four container ports were dedicated in 1972 Hong Kong has continually expanded its port capacity. Seven container ports are now in operation, and three others are under way or scheduled for construction in the near future. All of this activity, along with the planned new airport, represents an enormous potential for the sale of cargo handling equipment.

With virtually no local production, Hong Kong relies completely on imports. In addition to heavy container handling equipment (large mobile cranes and rubber-tire gantries), manually operated equipment used by small cargo handlers is in high demand. The need for increasingly sophisticated computerized tracking systems makes cargo handling hardware and software another growth area in which foreign suppliers can gain market share. Air freight and cargo handling services should also be considered by foreign providers.

Some of the HOT items:

- automated warehouse container-moving robots
- computer scheduling systems for container movement and placement
- heavy duty forklifts
- mobile container cranes (on tracks)
- parts and accessories for cargo handling equipment
- pneumatic elevators and conveyers
- pulleys and derricks
- rubber-tire gantry cranes
- works trucks

COSMETICS AND TOILETRIES

Featuring an increasingly affluent population, a cosmopolitan lifestyle, and over six million visitors a year, Hong Kong has become an important market for high-quality beauty products. Tourism and cosmetics complement each other: the more tourists Hong Kong attracts, the higher the sales of cosmetics and perfume.

Hong Kong consumers and international travelers alike now have a wide range of well-known perfumery and cosmetics products from which to choose. These buyers desire high-quality products that are easy to use, pleasant in fragrance, and appealing in texture. There is a growing awareness of health products and products made from organic ingredients. Environmentally friendly products and packaging are also gaining in popularity.

Use and frequency of use of beauty products—including skin care, hair care, and makeup—are increasing in Hong Kong. For example, more women now incorporate the use of skin care products into their daily routine. Shampoo is also being used with greater frequency. Once again, health, environment, and convenience are the primary selling points in a market that offers enormous potential for sales.

A final point: Chinese people in Hong Kong generally use perfume only for special occasions. However, perfume is often purchased as a gift, which encourages buyers to be brand conscious.

Some of the HOT items:

- brand name perfumes and fragrances
- lipsticks
- manicure preparations
- rouges and powders
- shampoos made from natural ingredients
- skin care products
- suntan preparations

TWELVE EXTRA PROSPECTS FOR EXPORTING TO HONG KONG

- audio and visual equipment
- construction equipment
- drugs and pharmaceuticals
- electronic production and test equipment
- food processing and packaging equipment
- hotel and restaurant equipment
- laboratory and scientific equipment
- office furniture
- pollution control equipment
- port and shipbuilding equipment
- security and safety equipment
- telecommunications equipment

OPPORTUNITIES FOR GROWTH

BANKING AND FINANCIAL SERVICES

Hong Kong's favorable regulatory environment, low taxes, and excellent telecommunications have spurred rapid growth in the banking industry. More than 360 banks as well as numerous other financial institutions operate in Hong Kong.

The growth of international trade through Hong Kong, most notably from China, has been a key factor in the growth of the banking industry and is the reason many foreign banks continue to come to Hong Kong. A strong real estate market and very profitable retail banking operations provide other attractive opportunities. Hong Kong's development into a major foreign exchange market in Asia has also been a boon to the banking industry.

As long as trade relationships remain unrestricted, the need for banking and financial services will continue to expand. In addition to the services already mentioned, project financing, mortgage financing, and commercial lending offer favorable prospects for foreign banks and investors.

INSURANCE

Hong Kong has some of the most liberal rules in the world regarding the operations of foreign insurance companies. Rising per capita income and expanding middle-class demand for insurance products have spurred industry growth, yet market penetration remains low. For example, only about 18 percent of adults under age 65 have any life insurance. Demand for life insurance coverage is expected to increase as economic prosperity makes Hong Kong's population more risk conscious. Hong Kong-based insurers also have strong opportunities to expand their portfolios throughout Asia.

In Hong Kong, life insurance companies commonly manage retirement plans. The government and the business community are actively working on an occupational retirement scheme ordinance. Estimates are that 20,000 to 50,000 additional retirement plans will need to be created following the enactment of such an ordinance. This new market will provide vast opportunities for life insurance providers who manage retirement plans.

Multinational insurers dominate the life insurance industry in Hong Kong. The top 11 companies account for approximately 90 percent of gross premiums. Economies of scale, market penetration, and the higher profiles of the larger companies give them distinct marketing advantages over smaller and generally less well-capitalized competitors.

REAL ESTATE

Property speculation is rampant in Hong Kong, and the end is not yet in sight. Indeed, speculation in Hong Kong seems pervasive: when new properties come on the market, long lines immediately form to take part in the lottery purchases, and the speculators range from multinational businesses to homemakers.

According to a recent worldwide survey, Hong Kong has slipped from fourth to sixth on the list of the most expensive cities in which to rent office space. Industry representatives believe that this change in relative cost will affect the relocation decisions of multinational corporations and strengthen Hong Kong's competitive position among international financial centers.

TELECOMMUNICATIONS

Hong Kong's telecommunications industry offers overseas firms many good prospects for business development. The presence of large corporate regional communications centers in Hong Kong has created a good market for building private networks. Attractive opportunities for foreign telecommunications companies include the provision of networking (local area network and wide area network systems) and such personal mobile communications equipment as CT2 (second generation, receive-only advanced cordless telephone systems).

Cable television networks may present a significant opportunity to foreign suppliers and buyers of data communications and electronic messaging equipment. Government officials are now discussing whether to allow a second telecommunications network to compete with Hong Kong Telecom. If competition is approved, sales of telecommunications equipment will increase in Hong Kong.

In the wake of a recent international value-added network services (IVANS) agreement, services employing satellite communications are likely to grow at an annual rate of 20 percent. Suppliers of components and systems in this sector should do well, consistent with the strong demand for satellite systems in the region. The Asian-Pacific market for IVANS is one of the fastest growing in the world. Revenues from such services could approach US$10 billion by the year 2000.

CONSUMER RETAIL

The heady days for shoppers in Hong Kong are a thing of the past. Several years of double-digit inflation have hurt Hong Kong's image as a tourists' shopping haven. Today, most visitors find prices in Hong Kong higher than those in their home countries.

Conditions may now be ripe in the retail sector for certain groups of exporters of consumer goods. The recent opening of a chain of Grand Mart stores in Hong Kong serves as a case in point. The idea of selling bulk packaged goods goes against standard marketing wisdom in Hong Kong. Because most apartments have limited storage space, retail analysts assumed that local consumers would not shop in bulk quantities. But almost from opening day, the Grand Mart stores have been jammed with shoppers lured by prices one half to one third of those in standard Hong Kong retail outlets.

The three Grand Mart stores have hardly saturated the Hong Kong consumer goods market. The consumer goods area as well as specialized markets (for example, office supplies and hardware) offer additional sales opportunities. The best opportunities are for high-quality products and those that fill specific niches.

TRAVEL AND TOURISM

Hong Kong is an attractive market for travel agencies and tour operators: Hong Kong's six million residents have relatively high incomes and most enjoy two weeks of annual paid leave and an average of 17 public holidays a year. And because Hong Kong itself is so small, international travel is extremely popular. Moreover, many residents speak English in addition to Cantonese, and they are therefore comfortable traveling to many countries in the world.

Competition for travelers is intense. With the advantages of both proximity and lower air fares, Asian Pacific countries attract the most tourists from Hong Kong. However, the United States and Europe are also popular destinations, and they could become even more popular through promotion.

The Hong Kong government imposes minimal regulations on the tourist industry. To qualify as a travel agent operating in Hong Kong, one must only be a member of the Travel Industry Council of Hong Kong. For foreign travel agents to be successful in Hong Kong, a good reputation and image are very important. The ideal way to establish a good reputation is by developing a strategic alliance with well-known travel agents.

Foreign tour operators have found participation in large trade events to be a cost-effective method of promotion. Well-organized tours for journalists and travel agents can also produce good results.

HOME HEALTH CARE

Hong Kong's population is provided with a comprehensive range of medical and health services by the public and private sectors. General affluence and the continual promotion of health awareness by the government have given a boost to the home health care industry.

The medical field in Hong Kong has historically been dominated by foreign suppliers. Providers from the United Kingdom, Taiwan, and the United States are among the strongest competitors. The aging of Hong Kong's population presents further opportunities to providers of health care services and products with proven practicality and ease of use. Demand among affluent consumers for products designed to provide comfort and support—for example, luxury lounges and back supports—is also strong.

Together, the elderly and physically disabled constitute nearly 50 percent of the home care equipment market in Hong Kong. Approximately one-third of medical apparatus and related products are used to care for the elderly.

Many new programs are under way to help mainstream the physically disabled. The Rehabilitation Program offers a variety of services, all of which are coordinated by the Commissioner for Rehabilitation. Some 1,300 day activity centers and 2,000 hostels serve those who cannot live independently or be adequately cared for by family. These day centers and hostels must meet government standards for health care services and products in order to remain in operation.

FRANCHISING

The market for franchised goods and services in Hong Kong has been quite strong in recent years. Increasingly affluent and savvy consumers appreciate the convenience, reliability, and moderate prices that many franchise operations provide. Strong growth in the retail sector and a long-standing entrepreneurial tradition have fueled investor interest in this sector. Increasing economic uncertainty in the territory should only enhance the appeal of a proven product and a short payback period.

The most successful Western franchise operations in Hong Kong have been fast-food restaurants. Convenience stores, repair shops, and car rentals services are also becoming popular. Other services likely to be popular are those that cater to leisure activities, including film rentals, music stores, and photography shops.

PUBLIC PROCUREMENT OPPORTUNITIES

In 1991 British and Chinese negotiators signed a memorandum of understanding pertaining to the construction of a new airport, a key component of Hong Kong's massive Port and Airport Development Strategy (PADS). Despite a subsequent yearlong political stalemate over financing proposals for the airport, progress has been made on various projects.

The initial go-ahead on the new airport and on PADS is a strong indication that Hong Kong's future growth and prosperity will be based on interdependence with China. The new airport and expanded port are expected to serve as a vital gateway for the successful processing trade that has developed so rapidly in the past decade between Hong Kong, China, and the rest of the world.

Hong Kong's program to build a new airport and expand its seaport represents significant commercial opportunities for foreign companies. The 10 core airport projects are:

Estimated Cost

(in 1991 US$ billions)

Chek Lap Kok Airport	5.66
North Lantau Expressway	0.56
Lantau Fixed Crossing	1.57
Right of Way	30.73
West Kowloon Expressway	0.22
Western Harbor Crossing	0.51
Airport Railway	2.86
Tung Chung New Town	0.34
West Kowloon Reclamation	1.17
Utilities	0.19

PADS calls for: a more passenger-friendly 24-hour airport; a threefold expansion of Hong Kong's container port; a new city designed to house 150,000 workers and staff; and an extensive transport web, including the world's second-longest suspension bridge, connecting the new port and airport with urban and industrial areas.

CONSTRUCTION

A host of overseas consultants were involved in the studies commissioned for PADS. Similarly, overseas advice will be sought in the construction, supply, and financing of PADS projects. Expenditures on planning, engineering, land reclamation, site investigation, and other activities have already exceeded US$1 billion and many billions more will be spent during the project's peak years from, 1993 through 1997.

The construction industry in Hong Kong is very competitive, with a large number of local and international companies vying to win contracts for core airport projects. While many of the primary contracts have been awarded, the need remains strong in the areas of engineering and construction services as well as in the supply of materials and specialized equipment. Analysts predict a yearly increase in demand of 30 to 40 percent in the market for building materials and supplies if the airport and port development projects move ahead as planned.

Hong Kong's construction industry is highly dependent on imports. China and Japan are Hong Kong's major sources of building materials and equipment. China supplies the most flagstones, bricks, glass, aluminum, nails, nuts, bolts, and spanners, while Japan supplies such items as cement, hand tools, electrical switches, mechanical shovels, excavators, and forklift trucks.

The United States holds a lucrative niche market in terms of large earth-moving equipment and drills, while European countries (primarily the United Kingdom, Italy, and Germany) dominate in the general market for building materials, and specialized construction and engineering equipment.

Overseas suppliers can expect to do well in high-tech, up-market areas, particularly if they offer training, after-sales service, and other incentives. The best subcontracting and supply opportunities for foreign firms include:

- **Electrical and mechanical equipment:** heating, ventilation, and air conditioning; switchgear; transformers, electrical power, and lighting; fire protection and alarms; public address systems; electrical distribution; refrigeration and boiler plants; hot and chilled water distribution; sprinkling systems; flight information systems; and security and building management control
- **Navigational aids and avionics:** runway approach lighting, taxiway lighting, heat and flood lighting, aircraft parking aids, ground power, road and car park lighting, and high-voltage distribution
- **Specialty equipment:** sensory detection devices, access control (bio-sensors), fare collection, traffic surveillance, lifts, escalators, baggage handling systems, people movers, and aircraft loading systems
- **Telecommunications and electronics:** flight information systems and computers, security, fiber optics, CCTV, and telephone materials.

For more information on the registration procedures for contractors and for lists of approved suppliers of materials, contact:

Planning, Environment and Lands Branch
Hong Kong Government
Murray Building
Garden Road, Hong Kong
Tel: [852] 8482111 Fax: [852] 8453489

For information on engineering and associated consultants, contact:

Engineering and Associated Consultants
Selection Board
Civil Engineering Services Department
9/F., Empire Centre
68 Mody Road
Kowloon, Hong Kong
Tel: [852] 7212527, 8481111 Fax: [852] 3110725

AIRPORT

Hong Kong's new airport is now under construction at Chek Lap Kok Island, off the northern coast of Lantau. The current estimated cost to bring the first runway into operation by mid-1997 is US$5.7 billion. Extensive private investment is expected to flow into the air freight and aircraft maintenance facilities as well as the passenger terminal.

The developer of the airport, the Provisional Airport Authority, is pushing forward on two reclamation projects for the airport site and on architectural and engineering design of the passenger terminal.

Once completed, the new airport will handle 35 million passengers annually and more than one million metric tons of air cargo. By 2040 the airport is expected to serve 87 million passengers a year and handle 8.9 million tons of air cargo.

Private sector investment will account for approximately 25 percent of the new airport and supporting infrastructure. In addition to the 10 core airport projects, US$310 million will be spent to keep the Kai Tak airport in operation until the new airport opens.

For general information on port and airport development, contact:

New Airport Project Coordinating Office
Works Branch, Hong Kong Government
7/F., Shui On Centre, 8 Harbour Road
Wanchai, Hong Kong
Tel: [852] 8023408, 8296774 Fax: [852] 8242008

For information regarding the airport, contact:

Provisional Airport Authority
25/F, Central Plaza
Wanchai, Hong Kong
Tel: [852] 8247111 Fax: [852] 8240717

PORT

Seven privately built and operated terminals are now in service at Hong Kong's Kwai Chung container port, handling upwards of 5 million TEUs (20-foot equivalent units) annually. An eighth terminal, off of Stonecutter's Island in Victoria Harbor, was scheduled for completion in 1993.

A ninth container terminal (CT9) is to be constructed on reclaimed land at nearby Tsing Yi Island. Plans for CT9, however, are on hold pending an agreement on land and franchise grants. The government of the Peoples' Republic of China insists that CT9 requires a land grant, which must be approved by the Sino-British Land Commission, as well as the grant of a franchise extending beyond 1997, which also requires the approval of the Sino-British joint liaison group. But the Land Commission had not yet allocated land for CT9, and the joint liaison group had yet to reach an agreement.

Expansion is also planned for Hong Kong's Western Harbor and on northern Lantau. Much of the infrastructure used by the new airport will link the Lantau port to Hong Kong and Kowloon. The budget for Lantau port development exceeds US$3 billion, with private enterprise taking the lead in both the construction and operation of these new terminals.

The overall port project comprises two bridges, five container terminals, four multipurpose berths, and supporting infrastructure, including a 5 km (3 mile) breakwater between Cheung Chau and Lamma Island.

For information regarding the port, contact:

Port Development Board
5/F., Yu Yuet Lai Building
Central, Hong Kong
Tel: [852] 8015825 Fax: [852] 8770583

TRANSPORTATION LINKS

The new airport and expanded port on Lantau require the construction of several high-capacity bridges, roads, and tunnels. These include the Lantau Fixed Crossing, consisting of two suspension bridges, the longer with a span of 1,377 meters; a third road tunnel across Hong Kong's Victoria Harbor, to be built entirely on a build-operate-transfer basis; and a passenger rail line to connect the airport to Hong Kong Island. Many dredging and land reclamation efforts are required to support these transportation projects, which also entail the design and implementation of highway interchanges, toll plazas, and traffic control systems.

Hong Kong will need capital, expertise, and equipment from all over the world to complete this vast undertaking. Hong Kong has long pursued a policy of private sector participation in infrastructure development. Just as important, the government wants "a level playing field for everyone" in the tendering and awarding of public projects. Almost all government purchases are conducted on the basis of "best value for the money," regardless of the source of supplies and services.

For information regarding transportation and infrastructure projects, contact:

Highways Department
10/F., Empire Centre
68 Mody Road
Kowloon, Hong Kong
Tel: [852] 7210564

AIRPORT RAILWAY

The Mass Transit Railway Corporation (MTRC) intends to select a main contractor and one or more subcontractors for each station and the depot to handle various support services, including the installation of air conditioning and ventilation systems, fire detection systems, security and access control, signs and advertising panels, and a traffic management system. The subcontractors will be employed directly by the main contractor.

The MTRC expects to open subcontractor bidding in early 1994; bidding will continue through 1995.

For information on airport railway prequalification for subcontractors for support services, contact:

Mass Transit Railway Corporation (MTRC)
Commercial/Contracts Department
14/F World Trade Square, Tower 1
123 Hoi Bun Road, Ngau Taua Kok
Kowloon, Hong Kong
Fax: [852] 7558127

FUTURE RAILWAY PLAN

The Transport Branch of the Hong Kong government is drawing up long-term plans for the development of railway systems through the year 2011. The railway development study proposes the following:

- Two strategic regional links—an improved Kowloon-Canton railway railway main line and a new western corridor connecting the urban areas with the New Territories and the border.
- Four principal north-south urban corridors through the metro area—the Tsuen Wan and Kwun Tong lines of the existing mass transit railway (MTR), the future airport railway, and the proposed east Kowloon route.
- East-west routes in the New Territories—a connection north of Sheung Shui between the two strategic regional links, interchanges in Kowloon between the various urban corridors,

and links on Hong Kong Island by the existing MTR island line and the proposed north Hong Kong Island line.
- Subregional links to connect the new northwest territories Ma On Shan, Tseung Kwan, Lantau (airport railway), and south Hong Kong Island.
- A port rail line to connect the border and the container port at Kwai Chung.

For information regarding the railroad development project, contact:

Transport Department
Government Secretariat
2-6/F, East Wing, Central Government Offices
Lower Albert Road
Hong Kong
Tel: [852] 810-2717 Fax: [852] 868-4643

WATER SUPPLY

While the development of the new airport receives much of the attention, billions of dollars are being spent on the expansion of Hong Kong's water supplies. One third of the territory is currently set aside as a sterilized catchment area. More than 200 km (125 miles) of catchments feed a system of reservoirs throughout the territory. Nonetheless, the domestic system can supply at most only two-thirds of the territory's needs for pure water.

As a result, 60 to 70 percent of Hong Kong's water is supplied from China's East River. An agreement signed in 1980 covers supplies from China until 1995. The agreement gives China a cost plus 10 percent return on its investment in piping water to Hong Kong. A new agreement is being negotiated to cover the period from 1995 through 2006.

Three major expansion projects are under the direction of the Water Supplies Department:

- By 1995 the present system of delivery (from Shenzhen) will be at full capacity and will not be able to meet Hong Kong's demand. A second pipeline is already under construction. The remaining project to be tendered is for a system of pumping stations.
- By 1997 a system must be in place to deliver water from China to the northern coast of Lantau Island and the new airport. This project is now in the design stage. The cost of construction is estimated at US$168 million.
- Projects are needed to supply water to Hong Kong's new towns. Tin Shui Wai and Tseung Kwan are the most recent of these eight satellite cities, each housing hundreds of thousands of people. Public works expenditures for new town developments are expected to be twice those of the above-mentioned two projects combined.

For information on water supplies department projects, contact:

Water Supplies Department
48/F Immigration Tower
7 Gloucester Road
Hong Kong
Tel: [852] 8294400 Fax: [852] 8240578

Inquiries may also be addressed to the New Works, Civil Engineering Division and the Mechanical and Engineering Division of the Water Supplies Department (same address, telephone and fax numbers).

WASTE MANAGEMENT

According to the Waste Management Policy Group, there are numerous opportunities for foreign suppliers of environmental products and services despite the temporary freeze on franchises and long-term projects extending beyond 1997. Four projects were scheduled to begin in 1993:

- Removal of the low-level radioactive waste stored in the Wanchai tunnel and the creation of a new storage facility. Some 1,000 cubic meters of water are to be treated and removed.
- Treatment and disposal of contaminated mud (23 million cubic meters) dredged up during the core airport projects. This mud is highly contaminated with lead, copper, and other toxic metals. At most, 13 million cubic meters can be dumped at special sites within Hong Kong waters.
- A treatment facility on Stonecutter's Island to handle sewage sludge. The enormous volume of sewage will come from western Hong Kong Island and virtually all of Kowloon. The project is delicate and complex: Stonecutter's Island sits in the middle of Victoria Harbor, and a new plant intended for construction on Stonecutter's Island is to use a lime treatment process.
- The design, construction, and operation of a central incinerator for all the medical waste, confidential waste (customs seizures), and animal carcasses originating within the territory.

For information on waste management projects, contact:

Waste Management Policy Group
Environmental Protection Department
25/F., Southorn Centre
130 Hennessy Road
Wanchai, Hong Kong
Tel: [852] 8351216 Fax: [852] 5910636

PUBLIC PROCUREMENT PROCESS

REGULATIONS

Hong Kong is a GATT member and signatory to the Government Procurement Code of the General Agreement on Tariffs and Trade (GATT) and conducts government procurements through competitive international offering and bidding. The Hong Kong government does not interfere in the market through price controls or subsidies of any kind.

AUTHORITY

The Hong Kong Government Supplies Department (GSD) is responsible for the procurement of government goods and services. The GSD usually purchases by open tender, with decisions based on price, quality, and delivery. Selective tender and single tender are rare. The GSD gives no preference to any particular source of supply, country, or organization.

GENERAL PROCEDURES

Bidders have six weeks to prepare their offers. Bidders are urged to submit offers with at least a 30 day validity period. Payment is usually made by check within 30 days of delivery. All bidders are entitled to receive an assessment of their bids, whether they are successful or not. Total bid prices and names of the successful bidders are published weekly in the government gazette.

Potential suppliers must prequalify with the GSD. A company must provide the GSD with background information about the goods and services it offers. The GSD evaluates the information and selects qualified suppliers for inclusion on its register. Registered suppliers regularly receive the GSD's tender notices.

For information about a subscription to the government gazette, contact:

HK Information Services Department
Beaconsfield House
4 Queen's Road Central
Hong Kong
Tel: [852] 8428777

For information regarding status or procurement procedures contact:

Government Supplies Department
12 Oil Street
North Point, Hong Kong
Tel: [852] 8026102 Fax: [852] 8072764

SPECIAL TRADE ZONES

Hong Kong has no free trade zones, as the territory itself is essentially a duty-free port, with the exception of duties on tobacco, certain alcoholic and nonalcoholic beverages, and certain hydrocarbons. Bonded warehouses are available for goods in transit and for certain products that are subject to import duties.

Hong Kong is firmly committed to an open market policy for trade in goods and services as well as investments in Hong Kong. Accordingly, foreign and locally owned companies receive equal treatment. Moreover, Hong Kong does not have any investment practices or policies favoring particular industries. Imported products are free to compete with locally made products.

Foreign Investment

INVESTMENT CLIMATE AND TRENDS

Hong Kong has long been a favorite spot for foreign investors in Asia. With the second highest per capita income in East Asia after Japan, minimal regulations, and low tax rates, Hong Kong remains as attractive as ever in most respects. Although Hong Kong's tight labor market and rising wages have diminished its standing as a manufacturing site, increasing trade with China and the explosion in banking and financial services, tourism, and retail trade, among other areas, afford many new investment opportunities.

Uncertainty over the transfer of sovereignty to China in 1997 is causing some investors to shy away and a number of Hong Kong-based firms to relocate. However, the increasing economic liberalization in China, which is fueling an even greater expansion of free market activity in that country's southern regions, will all but guarantee lucrative, new commercial prospects for firms based in Hong Kong.

Hong Kong has already become the main transit and shipping point for goods partially and fully manufactured in southern China. Chinese-made goods, which enter Hong Kong's customs territory for final assembly and shipment to other countries, are classified as reexports. Reexports, which have driven Hong Kong's external trade in recent years, increased by 31 percent in 1992 over the previous year and accounting for 74.7 percent of Hong Kong's total exports. China is also the main destination for goods produced or assembled in Hong Kong, accounting for 29.6 percent of its total exports in 1992. The United States was the second most important destination for Hong Kong's exports, with 23 percent of the total.

Increasingly, Hong Kong and southern China are becoming a single large integrated market of more than 70 million consumers. Low-end manufacturing, assembly operations, and investment capital continue to move across the border from Hong Kong. An estimated three million workers in southern China are now employed as a result of business generated by Hong Kong firms. Massive capital investment in infrastructure projects by the PRC government, the Hong Kong government, and private investors is creating a highly developed and integrated series of ports, airports, highways, and power plants. As a result, there has been no letup in Guangdong Province's breakneck growth rate of 25 percent a year, and per capita incomes there are now at the level of many newly industrialized economies.

Some of Hong Kong's best investment prospects are in industries producing the following goods and services: telecommunications equipment, construction equipment, computers and peripherals, pollution control equipment and services, banking and financial services, medical equipment, plastics, avionics and ground support equipment, household consumer goods, and food commodities.

The American Chamber of Commerce in Hong Kong sums up the reasons why so many foreign companies have selected Hong Kong as an investment location: location, communications, infrastructure, low taxes, favorable regulatory environment, and human resources, in that order.

Location No center is better situated than Hong Kong to support commercial activities in China, Southeast Asia, and East Asia. Known as the Gateway to China, Hong Kong is the leading investor in China, the entrepôt for more than one-third of China's external trade, and a base for a large number of PRC-controlled companies, banks, agencies, and organizations.

Communications Network All domestic and international communications services in Hong Kong are modern, efficient, and relatively inexpensive.

Infrastructure Hong Kong has the world's largest container port and the second busiest international airport. Hong Kong offers sophisticated financial, educational, manufacturing, and recreational facilities.

Low Taxes Hong Kong taxes corporate profits at 17.5 percent and personal income and property at a an average rate of 15 percent. There is no withholding tax on interest.

Favorable Regulatory Environment Hong Kong's economy is largely free from government control and regulation. The government's policy is usually to allow market forces to determine economic and commercial practices. There is very little use of centrally directed incentives and disincentives, entitlements, or restrictions to control the economy. Business activity, especially activity regarding foreign investment, requires very little governmental, bureaucratic, or administrative approval. An extensive body of commercial and company law ensures that contracts are enforced and rights protected. An established and comprehensible legal and judicial system can settle virtually any disputes that arise. Company law has been structured to facilitate a wide range of trading and investment activities, and it makes no distinction between local and foreign-owned firms. Foreign and domestically owned companies are allowed to set up offices, incorporate, and register branches without strict government guidelines defining the future scope of their activities or mandating levels of performance. Companies may be structured without conditions on ownership, management, and composition of boards. No quota system governs foreign investment, staffing, or management of foreign-owned operations.

Human Resources Hong Kong's labor and professional forces have long enjoyed a reputation for hard work, innovation, efficiency, and reliability. Companies have direct access to labor and the freedom to employ workers without interference by intermediate organizations. Although a labor shortage and emigration among young professionals have increased human resource problems, labor-employer relations in Hong Kong are generally harmonious.

INVESTMENT POLICY

Hong Kong welcomes foreign investment to diversify its industrial base and develop high-technology industries. The government maintains a policy of minimum interference in the economy. There are no export performance requirements, and there are no distinctions based on the source of investment. Hong Kong has a freely convertible currency and allows complete freedom of movement of capital. Foreign companies are not restricted in any way from repatriating capital and profits, including dividends, interest, royalties, service fees, and branch profits. There are no import tariffs or duties (although excise levies exist to control the import of certain commodities), nor are there laws or regulations to encourage or discourage investment or determine its character. As a result, the territory's markets are arguably the most open in the world.

Foreign Ownership and Control of Business Hong Kong does not require local participation in ownership or management. No industries are closed to foreign investors, and the government permits 100 percent foreign ownership in most industries. The only enterprises and areas of the economy that the government controls and that as a result are not generally open to investment are the postal system, public utilities, the port, the airport, the Mass Transit Railway Corporation, the Kowloon-Canton Railroad, and Radio Television Hong Kong.

Registering a Company There is generally no approval or screening procedure for foreign investment. However, foreign companies must register with the Companies Registry within one month of establishing a business in Hong Kong and with the Inland Revenue Department's Business Registration Office. To register a branch with the Companies Registry, the parent company must submit its articles of incorporation, information about the directors, and the name of at least one official contact person in Hong Kong. Finally, there are no specific registration or reporting requirements for foreign capital, loans, technology agreements, or other types of commercial agreements. (See "Business Entities & Formation" chapter for further information on registration procedures).

The Joint Declaration and Life After 1997 Under the Joint Declaration between the United Kingdom and China, China has agreed to keep Hong Kong's current laws in force and leave its social and economic institutions intact for a period of at least 50 years after sovereignty over Hong Kong is transferred to the PRC in 1997. However, recent statements by Chinese officials cast doubt on China's sincerity about adhering to the agreement.

While Hong Kong has been under British control, there has never been a threat of nationalization. A series of statements by China in reaction to democratization proposals advanced by Governor Chris Patten precipitated a sharp decline on Hong Kong's stock market in December 1992. China said that it would dismantle the legislative council if its manner of selection was inconsistent with its interpretation of the Basic Law, which the PRC drafted. Britain has made an effort to push a more democratic legislative body than it has allowed in the past, giving China some cause to cry foul.

China expressed loud disapproval in 1992 over financing of the airport project, which involves considerable government borrowing and threatens to accelerate inflation. China's stance on the airport project increases the likelihood that it will not be completed as scheduled in 1997.

Even more disconcerting to the local business community, Chinese officials have said they will not honor commercial contracts in the private sector that they have not approved prior to 1997. But the general consensus among leading businesspeople as well as the heads of business and trade organizations in Hong Kong is that such threats are not as serious as they sound. They believe that China will do little to disrupt economic activity in Hong Kong, especially when the territory is such an important source of growth and opportunity, attracting trade and investment from around the world.

INVESTMENT INCENTIVES

There are no special incentives to attract foreign investment to Hong Kong. The low corporate tax rate and the minimal government regulation are incentive enough. As mentioned earlier, the current tax rate for corporate profits is 17.5 percent, and the average rate on personal income is 15 percent. Property is taxed, but interest, royalties, dividends, capital gains, and sales are not. The Hong Kong government makes no distinction in law or practice between foreign and domestic companies. There are no restrictions on foreign ownership, nor are there export performance or local content requirements. Hong Kong-based businesses are free to remit or repatriate capital and profits to nonresident investors.

LEADING INVESTORS

China, Japan, and the United States have the largest investments in Hong Kong. Figures for US direct investment are the most accurate and complete, followed by the figures for Japan; China's are the least reliable. In 1992 China's total investment in Hong Kong was approximately US$20 billion, Japan's direct investment was US$11.2 billion, and US direct investment was US$7.1 billion. Because there is no approval process and no need to register capital for future repatriation, Hong Kong does not keep statistics on foreign investment.

Differences in methods of data collection make these figures misleading. The figures for Japan are based on reports to Japan's Ministry of Finance (MOF) by firms planning outward remittances in connection with overseas investment. But the figures do not necessarily represent the funds actually invested in any given year, because they only record intention and the total projected investment amount. Furthermore, the figures do not account for delayed or canceled investment plans. Even so, they are probably fairly accurate on an aggregate basis.

As the *China Daily* reported in February 1993, China's investment in Hong Kong on an assets basis *(caichan)* was US$20 billion in 1992. Unfortunately, there is no information about the method of calculation. If we assume that it is a total assets figure (including debt) and that it includes investment categories not counted by the US Department of Commerce or Japan's Ministry of Finance, then the fig-

ure is significantly overstated relative to US and Japanese direct investment.

On the basis of estimated nonproperty assets, Japan was the leading investor in 1992 with US$22.4 billion, followed by the US and China with US$19.7 billion and US$15 billion respectively.

Notwithstanding these results, current trends suggest that China will soon be the number one foreign investor in Hong Kong. Its rapidly growing economy, its proximity to Hong Kong, and its pending takeover virtually guarantee such a development. Of course, after 1997 China will have sovereignty over Hong Kong, essentially making comparisons between China's investment in the territory and those of other countries irrelevant.

Leading Foreign Investors by Company and Country Origin

United States Sea-Land, Exxon, Citibank, Motorola, Caltex, AT&T, IBM, Digital Equipment Corp., Williamette Industries, Kodak, Bank Of America, Dun and Bradstreet, American International Group

Japan Kumagai-Gumi, Yaohan, Jusco, Daimaru, Mitsubishi, Uny, Nishimatsu, Seibu, Daido Concrete, C. Itoh

United Kingdom Inchcape Pacific, Cable and Wireless, Standard Chartered Bank, Jardine Matheson (UK Controlled), Swire (UK Controlled)

Western Europe Philips (Netherlands), Dragages (France), Carlsberg Brewery (Denmark), Phonopress (Hong Kong JV with Bertelsmann of Germany), Hong Kong Petrochemical (Italian/Korean/Chinese JV), Melitta (Germany)

China China International Investment and Trust Corp. (CITIC), China Resources, China Travel Service, China Merchants, Guangdong Enterprises, China Everbright

Asia San Miguel Brewery (Philippines), Shangrila/Kerry (Malaysia's Robert Kuok, Hotels and Real Estate), Chyau Fwu Properties (Taiwan), Paladin (Taiwan), Lippo Group (Indonesia, Banking and Real Estate), C.P. Pokphand (Thailand, Agribusiness), Pioneer (Australia, Construction)

REGULATORY AGENCIES

In keeping with the Hong Kong government's general policy of noninterference in the economy, the number of regulatory agencies is minimal, as is the control that they exercise over commercial activity. This section lists the agencies directly related to foreign investment.

In addition to collecting corporate and personal income taxes, the Inland Revenue Department's Business Registration Office is responsible for registering locally and foreign-owned enterprises conducting business in Hong Kong. An annual fee of HK$1,000 (about US$130) is payable in advance.

Business Registration Office
Inland Revenue Department
Wanchai Tower
5 Gloucester Road
Wanchai, Hong Kong
Tel: [852] 5490888

Within one month of establishing a business in Hong Kong, foreign business owners must register with the Companies Registry. In registering a branch with the Companies Registry, the parent company must submit its articles of incorporation, information about the directors, and the name of at least one official contact person in Hong Kong.

Companies Registry
13/F., Queensway Government Offices
66 Queensway
Wanchai, Hong Kong
Tel: [852] 8672600 Fax: [852] 8690423

The Securities and Futures Commission (SFC) oversees the Hong Kong stock exchange and regulates the promotion of investments outside Hong Kong. Thus, individuals and companies in Hong Kong involved in promoting commercial real estate in another country may be required to have SFC clearance.

Securities and Futures Commission (SEC)
Exchange Square
38/F., Tower II
Hong Kong
Tel: [852] 8409222 Fax: [852] 8459553

LOANS AND CREDIT AVAILABILITY

Because trade is such an important part of Hong Kong's economic livelihood, banks tend to specialize in the financing of international trade. A banking network enables Hong Kong banks to maintain extensive contacts with local business organizations and introduce investors to traders and manufacturers in Hong Kong. Foreign investors can usually obtain local financing without difficulty. (Refer to "Important Addresses" chapter for a list of banks and their addresses.)

COMMERCIAL AND INDUSTRIAL SPACE

Land Prices and Availability Virtually all land in Hong Kong is owned by the British Crown, which grants or sells permission to hold an interest in a lease for a term of 75 years in the Hong Kong and Kowloon areas and a term of 15 years in the New Territories. Once these rights have been obtained, leases can be sold without government approval. As a result of a 1985 accord between the United Kingdom and the People's Republic of China, most leases

in the New Territories can be extended for an additional 50 years beyond 1997.

Commercial and industrial land is generally expensive, but prices vary with location, demand, and other factors. At regular intervals, the government auctions interests to hold the leases of commercial, industrial, and residential land in urban areas. The government also offers land for sale by tender and private treaty when it considers attaching restrictions to leases in certain areas to be advantageous to Hong Kong's economy. For example, lease restrictions can be structured to attract high-technology industries that have operations unsuitable for normal factory buildings.

The government publishes a biennial forecast of provisional Crown land sales. Investors wishing to lease Crown land should state in the lease application their requirements and the use that they intend to make of the land. If the government is willing to sell the lease, then the site is auctioned. Commercial and factory space can also be purchased from private developers.

The Land Registry and the district Land Offices maintain records of all Crown leases and advise the government on all land matters. The central government's Land Office is responsible for settling conditions of land sales, land registration, apportionment of Crown rents and premiums, and enforcement of lease conditions.

The Land Registry
K.T.W. Pang, Land Registrar
Queensway Government Offices
66 Queensway
Wanchai, Hong Kong
Tel: [852] 8672811 Fax: [852] 5960281

Factory Space More than 60 percent of Hong Kong's factory space is situated in the New Territories and Kowloon. What little factory space there is on Hong Kong Island is usually very expensive. Tai Po and Yuen Long are two industrial estates that the government has targeted for high-technology medium and heavy industries that cannot operate in multistory buildings. The development of these areas was completed recently, and they are now fully operational. Another industrial estate is currently being developed at Tseung Kwan O in southeastern Kowloon near Junk Bay. Most of Hong Kong's light industries occupy high-rise factory buildings, many in the vicinities of Tsuen Wan and Kwai Chung. These areas are well developed with such community facilities as clinics, schools, police stations, and banks.

Prices for factory space in the New Territories run about HK$161 (US$21) per square meter. Rates in Kowloon range upward from HK$215 (US$28) per square meter.

Office Space The offices of most large corporations in Hong Kong are located in and around the Central District, in Wanchai, or in Tsimshatsui. Due to limited supplies, prime office space in Central is expensive, with monthly rental rates around HK$549 (US$71) per square meter. Rentals in Wanchai range from HK$269 to HK$431 (US$35 to US$56) per square meter; in Tsimshatsui they run between HK$280 and HK$344 (US$36 and US$44) per square meter.

A 1992 report on office rental prices around the world reveals that Hong Kong has fallen to sixth place, from fourth, on the list of the world's most expensive urban areas. It is preceded by Tokyo, London, Paris, Madrid, and Frankfurt, in that order. The biennial report, which is produced in London, compares total office occupancy costs (rents plus service charges and property tax rates) in 30 major commercial centers.

The downturn in office prices results from a combination of decreased demand, slowed economic growth, and the overall consolidation of property markets after several years of rapid expansion. Industry analysts believe that Hong Kong's current ranking does not indicate a slump in the Hong Kong market. Rather, because the cost of office space is a significant factor in an international firm's decision to relocate, the downward adjustment is likely to strengthen Hong Kong's competitive position among world commercial centers.

BILATERAL INVESTMENT AGREEMENTS

While the Sino-British Joint Declaration states that the free enterprise and liberal investment regimes in Hong Kong will be preserved after 1997, foreign investors have turned to bilateral agreements in an attempt to secure additional protection. Based on a model text approved by the United Kingdom and China, these so-called investment promotion and protection agreements (IPPAs) are arranged individually between Hong Kong and investor countries. Agreements have already been reached with Australia, Canada, Denmark, Germany, the Netherlands, Sweden, and Switzerland, and negotiations have been scheduled with France, Italy, New Zealand, and Singapore.

The first meeting with the United States was held late in 1991, but progress has been stymied by the insistence of each side on using its own model text as a basis for negotiation. Moreover, the United States wants to link a bilateral investment treaty with an intellectual property rights agreement. However, Hong Kong continues to advocate a multilateral approach in the area of intellectual property protection.

INVESTMENT ASSISTANCE

The Hong Kong government's Industry Department promotes foreign investment in Hong Kong, and it can provide information on potential joint venture partners, suppliers, rental costs, labor, and other matters of importance to investors.

Industry Department
14/F., Ocean Centre
5 Canton Road
Kowloon, Hong Kong
Tel: [852] 7372573, 7372208 Fax: [852] 7304633

The Trade Department supplies information on import and export licensing requirements.

Trade Department
Trade Department Tower
700 Nathan Road
Kowloon, Hong Kong
Tel: [852] 7897555 Fax: [852] 7892491

Foreign businesses are also advised to obtain a copy of the Companies Ordinance, because they will have to comply with its provisions. A copy can be purchased for HK$94 plus postage (about US$13) from the government printing office:

Information Services Department
Beaconsfield House
4 Queen's Road Central
Hong Kong
Tel: [852] 8428777

The American Chamber of Commerce in Hong Kong is an excellent source of information for businesspeople and other investors. It publishes brochures and books about investing in Hong Kong and in nearby Guangdong Province in China. Membership in the American Chamber of Commerce is not limited to American companies. Many companies owned by Hong Kong citizens and nationals from other countries are members of the chamber.

American Chamber of Commerce, Hong Kong
1030 Swire House
6 Chater Road
Central, Hong Kong
Tel: [852] 5260165 Fax: [852] 8101289, 5960911
Tlx: 83664 AMCC

Foreign Trade

Hong Kong has depended on trade since its founding by the British in 1841. With a limited area, consisting mostly of rocky islands and a chunk of the adjacent mainland, and no natural resources to speak of, its only real advantages are its first-class harbor and its location as a natural gateway to south-eastern China. First the British and now other traders have been eager to seize on these factors to turn this otherwise unpromising piece of real estate into a thriving trading port and business center.

Hong Kong's economy has been determined by two major factors: its dependence on trade, which places its economy at the mercy of external factors, and its position as an adjunct to China. Both mean that Hong Kong has had to become good at placating and finessing forces greater than itself. It has had to get itself noticed in a positive way by the outside world in order to sustain itself, and it has had to reach a modus vivendi with China by making itself indispensable.

Hong Kong, a free port with few import restrictions, tariffs, and other barriers, is the world's 10th largest trading power. Taxation and licensing are also kept at minimal levels, as are incentives: Hong Kong figures that maintenance of a favorable business environment is incentive enough. It has no exchange controls, making it a mecca for businesses used to onerous foreign exchange restrictions in many other countries, especially in Asia, and it allows a wide range of financial transactions with minimal oversight and high levels of confidentiality. In recent years Hong Kong has had to impose some export restrictions, primarily those required by trading partners as part of international agreements that set quotas, particularly for apparel and textiles. Because of this, certificates of origin and export licenses have become important in certain areas of operation, and the need for these approvals affects business, but does not hamper it unduly. Hong Kong does use hefty import duties and excise levies to control certain items, such as automobiles. Nevertheless, Hong Kong is the closest approximation there is in the real world

to a capitalist paradise.

That Hong Kong exists cheek by jowl with the People's Republic of China (PRC) is an irony and an area of concern for those interested in its future. The accord by which Great Britain agreed to return Hong Kong to Chinese sovereignty in 1997 ostensibly protects the capitalist system for 50 years, although many wonder whether the control-oriented Chinese government will be able to refrain from meddling in Hong Kong's freewheeling commercial affairs and allow it to continue doing what it does so well. Because of the mutual dependency of China and Hong Kong—and in many respects China, despite its greater size, is more dependent than is Hong Kong—most observers remain cautiously optimistic that the two entities will be able to maintain a functioning version of the status quo that will allow trade to continue in a relatively unrestricted fashion.

Hong Kong must import virtually everything it consumes, including half of its water, all of its energy, about 80 percent of its food, and essentially all of its raw materials and consumer goods. As a financial center it even imports money. To pay for these imports it must export vast quantities of value-added items and process large volumes of third-party trade for which it gets paid as an intermediary. During the 1950s and 1960s Hong Kong was noteworthy as a producer of light manufactured goods in its own right, such as apparel, electronics, and toys, and it continues to be a power in many of these product areas. For instance, Hong Kong is the world's largest manufacturer and exporter of toys and games, textiles, apparel, watches and clocks, radios, hairdryers, flashlights, furs, and costume jewelry.

However, as China began to open to the world in the late 1970s, Hong Kong's primary role shifted from that of independent producer to that of broker for the China trade. It has also lost its cost advantage to a more accessible China, so that Hong Kong's primary production increasingly is moving offshore in search of lower cost structures on the mainland. In compensation, Hong Kong interests provide a great

Hong Kong's Major Exports by Commodity
(in HK$ billions)
Domestic Exports

Commodity	1992	1991	% change
Apparel	$77,156	$75,525	2%
Textiles	17,226	17,595	-2
Watches & clocks	15,476	17,037	-15
Computers, office machines & parts	15,239	12,372	23
Telecommunications equipment & parts	10,991	11,519	[5
Semiconductors, electronic values & tubes, etc.	7,669	5,890	30
Jewelry	5,047	5,668	-11
Printed matter	4,414	3,937	12
Plastic articles	4,064	4,228	-4
Electrical apparatus (resistors, switches, etc.)	3,626	3,465	5
Plastics in primary forms	3,367	3,576	6
Electric power machinery & parts	3,322	2,970	12

Reexports

Commodity	1992	1991	% change
Apparel	$78,095	$63,577	23%
Textiles	67,744	58,159	16
Toys, games & sporting goods	57,890	41,791	38
Footwear	35,327	24,951	42
Travel goods & handbags	23,831	19,934	20
Telecommunication equipment & parts	22,222	17,466	27
Watches & clocks	21,077	15,764	38
Radios	19,476	18,291	6
Semiconductors, electronic valves & tubes, etc.	16,752	14,297	16
Misc. manufactured articles	16,223	13,237	23
Plastics in primary forms	14,218	11,344	25
Computers, office machines & parts	11,576	7,425	56

Total Exports

Commodity	1992	1991	% change
Apparel	$155,251	$139,102	12%
Textiles	84,970	75,754	12
Toys, games & sporting goods	57,890	41,791	38
Watches & clocks	36,553	32,801	11
Footwear	35,327	24,951	42
Telecommunications equipment & parts	33,213	28,985	15
Computers, office machines & parts	26,815	19,798	35
Semiconductors, electronic valves & tubes, etc.	24,421	20,187	21
Travel goods & handbags	23,831	19,934	20
Radios	19,476	18,291	6
Plastics in primary forms	17,585	14,620	20
Misc. manufactured articles	16,223	13,237	23
Automobiles	5,799	7,850	213

Source: Hong Kong Trade Development Council

deal of the managerial and technical expertise and support systems for China's industrial enterprises.

Nearly 50 percent of China's foreign trade and 70 percent of its foreign investment is channeled through Hong Kong, and China earns between 30 and 40 percent of its foreign exchange from Hong Kong-related activities. As of 1990 about one-quarter of Hong Kong's economy depended directly on China, and the proportion is growing rapidly. Some analysts reckon that the two economies are so closely linked that an economic slowdown in China would cause Hong Kong's gross domestic product (GDP) to drop by as much as two percentage points. Others fear that a relatively minor international shift, such as an alteration in the terms of the international Multi-Fiber Arrangement (MFA) affecting textiles or of China's Most Favored Nation (MFN) trade status with the United States, could send the Hong Kong economy into a tailspin.

Hong Kong's Reexports by Country of Origin (in HK$ billions)

Country	1992	1991	% change
China	$404	$316	28%
Japan	85	57	50
Taiwan	54	42	29
United States	32	27	19
South Korea	19	15	27
Germany	9	7	29
Singapore	8	6	33
United Kingdom	7	6	17
France	6	5	20
Switzerland	5	6	-17

Source: Foreign Trade Magazine

REEXPORTS

Hong Kong has become a reexport, or transshipment, center primarily for the China trade, bringing in goods destined for China from elsewhere and shipping out goods from China to the rest of the world, often without performing any intermediate processing on the products involved. This role has been growing at a rapid rate since the late 1980s. In 1988 55 percent of Hong Kong's total exports represented reexports, while 45 percent were of domestically manufactured goods. By 1990 64.7 percent represented reexports and 35.3 percent domestically produced goods. By 1992 reexports were 74.7 percent of the total and during the first quarter of 1993, domestic exports fell even further—to 21.9 percent—while reexports rose to 78.1 percent. In 1990, 64.4 percent of total imports were destined for reexport,

Hong Kong's Reexports by Country of Destination (in HK$ billions)

Country	1992	1991	% change
China	$212	$153	39%
United States	149	111	34
Japan	37	30	23
Germany	33	32	3
Taiwan	26	25	4
United Kingdom	21	15	40
South Korea	14	15	-7
Singapore	14	12	17
France	11	9	22
Canada	11	8	27

Source: Foreign Trade Magazine

with only 35.6 percent being destined for local consumption. By 1992, reexported imports had risen to 72.3 percent and local use of imports had dropped to 27.7 percent. The trend strengthened in the first quarter of 1993 with 74.7 percent of imports being reexported, while only 25.3 percent were consumed locally. In just over three years since 1990, reexports have jumped from just under two-thirds to nearly four-fifths of all exports, while reexported imports have risen from about two-thirds to almost three-fourths of all imports.

Reexports also muddy the waters when assessing the status of Hong Kong's trading partners. China is the primary destination for goods transshipped through Hong Kong, accounting for 30 percent of all such activity in 1992 (the United States was second, representing 22 percent). China is also the main source of Hong Kong imports destined for reexport, providing 58 percent of all such products in 1992. In 1990 50 percent of all reexports went to Asian destinations, primarily China, Japan, Taiwan, South Korea, and Singapore. Besides the United States, other major destinations included Germany, the United Kingdom, France, and Italy.

Although no hard figures are available to evaluate the scope of the trade, Hong Kong also functions as an important intermediary between China and Taiwan. It is still illegal for Taiwanese to have direct commercial dealings with China, although observers estimate that perhaps 10 percent of Taiwan's total trade is actually carried on with the mainland, and Taiwan is one of the biggest foreign investors in the PRC. Hong Kong has been able to capitalize on such activity by serving as broker between the two. In general, Taiwan's refusal to openly acknowledge its cross-straits sibling has resulted in Hong Kong's garnering a virtual monopoly in serving as the gateway to China for the rest of the world.

Reexports also add to the phenomenon that total trade, instead of being a fraction of GDP as it is in most other, better diversified economies, is a multiple of GDP in Hong Kong. In 1992, Hong Kong's total trade was equal to 246 percent of its gross domestic product (GDP), second only to that of Singapore, which had trade equal to 274 percent of its GDP. Hong Kong's total exports were equal to 121 percent of Hong Kong's economy, while imports were equal to 125 percent of GDP, a further indication of the colony's dependence on trade. By comparison, exports represent only about 9 percent of Japan's economy, 8 percent of that of the United States, and 26 percent of that of South Korea and 41.5 percent of that of Taiwan, two Asian nations that ostensibly base their economies on foreign trade. Imports account for about 6.2 percent of Japan's economy and 9.5 percent of that of the United States; they make up about 35.4 percent of Taiwan's and about 27.8 percent of South Korea's economy.

The structural shift in the external trade sector is a reflection of the strong production links established by Hong Kong firms in China over the past few years. These firms have taken advantage of the mainland's low-cost land and labor to produce goods for world markets. The expansion in reexports thus confirms the competitive advantage of combining China's production capabilities with Hong Kong's design, marketing, and management expertise and underscores Hong Kong's role as a strategic entrepôt serving China and the Asia-Pacific region.

The PRC lacks the infrastructure and technical support to accommodate large container ships at most of its ports. It also lacks the necessary equipment to off-load goods and the warehousing space to store them. Internal transportation networks are insufficient to move goods in volume within China. Thus goods are consigned to Hong Kong where freight-forwarding agents can best determine how to dispatch them to or from China. Hong Kong also provides similar logistical services for Taiwan and South Korea.

EXPORTS

Although Hong Kong's economy is relatively diversified, the top six categories—apparel; textiles; watches and clocks; computers, office machinery, and parts; telecommunications equipment and parts; and semiconductors and other electronic parts—accounted for 61.5 percent of its domestic exports in 1992. The next six categories accounted for an additional 10.1 percent. By contrast, when total exports—domestic exports and reexports combined—were taken into account, the top ten categories represented only 57.7 percent, and the next eight categories added only 6.5 percent to exports. This disparity indicates the vastly broader scope of China's less developed economy and the effect it has in swamping Hong Kong's more focused economy.

As noted, Hong Kong's export orientation overshadows its domestic economy. Some 90 percent of domestic manufactures are designated for export, and the bulk of its imports go to support the export economy. Total trade has risen every year since the 1950s, and since the 1970s has grown at double the rate of trade in the developed world. Since 1987 it has increased at an average rate of 16.4 percent per year in real terms. Total exports reached a high of US$118.6 billion in 1992, up 20.8 percent from the previous year and up 144 percent in cumulative nominal terms since 1988. Imports, up 153 percent be-

Hong Kong's Re-exports to China*
(in HK$ millions)

Commodity	1992	1991	% change
Textile yarns, fabrics & related products	$42,792	35,619	20%
Telecommunications parts & equipment	7,718	6,010	28
Textile & leather machinery	5,721	3,433	67
Thermionic, cold cathode & photocathode valves; transistors & semiconductors	4,910	4,316	14
Leather	4,906	3,450	42
Polymers of styrene	4,506	3,891	16
Oil	4,454	3,567	25
Paper & paperboard	4,386	3,302	33
Automobiles	4,186	1,478	183

* Goods sent to China through Hong Kong by third countries   *Source: Foreign Trade Magazine*

tween 1987 and 1992, reached US$122.5 billion in 1992, a rise of 22.6 percent from the year before.

Textiles and apparel, electronics, plastics, toys, and watches and clocks account for about 60 percent of Hong Kong's domestic exports. Exports of clothing are the largest foreign exchange earner—the Hong Kong market is second only to that of all of Italy in apparel—and together textiles and apparel account for 40 percent of all domestic exports and 26 percent of total exports.

One of Hong Kong's more recent exports has been jobs. In 1988 there were about 845,000 manufacturing jobs in the colony. By 1991 this figure had fallen to 735,000, and in mid-1993 manufacturing employment had fallen to 522,000. Not only has there been an overall drop of 38 percent, but the rate of erosion has also been accelerating, from a 3.4 percent annual rate between 1988 and 1991 to a 10.8 percent rate between 1991 and 1993. Virtually all of this outflow represents the relocation of operations to nearby lower-wage Chinese venues.

IMPORTS

Hong Kong is the world's 11th largest importer. Its gross import value surpasses that of such larger entities as Australia, Brazil, China, India, Iran, Mexico, Malaysia, and Sweden. Per capita imports are seven times what they are in Japan and five times what they are in the United States.

In 1990 the largest share of Hong Kong's imports—38.7 percent—consisted of raw and intermediate materials to support its manufacturing industries. These were primarily electrical components—such as semiconductors, integrated circuits, printed circuit boards—and textiles and plastic feedstocks.

In recent years the nature of these inputs has shifted from lower-grade bulk commodities to more sophisticated, higher-quality, higher-value intermediate items. Consumer goods, at 38.6 percent, make up the next category. Small, inexpensive items usually come from China, while more expensive items come from suppliers in developed countries, such as the United States and Japan. Although Hong Kong's population is small in absolute numbers, it has a high per capita income and is very consumption-oriented, meaning that it presents a rich market for a variety of upscale goods. The next largest functional import category is capital goods, primarily machinery and equipment, at 14.7 percent, followed by foodstuffs with a 5.8 percent share. Fuels, mostly refined petroleum products, make up the remaining 2.2 percent of imports.

Industrial inputs used to account for 40 percent or more of imports, while consumer items accounted for 35 percent or less. Between 1990 and 1992 local consumption of imported goods rose at an average annual rate of 5 percent, while domestic export production barely eked out a 1.1 percent gain. Given the continuing structural decline of onshore industry and the maturing of the consumer economy, consumer imports should surpass industrial inputs in the near future. With the exception of the changing positions of inputs and consumer items, the structure of imports has been fairly stable for the last several years.

Hong Kong has traditionally maintained a close equivalence between its imports and exports, so that it has not experienced the problem of trading partners irate over mounting trade surpluses that is faced by many other growing Asian economies. In fact, in recent years Hong Kong's trade has shown a tendency to develop a small and slightly growing merchandise trade deficit. So far, this deficit has remained relatively small.

Hong Kong's Major Imports by Commodity (in HK$ billions)

Commodity	1992	1991	% change
Textile yarns, fabrics & made-up articles	$101,322	$93,678	8%
Electrical machinery, apparatus & appliances & parts	95,434	77,791	23
Apparel	80,078	66,507	20
Telecommunications, audio & video equipment	75,629	60,094	26
Food & live animals	43,469	39,496	10
Office machines & computers	33,921	23,739	43
Watches & clocks	32,292	28,014	15
Footwear	31,689	22,338	42
Toys, games & sporting goods	31,145	23,157	34
Automobiles	16,497	5,912	179

Source: Hong Kong Trade Development Council

Hong Kong's Leading Trade Partners

Exports - 1992

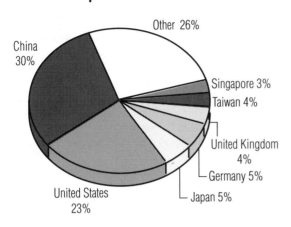

Total 1992 Exports: US$ 118.6 Billion

Imports - 1992

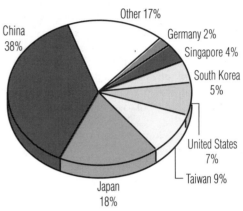

Total 1992 Imports: US$ 122.5 Billion

Source: Hong Kong Trade Development Council
Note: rounded to the nearest percent

However, during the first quarter of 1993 Hong Kong's trade deficit amounted to US$1.3 billion, 2.2 percent of total trade (the deficit previously had not topped 1 percent of the total).

The reasons for this growth are fairly easy to delineate. First, as Hong Kong moves more production offshore, it produces fewer goods to export. Second, its affluent populace is consuming more, both in terms of domestically produced goods— which cannot then be exported—and in terms of high-value imports, which adds weight to the other side of the equation. Finally, the trade deficit mimics the general deficit position as the government for the first time has begun to issue debt to fund the large infrastructure projects that are to be its legacy after it leaves in 1997.

However, the negative merchandise trade balance fails to take into account trade in intangibles, that due to profitable growth in the financial and business service sectors, are in a heavy surplus position, offsetting the effects of lagging trade in goods. Any residual concerns over the strength of Hong Kong's financial position were put to rest in 1991, when the government, at the behest of China—nervous about deficit financing of construction projects—released for the first time its level of international reserves. These stood at US$28.9 billion, more than double the estimates of the most optimistic analysts. Hong Kong seems well able to subsidize any trade deficit that it might accrue.

TRADING PARTNERS

In 1992 Hong Kong's largest trading partner was, not surprisingly, China, which took 29.8 percent of total exports and provided 37.1 percent of total imports. The United States took 23.2 percent of exports, so between them, these two large markets accounted for more than half of all exports. Other buyers took around 5 percent or less of exports: Germany (5.3 percent), Japan (5.3 percent), the United Kingdom (3.9 percent), Taiwan (3.5 percent), Singapore (2.6 percent), Canada (1.7 percent), the Netherlands (1.6 percent), and South Korea (1.6 percent). Together these ten countries accounted for more than three-quarters of all of Hong Kong's export trade. Remaining customers each accounted for less than 1.5 percent of the total.

Hong Kong's domestic exports show a definite trend. Between 1989 and the first quarter of 1993 the share of exports destined for Asian countries, primarily China, rose from 34.9 percent to 49.2 percent, while the share headed for North America, primarily the United States, fell from 35 percent to 26 percent. Europe's share also declined from 23.8 percent to 19.4 percent. During this period these three regions of the world accounted for between 93.7 percent and 94.9 percent of Hong Kong's total export trade, suggesting that despite Hong Kong's stated desire to diversify its products and partners, it has continued to market to essentially the same customers while becoming more enmeshed with China.

In 1992 Hong Kong's major import trade partners—the source markets for the goods it bought—

Hong Kong's Imports by Country (in HK$ billions)

Country	1992	1991	% change
China	$354	$293	21%
Japan	166	127	31
Taiwan	87	75	16
United States	71	59	20
South Korea	44	35	26
Singapore	39	32	22
Germany	22	17	30
United Kingdom	19	17	12
Italy	15	12	25
Switzerland	12	11	9

Source: Foreign Trade Magazine

INTERNATIONAL TRADE ORGANIZATION MEMBERSHIPS

As a dependency, Hong Kong has no international standing as a separate governmental unit. However, because of its prominence in world trade it has been active in and extended recognition by a variety of international organizations. Hong Kong participates in about 40 international organizations and maintains trade offices in major cities worldwide. The official Trade Department and the statutory Hong Kong Trade Development Council (HKTDC) are its primary internal trade organizations. The Trade Department is responsible for setting and enforcing official policy, while the HKTDC is a quasi-official body that promotes trade.

Hong Kong initially participated in negotiations on the General Agreement on Tariffs and Trade (GATT) as part of the British delegation, but was granted independent contracting party status in 1986 at the beginning of the Uruguay round. Hong Kong is also a principal in the Multi-Fiber Arrangement, which sets textile quotas between it and such major markets as the United States, the European Community, Canada, Austria, Finland, and Norway.

Hong Kong participates in several United Nations organizations such as the Conference on Trade and Development and the Economic and Social Commission for Asia and the Pacific. It is a full member of the Asian Development Bank, the Organization for Economic Cooperation and Development, the Customs Cooperation Council, the Asian Productivity Organization, the Asia Pacific Economic Cooperation group, and the Pacific Economic Cooperation Conference. Hong Kong participates in the General System of Preferences and the Harmonized Commodity Description and Coding System.

included China (37.4 percent), Japan (17.6 percent), Taiwan (9.1 percent), the United States (7.4 percent), South Korea (4.7 percent), Singapore (4.2 percent), Germany (2.3 percent), the United Kingdom (2 percent), and Italy (1.6 percent). Together these nine countries accounted for 86.3 percent of all of Hong Kong's imports. The remaining 13.7 percent came from countries that each accounted for less than 1.5 percent of Hong Kong's total imports.

During the first quarter of 1993 Hong Kong bought slightly less from China and Taiwan and somewhat more from Singapore (primarily refined petroleum products) and the Western European countries, although the same nine countries continued to account for 84.7 percent of total import purchases and the short-term changes were not significant. Hong Kong's buying patterns have remained relatively stable since the late 1980s.

DEVELOPMENT PLANS

Hong Kong does not operate with a planned economy or with significant incentives to direct investment into any particular avenues. However, the British colonial government, as part of its plans for handing over Hong Kong to China in 1997, has instituted an ambitious infrastructure development and improvement program. Projects include the construction of a major new airport on landfill, port improvements, and other transportation—highway and rail—projects. Chinese concerns over deficit financing for these projects has slowed them down, but observers expect the majority of them to be bid and finished, providing a significantly increased domestic market for materials, equipment, and expertise over the next several years.

Hong Kong's Exports by Country (in HK$ billions)

Country	1992	1991	% change
United States	$65	$63	3%
China	62	54	15
Germany	16	19	[16]
United Kingdom	16	14	14
Japan	11	12	[8]
Singapore	10	9	11
Taiwan	7	6	17
Netherlands	5	5	0
Canada	5	5	0
France	3	4	[25]

Source: Foreign Trade Magazine

Import Policy & Procedures

INTRODUCTION

It is well known that Hong Kong is a major exporter of light consumer products, but the territory is also a major importer of foreign products and services. Hong Kong relies on imports of almost all essential products—foodstuffs, energy, machinery, and components—and its consumers have become increasingly affluent and sophisticated, demanding a wide selection of goods. Hong Kong was the eleventh largest import market in the world in 1990, and its per capita import rate is one of the highest in the world, seven times the level in Japan and five times the level in the United States.

Hong Kong is thoroughly committed to free trade. There are no significant import taxes, and only a few items are restricted. Licensing formalities are kept to a minimum, and import licenses are required only for a few categories of products governed by international obligations or for reasons of health, safety, and security.

REGULATORY AUTHORITY

The Trade Department directs and implements Hong Kong's trade policy. Its functions include administering quotas, issuing import and export licenses, and issuing certificates of Hong Kong origin.

Trade Department
Trade Department Tower
700 Nathan Road
Kowloon, Hong Kong
Tel: [852] 7897555 Fax: [852] 7892491
Tlx: 45126 CNDI

IMPORT POLICY

There are import restrictions on a few commodities, based on health, safety, environmental, and security concerns. Import licenses are required for some items.

Customs Classification

Hong Kong classifies goods according to the standard international Harmonized Commodity Description and Coding System.

Tariffs, Duties, and Excise Taxes

Hong Kong is a free port and has no general tariff. However, excise duties, also called taxes, are levied on the certain commodities unless they are exported directly from bond or factory, or qualify as transshipment cargo that has been stored in Hong Kong. The following commodities are taxed:

- cosmetics
- hydrocarbon oils
- motor vehicles
- soft drinks
- tobacco and tobacco products
- wine, beer, and liquors, including certain industrial alcohol products

A 100 percent tax is levied on tobacco products. A tax is assessed on motor vehicles when first registered in Hong Kong. The registration tax on private cars is 90 percent of the CIF (cost, insurance, and freight) value; on trucks (including semi-tractor trailers) and public buses, 15 percent of the CIF value.

The Department of Trade determines eligibility for refund or drawback of taxes on the following basis:

- A refund is granted if goods are reexported, damaged in transit, or destroyed before use.
- A drawback is permitted if goods are reexported after undergoing a recognized manufacturing process in Hong Kong, provided the taxable material content can be accurately measured by analysis immediately before the finished product is shipped.

Restrictions

Hong Kong restricts imports primarily for health, safety, and security reasons, or to fulfill obligations under international trade agreements. The primary restrictions are as follows:

- A license is required for all imports of halons and chemicals that deplete the ozone layer. Under the 1987 Montreal protocol on substances that deplete the ozone layer, Hong Kong bans the import of chlorofluorocarbons and halons from nonparticipating countries and has frozen its consumption of halons at the 1986 level.
- Artificial sweeteners intended for human consumption, other than saccharin, saccharin sodium, and saccharin calcium, are prohibited. This ban applies also to products containing such sweeteners.
- A Wholesale Poisons License is required for the possession, storage, and sale of poisons.
- The import of acetic anhydride is restricted.
- Importers of antibiotics must first register with the Hong Kong Medical and Health Department.
- Pharmaceutical firms must be registered, and all pharmaceuticals, both imported and domestic, must be registered and licensed before entering the Hong Kong market.
- A license is required for the import of all agricultural pesticides, except for those in aerosol containers or in forms other than liquid, powder, or granular.
- Poisonous insecticides may be imported only under license, which must have the prior endorsement of the Hong Kong Agriculture and Fisheries Department.
- There are regulations governing radioactive substances and irradiating apparatus.
- Narcotics and drugs may be imported only under Medical and Health Department Special Import License.
- A Royal Hong Kong Police Special Permit is required for the import of arms and ammunition, including parts and imitations. This permit may be obtained after the shipment's arrival in Hong Kong, but customs officials will detain the goods until the permit is issued.

Valuation

Hong Kong adheres to the GATT Customs Valuation Agreement, which provides detailed rules for fair methods of valuation.

Countertrade

There are no specific government regulations or requirements governing countertrade transactions. An importer wishing to engage in this type of commerce may request a ruling for a specific transaction.

Samples and Advertising Matter

Hong Kong permits the importation of samples and advertising material in accordance with terms of the International Convention to Facilitate the Importation of Commercial Samples and Advertising Material. Samples enter duty free, except for valuable samples of dutiable goods. No duties or restrictions apply to the importation of advertising material.

ATA Carnets

Hong Kong is a signatory to the ATA Carnet Convention, which enables one to bring several different products into the territory with a single customs document (carnet). The carnet allows expeditious and duty-free entry of articles that are intended for display at trade fairs, exhibitions, seminars, and similar events. Such goods may remain in Hong Kong for up to 12 months.

The carnet assures customs officials in countries that are members of the ATA Carnet Convention that the carnet holder will pay duties, taxes, and other expenses should the conditions of the agreement be violated. For example, if the products covered by the carnet are lost or stolen, the carnet holder is liable for all applicable taxes and duties. Extensions and renewals are not granted. However, there is no limit to the number of times goods or parts of goods listed in a carnet may be exported and reimported during the 12 months. Only the Hong Kong General Chamber of Commerce can issue and guarantee carnets in Hong Kong. The fee for one set is HK$300 (about US$40) for members, and HK$100 (about US$13) for each additional country, with a HK$100-per-country charge for reuse within the validity period. Carnets are not issued for goods whose value exceeds HK$5 million (about US$650,000).

ATA carnets can be used to take samples to Australia, Japan, Korea, New Zealand, the United States, and many countries in Europe. It takes approximately two days for a carnet to be processed. For further information or to apply for an ATA carnet in Hong Kong, contact:

General Chamber of Commerce
22nd Floor, United Square
95 Queensway
Hong Kong
Tel: [852] 5279843 Fax: [852] 5279843
Tlx: 83535 TRIND

Marking and Labeling

The following marking and labeling requirements apply to imports of certain products:

- Sausages and sausage meats, liquid extracts of coffee and tea, pickles and sauces, certain unfermented grape juice products, and foods containing an antioxidant must bear English labels stating the preservative or antioxidant content. If the food is Chinese-style, the labeling should be in Chinese.

- Special regulations apply to margarine.
- Containers of frozen confection must bear the name and address of the manufacturer of the contents, clearly and legibly marked, in English.

The following dangerous goods must bear descriptive labels in both Chinese and English:

- compressed gases
- explosives
- flammable, combustible, corrosive, and poisonous substances

Penalties for false descriptions of quantity, origin, material, method of manufacture, patents, or copyrights include fines, imprisonment, and forfeiture of goods.

Packaging Weights and Measures

The size and contents of all locally produced and imported household products should be declared in SI units.

Electric Current

The electric current used in Hong Kong is AC, 50 cycle, 200/346 volts, 1, 3 phases, 2, 3, 4 wires.

Entry and Warehousing

Dutiable shipments must be stored in either a general bonded warehouse or in a licensed warehouse belonging to the importer until the duty is paid or the goods are reexported.

One of three permits is required to move a taxable commodity within Hong Kong:

- A removal permit for taxable goods covers movement before the tax is paid.
- A tax-paid removal permit covers taxable and tax-paid goods to be exported directly from a bonded or licensed warehouse or from a factory or firm authorized to receive drawback or refund.
- An export permit covers shipment of goods. Commercial firms that use such a permit are required to have a certificate issued by the authorities in charge at the shipping destination verifying that the goods have arrived. An export permit is not required if tax-paid goods are being exported and no drawback is claimed at a later date.

IMPORT PROCEDURES

Import Declaration

For all goods imported into Hong Kong, an import declaration must be filed with the Customs and Excise Department of the Trade Department within 14 days of entry. Import declaration fees are HK$2 (about US$0.25) for goods valued at HK$4,000 (aboutUS$520) and under, with an additional HK$0.50 (about US$0.07) for each HK$1,000 (about US$130) over. This charge is not levied on:

- advertising material of no commercial value
- aircraft stores
- personal effects
- personal gifts
- postal packages
- ship's stores
- transit or transshipment cargo (cargo consigned on a through bill of lading)

Import License

Licenses issued by the Trade Department are required for articles covered under international trade agreements, such as textiles, articles restricted or controlled for health, safety, or security reasons, and articles subject to excise tax. Licenses for textile imports are valid for 28 days; licenses for nontextile imports are valid for six months.

Preshipment Inspection

The government of Hong Kong does not require preinspection of import shipments, but individual importers may request it.

DOCUMENTATION

A commercial invoice and bill of lading (or air waybill) are required, but no special customs invoice or consular invoice is needed. Inclusion of a packing list with the entry documents can greatly facilitate customs clearance. Other documents may be required, depending upon the nature of the shipment. Hong Kong does not generally require documents to be legalized.

A brief description of the necessary documents for customs clearance follows.

Commercial Invoices

There are no requirements regarding the form of a commercial invoice. The document should contain a complete description of the goods being shipped, including shipping marks, price, quantity of goods, the number of packages, place of origin, freight, insurance, and any other relevant details. Facsimile signatures should not be used.

Bill of Lading

There are no special requirements regarding the form of a bill of lading, but all marks and case numbers appearing on the packages in the shipment must appear on it. Grouping of marks or numbers on shipments of mixed commodities is not permitted. For shipments coming by air, air waybills replace bills of lading. Bills of lading and air waybills must conform strictly to the conditions and terms of the buyer's letter of credit.

Packing List

Packing lists may be required for customs clearance of piece-goods imported into Hong Kong and subsequently reexported. In general, however, they are not required. Nevertheless, it is recommended that packing lists be included with the entry documents in order to expedite customs clearance.

Certificates of Origin

Hong Kong does not usually require certificates of origin for import goods. When a certificate of origin is specified in the transaction, the standard form available in stationery stores should be used. The certificate should agree with the other documents, be certified by a chamber of commerce, be issued in duplicate, and be signed by a responsible member of the exporting firm.

Insurance Certificate

Normal commercial practices apply.

Other Documents

Special documentation may be required for certain types of products, and in some cases in advance of the shipment. For example:

- Foodstuffs containing preservatives or antioxidants: documentation verifying the quantity of additives is required.
- Game bird, game meat, and prohibited meat: a permit from the Hong Kong Department of Health is required before shipment.
- Meat and poultry: an official and valid health certificate issued by a competent authority in the country of origin. The exporter should forward the health certificate with the order.
- Milk, frozen confections and prepackaged food: documentation of compliance with applicable Hong Kong law must be forwarded before shipping.
- Plant material and live plants: an official phytosanitary certificate issued by the competent authority in the country of origin may be required.

Export Policy & Procedures

INTRODUCTION

Hong Kong is one of the world's leading producers and exporters of consumer products. Although many labor-intensive assembly operations have been moved to southern China in recent years, the bulk of all consumer products—such as garments, toys, watches, and electronic goods—return to Hong Kong for final processing or storage before being reexported. It is estimated that as much as to 90 percent of Hong Kong's light manufacturing output is exported.

The government restricts the export of only a few commodities, although most restricted items can be exported with a proper license. Other export restrictions arise from the requirements of other countries and various international agreements.

REGULATORY AUTHORITY

The Trade Department directs and implements Hong Kong's trade policy. Its functions include administering quotas, issuing import and export licenses, and issuing certificates of Hong Kong origin.

Trade Department
Trade Department Tower
700 Nathan Road
Kowloon, Hong Kong
Tel: [852] 7897555 Fax: [852] 7892491
Tlx: 45126 CNDI

EXPORT POLICY

For the most part, Hong Kong places few restrictions on exports, other than for reasons of security, public health, and safety. However, even restricted items may be exported with a proper license. In addition, various documentation and licensing requirements reflect international trade agreements and the policies of the importing countries.

Countertrade

There are no specific regulations or requirements governing countertrade transactions. Businesses wishing to engage in this type of commerce may request a ruling for a specific transaction.

EXPORT PROCEDURES

Export Declarations

An exporter must file a declaration with the Hong Kong Customs and Excise Department for every export or reexport shipment. There are two forms:

- Export Declaration Form 2, for all exports and reexports except Hong Kong-made clothing and footwear, and certain articles exempted by regulation
- Export Declaration Form 2A, for Hong Kong-manufactured clothing

Filing fees are the exporter's responsibility, and are assessed on the value of the merchandise:

- For goods valued at HK$10,000 (about US$1,3000) or less—HK$5 (about US$0.65)
- For each additional HK$1,000 (about US$130) (up to and including)—HK$0.50 (about US$0.07)
- For each HK$1,000 (up to and including) of clothing—HK$0.30 (about US$0.04)

For more information, contact:

Hong Kong Customs and Excise Department
8th Floor, Harbour Building
38 Pier Road
Central, Hong Kong
Tel: [852] 8521411 Fax: [852] 5423334

Export Licenses

Export licenses are required for articles in the following categories:

- certain electrical products
- certain processed or manufactured foodstuffs
- footwear
- garments
- medicines
- ozone-depleting substances
- pesticides
- pharmaceutical products (except for products for personal use that are transported in accompanying personal luggage)
- reserved commodities (such as rice, frozen or chilled beef, mutton and pork, and frozen poultry)
- strategic commodities (such as computers, fiber-optics communication systems, biological agents, arms, ammunition, and explosives)
- textiles (except for textile articles for personal use that are transported in accompanying personal luggage)

Such articles may not be shipped out until the valid export license has been issued and the exporter has delivered it to the owner of the transport vessel. Export license forms are available from:

Trade Department, Collection Office
Trade Department Tower
700 Nathan Road
Kowloon, Hong Kong
Tel: [852] 3985333

Application for Export License

Application for an export license is made to the Trade Department; application forms are available from the Trade Department Collection Office. If export authorization by other departments or organizations is needed, it should be obtained before applying to Trade Department. In most cases, license approval takes one to three working days. The applicant receives a reference number and receipt, which he should present to the Issuing Counters where the application was made.

Licensing is immediate in the following cases:

- textile exports and most reexports to nonrestricted markets
- textile reexports to all European markets
- exports of textile samples
- unaccompanied personal effects and gifts to all markets (application must be submitted to Trade Department Tower)

Only the Trade Department may make changes to an approved license. Requests to amend a license should be made to the Department in writing and should include a copy of the license and any other supporting documents.

For further information regarding licenses for non-textile products, contact:

Non-Textiles Controls Division
Hong Kong Trade Department
13th Floor, Ocean Centre, Canton Road
Kowloon, Hong Kong
Tel: [852] 7372255

For information about textile export licenses and quota requirements and availability, contact:

Textile Controls Division
Hong Kong Trade Department
15th Floor, Ocean Centre, Canton Roa
Kowloon, Hong Kong
Tel: [852] 7372388 (for EC licenses), 7372345 (for US licenses)

Textile Export Control

Hong Kong has a textile restraint agreement, the Multi-Fiber Arrangement (MFA) with a number of countries. The Trade Department implements the MFA under its Textiles Export Control System. Quota allotment and license are required to export MFA textiles. For further information, contact the Trade Department.

DOCUMENTATION

Only registered Hong Kong companies are eligible to obtain official documents from the Hong Kong government.

Invoice

An invoice must accompany all other export documents so that customs can determine the value of the shipment. The Hong Kong supplier makes out the invoice in accordance with the terms of the purchase order and letter of credit. In general, an invoice should show:

- name and address of buyer
- name and address of seller
- general description of the merchandise, including quantity, unit price, and total price
- import license number, contract number, or any other number stipulated in the letter of credit
- statement to the effect that any special packaging requirements requested in the letter of credit have been met
- shipping method (terms of payment) and ports of shipment and discharge
- name of the issuing bank
- letter of credit number
- identifying shipping marks, gross and/or net weight, and other details required under the terms of the letter of credit

The invoice should be dated and signed.

Invoice Certification

Many countries require the Hong Kong government's endorsement of commercial invoices for importation. Others require that their consulate in Hong Kong endorse the commercial invoice. When either of these conditions pertains, the requirements should be clarified in the initial negotiation and included in the letter of credit. The Hong Kong Trade Department provides government endorsement at a minimal fee, as do five other bodies that are authorized to issue trade documents. Consulates usually charge a fee based on a percentage of the invoice value. Responsibility for the payment of this fee should be determined by the supplier and the importer when the order is placed and should be included in the letter of credit.

Special Customs Invoices

If the country of import requires a special customs declaration certificate, the Hong Kong supplier should provide a statement to the effect that the goods are valued as stated in the commercial invoice.

Bill of Lading

The bill of lading (or, for air shipments, the air waybill) constitutes the document of title to the merchandise, and it must conform strictly with the terms in the letter of credit. When shipping under cost, insurance, and freight (CIF), cost, freight/carriage, and insurance paid (CIP), or other related methods, the supplier contracts and pays for the freight. However, many buyers prefer to arrange for the shipment themselves in cooperation with a local freight forwarder, consolidator, or shipping line. In this case, payment is made under such terms as free alongside ship (FAS), free on board (FOB), free on board airport (FOA), or other related methods. The shipping agent should be informed of the correct terms and how the freight charges will be paid so that the carrier can prepare the bill of lading in accordance with the conditions of the letter of credit, purchase contract, and other documents.

The bill of lading lists the port of departure, port of discharge, name of the carrying vessel, and date of issue. The date of issue is very important because it indicates whether goods have been shipped within the time period required in the letter of credit. The supplier must submit all required documents on time to receive payment under the terms of the credit.

Bills of lading can be either negotiable or nonnegotiable. A negotiable bill of lading is made to the order of the shipper, who makes a blank endorsement on the back, or it is endorsed to the order of the bank that issues the letter of credit. A nonnegotiable bill of lading is consigned to a specific party (to the buyer or buyer's representative) and endorsement by the shipper is not required. In this case, the consignee must produce the original bill of lading in order to take delivery.

Certificates of Hong Kong Origin

Many countries require certificates of origin (that is, of actual manufacture) for imported goods. In order to obtain certificates of origin for its products, a Hong Kong factory must be registered with the Trade Department. Registration is product-specific: A factory registered for one item is not necessarily registered for another. Because not all Hong Kong factories are registered, and not all factories are registered for every product, foreign importers of goods that need certificates of origin should ascertain a supplier's status before placing an order.

The criteria for issuing certificates of origin depend on the product and the country to which it is being exported. When a foreign country's regulations are stricter than Hong Kong's, that country's criteria will govern the requirements for the certificate. Six organizations are authorized to issue certificates of origin:

- Hong Kong Trade Department
- Hong Kong General Chamber of Commerce
- Federation of Hong Kong Industries
- Indian Chamber of Commerce
- Chinese Manufacturer's Association of Hong Kong
- Hong Kong Chinese General Chamber of Commerce

Several types of endorsed certificates of origin can be requested, depending on the nature and origin of the merchandise. The following is a brief description of these certificates and their uses.

- A *Certificate of Hong Kong Origin* is issued only for products in which the Hong Kong manufacturing process has made substantial and permanent changes in either the shape, nature, form, or utility of the basic materials.
- A *Certificate of Hong Kong Origin—Form A* is required for entry of Hong Kong products under an importing country's Generalized System of Preferences (GSP). Hong Kong is currently accorded GSP benefits by Australia, Canada, the European Community, Finland, Japan, Norway, Sweden, and Switzerland. Each GSP country has individual origin criteria, and GSP-eligible products differ from country to country. Exporters wishing to take advantage of GSP benefits should contact the Hong Kong Trade Department for specifics. Application to the Trade Department for a Form A should be made at least two working days before the vessel is scheduled to leave Hong Kong. Form A is normally issued within four working days of

application, and a fee of HK$45 (about US$6) is charged.

- An *Endorsed Certificate of Hong Kong Origin* is issued for GSP-eligible products exported to Austria, Canada, Japan, Norway, and Switzerland, and for Hong Kong products that meet country-specific criteria for special tariff rate entry into Mauritius and St. Helena.
- A *Certificate of Hong Kong Processing* is issued for goods having undergone non-origin-conferring manufacturing in Hong Kong.
- A *Certificate of Hong Kong Reexport* applies to products reexported from Hong Kong that have not undergone manufacturing while in the territory.
- A *Certificate of Origin Without Transit/Transshipment* is used for transshipments being invoiced from Hong Kong without having entered or left the territory.
- *Outward Processing Arrangements (OPAs)* apply to Hong Kong products that are sent abroad for subsidiary manufacturing processing but that retain Hong Kong origin status. OPA Arrangement A governs goods requiring a Certificate of Origin and is available only to registered factories. OPA Arrangement B governs the reimportation of Hong Kong-origin goods not requiring a Certificate of Origin and is available regardless of supplier's registration status. Under both OPA arrangements, the applicant must establish that the finished goods meet the origin criteria for a Certificate of Origin.

Inspection Certificates

Hong Kong has no requirements for preexport inspection, except for consignments for which certificates of origin are being requested. Foreign buyers needing inspection certificates for Hong Kong goods should always stipulate their specific requirements in the purchase contract and in the letter of credit. Hong Kong suppliers and independent third parties can issue certificates of inspection, analysis, weight, or quality. For certification that the goods comply with the terms of the purchase order, an agent or supplier can perform an inspection and issue a control certificate. Independent laboratories are available to perform special analysis or tests and can issue certificates of inspection, analysis, or testing.

Industry Reviews

This chapter describes the status of and trends in major Hong Kong industries. It also lists key contacts for finding sources of supply, developing sales leads and conducting economic research. We have grouped industries into 11 categories, which are listed below. Some smaller sectors of commerce are not detailed here, while others may overlap into more than one area. If your business even remotely fits into a category don't hesitate to contact several of the organizations listed; they should be able to assist you further in gathering the information you need. We have included industry-specific contacts only. General trade organizations, which may also be very helpful, particularly if your business is in an industry not covered here, are listed in the "Important Addresses" chapter at the end of this book.

Each section has two segments: an industry summary and a list of useful contacts. The summary gives an overview of the range of products available in a certain industry and that industry's ability to compete in worldwide markets. The contacts listed are government departments, trade associations, publications, and trade fairs which can provide information specific to the industry. An entire volume could likely be devoted to each area, but such in-depth coverage is beyond the scope of this book. Our intent is to give you a basis for your own research.

All addresses and telephone numbers given are located in Hong Kong, unless otherwise noted. The telephone country code for Hong Kong is [852]; other telephone country codes are shown in square brackets where appropriate. Telephone city codes, if needed, appear in parentheses.

We highly recommend that you peruse the chapters on "Trade Fairs" and "Important Addresses." where you will find additional resources including a variety of trade promotion organizations, chambers of commerce, business services, and media.

INDUSTRY REVIEWS
TABLE OF CONTENTS

Computers and Other
    Information Products 67
Electronic Consumer and
    Component Products 69
Footwear 71
Furniture 72
Housewares and
    Household Appliances 73
Jewelry and Timepieces 74
Plastic Goods 75
Security and Safety Devices 76
Telecommunication
    Equipment 77
Textiles and Apparel 78
Toys 80

COMPUTERS AND OTHER INFORMATION PRODUCTS

Computers and computer peripherals are among Hong Kong's largest exports. Most computer products are shipped to the United States, but Hong Kong also exports to Europe, China, Canada, Japan, Australia, Singapore, and Taiwan.

Production of computers and peripherals is largely on an original equipment manufacturer (OEM) basis and is limited to small- to mid-sized systems. A majority of Hong Kong's computer firms employ fewer than 60 workers, and a large number of foreign-invested computer assemblers are operating in Hong Kong.

Personal Computers Approximately 80 percent of personal computers (PCs) produced in Hong Kong are exported. These PCs are generally low-price units intended for home or small business use. Most of

Hong Kong's PC firms assemble the units from imported parts, primarily obtained from US companies. Some US computer firms also manufacture PCs in Hong Kong to gain a larger share of Hong Kong's domestic market.

Hong Kong's computer manufacturers have pursued a strategy of labor-intensive production, which allows flexibility in meeting changing market demands. Beset by the resulting high production costs, most of Hong Kong's computer firms have relocated their manufacturing operations to China.

Software Many businesses in Hong Kong run custom applications software written by inhouse programmers or local software houses. Most software produced in Hong Kong is sold domestically to such businesses as retail and wholesale outlets, trading and shipping companies, banking and financial organizations, hotels and travel agencies, government entities, and manufacturers. These PC users require software tailored to Hong Kong's tax structure, accounting and payroll systems, inventory control processes, customs declarations, and other requirements business practices. Industry-specific inventory control software packages are of particular importance to businesses in Hong Kong, which is one of the world's largest trading centers for imports and reexports.

Software produced in Hong Kong is less sophisticated in design and documentation than imported software. However, software engineers in Hong Kong are experienced in writing applications for international business, and therefore can develop software for export. A few firms also have sufficient resources to develop software for mainframes and minicomputers. However, Hong Kong's software developers face difficulties in promoting their products internationally because the domestic market is not yet large enough to allow for testing and improvement of locally developed programs, and Hong Kong's firms are reluctant to expend R&D without a guaranteed worldwide market.

Government Agencies

Electrical & Mechanical Services Department
98 Caroline Hill Road
Hong Kong
Tel: 8958620 Fax: 8907493, 8685916

Information Technology Services Department
15/F., Wanchai Tower II
12 Harbour Road
Wanchai, Hong Kong
Tel: 8234520 Fax: 8656549

Trade Associations

Hong Kong Computer Society
14/F., Evernew House
485 Lockhart Road
Causeway Bay, Hong Kong
Tel: 8342228 Fax: 8343003

Hong Kong Information Technology Federation
1/F., Centre Point
181 Gloucester Road
Wanchai, Hong Kong
Tel: 8363356 Fax: 5910975

Directories/Publications

Asia Computer Weekly
(Bimonthly)
Asian Business Press Pte., Ltd.
100 Beach Road, #26-00 Shaw Towers
Singapore 0718
Tel: [65] 2943366 Fax: [65] 2985534

Asian Computer Directory
(Monthly)
Washington Plaza
1/F., 230 Wanchai Road
Wanchai, Hong Kong
Tel: 8327123 Fax: 8329208

Asian Computer Monthly
(Monthly)
Computer Publications Ltd.
Washington Plaza, 1/F.
230 Wanchai Road
Wanchai, Hong Kong
Tel: 9327123 Fax: 8329208

Asian Sources: Computer Products
(Monthly)
Asian Sources Media Group
22/F., Vita Tower
29 Wong Chuk Hang Road
Wong Chuk Hang, Hong Kong
Tel: 5554777 Fax: 8730488

Computer-Asia Software Guide
(Annual)
Syme Media Enterprises
6-12 Wing Kut Street
Central, Hong Kong

Computerworld Hong Kong
(Weekly)
Asia Computerworld Communications, Ltd.
701-4 Kam Chung Building
54 Jaffe Road
Wanchai, Hong Kong
Tel: 86132258 Fax: 8610953

What's New in Computing
(Monthly)
Asian Business Press Pte., Ltd.
100 Beach Road #26-00
Shaw Towers
Singapore 0718
Tel: [65] 2943366 Fax: [65] 2985534

Trade Fairs

Refer to the "Trade Fairs" chapter for complete listings, including contact information, dates, and venues. Trade fairs with particular relevance to this industry include the following, which are listed in that chapter under the heading given below:

Computer & Information Industries

- Auto-ID Hong Kong—The International Automatic Identification and Bar Code Technology and Equipment Exhibition
- Cenit Asia—Asian Centre and Conference for Information and Telecommunication Technologies
- Computer Expo—The International Computer Expo and Conference for Asia
- EDI Asia
- International Hi-Tech Show
- Software Exhibition
- Technology Showcase
- XII Conference of South East Asia Regional Computer Confederation (SEARCC)

For other trade fairs that may be of interest, we recommend that you also consult the heading Electronic & Electric Equipment.

ELECTRONIC CONSUMER AND COMPONENT PRODUCTS

Electronic products are among Hong Kong's top five exports in terms of value, accounting for at least 25 percent of total exports. Nearly all of Hong Kong's electronic exports are finished consumer products, and Hong Kong ranks among the world's top exporters of consumer electronic goods. Hong Kong's major export market is the United States, followed by Europe, China, Canada, Australia, the Philippines, Japan, Singapore, and Taiwan.

Hong Kong's electronic industry is largely an assembly center for electronic products of medium-range technology. Hong Kong's firms produce mostly low-end electronic parts and components. Upper-end components are imported to Hong Kong on an original equipment manufacturer (OEM) basis.

Electronic Consumer Products More than 1,700 electronic firms in Hong Kong assemble and export a broad variety of consumer goods: television sets, audio systems, calculators, electronic toys and games, videocassette recorders, video cameras, compact disc players, blank cassette and videotapes, and photocopying machines. Nearly 80 percent of the electronic parts and components used in these products including high-tech chips and specialty integrated circuits (ICs) for televisions are imported.

Electronic Parts and Components Hong Kong's electronic parts and components companies are unable to meet domestic market demands. Their output consists mainly of basic low-tech items. Principal electronic exports include low-end printed circuit boards (PCBs) and integrated circuits (ICs), which Hong Kong's three semiconductor manufacturers mass produce. The ICs made in Hong Kong include watch and clock ICs, voice and melody ICs, and electronic toy ICs for export to China and for

sale in domestic markets. However, Hong Kong-made ICs hold only about a 1 percent share of the domestic market. Imports of more technologically advanced ICs are high, and nearly 30 percent of imported ICs are reexported. In addition, several multinational IC manufacturers operate in Hong Kong; most of their production is designated for export to the United States.

Competitive Situation

Hong Kong's electronic product manufacturers face increasing competition in the low-end market from Southeast Asia and China, where labor is cheaper and generous incentives are being offered to attract foreign investment. To reduce production costs, many of Hong Kong's component manufacturers are making large varieties of parts in small lot sizes. Some electronic firms have relocated their assembly lines to China to take advantage of lower wages, and many have automated their production processes and reduced factory size. A few companies in Hong Kong are shifting their product lines to fast-growing market sectors, such as electronic components for computer network systems. Only a few companies, all of which have technology transfer arrangements with foreign investors, are investing in R&D to develop new products.

Hong Kong's electronic product manufacturers have lagged technologically, both in product development and manufacturing upgrades. A major problem for producers of components has been the volatility of Hong Kong's domestic market. Intense competition among international computer producers has slashed prices for low-end products. Because it has no trade barriers, Hong Kong has been a favorite dumping ground for low-end components used in consumer electronics, toys, telephones, and inexpensive computers and word processors.

Hong Kong's electronic components manufacturers are hoping to move into the less volatile, and more profitable, upper-end market. Thus, Hong Kong's semiconductor manufacturers are beginning to produce dynamic random access memory (DRAM) and static random access memory (SRAM) chips. With the introduction of surface mount technology (SMT), very large scale integration (VLSI) chips, and gate arrays, Hong Kong manufacturers have shifted to production of half-size mother boards, which cost less to make than full-size mother boards. The semiconductor companies are also responding to shortened chip technology life cycles by designing mother boards that use chips currently in development. This tactic allows Hong Kong IC suppliers to shorten the production cycle and to avoid some market price fluctuations by purchasing and mounting ICs just before the boards are ready to ship. To stimulate local manufacturing technology and product development, the Hong Kong government is providing R&D funding that encourages domestic semiconductor companies to link with university research centers. Several Hong Kong firms are also negotiating joint ventures with US firms for technology transfer and with Chinese firms for production of upper-end ICs.

Government Agencies

Electrical & Mechanical Services Department
98 Caroline Hill Road
Hong Kong
Tel: 8958620 Fax: 8907493, 8685916

Information Technology Services Department
15/F., Wanchai Tower II
12 Harbour Road
Wanchai, Hong Kong
Tel: 8234520 Fax: 8656549

Trade Associations

Hong Kong & Kowloon Electric Trade Association
6/F., 350-354 Hennessy Road
Wanchai, Hong Kong
Tel: 5737007, 5737005 Fax: 8345885

Hong Kong & Kowloon Electrical Appliances
Merchants Association Ltd.
4/F., 732 Nathan Road, Mongkok
Kowloon, Hong Kong
Tel: 3949991, 3942135 Fax: 3980147

Hong Kong Electronics Association
Rm. 1806-8, Beverly House
93-107 Lockhart Road
Wanchai, Hong Kong
Tel: 8662669 Fax: 8656843

Directories/Publications

Asian Electricity
(11 issues per year)
Reed Business Publishing Ltd.
5001 Beach Road #06-12
Golden Mile Complex
Singapore 0719
Tel: [65] 2913188 Fax: [65] 2913180

Asian Electronics Engineer
(Monthly, English, Chinese, Korean)
Trade Media Ltd.
29 Wong Chuck Hang Road
Hong Kong
Tel: 5554777 Fax: 8700816

Asian Sources: Electronic Components
(Monthly)
Asian Sources Media Group
22/F., Vita Tower
29 Wong Chuk Hang Road
Wong Chuk Hang, Hong Kong
Tel: 5554777 Fax: 8730488

Electronic Business Asia
(Monthly)
Cahners Publishing Company
249 West 17th Street
New York, NY 10011-5301, USA
Subscription Address: PO Box 173306
Denver, CO 80217-3306, USA

Electronic Product News-Asia
(7 issues per year)
Pan Asian Publishing Co.
c/o Elsevier Librico N.V.
Taman Warna, P.O. Box 0092
Singapore 9127

Electronics Bulletin
(Monthly)
Information Services Division
Hong Kong Productivity Council
HKPC Building
78 Tat Chee Avenue, Yau Yat Chuen
Kowloon, Hong Kong
Tel: 7885964 Fax: 7885900

Hong Kong Electronics
(Quarterly)
Hong Kong Trade Development Council
38/F., Convention Plaza
1 Harbour Road
Wanchai, Hong Kong
Tel: 5844333 Fax: 8240249 Tlx: 73595 CONHK

Trade Fairs

Refer to the "Trade Fairs" chapter for complete listings, including contact information, dates, and venues. Trade fairs with particular relevance to this industry include the following, which are listed in that chapter under the heading given below:

Electronic & Electric Equipment
- BROADCAST—The Hong Kong International Broadcasting, Sound, Film and Video Exhibition
- ECA—The International Electronic Component Exhibition for Asia
- EIE—The International Electronics Industry, Testing Equipment & Instrument Exhibition for Asia
- Elenex—The Asian International Electrical & Electronic Engineering Show
- Hong Kong Electronics Fair
- International Audio & Visual Show
- International Hi-Tech Show
- INTERNEPCON/SEMICONDUCTOR Hong Kong
- Securitex
- SMT—The International Surface Mount Technology Exhibition for Asia

For other trade fairs that may be of interest, we recommend that you also consult the heading Computer & Information Industries.

FOOTWEAR

Footwear is among Hong Kong's top exports. About 75 percent of Hong Kong's total footwear production value is shipped overseas. The largest export market is the United States, followed closely by East Asian and European countries.

Approximately 400 footwear manufacturers operate in Hong Kong, only a few of which are foreign-invested. The industry is dominated by small firms, which on average employ fewer than 20 workers.

Products Hong Kong's footwear industry mainly produces mid- to low-priced shoes of good quality. The most significant exports are leather shoes, which account for nearly 50 percent of export value, although plastic footwear holds the largest share of total production. Textile and rubber footwear are also significant exports. The footwear manufacturers are dependent on imports of raw materials, primarily leather, rubber, and plastic.

Competitive Situation

Footwear companies in Hong Kong face stiff competition from China, Indonesia, and Thailand in low-priced shoes, from Taiwan and Korea in mid-priced shoes, and from Italy and Switzerland in upper-end footwear. As a highly labor-intensive industry, Hong Kong's footwear manufacturing has been hurt in recent years by labor shortages and escalating production costs. In response, many of the manufacturers have relocated their plants to China.

To remain profitable and competitive in worldwide markets, Hong Kong's shoemakers are expanding their production of upper-end, higher-priced products, such as women's leather dress shoes, while reducing production of lower-priced plastic and rubber shoes. Hong Kong's footwear industry is also targeting new markets, particularly in Eastern Europe.

Trade Associations

Hong Kong Hide & Leather Traders Association Ltd.
1/F., 33 Portland Street
Kowloon, Hong Kong
Tel: 3887644 Fax: 7830804

Hong Kong Leather Goods Manufacturers Trade Association Ltd.
Unit 1-2, 4/F., Kai Fuk Industrial Centre
1 Wang Tung Road, Kowloon Bay
Kowloon, Hong Kong
Tel: 7953883 Fax: 7998745

Hong Kong Leather Shoe Merchants Association Ltd.
Flat E, 5/F., 88 Argyle Street
Kowloon, Hong Kong
Tel: 3955302 Fax: 3966020

Hong Kong Rubber & Footwear Manufacturers Association Ltd.
Block A, 2/F., 185 Prince Edward Road
Kowloon, Hong Kong
Tel: 3822297 Fax: 3976927

Directories/Publications

Asia Pacific Leather Directory
(Annual)
Asia Pacific Leather Yearbook
(Annual)
Asia Pacific Directories, Ltd.
6/F., Wah Hen Commercial Centre
381 Hennessy Road
Hong Kong
Tel: 8936377 Fax: 8935752

Fashion Accessories
(Monthly)
Asian Sources Media Group
22/F., Vita Tower
29 Wong Chuk Hang Road
Wong Chuk Hang, Hong Kong
Tel: 5554777 Fax: 8730488

Trade Fairs

Refer to the "Trade Fairs" chapter for complete listings, including contact information, dates, and venues. Trade fairs with particular relevance to this industry include the following, which are listed in that chapter under the headings given below:

Leather Goods, Footwear & Fur
- Hong Kong International Footwear Fair
- Hong Kong International Fur And Leather Fair
- Hong Kong International Handbags & Leather Goods Fair
- Hong Kong International Leather Exhibition
- Leather & Fur Products Showcase
- Shoe Vision

Textiles & Apparel
- Asia and World Textiles Conference
- Garmentec—The International Garment Machinery, Materials and Accessories Exhibition for Asia
- Hong Kong Fashion Week
- Hong Kong International Sporting Goods Fair
- Interstoff Asia

FURNITURE

Hong Kong's furniture industry is relatively small. Much of Hong Kong's trade in furniture consists of reexports of Western-style furniture to China and Southeast Asian furniture to Europe and the United States.

Approximately 1,050 manufacturing establishments produce furniture in Hong Kong, most of which employ fewer than 10 people. Some of Hong Kong's furniture companies are foreign-invested. Hong Kong furniture manufacturers specialize in producing low- to medium-end items.

Products Most of Hong Kong's furniture products are made of wood, metal, or a combination of these materials, but the industry also produces furniture of plastic, glass, fabric, and leather. Nearly all the raw materials hardwood, veneers, plywood, rattan, iron, steel, and fabric are imported from Southeast Asia, Japan, China, or Taiwan. Hong Kong's finished furniture products, made in both Western and Oriental styles, include office tables, desks, chairs, panels, partitions, filing systems, and cabinets; household items; outdoor patio furnishings; and specialty items for restaurants, stadiums, and educational and government institutions.

Competitive Situation

Hong Kong's furniture industry is renowned for flexibility, low prices, and availability of products. Most of the manufacturers produce their own designs and, depending on contract size, will meet specific customer requirements. Some larger manufacturers have invested in computer-aided design equipment to improve design capability.

High storage and production costs in Hong Kong have led about 90 percent of Hong Kong's furniture manufacturers to enter into licensing arrangements with Chinese firms. Various stages of production are done in China but, to ensure quality, the final finishing processes are completed in Hong Kong. Labor shortages are also a problem. Younger workers tend to be discouraged from entering the industry because of the harsh working conditions and the lengthy training period, usually three to five years.

Most furniture firms in Hong Kong are so small that mechanization is not affordable and shifting production to higher-quality goods is not feasible. These firms thus focus on cheaper products and quantity over quality, which places them in direct competition with furniture makers in Taiwan, Singapore, and Southeast Asia.

Trade Associations

Federation of Hong Kong Furniture Manufacturers
13/F., Flat A, 740 Nathan Road
Kowloon, Hong Kong
Tel: 3949162

Hong Kong & Kowloon Art Carved Furniture & Camphor-Wood Chests Merchants Association
Flat A, 13/F., Lee Wah Building
740 Nathan Road
Kowloon, Hong Kong
Tel: 3949162

Hong Kong & Kowloon Bamboo Goods Merchants Association
2/F., 128 Yee Kuk Street
Kowloon, Hong Kong
Tel: 3869917

Hong Kong & Kowloon Furniture & Shop Fittings Merchants Association
Flat A, 13/F., Lee Wah Building
740 Nathan Road
Kowloon, Hong Kong
Tel: 3949162

Hong Kong Furniture Dealers & Decorators General Association Ltd.
10/F., Kwong Ah Building
114 Thomson Road
Wanchai, Hong Kong
Tel: 5752755 Fax: 8344643

Hong Kong Office Equipment Association Ltd.
c/o Kodak (Far East) Ltd.
Kodak House, 321 Java Road
North Point, Hong Kong
Tel: 5649333 Fax: 5657474

Hong Kong Rattan Merchants Association
1/F., 314 Des Voeux Road West
Hong Kong
Tel: 5472900

Directories/Publications

Asian Sources: Gifts & Home Products (Monthly)
Asian Sources Media Group
22/F., Vita Tower
29 Wong Chuk Hang Road
Wong Chuk Hang, Hong Kong
Tel: 5554777 Fax: 8730488

Hong Kong Household
Hong Kong Trade Development Council
38/F., Convention Plaza
1 Harbour Road
Wanchai, Hong Kong
Tel: 5844333 Fax: 8240249 Tlx: 73595 CONHK

Trade Fairs

Refer to the "Trade Fairs" chapter for complete listings, including contact information, dates, and venues. Trade fairs with particular relevance to this industry include the following, which are listed in that chapter under the headings given below:

Construction & Housing
- International Building Exhibition (IBEX Hong Kong)

Furniture & Housewares
- Homefex & Invest

- Hong Kong International Furniture Fair
- Ideal Home Expo (held concurrently with Electrical Home Appliances Expo)

For other trade fairs that may be of interest, we recommend that you also consult the heading Gifts, Jewelry & Stationery.

HOUSEWARES AND HOUSEHOLD APPLIANCES

Housewares and household appliances account for a small but growing share of Hong Kong's exports. Exports are primarily shipped to other Asian countries.

Most of Hong Kong's factories for housewares and household appliances have fewer than 50 employees. Approximately 90 percent of the industry's output comes from a few large factories.

Products Hong Kong's production of household appliances is limited to small items, such as microwave ovens, standing and ceiling fans, electric frying pans, coffee pots, toasters, irons, vacuum cleaners, and space heaters. Housewares made in Hong Kong include medium-priced glass, plastic, aluminum, brass, and tinplate products, such as glassware, cooking utensils and pans, tableware, and cutlery. Decorative household goods include lamps, baskets, planters, bathroom accessories, and rattan and wicker items.

Competitive Situation

Manufacturers of household products in Hong Kong face strong competition from other Asian countries. Hong Kong's household goods industry has been contracting in recent years, both in the number of firms and in overall production.

Trade Associations

Air Conditioning & Refrigeration Association
Hong Kong
GPO Box 10158
Hong Kong
Tel: 6945359 Fax: 6919113

Design Council of Hong Kong
Rm. 407, Hankow Centre
5-15 Hankow Road, Tsimshatsui
Kowloon, Hong Kong
Tel: 7230818 Fax: 7213494

Hong Kong & Kowloon Bamboo Goods Merchants Association
2/F., 128 Yee Kuk Street
Kowloon, Hong Kong
Tel: 3869917

Hong Kong & Kowloon Electrical Appliances Merchants Association Ltd.
4/F., 732 Nathan Road, Mongkok
Kowloon, Hong Kong
Tel: 3949991, 3942135 Fax: 3980147

Hong Kong Designers Association
Rm. 407-411, Hankow Centre
5-15 Hankow Road, Tsimshatsui
Kowloon, Hong Kong
Tel: 7230818 Fax: 7213494

Hong Kong Furniture Dealers & Decorators General Association Ltd.
10/F., Kwong Ah Building
114 Thomson Road
Wanchai, Hong Kong
Tel: 5752755 Fax: 8344643

Directories/Publications

Asian Sources: Gifts & Home Products (Monthly)
Asian Sources Media Group
22/F., Vita Tower
29 Wong Chuk Hang Road
Wong Chuk Hang, Hong Kong
Tel: 5554777 Fax: 8730488

Hong Kong Household
Hong Kong Trade Development Council
38/F., Convention Plaza
1 Harbour Road
Wanchai, Hong Kong
Tel: 5844333 Fax: 8240249 Tlx: 73595 CONHK

Trade Fairs

Refer to the "Trade Fairs" chapter for complete listings, including contact information, dates, and venues. Trade fairs with particular relevance to this industry include the following, which are listed in that chapter under the headings given below:

Construction & Housing
- Airvex
- The Asian International Airconditioning, Ventilation, Heating & Refrigeration Show
- International Building Exhibition (IBEX Hong Kong)
- Luminex-The Asian International Lighting, Lighting Technology, Fittings & Systems Show
- World Plumbing Conferences and Expo

Furniture & Housewares
- Electrical Home Appliances Expo (held concurrently with Ideal Home Expo)
- Homefex & Invest
- Ideal Home Expo (held concurrently with Electrical Home Appliances Expo)

For other trade fairs that may be of interest, we recommend that you also consult the heading Gifts, Jewelry & Stationery.

JEWELRY AND TIMEPIECES

Hong Kong is one of the world's leading suppliers of designer jewelry, and its timepiece industry ranks as one of its top five export-earners. Hong Kong exports more complete watches than any other country; in dollar volume of exports, it ranks second in the world. Major export markets are in Western Europe, Japan, Canada, and the United States.

Over 2,000 jewelry and timepiece factories operate in Hong Kong. Most companies are small, labor-intensive enterprises, employing fewer than 50 workers.

Jewelry Hong Kong's jewelers produce an elaborate array of jewelry, primarily high-end pieces. Items include rings, bracelets, necklaces, tie clips and pins, brooches, and matched sets. Jewelry makers offer precious metal, semi-precious metal, and costume jewelry with and without precious or semi-precious stones. Styles vary from sophisticated and simple to elaborate and avant garde. Other Asian countries constitute a major market for Hong Kong's exports of gold and diamond jewelry. Hong Kong is also world renowned for its jade jewelry, primarily offered as bracelets, rings, and pendants.

As a chief world market for gems and precious metals, Hong Kong has nearly an endless supply of raw materials for its jewelry manufacturers. Hong Kong's jewelers remain competitive in international markets by emphasizing quality workmanship, diversity of high-quality designs, reasonable prices, genuine reliability, and attentive customer service. In addition, these jewelers deftly adjust their designs and manufacturing to meet consumers' changing tastes. To reduce manufacturing costs, many jewelry producers are having stones cut in China for setting in Hong Kong.

Timepieces Hong Kong's timepiece makers produce electronic and mechanical watches and clocks in a broad variety of styles, including desk and office clocks, novelty and decorative clocks, wall clocks, and mechanical, travel, and radio alarm clocks. They also offer high-quality components and accessories, such as watch and clock movements, metal watchcases, dials, and watchbands.

Timepiece manufacturers in Hong Kong remain near the top of the industry by focusing on product design. Although much of the production remains on an original equipment manufacturing (OEM) basis, some companies are beginning to market directly under their own brand names. Faced with rising competition from Southeast Asian countries, Hong Kong's timepiece producers are concentrating on mid- to high-end products. They are also upgrading their technology in the production of watch movements in order to reduce their dependence on imports.

Trade Associations

Chinese Gold & Silver Exchange Society
1/F., 12-18 Mercer Street
Hong Kong
Tel: 5441945 Fax: 8540869

Diamond Importers Association Ltd.
Rm. 1102, Parker House
72 Queen's Road
Central, Hong Kong
Tel: 5235497, 5260561 Fax: 8459649

Federation of Hong Kong Watch Trades & Industries Ltd.
Rm. 604, Peter Building
58-62 Queen's Road
Central, Hong Kong
Tel: 5233232 Fax: 8684485

Hong Kong & Kowloon Ivory Manufacturers Association Ltd.
B1, 3/F., Mirador Mansion
58 Nathan Road
Kowloon, Hong Kong
Tel: 3675336

Hong Kong Jade & Stone Manufacturers Association
16/F., Hang Lung House
184-192 Queen's Road
Central, Hong Kong
Tel: 5430543 Fax: 8150164

Hong Kong Jewellers & Goldsmiths Association Ltd.
13/4, Hong Kong Jewellery Building
178-180 Queen's Road
Central, Hong Kong
Tel: 5439633 Fax: 8507361

Hong Kong Jewellery Manufacturers Association
Unit 5, 1/F., Hunghom Square
37 Ma Tau Wai Road, Hunghom
Kowloon, Hong Kong
Tel: 7663002 Fax: 3623647

Hong Kong Watch Importers Association
GPO Box 5311
Hong Kong
Tel: 7354248 Fax: 7304570

Hong Kong Watch Manufacturers Association Ltd.
11/F., Yu Wing Building
64-66 Wellington Street
Central, Hong Kong
Tel: 5253902 Fax: 8106614

Kowloon Pearls, Precious Stones, Jade, Gold & Silver Ornament Merchants Association
6/F., Front Section, 506-508 Nathan Road
Kowloon, Hong Kong
Tel: 3843105, 3846863

Directories/Publications

Asian Sources: Timepieces (Monthly)
Asian Sources Media Group
22/F., Vita Tower
29 Wong Chuk Hang Road
Wong Chuk Hang, Hong Kong
Tel: 5554777 Fax: 8730488

Hong Kong Jewellery
(Quarterly)
Ridgeville Ltd.
Flat A, 12/F., Kaiser Estate Phase 1
41 Man Yue Street
Hunghom, Kowloon, Hong Kong
Tel: 3344311 Fax: 7641956

Hong Kong Watches & Clocks
(Semiannual)
Hong Kong Trade Development Council
38/F., Convention Plaza
1 Harbour Road
Wanchai, Hong Kong
Tel: 8334333 Fax: 8240249 Tlx: 73595 CONHK

Jewellery News Asia
(Monthly)
Jewellery News Asia Ltd.
Rm. 601-603, Guardian House
32 Oi Kwan Road
Wanchai, Hong Kong
Tel: 8322011 Fax: 8329208

Jewellery Review
(Bimonthly)
Brilliant-Art Publishing Ltd.
1101 Tung Wai Commercial Building
111 Gloucester Road
Wanchai, Hong Kong
Tel: 5116077 Fax: 5075855

World Jewelogue
(Annual)
Headway International Publications Co.
907 Great Eagle Centre
23 Harbour Road
Hong Kong
Tel: 8275121 Fax: 8277064

Trade Fairs

Refer to the "Trade Fairs" chapter for complete listings, including contact information, dates, and venues. Trade fairs with particular relevance to this industry include the following, which are listed in that chapter under the heading given below:

Gifts, Jewelry, & Stationery
- Christmas Showcase
- Hong Kong Gifts & Housewares Fair
- Hong Kong International Coin Show
- Hong Kong International Fashion Jewellery & Accessories Fair
- Hong Kong International Jewellery Show
- Hong Kong International Toy & Gift Show
- Hong Kong Jewellery & Watch Fair
- Hong Kong Premium Show
- Hong Kong Watch & Clock Fair
- Timepiece Gallery
- WatchTech

For other trade fairs that may be of interest, we recommend that you also consult the headings Furniture & Housewares.

PLASTIC GOODS

Hong Kong's plastic goods industry is a top world supplier of plastic products. The industry is also one of Hong Kong's top 10 domestic exporters. Major markets are in Europe, Asia, Canada, Japan, and the United States.

More than 5,500 manufacturers of plastic goods are located in Hong Kong. Most are small firms with fewer than 50 employees.

Products Approximately one-third of Hong Kong's plastic manufacturers make plastic toys, which are the industry's most significant export. Other plastic goods include straws, bottles, bags, flowers, wrapping films, household products, telecommunication components and equipment, and sporting goods. Local production of plastics is very limited, and all manufacturers are heavily dependent on imports of such plastics as polystyrene, polyethylene, polyvinyl chloride, and polypropylene. They also import high-quality resins, including acrylonitailebutadiene styrene, polycarbonate, linear-low density polyethylene, and nylon.

Competitive Situation

Many of Hong Kong's plastic goods manufacturers have moved their production operations particularly the processing and molding of simple products, to China. Firms that have stayed in Hong Kong are able to compete because of high worker productivity. Many of these firms are shifting to complex product design and mold and tool making. To remain competitive in international markets despite shortages of skilled labor, rising labor costs, and increasing production expenses, Hong Kong's plastic goods firms are automating their production lines, both in China and in Hong Kong, with plastic injection robots and runnerless molds. Some manufacturers are also exploring various advanced technologies: multilayer film coextrusion, gas injection molding, polymer alloying and compounding, and linked computer-aided design and manufacturing (CAD/CAM) systems for direct transfer of design data into machining instructions.

Trade Associations

Hong Kong & Kowloon Plastic Products Merchants United Association Ltd.
13/F., 491 Nathan Road
Kowloon, Hong Kong
Tel: 3840171 Fax: 7810107

Hong Kong Plastic Material Suppliers Association Ltd.
1/F., 11 Lai Yip Street, Kwun Tong
Kowloon, Hong Kong
Tel: 7579331 Fax: 7968885

Hong Kong Plastics Manufacturers Association Ltd.
Rm. 302, Red A Central Building
37 Wellington Street
Central, Hong Kong
Tel: 5232229 Fax: 8400704

Hong Kong Polyethylene Tubing Manufacturers'
Association
10/F., Lee Fat Building
40 Bute Street, Mongkok
Kowloon, Hong Kong
Tel: 3945912 Fax: 3990152

Directories/Publications

Asian Manufacturing
Far East Trade Press Ltd.
2/F., Kai Tak Commercial Building
317 Des Voeux Road
Central, Hong Kong
Tel: 5453028 Fax: 5446979

Asian Plastic News
(Quarterly)
Reed Asian Publishing Pte., Ltd.
5001 Beach Road #06-12
Golden Mile Complex
Singapore 0719
Tel: [65] 2913188 Fax: [65] 2913180

Trade Fairs

Refer to the "Trade Fairs" chapter for complete
listings, including contact information, dates, and
venues. Trade fairs with particular relevance to this
industry include the following, which are listed in
that chapter under the headings given below:

Hobbies, Recreation & Travel
* Hong Kong International Sporting Goods Fair
* Hong Kong International Toy & Gift Show
* Hong Kong Toys & Games Fair

Industrial Materials & Metals
* InterplasAsia—The International Plastics
  Machinery, Materials, Production Technology
  and Ancillary Equipment Exhibition for Asia
* MetalTech
* The International Mould & Die Exhibition
* Tube & Pipe—Hong Kong
* World Plumbing Conferences and Expo

For other trade fairs that may be of interest, we
recommend that you also consult the headings Construction & Housing; Furniture & Housewares; Gifts,
Jewelry & Stationery; and Machines & Instruments.

SECURITY AND SAFETY DEVICES

Hong Kong's security and safety industry is composed of fewer than 70 manufacturers, many of which
are medium- to large-size companies. Almost all production is exported on an original equipment manufacturer (OEM) basis for overseas manufacturers or
distributors. China is a major export market for security and safety equipment.

Products Security and safety devices produced
in Hong Kong range from low- to high-priced mod-
els. Low-priced devices include stand-alone or modu-
lar burglar alarms, fire alarms, and smoke and gas
detectors. Mid-price, mid-technology products include portable devices for protecting valuables or
vehicles. The high end consists mostly of surveillance systems with central control panels for residential and commercial premises.

Competitive Situation

Hong Kong's security and safety devices industry is growing industry, spurred particularly by demands in China's business sector, which is facing
rapid increases in crime.

Trade Associations

Society of Builders Hong Kong
Rm. 801/2, On Lok Yuen Building
25 Des Voeux Road
Central, Hong Kong
Tel: 5232081/2 Fax: 8454749

Hong Kong E&M Contractors' Association
Quarry Bay Reclamation Area
Hoi Tai Street
Quarry Bay, Hong Kong
Tel: 5655411

Hong Kong & Kowloon Electrical Appliances
Merchants Association Ltd.
4/F., 732 Nathan Road, Mongkok
Kowloon, Hong Kong
Tel: 3949991, 3942135 Fax: 3980147

Directories/Publications

Asian Architect And Contractor
(Monthly)
Thompson Press Hong Kong Ltd
Tai Sang Commercial Building, 19/F.
24-34 Hennessy Road
Hong Kong

Asian Electronics Engineer
(Monthly)
Trade Media Ltd.
29 Wong Chuck Hang Road
Hong Kong
Tel: 5554777 Fax: 8700816

Asian Security & Safety Journal
(Bimonthly)
Elgin Consultants, Ltd.
Tungnam Building
Suite 5D, 475 Hennessy Road
Causeway Bay, Hong Kong
Tel: 5724427 Fax: 5725731

Building & Construction News
(Weekly)
Al Hilal Publishing (FE) Ltd.
50 Jalan Sultan #20-06
Jalan Sultan Centre
Singapore 0719
Tel: [65] 2939233 Fax: [65] 2970862

Building Journal
(Monthly)
Trend Publishing (HK) Ltd.
19/F., Washington Plaza
230 Wanchai Road
Wanchai, Hong Kong
Tel: 8329298 Fax: 8329667

International Construction
(Monthly)
Reed Business Publishing, Ltd.
Reed Asian Publishing Pte
5001 Beach Road #06-12
Golden Mile Complex
Singapore 0719
Tel: [65] 2913188 Fax: [65] 2913180

Trade Fairs

Refer to the "Trade Fairs" chapter for complete listings, including contact information, dates, and venues. Trade fairs with particular relevance to this industry include the following, which are listed in that chapter under the heading given below:

Miscellaneous
- Hong Kong International Exhibition on Peaceful Use of Military Industry Technology
- Securitex

For other trade fairs that may be of interest, we recommend that you also consult the headings Computer & Information Industries; and Electronic & Electric Equipment.

TELECOMMUNICATION EQUIPMENT

Hong Kong is the telecommunication center for East Asia. Hong Kong's satellite transmission company, which is jointly owned with a Chinese venture, is Asia's premier transmission company, with more than 20 transmitters broadcasting television and radio signals throughout the Middle East, South and Southeast Asia, and East Asia.

In addition to the system operated by Hong Kong's government, three telecommunication operators provide high-tech services. Many major international telecommunication manufacturers have partnerships, joint ventures, or subsidiaries in Hong Kong making parts or building entire systems under license. Almost all production of telecommunication equipment in Hong Kong is on an original equipment manufacturer (OEM) basis. A large percentage of Hong Kong's exports of telecommunication products are reexports; key reexports are Chinese-made cellular phones and phone parts.

Products Hong Kong suppliers of telecommunication products assemble corded, cordless, and cellular telephones, modems, and facsimile machines. Local production is relatively small, and reexports dominate Hong Kong's telecommunication equipment industry.

Competitive Situation

As a result of Hong Kong's technologically progressive telecommunication authority, Hong Kong end-users have a first-rate fiber-optic system featuring four cellular networks and four second-generation cordless telephone (CT2) systems. In an effort to further boost volume and sales, the government is now shifting its focus from developing high-technology systems to encouraging lower costs, improved services, and deregulation of the domestic telecommunication equipment and services sectors. Three of Hong Kong's cellular systems are analog, and plans are under way to upgrade them to cellular networks. Chinese investors have joined with Hong Kong's telecommunication industry to expand access for cellular telephone users to every major mainland China city. In addition, Hong Kong's telecommunication operators are switching to digital systems to reduce installation and operating costs and to accelerate the expansion of high-speed data, facsimile, and cellular radio services.

Government Agencies

Information Services Department
Beaconsfield House
4 Queen's Road Central
Hong Kong
Tel: 8428777

Information Technology Services Department
15/F., Wanchai Tower II
12 Harbour Road
Wanchai, Hong Kong
Tel: 8234520 Fax: 8656549

Radio Television Hong Kong
Broadcasting House
30 Broadcast Drive
Kowloon, Hong Kong
Tel: 3396441 Fax: 3380279

Television and Entertainment Licensing Authority
National Mutual Centre, 9/F.
151 Gloucester Road
Wanchai, Hong Kong
Tel: 5743130 Fax: 8382219

Trade Associations

Hong Kong Information Technology Federation
1/F., Centre Point
181 Gloucester Road
Wanchai, Hong Kong
Tel: 8363356 Fax: 5910975

Hong Kong Telecom Association
GPO Box 13461
Hong Kong
Tel: 8770781 Fax: 8779115

Publications

Asia Pacific Broadcasting & Telecommunications
(Monthly)
Asian Business Press Pte., Ltd.
100 Beach Road
#26-00 Shaw Towers
Singapore 0718
Tel: [65] 2943366 Fax: [65] 2985534

Asiatechnology
(Monthly)
Review Publishing Company Ltd
6-7/F., 181-185 Gloucester Road
GPO Box 160
Hong Kong
Tel: 8328381 Fax: 8345571

Electronic Business Asia
(Monthly)
Cahners Publishing Company
249 West 17th Street
New York, NY 10011-5301, USA
Subscription Address: PO Box 173306, Denver, CO
80217-3306, USA

Electronic Product News-Asia
(7 issues per year)
Pan Asian Publishing Co.
c/o Elsevier Librico N.V.
Taman Warna, P.O. Box 0092
Singapore 9127

Electronics Bulletin
(Monthly)
Information Services Division
Hong Kong Productivity Council
HKPC Building
78 Tat Chee Avenue, Yau Yat Chuen
Kowloon, Hong Kong
Tel: 7885964 Fax: 7885900

Telecom Asia
(Bimonthly)
CCI Asia-Pacific (HK)
Suite 905, Guardian House
32 Oi Kwan Road
Wanchai, Hong Kong
Tel: 8332181 Fax: 8345620

Trade Fairs

Refer to the "Trade Fairs" chapter for complete listings, including contact information, dates, and venues. Trade fairs with particular relevance to this industry include the following, which are listed in that chapter under the headings given below:

Computer & Information Industries
- Asian Centre and Conference for Information and Telecommunication Technologies (Cenit Asia)
- EDI Asia
- Technology Showcase

Electronic & Electric Equipment
- Broadcast
- International Hi-Tech Show

TEXTILES AND APPAREL

Hong Kong-produced textiles and clothing are among the country's top five exports in terms of value, and Hong Kong ranks as one of the world's largest clothing exporters in terms of value. Major export markets are in Western Europe, Canada, Japan, China, and the United States.

More than 14,000 factories produce textiles and clothing in Hong Kong. Over 9,700 of those produce clothes, making apparel Hong Kong's largest manufacturing sector. A few foreign apparel firms have established production facilities in Hong Kong as well. Hong Kong is also a major regional sourcing center for garments.

Textiles Hong Kong's textile industry has four sectors: spinning, weaving, knitting, and finishing. Yarns available from the spinning sector include cottons, blended cottons, woolens, and worsteds. Production of man-made fiber-blended yarns has increased dramatically. Most of Hong Kong's yarns are used by domestic weaving and knitting firms to make canvas, sheeting, poplin, knits, denim, silk, and other fabrics.

Apparel Hong Kong's apparel manufacturers produce a wide array of goods, ranging from basic accessories to expensive, high-quality fashions for men, women, and children. Products include woven outer garments, knit outerwear, leather and fur clothing, shirts, blouses, T-shirts, suits, dresses, slacks, gloves, and headgear. In recent years, strong gains in the production and reexport of women's lingerie and nightwear have made Hong Kong one of the world's top suppliers, with exports accounting for 60 percent of local production.

Competitive Situation

Domestic labor shortages and rising production costs have led many of Hong Kong's major textile and apparel manufacturers to move labor- and land-intensive production facilities to countries where costs are lower, primarily China. Their R&D departments, however, remain in Hong Kong. To lower production costs, textile and apparel firms have also updated design and pattern development through computer-aided design, manufacturing, and engineering (CAD/CAM/CAE) technology.

Trade Associations

Association of Hong Kong Gloves Manufacturers Ltd.
c/o Action Secretarial Ltd.
Rm. D, 10/F., Harvard House
111 Thompson Road
Wanchai, Hong Kong
Tel: 5728224 Fax: 8382229

Federation of Hong Kong Cotton Weavers
Flat B, 14/F., Astoria Building
23-34 Ashley Road
Kowloon, Hong Kong
Tel: 3672383 Fax: 7213233

Federation of Fur Manufacturers & Dealers (Hong Kong) Ltd.
Rm. 603, Chevalier House
45-51 Chatham Road South, Tsimshatsui
Kowloon, Hong Kong
Tel: 3674646 Fax: 7390799

Federation of Hong Kong Garment Manufacturers
4/F., 25 Kimberley Road
Kowloon, Hong Kong
Tel: 7211383

Hong Kong Association of Textile Bleachers, Dyers, Printers & Finishers Ltd.
3/F., C.M.A. Building
64 Connaught Road Central
Central, Hong Kong
Tel: 5428600 Fax: 5414541

Hong Kong Cotton Made Up Goods Manufacturers Association Ltd.
12/F., Flat D, 739 Nathan Road
Kowloon, Hong Kong
Tel: 3944546 Fax: 3418582

Hong Kong Garment Manufacturers Association
Rm. 708, Universal Commercial Bldg.
69 Peking Road
Kowloon, Hong Kong
Tel: 3673392 Fax: 7217537

Hong Kong Hide & Leather Traders Association Ltd.
1/F., 33 Portland Street
Kowloon, Hong Kong
Tel: 3887644 Fax: 7830804

Hong Kong Knitted Fabrics Dyeing & Finishing Manufacturers' Association Ltd.
20/F., Wah Kit Commercial Centre
300 Des Voeux Road Central
Central, Hong Kong
Tel: 5453222 Fax: 5433622

Hong Kong Knitwear Exporters & Manufacturers Association Ltd.
Hang Pont Commercial Building
12/F., 31 Tonkin Street
Kowloon, Hong Kong
Tel: 7290111

Hong Kong Leather Goods Manufacturers Trade Association Ltd.
Unit 1-2, 4/F., Kai Fuk Industrial Centre
1 Wang Tung Road, Kowloon Bay
Kowloon, Hong Kong
Tel: 7953883 Fax: 7998745

Hong Kong Silk Piece-Goods Merchants Association
Flat 5D, Wing Cheong Commercial Building
19-25 Jervois Street
Hong Kong
Tel: 3845570, 5441143

Hong Kong Woollen & Synthetic Knitting Manufacturers Association Ltd.
Rm. 506C, Harbor Crystal Centre
100 Granville Road, Tsimshatsui East
Kowloon, Hong Kong
Tel: 3682091 Fax: 3691720

Textile Council of Hong Kong Ltd.
Rm. 744, Star House
3 Salisbury Road, Tsimshatsui
Kowloon, Hong Kong
Tel: 7357793 Fax: 7357795

Directories/Publications

Asia Pacific Leather Directory
(Annual)
Asia Pacific Leather Yearbook
(Annual)
Asia Pacific Directories, Ltd.
6/F., Wah Hen Commercial Centre
381 Hennessy Road
Hong Kong
Tel: 8936377 Fax: 8935752

ATA Journal: Journal for Asia on Textile & Apparel
(Bimonthly)
Adsale Publishing Company
Tung Wai Commercial Building, 21/F.
109-111 Gloucester Road
Wanchai, Hong Kong
Subscriptions: Hennessy Road
PO Box 20032, Hong Kong
Tel: 8920511 Fax: 8384119

Fashion Accessories
(Monthly)
Asian Sources Media Group
22/F., Vita Tower
29 Wong Chuk Hang Road
Wong Chuk Hang, Hong Kong
Tel: 5554777 Fax: 8730488

Textile Asia Index
(Annual)
Business Press Ltd
Tak Yan Commercial Building, 11/F.30-32 d'Aguilar Street
GPO Box 185
Central Hong Kong
Tel: 5247441 Tlx: 60275 TEXIA

Textile Asia: The Asian Textile And Apparel Monthly
(Monthly)
Business Press Ltd.
11/F., California Tower
30-32 d'Aguilar Street
Central, Hong Kong
Tel: 5247467 Fax: 8106966

Trade Fairs

Refer to the "Trade Fairs" chapter for complete listings, including contact information, dates, and venues. Trade fairs with particular relevance to this industry include the following, which are listed in that chapter under the headings given below:

Leather Goods, Footwear & Fur
- Hong Kong International Footwear Fair
- Hong Kong International Fur And Leather Fair
- Hong Kong International Handbags & Leather Goods Fair
- Hong Kong International Leather Exhibition
- Leather & Fur Products Showcase
- Shoe Vision

Textiles & Apparel
- Apparel from France
- Asia and World Textiles Conference
- Clothing Industry Fair
- Garmentec—The International Garment Machinery, Materials and Accessories Exhibition for Asia
- Hong Kong Fashion Week
- Hong Kong International Apparel Fair
- Hong Kong International Sporting Goods Fair
- Hong Kong Optical
- Interstoff Asia
- Textile Machine Expo—The International Textile Machinery, Ancillary Equipment, Materials and Technology Exhibition for Asia
- Wedding Apparel

For other trade fairs that may be of interest, we recommend that you also consult the headings Furniture & Housewares; Gifts, Jewelry & Stationery; and Hobbies, Recreation & Travel.

TOYS

Toys are among Hong Kong's top ten total exports. Key export markets are Europe, Japan, Canada, Australia, and the United States. More than 75 percent of Hong Kong's total toy exports are reexports to China.

More than 1,700 toy makers operate in Hong Kong. The bulk of production is for foreign companies under licensing and contract manufacturing arrangements.

Products Hong Kong toy makers offer products of great variety, including stuffed, plastic, electronic, wooden, and metal toys. Over half of Hong Kong's exported toys are plastic. Among the most popular exports are dolls, guns and water pistols, miniature household utility sets, role-playing gimmicks, cars, robots, and airplanes. Electronic toys include battery-operated items, robots, handheld and television electronic games, train sets, and remote-control cars, and airplanes. Hong Kong toy companies offer games for adults and children: chess and checkers, darts, poker accessories, card decks, backgammon, puzzles, and other board and educational games.

Competitive Situation

In recent years, production in Hong Kong's toy industry has declined slightly, mainly because firms are shifting their operations to China to take advantage of lower labor and production costs. To retain a competitive edge, several major Hong Kong toy makers are initiating quality control systems, direct marketing, and product design processes. Toy makers also are striving to remain flexible to meet, and even anticipate, market trends, and they are producing toys that comply with international safety standards.

Trade Associations

Hong Kong & Kowloon Bamboo Goods Merchants Association
2/F., 128 Yee Kuk Street
Kowloon, Hong Kong
Tel: 3869917

Hong Kong & Kowloon Plastic Products Merchants United Association Ltd.
13/F., 491 Nathan Road
Kowloon, Hong Kong
Tel: 3840171 Fax: 7810107

Hong Kong Plastics Manufacturers Association Ltd.
Rm. 302, Red A Central Building
37 Wellington Street
Central, Hong Kong
Tel: 5232229 Fax: 8400704

Hong Kong Rattan Merchants Association
1/F., 314 Des Voeux Road West
Hong Kong
Tel: 5472900

Hong Kong Toys Council
4/F., Hankow Centre
5-15 Hankow Road, Tsimshatsui
Kowloon, Hong Kong
Tel: 7230818 Fax: 7213494

Directories/Publications

Asian Manufacturing
Far East Trade Press Ltd.
2/F., Kai Tak Commercial Building
317 Des Voeux Road
Central, Hong Kong
Tel: 5453028 Fax: 5446979

Asian Plastic News
(Quarterly)
Reed Asian Publishing Pte., Ltd.
5001 Beach Road #06-12
Golden Mile Complex
Singapore 0719
Tel: [65] 2913188 Fax: [65] 2913180

Asian Sources: Gifts & Home Products
(Monthly)
Asian Sources Media Group
22/F., Vita Tower
29 Wong Chuk Hang Road
Wong Chuk Hang, Hong Kong
Tel: 5554777 Fax: 8730488

Hong Kong Gifts & Premiums
(Biennial)
Hong Kong Trade Development Council
38/F., Convention Plaza
1 Harbour Road
Wanchai, Hong Kong
Tel: 5844333 Fax: 8240249 Tlx: 73595 CONHK

Trade Fairs

Refer to the "Trade Fairs" chapter for complete listings, including contact information, dates, and venues. Trade fairs with particular relevance to this industry include the following, which are listed in that chapter under the heading given below:

Hobbies, Recreation & Travel
- Hong Kong Book Fair
- Hong Kong International Coin show
- Hong Kong International Sporting Goods Fair
- Hong Kong International Toy & Gift Show
- Hong Kong Stamp Exhibition
- Hong Kong Toys & Games Fair

For other trade fairs that may be of interest, we recommend that you also consult the headings Computer & Information Industries; Electronic & Electric Equipment; and Gifts, Jewelry & Stationery.

Trade Fairs

Hong Kong hosts a wide range of trade fairs and expositions that should interest anyone who seeks to do business in this dynamic and expanding economy. Whether you want to buy Hong Kong goods or exhibit your own goods and services for sale in Hong Kong or the markets it serves, you will almost undoubtedly find several trade fairs to suit your purposes.

The listing of trade fairs in this section is designed to acquaint you with the scope, size, frequency, and length of the events held in Hong Kong and to give you contact information for the organizers. While every effort has been made to ensure that this information is correct and complete as of press time, the scheduling of such events is in constant flux. Announced exhibitions can be canceled and dates and venues are often shifted. If you're interested in attending or exhibiting at a show listed here, we urge you to contact the organizer well in advance to confirm the venue and dates and to ascertain whether it is appropriate for you. (*See* Tips for Attending a Trade Fair, following this introduction, for further suggestions on selecting, attending, and exhibiting at trade fairs.) The information in this volume will give a significant head start over others who have considered participating in a trade fair as an exhibitor or attendee.

In order to make access to this information as easy as possible, fairs have been grouped alphabetically by product category and within product category, alphabetically by name. Product categories, with cross references, are given following this introduction in a table of contents. Note that the first and last headings listed are out of alphabetical order. Trade fairs listed under Comprehensive do not focus on a single type of product, but instead show a broad range of goods that may be from one geographic area or centered around a particular theme. The final category, Others, is a miscellaneous listing of fairs that do not fit easily into one of the other categories. When appropriate, fairs have been listed in more than one category. The breadth of products on display at a given fair means that you may want to investigate categories that are not immediately obvious. Many exhibits include the machinery, tools, and raw materials used to produce the products associated with the central theme of a fair; anyone interested in such items should consider a wide range of the listings.

The list gives the names and dates of both recent and upcoming events, together with site and contact information; for some fairs, the listing also describes the products to be exhibited. Many shows take place on a regular basis. Annual or biennial schedules are common. When we were able to confirm the frequency of a show through independent sources, it has been indicated. Many others on the list may also be regular events. Some are one-time events. Because specifics on frequency are sometimes difficult to come by, and because schedules for some 1994 and many 1995 shows were not available at press time, we have given both recent and future dates. It is quite possible that a fair listed for 1993 will be held again in 1994 or 1995, so it would be worthwhile getting in touch with the contact listed for any show that looks interesting. Even if we were not able to confirm the frequency, you can infer a likely time cycle if several dates are given for a fair.

As you gather further information on fairs that appeal to you, do not be surprised if the names are slightly different from those listed here. Some large trade fairs include several smaller exhibits, some use short names or acronyms, and Chinese names can be translated in a variety of ways. Dates and venues, of course, are always subject to change.

For further information The Hong Kong Trade Development Council (HKTDC) is the best source of information on trade fairs in Hong Kong. HKTDC publishes "Businessmen's Calendar: Trade Exhibitions & Conferences in Hong Kong" quarterly in January, March, June, and September. Besides giving the name, dates, and organizer, it sometimes includes descriptive information. Branch offices of HKTDC outside Hong Kong may carry copies of this publica-

TRADE FAIRS
TABLE OF CONTENTS

Comprehensive .... p. 88
  Trade fairs exhibiting a wide range of goods
  See also: Chinese Product Trade Fairs
Automobiles & Automotive Parts .... p. 88
Chinese Product Trade Fairs .... p. 88
  Trade fairs exhibiting a wide range of goods from various cities
  and provinces in China
Computer & Information Industries .... p. 90
  Includes communications
  See also: Electronic & Electric equipment
Construction & Housing .... p. 92
  See also: Furniture & Housewares
Electronic & Electric Equipment .... p. 93
  Includes Audiovisual equipment
  See also: Computer & Information Industries
Food, Beverages & Food Processing .... p. 94
Furniture & Housewares .... p. 96
  See also: Construction & Housing
Gifts, Jewelry & Stationery .... p. 96
  Includes timepieces
Health & Beauty .... p. 99
Hobbies, Recreation & Travel .... p. 99
  Includes books, sporting goods, toys
Industrial Materials & Metals .... p. 101
Investment & Business Services .... p. 102
Leather Goods, Footwear & Fur .... p. 106
  See also: Textiles & Apparel
Machines & Instruments .... p. 107
  Includes factory automation
  See also: Tools: Precision & Measuring, other categories which may
  include exhibitions with machines specific to those industries
Packaging & Printing .... p. 108
Textiles & Apparel .... p. 108
  See also: Leather Goods, Footwear & Fur
Tools: Precision & Measuring .... p. 110
  See also: Machines & Instruments, other categories which
  may include exhibitions with tools specific to those industries
Others .... p. 110
  Miscellaneous trade fairs

tion, but it is likely that you will need to contact the main office for the most recent edition. The Trade Development Council also maintains an on-line trade information system called TDC-link. Contact the main office in Hong Kong at [852] 5844383 or a Hong Kong Trade Development Council office in your country for more information. (Refer to "Important Addresses" chapter for Hong Kong Trade Development Council offices.)

Hong Kong Trade Development Council
38/F., Convention Plaza, 1 Harbour Road
Wanchai, Hong Kong
Tel: [852] 5844333 Fax: [852] 8240249
Tlx: 73595 CONHK

The Hong Kong Trade Development Council also compiles the following trade exhibition calendars: "China & Other Asian Countries"; "International Exhibitions on Electronics & Electrical Products";

"Giftware, Toys & Sporting Goods"; "Jewellery, Watches & Clocks"; "Leather & Leather Goods"; and "Textiles & Clothing."

Other valuable sources of information include the commercial section of the embassy or consulate of your own country located in Hong Kong, chambers of commerce, and other business organizations dedicated to trade between your country and Hong Kong. Professional and trade organizations in Hong Kong involved in your area of interest may also be worth contacting. (Refer to "Important Addresses" chapter for chambers of commerce and business organizations, diplomatic missions located in Hong Kong, and trade organizations.)

While the annual directory *Trade Shows Worldwide* (Gale Research Inc., Detroit, Michigan) is far from comprehensive, it may provide further information on some trade fairs in Hong Kong, and it is worth seeking out at your local business library.

Tips for Attending a Trade Fair

Overseas trade fairs can be extremely effective for making face-to-face contacts and sales or purchases, identifying suppliers, checking out competitors, and finding out how business really works in the host country. However, the cost of attending such fairs can be high. To maximize the return on your investment of time and money, you should be very clear about your goals for the trip and give yourself plenty of time for advance research and preparation. You should also make sure that you are aware of the limitations of trade fairs. The products on display probably do not represent the full range of goods available on the market. In fact, some of the latest product designs may still be under wraps. And while trade fairs give you an opportunity to make face-to-face contact with many people, both exhibitors and buyers are rushed, which makes meaningful discussions and negotiations difficult. These drawbacks can easily be minimized if you have sufficient preparation and background information. Allow at least three months for preparation—more if you also need to identify the fair that you will attend. Under ideal circumstances, you should begin laying the groundwork nine to 12 months in advance.

Selecting an appropriate trade fair

Consult the listings of trade fairs here to find some that interest you. Note the suggestions for finding the most current calendars of upcoming fairs. Once you have identified some fairs, contact their organizers for literature, including show prospectus, attendee list, and exhibitor list. Ask plenty of questions. Do not neglect trade organizations in the host country, independent show-auditing firms, and recent attendees. Find out whether there are "must attend" fairs for your particular product group. Fairs that concentrate on other but related commodities might also be a good match. Be aware that there may be preferred seasons for trade in certain products. Your research needs to consider a number of points.

Audience • Who is the intended audience? Is the fair open to the public or only to trade professionals? Are the exhibitors primarily foreigners looking for local buyers or locals looking for foreign buyers? Many trade fairs are heavily weighted to one or the other. Decide whether you are looking for an exposition of general merchandise produced in one region, a commodity-specific trade show, or both.

Tips for Attending a Trade Fair (cont'd.)

Statistics • How many people attended the fair the last time it was held? What were the demographics? What volume of business was done? How many exhibitors were there? How big is the exhibition space? What was the ratio of foreign to domestic attendees and exhibitors?

Specifics • Who are the major exhibitors? Are particular publications or organizations associated with the fair? On what categories of products does the fair focus? Are there any special programs, and do they require additional fees? Does the fair have particular themes that change each time? How long has the fair been in existence? How often is it held? Is it always in the same location, or does it move each time? How much does it cost to attend? To rent space?

Before you go

- If you have not already spoken with someone who attended the fair in the past, make sure to seek someone out for advice, tips, and general information.
- Make your reservations and travel arrangements well in advance, and figure out how you are going to get around once you get there. Even if the fair takes place in a large city, do not assume that getting around will be easy during a major trade fair. If the site is a small city or less-developed area, the transportation and accommodation systems are likely to be saturated even sooner than they can be in metropolitan areas.
- Will you need an interpreter for face-to-face business negotiations? A translation service to handle documents? Try to line up providers well in advance of your need for their services.
- Do you need hospitality suites and/or conference rooms? Reserve them as soon as you can.
- Contact people you'd like to meet before you go. Organize your appointments around the fair.
- Familiarize yourself with the show hours, locations (if exhibits and events are staged at several different venues), and schedule of events. Then prioritize.

While you are there

- Wear businesslike clothes that are comfortable.
- Immediately after each contact, write down as much information as you can. Do not depend on remembering it.

After the fair

- Within a week after the conclusion of the fair, write letters to new contacts and follow up on requests for literature. If you have press releases and questionnaires, send them out quickly as well.
- Write a report evaluating the experience while it is still fresh in your mind. Even if you don't have to prepare a formal report, spend some time organizing your thoughts on paper for future reference and to quantify the results. Did you meet your goals? Why or why not? What would you do differently? What unforeseen costs arose?
- With your new contacts and your experience in mind, start preparing for your next trade fair.

If you are selling

- Set specific goals for sales leads, developing product awareness, selling and positioning current customers, and gathering industry information; for example, number of contacts made, orders written, leads converted into sales, visitors at presentations, brochures or samples distributed, customers entertained, seminars attended. You can also set goals for total revenue from sales, cost-to-return benefit ratio, amount of media coverage, and amount of competitor information obtained.

- Review your exhibitor kit, paying particular attention to show hours and regulations, payment policies, shipping instructions and dates, telephone installation, security, fire regulations, union regulations, and extra-cost services. Is there a show theme that you can tie into?

- Gear your advertising and product demonstrations to the audience. Should you stress certain aspects of your product line? Will you need brochures and banners in different languages? Even if you do not need to translate the materials currently in use into another language, do you need to re-write them for a different culture? Consider advertising in publications that will be distributed at the fair.

- Plan the display in your booth carefully; you will have only a few seconds to grab the viewer's attention. Secure a location in a high-traffic area—for example, near a door, restroom, refreshment area, or major exhibitor. Use banner copy that is brief and effective. Focus on the product and its benefits. Place promotional materials and giveaways near the back wall so that people have to enter your area, but make sure that they do not feel trapped. If you plan to use videotapes or other multimedia, make sure that you have enough space. Such presentations are often better suited to hospitality suites, because lights are bright and noise levels high in exhibition halls.

- Do not forget about the details. Order office supplies and printed materials that you will need for the booth. If you ordered a telephone line, bring your own telephone or arrange to rent one. Have all your paperwork—order forms, business cards, exhibitor kit and contract, copies of advance orders and checks, travel documents, and so on—in order and at hand. Draw up a schedule for staffing the booth.

- Plan and rehearse your sales pitch in advance, preferably in a space similar to the size of your booth.

- Do not sit, eat, drink, or smoke while you are in the booth.

- If you plan to return to the next show, reserve space while you're still at the fair.

- Familiarize yourself with import regulations for products that you wish to exhibit at the fair.

If you are buying

- Set specific goals for supplier leads and for gathering industry information; for example, number of contacts made, leads converted to purchases, seminars and presentations attended, booths visited. Other goals might be cost-to-return benefit ratio, amount of competitor information gathered, and percentage of projected purchases actually made.

- List all the products that you seek to purchase, their specifications, and the number of units you plan to purchase of each.

- Know the retail and wholesale market prices for the goods in your home country and in the country where you will be buying. List the highest price you can afford to pay for each item and still get a worthwhile return.

- List the established and probable suppliers for each of the products or product lines that you plan to import. Include their addresses and telephone numbers and your source for the information. Contact suppliers before you go to confirm who will attend and to make appointments.

- Familiarize yourself with customs regulations on the products that you seek to purchase and import into your own country or elsewhere. Be sure to include any products that you might be interested in.

Trade Fair	Site	Exhibition Profile	Organizer
COMPREHENSIVE Trade fairs exhibiting a wide range of goods See also Chinese Product Trade Fairs			
Asia Pacific Duty-Free Conference and Exhibition Last held: May 11-14, 1993	Hong Kong Convention & Exhibition Centre		Int'l Trade Publications 2 Queensway House Redhill, Surry, RH1 1QS U.K. Tel: [44] (0737) 768611 Fax: [44] (0737) 761989 Tlx: 948669 Topjnl G
Christmas Showcase December 17-21, 1993 December 16-20, 1994	Hong Kong Convention & Exhibition Centre	Consumer goods for spot sales.	Hong Kong Trade Development Council 36-39th Floor, Office Tower Convention Plaza, 1 Harbour Road Wanchai, Hong Kong Tel: 5844333 Fax: 8240249 Tlx: 73595 CONHK HX
Elenex **The Asian International Electrical &** **Electronic Engineering Show** Every 2 years June 8-11, 1994	Hong Kong Convention & Exhibition Centre	Power generation and distribution, electrical accessories and systems, building automation, electrical appliance manufacturing.	Hong Kong Exhibition Services Unit 902 Shiu Lam Building 23 Laurd Road Wanchai, Hong Kong Tel: 8041500 Fax: 5283103 Tlx: 65646 HKEXH HX
AUTOMOBILES & AUTOMOTIVE PARTS			
Hong Kong International Auto & Accessories Fair November 26-29, 1994	Hong Kong Convention & Exhibition Centre	Passenger cars, sports cars, trucks, lorries, vans, motorcycles, scooters, parts and accessories. Estimated Exhibitors: 90	Headway Trade Fairs 907 Great Eagle Centre 23 Harbour Road Wanchai, Hong Kong Tel: 8275121 Fax: 8277064 Tlx: 72554 HEWAY HX
CHINESE PRODUCT TRADE FAIRS Trade fairs exhibiting a wide range of goods from various cities and provinces of China			
Gansu Province Trade Fair Last held: April 6-10, 1993	Hong Kong Convention & Exhibition Centre		Gansu Provincial Foreign Economic Relations & Trade Commission c/o China Resources Advertising Co. 4/F., Low Block, China Resources Bldg. 26 Harbour Road Wanchai, Hong Kong Tel: 5938831 Fax: 8275453 Tlx: 76757 CRACL HX

Guangdong Province Trade Fair
Last held: June 10-13, 1993

Hong Kong Convention & Exhibition Centre

Guangdong Provincial Foreign Economic Relations & Trade Commission
c/o China Resources Advertising Co.
4/F., Low Block, China Resources Bldg.
26 Harbour Road
Wanchai, Hong Kong
Tel: 5938831 Fax: 8275453 Tlx: 76757 CRACL HX

Hubei Province Trade Fair
Last held: June 29-July 3, 1993

Hong Kong Convention & Exhibition Centre

Hubei Provincial Foreign Economic Relations & Trade Dept.
c/o China Resources Advertising Co.
4/F., Low Block, China Resources Bldg.
26 Harbour Road
Wanchai, Hong Kong
Tel: 5938831 Fax: 8275453 Tlx: 76757 CRACL HX

Jiangsu Province Food-Techno Cooperation Fair
Last held: May 11-15, 1993

Hong Kong Convention & Exhibition Centre

Jiangsu Provincial Foreign Economic Relations & Trade Commission
c/o China Resources Advertising Co.
4/F., Low Block, China Resources Bldg.
26 Harbour Road
Wanchai, Hong Kong
Tel: 5938831 Fax: 8275453 Tlx: 76757 CRACL HX

Jiangxi Province Trade Fair
Last held: July 21-26, 1993

Hong Kong Convention & Exhibition Centre

Jiangxi Provincial Foreign Economic Relations & Trade Commission
c/o China Resources Advertising Co.
4/F., Low Block, China Resources Bldg.
26 Harbour Road
Wanchai, Hong Kong
Tel: 5938831 Fax: 8275453 Tlx: 76757 CRACL HX

Shandong Province Trade Fair
Last held: March 27-April 1, 1993

Hong Kong Convention & Exhibition Centre

Shandong Provincial Foreign Trade Department
c/o China Resources Advertising Co.
4/F., Low Block, China Resources Bldg.
26 Harbour Road
Wanchai, Hong Kong
Tel: 5938831 Fax: 8275453 Tlx: 76757 CRACL HX

Note: Country codes for telephone and fax numbers are not displayed unless they are *outside* of Hong Kong. All country codes have square brackets around them, while city codes have parentheses. The country code for Hong Kong is [852]. Hong Kong does not use city codes.

Trade Fair	Site	Exhibition Profile	Organizer
Shanghai Export Commodities Trade Fair Last held: June 18-23, 1993	Hong Kong Convention & Exhibition Centre		Shanghai Municipal People's Government Foreign Economic Relations & Trade Commission c/o China Resources Advertising Co. 4/F., Low Block, China Resources Bldg. 26 Harbour Road Wanchai, Hong Kong Tel: 5938831 Fax: 8275453 Tlx: 76757 CRACL HX
Shenyang City Econ-Techno Trade Fair Last held: May 14-19, 1993	The Museum of Chinese Historical Relics		Shenyang City Foreign Economic Relations & Trade Commission c/o China Resources Advertising Co. 4/F., Low Block, China Resources Bldg. 26 Harbour Road Wanchai, Hong Kong Tel: 5938831 Fax: 8275453 Tlx: 76757 CRACL HX
Sichuan Province Trade Fair Last held: April 16-21, 1993	Hong Kong Convention & Exhibition Centre		Sichuan Provincial Foreign Economic Relations & Trade c/o China Resources Advertising Co. 4/F., Low Block, China Resources Bldg. 26 Harbour Road Wanchai, Hong Kong Tel: 5938831 Fax: 8275453 Tlx: 76757 CRACL HX
Xi'an Municipal Econ-Tech Symposium & Trade Fair Last held: June 1-6, 1993	Hong Kong Convention & Exhibition Centre		Xi'an City Foreign Economic Relations & Trade Commission c/o China Resources Advertising Co. 4/F., Low Block, China Resources Bldg. 26 Harbour Road Wanchai, Hong Kong Tel: 5938831 Fax: 8275453 Tlx: 76757 CRACL HX

COMPUTER & INFORMATION INDUSTRIES Includes communications
See also Electronic & Electric Equipment

Trade Fair	Site	Exhibition Profile	Organizer
Auto-ID Hong Kong **The International Automatic Identification and Bar Code Technology and Equipment Exhibition** May 12-15, 1993 May 11-14, 1994	Hong Kong Convention & Exhibition Centre	Bar-coding and scanning equipment, data communication equipment, OCR, label design and printing, radio frequency identification, POS systems, printers, voice data entry, machine vision, magnetic stripe (smart cards).	Business & Industrial Trade Fairs 18/F., First Pacific Bank Centre 51 Gloucester Road Wanchai, Hong Kong Tel: 8652633 Fax: 8661770 Tlx: 64882 ASIEX HX

Name / Date	Venue	Description	Contact
Cenit Asia Asian Centre and Conference for Information and Telecommunication Technologies Annual October 5-8, 1993 September 28-October 1, 1994	Hong Kong Convention & Exhibition Centre	Information, telecommunications, office and organizational technology. Research and development, application-related problem solving and services. Estimated Exhibitors: 150	Hannover-Messe International c/o Adsale Exhibition Services 14/F., Devon House Taikoo Place 979 King's Road Quarry Bay, Hong Kong Tel: 5110511 Fax: 5165204
Computer Expo The International Computer Expo and Conference for Asia May 12-15, 1993 May 11-14, 1994	Hong Kong Convention & Exhibition Centre	Computers, peripherals, software, accessories and services.	Business & Industrial Trade Fairs 18/F., First Pacific Bank Centre 51 Gloucester Road Wanchai, Hong Kong Tel: 8652633 Fax: 8661770 Tlx: 64882 ASIEX HX
EDI Asia Last held: September 27-30, 1993	Hong Kong Convention & Exhibition Centre	Electronic document equipment and services.	Tradelink Electronic Document Service Standard Chartered Bank Bldg., 12/F. 4 Des Vouex Road, C. Central, Hong Kong Tel: 5300600 Fax: 8778980
International Hi-Tech Show Last held: August 19-22, 1993	Hong Kong Convention & Exhibition Centre	High technology products including consumer electronics, computer hardware and software, electrical appliances, security systems, office automation, hi-end audio and visual equipment.	Hong Kong Exhibition Production 10/F., Kiu Yin Commercial Bldg. 361-363 Lockhart Road Wanchai, Hong Kong Tel: 8330186 Fax: 8335445
Software Exhibition Last held: December 8-11, 1993	Hong Kong Convention & Exhibition Centre	Computer software and related products.	Hong Kong Productivity Council HKPC Building 78 Tat Chee Avenue Kowloon Tong Kowloon, Hong Kong Tel: 7885678 Fax: 7885011 Tlx: 32842 HKPC HX
Technology Showcase Last held: November 18-20, 1993	HKPC Building	Technology from China related to network computing, ISDN, wireless telephones, video-phones, paging systems, mobile communication, global communication systems.	Hong Kong Productivity Council HKPC Building 78 Tat Chee Avenue Kowloon Tong Kowloon, Hong Kong Tel: 7885678 Fax: 7885011 Tlx: 32842 HKPC HX

Note: Country codes for telephone and fax numbers are not displayed unless they are *outside* of Hong Kong. All country codes have square brackets around them, while city codes have parentheses. The country code for Hong Kong is [852]. Hong Kong does not use city codes.

Trade Fair	Site	Exhibition Profile	Organizer
XII Conference of South East Asia Regional Computer Confederation (SEARCC) Last held: October 5-8, 1993	Hong Kong Convention & Exhibition Centre		South East Asian Regional Computer Confederation Hong Kong Computer Society c/o BDG Communications Management Suite 1104-5 East Town Building 41 Lockhart Road Wanchai, Hong Kong Tel: 5286136 Fax: 8651528

CONSTRUCTION & HOUSING
See also Furniture & Housewares

Trade Fair	Site	Exhibition Profile	Organizer
Airvex **The Asian International Airconditioning, Ventilation, Heating & Refrigeration Show** Every 2 years June 8-11, 1994	Hong Kong Convention & Exhibition Centre	Air conditioning, ventilation, heating and refrigeration equipment, components, controls and systems.	Hong Kong Exhibition Services Unit 902 Shiu Lam Building 23 Laurd Road Wanchai, Hong Kong Tel: 8041500 Fax: 5283103 Tlx: 65646 HKEXH HX
International Building Exhibition (IBEX Hong Kong) Last held: June 16-19, 1993	Hong Kong Convention & Exhibition Centre	Building materials, supplies and equipment maintenance and services. Estimated Exhibitors: 600	Reed Exhibitions 2805 Office Tower Convention Plaza 1 Harbour Road Wanchai, Hong Kong Tel: 8240330 Fax: 8240246 Tlx: 62270 CEG HX
International Conference and Exhibition of Signs and Signmaking Last held: December 3-5, 1993	Hong Kong Convention & Exhibition Centre	Signs and signmaking equipment, materials, accessories and services.	Expoconsult Int'l Exhibitions & Conferences 46A Horne Road Singapore 0820 Tel: [65] 2999273 Fax: [65] 2999782
Luminex **The Asian International Lighting, Lighting Technology, Fittings & Systems Show** Every 2 years June 8-11, 1994	Hong Kong Convention & Exhibition Centre	Contract lighting, industrial, commercial and retail lighting, decorative lighting, lamps, fixtures, fittings and components.	Hong Kong Exhibition Services Unit 902 Shiu Lam Building 23 Laurd Road Wanchai, Hong Kong Tel: 8041500 Fax: 5283103 Tlx: 65646 HKEXH HX
Tube & Pipe - Hong Kong Last held: November 17-19, 1993	Hong Kong Convention & Exhibition Centre	Estimated Exhibitors: 120	International Wire & Machinery Association 46 Holly Walk Leamington Spa Warwickshire CV32 4HY U.K. Tel: [44] (926) 334137 Fax: [44] (926) 314755 Tlx: 312598 INTRAS G

World Plumbing Conferences and Expo
Last held: June 15-18, 1993

Hong Kong Convention & Exhibition Centre

World Plumbing Council
Lee May Bldg., 4/F.
788-790 Nathan Road
Mong Kok
Kowloon, Hong Kong
Tel: 8662889 Fax: 3971947

ELECTRONIC & ELECTRIC EQUIPMENT Includes Audiovisual equipment
See also Computer & Information Industries

BROADCAST
The Hong Kong International Broadcasting, Sound, Film and Video Exhibition
Last held: July 8-10, 1993

Hong Kong Convention & Exhibition Centre

Radio, television, studio and outside broadcast equipment; higher definition television systems.

Hong Kong Exhibition Services
Unit 902 Shiu Lam Building
23 Laurd Road
Wanchai, Hong Kong
Tel: 8041500 Fax: 5283103 Tlx: 65646 HKEXH HX

ECA
The International Electronic Component Exhibition for Asia
June 9-12, 1993
July 7-10, 1994

Hong Kong Convention & Exhibition Centre

Business & Industrial Trade Fairs
18/F., First Pacific Bank Centre
51 Gloucester Road
Wanchai, Hong Kong
Tel: 8652633 Fax: 8661770 Tlx: 64882 ASIEX HX

EIE
The International Electronics Industry, Testing Equipment & Instrument Exhibition for Asia
June 9-12, 1993
July 7-10, 1994

Hong Kong Convention & Exhibition Centre

Equipment, materials and products for manufacturing and inserting PCB semiconductor and hybrid components. Automatic assembly equipment, CAD/CAM, measuring, control and testing equipment, electronic components, surface mount technology.

Business & Industrial Trade Fairs
18/F., First Pacific Bank Centre
51 Gloucester Road
Wanchai, Hong Kong
Tel: 8652633 Fax: 8661770 Tlx: 64882 ASIEX HX

Elenex
The Asian International Electrical & Electronic Engineering Show
Every 2 years
June 8-11, 1994

Hong Kong Convention & Exhibition Centre

Power generation and distribution, electrical accessories and systems, building automation, electrical appliance manufacturing.

Hong Kong Exhibition Services
Unit 902 Shiu Lam Building
23 Laurd Road
Wanchai, Hong Kong
Tel: 8041500 Fax: 5283103 Tlx: 65646 HKEXH HX

Hong Kong Electronics Fair
Annual
October 13-16, 1993
October 18-21, 1994
October 17-20, 1995
October 15-18, 1996

Hong Kong Convention & Exhibition Centre

Consumer electronics, office automation systems, electronic parts and components, original equipment manufacturing, supplies and services, production equipment.
Estimated Exhibitors: 600

Hong Kong Trade Development Council
36-39th Floor, Office Tower
Convention Plaza, 1 Harbour Road
Wanchai, Hong Kong
Tel: 5844333 Fax: 8240249 Tlx: 73595 CONHK HX

Note: Country codes for telephone and fax numbers are not displayed unless they are *outside* of Hong Kong. All country codes have square brackets around them, while city codes have parentheses. The country code for Hong Kong is [852]. Hong Kong does not use city codes.

Trade Fair	Site	Exhibition Profile	Organizer
International Audio & Visual Show October 27-31, 1993 October 26-30, 1994	Hong Kong Convention & Exhibition Centre	Audio and visual products for home entertainment, televisions, hi-fi systems, karaoke, cameras, camcorders, binoculars, photo accessories, compact discs, laser video, high-end systems, car stereos, electronic musical organs.	Radio Assn. of Hong Kong, Hong Kong & Kowloon Photographic Merchant Assn. c/o Hong Kong Trade Development Council 36-39th Floor, Office Tower Convention Plaza, 1 Harbour Road Wanchai, Hong Kong Tel: 5844333 Fax: 8240249 Tlx: 73595 CONHK HX
International Hi-Tech Show Last held: August 19-22, 1993	Hong Kong Convention & Exhibition Centre	High technology products including consumer electronics, computer hardware and software, electrical appliances, security systems, office automation, hi-end audio and visual equipment.	Hong Kong Exhibition Production 10/F., Kiu Yin Commercial Bldg. 361-363 Lockhart Road Wanchai, Hong Kong Tel: 8330186 Fax: 8335445
INTERNEPCON / SEMICONDUCTOR Hong Kong Every 2 years September, 1993 September, 1995	Hong Kong Convention & Exhibition Centre	Production and test equipment, materials, chemicals, and hardware for semiconductor and electronics manufacturing.	Cahners Exhibitions (HK) 2808 Office Tower, Convention Plaza 1 Harbour Road Wanchai, Hong Kong Tel: 8240330 Fax: 8240271 Tlx 62270 CEGHX
Securitex Every 2 years June 8-11, 1994	Hong Kong Convention & Exhibition Centre	Access control systems, alarm equipment, fire and smoke detectors, locks, sprinkler systems, security glass, gates and doors, control panels, CCTV, intruder detection, personal security equipment.	Hong Kong Exhibition Services Unit 902 Shiu Lam Building 23 Laurd Road Wanchai, Hong Kong Tel: 8041500 Fax: 5283103 Tlx: 65646 HKEXH HX
SMT **The International Surface Mount Technology Exhibition for Asia** Annual June 9-12, 1993 July 7-10, 1994	Hong Kong Convention & Exhibition Centre		Business & Industrial Trade Fairs 18/F., First Pacific Bank Centre 51 Gloucester Road Wanchai, Hong Kong Tel: 8652633 Fax: 8661770 Tlx: 64882 ASIEX HX

FOOD, BEVERAGES & FOOD PROCESSING

Trade Fair	Site	Exhibition Profile	Organizer
Bakery & Confectionery **The Hong Kong International Bakery, Confectionery, Snack Food & Ice Cream Industries Show** Last held: May 4-7, 1993	Hong Kong Convention & Exhibition Centre	Biscuits, chocolate, ice-cream makers, ingredients, ovens, burners, packaging forming, whipping, cleaning machines, steam appliances.	Hong Kong Exhibition Services Unit 902 Shiu Lam Building 23 Laurd Road Wanchai, Hong Kong Tel: 8041500 Fax: 5283103 Tlx: 65646 HKEXH HX

Event	Venue	Description	Organiser / Contact
Food Expo August 11-15, 1993 August 10-14, 1994	Hong Kong Convention & Exhibition Centre	General food and drink products, wines and spirits, preparation ingredients, natural food, health food, baby food, restaurant and catering outlets, kitchen utensils and food preparation apparatus. Estimated Exhibitors: 250	Hong Kong Trade Development Council 36-39th Floor, Office Tower Convention Plaza, 1 Harbour Road Wanchai, Hong Kong Tel: 5844333 Fax: 8240249 Tlx: 73595 CONHK HX
HOFEX **The Asian International Exhibition of Hotel, Restaurant and Catering Systems, Supplies, Equipment, Food and Drink** Every 2 years Last held: May 4-7, 1993	Hong Kong Convention & Exhibition Centre	Hotel, catering, food and beverage equipment, and services. Estimated Exhibitors: 750	Hong Kong Exhibition Services Unit 902 Shiu Lam Building 23 Laurd Road Wanchai, Hong Kong Tel: 8041500 Fax: 5283103 Tlx: 65646 HKEXH HX
Holland in Hong Kong Last held: November 5-14, 1993	Kowloon Park	Food and agricultural products from Holland.	Consulate General of the Netherlands China Building, 3/F. 29 Queen's Road Central Central, Hong Kong Tel: 5248187 Fax: 5249419
Inflight Services **The Asian International Inflight and Onboard Services Show & Conference** Last held: May 4-7, 1993	Hong Kong Convention & Exhibition Centre	Food, beverages, equipment and supplies for airline inflight and onboard services.	Hong Kong Exhibition Services Unit 902 Shiu Lam Building 23 Laurd Road Wanchai, Hong Kong Tel: 8041500 Fax: 5283103 Tlx: 65646 HKEXH HX
Jiangsu Province Food-Techno Cooperation Fair Last held: May 11-15, 1993	Hong Kong Convention & Exhibition Centre		Jiangsu Provincial Foreign Economic Relations & Trade Commission c/o China Resources Advertising Co. 4/F., Low Block, China Resources Bldg. 26 Harbour Road Wanchai, Hong Kong Tel: 5938831 Fax: 8275453 Tlx: 76757 CRACL HX

Note: Country codes for telephone and fax numbers are not displayed unless they are *outside* of Hong Kong. All country codes have square brackets around them, while city codes have parentheses. The country code for Hong Kong is [852]. Hong Kong does not use city codes.

FURNITURE & HOUSEWARES
See also Construction & Housing

Trade Fair	Site	Exhibition Profile	Organizer
Electrical Home Appliances Expo (held concurrently with Ideal Home Expo) April 9-12, 1993 April 1-4, 1994	Hong Kong Convention & Exhibition Centre	Electrical home appliances. Estimated Exhibitors: 50	H.K. Kowloon Electrical Appliances Mer. Assn. c/o Hong Kong Trade Development Council 36-39th Floor, Office Tower Convention Plaza, 1 Harbour Road Wanchai, Hong Kong Tel: 5844333　Fax: 8240249　Tlx: 73595 CONHK HX
Homefex & Invest Last held: December 14-17, 1993	New World Plaza	Household products & property investment. Estimated Exhibitors: 80	Hong Kong Exhibition Production 10/F., Kiu Yin Commercial Bldg. 361-363 Lockhart Road Wanchai, Hong Kong Tel: 8330186　Fax: 8335445
Hong Kong International Furniture Fair Last held: October 29-November 1, 1993	Hong Kong Convention & Exhibition Centre	Furniture, lighting and fixtures, interior furnishings, bathroom accessories, fabrics and upholstery, decorative items for home, offices, hotels, restaurants and special projects.	Headway Trade Fairs 907 Great Eagle Centre 23 Harbour Road Wanchai, Hong Kong Tel: 8275121　Fax: 8277064　Tlx: 72554 HEWAY HX
Ideal Home Expo (held concurrently with Electrical Home Appliances Expo) April 9-12, 1993 April 1-4, 1994	Hong Kong Convention & Exhibition Centre	Furniture, lighting, fixtures, home furnishings, bathroom accessories, fabrics and upholstery, decorative items, kitchenware. Estimated Exhibitors: 120	H.K. Furniture Dealers & Decorators Gen. Assn. c/o Hong Kong Trade Development Council 36-39th Floor, Office Tower Convention Plaza, 1 Harbour Road Wanchai, Hong Kong Tel: 5844333　Fax: 8240249　Tlx: 73595 CONHK HX
Luminex **The Asian International Lighting, Lighting Technology, Fittings & Systems Show** Every 2 years June 8-11, 1994	Hong Kong Convention & Exhibition Centre	Contract lighting, industrial, commercial and retail lighting, decorative lighting, lamps, fixtures, fittings and components.	Hong Kong Exhibition Services Unit 902 Shiu Lam Building 23 Laurd Road Wanchai, Hong Kong Tel: 8041500　Fax: 5283103　Tlx: 65646 HKEXH HX

GIFTS, JEWELRY, & STATIONERY　Includes timepieces

Trade Fair	Site	Exhibition Profile	Organizer
Christmas Showcase December 17-21, 1993 December 16-20, 1994	Hong Kong Convention & Exhibition Centre	Consumer goods for spot sales.	Hong Kong Trade Development Council 36-39th Floor, Office Tower Convention Plaza, 1 Harbour Road Wanchai, Hong Kong Tel: 5844333　Fax: 8240249　Tlx: 73595 CONHK HX

Hong Kong Book Fair
July 22-26, 1993
July 21-25, 1994

Hong Kong Convention & Exhibition Centre

Printed materials, including catalogs, text and reference books, publications and journals, magazines, calendars, cards, art prints, office supplies, and stationery. Estimated Exhibitors: 500

Hong Kong Trade Development Council
36-39th Floor, Office Tower
Convention Plaza, 1 Harbour Road
Wanchai, Hong Kong
Tel: 5844333 Fax: 8240249 Tlx: 73595 CONHK HX

Hong Kong Gifts & Housewares Fair
Annual
April 19-22, 1993
April 11-14, 1994
April 10-13, 1995
April 17-20, 1996

Hong Kong Convention & Exhibition Centre

Housewares, tableware, ceramics, consumer electronics, watches and clocks, furniture, decorations and crafts, travel goods, handbags, sporting goods, stationery, printed matter, fashion accessories, toys, Christmas decorations. Estimated Exhibitors: 680

Hong Kong Trade Development Council
36-39th Floor, Office Tower
Convention Plaza, 1 Harbour Road
Wanchai, Hong Kong
Tel: 5844333 Fax: 8240249 Tlx: 73595 CONHK HX

Hong Kong International Coin Show
Last held: September 3-5, 1993

Holiday Inn Golden Mile

Antique watches, coins and notes.

Taisei Stamps & Coins (HK)
Shop no. UG 45-47
Wing On Plaza, Upper Ground Fl.
62 Mody Road, Tsim Sha Tsui
Kowloon, Hong Kong
Tel: 3111699 Fax: 3113928

Hong Kong International Fashion Jewellery & Accessories Fair
Annual
June 16-19, 1993
June 30-July 3, 1994

Hong Kong Convention & Exhibition Centre

Fashion jewelry and ornaments, accessories, related materials and beauty products.

Headway Trade Fairs
907 Great Eagle Centre
23 Harbour Road
Wanchai, Hong Kong
Tel: 8275121 Fax: 8277064 Tlx: 72554 HEWAY HX

Hong Kong International Jewellery Show
Annual
March 16-19, 1994
March 18-20, 1995
March 16-19, 1996

Hong Kong Convention & Exhibition Centre

Gold, platinum, silver, gold plated, pearl and gemset jewelry. Jewelry sets, carvings, ornaments, precious and semi-precious stones, parts and accessories. Allied trades.

Hong Kong Trade Development Council
36-39th Floor, Office Tower
Convention Plaza, 1 Harbour Road
Wanchai, Hong Kong
Tel: 5844333 Fax: 8240249 Tlx: 73595 CONHK HX

Hong Kong International Stationery & Premium Fair
Annual
Last held: June 16-19, 1993

Hong Kong Convention & Exhibition Centre

Stationery and office supplies, premiums, gift wrap and accessories, vanity products, consumer electronics, toys and games, materials and parts.

Headway Trade Fairs
907 Great Eagle Centre
23 Harbour Road
Wanchai, Hong Kong
Tel: 8275121 Fax: 8277064 Tlx: 72554 HEWAY HX

Note: Country codes for telephone and fax numbers are not displayed unless they are *outside* of Hong Kong. All country codes have square brackets around them, while city codes have parentheses. The country code for Hong Kong is [852]. Hong Kong does not use city codes.

Trade Fair	Site	Exhibition Profile	Organizer
Hong Kong International Toy & Gift Show Last held: October 20-22, 1993	Hong Kong Convention & Exhibition Centre		Kenfair International Limited 1002 Perfect Commercial Bldg. 20 Austin Avenue Tsim Sha Tsui Kowloon, Hong Kong Tel: 3118216 Fax: 3116629
Hong Kong Jewellery & Watch Fair Twice a year (June and September) June 3-6, 1993; September 20-24, 1993 June 30-July 3, 1994; September 19-23, 1994	Hong Kong Convention & Exhibition Centre	Jewelry, timepieces, gemstones, accessories, machinery and equipment.	Headway Trade Fairs 907 Great Eagle Centre 23 Harbour Road Wanchai, Hong Kong Tel: 8275121 Fax: 8277064 Tlx: 72554 HEWAY HX
Hong Kong Premium Show April 19-22, 1993 April 11-14, 1994	Hong Kong Convention & Exhibition Centre	Premium items for advertising, promotional and souvenir purposes. Estimated Exhibitors: 170	Hong Kong Exporters' Association c/o Hong Kong Trade Development Council 36-39th Floor, Office Tower Convention Plaza, 1 Harbour Road Wanchai, Hong Kong Tel: 5844333 Fax: 8240249 Tlx: 73595 CONHK HX
Hong Kong Watch & Clock Fair September 9-13, 1993 September 9-13, 1994 September 11-14, 1995 September 5-8, 1996	Hong Kong Convention & Exhibition Centre	Complete watches, clocks, accessories and components. Checking and measuring instruments, machines, equipment and tools for after-sales service of watches. Estimated Exhibitors: 600	Federation of H.K. Watch Trades & Industries, Ltd., H.K. Watch Manufacturers Assoc. c/o Hong Kong Trade Development Council 36-39th Floor, Office Tower Convention Plaza, 1 Harbour Road Wanchai, Hong Kong Tel: 5844333 Fax: 8240249 Tlx: 73595 CONHK HX
Timepiece Gallery Last held: September 9-13, 1993	Hong Kong Convention & Exhibition Centre	Branded timepieces. Estimated Exhibitors: 100	Federation of H.K. Watch Trades & Industries, Ltd., H.K. Watch Manufacturers Assoc. c/o Hong Kong Trade Development Council 36-39th Floor, Office Tower Convention Plaza, 1 Harbour Road Wanchai, Hong Kong Tel: 5844333 Fax: 8240249 Tlx: 73595 CONHK HX
WatchTech March 3-5, 1994	HKPC Building	Watch movements, cases, dials, bands, hands and crowns, machines and equipment, packaging, electroplating and other technologies.	H.K. Watch Manufacturers Association c/o Hong Kong Productivity Council HKPC Building 78 Tat Chee Avenue Kowloon Tong Kowloon, Hong Kong Tel: 7885678 Fax: 7885011 Tlx: 32842 HKPC HX

Wedding Apparel
1993 dates: April 30-May 3; October 14-17

New World Plaza

Wedding gowns, studio service, flower arrangement, jewelry, skin care and cosmetics, hotel and travel agency services.
Estimated Exhibitors: 80

Hong Kong Exhibition Production
10/F., Kiu Yin Commercial Bldg.
361-363 Lockhart Road
Wanchai, Hong Kong
Tel: 8330186   Fax: 8335445

HEALTH & BEAUTY

Asia Pacific Cosmetic Conference
Last held: June 26, 1993

Hong Kong Convention & Exhibition Centre

Hong Kong Trade Fair Group
China Resources Building, 44/F.
26 Harbour Road
Wanchai, Hong Kong
Tel: 8276211   Fax: 8277831   Tlx: 68444 HKTF HX

Cosmetics, Hair & Beauty
The Cosmetics Hair and Beauty Exhibition
Last held: June 27-30, 1993

Hong Kong Convention & Exhibition Centre

Raw materials, cosmetics and perfumes, skin care products, hair accessories and equipment, packaging machinery, equipment for beauty salon.

Hong Kong Trade Fair Group
China Resources Building, 44/F.
26 Harbour Road
Wanchai, Hong Kong
Tel: 8276211   Fax: 8277831   Tlx: 68444 HKTF HX

Wedding Apparel
1993 dates: April 30-May 3; October 14-17

New World Plaza

Wedding gowns, studio service, flower arrangement, jewelry, skin care and cosmetics, hotel and travel agency services.
Estimated Exhibitors: 80

Hong Kong Exhibition Production
10/F., Kiu Yin Commercial Bldg.
361-363 Lockhart Road
Wanchai, Hong Kong
Tel: 8330186   Fax: 8335445

HOBBIES, RECREATION & TRAVEL Includes books, sporting goods, toys

Hong Kong Book Fair
July 22-26, 1993
July 21-25, 1994

Hong Kong Convention & Exhibition Centre

Printed materials, including catalogs, text and reference books, publications and journals, magazines, calendars, cards, art prints, office supplies, and stationery.
Estimated Exhibitors: 500

Hong Kong Trade Development Council
36-39th Floor, Office Tower
Convention Plaza, 1 Harbour Road
Wanchai, Hong Kong
Tel: 5844333   Fax: 8240249   Tlx: 73595 CONHK HX

Hong Kong International Coin Show
Last held: September 3-5, 1993

Holiday Inn Golden Mile

Antique watches, coins and notes.

Taisei Stamps & Coins (HK)
Shop no. UG 45-47
Wing On Plaza, Upper Ground Fl.
62 Mody Road, Tsim Sha Tsui
Kowloon, Hong Kong
Tel: 3111699   Fax: 3113928

Note: Country codes for telephone and fax numbers are not displayed unless they are *outside* of Hong Kong. All country codes have square brackets around them, while city codes have parentheses. The country code for Hong Kong is [852]. Hong Kong does not use city codes.

Trade Fair	Site	Exhibition Profile	Organizer
Hong Kong International Sporting Goods Fair Annual Last held: July, 1993	Hong Kong Convention & Exhibition Centre	Equipment and accessories for indoor and outdoor gyms, sportswear and accessories, shoes, related services and publications. Estimated exhibitors: 350	Headway Trade Fairs 907 Great Eagle Centre 23 Harbour Road Wanchai, Hong Kong Tel: 8275121 Fax: 8277064 Tlx: 72554 HEWAY HX
Hong Kong International Toy & Gift Show Last held: October 20-22, 1993	Hong Kong Convention & Exhibition Centre		Kenfair International Limited 1002 Perfect Commercial Bldg. 20 Austin Avenue Tsim Sha Tsui Kowloon, Hong Kong Tel: 3118216 Fax: 3116629
Hong Kong Stamp Exhibition February 18-21, 1994	Hong Kong Convention & Exhibition Centre	Estimated Exhibitors: 80	Hong Kong Philatelic Society c/o Secretary General HK'94 Organising Committee General Post Office Central, Hong Kong Tel: 5221071 Fax: 5302618
Hong Kong Toys & Games Fair Annual January 12-15, 1994 January 11-14, 1995 January 10-13, 1996	Hong Kong Convention & Exhibition Centre	B/O toys, dolls, soft and inflatable toys, non-electronic games and toys, carnival items, model kits, hobby products, toy parts and accessories. Allied trades.	Hong Kong Trade Development Council 36-39th Floor, Office Tower Convention Plaza, 1 Harbour Road Wanchai, Hong Kong Tel: 5844333 Fax: 8240249 Tlx: 73595 CONHK HX
Incentive Travel & Corporate Meetings Asia IT & CMA Last held: December 7-9, 1993	Hong Kong Convention & Exhibition Centre		Expoconsult Int'l Exhibitions & Conferences 46A Horne Road Singapore 0820 Tel: [65] 2999273 Fax: [65] 2999782
Intertour Hong Kong **The Annual International Travel Exposition of Asia** Last held: June 3-6, 1993	Hong Kong Convention & Exhibition Centre	National tourist organizations, airlines, cruise shipping companies, hotels, airlines, car rental firms, travel related services. Estimated Exhibitors: 450	Trend Exhibition 1203 Shanghai Industrial Bldg. 48-62 Hennessy Road Wanchai, Hong Kong Tel: 5272601 Fax: 8651709 Tlx: 84784 TPP HX

INDUSTRIAL MATERIALS & METALS

Event	Venue	Description	Contact
Diecasting Exhibition Last held: April 22-24, 1993	HKPC Building	Diecasting machines, spin casting machines, industrial and diecasting hardware, vacuum diecasting system, zinc, lead, silver, cadmium, copper sulfate and diecasted parts and equipment.	Hong Kong Diecasting Association c/o Hong Kong Productivity Council HKPC Building 78 Tat Chee Avenue Kowloon Tong Kowloon, Hong Kong Tel: 7885678 Fax: 7885011 Tlx: 32842 HKPC HX
Hong Kong Linkage Industry International Machine Tool March 24-27, 1994	Hong Kong Convention & Exhibition Centre	Mold and tool making, surface finishing, plastics, hot and cold workings, metal machining, machinery repair and maintenance.	Paper Communication Exhibition Services Room 16, Wah Shing Centre, 12/F. 11 Shing Yip Street Kwun Tong Kowloon, Hong Kong Tel: 7639011 Fax: 3410379
InterplasAsia **The International Plastics Machinery, Materials, Production Technology and Ancillary Equipment Exhibition for Asia** May 21-25, 1993 May 20-23, 1994	Hong Kong Convention & Exhibition Centre	Plastics processing machinery, materials, ancillary equipment.	Business & Industrial Trade Fairs 18/F., First Pacific Bank Centre 51 Gloucester Road Wanchai, Hong Kong Tel: 8652633 Fax: 8661770 Tlx: 64882 ASIEX HX
MetalTech Last held: September 16-19, 1993	HKPC Building	Precision plastic injection molds, precision sheet metal dies, CAD/CAM/CAE systems, mold and die fabrication machinery, equipment and tooling, plastic injection machines and accessories, sheet metal and plastic parts processing automation systems.	Hong Kong Productivity Council HKPC Building 78 Tat Chee Avenue Kowloon Tong Kowloon, Hong Kong Tel: 7885678 Fax: 7885011 Tlx: 32842 HKPC HX
MEX **The International Machinery & Materials Exhibition for Asia** Annual June 9-12, 1993 July 7-10, 1994	Hong Kong Convention & Exhibition Centre	Machine tools, metalworking machinery, production machinery, materials handling and storage equipment, surface treatment equipment, pneumatics and hydraulics, tools, instrumentation, other factor automation equipment.	Business & Industrial Trade Fairs 18/F., First Pacific Bank Centre 51 Gloucester Road Wanchai, Hong Kong Tel: 8652633 Fax: 8661770 Tlx: 64882 ASIEX HX

Note: Country codes for telephone and fax numbers are not displayed unless they are *outside* of Hong Kong. All country codes have square brackets around them, while city codes have parentheses. The country code for Hong Kong is [852]. Hong Kong does not use city codes.

Trade Fair	Site	Exhibition Profile	Organizer
Mould & Die **The International Mould & Die Exhibition** June 9-12, 1993 July 7-10, 1994	Hong Kong Convention & Exhibition Centre	Mold and die, CAD/CAM/CAE, surface treatment, mold and die processing machines, parts and component manufacturing machines, standard components and supplies, metal finishing, measuring/texting and control equipment, auxiliary equipment.	Business & Industrial Trade Fairs 18/F., First Pacific Bank Centre 51 Gloucester Road Wanchai, Hong Kong Tel: 8652633 Fax: 8661770 Tlx: 64882 ASIEX HX
Tube & Pipe - Hong Kong Last held: November 17-19, 1993	Hong Kong Convention & Exhibition Centre	Estimated Exhibitors: 120	International Wire & Machinery Association 46 Holly Walk Leamington Spa Warwickshire CV32 4HY U.K. Tel: [44] (926) 334137 Fax: [44] (926) 314755 Tlx: 312598 INTRAS G
Wire, Cable & Fastener Hong Kong Last held: November 17-19, 1993	Hong Kong Convention & Exhibition Centre	Estimated Exhibitors: 150	International Wire & Machinery Association 46 Holly Walk Leamington Spa Warwickshire CV32 4HY U.K. Tel: [44] (926) 334137 Fax: [44] (926) 314755 Tlx: 312598 INTRAS G
World Plumbing Conferences and Expo Last held: June 15-18, 1993	Hong Kong Convention & Exhibition Centre		World Plumbing Council Lee May Bldg., 4/F. 788-790 Nathan Road, Mong Kok Kowloon, Hong Kong Tel: 8662889 Fax: 3971947

INVESTMENT & BUSINESS SERVICES

Trade Fair	Site	Exhibition Profile	Organizer
Annual Business & Industry Environment Week Last held: June 7-11, 1993	Hong Kong Convention & Exhibition Centre		Centre of Environmental Technology 83 Tat Chee Avenue, Kowloon Tong Kowloon, Hong Kong Tel: 7887097 Fax: 7887090
China and Overseas Properties Exhibition Last held: July 7-11, 1993	Hong Kong Convention & Exhibition Centre		Oriental Wesley Promotions China Harbour Bldg., 6/F. 370 King's Road North Point, Hong Kong Tel: 8077633 Fax: 5705903 Tlx: 89587 SHKIS HX

Fair	Venue	Description	Contact
Education & Careers Expo February 24-27, 1994	Hong Kong Convention & Exhibition Centre	Education and careers development opportunities.	Hong Kong Trade Development Council 36-39th Floor, Office Tower Convention Plaza, 1 Harbour Road Wanchai, Hong Kong Tel: 5844333 Fax: 8240249 Tlx: 73595 CONHK HX
Europe / East Asia Economic Forum Last held: October 13-15, 1993	Hong Kong Convention & Exhibition Centre		World Economic Forum 53 Chemin des Hauts-Crets CH-1223 Cologny Geneva, Switzerland Tel: [41] (22) 7362043 Fax: [41] (22) 7862744 Tlx: 413280
Franchising **The Exhibition and Forum on Franchising** **Business in Hong Kong** November 10-13, 1993 November 10-13, 1994	Hong Kong Convention & Exhibition Centre	Franchising and licensing.	Adsale Exhibition Services c/o Hong Kong Productivity Council HKPC Building 78 Tat Chee Avenue Kowloon Tong Kowloon, Hong Kong Tel: 7885678 Fax: 7885011 Tlx: 32842 HKPC HX
Hebei Province Investment Project Trade Fair Last held: July 16-21, 1993	Hong Kong Convention & Exhibition Centre		Hebei Provincial Foreign Economic Relations & Trade Commission c/o China Resources Advertising Co. 4/F., Low Block, China Resources Bldg. 26 Harbour Road Wanchai, Hong Kong Tel: 5938831 Fax: 8275453 Tlx: 76757 CRACL HX
Hefei City (Anhui Province) Investment Projects Fair Last held: June 29-July 2, 1993	The Museum of Chinese Historical Relics		Hefei City Foreign Economic Relations & Trade Commission c/o China Resources Advertising Co. 4/F., Low Block, China Resources Bldg. 26 Harbour Road Wanchai, Hong Kong Tel: 5938831 Fax: 8275453 Tlx: 76757 CRACL HX
Homefex & Invest Last held: December 14-17, 1993	New World Plaza	Household products & property investment. Estimated Exhibitors: 80	Hong Kong Exhibition Production 10/F., Kiu Yin Commercial Bldg. 361-363 Lockhart Road Wanchai, Hong Kong Tel: 8330186 Fax: 8335445

Note: Country codes for telephone and fax numbers are not displayed unless they are *outside* of Hong Kong. All country codes have square brackets around them, while city codes have parentheses. The country code for Hong Kong is [852]. Hong Kong does not use city codes.

Trade Fair	Site	Exhibition Profile	Organizer
Hong Kong Quality Circles Convention Last held: August 21-24, 1993	Hong Kong Cultural Centre, HKPC Building		Hong Kong Quality Management Association Federation of Hong Kong Industries c/o Hong Kong Productivity Council HKPC Building 78 Tat Chee Avenue, Kowloon Tong Kowloon, Hong Kong Tel: 7885678 Fax: 7885011 Tlx: 32842 HKPC HX
Incentive Travel & Corporate Meetings Asia **IT & CMA** Last held: December 7-9, 1993	Hong Kong Convention & Exhibition Centre		Expoconsult Int'l Exhibitions & Conferences 46A Horne Road Singapore 0820 Tel: [65] 2999273 Fax: [65] 2999782
International Convention on Quality Control Circles October 25-29, 1994	Hong Kong Convention & Exhibition Centre		Hong Kong Quality Management Association Federation of Hong Kong Industries c/o Hong Kong Productivity Council HKPC Building 78 Tat Chee Avenue, Kowloon Tong Kowloon, Hong Kong Tel: 7885678 Fax: 7885011 Tlx: 32842 HKPC HX
Investment & Trade **The International Forum on Investment &** **Trade for the Asia Pacific Region** Annual November 10-13, 1993 November 10-13, 1994	Hong Kong Convention & Exhibition Centre	Industrial and commercial investment and trade promotion. Estimated Exhibitors: 100	Adsale Exhibition Services 14/F., Devon House Taikoo Place 979 King's Road Quarry Bay, Hong Kong Tel: 5110511 Fax: 5165204
Money **The Hong Kong Money Show** Annual November 10-13, 1993 November 10-13, 1994	Hong Kong Convention & Exhibition Centre	Personal investment products and services. Estimated Exhibitors: 100	Adsale Exhibition Services 14/F., Devon House Taikoo Place 979 King's Road Quarry Bay, Hong Kong Tel: 5110511 Fax: 5165204
Real Estate **Hong Kong International Real Estate** **Exhibition** Annual November 10-13, 1993 November 10-13, 1994	Hong Kong Convention & Exhibition Centre	Real estate, land and property investment. Estimated Exhibitors: 100	Adsale Exhibition Services 14/F., Devon House Taikoo Place 979 King's Road Quarry Bay, Hong Kong Tel: 5110511 Fax: 5165204

Seminar on "Single European Market"
Last held: June 2, 1993

Hong Kong Convention & Exhibition Centre

Hong Kong Trade Development Council
36-39th Floor, Office Tower
Convention Plaza, 1 Harbour Road
Wanchai, Hong Kong
Tel: 5844333 Fax: 8240249 Tlx: 73595 CONHK HX

Symposium on Projects with Foreign Investment in Jiujiang City
Last held: May 25-28, 1993

The Museum of Chinese Historical Relics

The People's Government of Jiujiang
c/o China Resources Advertising Co.
4/F., Low Block, China Resources Bldg.
26 Harbour Road
Wanchai, Hong Kong
Tel: 5938831 Fax: 8275453 Tlx: 76757 CRACL HX

The Hong Kong Quality Circles Convention
Last held: August 21-24, 1993

Hong Kong Cultural Centre, HKPC Building

Hong Kong Quality Management Association
Federation of Hong Kong Industries
c/o Hong Kong Productivity Council
HKPC Building
78 Tat Chee Avenue, Kowloon Tong
Kowloon, Hong Kong
Tel: 7885678 Fax: 7885011 Tlx: 32842 HKPC HX

World Chinese Entrepreneurs Convention
Last held: November 22-24, 1993

Hong Kong Convention & Exhibition Centre

Chinese Gen. Chamber of Commerce of Hong Kong
7/F., 24 Connaught Road Central
Central, Hong Kong
Tel: 5256385 Fax: 8452610 Tlx: 89854 CGCC HX

World Leasing Convention
Last held: May 23-26, 1993

Island Shangri-La Hotel

Hong Kong Equipment Leasing Association
c/o BOT Lease Hong Kong Co.
Far East Finance Center, 3/F.
16 Harcourt Road
Central, Hong Kong
Tel: 5276265 Fax: 8650231

World Property Market
Last held: September 27-30, 1993

Hong Kong Convention & Exhibition Centre

Cathay Int'l Trade Fairs
Suite 1203, Shanghai Industrial Investment Building
48 Hennessy Road
Wanchai, Hong Kong
Tel: 5272601 Fax: 8651709

Note: Country codes for telephone and fax numbers are not displayed unless they are *outside* of Hong Kong. All country codes have square brackets around them, while city codes have parentheses. The country code for Hong Kong is [852]. Hong Kong does not use city codes.

LEATHER GOODS, FOOTWEAR & FUR
See also Textiles & Apparel

Trade Fair	Site	Exhibition Profile	Organizer
Hong Kong International Footwear Fair Annual Last held: October 22-25, 1993	Hong Kong Convention & Exhibition Centre	Footwear, materials, machinery, equipment and accessories.	Headway Trade Fairs 907 Great Eagle Centre 23 Harbour Road Wanchai, Hong Kong Tel: 8275121 Fax: 8277064 Tlx: 72554 HEWAY HX
Hong Kong International Fur and Leather Fair February 28-March 3, 1994	Hong Kong Convention & Exhibition Centre	Fur and leather garments, accessories, machinery.	Federation of Fur Manufacturers & Dealers (HK) 603, 6/F., Chevalier House 45-51 Chatham Road, South Tsim Sha Tsui Kowloon, Hong Kong Tel: 3674646 Fax: 7390799 Tlx: 48958 FURFD HX
Hong Kong International Handbags & Leather Goods Fair Annual Last held: October 22-25, 1993	Hong Kong Convention & Exhibition Centre	Handbags, luggage, cases, travel accessories, leather goods, materials, machinery and equipment.	Headway Trade Fairs 907 Great Eagle Centre 23 Harbour Road Wanchai, Hong Kong Tel: 8275121 Fax: 8277064 Tlx: 72554 HEWAY HX
Hong Kong International Leather Exhibition April 26-29, 1993 April 25-28, 1994	Hong Kong Convention & Exhibition Centre	Raw materials, shoe and tanning machinery, chemicals and dyes, components and accessories plus finished products.	Hong Kong Trade Fair Group China Resources Building, 44/F. 26 Harbour Road Wanchai, Hong Kong Tel: 8276211 Fax: 8277831 Tlx: 68444 HKTF HX
Leather & Fur Products Showcase December 24, 1994-January 2, 1995	World Trade Centre	Leather and furs.	Oriental Wesley Promotions China Harbour Bldg., 6/F. 370 King's Road North Point, Hong Kong Tel: 8077633 Fax: 5705903 Tlx: 89587 SHKIS HX
Shoe Vision Last held: November 4-6, 1993	Hong Kong Convention & Exhibition Centre	High quality leather fashion shoes.	Hong Kong Trade Fair Group China Resources Building, 44/F. 26 Harbour Road Wanchai, Hong Kong Tel: 8276211 Fax: 8277831 Tlx: 68444 HKTF HX

MACHINES & INSTRUMENTS Includes factory automation

See also Tools: Precision & Measuring, other categories which may include exhibitions with machines specific to those industries

Fair	Venue	Categories	Contact
Asia Pacific Manufacturing Technology Fair Last held: June 23-25, 1993	Hong Kong Convention & Exhibition Centre	Electrical manufacturing and coil winding, assembly technology and quality.	Hong Kong Trade Fair Group China Resources Building, 44/F. 26 Harbour Road Wanchai, Hong Kong Tel: 8276211 Fax: 8277831 Tlx: 68444 HKTF HX
Asian Industrial Technology Congress Last held: May 21-23, 1993	Hong Kong Convention & Exhibition Centre		Hong Kong Polytechnic Industry Department Hong Kong Government c/o BDG Communications Management Suite 1104-5 East Town Building 41 Lockhart Road Wanchai, Hong Kong Tel: 5286136 Fax: 8651528
Hangzhou Light Industrial Trade Fair Last held: April 6-8, 1993	The Museum of Chinese Historical Relics		China Int'l Advertising Corporation c/o China Resources Advertising Co. 4/F., Low Block, China Resources Bldg. 26 Harbour Road Wanchai, Hong Kong Tel: 5938831 Fax: 8275453 Tlx: 76757 CRACL HX
Hong Kong International Exhibition on Peaceful Use of Military Industry Technology Last held: July 5-11, 1993	Hong Kong Convention & Exhibition Centre		China Association for Peaceful Use of Military c/o China Resources Advertising Co. 4/F., Low Block, China Resources Bldg. 26 Harbour Road Wanchai, Hong Kong Tel: 5938831 Fax: 8275453 Tlx: 76757 CRACL HX
Hong Kong Linkage Industry International Machine Tool March 24-27, 1994	Hong Kong Convention & Exhibition Centre	Mold and tool making, surface finishing, plastics, hot and cold workings, metal machining, machinery repair and maintenance.	Paper Communication Exhibition Services Room 16, Wah Shing Centre, 12/F. 11 Shing Yip Street Kwun Tong Kowloon, Hong Kong Tel: 7639011 Fax: 3410379

Note: Country codes for telephone and fax numbers are not displayed unless they are *outside* of Hong Kong. All country codes have square brackets around them, while city codes have parentheses. The country code for Hong Kong is [852]. Hong Kong does not use city codes.

Trade Fair	Site	Exhibition Profile	Organizer
MEX **The International Machinery & Materials Exhibition for Asia** Annual June 9-12, 1993 July 7-10, 1994	Hong Kong Convention & Exhibition Centre	Machine tools, metalworking machinery, production machinery, materials handling and storage equipment, surface treatment equipment, pneumatics and hydraulics, tools, instrumentation, other factory automation equipment.	Business & Industrial Trade Fairs 18/F., First Pacific Bank Centre 51 Gloucester Road Wanchai, Hong Kong Tel: 8652633 Fax: 8661770 Tlx: 64882 ASIEX HX

PACKAGING & PRINTING

Trade Fair	Site	Exhibition Profile	Organizer
Pack & Print Asia **The International Packaging & Printing Machinery & Materials Exhibition for Asia** May 21-25, 1993 May 20-23, 1994	Hong Kong Convention & Exhibition Centre	Packaging machinery and materials, converting machinery, printing machinery, print-related equipment, materials and supplies.	Business & Industrial Trade Fairs 18/F., First Pacific Bank Centre 51 Gloucester Road Wanchai, Hong Kong Tel: 8652633 Fax: 8661770 Tlx: 64882 ASIEX HX

TEXTILES & APPAREL

Trade Fair	Site	Exhibition Profile	Organizer
Apparel From France Last held: August 19-20, 1993	Kowloon Shangri-La Hotel	High fashion, ready-to-wear, leather goods, furs, fashion accessories for ladies, men and children.	French Textile Office Rich Tower, 3/F. 2 Blenheim Avenue, Tsim Sha Tsui Kowloon, Hong Kong Tel: 3120331 Fax: 7398073 Tlx: 37077 TEXIM HX
Asia and World Textiles Conference Last held: May 25-27, 1993	Hong Kong Convention & Exhibition Centre		Textile Institute (Hong Kong Section) c/o 11/F., California Tower 30 D'Aquilar Street Central, Hong Kong Tel: 5233744 Fax: 8106966
Clothing Industry Fair March 10-13, 1994	Hong Kong Convention & Exhibition Centre	Clothing manufacturing, machinery and related equipment.	Hong Kong Productivity Council HKPC Building 78 Tat Chee Avenue, Kowloon Tong Kowloon, Hong Kong Tel: 7885678 Fax: 7885011 Tlx: 32842 HKPC HX
Garmentec—The International Garment Machinery, Materials and Accessories Exhibition for Asia May 19-22, 1993 May 19-22, 1994	Hong Kong Convention & Exhibition Centre	Garment manufacturing machinery, garment accessories, computer systems and fabrics.	Business & Industrial Trade Fairs 18/F., First Pacific Bank Centre 51 Gloucester Road Wanchai, Hong Kong Tel: 8652633 Fax: 8661770 Tlx: 64882 ASIEX HX

Fair	Location	Description	Contact
Hong Kong Fashion Week Annual January 19-22, 1994 January 18-21, 1995 January 17-20, 1996	Hong Kong Convention & Exhibition Centre	Ladies' wear, men's wear, children's wear, casual wear, young fashion, sportswear, evening dresses, bridal gowns, lingerie and designers' collections. Fashion accessories, garment accessories and fabrics.	Hong Kong Trade Development Council 36-39th Floor, Office Tower Convention Plaza, 1 Harbour Road Wanchai, Hong Kong Tel: 5844333 Fax: 8240249 Tlx: 73595 CONHK HX
Hong Kong International Apparel Fair Annual Last held: June 16-19, 1993	Hong Kong Convention & Exhibition Centre	Ready-to-wear clothing, accessories, material and machinery.	Headway Trade Fairs 907 Great Eagle Centre 23 Harbour Road Wanchai, Hong Kong Tel: 8275121 Fax: 8277064 Tlx: 72554 HEWAY HX
Hong Kong International Sporting Goods Fair Annual Last held: July, 1993	Hong Kong Convention & Exhibition Centre	Equipment and accessories for indoor and outdoor gyms, sportswear and accessories, shoes, related services and publications. Estimated exhibitors: 350	Headway Trade Fairs 907 Great Eagle Centre 23 Harbour Road Wanchai, Hong Kong Tel: 8275121 Fax: 8277064 Tlx: 72554 HEWAY HX
Hong Kong Optical November 3-5, 1994	Hong Kong Convention & Exhibition Centre	Optical frames, lenses, sunglasses, contact lenses, spare parts and accessories as well as tools and equipment for optical goods.	Hong Kong Trade Development Council 36-39th Floor, Office Tower Convention Plaza, 1 Harbour Road Wanchai, Hong Kong Tel: 5844333 Fax: 8240249 Tlx: 73595 CONHK HX
Interstoff Asia Last held: November 4-6, 1993	Hong Kong Convention & Exhibition Centre	Fabrics and yarns. Estimated Exhibitors: 350	Messe Frankfurt Rep. Office for HK, China & Macao c/o The Delegate of German Industry and Commerce 22/F., 19 Des Voeux Road Central Central, Hong Kong Tel: 5267203 Fax: 8106093 Tlx: 60128 VDKHK HX
Textile Machine Expo **The International Textile Machinery, Ancillary Equipment, Materials and Technology Exhibition for Asia** Annual May 19-22, 1993 May 19-22, 1994	Hong Kong Convention & Exhibition Centre	Textile machinery and accessories, computer systems, materials, testing and measuring equipment.	Business & Industrial Trade Fairs 18/F., First Pacific Bank Centre 51 Gloucester Road Wanchai, Hong Kong Tel: 8652633 Fax: 8661770 Tlx: 64882 ASIEX HX

Note: Country codes for telephone and fax numbers are not displayed unless they are *outside* of Hong Kong.
All country codes have square brackets around them, while city codes have parentheses.
The country code for Hong Kong is [852]. Hong Kong does not use city codes.

Trade Fair	Site	Exhibition Profile	Organizer
Wedding Apparel 1993 dates April 30-May 3; Oct. 14-17	New World Plaza	Wedding gowns, studio service, flower arrangement, jewelry, skin care and cosmetics, hotel and travel agency services. Estimated Exhibitors: 80	Hong Kong Exhibition Production 10/F., Kiu Yin Commercial Bldg. 361-363 Lockhart Road Wanchai, Hong Kong Tel: 8330186 Fax: 8335445

TOOLS: PRECISION & MEASURING
See also Machines & Instruments, other categories which many include exhibitions with tools specific to those industries

Trade Fair	Site	Exhibition Profile	Organizer
E I E **The International Electronics Industry,** **Testing Equipment & Instrument Exhibition** **for Asia** June 9-12, 1993 July 7-10, 1994	Hong Kong Convention & Exhibition Centre	Equipment, materials and products for manufacturing and inserting PCB semiconductor and hybrid components, automatic assembly equipment, CAD/CAM, measuring, control and testing equipment, electronic components, surface mount technology.	Business & Industrial Trade Fairs 18/F., First Pacific Bank Centre 51 Gloucester Road Wanchai, Hong Kong Tel: 8652633 Fax: 8661770 Tlx: 64882 ASIEX HX
Exhibition of Modern Laboratory **Equipment, Supplies and Services** March 24-27, 1994	Hong Kong Convention & Exhibition Centre	Analytical instrumentation, electronic balance, measuring instruments, laboratory supplies and accessories, universal testing machines and laboratory services.	Paper Communication Exhibition Services Room 16, Wah Shing Centre, 12/F. 11 Shing Yip Street Kwun Tong Kowloon, Hong Kong Tel: 7639011 Fax: 3410379
Hong Kong Optical November 3-5, 1994	Hong Kong Convention & Exhibition Centre	Optical frames, lenses, sunglasses, contact lenses, spare parts and accessories as well as tools and equipment for optical goods.	Hong Kong Trade Development Council 36-39th Floor, Office Tower Convention Plaza, 1 Harbour Road Wanchai, Hong Kong Tel: 5844333 Fax: 8240249 Tlx: 73595 CONHK HX

OTHERS Miscellaneous trade fairs

Trade Fair	Site	Exhibition Profile	Organizer
Hong Kong International Exhibition on **Peaceful Use of Military Industry Technology** Last held: July 5-11, 1993	Hong Kong Convention & Exhibition Centre		China Association for Peaceful Use of Military c/o China Resources Advertising Co. 4/F., Low Block, China Resources Bldg. 26 Harbour Road Wanchai, Hong Kong Tel: 5938831 Fax: 8275453 Tlx: 76757 CRACL HX

International Conference and Exhibition of Signs and Signmaking Last held: December 3-5, 1993	Hong Kong Convention & Exhibition Centre	Signs and signmaking equipment, materials and accessories, services.	Expoconsult Int'l Exhibitions & Conferences 46A Horne Road Singapore 0820 Tel: [65] 2999273 Fax: [65] 2999782
Sanitary Fair Last held: September 22-25, 1993	Hong Kong Convention & Exhibition Centre	Estimated Exhibitors: 80	Hong Kong Exhibition Services Unit 902 Shiu Lam Building 23 Laurd Road Wanchai, Hong Kong Tel: 8041500 Fax: 5283103 Tlx: 65646 HKEXH HX
Securitex Every 2 years June 8-11, 1994	Hong Kong Convention & Exhibition Centre	Access control systems, alarm equipment, fire and smoke detectors, locks, sprinkler systems, security glass, gates and doors, control panels, CCTV, intruder detection, personal security equipment.	Hong Kong Exhibition Services Unit 902 Shiu Lam Building 23 Laurd Road Wanchai, Hong Kong Tel: 8041500 Fax: 5283103 Tlx: 65646 HKEXH HX

Note: Country codes for telephone and fax numbers are not displayed unless they are *outside* of Hong Kong. All country codes have square brackets around them, while city codes have parentheses. The country code for Hong Kong is [852]. Hong Kong does not use city codes.

Business Travel

To the uninitiated business traveler, Hong Kong is business on such a scale that it can be alternately intimidating and infuriating, confusing and amusing, hectic and time-wasting, fascinating and fatiguing, and generally unnerving. Hong Kong is never boring. It's never at a loss. Whether you're being jostled in the streets, or your money is being practically grabbed out of your hand by a shopkeeper, or you're being pampered by the staff in the hotel that you (or your company) are paying dearly for, Hong Kong sweeps you up into a whirlwind of activity the intensity of which doesn't let up until you're on the plane heading for someplace with a slower pace—Tokyo, for example. The sheer pace at which the city operates amazes and exhausts you, and the sensory overload hits from all directions.

Luckily for the traveler, Hong Kong's many first-class hotels and restaurants can help you slow down, relax, get your bearings, and regain your perspective. When you're in Hong Kong, especially for the first time, it's best not to try to do too much too soon all by yourself. Take time to get the lay of the land, and make an entry in your travel budget for self-indulgence in simple luxuries that can ease the body and soul. You'll find it's money well spent.

NATIONAL TRAVEL OFFICES WORLDWIDE

The Hong Kong Tourist Association (HKTA) comes close to equaling Korea's National Tourism Corporation in its enthusiasm for its mission and the quality of its product. HKTA offices worldwide have all the information—free or at nominal cost—that you need to plan your trip. And once you arrive in Hong Kong, a visit to one of its offices is well worth your time.

Europe

Barcelona c/o Sergat España S.L., Apdo. Correos 30266, 08080 Barcelona, Spain; Tel: (93) 280-5838 Fax: (93) 280-4520 Tlx: 54687 FGCE.

Frankfurt Wiesenau 1, 6000 Frankfurt am Main 1, Germany; Tel: (69) 722-841 Fax: (69) 72-12-44 Tlx: 041-412402.

London 125 Pall Mall, London, England SW1Y 5EA; Tel: (71) 930-4775 Fax: (71) 930-4777 Tlx: 051-895-0160.

Paris 38 Avenue George V (entrée 53 rue Francois 1er, 7ème étage), 75008 Paris, France; Tel: (1) 47-20-39-54 Fax: (1) 47-23-09-65 Tlx: 042-650055.

Rome c/o Sergat Italia, s.r.l., Piazza dei Cenci 7/A, 00186 Rome, Italy; Tel: (6) 688-013-36 Fax: (6) 687-3644 Tlx: 623033.

North America

Chicago 333 North Michigan Avenue, Suite 2400, Chicago, IL 60601; Tel: (312) 782-3872 Fax: (312) 782-0864.

Los Angeles 10940 Wilshire Boulevard, Suite 1220, Los Angeles, CA 90024; Tel: (310) 208-4582 Fax: (310) 208-1869.

New York 590 Fifth Avenue, 5th Floor, New York, NY 10036; Tel: (212) 869-5009 Fax: (212) 730-2605.

Toronto 347 Bay Street, Suite 909, Toronto, ON M5H 2R7; Tel: (416) 366-2389 Fax: (416) 366-1098.

Pacific Asia

Osaka 4th Floor, 6-1 Awaji-machi 3-chome, Chuo-ku, Osaka 541, Japan; Tel: (6) 229-9240 Fax: (6) 229-9648.

Singapore 13-08 Ocean Building, 10 Collyer Quay, Singapore 0104, Singapore; Tel: 532-3668 Fax: 534-3592 Tlx: 087-28515.

Sydney Level 5, Harrington Street, The Rocks, Sydney NSW, Australia 2000; Tel: (2) 251-2855 Fax: (2) 247-8812 Tlx: 071-24668.

Taipei 7th Floor, 18 Chang An East Road, Section 1, Taipei; Tel: (2) 581-2967 Fax: (2) 581-6062.

Tokyo Toho Twin Tower Building, 1-5-2 Yurakucho, Chiyoda-ku, Tokyo 100, Japan; Tel: (3) 3503-0731 Fax: (3) 3503-736 Tlx: 072-0222-5678.

Hong Kong

Central Shop 8, Basement, Jardine House, 1 Connaught Place; Tel: [852] 8017177.

Kai Tak Airport Buffer hall information counter; Tel: [852] 8017177.

Kowloon Star Ferry Terminal, Tsim Sha Tsui; Tel: [852] 8017177.

VISA AND PASSPORT REQUIREMENTS

No matter what country you're from, you need a valid passport to enter Hong Kong. Visa policies are very liberal. British citizens can stay for up to 12 months without visas, while those from other Commonwealth countries and most western European nations can stay three months. US citizens can stay one month without visas. Legally, you have to show that you have a ticket to leave Hong Kong, but it's doubtful anyone will ever ask you for it—they don't have time. If you're traveling on business for your company, it's wise to carry a letter stating your business and that your company is responsible for your expenses and activities.

Work visas are another story. If you want to work in Hong Kong, you need to submit a letter of employment in the form of a contract from the Hong Kong firm that you're working for, along with a visa application to the nearest visa-issuing office of the British government. The process normally takes eight weeks because your application goes through the Hong Kong immigration office. If you want to go to Hong Kong to establish a business, again you need to apply for a visa that is processed by Hong Kong Immigration. British citizens don't need work visas.

IMMUNIZATION

You need no proof of vaccination unless you're arriving from an infected area—for example, tropical South America (cholera and yellow fever) or tropical Africa (yellow fever).

CLIMATE

Don't let Hong Kong's tropical latitude fool you. The weather is tropical—hot, humid, and rainy—only in the summer (and like Singapore, the city is thoroughly air conditioned). Winter weather comes courtesy of Siberia—no frost or snow but plenty of cloudy, windy, chilly spells, sometimes accompanied by a seemingly never-ending drizzle. The average January temperature range is 8°C to 23°C (47°F to 74°F). The winds stop suddenly in March, and Hong Kong enjoys a pleasant spring, complete with April showers and mild temperatures.

Big, crashing thunderstorms arrive towards the end of May, and in June the temperature begins rising, reaching an average high of 34°C (94°F) from July through September. Typhoon season begins in July and lasts through October. The Hong Kong civil defense system is well-prepared, and so should you be with flashlights, candles and batteries when you hear a typhoon is imminent (large hotels should be able to help you if you are caught while a guest). November settles down into the best month of the year to visit Hong Kong.

BUSINESS ATTIRE

Hong Kong is king of the business suit, and as in Shanghai and Singapore, you can quickly get exactly what you need in cut, quality, fabric, color, and weight within a few days. You are, however, warned to avoid the 24 hour custom-made suit. These days, most Hong Kong business has to do with finance, trade, or shipping, so dress as you would on Wall Street or the City of London. Or Milan: Hong Kong is probably the only place in East Asia where standards of attire are so relaxed that fashion is appreciated as much as tradition. High quality, expert tailoring, dark colors, and expensive, tasteful accessories fit well with the all-important concept of face. Although women have more power here than anywhere else in East Asia, men still dominate society and women should take care to dress conservatively—hemlines, necklines, sleeve lengths, and makeup are conservative, and pantsuits are out. Feel free to dress more casually if you're doing business on a small scale in light manufacturing or in the arts and crafts, fashion, fabrics, jewelry, or similar industries.

Dress for cool and humid winter weather—you'll never need heavy-duty winter wear—and change to tropical-weight attire for the hot, rainy spring and summer and the warm, sunny fall. As with suits, raingear is readily available.

CUSTOMS ENTRY

Hong Kong customs inspectors are on the lookout for narcotics, which feed the colony's tens of thousands of heroin addicts. But other than this, you can bring just about anything that isn't dangerous into Hong Kong.

Duty-free for personal use

- 200 cigarettes or 50 cigars or 250 grams of tobacco
- 1 liter of alcohol
- 60 ml of perfume
- 250 ml of toilet water
- Personal effects
- ATA carnet items—professional equipment, commercial samples, and advertising material

Cash
- no limit

Prohibited
- Narcotics and other illegal drugs
- Fireworks
- Arms and ammunition

FOREIGN EXCHANGE

The Hong Kong dollar (HK$) comes in coin denominations of 10, 20 and 50 cents, and 1, 2 and 5 dollars. Notes come in denominations of 10, 20, 50, 100, 500, and 1,000 dollars. At year-end 1993, the Hong Kong dollar was HK$7.73 to US$1, and it generally holds steady at around 7.8. The currency is freely convertible, and in Hong Kong any foreign currency may be bought and sold on the open market.

The first place to change money is at Kai Tak Airport's money changing counters, but don't change too much because the commission can be more than 5 percent. As always, hotels give you the poorest rate, banks are somewhere in the middle, and foreign exchange houses, such as Thomas Cook, and private money changers will offer the most favorable rates. But watch out for private money changers who neglect to mention their commission: They often advertise as having no sales commission, but don't tell you about the buying commission, which you must pay, and which can also be more than 5 percent. To get the best rate from a money changer, you must bargain. In fact, money changers' hidden commissions can often mean that such banks as Wing Lung or Hang Seng actually give better rates. Many shops and stores accept payment in US dollars or other major currencies for large purchases, although you'll find that you don't get the official rate in change in Hong Kong dollars.

Hong Kong's position as Asia's leading financial center means that it's very easy to change money; have money wired or transferred to you; buy, sell, and replace traveler's checks; and use credit cards. With so much money floating around, there is no need for a black market.

TIPPING

Hong Kong has become fully Westernized on the subject of tipping. Whereas this custom is absent or poorly developed in most of Asia, it is the expected norm in Hong Kong. Not only do major restaurants tack on a 10 percent service charge, but you're expected to leave an additional 10 percent on the table or on your credit card as well. Hotels, of course, add the 10 percent charge, and it's customary to tip taxi drivers and beauticians 10 percent. Tip the doormen or porters HK$5 (about US$0.65) per item, the concierge HK$10 (about US$1.30) for services rendered, and room service waiters 10 percent. If you have anything left, order a stiff drink (cocktail waiters also get 10 percent).

AIRLINES

Every major airline flies to Hong Kong's Kai Tak International Airport, including Air China, Air France, Air India, Air New Zealand, Alitalia, British Airways, Canadian Airlines International, Cathay Pacific, Continental, Delta, Dragonair, Garuda Indonesia, Japan Airlines, KLM, Korean Air, Lufthansa, Malaysia Airlines, Northwest, Philippine Airlines, Qantas, SAS, Singapore Airlines, South African Airways, Swissair, Thai Airways, and United.

Air Travel Time to Hong Kong

- From Auckland nonstop on Air New Zealand: 11 hrs.
- From Bangkok nonstop on Thai Airlines: 2 hrs. 40 min.
- From Beijing nonstop on Air China: 3 hrs.
- From Frankfurt nonstop on Lufthansa: 12 hrs.
- From Jakarta nonstop on Garuda Indonesia: 4 hrs. 50 min.
- From Kuala Lumpur nonstop on Malaysia Airlines: 2 hrs. 40 min.
- From London nonstop on British Airways: 13 hrs. 15 min.
- From Manila nonstop on Philippine Airlines: 1 hour 50 min.
- From New York nonstop to San Francisco on United: 6 hrs. 20 min. (see San Francisco for remainder of route)
- From San Francisco nonstop on United: 14 hrs.
- From Seoul nonstop on Korean Airlines: 3 hrs. 15 min.
- From Singapore nonstop on Singapore Airlines: 3 hrs. 40 min.
- From Sydney nonstop on Qantas: 9 hrs.
- From Taipei nonstop on China Airlines: 1 hour 30 min.
- From Tokyo nonstop on Japan Airlines: 4 hrs.

TIME CHANGES

Hong Kong shares its time zone, 8 hours ahead of Greenwich Mean Time, with China, Malaysia, Singapore, Taiwan, the Philippines, central Indonesia, and Western Australia. When you're in Hong Kong, you can determine what time it is in any of the cities listed below by adding or the subtracting the number shown to or from Hong Kong time.

Bangkok	-1
Beijing	0
Frankfurt	-7
Jakarta	-1
Kuala Lumpur	0
London	-8
Manila	0
New York City	-13
San Francisco	-16
Seoul	+1
Singapore	0
Sydney	+2
Taipei	0
Tokyo	+1

ACCESS TO CITY FROM AIRPORT

Kai Tak International Airport is on the harbor in a crowded high-rise residential area of Kowloon Peninsula, only 7 km (4.4 miles) northeast of Kowloon's Tsim Sha Tsui business district and 12 km (7.5 miles) northeast of Central, Hong Kong Island's business district. When you land or take off, be prepared to feel as if your plane will crash into dozens of apartment buildings.

The main form of mass transportation to and from the airport is the Airbus. There are four Airbus routes, two to Hong Kong Island and two to Kowloon. Just follow the signs to the main entrance. The buses, which are comfortable and have ample luggage space, run every 15 to 20 minutes. Bus A1 serves 15 hotels in Kowloon—Ambassador, Empress, Grand, Holiday Inn Golden Mile, Hyatt Regency, Imperial, International, Kowloon, Miramar, New World, Park, Peninsula, Regent, Shangri-La, and Sheraton—as well as the YMCA, Chungking Mansions, and the Star Ferry for fares of about HK$8 (about US$1) for the 20-minute trip. Buses A2 and A3 take about 40 minutes and charge HK$12 (about US$1.50) to hit Hong Kong Island hotels. The A2 serves Harbour View International House, Furama, Hilton, Mandarin, and Victoria, while the A3 serves the Causeway Bay hotels near Victoria Park—Caravelle, Excelsior, Lee Gardens, and Park Lane Radisson. From all of these hotels you can either walk or take a taxi to your destination.

Taxis are a more convenient airport transfer, with fares of about HK$60 (about US$7.75) to the Kowloon hotel or business districts and HK$80-100 (about US$10.35 to 13) to the island, but lines for taxis are long. Some hotels have pre-arranged airport limousine service—again, follow the signs. But all forms of transport take the same amount of time in the city's snarled traffic, which is worse than Tokyo's. During rush hour, figure your trip will take another half-hour.

ACCOMMODATIONS

If possible, strike up a pen pal relationship with a Hong Kong resident, and invite this pen pal to your country for a visit, all expenses paid. Then invite yourself to stay with your pen pal in Hong Kong for a week. Pay your own airfare, and your total cost is still bound to be cheaper than a one-week stay in a first-class Hong Kong hotel.

On the other hand, while a Hong Kong hotel can bust the budget of a traveler concerned with the bottom line, it is nothing less than expense account heaven. The average room of international-class standards will cost at least HK$700 (about US$90) a night. For that price, you will get an international direct-dial phone, TV, radio, refrigerator, minibar, air-conditioning, and travel services. Room service, same-day laundry service and business services are available for extra fees. The typical deluxe hotel room will cost at least HK$1,400 (about US$180), with rooms on executive floors costing even more. The difference is in the larger and more luxurious room, the huge number of amenities, and the added cachet—invaluable in East Asian business—of staying in the best place money can buy. Overall, service is superb—not even Japan surpasses Hong Kong in the quality of service. In addition, many hotels give discounts to corporate travelers, children sharing their parents' room, honeymooners, and seniors.

Book your hotel room early, especially if you're going to be in Hong Kong during the high season—September through early December—when hotel rooms are scarce despite there being 36,000 of them. If you don't have a booking when you arrive, you might be able to arrange one through the Hong Kong Hotel Association's airport reservations office, which is just beyond the customs area.

Don't forget where your hotel is. Hong Kong is a vast forest of highrise buildings. You will never be able to see your hotel until you're standing in front of it.

The rates quoted here are accurate as of January 1993; prices have certainly risen since then. Rates are the same for single or double occupancy, unless otherwise noted, and are only the starting rates.

Hong Kong Island–Top-end

Grand Hyatt 1 Harbour Road, Wanchai; business district, on waterfront, adjoining Hong Kong Convention and Exhibition Centre. Business center, computer rentals, banquet and conference facilities, health club, pool, tennis, jogging track, travel desk, doctor, restaurants. Rates: double/twin HK$1,800 (about US$233); suite HK$4,300 (about US$556). Tel: [852] 5881234, (800) 2331234 (US) Fax: [852] 8020677 Tlx: 68434.

Hilton 2 Queen's Road, Central; in financial district. Executive floors, business center, computer rentals, banquet and conference facilities, health club, pool, doctor, travel desk, restaurants, shops. Rates: double/twin HK$1,950 (HK$1,800 single occupancy); suite HK$3,000 (about US$233 to US$388). Tel: [852] 5233111, (800) 4458667 (US) Fax: [852] 8452590 Tlx: 73355 HILTL.

Mandarin Oriental 5 Connaught Road, Central; in financial district, next to Star Ferry concourse. Consistently on world's-best lists. Business center, computer rentals, banquet and conference facilities, health club, pool, travel desk, Rolls Royce fleet, doctor, restaurants, shops. Rates: double/twin HK$1,750; suite HK$3,500 (about US$226 to US$453). Tel: [852] 5220111 Fax: [852] 8106190 Tlx: 73653 MANDA.

New World Harbor View 1 Harbour Road, Wanchai; in business district, adjoins Hong Kong Convention and Exhibition Centre, next to Grand Hyatt. Business center, computer rentals, executive floors, banquet and conference facilities, health club, pool, tennis, doctor, restaurants, shops, shuttle to Central and Causeway Bay. Rates: double/twin HK$1,630 (HK$1,480 single occupancy); suite HK$3,300 (about US$211 to 427). Tel: [852] 8028888 Fax: [852] 8028833.

Ritz-Carlton Connaught Road, Central; in financial district. Small (187 rooms), brand new (1993) art deco townhouse on waterfront. Business center, health club, pool, restaurants. Rates: double/twin HK$2,250; suite HK$7,200 (about US$291 to 931). Tel: [852] 8776666, 800/2413333 (US) Fax: [852] 8776778.

Expensive

Century Hong Kong 238 Jaffe Road, Wanchai; in business district, near Hong Kong Convention and Exhibition Centre. Business center, banquet and conference facilities, health club, pool, travel desk, doctor, restaurants. Rates: double/twin HK$1,150; suite HK$2,400 (about US$149 to 310). Tel: [852] 5988888 Fax: [852] 5988866.

Charterhouse 209-219 Wanchai Road, Wanchai; in business district, near Hong Kong Convention and Exhibition Centre. Business center, health club, restaurants. Rates: double/twin HK$1,100; suite HK$1,500 (about US$142 to US$194). Tel: [852] 8335566 Fax: [852] 8335888 Tlx: HX78123.

Excelsior 281 Gloucester Road, Causeway Bay; next to World Trade Centre, near Victoria Park and financial and business districts. Business center, computer rentals, banquet and conference facilities, indoor tennis, travel desk, doctor, restaurant, shops. Rates: double/twin HK$1,150; suite HK$2,500 (about US$149 to US$323). Tel: [852] 8948888 Fax: [852] 8956459 Tlx: 74550 EXCON.

Wharney 57-73 Lockhart Road, Wanchai; formerly Ramada Inn; in business district, near Hong Kong Convention and Exhibition Centre. Business center, banquet and conference facilities, health club, pool, travel desk, doctor, restaurants. Rates: double/

twin HK$1,050; suite HK$2,500 (about US$136 to US$323). Tel: [852] 8611000 Fax: [852] 8656023 Tlx: 82590 WHARN.

Moderate

China Merchants 160-161 Connaught Road West, Western District; west of financial district, near tram line. Business center, banquet and conference facilities, health club, travel desk, doctor, restaurants, shuttle bus to Central. Rates: double/twin HK$650; suite HK$1,800 (about US$84 to 233). Tel: [852] 5596888 Fax: [852] 5590038 Tlx: 66701 CMHTL

Emerald 152 Connaught Road West, Western District; west of financial district, near tram line. Banquet and conference facilities, travel desk, doctor, restaurants. Rates: single HK$500; double/twin HK$600; suite HK$850 (about US$65 to US$110). Tel: [852] 5468111 Fax: [852] 5590255 Tlx: 84847 EMERA.

Grand Plaza 2 Kornhill Road, Quarry Bay; 5 km west of Central, directly on top of Taikoo Shing MTR Station, connected to massive Kornhill Shopping Center. Business center, banquet and conference facilities, health club (one of the best), pool, tennis, jogging track, putting green, doctor, travel desk, restaurants, shops. Rates: double/twin HK$860; suite HK$1,780 (about US$111 to US$230). Tel: [852] 8860011 Fax: [852] 8861738 Tlx: 67645 GPH.

Harbour View International House 4 Harbour Road, Wanchai; YMCA, on waterfront in business district, near Hong Kong Convention and Exhibition Centre. Banquet and conference facilities, doctor, travel desk, free shuttle to Causeway Bay and Star Ferry. Rates: double/twin HK$620; suite HK$950 (about US$80 to US$123). Tel: [852] 8020111 Fax: [852] 8029063 Tlx: 61073 CYMCA.

Wesley 22 Hennessy Road, Wanchai; in business district, near Hong Kong Convention and Exhibition Centre. Business center, travel desk, doctor, restaurant. Rates: double/twin HK$650 (about US$84). Tel: [852] 8666688 Fax: [852] 8666633 Tlx: 47666 WESHK.

Kowloon–Top-end

Hyatt Regency 67 Nathan Road, Tsim Sha Tsui. Executive floors, business center, conference facilities, travel desk, doctor, restaurants, shops. Rates: double/twin HK$1,600; triple HK$1,900; suite HK$4,500 (about US$207 to 582). Tel: [852] 3111234, 800/2231234 (US) Fax: [852] 7398701 Tlx: 43127 HYATT.

Peninsula Salisbury Road, Tsim Sha Tsui. Legendary waterfront grand hotel, small (156 rooms), total elegance. Business services, computer rentals, banquet and conference facilities, high tea, chandeliered rooms, in-room fax, two-line phones, 3-1 staff-to-guest ratio, valets, Rolls Royce fleet, travel desk, doctor, restaurants, shops. Rates: double/twin HK$2,350; suite HK$7,000 (about US$304 to US$906). Tel: [852] 366-6251 Fax: [852] 7224170 Tlx: 43821 PEN.

Regent Salisbury Road, Tsim Sha Tsui; on harbor edge, unobstructed view. Superior hotel. Business center, computer rentals, banquet and conference facilities, 24-hour butler for every six rooms, health club, pool, tennis, doctor, restaurants, shops. Rates: double/twin HK$ 1,650; suite HK$2,800 (about US$213 to US$362); Tel: [852] 7212111 Fax: [852] 7394546 Tlx: 37134 REG.

Shangri-La 64 Mody Road, Tsim Sha Tsui East. Often on top-10 lists. Executive floor, business center, computer rentals, banquet and conference facilities, health club, pool, doctor, travel desk, restaurants. Rates: double/twin HK$1,600; suite HK$3,300 (about US$207 to US$427). Tel: [852] 7212111 Fax: [852] 7238686 Tlx: 36718 SHALA.

Expensive

Holiday Inn Golden Mile 46-52 Nathan Road, Tsim Sha Tsui. Lobby and restaurants are popular meeting places. Executive floors, business center, banquet and conference facilities, health club, pool, travel desk, doctor, restaurants, shops. Rates: double/twin HK$1,160 (HK$1,060 single occupancy); suite HK$2,500 (about US$137 to US$323). Tel: [852] 369-3111, (800) HOLIDAY (US) Fax: [852] 3698016 Tlx: 56332 HOLIN.

Holiday Inn Crowne Plaza Harbour View 70 Mody Road, Tsim Sha Tsui East; waterfront. Executive floor, business center, computer rentals, banquet and conference facilities, health club, pool, restaurants, shops. Rates: double/twin HK$1,360 (HK$1,260 single occupancy); suite HK$3,500 (about US$176 to US$453). Tel: [852] 7215161, (800) HOLIDAY (US) Fax: [852] 3695672 Tlx: 38670 HIHV.

New World 22 Salisbury Road, Tsim Sha Tsui; in New World Shopping Center. Executive floors, business center, banquet and conference facilities, health club, pool, travel desk, doctor, restaurants, shops. Rates: double/twin HK$1,500 (HK$1,400 single occupancy); suite HK$2,200 (about US$194 to US$285). Tel: [852] 3694111 Fax: [852] 3699387 Tlx: 35860 NWHTL.

Sheraton 20 Nathan Road, Tsim Sha Tsui; across from Peninsula Hotel and Space Museum. Executive floors, business center, banquet and conference facilities, health club, pool, travel desk, doctor, restaurants, shops. Rates: double/twin HK$1,530 (HK$1,430 single occupancy); suite HK$2,330 (about US$198 to US$301). Tel: [852] 3691111, (800) 3253535 (US) Fax: [852] 7398707 Tlx: 45813.

Moderate

Ambassador 26 Nathan Road, Tsim Sha Tsui; across from Peninsula Hotel. Executive floors, business center, travel desk, doctor, restaurants. Rates: double/twin HK$880; suite HK$2,380 (about US$4 to US$308). Tel: [852] 3666321 Fax: [852] 3690663 Tlx: 43840 AMHOC.

Eaton 380 Nathan Road, Yau Ma Tei; 3 km north of Peninsula Hotel. Business center, banquet and conference facilities, restaurants. Rates: double/twin HK$630; suite HK$1,450 (about US$82 to US$188). Tel: [852] 7821818 Fax: [852] 7825563 Tlx: 42862 EATHK.

Kowloon 19-21 Nathan Road, Tsim Sha Tsui; across from Peninsula Hotel (same management). Business oriented. Executive floors, business center, computer rentals, doctor, restaurants, shops. Rates: double/twin HK$930 (HK$900 single occupancy); suite HK$1,700 (HK$1,640 single occupancy) (about US$116 to US$220). Tel: [852] 3698698, 800/ 2629467 (US) Fax: [852] 3698698 Tlx: 47604 KLNHL.

Budget

Booth Lodge 11 Wing Sing Lane, Yau Ma Tei; 4 km north of Peninsula Hotel. Salvation Army-operated. Conference facilities, travel desk, restaurants. Rates: single HK$360; double/twin HK$380 (about US$47 to US$49). Tel: [852] 7719266 Fax: [852] 3851140 Tlx: 57091 SALVO.

Caritas Bianchi Lodge 4 Cliff Road, Yau Ma Tei; 4 km north of Peninsula Hotel, around corner from Booth Lodge, near Jade and Temple Street markets. Restaurants. Rates: single HK$450; double/twin HK$520; triple HK$640; suite HK$690 (about US$58 to US$89). Tel: [852] 3881111 Fax: [852] 7706669 Tlx: 39762 CBLOD.

Salisbury YMCA 41 Salisbury Road, Tsim Sha Tsui; across from Peninsula Hotel. Business center, banquet and conference facilities, instant business card machine, health club, pools, tennis, travel desk, restaurants. Rates: single HK$590; double/twin HK$690; suite HK$1,150 (about US$76 to US$149). Tel: [852] 3692211 Fax: [852] 7399315 Tlx: 31724 HYMCA.

Shamrock 223 Nathan Road, Yau Ma Tei; 2.5 km north of Peninsula Hotel, near MTR. Travel desk, restaurants. Rates: double/twin HK$450 (HK$380 single occupancy); suite HK$800 (about US$49 to 103). Tel: [852] 7352271 Fax: [852] 7367354 Tlx: 50561 SHAMH.

YMCA International House 23 Waterloo Road, Yau Ma Tei; 4 km north of Peninsula Hotel. Banquet and conference facilities, travel desk, restaurant. Rates: single HK$150; double/twin HK$550 (HK$450 single occupancy); suite HK$800 (about US$19 to US$103). Tel: [852] 7719111 Fax: [852] 3885926 Tlx: 39012 CYMCA.

New Territories

Kowloon Panda 3 Tsuen Wah Street, Tsuen Wan; near MTR station. Business center, banquet and conference facilities, health club, pool, travel desk, airport transfer, doctor, restaurants, shops. Rates: double/twin HK$800; suite HK$1,600 (about US$103 to US$207). Tel: [852] 4091111 Fax: [852] 4091818 Tlx: 47611 KPHHK.

Regal Riverside Tai Chung Kiu Road, Sha Tin; overlooks Shing Mun River, 0.8 km to train station. Resort atmosphere but with many long-term business guests. Business center, banquet and conference facilities, health club, pool, travel desk, doctor, restaurants, shops. Rates: double/twin HK$900; suite HK$1,750 (about US$116 to US$226). Tel: [852] 6497878 Fax: [852] 6374748 Tlx: 30013 RERIV.

Royal Park 8 Pak Hok Ting Street, Sha Tin; adjoins Town Plaza and train station. Business center, banquet and conference facilities, health club, pool, tennis, travel desk, doctor, restaurants. Rates: double/twin HK$950; suite HK$2,050 (about US$123 to US$265). Tel: [852] 6012111 Fax: [852] 6013666 Tlx: 45776 RPARK.

EATING

No matter what you want to eat—anything, anything at all—you'll find it in Hong Kong. Besides the usual Chinese, French, Italian, Japanese, Mexican, Korean, Indian, Thai, Vietnamese, Burmese, Malaysian, Indonesian, Filipino, and various and sundry other cuisines, and cooking styles with doubtful claims to the word cuisine—such as English, German, Australian, and American—you may find dishes you've never even dreamed of, nor wanted to. Hong Kong, after all, is the City of Possibilities. Thus, it's possible you'll find a little hole-in-the-wall serving the world's best dim sum, and even more likely that you'll find one serving the world's worst.

With tens of thousands of restaurants and vendors to choose from, the choices are endless. We've tried to select five of the best restaurants on Hong Kong Island and in Kowloon, each serving one kind of cuisine. Some are eminently suitable for lunchtime business discussions, some for dinner entertaining; some are meant to impress, others to save money on excellent food. All have received excellent reviews.

If you really want to impress your Hong Kong business clients, rent the Hilton Hotel's brigantine Wan Fu for a private party. Cost: HK$1,400 (about US$181) per hour, minimum 2 hours, plus food and drink. Note: Chinese love to drink. Be sure to plan accordingly, although most restaurants will make the necessary allowances automatically.

Whatever restaurant you favor with your palate, be sure to check the prices, which can range from unreasonably cheap to unreasonable. Take special care when the menu reads "market price." As any businessperson or investor knows, the market often bears unpleasant surprises.

Hong Kong

East Ocean Seafood Restaurant Cantonese-California cuisine. A business favorite. Specialties: fried spare ribs, drunken prawns, coconut-custard dumplings. Dinner: HK$275 (about US$36) and up. Reservations advised. Dress: jacket and tie. Harbour Centre 3F, 25 Harbour Road, Wanchai; Tel: [852] 8938887.

Harcourt Kitchen Caribbean cuisine. Specialties: Havana chicken, smoked over coffee beans; Haiti "starfish." Dinner: up to HK$120 (about US$16). Reservations advised. Dress: casual. Harcourt House, Fenwick Street and Gloucester Road, Wanchai; Tel: [852] 8650965.

Le Café de Paris French cuisine. Specialties: Barbarie duck breast, quail with raisins. Dinner: HK$125 (about US$16) and up. Reservations advised. Dress: business or elegant casual. 30-32 D'Aguilar Street, Central; Tel: [852] 5247521.

Mandarin Grill Continental cuisine. A favorite of movers and shakers. Specialties: lobster, Kobe steak, wine list. Dinner: HK$550 (about US$71) and up. Reservations required. Dress: jacket and tie. Mandarin Oriental Hotel, 5 Connaught Road, Central; Tel: [852] 5220111.

Tandoor Indian cuisine. Specialties: roast lamb sagwalla, tandoori dishes. Dinner: HK$125 (about US$16) and up. Reservations required. Dress: elegant casual. Carfield Commercial Building, 75-77 Wyndham Street, Central; Tel: [852] 8456313.

Kowloon

Capriccio Italian cuisine. Best Italian in Hong Kong; good place for business discussions. Specialties: four-course set-price business lunch, fettucine with sautéed prawns. Dinner: HK$550 (about US$71) and up. Reservations advised. Dress: jacket and tie. Ramada Renaissance Hotel, 8 Peking Road, Tsim Sha Tsui; Tel: [852] 3751133.

Chalet Swiss cuisine. Small and quiet. Specialties: fillet of beef Helvetia stuffed with goose liver, cheese raclette. Dinner: up to HK$275 (about US$36). Reservations accepted. Dress: casual. Royal Pacific Hotel, 33 Canton Road, Tsim Sha Tsui; Tel: [852] 7361188.

Gaddi's French cuisine. Colony's most prestigious restaurant; princely luxury. Specialties: soufflés, and everything else. Dinner: HK$550 (about US$71) and up. Reservations required. Dress: the finest, black tie if possible. The Peninsula Hotel, Salisbury Road, Tsim Sha Tsui; Tel: [852] 3666251 ext. 3989.

Lai Ching Heen One of the best Cantonese restaurants. Luxurious. Specialties: based on Chinese lunar months. Dinner: HK$550 (about US$71) and up. Reservations required. Dress: jacket and tie advised. Regent Hotel, Salisbury Road, Tsim Sha Tsui; Tel: [852] 7211211.

Three-Five Korean Restaurant Korean cuisine. Specialities: Korean barbeque, kimchi. Dinner: under HK$120 (about US$16). Reservations advised (make them in Chinese or Korean, if possible). Dress:

casual. 6 Ashley Road, Tsim Sha Tsui (near Peninsula Hotel and Hankow Centre); Tel: [852] 3762993.

LOCAL CUSTOMS OVERVIEW

The Chinese are among the world's hardest workers and most adventurous entrepreneurs. Some day, anthropologists may trace the origins of business to ancient China. Westerners, in their cultural conceit, often think that they invented capitalism and determine its practice, yet the Chinese way of doing business is distinctly non-Western and equally successful. If foreigners expect to have the best chances for business success in Hong Kong, they must bear in mind several important facets of Chinese culture.

- The Chinese observe Confucian precepts. Dignity, mutual respect, humility, courtesy, and deference are the most prized human traits. This is called face, which you can have, create, and lose. Face applies to every facet of human interaction. Criticism delivered or received in front of others is anathema, while moderate and appropriate praise is invaluable.
- The Confucian culture is a collective one. One must belong to a group, whether it's a family, village, government agency, or company. Independent action is abhorred as subversive to the collective good—a facet of Confucian culture that explains its attraction to totalitarian governments (although Hong Kong's people make up the freest of Confucian societies). All decisions are made by consensus, reached through seemingly endless meetings, leaving each individual blameless if anything goes wrong, and yet partaking in the success if all goes well.
- The Confucian society is patriarchal, another trait of totalitarian governments. Every person in charge of others is a supposedly benevolent despot whose every word is law and who cares about the most personal details of the workers' lives as if they were family. To break into this "family" circle, you need an intermediary—a matchmaker—who will help you begin the personal kind of relationship that the Chinese value and that is essential in any kind of business relationship.
- Chinese almost never say "no." Such directness is seen as hostile or disrespectful. You will have to learn to read between the lines of discussions. Any answer but yes could mean no.
- If you're meeting a business contact for the first time, shake hands and exchange business cards. Present and receive the cards with both hands; carefully and respectfully study the card you receive, and put it in a pocket above your waist. Further meetings need just the handshake.
- Be prepared to attend and give banquets. Gift giving is also appreciated, but not too early in the relationship and not too lavishly else it seem like a bribe or as if you're trying to put the recipient in your debt.
- Nothing you can give will be better than understanding how the Chinese think and trying your best to adapt to it. They do not expect you to learn all the rules, and will accommodate your Western ways, but they will also appreciate fully your best efforts.
- Despite Confucianism, Hong Kong people often seem appallingly rude. Western travelers' most common complaint is that store clerks, waiters, concierges, and taxi drivers not only just want their money, but are pushy and impatient about it. Bustling pedestrians elbow you right off the sidewalk into the street—and in Hong Kong that's dangerous. The Hong Kong Tourist Association is trying to educate the citizens about the importance of manners, but the lessons don't seem to have helped much. It's important to know that your Chinese business contacts are often just as upset by the lack of civility as you are, and you shouldn't allow the impersonal rudeness to interfere with your budding personal business relationships.

(Refer to "Business Culture" chapter for an in-depth discussion.)

DOMESTIC TRANSPORTATION

Hong Kong's traffic ranks with the world's worst, but its transport systems rank with the world's best. Just try to avoid going anywhere during rush hours. It's likely that your hometown rush hour compares favorably to Hong Kong's normal traffic. Buses and minibuses aren't a good way for the non-Chinese-speaking business traveler to get around because the routes are confusing and the drivers rarely speak English.

Ferry The Star Ferry is the fastest, cheapest and most visually stimulating way to travel between Central in Hong Kong and Tsim Sha Tsui in Kowloon. The ferries cross the harbor hundreds of times a day for a fare of only HK$1.20 for the upper deck and HK$1 for the lower deck (about US$0.16 to 0.13). The ferry also runs between Hunghom and Wanchai, Central and North Point on the island, and between Wanchai and Tsim Sha Tsui in Kowloon.

Ferries also serve the New Territories and the outer islands.

Subway The Mass Transit Railway (MTR) is fast, clean, and efficient, connecting Hong Kong Island with Kowloon and with the New Territories as far as Tsuen Won. The trains run every 2 to 6 minutes; fares range

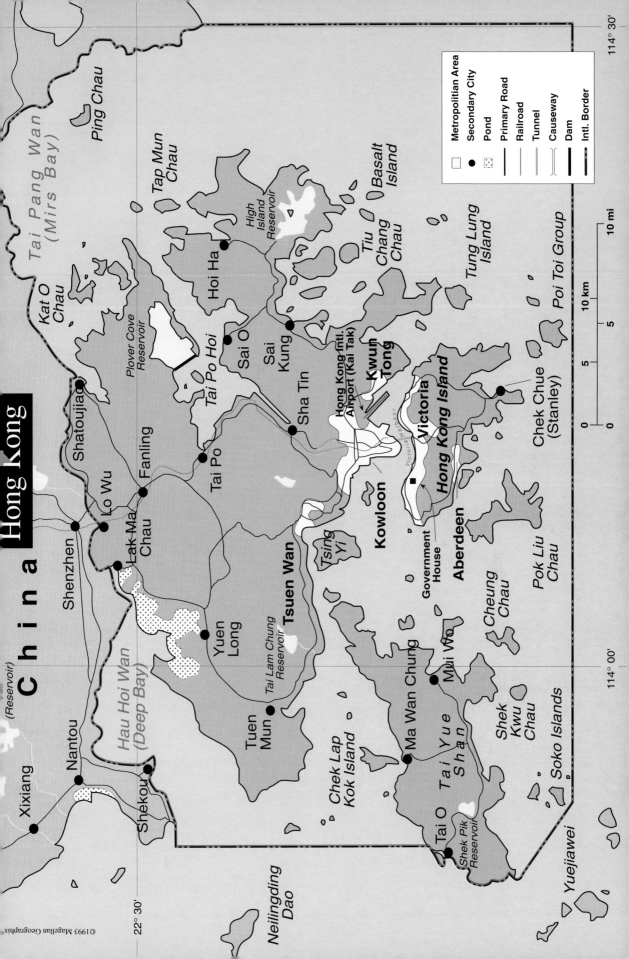

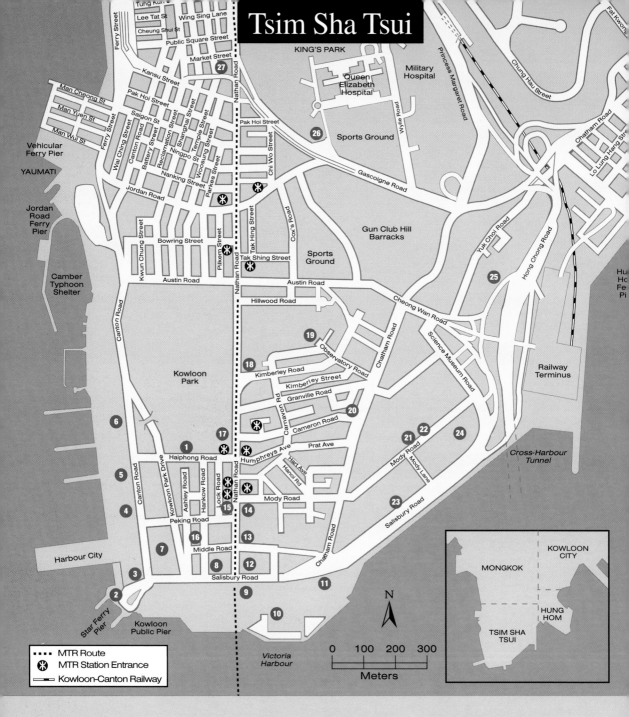

Tsim Sha Tsui

KING'S PARK

Queen Elizabeth Hospital

Military Hospital

Sports Ground

Gun Club Hill Barracks

Sports Ground

Kowloon Park

Railway Terminus

Cross-Harbour Tunnel

Harbour City

YAUMATI

Vehicular Ferry Pier

Jordan Road Ferry Pier

Camber Typhoon Shelter

Star Ferry Pier

Kowloon Public Pier

Victoria Harbour

Streets:
Tung Kun St, Wing Sing Lane, Lee Tat St, Cheung Shui St, Wing Sing Lane, Public Square Street, Market Street, Ferry Street, Kansu Street, Man Cheong St, Pak Hoi Street, Saigon St, Man Yuen St, Shanghai Street, Temple Street, Woosung Street, Man Wui St, Nanking Street, Ningpo St, Canton Road, Battery Street, Reclamation Street, Jordan Road, Parkes Street, Kwun Chung Street, Bowring Street, Wai Ching Street, Austin Road, Pilkem Street, Nathan Road, Chi Wo Street, Pak Hoi Street, Tak Hing Street, Cox's Road, Tak Shing Street, Gascoigne Road, Wylie Road, Princess Margaret Road, Chung Hau Street, Chatham Road, Lo Lung Hang Street, Fat Kwong, Austin Road, Hillwood Road, Cheong Wan Road, Yuk Choi Road, Hong Chong Road, Science Museum Road, Observatory Road, Kimberley Road, Kimberley Street, Carnarvon Rd, Granville Road, Chatham Road, Cameron Road, Humphreys Ave, Prat Ave, Hart Ave, Mody Road, Mody Lane, Haiphong Road, Hanoi Rd, Canton Road, Ashley Road, Hankow Road, Lock Road, Nathan Road, Mody Road, Salisbury Road, Peking Road, Middle Road, Salisbury Road, Kowloon Park Drive

Inset map: MONGKOK, KOWLOON CITY, TSIM SHA TSUI, HUNG HOM

Scale: 0 100 200 300 Meters

N

Legend

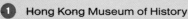

- ••• MTR Route
- ✳ MTR Station Entrance
- ▭ Kowloon-Canton Railway

1. Hong Kong Museum of History
2. Tourist Information Center
3. Star House / Hong Kong Exporters' Association
4. Ocean Center / Industry Department
5. Omni Marco Polo Hotel
6. Omni Prince Hotel
7. Tsim Sha Tsui Police Station
8. Peninsula Hotel
9. Hong Kong Space Museum
10. Regent Hotel
11. New World Center
12. Sheraton Hotel
13. Ambassador Hotel
14. Holiday Inn Golden Mile
15. Hyatt Regency Hotel
16. Hankow Center / Federation of Hong Kong Industries
17. Kowloon Mosque
18. Miramar Hotel
19. Royal Observatory
20. Park Hotel
21. Royal Garden Hotel
22. Regal Meridien Hotel
23. Shangri-La Hotel
24. Holiday Inn Harbour View
25. Hong Kong Polytechnic
26. Kowloon District Court
27. Kowloon Central Post Office

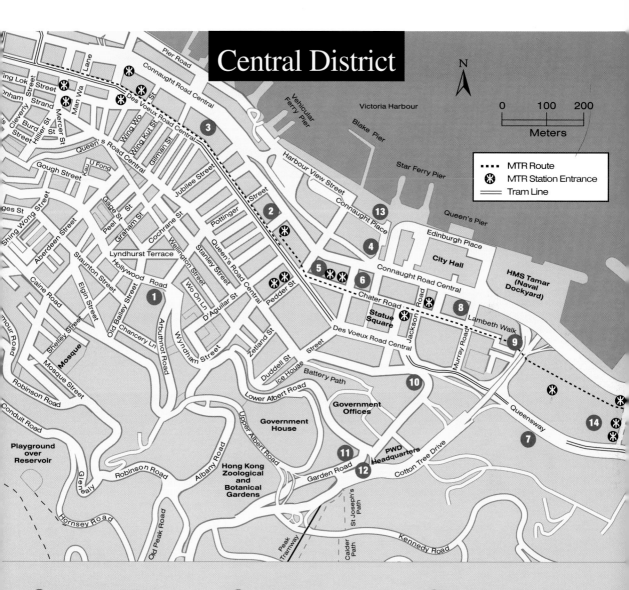

Central District

Legend
- ···· MTR Route
- ✳ MTR Station Entrance
- — Tram Line

1. Central Police Station
2. Chinese General Chamber of Commerce
3. Chinese Manufacturers' Association
4. Jardine House Hong Kong Tourist Association
5. Swire House American Chamber of Commerce
6. Mandarin Oriental Hotel
7. Supreme Court
8. Hotel Furama Kempinski
9. Japanese Consulate General British Trade Commission
10. Hilton Hotel
11. United States Consulate General
12. Peak Tram Terminal
13. General Post Office
14. United Center Hong Kong General Chamber of Commerce

Mongkok

Yu Chau Street
Boundary Street
Sycamore Street
Willow Street
Tung Chau Street
Ki Lung Street
Tai Nan Street
Lai Chi Kok Road
Portland Street
Playing Field Road
Flower Market Road
Prince Edward Road
Tat Chee Ave
Fa Hui Park
Boundary Street
Embankment Rd
Cumberland Rd
Duke Street
Knight St
Belfran Rd
Prince Edward Road
Waterloo Road
Chung Wui St
Tai Tsun St
Larch Street
Bedford Road
Fuk Tsun Street
Arran Street
Nullah Road
Kadoorie Avenue
Braga Circuit
Lai Tak St
Fuk Chak St
Ivy Street
Pine St
Anchor Street
Bute Street
Tung Choi Street
Fa Yuen Street
Sai Yee Street
Kadoorie Avenue
Argyle
Ka Shin St
Pok Man Street
Tai Kok Tsui Road
Beech Street
Oak Street
Cherry Street
Tong Mei Road
Nathan Road
Mongkok Road
Fife Street
Argyle Street
Argyle Street
Waterloo Road
Man Fuk Rd
Man Wan Rd
Victory Avenue
Soares Avenue
Pui Ching Road
TAI KOK TSUI
Nelson Street
Shantung Street
Sai Yeung Choi Street
Tung Choi Street
Fa Yuen Street
Sai Yu Street
Kwong Wa St
Yim Po Fong Street
Peace Avenue
Ho Man Tin Street
HO MAN TIN
Soy Street
Yaumati Typhoon Shelter
Ferry Street
Canton Road
Reclamation Street
Shanghai Street
Portland Street
Dundas Street
Waterloo Road
Wylie Road
Princess Margaret Road
Ho Man Tin Hill Road
Carmel Village
Oi Man Estate
N
Hamilton Street
Pitt Street
0 100 200 300
Meters
Waterloo Road
Shek Lung St
Man Ming Lane
KING'S PARK
Oi Man Estate
Chung Hau Street
MTR Route
MTR Station Entrance
Kowloon-Canton Railway
Tung Kun St
Hi Lung Lane
Lee Tat St
Wing Sing Lane
Cheung Shui St
Public Square Street

1. Meteorological Station
2. Housing Department
3. YMCA
4. Kwong Wah Hospital
5. Tai Kok Tsui Ferry Pier
6. Kowloon Chamber of Commerce
7. Mongkok Post Office
8. Mongkok Police Station
9. Mongkok Railway Station
10. Kowloon Hospital

from HK$3 to HK$7 (about US$0.40 to US$0.90). Ticket purchases, turnstiles, doors—everything is automated and easy to use. Signs are in English and Chinese, and since there are only four routes, it's hard to get lost. The tickets are the size of credit cards and have magnetic strips on the back—when you exit the train, the turnstile reads your card, figures out how far you went and deducts the amount from your ticket. Single-trip tickets must be used the same day; in fact, once you pass through the entrance turnstile, they must be used within 90 minutes. One way to save money is to buy Common Stored Value Tickets in denominations of HK$50, HK$100 and HK$200 (about US$6.50 to US$26), available at MTR station minibanks.

If your business takes you to Tsuen Wan in the New Territories, the MTR is the best and cheapest way to get back to Kowloon and Hong Kong.

Confucian ethics allow for what seems to Westerners to be incredible rudeness in mass transit behavior. Try to avoid rush hours, when the MTR becomes very crowded and there are pushing and shoving matches to get on. You will probably have to wait until a few trains pass before you can work your way onto a train.

Train The Kowloon-Canton Railway (KCR) runs from Kowloon to the Chinese border. Special express trains make the 3-hour trip to Guangzhou (Canton). The KCR is the best way to get to and from Sha Tin in the New Territories. The fare is less than HK$20 (about US$2.60), which is far less than a taxi fare.

Tram The tram line runs along Hong Kong Island's north shore from Kennedy Town west of Central to Shaukiwan east of Quarry Bay. In fact, it used to run along the shoreline, so if you look north on your ride, you can see the vast land reclamation projects that have enlarged the island. The tram is slow, makes a lot of stops, and is impossibly crowded during rush hour, but it's a pleasant and cheap (HK$1—US$0.13) way to get around the island, especially if you're staying in the Western District or Quarry Bay. Each tram has a sign showing its destination. You board in the rear, work your way towards the front as you near your stop, and pay as you get off.

Taxi Taxis are hard to miss in Hong Kong—they're red with an illuminated roof-sign reading "TAXI." And they're easy to get, too, unless it's rush hour, or raining, or you're standing in a no-stopping zone (the curb is painted yellow), or the driver doesn't feel like picking you up. All cabs must have working meters, and you'll notice the fare is already HK$9 (about US$1.16) before you've even sat down. The fare thereafter will rise 90¢ for every 2-tenths of a kilometer you travel. Be prepared for the HK$1 surcharge for a radio-summoned taxi, the HK$4 surcharge for each large piece of luggage and the HK$20 surcharge for going through the Cross-Harbour Tunnel. As a tip you should leave the odd change, or, for a large fare, from 50¢ to HK$1.

If you're traveling to or staying in the New Territories, be aware that cabs stationed there cannot travel into Kowloon or Hong Kong, although the urban cabs can pick you up and drop you off in the New Territories.

Many Hong Kong taxi drivers don't speak much English so to prevent confusion, have your hotel staff write down your destination in Chinese. All cabs are equipped with a card listing the 50 most popular destinations in Chinese, English, and Japanese.

Because taxi licenses are issued through competitive bidding that has driven the price up to at least HK$600,000 (about US$77,620), and with severe penalties for cheating, most taxi drivers are honest. If you think you've been cheated or otherwise mistreated, call the hot line (5776866) and report the taxi license number, which you can find on the dashboard.

Hired car and driver You don't want to drive yourself around Hong Kong. For a fee approximating that of your first-class hotel room, your concierge can arrange a rented car and chauffeur for you. For example, Goodway Express Tours, Ltd., offers a Mercedes 300SE with driver for HK$230 (about US$30) per hour for a minimum of three hours, plus driver's tip, parking fees, and tunnel tolls. It will impress your Chinese business contacts beyond belief if you engage one of the Peninsula or Mandarin Oriental's Rolls Royces.

HOLIDAYS/BANK HOLIDAYS

Hong Kong has several public holidays, many based on the Chinese lunar calendar (signified by * on the list on the following page). Almost everything closes for the first three days of Chinese New Year, the only holiday that everyone observes. Businesses and workers seem to take other holidays less seriously, although workers are guaranteed 11 per year. If a holiday falls on a Sunday or other normal rest day, the day after is observed as the holiday. Employees of the government, banks, and most professional offices receive full pay. Some shops and factories recognize only the Chinese festivals.

BUSINESS HOURS

Most businesses open at 9 am and close at 5 or 6 pm Monday through Friday—taking lunch from 1 to 2 pm—and are open Saturday from 9 am to 1 pm. Banks are open weekdays from 9 am to 4:30 pm and Saturday from 9:30 am to 12:30 pm. Shops and stores are open every day from 10 am to 6 pm in Central; 10 am to 9:30 pm in Wanchai and Causeway; and 10 am to 9 pm in Tsim Sha Tsui.

Hong Kong Holidays and Bank Holidays

New Year's Day – First weekday in January

Lunar or Chinese New Year* – First 3 days of lunar New Year, late January or early February

Good Friday through Easter – Monday, March or April

Easter – 3 days

Ching Ming Festival* – 1 day, usually early April

Tuen Ng or Dragon Boat Festival* – 1 day, usually early June

Queen's Birthday – June 11; celebrated on closest Saturday, observed on following Monday

Liberation Day – Last Monday in August

Mid-Autumn Festival* – 1 day, usually September

Chung Yeung Festival* – 1 day, mid- to late October

Christmas – December 25

Boxing Day – December 26

2 floating holidays – Designated in advance by employer

COMMUNICATIONS

Hong Kong didn't get as rich as it is by having third-rate telecommunications, mail service, and media. Hong Kong swims in a sea of spoken and written information, all of it transmitted quickly and efficiently.

Telephones Local calls are free, although calls from public phones cost HK$1. There aren't many public phones on the street—you can find them in hotel lobbies, post offices, the ferry terminals, Hong Kong Telecom offices (listed in the phone books), offices of Cable & Wireless (affiliated with Hong Kong Telecom, and also listed), and the airport—but it's perfectly all right to walk into a shop and ask to use the phone to make a local call. Shopkeepers usually have their phones right on the counter in plain view from the street; after all, if they can lure you into their store with a free local phone call, you might just buy something.

Almost every hotel room has an international direct-dial (IDD) phone. IDD calls are supposed to be cheaper than operator-assisted, but beware of hotel surcharges. As an alternative, you can use a Phonecard or AT&T World Connect service. You can use the Phonecard in pay phones; buy it in denominations of HK$40, HK$100 or HK$250 (about US$5.20 to US$32.50) in shops or at one of the 24-hour Hong Kong Telecom/Cable & Wireless offices—10 Middle Road, Tsim Sha Tsui, Kowloon (behind the Sheraton Hotel); or Room 102A Tower One, Exchange Square, Central, Hong Kong Island (on Harbour View Street

just west of the Star Ferry pier). Without a Phonecard, you need a pocketful of HK$5 coins unless your call is going to be brief.

For World Connect service instructions, see below.

Useful Telephone Numbers

- AT&T USADirect or AT&T World Connect 800-1111
- International direct dial access 001
- International calling assistance 013
- Operator-assisted international calls 010
- International collect or conference calls ... 011
- Local directory service 1081
- Taxi complaints 577-6866
- Time and weather 1852
- Hong Kong Information Services Department 8428777
- Lost or stolen credit cards
  (International collect calls only to US regardless of which country issued your card)
  Amex 919-333-3211
  Diners Club 303-799-1504
  MasterCard 314-275-6690
  Visa 410-581-7931

To direct-dial internationally Dial the international access code—001—then the country code, then the area code (if there is one), and the local phone number. For example, to call World Trade Press direct, dial 001-1-415-454-9934.

To use AT&T USADirect or AT&T World Connect Hong Kong has AT&T World Connect service (known as Home Country Direct in some countries). A cooperative venture among large phone companies, including AT&T, the service allows you to bypass Hong Kong Telecom (or the local system of the country you're in) and hook directly into the phone company of the country you're calling—if that country is also a member of World Connect. World Connect is much cheaper than IDD because you're not using your hotel's long-distance equipment, and so the hotel can assess only the local call surcharge (and in Hong Kong local calls are free). You'll find out if your country is a member by trying to make the call. This is how to do it:

- Dial the access number: 800-1111.
- Wait for the recorded voice prompt, which offers you the option of using your home country calling card, a credit card (except US), or an operator for collect calls. Then follow the instructions for the option you choose.
- If you're calling the US on your calling card, follow the instructions for that procedure, then dial just the area code and the local phone number; you don't need to dial the country code.
- If you're calling another country that is a

member of World Connect, dial 01, then the country code, then the area code, and then the local phone number.

- If you're making more than one call, don't hang up after the first call, or if there's a busy signal or no answer—simply press # and wait for the voice prompt, and redial or dial the number.
- If you don't know if the country you want to call is a member of World Connect, wait for an operator to come on the line, and ask him or her.

Country Codes of Major Countries

Country	Code
Australia	61
Brazil	55
Canada	1
China	86
France	33
Germany	49
Hong Kong	852
India	91
Indonesia	62
Italy	39
Japan	81
Korea	82
Malaysia	60
Mexico	52
New Zealand	64
Pakistan	92
Philippines	63
Russia	7
Singapore	65
South Africa	27
Spain	34
Taiwan	886
Thailand	66
United Kingdom	44
United States	1

Electronic data services Hong Kong Telecom has linkups to the International Database Access Service (IDAS); Dialcom electronic mail and data base access system; Infonet, the single-source, worldwide data communications and information network; and International High-Speed Document Transfer Service. For information, call either of the two 24-hour offices (listed in the phone book).

Fax and telex Since local calls are free and Chinese characters can be transmitted on fax, fax machines have taken over Hong Kong. Most hotels and businesses have them, and the Post Office and Cable & Wireless have joined forces to offer Postfax, available at all main post offices and at C&W's two 24-hour offices. Call the General Post Office (5231071) to learn which branches have Postfax.

For a hefty surcharge your hotel will send telex messages, or you can visit any C&W office (listed in the directories).

Post Office Hong Kong's mail service is fast and efficient. Mail is delivered twice a day, six days a week, and overnight delivery in the main business areas is standard. Aerograms cost HK$1.80 (about US$0.23), while postcards and letters under 10 grams destined for Europe or North America cost HK$2.30 (about US$0.30). The most convenient way to mail letters is at your hotel front desk.

English-language media Hong Kong is publisher's central for East Asian English-language print media. Among the newspapers, magazines and journals available are the *Asian Wall Street Journal,* the *International Herald Tribune,* the *South China Morning Post,* the *Hongkong Standard,* the *Far Eastern Economic Review, Asiaweek, Newsweek,* and *Time.* In addition, periodicals from a variety of foreign countries are readily available at the major hotels and from the newstands in the Star Ferry concourse in Kowloon. The government has censorship power which it does use infrequently to avoid offending mainland China.

There are at least four telephone directories printed in English, three of them bilingual English and Chinese. Look through the *Yellow Pages Buying Guide,* the *Yellow Pages Commercial and Industrial Guide,* the *Business Telephone Directory,* and the *Residential Directory.*

Hong Kong is rich with libraries, including the Hong Kong Trade Development Council's Reference Library and China Trade Library in the HKTDC main office at Hong Kong Convention and Exhibition Centre, 1 Harbour Road, Wanchai (in same complex as the Grand Hyatt and New World Harbour View hotels).

Radio Television Hong Kong (RTHK) broadcasts news and information in English on Radio 3 at am 567 and 1584, and FM 97.9 and 98.9. You can hear classical music on Radio 4 at FM 97.6 and 98.9, and the BBC World Service on bilingual Radio 6 at am 675.

The two English-language television stations are Channel 3 and Channel 4.

Videoconferencing Hong Kong Telecom offers a videoconferencing service at its two studios.

COURIER SERVICES

All major international courier services know a good thing when they see it, so they operate in Hong Kong. All are listed in the directories.

Federal Express Shop 127B, 1/F, Shopping Arcade, New Mandarin Plaza, Tsim Sha Tsui East, Kowloon; Tel: [852] 3661889.

TNT 6th Floor, Chung Nam Centre, 414 Kwun Tong Road, Kwun Tong, Kowloon; Tel: [852] 3895279/88, 3898292/8 Fax: [852] 3432714 Tlx: 38811 SKYHK.

UPS Suite 602 North Tower, World Finance Center, Harbour City, Tsim Sha Tsui, Kowloon; Tel: [852] 7353535 Fax: [852] 7385073.

LOCAL SERVICES

Every possible type of business service is available in Hong Kong.

Business centers

All major hotels have these centers, which gather under one roof secretarial and translation services, computer, fax and telex capabilities, business-card printing services, and a host of others. Some hotel center fees can border on the unconscionable, so you may want to check out business centers outside the hotels. These centers will not only rent you a private desk for HK$3,500 (about US$453) per month and up but provide you with a private address, answering and forwarding services, and lawyers and accountants to help you register your company.

Try one of the following business centers:

Asia Business Centre 3rd Floor, The Centremark, 287-299 Queen's Road, Central; Tel: [852] 5448773 Fax: [852] 8540203 Tlx: WINGP

Central Executive Business Centre 11/F Central Building, Pedder Street, Central; Tel: [852] 8417888.

China Traders Centre Regal Airport Hotel; offices and conference rooms by the hour, day, week or month.

Secretarial and translation services

Several firms offer the talents of bilingual secretaries and translators, and some even can print your business cards, offer language courses, or organize seminars or conferences for you.

A-Tech Translation Services 1504 Kelly Communications Centre, 570 Nathan Road, Tsim Sha Tsui, Kowloon; Tel: [852] 3881662 Fax: [852] 3854522.

Chang Jiang Translanguage Centre 3/F Wai Hing Communications Building, 17 Wing Ho Street, Hong Kong; Tel: [852] 8153145 Fax: [852] 8541620.

China Communication Translation Services 1/F, 129 Queen's Road, Central; Tel: [852] 5418585 Fax: [852] 8540549.

International Information Service, Ltd. 10-3 Wing On Plaza, 62 Mody Road, Tsim Sha Tsui, Kowloon; Tel: [852] 7391818 Fax: [852] 7213692 Tlx: 30431 NTEDL.

Margaret Sullivan Secretarial Services 33 Duddell Street, Central; Tel: [852] 5265946 Fax: [852] 8450989 Tlx: 63210 ALAYE.

Translanguage Centre, Ltd. 1604 Tung Wah Mansion, 199 Hennessy Road, Wanchai; Tel: [852] 5732728 Tlx: 76579 TRLAN.

STAYING HEALTHY

Hong Kong is fairly easy on your health and safety. The government says that the tap water is safe to drink, but most Chinese boil it anyway. The food may sometimes be strange, but even when it's from street vendors, it's still safe to eat.

Crime Like most hotbeds of democratic capitalism, Hong Kong has a crime problem. Organized gangs known as the Triads run drugs, gambling, prostitution, weapons, extortion, and loan sharking. It all has a familiar ring to those from Western cities. Yet unlike many Western cities, Hong Kong is relatively safe. The heavy police presence makes it unlikely that you'll encounter any problem at all, and if you do, that problem will more than likely be pickpocketing, an easy career to pursue in the crowded streets, rather than mugging. There are occasional purse snatchings as well. But there are ways you can help prevent yourself from becoming a victim.

- Check in with your embassy or consulate on your arrival, both to let them know you're there and to ask about crime conditions.
- Avoid displays of flashy jewelry and watches; dress and behave conservatively.
- Be aware that pickpockets like crowds, and don't give them a chance. Don't carry much cash, and keep it in a money belt. Use credit cards or traveler's checks for most of your transactions.
- Ask at your hotel about the safety of the surrounding streets.
- Behave and walk as if you know where you are and where you're going. Muggers are as drawn to the lost and confused as they are to Rolex watches and rolls of cash.
- Walk with your briefcase or shoulder bag to the side away from the street to keep motorcycling thieves from grabbing it.

Personal care products Most of the personal care products you're accustomed to can be found in Hong Kong, but bring your own shaving lotion, dental floss, vitamins, deodorant, sunscreen, cosmetics, and mosquito repellent—these are often extremely expensive or not available in your preferred brands. You should also bring a sufficient supply of your prescription medications. And while toilet paper is readily available in stores and hotels, most public restrooms don't have it, so take a supply of your own when you're out and about.

EMERGENCY INFORMATION

Police, fire or ambulance 999

Royal Hong Kong Police Visitor Hot Line to report a non-emergency crime: 5277177.

Doctors and hospitals

Most major hotels have a house doctor or one on call, or can arrange for a doctor to visit you. The typical doctor's fee ranges from HK$120 to HK$350 (about US$15.50 to US$45.25). Hong Kong has several hospitals that are operated by the British government, and some excellent private hospitals as well.

Adventist Hospital private; 40 Stubbs Road, Wanchai; Tel: [852] 5746211.

Princess Margaret Hospital public; Lai Chi Kok, Kowloon; Tel: [852] 7427111.

Queen Elizabeth Hospital public; Wylie Road, Yau Ma Tei, Kowloon; Tel: [852] 7102111.

St. Paul's Hospital private; 2 Eastern Hospital Road, Causeway Bay; Tel: [852] 6906008.

DEPARTURE FORMALITIES

Formalities are just that. All you need to leave Hong Kong is a ticket to someplace else. You can take any amount of money in any currency you want, and anything else except for arms and ammunition, narcotics, and fireworks.

BEST TRAVEL BOOKS

No travel book can possibly keep up to date with all the changes occurring so rapidly in Hong Kong's neck of the woods, so don't judge them (or us) too harshly when prices, phone numbers, and addresses are wrong. The following three books are about as informative and practical as any you can buy.

Fodor's 93 Hong Kong, edited by Caroline Haberfeld. New York: Fodor's Travel Publications, 1993. ISBN 0-679-02302-X. 220 pages, US$12.00. Oriented towards the tourist and shopper, but strong on transportation, hotels, and restaurants. Includes excursions to Macao and China. Good maps.

The Four Dragons Guidebook, by Fredric M. Kaplan. Boston: Houghton Mifflin, 1991. ISBN 0-395-58577-5. 688 pages, US$18.95. 172 pages devoted to Hong Kong (the rest to Singapore, Taiwan, and Thailand), including 19 pages on doing business in Hong Kong. Good basic information on travel; needs updating.

Hong Kong, Macao & Canton, by Robert Story. Hawthorn, Victoria, Australia: Lonely Planet Publications, 1992. ISBN 0-86442-142-7. 357 pages, US$14.95. The usual somewhat quirky Lonely Planet guide for the independent, budget-minded traveler: thorough, insightful, irreverent, practical, especially for backpacking wanderers and those who want to spend like them. Very good maps.

Typical Daily Expenses in Hong Kong

All prices are in Hong Kong dollars (HK$) unless otherwise noted.

At press time, the exchange rate was US$1 = HK$7.73.

Expense	LOW	MODERATE	HIGH
Hotel	660	1,350	2,200
Local transportation *	12	50	130
Food	200	600	1000
Local telephone †	5	20	40
Tips	5	50	80
Personal entertainment **	50	200	450
TOTAL	**932**	**2,270**	**3,900**
One-way airport transportation	10	80	80

US Government per diem allowance as of December, 1993 was US$179 for lodgings and US$100 for meals and incidentals (approximately HK$2,156).

* Based on 2 bus rides for low cost, 2 medium length taxi rides for moderate cost and 4 medium to longer taxi rides for high cost.
† Based on 2 telephone calls from pay phones for low cost, 4 calls from the hotel room for moderate cost and 6 calls from the hotel room for high cost.
** Based on a movie ticket and refreshments for low cost, a visit to a disco with a drink for moderate cost and a live floor show for high cost.

Business Culture

Hong Kong, called The Pearl of the Orient, is by any standards one of the world's leading business centers and the preeminent trade center in East Asia. Comparable to New York, London, and Tokyo in commerce, development, and wealth, Hong Kong is the meeting place of two great cultural traditions: East and West. The resulting blend makes Hong Kong not only one of the greatest cities on earth but also one of the most exciting and interesting.

Hong Kong is the financial capital of mainland East Asia for a number of reasons: situated at the mouth of the Pearl River, it has one of the world's finest natural harbors. Its communications and transportation infrastructures are well developed. Its legal system, founded on British common law, is designed for trade. The number one port of entry to its giant neighbor, China, it is the conduit for trade between Taiwan and China, two old enemies whose economic interdependence is increasing. Its people are culturally disposed toward business. It has been and continues to be the center of Western business interests in East Asia. Finally, English is spoken widely as a second language, making it highly accessible to Westerners.

The Foundation of Trade

Modern Hong Kong was founded for the sole purpose of trade. In the 1840s traders from the British East India Company established Hong Kong as a trading outpost. The British used Hong Kong as their port of entry to China and declared it a free port in 1841. From there they sold huge amounts of opium produced in India to the locals, depleting Chinese silver reserves and creating a drug problem of epidemic proportions. The Opium War of 1842, fought between the British and Chinese, resulted in the ceding of Hong Kong Island to the British in perpetuity. In 1898 the Kowloon Peninsula, various islands, and a large tract on the mainland called the New Territories were signed over to Britain under a 99-year lease, one of the many unequal treaties forced on the weak and corrupt Q'ing Dynasty.

In the first half of the 20th century, Hong Kong's position as a trade center declined in relative importance to Shanghai, and it was not until the Communist takeover of mainland China in 1949 that the colony once more began to grow. Millions of refugees from Guangdong Province poured into Hong Kong, providing cheap labor for the colony's many foreign-owned factories.

The Rebirth of Hong Kong

But the refugees brought more than cheap labor; they also brought dreams of starting new lives and a determination to succeed. For the next several decades, while mainland China stagnated under Communist mismanagement and the chaos of the Cultural Revolution, Hong Kong steadily developed into a regional industrial center, providing the West with low-cost goods. With few natural resources, Hong Kong's people had no other option than to turn to business and manufacturing for survival. Many of the local people and immigrants from China began to make fortunes through shrewd investments and savvy management styles, gradually usurping financial dominance from foreign capitalists. The people of Hong Kong embraced business not only as a means to survival but as a way of life.

Aspiring to Greatness

Hong Kong's leap into world-class status as a financial center was spurred by China's "Open Door" policies initiated by Deng Xiaoping in 1978. As the only capitalist city on China's coast, Hong Kong was naturally suited to provide the business skills that China desperately needed, and its well-developed port facilities were ready to handle South China's export commodities. Guangdong Province in turn provided cheap labor and investment opportunities, and Hong Kong entrepreneurs threw themselves into the China market with zeal. As industrial jobs moved inland, Hong Kong business focused on providing the finance, shipping, and marketing services needed to fuel the area's booming economy. Aided by the colony's long experience of dealing with the outside world and its use of English as the language of business, Western companies set up shop in Hong Kong for easy access to China.

The Capital of Greater China

Today Hong Kong sits at the center of a huge economic dynamo commonly called Greater China which includes the combined economic resources of China's southern coast, Taiwan, Hong Kong, and the overseas Chinese communities of Southeast Asia. Transcending geopolitical boundaries, Greater China includes hundreds of millions of producers and consumers bound by a common cultural tradition and racial homogeneity. This region's continued development promises to make it an economic bloc more powerful than Japan and on a par with North America and the European Community. Hong Kong is the undisputed capital of Greater China.

UNDERSTANDING THE CHINESE MENTALITY

Although Hong Kong has a huge foreign population of expatriate businesspeople, its population is 98 percent Chinese. Although their traditions and values have been influenced by the Western presence, they are still essentially Chinese, and Hong Kong inhabitants possess many characteristics which are difficult for Westerners to understand. Moreover, Hong Kong business is inextricably bound to business in mainland China and other Chinese areas less affected by Western culture. Foreign businesspeople operating in Hong Kong must therefore grasp the moral values and traditional concepts which shape the Chinese mentality if they are to operate successfully in a Chinese business environment, all the more so because Hong Kong reverts to mainland Chinese control in 1997.

Confucianism

The mentality of modern Chinese is still shaped largely by the teachings of Confucius, who lived more than 2,500 years ago. Confucianism is more of a social code for behavior than it is a religion. The basic tenets of Confucian thought are obedience to and respect for superiors and parents, duty to family, loyalty to friends, humility, sincerity, and courtesy. Confucius identified five types of relationships, each with very clear duties. They are: ruler to people, husband to wife, parent to child, older to younger, and friend to friend.

Ruler to People In the Confucian view, the ruler commands absolute loyalty and obedience from his people. They are never to question his directives or his motives. In return, the ruler is to be wise and work for the betterment of his people. He should always take their needs and desires into account—

Husband to Wife The Confucian husband rules over his wife as a lord rules over his people. The wife is to be obedient and faithful, and she has a duty to bear her husband sons. The husband has the duty of providing his wife with all the necessities of life.

Parent to Child Children must be loyal to their parents and obey their wishes without question. While the parents must raise and educate their children, the children must care for their parents in old age and always love and respect them.

Older to Younger Respect for age and obedience to all older family members is a key element of the Confucian ethic. Grandparents receive deferential treatment from grandchildren as well as from children.

Friend to Friend The relationship between two friends is the only equal relationship in Confucianism. Friends have a duty to be loyal, trustworthy, and willing to work for each other's benefit. Dishonesty between friends is a social crime and demands punishment.

In modern Hong Kong, westernization and competing philosophies have diluted Confucianism somewhat, but its ethic is still manifest in people's behavior. The remainder of this section examines some characteristics of Hong Kong's people that result directly from the continuing influence of Confucianism.

In many Hong Kong companies, the boss is a ruler and father to his subordinates. Workers have a duty to obey the boss and work diligently to help the company succeed. In return, the boss must concern himself with the daily affairs of his workers and make sure that all their basic needs are met.

Age and rank are well respected in Hong Kong, and young people are expected to obey their elders unquestioningly. Among coworkers, those with greater status and age command the respect of their juniors. Younger people are expected to defer to their elders in speech and manner, by opening doors and so on. In return, elders are expected to reward their juniors for work well done and to assure that their subordinates benefit from any personal successes or promotions that the elders receive.

The family is the preeminent institution in Hong Kong. One's first duty is to the welfare of one's family, and working family members often pool their financial resources. In many ways, Chinese people view themselves more as parts of the family unit than as individuals. Grown children typically live with their parents even if they are married (often with the husband's parents).

There is a strong bond among friends in Hong Kong society. Chinese who have established mutual trust and respect with each other will work hard to make each other successful. Favors and gifts between friends must constantly be reciprocated.

Humility remains an honored Confucian trait.

Hong Kong Chinese are seldom boastful or self-satisfied, even if their accomplishments are laudable. When Chinese are being polite, they can seem excessively self-deprecating.

Chinese can be the most courteous people in the world toward their friends. When a Hong Kong friend visits a friend, every detail of his or her stay may be prearranged, and the guest may not be allowed to spend money on even the smallest items. For individualists from the West, this form of courtesy can be overwhelming. However, when Chinese in Hong Kong deal with strangers, they are often rude or uncaring. Such behavior is a psychological necessity in a city as densely populated as Hong Kong (or New York or Paris). Crowds everywhere push and shove; no apologies are given, and none are expected.

The effect of Confucianism on Hong Kong businesses has been to develop a hierarchical working environment in which workers are dedicated and industrious. As in most Confucian societies in the Far East, productivity is high, and labor relations are generally harmonious.

Face Value

No understanding of the Chinese mentality is complete without a grasp of the concept of face. Having face means having a high status in the eyes of one's peers, and it is a mark of personal dignity. Chinese are acutely sensitive to having and maintaining face in all aspects of social and business life. Face can be likened to a prized commodity: it can be given, lost, taken away, or earned. You should always be aware of the face factor in your dealings with Chinese and never do or say anything that could cause someone to lose face. Doing so could ruin business prospects and even invite retaliation.

The easiest way to cause someone to lose face is to insult the individual or to criticize him or her harshly in front of others. Westerners can offend Chinese unintentionally by making fun of them in the good-natured way that is common among friends in the West. Another way to cause someone to lose face is to treat him or her as an underling when his or her official status in an organization is high. People must always be treated with proper respect. Failure to do so makes them and the transgressor lose face for all others aware of the situation.

Just as face can be lost, it can also be given by praising someone for good work in front of peers or superiors or by thanking someone for doing a good job. Giving someone face earns respect and loyalty, and it should be done whenever the situation warrants. However, it is not a good idea to praise others too much, as it can make you appear to be insincere.

You can also save someone's face by helping him to avoid an embarrassing situation. For example in playing a game you can allow your opponent to win even if you are clearly the better player. The person whose face you save will not forget the favor, and he will be in your debt.

A person can lose face on his own by not living up to other's expectations, by failing to keep a promise, or by behaving disreputably. Remember in business interactions that a person's face is not only his own but that of the entire organization that he represents. Your relationship with the individual and the respect accorded him is probably the key to your business success in Hong Kong.

It's Not What You Know . . .

Personal connections are the key element of doing business in Hong Kong. As in mainland China and Taiwan, little or no distinction is made between business and personal relationships. This point cannot be overemphasized. For a foreign businessperson to succeed with Hong Kong Chinese, he must cultivate close personal ties with business associates and earn their respect and trust. Attempts to establish long-term businesses in the colony have failed because foreigners did not recognize that business relationships were also personal relationships. Any successful person in Hong Kong, Chinese or Western, will be a member of a loose network of personal friends, friends of friends, former classmates, relatives and associates with shared interests. These people do favors for one another and always seek a rough balance between help given and received.

Money Talks The one area of business in Hong Kong where the importance of personal connections is minimal is export trade. Because Hong Kong has been exporting to the West for decades, Hong Kong businessmen understand that foreigners have little understanding of their society and traditions. Selling goods to foreigners is now itself a tradition, and since it usually does not involve close cooperation between the two sides, it can be conducted impersonally. But to market products or engage in cooperative ventures in Hong Kong, foreign businessmen must cultivate connections.

Clan Connections The importance of personal connections has its roots in the traditional concept of family. For the Chinese, individuals are parts of the collective family whole. The family is the source of identity, protection, and strength. In times of hardship, war, or social chaos, the Chinese family structure was a bastion against the brutal outside world, in which no one and nothing could be trusted. As a result, trust, and cooperation were reserved for family members and extremely close friends. Moreover, ancient China was ruled more by decree than by laws. A high official could act with impunity, and innocent people could get hurt unless they had powerful friends to protect them. By establishing close connections with other households and persons of higher rank,

Chinese could survive and perhaps even prosper.

The social situation in Hong Kong today is more secure than it was in the past, but the tradition of personal connections is as strong as ever. In essence, the Chinese possess a clan mentality under which those inside the clan work cooperatively and those outside the clan are seen either as inconsequential or as potential threats. To be accepted into a network of personal or business relationships in Hong Kong entails responsibility and commitment to the members of the network.

Connecting to Profits In the fast-paced, competitive business environment of Hong Kong, executives and entrepreneurs work constantly to maintain and expand their networks of connections. These networks extend to Guangdong Province in the PRC, to Taiwan, and abroad to Southeast Asia, Europe, and the Americas. While the purpose of such contacts is often mutual financial profit, the criteria are the same as for personal networks: trustworthiness and loyalty. Cultivating friendships in the business world is an art learned through practice and close attention to the needs and expectations of others. You form such relations by doing favors and demonstrating integrity.

Cultivating Relationships

For the foreign businessperson, the difficulties in cultivating solid relationships can be the biggest obstacle to success in Hong Kong. A Chinese who does not already know a potential business associate will hesitate to do business with him until he has had time to get acquainted and size up his associate's character and intentions.

Find a Matchmaker The best way to make contact with potential Hong Kong business associates is to have a mutual friend serve as an intermediary and introducer. If the third party has close relationships with both sides, that alone may constitute solid grounds for the conduct of business. Finding a third party may be as simple as asking an overseas Chinese if he or she has any family members in Hong Kong who could be potential associates. Anyone who has worked in Hong Kong or who has cooperated with Hong Kong businesspeople in the past could be a key source of business contacts. There are also many business consultants who can provide assistance for a fee. Chambers of commerce, small business associations, and Hong Kong international trade offices may also help you to find contacts.

Go to the Source If finding a third party for introductions in your home country proves impossible, consider making a fact-finding trip to Hong Kong. A trade show in Hong Kong that would allow you to display your goods or services gives you a good opportunity to gauge your business prospects, or you could spend time meeting people in your area of business. Before leaving for Hong Kong, fax businesses there with which you would consider working with to make appointments for visits. However, don't be surprised if some businesses ignore your request: they do not know you, and therefore they may consider you to be a non-entity.

Patience! On your first and perhaps even your second trip to Hong Kong, you may accomplish nothing more than getting to know several possible candidates for business relationships. Rushing into business before you have established a personal relationship is a prescription for failure. After drawing up a list of possible candidates, take time to evaluate each person carefully. Weigh his or her strengths and weaknesses before you decide who to follow up on. Don't underestimate your gut feelings or your comfort level with various individuals, but appraise their business abilities realistically and, of course, evaluate them from the standpoint of whom they know.

After making your first contacts with businessmen in Hong Kong, be prepared to spend a lot of time deepening and strengthening relationships through visits, dinners, gift giving, and many small favors. While this can be costly and time-consuming, Chinese appreciate all sincere efforts in this area, and no favor done goes unnoticed. Likewise, keep a running account of all favors done for you, all small gifts received, and the like. The odds are good that you will be expected to reciprocate in the future. Remember this aspect of Hong Kong business culture whenever someone offers you a favor, dinner, or gift. If you absolutely do not want to be in the person's debt, be creative and find some polite excuse for declining the offer. And decline it only if you have no intention of having a relationship, because such rejections can be insulting to Hong Kong Chinese.

Maintain Your Perspective Finally, foreign businesspeople will benefit from the process of cultivating personal connections by keeping in mind that it gives them an opportunity to learn about the people with whom they are dealing. Getting to know your business associates has practical value regardless of your culture. Learning about the personality of an associate can make communication and understanding smoother, and the resulting knowledge can be critical when it comes time to decide how far to take the business relationship.

The Company Face A foreign business should designate a personable member of the company to act as the face man for the organization in Hong Kong, and that individual should continue to represent the business on a long-term basis. Whether they are dealing with a large foreign company or an individual, Hong Kong Chinese like to deal with the same individual, and they treat every interaction as a personal one. Over time, if the business relationship is a success, Hong Kong associates may come to regard the face man as a close personal friend. Replacing that individual could jeopardize the business relationship, unless the current representative introduces the new representative and spends some time bringing him closer to Hong Kong associates.

THE HONG KONG BUSINESS ENVIRONMENT

Although Hong Kong is relatively small and almost all its people are ethnic Chinese, it is not easy to generalize about work styles and office environments. Management styles can range from traditional Confucian to ultramodern and Western, but they are usually a combination of the two. Everything depends upon the executive's personal background and degree of Western influence.

But at the risk of oversimplifying, business in Hong Kong is conducted formally, often in emulation of the British style. Punctuality, efficiency, and frugality are usually present in business environments. Because Hong Kong is one of the world's most densely packed cities, working spaces are often cramped.

In contrast to Korea and Japan, companies in Hong Kong are characteristically small and rather entrepreneurial in spirit. Thousands of offices conduct the bulk of trade to and from China, and small back-alley garment shops employing ten people or fewer produce most of the colony's textiles for export. This small scale of operation gives overseas businesspeople looking for Hong Kong associates many opportunities. Because so many different interests are clamoring for a piece of the business action, it is difficult for larger companies to lock out their smaller competitors. The embarrassment of riches also causes headaches in narrowing down who you will actually do business with.

Naturally, the number of businesses is directly proportional to the intensity of competition. Prices are very competitive, and markups on production costs are minimal. These are two of many reasons why Hong Kong is a shopper's bonanza and a business purchaser's cornucopia. As one expert said, "In Hong Kong, you can buy anything, with the possible exception of a nuclear bomb." This may be only a slight overstatement.

Business Hours

There are no hard-and-fast business hours in Hong Kong, with the exception of banks and government offices. Banks are open Monday to Friday from 9:30 am to 4:00 pm; Saturday hours are from 9:30 am to noon. Government offices are open Monday through Friday between 9:00 am and 1:00 pm and between 2:00 and 5:00 pm; Saturday hours are 9:00 am to 1:00 pm. Factories and shops are often open seven days a week. Small family operated shops can be open from early in the morning until late at night.

To many foreigners, the long hours and sometimes frenzied pace of work in Hong Kong can seem less than humane, and the lives of poor factory workers can be drab. But for many people, hard work is an accepted way of life, and they would often rather be working than doing anything else, especially given the alternatives. The Western concept of leisure does not appeal to many and, likely as not, it is interpreted as laziness. Making money is what matters to the majority of Hong Kong's residents; it is an end in itself, not just a means to a better life.

Appropriate Dress

Businesspeople in Hong Kong should dress just as they would in major business venues in Western countries. Because summers are very hot and humid, summer dress needs to be as light as possible while still remaining formal. During monsoon season, raincoats and umbrellas are necessary. Winter weather can be a bit nippy, but very heavy winter wear is not needed.

Women in the Workplace

Women are treated far better in Hong Kong businesses than they are in many other places, but they have yet to reach equality with men. Exceptions do exist, but most executives are male, and their secretaries are female. Skilled women in good social standing do have opportunities for advancement. Many travel agents, public relations executives, and sales personnel are female.

Foreign businesswomen coming to Hong Kong should not encounter any overt discrimination. Sexual harassment is virtually unknown. Nevertheless, a woman on business in Hong Kong should maintain very businesslike in manner, and her attire should be formal. By displaying self-confidence and poise, she may in fact be able to accomplish things much faster than a male counterpart.

Chinese men sometimes feel in awe of tall, blond Western women. Women should not consider this to be a disadvantage. On the contrary, if a woman represents a company in Hong Kong, Chinese may feel that she is a person of exceptional competence, since she has been given such an important job.

Learning the Chinese Way

A knowledge of Chinese etiquette and rules for social behavior is a major asset for foreigners doing business in Hong Kong. Body language, subtle remarks, and patterns of conduct can tell you more about a situation than blunt verbal communication. In contrast to Americans and other Westerners who value straight unambiguous dialogue, Chinese are masters of the oblique. In conversation, what is not said can be more important than what is said. Even the seating arrangements can tell you how the Chinese view a certain meeting. Knowing how to respond to situations appropriately can mean the difference between success and failure.

Hong Kong Chinese will not expect you to understand all the nuances of their behavior. But knowing how to read between the lines can give you an inside view into what is going on, whether the Chinese wish you to know it or not. And, by displaying a sensitivity to the native way of doing things, you can make the Chinese respect you more and feel more comfortable interacting with you.

Meeting the Hong Kong Chinese

When meeting Hong Kong businesspeople, foreigners should display sincerity and respect. Handshaking, imported from the West, is generally the accepted form of salutation. However, Hong Kong handshakes differ in two ways from those common in the West. First, Chinese tend to shake hands very lightly, without the Western custom of gripping the hand firmly and pumping vigorously. Second, a handshake can last as long as ten seconds, instead of the brisk three-second contact common in the West.

The handshake is always followed by a ritualistic exchange of business cards. Foreigners should always carry an ample supply of business cards, preferably with English text on one side and Chinese on the other. Seek the advice of a knowledgeable person on the choice of characters for your name and company, as some characters have more favorable connotations than others.

The proper procedure for exchanging business cards is to give and receive cards with both hands, holding the card corners between thumb and forefinger. When receiving a card, do not simply pocket it immediately, but take a few moments to study the card and what it says. The name card represents the person who presents it, and it should be given respect accordingly.

When the Chinese greet someone, they do not look a person straight in the eye, but lower their eyes slightly. This is a sign of deference and respect. A visitor should refrain from looking intensely into a person's eyes, as this can make a Chinese person feel uncomfortable.

Presenting letters of introduction from well-known business leaders, overseas Chinese, or former government officials who have dealt with Hong Kong is an excellent way of showing both that you are a person of high standing and that you mean business. Chinese are very concerned about social standing, and anything that you can do to enhance their regard for you is a plus. But be careful not to appear arrogant or haughty, as Confucian morality condemns such behavior.

Giving and Receiving Gifts

Chinese are inveterate gift givers. Gifts express friendship, and they can symbolize hopes for good future business, the successful conclusion of an endeavor, or appreciation for a favor done. Foreign businesspeople should spend some time choosing appropriate presents before embarking on a trip to Hong Kong. The Chinese consider the Western habit of simply saying thank you for a favor glib and perhaps less than sincere. Favors should be rewarded materially, although gifts can have more symbolic than monetary value. Avoid very expensive gifts unless the recipient is an old associate who has proved to be particularly important in business dealings. Gifts are not expected on the first visit, but they can be given if you feel that the beginnings of a relationship have been established.

In an office or business environment, it is best to present business-related gifts, such as pens or paperweights with your company logo. If only one gift is to be given, it should be presented to the head of the Hong Kong group at a dinner or on the conclusion of a successful meeting. If gifts are to be given to several individuals, be sure that each person receives a gift of roughly equal value or else that the chief executive receives a gift of greater value. Omit no one with whom you have a relationship when giving several gifts at the same time.

If you are invited to a Hong Kong person's home, it is courteous to arrive with a small gift. Suitable presents include a basket of fruit, tea, flowers, or any memento from your home country that the host can associate with you. Picture books of your home area make good presents. Presenting a wife with perfume or children with toys is likely to be appreciated. Such presents show that you are concerned about the welfare of the entire family, not just the business relationship. Foreign liquor is another gift that is much appreciated. French cognac is the most prized, although it can be rather expensive, and it should only be given to those with whom you already have a personal relationship.

As in the case of business cards, the polite way to present and receive gifts is with both hands outstretched.

It is polite for the recipient to refuse a gift two or three times before finally accepting it. For Westerners, the process can be tricky. If the Chinese person appears embarrassed when he refuses your gift and says that he cannot possibly receive such a nice item, the proper thing to do is to insist that your gift is only a small token and to add that you would be honored if it were accepted. As a rule, after some hemming and hawing, the Hong Kong Chinese will accept the present graciously. If your attempts to give a present are rejected several times and it is evident that the intended recipient is serious about not wishing to accept it, it may be that he is sincere and that your offer should be withdrawn. He may refuse your gift because he does not want to be in your debt or because he has no intentions of having a relationship with you.

When a gift is offered to you, it is not necessary for you to refuse it ceremonially as the Chinese do. Humble acceptance and a few choice words of appreciation are enough. A gift from a Hong Kong businessperson may simply be a courtesy that he accords to all visitors, but it can also be an acknowledgment that a relationship with you exists. Or it may indicate that you will be asked for a favor. In any case, if someone presents you with a gift, you are expected to reciprocate in kind or through a favor.

If the gift is wrapped, it is considered impolite to open it in front of the giver unless he or she encourages you to do so. Tearing the wrappings off hastily is a sign of greediness. Any gift that you give wrapped to an individual should be wrapped in the traditional lucky colors of gold or red. White and black are considered colors of mourning.

Conversation

Cultural differences can cause trouble for Chinese and foreigners over the simple matter of small talk. Expect people whom you don't know well to ask questions concerning personal matters, such as your age, the amount of money you make, or the members of your family. It is obviously not polite to tell people such matters are none of their business, and with associates, frank answers are a sign of familiarity and closeness. The basic rule of thumb in conversation is not to say anything that the Chinese would find offensive or insulting. Chinese are often curious about foreigners and their habits, and their questions are usually related to what they consider to be important in life. Often this involves money. For example, a Chinese may ask how much your watch cost or what kind of car you have and how much it is worth.

Family Matters Family members can be an important topic of conversation, because Chinese who are getting to know you may evaluate you as the member of a family as much as an individual. Asking Chinese about their families is readily acceptable, and they may go into great detail about the lives of brothers, sisters, parents, spouses, and children. If you are divorced or unmarried, the topic of family may be uncomfortable to you. Because Hong Kong has one of the world's lowest divorce rates, it is not an acceptable discussion topic. In a tense situation, it may be better to skirt the truth rather than to be open about something that could jeopardize a relationship.

Money Matters If people ask you about your income, it is fine to tell them the truth. Remember that Hong Kong is a wealthy place, and there will be no feelings of resentment if you report a decent income. If you are really uncomfortable about this topic, you can give a figure that is neither too high nor too low, or you can simply laugh and say that you don't make as much as you would like to.

Jokes It is fine to tell jokes during informal situations, but they are best avoided if you are delivering a speech to a group. Sexual jokes are taboo. Also, cross-cultural humor is hard to find, and jokes concerning persons or events specific to your country are not likely to be understood.

Saying No When asked for a favor, Hong Kong Chinese will usually avoid saying no, as to do so causes embarrassment and loss of face. If a request cannot be met, Chinese may say it is inconvenient or under consideration. This generally means no. Another way of saying no is to ignore a request and pretend it wasn't asked. Unless a request is really urgent, its best to respect these subtleties and not to press the issue.

Sometimes a Chinese will respond to a request by saying, "Yes, but it will be difficult." To a Westerner, this response may seem to be affirmative, but in Hong Kong it may well mean no or probably not. If a person says yes to a question and follows by making a hissing sound of sucking breath between his teeth, the real answer could be no

The Chinese also have the habit of telling a person whatever they believe he or she wants to hear, whether or not it is true. They do this as a courtesy, rarely with malicious intent, although it can be a real problem in the workplace. If bad news needs to be told, Chinese will be reluctant to break it. Sometimes they will use an intermediary for communication, or perhaps they will imply bad news without being blunt. To cut through such murkiness, it is best to explain to your Chinese coworkers that you appreciate direct communication, and that you will not be upset at bearers of bad news.

Body Language and Other Courtesies

Chinese often use body language that can be incomprehensible to uninitiated Westerners, and some Western body language or positions can also be misunderstood. This section reviews a few key examples to keep in mind when you visit Hong Kong.

- When Chinese want someone to approach, they extend the hand palm down and curl the fingers, as if scratching an imaginary surface.
- Holding one's hand up near the face and slightly waving means no; it can also represent a mild rebuke.
- Pointing at someone with the forefinger is an accusatory motion considered rude or hostile. When you point, use the entire hand, palm open.

- Winking is impolite and it can have a negative connotation.
- Laughing or smiling among Chinese can be confusing and means different things according to the situation. When nervous or embarrassed, Chinese will smile or laugh nervously and cover their mouths with their hands. This can be in response to an inconvenient request, a sensitive issue that has been brought up, or a social faux pas committed by the smiler or another person nearby.
- While shaking hands is now the standard form of greeting, traditional etiquette calls for making a fist with the left hand, covering it with the right palm, and shaking the hands up and down. Some Chinese still do this, especially with close friends. It is also a formal way of saying thank you and a sign of reverence.
- When Chinese are embarrassed, they cover their faces with their hands.
- Hissing is a sign of difficulty or uncomfortableness.
- When Chinese yawn, cough, or use a toothpick, they cover their mouths.
- It is impolite to point one's feet at another person. Chinese sit upright in chairs with both feet on the floor.
- Unlike some other places in Asia, Hong Kong people do not remove their shoes when they enter a home.
- Chinese are not given to physical displays, and they rarely hug in public. Lightly touching another person's arm when speaking is a sign of close familiarity. Men and women rarely hold hands in public, but it is not uncommon for friends of the same sex to hold hands or clasp each other by the shoulders.

Language

The mother tongue of the Hong Kong people is Cantonese, and it is one of the colony's two official languages. English, the other official language, is used in business interchangeably with Cantonese. The vast majority of the people in Hong Kong, especially businesspeople, are bilingual in these two languages, although older people, children, and the undereducated may only know a little English.

Foreign businesspeople in Hong Kong should have no trouble communicating in English, although factory workers and other unskilled employees may not speak English well. It is therefore practical for any long-term resident of Hong Kong to learn some Cantonese.

In preparation for Hong Kong's return to Chinese sovereignty, many people are learning Mandarin Chinese, the PRC's national language. Though both Mandarin and Cantonese are Chinese dialects, they are mutually incomprehensible. However, they both use the same written Chinese characters (pronounced differently in the two dialects), so that native Cantonese and Mandarin speakers can communicate fluently in writing. The unified writing system in China is one of the major forces for social cohesion in that immense country.

Names and Forms of Address

In Chinese, an individual's family name precedes his or her personal name. The family name is almost always monosyllabic, and the personal name usually has two syllables, although one-syllable personal names are not uncommon. For example, Deng Xiaoping's family name is Deng, and his personal name is Xiaoping. Lu Xun, a famous author of the early twentieth century, has a one-syllable personal name: Xun. Each syllable is the pronunciation of a single written character.

Hong Kong Chinese often adopt English names, since they know it is difficult for foreigners to remember Chinese names. Sometimes they invert their names so that the family name follows the personal name as in Western practice. This can be confusing, since you may not know if a name has been inverted. As a general rule, assume that a name has not been inverted.

People outside the family almost never call each other by their personal names, often even if they are very close. Westerners should use Mister, Miss, or Mrs. when addressing Chinese, just as they do in Western society. Although a woman does not take her husband's family name when she marries, it is acceptable for Westerners to address a married woman in the Western form, such as Mrs. Hu if the woman's husband is Mr. Hu.

Another common form of address is to use a person's designated position in society. For example, a teacher with the family name Yuan can be referred to as Teacher Yuan. This form of address also applies to company managers, directors, and higher-ranking officials.

Trade Delegations

There are a few important points to remember when you send a trade delegation to Hong Kong. First, keep in mind that the Hong Kong Chinese are a group-oriented people and that they are more comfortable functioning as members of a group than as individuals. Generally, they assume that this is true of all people. They are confused when members of a visiting group speak as individuals and make statements that are contradictory or inconsistent with the stated views of the group as a whole. Differing individual opinions are not wanted. Therefore, every trade delegation should have a designated speaker, who is also its most senior member. The

Chinese will look to that member for all major communication and accept his words as the words of the entire organization.

The Importance of Status Hong Kong Chinese are quite concerned about the status that an individual holds in a company or organization. They will evaluate the seriousness of a trade delegation by the rank of its members, and a delegation is not likely to succeed if the Chinese know that its head is a junior executive. Likewise, they will wish to match your delegation with executives of similar status from their own organization. It is wise to send them a list of the delegates who will attend that gives their ranks in the company and to request that they do the same. If the Hong Kong company sends someone to a meeting who is obviously of lower rank, the chances are good that it is not particularly interested in you, or that it is unaware of the status of the members of your delegation, which is functionally much the same thing.

Delegation Leaders A trade delegation should be led by older members of the company who have at least middle-level executive rank. They should be patient, genial, and persistent, and have extensive cross-cultural experience. Ideally, they have already had some experience in Hong Kong or Asia, and have enough rank to make decisions on the spot without fear of repercussions from the home office.

Foreign Businesswomen In contrast to many other cultures, Hong Kong accepts doing business with foreign women, and a trade delegation should have no problem having women members. However, women have not traditionally headed trade delegations. Outside of the cosmetics and fashion industries, companies should consider balancing delegations with men if the leader is a woman.

First Day Protocol Little in the way of serious business will be accomplished on the first day of a delegation's visit to Hong Kong. This is a time for getting to know one another and for feeling out the personalities who will be involved in more serious negotiations later. Use this time to get to know the Hong Kong side, and try to determine the status of all the members and their likely relations with one other. Because most Hong Kong companies are small, the person who heads the Hong Kong group may be the company's senior executive. He will be the only spokesman for the group on substantive issues, but other members will probably have some say in decision making. Chinese place great stock in consensus. Most likely they will debate their position on the business at hand among themselves, but never in front of the foreign delegation.

As hosts, the Hong Kong Chinese will have an itinerary of events for your delegation, and most of your time will be taken up doing what they have planned. The first day may include a factory tour, followed in the evening by a traditional Chinese banquet, which may be followed by a trip to a popular karaoke club.

Banqueting and Dinner Etiquette

Business and eating compete for the place of number one pastime in Hong Kong. As one Chinese said, "When foreigners are happy, they dance. When we're happy, we eat!" If you like Chinese food, going to a traditional banquet may be your most pleasant experience in Hong Kong. The form of the meal is ancient, and thus there are rules of etiquette, which should be followed. Although your Hong Kong host will not expect you to know everything about proper banquet behavior, he will greatly appreciate your displaying some knowledge of the subject, because it shows that you have respect for Chinese culture and traditions.

Arrival Banquets are usually held in restaurants in private rooms that have been reserved for the purpose. All members of your delegation should arrive together and on time. You will be met at the door and escorted to the banquet room, where the hosts are likely to have assembled. Traditionally, and as in all situations, the head of your delegation should enter the room first. Do not be surprised if your hosts greet you with a loud round of applause. The proper response is to applaud back.

Seating and Settings The banquet table is large and round and can seat up to twelve people. If there are more than twelve people, guests and hosts will have been divided equally among tables. Seating arrangements, which are based on rank, are stricter than in the West. This is another reason why you should give your host a list of delegation members that clearly identifies their rank. The principal host is seated facing the entrance and farthest from the door, usually with his back to the wall. The principal guest sits to the host's immediate right. If there are two tables, the second-ranking host and guest sit at the other table facing the principal host and guest. Interpreters sit to the right of the principal and second-ranking guests if there are two tables. Lower-ranking delegation members are seated in descending order around the tables, alternating with Hong Kong hosts. Guests should never assume that they may sit where they please and should wait for hosts to guide them to their places.

Each place setting at the table contains a rice bowl, a dish for main courses, a dessert dish, a spoon, and chopsticks on a chopstick rest; usually there is a napkin. Two glasses are customary: a larger glass for beer or soda and a small thin glass for hard liquor. In the middle of the table is a revolving tray on which entrees are placed. During the meal it can be spun at will to gain access to the dishes that it holds.

Chopsticks Your host may politely ask if you are able to use chopsticks or if silverware would be more convenient. It is advisable to learn how to use chopsticks before you come to Hong Kong. One good method of learning is to practice picking up peanuts from a bowl. If you are able to pick up a bowlful of peanuts with relative ease, then you should have no trouble at a banquet. If you absolutely cannot master chopsticks, silverware will be provided. This involves some loss of face. However, it is less than if you make a mess through totally inept use of chopsticks.

Smoking and Drinking It is probable that your host will offer cigarettes throughout the banquet. Many Hong Kong men smoke, but it is perfectly acceptable to decline the invitation to light up. It is rude to light a cigarette without first offering cigarettes to others. If at all possible, bear with the secondhand smoke. It would be quite rude to ask the host not to smoke while enjoying a banquet.

Beer is the standard drink of choice at banquets, but you may feel free to substitute soda. Hard liquor usually rice wine or perhaps brandy is served ceremonially and reserved for toasts. It is impolite to drink liquor alone.

Beginning the Feast The first round of food at a banquet consists of small plates of coldcuts. They may already be on the revolving tray when you sit down. The dishes may contain pork, chicken, pickled vegetables, codfish, scallops, tofu, or any number of different foods. It is polite, but certainly not mandatory, to try a taste of each dish. It is better not to partake of foods that you cannot eat than to gag at the table, but if you find something on your plate that you dislike, you may simply push it around on your plate to make it look as if you have at least tasted it.

It is the host's responsibility to serve the guests, and at very formal banquets people do not begin to eat until the principal host has broken into the dishes by serving a portion to the principal guest. Or, the host may simply raise his chopsticks and announce that eating has begun. After this point, one may serve oneself any food in any amount, although it is rude to dig around in a dish in search of choice morsels. There is a fine line between showing appreciation by taking ample portions and showing greed by taking excessive portions. Appreciative restraint is usually best, especially given the fact that there are usually many more dishes to follow. Proper etiquette requires that serving spoons or a set of large chopsticks be used to transport food to one's dish, but in fact many Chinese use their eating chopsticks for this purpose. Watch your host to determine which procedure to use.

After the first course of coldcuts comes a succession of delicacies. Waiters will constantly remove and replace dishes as they are soiled or emptied, so that it is hard to tell exactly how many courses are served through the event. Some banquets can include more than twelve courses, but ten are more

likely. Remember to go slow on eating. Don't fill yourself up when five courses are left to go. To stop eating in the middle of a banquet is rude, and your host may incorrectly think that something has been done to offend you.

Manners Table manners at Chinese banquets often have no relation to manners in the West. There are no prohibitions on putting one's elbows on the table, reaching across the table for food, or making loud noises when eating. Usually it is impolite to touch one's food with anything except chopsticks, but when eating chicken, shrimp, or other hard-to-handle food, Chinese use their hands. Bones and shells are usually placed directly on the tablecloth next to the eating dish, although in more formal banquets a small plate may be provided for this purpose. Waiters periodically come around and unceremoniously rake the debris into a bowl or small bucket. Although banquets have their prescribed methods for behavior, manners conform more to practicality than they do in the West. In fact, banquet time is when businesspeople tend to be the most relaxed and comfortable.

Liquor and Toasts One reason is that drinking figures prominently in Chinese banquets. Toasting is mandatory, and the drinking of spirits commences only after the host has made a toast at the beginning of the meal. It is likely that he will stand and hold his glass out with both hands while saying a few words to welcome the guests, after which all present should drain their glasses. After this initial toast, drinking and toasting are open to all, but the head of the visiting group will be expected to toast the well-being of his hosts in return. Subsequent toasts can be made from person to person or to the group as a whole. No words are needed to make a toast, and it is not necessary to drain your glass, although to do so is more respectful.

Remember that hard liquor should never be drunk alone. If you are thirsty, you can sip beer or a soft drink individually, but if you prefer to drink hard liquor, be sure to catch the eye of someone at your table, smile and raise your glass, and drink in unison. Beer or soft drinks can also be used for toasting, but do not switch from alcohol to a soft drink in the middle of the banquet lest the host think that something has offended you.

Also, it is impolite to fill your own glass without first filling glasses of all others. This applies to all drinks and not just to alcohol. If your glass becomes empty and your host is observant, it is likely that he will fill it for you immediately. When filling another's glass, it is polite to fill it as full as you can without having the liquid spill over the rim. This symbolizes full respect and friendship.

It is a matter of courtesy for the host to try to get his guests drunk. If you do not intend to drink alcohol, make it known at the very beginning of the meal to prevent embarrassment. Even then, the host may good-naturedly try to goad you into drinking. One way to eliminate this pressure is to tell your host that you are allergic to alcohol.

In the course of drinking at banquets, it is not unusual for some Hong Kong Chinese to become inebriated, although vomiting or falling down in public entails loss of face. After a few rounds of heavy drinking, you may notice your hosts excusing themselves to the bathroom, from whence they often return a bit lighter and rejuvenated for more toasting! Also, many Asians are unable to metabolize alcohol as fast many Westerners do. The result is that they often get drunk sooner, and their faces turn crimson, as if they were blushing.

The Main Dish The high point of a Chinese banquet is often the presentation of a large whole cooked fish. In formal situations, the fish is placed on the revolving tray with its head pointing toward the principal guest. The guest should accept the first serving, after which everyone helps himself.

The final rounds of food follow, usually a soup followed by rice, concluding with fresh fruit. Chinese consider soup to be conducive to digestion. Rice is served at the end so that guests can eat their fill, as if the preceding courses had not been enough. It is polite to leave some rice and other food on your plate; to finish everything implies that you are still hungry and that you did not have enough to eat. Fruit is served to cleanse the palate.

Concluding the Banquet When the fruit is finished, the banquet has officially ended. There is little ceremony involved with its conclusion. The host may ask if you have eaten your fill, which you undoubtedly will have done. Then, without further ado, the principal host will rise, signaling that the banquet has ended. Generally, the principal host will bid good evening to everyone at the door and stay behind to settle the bill with the restaurateur. Other hosts usually accompany guests to their vehicles and remain outside waving until the cars have left the premises.

Reciprocity

After you have been entertained by your Hong Kong associates, it is proper to return the favor unless time or other constraints make it impossible. A good time to have a return banquet is on the eve of your departure from Hong Kong or at the conclusion of the business at hand. If possible, a third party should relay your invitations to the Hong Kong Chinese. If for some reason they must refuse the invitation, they will feel more comfortable telling the third party than speaking directly to you.

It is advisable to make reservations at a Chinese restaurant where you are sure to get good service and food. Your guests are likely to appreciate it more than Western fare. Banquets are priced per person and cover all expenses except alcohol. There is no need to order specific dishes, although you may do so. Good restaurateurs know how to prepare adequately for a banquet.

Karaoke

After a banquet, a hardy Hong Kong host may invite you to go singing at a karaoke club. Karaoke clubs began in Japan, but in recent years the craze has spread to all other countries in East Asia. For Chinese, the karaoke phenomenon is a technological extension of their cultural propensity to sing with close friends.

Karaoke clubs feature a raised platform with a microphone above which is a monitor. The monitor displays preselected music videos with accompanying music but without vocals. The words of the song are displayed at the bottom of the screen. The designated singer will then sing the words. Most karaoke clubs in Hong Kong have Cantonese, Japanese, and English songs. Expect to be forced to sing at least one song when you visit a karaoke. For Chinese, being a competent singer enhances face, because one's close friends will be watching. In higher-class karaoke clubs, large private rooms with big-screen television sets are the norm. Groups of friends can use these rooms to sing until the sun comes up, attended all the while by beautiful hostesses. It is an experience that you are not likely have in the West, although some foreigners find it rather boring.

Many observers have wondered why karaoke has become so popular in the collectivist cultures of Asia. One answer is that singing in front of one's peers is one of the very few socially acceptable ways in which an individual can display his or her talent and individuality without being branded arrogant or self-centered. It fulfills the latent desire to gain credit as an individual without jeopardizing the need to be accepted by the whole group. Of course, no one goes to a karaoke club alone, and it usually is a meeting place for the closest of friends. If you wish to establish close relations with Chinese, going to karaoke is one of the best ways of doing it. However, some Hong Kong Chinese regard karaoke as somewhat déclassé, so you should avoid mention of karaoke unless you are invited to go.

BUSINESS NEGOTIATIONS

After banqueting and singing with Hong Kong businesspeople, foreigners may begin to believe that their business dealings will be equally smooth. This is possible but not likely. Hong Kong Chinese are known to be tough negotiators. Almost every aspect of a business deal is subject to the give-and-take of the negotiating process. Before going into negotiations, foreigners must be prepared for subtle and aggressive tactics from the Hong Kong side. In fact, the lavish entertainment heaped on foreign businesspeople before everyone sits down at the negotiating table is partly an attempt to soften up the delegation psychologically and gain maximum advantage in the process that arrives at a business agreement.

Negotiation Etiquette When arranging for negotiations with Hong Kong Chinese, it is customary to give them as much detail on the issue to be discussed as reasonable, plus notice of all delegation members who will be present. The team leader's name should be listed first. Other members should be listed in order of seniority or importance to the deal. The number of negotiation members can vary from two to ten, depending on the nature of the business. The Hong Kong side will try to match their team members with the visiting team.

Beginning the Meeting Negotiations are often held in meeting rooms at the Hong Kong place of business. A functionary escorts the members of the visiting delegation to the meeting room as soon as they arrive. The Hong Kong team is already there. The head of the visiting delegation should enter the meeting room first. This is Chinese custom, and not to observe it could confuse the Chinese about the identity of the delegation leader.

After a round of handshaking and smiles, the visitors are seated at the negotiation table. The table is usually rectangular, and teams sit opposite each other, with the heads of delegations sitting eye to eye. Other team members are arrayed next to delegation heads, often in descending order of importance. Most likely, the guest delegation will be seated facing the door, a common Chinese courtesy. Tea or other drinks are provided.

Hong Kong Chinese do not expect to jump into substantive negotiations right away. Some small talk is usually necessary in order to get the ball rolling, and this time can also be used to get a feel for those present. Chinese like to know who they are dealing with. The subject of business usually comes up naturally after the participants feel comfortable enough to begin.

Entering Substantive Talks After initial courtesies, the head of the host delegation usually delivers a short welcoming speech and then turns the floor over to the head of the guest delegation. Hong Kong Chinese customarily allow visitors to speak first in negotiations. In some ways, this can be to their advantage, but participants usually know enough about each other's positions through prior communication that there are few surprises. As noted earlier of trade delegations, Hong Kong Chinese look to the senior leader for all meaningful dialogue. Conflicting statements from different team members are to be avoided, and guest team members should speak only when they are asked to do so. When speaking, the visiting delegation leader should look toward the head of the Hong Kong team.

The Chinese do not like surprises in negotiations, so it may be wise to lay out your basic position at this time. It can also be useful to distribute sheets stating your main points in Chinese. When tackling a business issue at the appropriate time, Hong Kong Chinese appreciate directness. Anything that you can do to clarify their understanding of your position is fine, but in the initial stage, your presentation may need to involve only the big picture. Details can be saved for later. However, in some forms of negotiations, the Hong Kong side will expect a very serious and in-depth presentation, covering all the major details and answering all foreseeable questions at the very outset of talks. A typical opening statement highlighting the major topics that need to be discussed can last between five and ten minutes.

After the visitor outlines his team's position, the Hong Kong team leader takes the floor and answers point by point, remedying any perceived omissions. From this point on, the negotiation process runs with the rhythm of a controlled conversation, not an open-ended chat. It is more like a formal debate than a free-for-all. The Hong Kong approach is often first to gain a holistic view of the entire proposal, then to break it down into specific chunks, at which time concrete issues and problems can be discussed. Use your own judgment in the talks, and adopt methods that are naturally suited to your particular subject.

Negotiating Tactics

Hong Kong negotiators are shrewd and use many tactics. This section reviews some of the most common ones.

- Controlling the schedule and location. When negotiations are held in Hong Kong, the Chinese are aware that foreigners must spend a good deal of time and money to come there, and that they do not want to go away empty-handed. The Chinese may appear at the negotiating table seemingly indifferent to the success or failure of the meeting, and then make excessive demands on the foreign side.
- Threatening to do business elsewhere. Chinese may tell you that they can easily do business with someone else for example, the Japanese or the Germans if you do not meet their demands.
- Using friendship as a way of gaining concessions. Hong Kong Chinese who have established relations with foreigners may remind them that true friends aim to work out an agreement of maximum mutual benefit. Be sure that the benefits in your agreement are not all one-way.

- Showing anger. Although the display of anger is not acceptable under Confucian morality, Chinese may show calculated anger to put pressure on the opposite side, which may be afraid of losing the contract.
- Sensing the foreigner's fear of failure. If the Chinese know that you are committed 100 percent to procuring a contract and that you are fearful of not succeeding, they are likely to increase their demands for concessions.
- Flattery. Chinese are not above heaping praise on foreigners either for personal attributes or business acumen. Don't let their skill at stroking your ego give them an advantage.
- Knowing when you need to leave. If the Hong Kong Chinese know the date of your departure, they may delay substantive negotiations until the day before you plan to leave in order to pressure you into a hasty agreement. If possible, make departure reservations for several different dates, and be willing to stay longer than anticipated if there is a real chance for success.
- Attrition. Hong Kong negotiators are patient and can stretch out the negotiations in order to wear you down. Excessive entertaining in the evening, especially when coupled with jet-lag, can also take the edge off a foreign negotiator's attentiveness.
- Using your own words and looking for inconsistencies. Chinese take careful notes at discussions, and they have been known to quote a foreigner's own words in order to refute his current position. You, of course, may do the same.
- Playing off competitors. Hong Kong Chinese may invite several competing companies to negotiate at the same time, and they will tell you about it to apply pressure.
- Inflating prices and hiding the real bottom line. Hong Kong negotiators may appear to give in to your demand for lower prices, but their original stated price may have been abnormally high.

Tips for Foreign Negotiators

A number of tactics may be helpful for foreign negotiators dealing with Hong Kong Chinese.

- Be absolutely prepared. The effective negotiator has a thorough knowledge of every aspect of the business deal. At least one member of your negotiating team should have an in-depth technical knowledge in your area and be able to display it to the Chinese. Be prepared to give a lengthy and detailed presentation on your side of the deal.

- Play off competitors. If the going gets tough, you may let the Chinese know that they are not the only game in town. Competition is cut-throat among Hong Kong producers, and you can probably find other sources in the colony for what your counterpart has to offer. Also, if price is the problem, you may be able to strike a cheaper deal in mainland China or Southeast Asia. If quality is the concern, Japanese companies can generally outperform Hong Kong producers.
- Be willing to cut your losses and go home. Let the Chinese know that failure to agree is an acceptable alternative to a bad deal.
- Cover every detail of the contract before you sign it. Talk over the entire contract with the Hong Kong side. Be sure that your interpretations are consistent and that everyone understands his duties and obligations. Assume nothing. Business practices and cultural perceptions are different.
- Take copious and careful notes. Review what the Hong Kong side has said, and ask for clarification on any possible ambiguities.
- Pad your price. Do as the Chinese do: Start out high, and be willing to give a little from there. If purchasing, do the opposite.
- Remain calm and impersonal during negotiations. Do not show your agitation, lest the Chinese know your sensitive areas. Even if you were good buddies the night before, a standoffish personal attitude in negotiations lets the Chinese know that your first priority is good business.
- Be patient. Chinese believe that Westerners are always in a hurry, and they may try to get you to sign an agreement before you have adequate time to review the details.
- State your commitment to work toward a fair deal. Tell the Chinese that your relationship can only be strengthened by a mutually beneficial arrangement.
- Be willing to compromise, but don't give anything away easily.
- Finally, approach negotiations and all business in Hong Kong from the standpoint of long-term involvement. Giving some leeway to the Chinese over a specific issue can result in far greater benefit in the future. Nevertheless, while it is important to be seen as flexible, it is also important not to be seen as weak or easy to take advantage of. You should always insist that concessions be matched.

The Hong Kong Approach to Contracts

A few years ago, many Hong Kong Chinese viewed written contracts as virtually meaningless compared to personal commitments between associates. This view still causes problems in mainland China, but Hong Kong business is based on the rule of law, and under Hong Kong law a contract is a legally binding document.

In contrast to the Western view, some Hong Kong Chinese still consider a contract to be a loose commitment to do business, not a document outlining every aspect of the business relationship. Some head executives would rather sign a short agreement in principle and allow subordinates to work out the details at a later time. Avoid this situation if you can, because it increases the chance of misunderstanding on both sides and necessitates further negotiations, which can be costly.

While negotiating a detailed contract is important, understand that the Hong Kong Chinese often view any deal with foreigners as only one component of a larger, ongoing relationship. They see the immediate issue as a sort of building block that allows them to measure and strengthen reliability and cooperation. This is a practical and realistic philosophy that any Westerner who wants to do business in Hong Kong over the long term should appreciate and adopt for his own ventures.

FURTHER READING

The preceding discussion of Hong Kong business culture and etiquette is by no means complete. The books listed here can give the reader additional insight. While some of these books focus mainly on business in mainland China, many of the customs discussed are equally applicable to Hong Kong.

Dealing With the Chinese, by Scott D. Seligman. New York: Warner Books, 1989. ISBN 0-446-38994-3. $12.95. A detailed examination of Chinese-foreign business relationships and etiquette. The author has extensive experience in mainland China and uses personal stories and examples to illustrate Chinese behavior.

Chinese Etiquette and Ethics in Business, by Boye De Mente. Lincolnwood, Ill.: NTC Business Books, 1989. ISBN 0-8442-8525-0. $14.95. A broad cultural survey of Chinese morals and values related to business interaction, mostly in mainland China.

Do's and Taboos Around the World, edited by Roger Axtell. New York: John Wiley and Sons, 1990. ISBN 0-471-52119-1. $10.95. A humorous and insightful bestseller compiled by the Parker Pen Company on social customs around the world that includes entries on Taiwan, China, and Hong Kong.

Gestures: The Do's and Taboos of Body Language Around the World, by Roger Axtell. New York: John Wiley and Sons, 1991. ISBN 0-471-53672-5. $9.95. A follow-up to the preceding book focused on body language in different cultures.

Demographics

AT A GLANCE

The figures given here are the best available, but sources vary in comprehensiveness, in definition of categories, and in reliability. Sources include the United Nations, the World Bank, the International Monetary Fund, and the Hong Kong government. The value of demographics lies not just in raw numbers but in trends, and the trends illustrated here are accurate.

POPULATION

Population	(1986 census):	5,495,488
	(1991 census):	5,674,114
	(1992 estimate):	5,754,800
Male	(1992 estimate):	2,942,400
Female	(1992 estimate):	2,812,400

Population density per sq. km. (**1991**): 5,385

POPULATION GROWTH RATE AND PROJECTIONS

Average annual growth rate (percent)

1970-80	1980-91	1991-2000
2.4%	1.2%	0.8%

Age structure of population (percent)

	1991	2025
Under 15 years old	20.6%	15.4%
15 - 64 years old	70.3%	61.4%
Over 64 years old	9.1%	23.2%

	1970	1991
Urban population (percent of total)	90%	94%

POPULATION

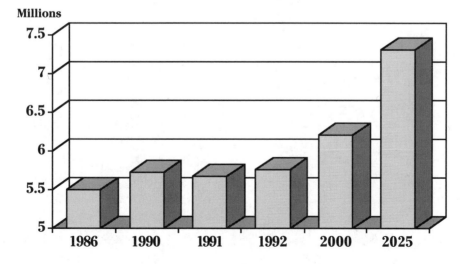

VITAL STATISTICS

Live births; marriages; and deaths
Rates per 1,000 persons

Year	Births	Rate	Marriages	Rate	Deaths	Rate
1985	76,126	14.0	45,056	8.3	25,258	4.6
1986	71,620	13.0	43,280	7.8	25,912	4.7
1987	69,958	12.6	48,561	8.7	26,916	4.8
1988	75,412	13.4	45,238	8.1	27,659	4.9
1989	69,621	12.3	43,947	7.8	28,745	5.1
1990	67,731	12.0	47,168	8.3	29,136	5.2
1991	68,281	12.0	42,568	7.5	28,429	5.0
1992	70,954	12.3	45,702	7.9	30,317	5.3

Child mortality rate (per 1,000 births)

1960	53
1975	17
1990	7

Life expectancy at birth

1960	64
1990	78

Fertility rate

1977	3.3%
1991	1.4%
2000	1.5%

Women of childbearing age (% of all women)

1965	45%
1991	56%

Divorces (1990): 157,000
            per 1,000: 1.3

POPULATION BY PRINCIPAL AREA

(1991 census)

Hong Kong Island	1,250,993
Kowloon	2,030,683
New Territories	2,374,818

POPULATION

by Age and Sex, 1990

Age	Total	Male	Female
All ages	5,728,500	51.1%	48.9%
0 - 1	72,100	36,900	35,200
1 - 4	309,100	160,400	148,700
5 - 9	435,300	226,300	209,000
10 - 14	428,400	223,100	205,300
15 - 19	437,200	229,500	207,700
20 - 24	487,700	247,700	240,000
25 - 29	621,800	311,700	310,100
30 - 34	618,600	315,400	303,200
35 - 39	495,400	255,700	239,700
40 - 44	389,100	207,000	182,100
45 - 49	236,600	128,900	107,700
50 - 54	260,100	139,600	120,500
55 - 59	263,400	139,500	123,900
60 - 64	235,200	120,400	114,800
65 - 69	191,000	93,200	97,800
70 - 74	138,700	63,800	74,900
75 - 79	95,500	39,800	55,700
80 - 84	48,400	16,200	32,200
85 +	37,000	8,700	28,300

MANUFACTURING WAGES, DAILY, IN HONG KONG DOLLARS

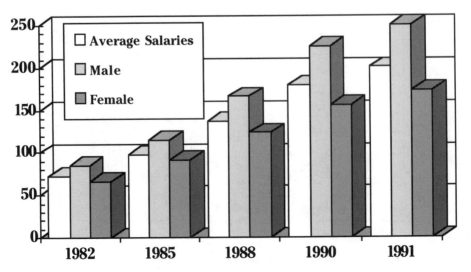

Hong Kong
Consumer Price Index (CPI)

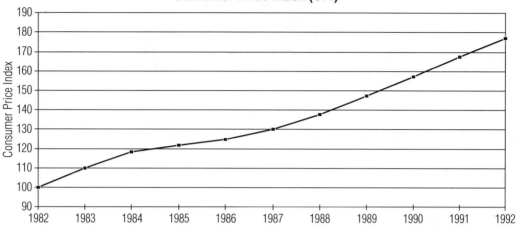

PRICE INDEX BY CATEGORY

(1990 = 100)

Category	1990	1991	1992
Food	100	114	124
Housing	100	117	132
Utilities and fuel	100	110	116
Clothing and footwear	100	108	118
Durable goods	100	105	107
Transportation	100	116	125
Services	100	116	130
ALL ITEMS	100	115	125

EXPENSES

percentage of total household consumption

Category	1985
Food	12
Clothing and footwear	9
Rent, utilities, fuel	15
Medical care & health	6
Transport & communications	9
Education	5
Other	44

AVERAGE ANNUAL RATE OF INFLATION

(percent)

1975-84	8.7%
1985	3.4%
1986	3.2%
1987	5.3%
1988	7.4%
1989	9.7%
1990	9.8%
1991	10.3%
1992	9.5%

EARNINGS

GDP per capita (1991) : US$13,430
Average annual growth rate 1980-91: 5.6 percent

Monthly Household Income Breakdown, 1991

Monthly household income	% of total
Under HK$4,000	12.1
$4,000 - $5,999	12.8
$6,000 - $7,999	13.8
$8,000 - $9,999	11.5
$10,000 - $14,999	19.9
$15,000 - $19,999	11.1
$20,000 - $29,999	9.9
$30,000 - $39,999	3.8
$40,000 and over	5.1

INCOME DISTRIBUTION, 1990

percent share of income

Lowest 20%	Second 20%	Third 20%	Fourth 20%	Top 20%	Top 10%
5.4	10.8	15.2	21.6	47.0	31.3

HONG KONG NUTRITION

Individual Daily Average Consumption

	Calories			% of Calories Requirements			Protein (grams)	
1980	1986	1990	1967/70	1980	1984/6	1980	1986	1990
2,652	2,788	2,857	114	127	121	84	87	85

HEALTH

Health expenditures (1990):
US$4 billion
Per capita: US$699.00

Health expenditures as a percentage
of GDP (1990):   Total: 5.7
                 Public: 1.1
                 Private: 4.6

Tobacco consumption per year
(kilograms per capita adult)

1974-76	1990	2000
2.0	1.6	1.8

COMMUNICATION CHANNELS

Daily Newspapers

	Circulation (millions)			Titles Per 1,000 Persons		
	1979	1986	1988	1979	1986	1988
	N.A.	3.6	3.1	82	46	40

Televisions and radios

	Number (millions)			Per 1,000 Persons		
	1980	1985	1989	1980	1985	1989
TVs	1,1	1,3	1,5	221	234	260
Radios	2.5	3.2	3.7	506	596	642

Telephones

	Number (millions)			Per 1,000 Persons		
	1987	1988	1990	1987	1988	1990
	2.7	2.9	3.3	47	50	56

EDUCATION ENROLLMENT

Category	1990	1991	1992
Kindergarten	196,466	193,658	189,730
Primary	526,720	517,137	501,625
Secondary	453,423	454,372	461,460
Post-secondary			
colleges	4,730	3,373	3,070
Teacher training	4,979	4,891	4,355
Special ed.	7,999	8,224	8,257
Technical	56,804	55,657	50,053
Polytechnics and			
Baptist College	39,718	43,170	44,233
Universities	17,946	19,697	24,556
Adult and others	105,932	94,501	88,011

ENERGY CONSUMPTION

(kilograms per capita of coal equivalent)

1980	1988	1990
1,447	2,071	1,792

MOTOR VEHICLES IN USE

(thousands)

	1982	1985	1988	1990
Passenger	197.3	160.9	177.4	214.9
Commercial	70.7	81.4	118.4	131.8

Marketing

Selling your product in Hong Kong is not a venture into the realm of the exotic. It's plain, hard-nosed common sense. Hong Kong is a market that you cannot afford to ignore. It's a free port and a voracious market virtually without restrictions, tariffs, or other barriers to trade. The market accepts products from around the world, and it is far from saturated. In fact, the market is so open and sophisticated that foreign products don't need a lot of special tweaking to sell in much the same way as they would at home. You can penetrate this potent market without placing large amounts of your company's assets or annual budget at risk. And unless you plan to ship three years of inventory to Hong Kong before you've sold anything there, 1997 isn't a financial threat. No company is too small, and no company is too large to make Hong Kong a profitable venture. All you need is a high-quality, competitively priced product, a well-managed market penetration program, and a moderate investment in market development. Agents, distributors, and end users are there to welcome you with open arms. Once you've gotten your foot in the door and returns start flowing in—and they'll start flowing in Hong Kong before they start flowing in any of your other East Asian markets—you can expand your horizons as you gain confidence and experience. Today Hong Kong, tomorrow China, because what you can't sell in Hong Kong, you can probably sell down the road (or up the river) in China, which needs just about everything.

Let's take a brief look at what makes Hong Kong the ideal jumping-off point for ventures into world trade:

- Geographic location: No center is better situated to support business inroads into China, Southeast Asia, and East Asia.
- Communications: All domestic and international services are modern, efficient, and relatively inexpensive.
- Infrastructure: Hong Kong has the world's largest container port and the second busiest international airport, which is also the world's eighth busiest cargo airport. A new 24-hour, state-of-the-art airport—the world's largest ongoing infrastructure project—is scheduled to open in 1997.
- Low taxes: Hong Kong's tax system is simple, efficient and fair. Corporate profits are taxed at 17.5 percent and personal income and property at an average of 15 percent. There is no withholding tax on interest.
- Favorable regulatory environment: Hong Kong's economy is laissez-faire and its current government is non-interventionist. Market forces rule. Foreign investment and business formation are virtually unrestricted. Contracts are backed by law. The civil service is well educated, well managed, and highly experienced and dedicated.
- Labor force: The people enjoy a well-deserved reputation for hard work, innovation, efficiency, and reliability.
- The gateway to China: Hong Kong leads the world in investment in China. It's the conduit for more than one-third of China's international trade and the base for many PRC-affiliated companies, banks, agencies, and organizations.

Hong Kong is not another New York, Paris, or London. Despite the glass highrises and the advanced telecommunications, it's still a Chinese society with Chinese superstitions, Confucian customs, and traditional values. The Chinese are extremely conformist, which can be a boon to Western marketers: if it is believed that "everyone" is buying a certain product, a great number of Hong Kong Chinese are likely to rush out to buy it. The idea of "keeping up with the Wongs" is even more important than "keeping up with the Joneses" is in the West. Moreover, the people are Westernized enough to appreciate Western culture and products, to which they often attach cachets of prestige and quality.

Now that you have a clue as to what Hong Kong can do for your company, let's look into some of the ways there are to open the door.

SEVEN WAYS TO ENTER THE HONG KONG MARKET

1. Establish a representative office

The preferred means for dealing with products needing heavy after-sales service and cultivation of close relationships with clients—for example, software, computers, appliances, and sophisticated or large-scale equipment.

Advantages: Allows you to retain a competitive edge in prompt service, customer commitment, and consulting aspects of a sale; suggests to your buyers that you have a permanent presence in domestic markets, promoting the image of stability and long-term availability; enables use of Hong Kong as a regional marketing and sales support base; Hong Kong tax incentives.

Disadvantages: Cost of office space and staff, plus added costs for specializing for customer's needs. Can't earn income or conduct other business.

2. Exhibit at trade fairs

Preferred for promotion of existing products and introduction of new products; available only if trade fair includes your product.

Advantages: Allows for contacts with major as well as smaller buyers and foreign and local industry representatives; hands-on demonstration techniques increase product awareness; very high attendance typical in Hong Kong.

Disadvantages: Prospective market limited to attendees; competition with other products targeted for same market may be intense; frenetic, difficult to make in-depth contacts and do serious business.

3. Hire a distributor or an agent

Usual route for imports, at least initially; preferred for medium-sized companies selling consumer products with well-established competitors or for nonconsumer products (such as business and vertical market applications software, industrial machinery, electronic parts) aimed at government or commercial institutions; good for products requiring before- and after-sales service; good for supervision of agents and distributors; (agents often act as distributors and vice versa) usually responsible for advertising and promotion.

Advantages: Types and practices of agents and distributors are similar to those in US and other Western countries; removes need for you to create your own marketing and distribution structure; agent knows local needs and customs; often aware of opportunities before bids are announced; knows ins and outs of bidding; monitors and promotes smaller sales, which can add up over time; maintains spare parts inventories; provides after-sales services; markets to both wholesalers and retailers.

Disadvantages: Middleman fees raise cost of product in market; marketing is limited by agent's preferences and biases; agents often drop clients in favor of competitors, taking client lists with them; large size and complexity of agencies or distributorships may limit their attention to your product; transfer of technical information can lead to copyright infringement (a serious problem in Hong Kong despite strong laws and vigorous enforcement).

4. Market direct

Preferred for consumer products (such as auto parts and accessories, small appliances, consumer electronic products) but also common among industries (including factories) that want to avoid middleman costs.

Contact local importers who market through warehouse stores or other retail outlets:

Advantages: Direct access to large consumer market.

Disadvantages: Extreme competition with other producers because such stores market a large number of products

Advertise in industry-specific trade journals or magazines:

Advantages: Economical and effective means to increase product awareness among large number of consumers; good for testing the market.

Disadvantages: Limited time period; costs of extended advertising can be high; effectiveness can vary.

5. Open your own distributorship or retail stores

Most likely for companies with a large array of products to offer (for example, auto accessories or household products).

Advantages: Direct market access, which allows you to keep prices low and competitive (by eliminating middlemen), control of sales environment (type of building, training of sales personnel), and improved quality and service (by reducing the gap between you and the end user).

Disadvantages: High cost to establish, maintain, and staff; need to overcome bias of consumers towards established local merchants; language and cultural barriers.

6. Negotiate a joint venture with a local company

Preferred for consumer products and food and for high-tech products that must be modified for sale in local market; that are in growing international demand; and that are protected by copyright, patent, or similar intellectual property laws (for example, high-tech software); also good for companies wanting to enter the China market through Hong Kong.

Advantages: Direct resource for creating specialized products aimed at particular needs of consumers in domestic market; allows use of local company's marketing and other contacts; foreign companies retain a say in decision making and a hold on intellectual property, become familiar with the target market.

Disadvantages: Allows for technology transfer, potential infringement on design and technology rights (a large risk in Hong Kong), and resulting enforcement problems (Hong Kong vigorously enforces its British-based copyright laws—if it can catch the thieves).

7. Enter a bid on projects

Primarily for sales to public organizations; best done through local representative or joint venture; plenty of niche-building room for subcontactors who carefully follow moves of major players.

Advantages: Successful bid may further your product's reputation in domestic markets; Hong Kong currently is (and will be for the next 10 years) site of world's biggest infrastructure projects, and has opened bidding to many foreign firms.

Disadvantages: Price concessions may be needed for success; uncertainty of continued Chinese sponsorship after 1997.

FOUR TIPS ON GETTING THE BEST FROM YOUR AGENT

Because contracting with an agent or distributor is the most efficient and least costly way for a company new to Hong Kong to enter the market, it's important to understand how the system can work against you and how to counteract it.

1. Don't grant exclusivity too soon

Before you agree to exclusivity, find out everything you can about your prospective partner. Many a foreign firm has discovered, that its agent wanted an exclusive agreement not because he planned to promote the product but to effectively block its sale. The agent, unbeknownst to the companies, already represented a competing firm and wanted to keep new competition to a minimum.

2. Be careful with technical and copyrighted information

Although Hong Kong has strong British copyright and contract enforcement laws, such piracy is still rife—especially in collusion with companies from the PRC—and legal action is expensive and often ineffective after the fact. Investigate your prospective agent's background. Be careful with any agent who asks for a lot of technical information, drawings, or specifications before an agreement has been signed. Supply technical data in increments as your nego-

tiations on the agreement progress. Provide only enough to determine the capability and sincerity of your potential partners.

3. Monitor your agent closely for the first few months

Make certain he or she is doing what you expect in sales and promotion. If you don't see the progress you expect, take immediate action. Warn your agent that you want more action, and terminate the agreement if nothing happens. Make sure that your agreement specifies how much and what kinds of activity should occur and that it specifies remedies—such as a probation period—to correct faulty performance. Always follow Confucian tenets in discussing performance with your agent and especially when you terminate a relationship.

4. Restrict the agent's activities in your industry after the agreement is terminated

Your agreement must have language that protects you from having the agent contract with you just to gain training in your technology and acquire your client list and then leave your company to work for a competitor. Include in your contract a period of time after termination of the agreement during which the agent cannot compete in your field after the contract is terminated—no matter why the termination occurs.

ADVERTISING

Hong Kong's advertising industry is fast-paced, money-driven, and sophisticated. Agencies and clients have to keep an eagle eye out for the competition, which is doing the same. Advertisers are demanding more slickness and polish from their agencies, who do cutthroat business to keep ahead of the pack.

Advertising in Hong Kong goes far beyond the colony's borders. China is responsible for an increasing share of advertising spending—one estimate was 10 percent in 1992—and all major advertising joint ventures in the PRC are managed out of Hong Kong.

Hong Kong's government, unlike most other East Asian governments, leaves its advertising industry mostly alone. Except for tobacco products, regulations are few. Those that exist are very specific:

- One product cannot be put up against its competitors in direct comparison advertising.
- Any claims to being "number one" must be substantiated.
- Doctors and lawyers are not allowed to advertise using mass media.
- Prescription medicines cannot be advertised.

The local Consumer Council has the authority to investigate allegedly false advertising.

Seven Rules for Selling Your Product

1. Respect the individuality of each market

The profit motive generally operates cross-culturally and the nationals of most countries, especially within a given region, will have much in common with one another. However, there will also be substantial differences, enough to cause a generic marketing program to fall flat on its face and even build ill-will in the process. You may have some success with this sort of one-size-fits-all approach, but you won't be able to build a solid operation or maximize profits this way. "Japan proves this point phenomenally," says Steve Provost, KFC's vice president of International Public Affairs. "Our first three restaurants in Tokyo were modeled after our American restaurants, and all three failed within six months. Then we listened to our Japanese partner, who suggested we open smaller restaurants. We've never looked back." However, what works in Japan doesn't necessarily work elsewhere. Hong Kong Chinese tastes may be more similar to US tastes than to Japanese, or may differ in other ways.

2. Adapt your product to the foreign market

Markets are individual, and you may well need to tailor your products to suit individual needs. As the United States' Big Three automakers have yet to learn, it's hard to sell a left-hand-drive car in a right-hand-drive country. Black may be a popular color in your country, but may also be seen as the color of death in your foreign market. Dress, styles, and designs considered fashionably tasteful at home can cause offense abroad. One major US computer manufacturer endured years of costly marketing miscalculations before it realized that the US is only one-third of its market, and that the other two-thirds required somewhat different products as well as different approaches.

You can avoid this company's multi-million dollar mistakes by avoiding lazy and culturally-biased thinking. A foreign country has official regulations and cultural preferences that differ from those of your own. Learn about these differences, respect them, and adapt your product accordingly. Often it won't even take that much thought, money, or effort. Kentucky Fried Chicken offers a salmon sandwich in Japan, fried plantains in Mexico, and tabouleh in the Middle East—and 450 other locally specific menu items worldwide. And even the highly standardized McDonald's serves pineapple pie in Thailand, teriyaki burgers and tatsuda sandwiches (chicken with ginger and soy) in Japan, spicy sauces with burgers in Malaysia (prepared according to Muslim guidelines), and a seasonal durian fruit shake in Singapore.

3. Don't get greedy

Price your product to match the market you're entering. Don't try to take maximum profits in the first year. Take the long-term view. It's what your competitors are doing, and they're in it for the long haul. Hong Kong Chinese can be very price-conscious. When you're pricing your product, include in your calculations the demand for spare parts, components, and auxiliary equipment. Add-on profits from these sources can help keep the primary product price down and therefore more competitive.

4. Demand quality

A poor-quality product can ambush the best-laid marketing plans. Hong Kong Chinese may look at price first, but they also want value and won't buy junk no matter how cheap. And there's just too much competition to make it worth your while to put this adage to the test. Whatever market you gain initially will rapidly fall apart if you have a casual attitude towards quality. And it is hard to come back from an initial quality-based flop. On then other hand, a product with a justified reputation for high quality and good value creates its own potential for market and price expansions.

5. Back up your sales with service

Some products demand more work than others—more sales effort, more after-sales service, more hand-holding of the distributor, and more contact with the end user. The channel you select is crucial here. Paradoxically in this age of ubiquitous and lightning-fast communications and saturation advertising, people rely more than ever on word of mouth to sort out the truth from hyperbole. Nothing will sink your product faster than a reputation for poor or nonexistent service and after-sales support. US firms in particular need to do some serious reputation building for such after-sales service. Although the Hong Kong Chinese often see US products as superior in quality and performance, they rate Japanese after-sales service as vastly better. And guess whose products they buy.

Consider setting up your own service facility. If

you're looking for a Hong Kong agent to handle your product, look for one who has qualified maintenance people already familiar with your type of product or who can handle your service needs with a little judicious training. And make sure that this partner understands how important service and support are to you and to your future relationship with him.

6. Notice that foreigners speak a different language

Your sales, service, and warranty information may contain a wealth of information but if it's not in their language, you leave the foreign distributors, sales and service personnel, and consumers out in the cold. English is an official language in Hong Kong, at least for the present, but you will get much broader exposure if you use Chinese. It's expensive to translate everything into Chinese, but it's necessary.

7. Focus on specific geographic areas and markets

To avoid wasteful spending, focus your marketing efforts. A lack of focus means that you're wasting your money, time, and energies. A lack of specificity means that your foreign operations may get too big too fast. Not only does this cost more than the local business can justify or support, it also can translate into an impersonal attitude towards sales and service and the relationships you've working so hard to build. Instead concentrate your time, money, and efforts on a specific market niche and work on building the all-important business relationships that will carry you over the many obstacles to successful export marketing.

If you want your advertising to reach Hong Kong's people—average per capita gross domestic product (GDP) was US$16,288 in 1992—it's essential to keep in mind that, although English is the language of business, 98 percent of the colony's 5.9 million people speak Cantonese as their first language.

In general, the client pays cost plus 17.65 percent for production work. Agencies charge a 15 percent commission on media advertising, while artwork fees were US$96 per hour in 1992.

Agencies

In 1992 there were 787 advertising agencies in Hong Kong, together employing almost 6,000 people. The impending return of Chinese sovereignty has caused a severe brain drain in the industry as upper- and middle-management people have left for Australia, Canada and the US. To fill their spots, agencies have promoted lower-level staff, who are often inexperienced. Still, advertising expenditures in Hong Kong soared to US$1.2 billion in 1992, a 25 percent increase over 1991. US advertising agencies are the biggest in the business—eight of the top 10 in billings and a 70 percent market share—and get the highest ratings for quality and creativity.

Television

Television accounts for almost half of all advertising expenditures in Hong Kong, yet its share of the total market dropped from 58 percent in 1986 to just under 50 percent in 1992. Market analysts cite two reasons for the steep decline:

- Although the stations won't admit it, program quality is deteriorating or at least not keeping up with audience expectations, and so people are tuning out.
- The way viewers use their TVs is changing: Home videos, laser discs, video games, and karaoke are becoming more popular at the expense of regular programming.

The upshot is that TV stations are having to fight hard to retain their viewers' attention. The Satellite Television Asia Region (STAR) system now carries Hong Kong programming to more than 11 million households in Asia, and subscription cable TV is being introduced, so TV may yet improve its hold on its own and other markets.

Of the four commercial channels, two are Chinese-language and two are English-language. Spending on English-language commercials is only one-tenth of that spent on Cantonese. And with almost 100 percent of Hong Kong's households owning at least one television set, media specialists say, a single prime-time spot run for one week will reach between 30 and 40 percent of the total population.

A major problem with advertising on Hong Kong television is the intense competition for time slots. Companies try to outbid each other for specific time slots, which means that rate cards are often nothing more than pieces of paper. The television station is required to notify the advertising agency or the client when its rights to a time slot have been preempted by a higher bid, but the station's obligations end there. This means that the ad agency or client must remain in constant touch with the station or risk being preempted right off the screen.

Another problem is the inability of advertisers to target their markets because the stations are so few in number and the programming is so general in nature. Advertisers find themselves reaching a far larger audience than they want and paying to reach people who aren't interested in what they have to sell.

Radio

Hong Kong has six commercial radio stations. Radio is grossly underused for advertising. Not only does it command a much lower percentage share of the market than it does in other countries, it isn't even taken seriously in Hong Kong. It used to be thought that the problem was a lack of competition, because radio audiences in Hong Kong are small, and until recently the choice was Commercial Radio, take it or leave it. Now, the launch of Metro Broadcast gives advertisers not only a choice but a new approach to programming that offers a wider audience—and a quality one in advertisers' eyes. The response has been good: radio advertising revenue jumped 60 percent from 1991 to 1992.

Print media

Newspapers and magazines claimed more than 40 percent of all advertising billings in 1992. Of the more than 600 publications, 51 are Chinese-language newspapers, while only two papers are English-language. Hong Kong's publications have a wide circulation among overseas Chinese in Asia and even North America and reach millions of affluent consumers. Of course print media—especially magazines—are much better adapted to target marketing than is East Asia television. This means that an advertiser has to choose outlets with care.

Direct mail

This form of advertising is still in its infancy, at least by Western standards. Industry analysts expect it to grow an average of 30 percent annually for the next few years.

Outdoor advertising

Except for the subways and a few well-established commuter routes, outdoor advertising is difficult to buy and is considered largely ineffective. The neon signs that make Hong Kong famous exist mainly to light up tourists' eyes. Space for posters, signs, and billboards is limited and expensive; negotiations are tough; and the results depend more often than not on personal connections.

HELPING YOUR COMPANY LEARN TO LOVE EXPORT MARKETING

Five In-House Rules

1. Eliminate as much guesswork as you can

Expert export consultation is usually time and money well spent. You need a well thought out marketing plan. You cannot get into successful exporting by accident. It's not a simple matter of saying, "Let's sell our product in Hong Kong." You need to know that your product will, in fact, sell and how you're going to sell it. First, do you need to do anything obvious to your product? Who is your buyer? How are you going to find him? How is he going to find you? Do you need to advertise? Exhibit at a trade fair? How much can you expect to sell? Can you sell more than one product? A plan may be the only way you can begin to uncover hidden traps and costs before you get overly involved in a fiasco. While you may be able to see an opportunity, knowing how to exploit it isn't necessarily a simple matter. You must plot and plan and prepare.

2. Just go for it

We're not suggesting you throw caution to the winds, but sometimes your "plan" may be to use a shotgun approach—rather than the more tightly targeted rifle approach—and just blast away to see if you hit anything. You can narrow things down later. If your product is new to the market, there may be precious little marketing information, and you may have essentially no other choice. Two scenarios illustrate these points: Two companies decide to begin selling similar products in East Asia, which has never seen such products before. Company A hires a market research firm, which spends six months and US$50,000 to come up with a detailed plan. Company Z sends its president to a trade fair—not to exhibit but just to look around and meet people. He follows that trip up with two others. On the last one his new associates present him with his first order. Company Z also spent six months and US$50,000 investigating doing export business, but it has an order to show for it, while Company A only has an unproven plan.

3. Get your bosses to back you up and stick with the program

Whether your company consists of 10, 50, 500, or 5,000 people—or just you—and whether you're the head of the company, the chief financial officer, or the person leading the exporting charge, there must be an explicit commitment to sustain the initial setbacks and financial requirements of export marketing. You must be sure that the firm is committed to the long-term: don't waste money by abandoning the project too early.

International marketing consultants report that because results don't show up in the first few months, the international marketing and advertising budget is *invariably* the first to be cut in any company that doesn't have money to burn. Such shortsighted budgetary decisions are responsible for innumerable premature failures in exporting.

The hard fact is that exports don't bring in money as quickly as domestic sales. It takes time and persistence for an international marketing effort to succeed. There are many hurdles to overcome—per-

Five Ways to Help Your Local Agent

1. Make frequent visits to Hong Kong to support your agent's efforts. This helps to build the relationship, without which no amount of effort can succeed in Hong Kong. Keep in mind that your competitors are also paying personal visits to their agents and customers. And invite your agent to your country to reciprocate his hospitality and to familiarize him with your country and your company.

2. Hold many demonstrations and exhibits of your products. For suppliers to Hong Kong manufacturers, the value of sales presentations at factories cannot be overemphasized. Factory engineers and managers are directly responsible for the equipment and machinery to be purchased, and they have much influence over the decision to buy. This is so highly effective—and so relatively easy and inexpensive—a sales booster that it's irresponsible for an exporter to ignore it.

3. Increase distribution of promotional brochures and technical data . Make literature available to potential buyers, libraries, and industry associations—in Chinese and English. When your agent makes personal sales calls, your potential customers won't be completely in the dark.

4. Improve follow-up on initial sales leads. Let your agent know you're backing him or her up with whatever is needed to pursue the lead. "All of our foreign partners know that they have the support of a large system behind them," McDonald's spokesman Brad Trask says. "The support system is available on request." Make it easy to request help.

5. Deliver on time. If you don't, you can bet that someone else will. Failure to deliver on time not only makes your agent lose face and thereby undermines your relationship, but it jeopardizes your sales. There's not much you can do to make ships go faster or airlines schedule more flights, but you can stockpile your products in Hong Kong to ensure that your agent has a steady supply. When you have to (and it's possible) forget the expense and airfreight the product for two-day delivery: the extra effort will go a long way in establishing and fortifying your reputation for the longer term.

sonal, political, cultural, and legal, among others. It will be at least 6 to 9 months before you and your overseas associates can even begin to expect to see glimmers of success. And it may be even longer. Be patient, keep a close but not a suffocating watch on your international marketing efforts, and give the venture a chance to develop.

4. Avoid an internal tug-of-war

Consultants report that one of the biggest obstacles to successful export marketing in larger companies is internal conflict between divisions within a company. Domestic marketing battles international marketing while each is also warring with engineering, and everybody fights with the bean counters. All the complex strategies, relationship building, and legal and cultural accommodations that export marketing requires mean that support and teamwork are crucial to the success of the venture.

5. Stick with export marketing even when business booms at home

Exporting isn't something to fall back on when your domestic market falters. Nor is it something to put on the back burner when business is booming at home. It is difficult to ease your way into exporting. All the complex strategies, relationship-building, legal and cultural accommodations, and financial and management investment, and blood, sweat, and tears that export marketing requires means that a clear commitment is necessary from the beginning. Any other attitude as good as dooms the venture from the start, and you may as well forget it. We can't overstress this aspect: take the long-range view or don't play at all. Decide that you're going to export and that you're in it for the long haul as a viable money-making full-fledged division within your company.

McDonald's Corporation spokesperson Brad Trask, commenting on his company's overwhelming international success, notes, "We're a very long-term focused company. We do things with patience; we're very deliberate. We're there to stay, not to take the money and run." And Texas Instruments, which has suffered recent losses in its semiconductor business, has made a considered move into long-term joint ventures in East Asia, banking that these investments will provide a big payoff five years down the road.

FIVE WAYS TO BUILD A GOOD OVERSEAS RELATIONSHIP

1. Be careful in choosing overseas distributors

This is crucial. Whether you choose to go with a subsidiary, agent, export trading company, export management company, dealer, distributor, or your own setup, you must investigate the potential and pitfalls of each. Pay personal visits to potential partners to assure yourself of their long-term commitment to you and your product, their experience, ability, reputation, and financial stability. You can still make mistakes, but you won't make obvious ones. Rather than relying on bank or credit sources for information on the prospective distributor's financial stability and resources, hire an independent expert to advise you.

The keys to McDonald's success, says spokesman Brad Trask, is a meticulous search for partners that focuses on "shared philosophies, past business conduct, and dedication. After all, we're asking a businessman to give up two years to be absorbed into the McDonald's way of business. We want to be sure we're right for each other."

2. Treat your overseas distributors as equals of their domestic counterparts

Your overseas distributors aren't some poor family relations entitled only to crumbs and handouts when you feel like it or remember to. They are an intergral part of your company's future success, a division equal to any domestic division. Offer them advertising campaigns, discount programs, sales incentives, special credit terms, warranty deals, and service programs that are equivalent to those you offer your domestic distributors but specifically tailored to meet the special needs of that country.

Also take into account the fact that distributors of export goods need to act more independently of manufacturers and marketers than do domestic distributors because of the differences in trade laws and practices, and the vagaries of international communications and transportation.

McDonald's partners in Hong Kong adhere to the company's overall standards of consistency and quality, Trask says, but in all other ways, the McDonald's Hong Kong partners staff and operate the restaurants the way they want to. "We're not operational police," Trask says. The company knows it has to leave well enough alone and trust its partners. "Those partners have purchased the rights to a formula for proven success. We've never found anyone foolish enough to fly in the face of success. Instead, they've adapted the formula to suit their needs." Kentucky Fried Chicken sees things the same way. "We mandate that our partners or licensees

have the Colonel up on the logo, and they have to serve original recipe chicken and cole slaw," says Steve Provost, KFC's vice president of International Public Affairs. "Beyond that it's up to them."

3. Learn the dos and taboos

Each country does business in its own way, a process developed over years to match the history, culture, and precepts of the people. Ignore these practices, and you lose. "McDonald's system has enough leeway in it to allow the local businessmen to do what they have to do to succeed," Trask says. Thus every new McDonald's in Thailand holds a "staff night" just before the grand opening. The families of the youthful employees descend en masse to be served McDonald's meals in an atmosphere that they can see for themselves is clean and wholesome. (Refer to "Business Culture" chapter for a detained discussion of local issues.)

4. Be flexible in forming partnerships

US companies in particular are notoriously obsessed with gaining majority share of a joint venture, the type of partnership most favored by East Asian governments. One reason is accounting: revenue can show up on the books at home only when the stake is more than 50 percent. Another reason is the US Foreign Corrupt Practices Act, which makes US citizens and companies liable for their conduct overseas. The idea, presumptuous at best, is that majority control translates into control over the minority partner.

Ownership is yet another area in which the Japanese have succeeded. They see a two-sided relationship where US partners often see themselves as the superior partner, in knowledge, finances, technology, and culture—in other words, know-it-alls. Westerners, and US businesspeople in particular, have a lot to learn about flexibility in such relationships. McDonald's has chosen the 50-50 joint-venture route, with great profitability—more than half its income now comes from outside the US. KFC is another US company that has found enormous success by being flexible. "We have a philosophy of relying heavily on our joint venture or franchise partners to guide us," says KFC's Provost. "We'd never dream of trying to impose our attitudes on them."

Finally, keep in mind that there is more than one way to do business overseas and that changing laws or market conditions will often force you to consider other options. Where a distributorship worked at first, a joint venture or a licensing agreement may be the way to go later.

5. Concentrate on the relationship

We cannot over emphasize this point: the Confucian culture of East Asia emphasizes personal relationships above all else. Building a good relationship takes time, patience, courtesy, reliability, dignity, honorable conduct, and farsightedness. A poorly developed relationship dooms even your best marketing efforts to failure. One US computer maker made a great mistake when it fired its Asian distributor after a falling-out. The dismissal, handled in a typically abrupt American way, caused the man to lose face, and ruined all the relationships the company had built through this man. For three years afterward, company executives couldn't find another distributor because no one would even talk to them. Not only did the company lose untold millions of dollars in sales, but it took US$40 million in advertising to create enough consumer-driven demand for local distributors to consider meeting with the firm.

So do your very best to build a sound, trusting, and profitable relationship with your overseas partners. They are putting themselves on the line for you, spending time, money, and energy in hopes of future rewards and a solid, long-term relationship.

And by all means, don't expect your foreign distributors to jump through hoops on a moment's notice. For example, they need price protection so they don't lose money on your price changes. If they buy your product for HK$100 and a month later you cut your price to HK$90, you have to give them credit so they don't get stuck with inventory at the higher price. If you raise your price, you have to honor your prior commitments while giving ample notice of the increase.

With their focus on long-term personal relationships and on mutual respect and trust, East Asians, in particular, make honorable partners once you have gained their confidence by showing them they have yours.

Business Entities & Formation

FORMS OF BUSINESS ORGANIZATION

Hong Kong offers residents and foreign nationals a wide range of options for establishing a business. Alternatives include setting up a variety of companies, partnerships, sole proprietorships, or foreign branch, representative, or liaison offices. Entities can be incorporated and registered under the provisions of the Companies Ordinance or established as a registered business under the Business Registration Ordinance. The specific type of business entity selected will be determined by the objectives, circumstances, degree of control desired, and anticipated duration of the investment as well as by other business considerations. However, the range of likely solutions to most business needs is fairly narrow.

Companies

A company is an entity that has been organized and registered for profit-seeking purposes. Under Hong Kong law, two or more persons may form an incorporated company by completing a memorandum of association to do so and by complying with registration requirements. Most Hong Kong companies are limited liability companies, and most foreign and local businesses select this structure. The legal concepts and regulatory frameworks governing Hong Kong companies follow British common law and are similar to those familiar in Western legal and business practice.

Companies Limited by Shares The company limited by shares is the corporate structure that Hong Kong and foreign firms most often use. Such a company can be 100 percent foreign owned. Most independent foreign operations and local subsidiaries of foreign companies are organized in this fashion. The company's initial capital and subsequent earnings can be repatriated. Earnings are taxable in Hong Kong. There is no withholding on dividends or interest paid to nonresidents.

A company limited by shares has members whose liability is limited to the amount of their paid-in and subscribed capital. Limited companies must have the word *Limited* or the abbreviation *Ltd.* at the end of their corporate name. Some types of associations that have incorporated as limited companies do not have to use these identifying terms, but they represent special cases that are not generally involved in commerce.

The remaining company formats are used primarily by trade and professional organizations that prefer a corporate to a partnership structure. These formats are relatively uncommon, and they are not likely to be of interest to foreigners doing business in Hong Kong.

Companies Limited by Guarantee A company limited by guarantee must have at least two members whose liability is limited to the actual amounts that they have contributed to company assets. This form of business entity is used by specialized organizations seeking corporate status, and it is not generally of interest to foreign investors.

Unlimited Companies An unlimited company requires a minimum of two shareholders each of whom bears both unlimited and joint and several liability for the company's obligations. This form of business entity is used by specialized organizations seeking the benefits of incorporation. As such, it will not generally be of interest to foreign investors, even if they are not deterred by the prospect of unlimited liability. An unlimited company can reregister as a limited company, but a limited company cannot convert to an unlimited company.

Public Versus Private Companies Limited companies can be either private or public entities. Most companies organized by foreign interests are public companies.

A private company must meet all the following criteria: it must have no more than 50 shareholders (it can get around this requirement by not counting current and former employees who hold shares in the company), it must restrict the right to transfer shares to outsiders, and it must not offer any of its shares or debt instruments to the public. If it fails to meet any

---

GLOSSARY

Business Registration Office To do business in the colony every entity, whether incorporated or unincorporated, must register with the Business Registration Office of the Inland Revenue Service to obtain a business certificate.

Hong Kong Trade Development Council (HKTDC) The Hong Kong Trade Development Council was set up to develop and expand Hong Kong's international trade by promoting Hong Kong's exports of goods and services and persuading foreign companies to use Hong Kong as their global trading hub. It provides information to foreign firms interested in doing business in Hong Kong.

Registrar of Companies An individual or company that wants to set up an incorporated business entity in Hong Kong must register with the Registrar of Companies. The registrar's index of companies is also the primary source of information on registered business entities.

---

of these criteria, it must register as a public company or, if it has already registered as a private company, it must convert to a public company. Conversely, a public company that meets all the standards set for a private company may convert to private status.

Private companies can be organized with a minimum of two shareholders. Public companies require a minimum of seven. In contrast to a private company, a public company must issue a prospectus upon organization and register to offer shares and debt to the public as part of its funding, or, if it does not intend to sell securities to the public at the time of formation, it can file a statement in lieu of prospectus. A public company can also apply for listing on the Hong Kong stock exchange, an option not open to a private company. A private company can begin operations immediately without the added delay and expense occasioned by this aspect of the registration procedures for public companies.

In general, a private company faces fewer regulatory requirements than a public company, and it is quicker, easier, and less expensive to set one up. Private company status is desirable because it relieves the company from the necessity of filing financial statements with the Registrar of Companies, where they are available for public inspection. A private company could provide a structure suitable for a foreign company that has relatively few shareholders and that does not plan to sell shares to or borrow funds from the public in Hong Kong.

Capital Requirements Hong Kong law sets no minimum requirements for capital or equity participation. In practice, private companies must have a minimum capitalization of HK$10,000 (about US$1,300) in order to register. Financial service firms have substantially higher initial capital requirements: Banks must have minimum capital of between HK$150 million and HK$25 million (between about US$19.5 million and US$3.25 million) depending on the category of their operating license. Minimum capital requirements are also relatively high for securities and insurance firms.

Hong Kong does not require any portion of a company's debt or equity capital to be held by legal residents of the colony. Corporate shareholders and their nominees are allowed. Authorized capital must be equal to or greater than issued capital, and the company can allow shareholders to carry an unpaid balance on shares subscribed but not fully paid. However, this practice is uncommon. Any increase in either authorized or issued capital must be voted by shareholders. Companies cannot pay dividends out of capital or otherwise reduce capital without a court order.

The government will revoke a company's registration if its membership falls below the minimum number of shareholders—two for private companies, seven for public companies—and continues below the minimum for six months. In such cases, the remaining shareholders are jointly and severally liable for any corporate obligations incurred after the six-month grace period unless they can demonstrate that they were unaware that the membership had lapsed.

Unless private or public company bylaws specify otherwise, shares can be transferred among existing shareholders or to new outside shareholders. Both parties pay a transfer stamp tax of 0.25 percent of the price paid or the net asset value, whichever is greater.

Companies can issue common and preferred stock, different classes of stock, and bonds, mortgages, convertible bonds, and other debt securities. Common shares of public companies usually carry voting rights, but preferred shares can be restricted with respect to voting, payment of dividends, and return of capital. All shares must have a par value, usually a minimal HK$1 to HK$10 (about US$0.13 to US$1.30). All shares must be issued in registered form, and details on all shareholders must be maintained in a company register showing the shareholder's name, address, occupation, and the dates and amounts of all share transactions.

Companies can issue shares at a premium above par with the excess going into a special capital reserve account or, with shareholder and court approval, at a discount. Reserve accounts can be used to pay for unissued shares to be distributed as a stock dividend. There are restrictions on using reserves to pay cash dividends. A company cannot use its share capital as collateral when it borrows. It cannot buy its own shares, nor can it offer financial assistance or incentives to anyone to buy its shares except in a limited way for employee share purchase assistance plans. Companies can issue preferred shares that are redeemable out of reserves established with funds that otherwise would have gone into dividends or from the issue of new common shares.

Shareholders, Directors, Officers, and Corporate Governance Unless otherwise provided for by law, every company may define the specific rights and responsibilities of its shareholders, directors, and officers through its bylaws. The Companies Ordinance specifies duties for directors with regard to fiduciary and other responsibilities—focusing mainly on record-keeping—but in general directors have wide discretionary powers in running a company.

Every company must have at least two directors and at least one secretary who is a Hong Kong resident. The secretary can be a corporate entity, in which case it must be registered and maintain an office in Hong Kong. There are no other limitations on or prescriptions for the nationality of officers. Directors and officers must be natural persons: a corporation cannot serve as a governing officer of a company except under very limited conditions. The company must maintain an official office in Hong Kong where it keeps all required books and records and where it can be served with legal and other official notices.

Directors are chosen by shareholders to serve for a stated term, the duration of which is specified in the bylaws. Terms of from one to three years are most common. Directors are not required to be shareholders unless the bylaws so specify. Directors appoint the officers of the company or, if the bylaws allow it, elect one of their number to act as executive officer. Individuals involved in a bankruptcy cannot serve as directors, and Hong Kong law prohibits insider trading and self-dealing among company directors and officers, although it has not specified penalties for such offenses.

Public companies must hold an annual general shareholders meeting every calendar year no more than 15 months after the last meeting. The initial meeting must be held no more than 18 months after the company is incorporated. Meetings do not need to be held in Hong Kong. However, the original minutes of meetings must be maintained at the company's Hong Kong office. The main order of business at such meetings is the disclosure of earnings and the company's financial condition. Special meetings can be called at the behest of either the directors or the shareholders. There are no quorum requirements, but all shareholders must be notified at least 21 days in advance of any meeting unless they unanimously waive this right.

Within 42 days after its annual meeting, a public company must file an annual report of the meeting with the Registrar of Companies. This report must include the following: data on the meeting, the company's capital structure, debt outstanding, a roster of shareholders that specifies their holdings, a roster of directors and officers, and the statutory audit of the financial statements of the company. Private companies must file all materials just enumerated except the audit. Dormant companies for which there have been no changes since the last filing are allowed to file a statement of no activity rather than a full annual report.

Every company incorporated under the Companies Ordinance must appoint certified outside auditors before the company's first meeting. Every registered public company must have its books audited by such accountants throughout its life. These books must record all inflows and outflows of cash, all sales and purchases, and all corporate assets and liabilities. Such records can be kept outside Hong Kong, but they must be updated and deposited in the company's Hong Kong office at least once every six months. Even when the Registrar of Companies does not require such audited books, as it does not in the case of private companies, tax authorities usually require them to establish tax liability.

Dissolution Under the Companies Ordinance, a company can dissolve voluntarily or as mandated by court order. Voluntary liquidation can be initiated by the board or shareholders, in which case it is known as a *members' voluntary winding-up.* A voluntary liquidation can only be undertaken if the company certifies that it can pay off all its obligations within 12 months. If dissolution is due to insolvency, it is known as a *creditors' voluntary winding-up,* and a liquidator is appointed in consultation with creditors. In either case, the company usually manages its own dissolution.

A *court winding-up* can be initiated by a creditor, by the directors or shareholders, or by the court under original jurisdiction, in which case a receiver is appointed to liquidate the company. A creditor can force a company into liquidation by filing a demand for payment for any sum exceeding HK$5,000 (about US$650). If the demand remains unpaid after three weeks, the creditor can move for liquidation, which is the most common route in involuntary court-ordered liquidations. It is illegal for a company to operate while insolvent, and directors and officers can be held personally liable for obligations incurred during insolvency.

Branch Offices

A branch office is any office that has been registered and maintained in Hong Kong for business pur-

Instant Offices, Shelf Companies, and Administrative Service Companies: Making Business Quick and Easy in Hong Kong

Hong Kong is the land of instant business gratification, and a whole range of services cater to the need to get down to business without delay. These services include hotel business centers, secretarial and translation services, and specialist consultants and advisers. Of particular interest to foreign businesses are specialized instant offices, shelf companies, and administrative service companies.

Instant Offices There are more than 20 business centers in Hong Kong that offer fully equipped instant offices complete with clerical support and the latest communications links. These range from bare-bones cubicles with minimal amenities and services to luxury suites complete with a view, a prestigious address, and a full range of services. Most are available by the week or the month. Some can be had by the day or for longer lease periods. It is usually possible to arrange for the use of such space within a few hours at most and with no advance notice. As might be expected, such service does not come cheap. Rates start at around US$4,000 per month and go up rapidly from there. Most prices are on an a la carte basis. That is, each service and use above the basic rent is priced separately.

Such centers allow a foreign entity or individual to maintain a presence in Hong Kong on a short- to intermediate-term or intermittent basis without the necessity and expense of setting up a permanent office. Most businesses use them for a short period while concluding a single deal or as an interim step while they are in the process of setting up their own permanent facilities.

Some legal, accounting, financial, and other firms may also be willing to provide office space and some support services for a limited term as an accommodation to clients. Their willingness will depend on the relationship and the circumstances.

Shelf Companies Some foreign entities may have projects requiring immediate action that won't wait while they go through the procedures required to form a company from scratch. To fill this need, many of the larger legal, financial, and accounting firms operating in Hong Kong maitain an inventory of so-called shelf or ready-formed companies that clients can purchase from them and use to begin doing business as a registered Hong Kong company with essentially no delay.

Such shelf companies are legally formed and registered but inactive companies, usually having general, innocuous names and fairly broad, standard memoranda of association (charters) and articles of association (bylaws). Hong Kong firms regularly dealing in specialized areas may have customized these charters and bylaws to suit the specific needs of their usual clientele, but in general such legal entities are fairly generic in nature. It is difficult to alter the charter or bylaws of a company, but it is a relatively simple matter to apply for a change of name. Most such companies will serve the immediate needs of a business that can't wait, but most businesses with a longer-term need will eventually want to set up their own entity.

Entities can use such shelf companies to exploit immediately opportunities that require an incorporated structure or as a stopgap measure while their own company is being formed. For instance, it is difficult to obtain an office lease unless one is a registered company, and a shelf company can allow an entity to begin setting up housekeeping before its active, official entry into the market.

Most firms that offer such shelf companies for sale say that they do so as an accommodation to their clients and that the costs to the client are roughly the same as the costs of forming a similar company from scratch.

Administrative Service Companies For foreign businesses that need more than a temporary office but less than their own local company, Hong Kong boasts several firms that provide rent-a-company services. These firms offer a registered business address, and they can handle all back-office services, such as bookkeeping and accounting, (including audit and tax services), commercial banking relationships, (including financial and investment planning), billing, payables and receivables, documentation, and shipping. They can also make appointments, handle communications, maintain files, and provide other clerical, secretarial, and support services. Such firms do not handle negotiations, business operations, or management, and so they do not act as surrogate companies, but they can free up expatriate personnel to concentrate on these matters. Again, those interested in such services should not expect them to be cheap.

poses for which the company's principal office holds ultimate responsibility. A branch office can carry on virtually any type of business activity, it can earn income, and it is free to repatriate earnings and capital. Branch earnings are taxed at the same rate as company earnings. The Registrar of Companies can preempt a branch from using its parent's name if that name is already in use in Hong Kong or the registrar determines that it would mislead the public.

A branch office is relatively easy to set up, and some foreign companies may realize home country tax advantages from operating a branch rather than a separate incorporated entity in Hong Kong. However, a branch usually bears greater potential liability than a limited company, because a company incorporated in Hong Kong is considered to be a separate entity, and its liability is limited to its local capital, while a branch is considered to be an entity dependent on its parent firm, and the parent firm is implicitly liable for the branch to the full extent of the parent's total capital.

Operating Requirements There are no minimum capital requirements and no local participation requirement for the establishment of a branch office. A branch office must maintain a physical location where it keeps its licenses and shareholder registry, and it must appoint an official local representative who is responsible for its operations and for accepting legal and other notices on its behalf. A branch office must register with the Registrar of Companies and follow the general requirements that apply to an incorporated company, including the filing of an annual report. A branch must also supply documentation on its parent company that includes annual financial statements.

If the parent firm is a private company or if it is not required to make public disclosure of its accounts in its home jurisdiction, the branch is not required to disclose financial information about the parent. It does have to apply annually to renew this exemption. Hong Kong branches do not have to file the customary statutory audit. However, the branch must maintain audited books to satisfy tax authorities.

There are no restrictions on or established procedures for the dissolution of a branch.

Representative and Liaison Offices

Representative and liaison offices are any offices operating in Hong Kong under the authorization of the company's principal office that engage in no direct commercial profit-making activities. In Hong Kong, a representative or liaison office must not constitute a place of business as defined by the Companies Ordinance; this basically means that the office is not authorized to create legal obligations for itself or its sponsoring parent entity. In practice, such offices are involved primarily in product and market research and in dealing with local agents.

A representative or liaison office generally has foreign managerial personnel and Hong Kong support staff. No registered capital is required to set up an office. Because an office does not earn income, it must be supported financially by its parent organization, which bears implicit liability for its activities, despite the stipulation that the office cannot create obligations for its parent. There are no special accounting requirements on funds transfers. As a nonearning entity, an office is not liable for income taxes. Taxes on employee and representative earnings are individual responsibilities.

Representative and liaison offices have no specific legal standing or recognition. However, they should register under the Business Registration Ordinance, which governs unincorporated entities. Registration, which is not required, allows the office to sign leases and obtain utility and other services as a separate entity instead of having the designated representative make the arrangements as an individual. There are no prescribed procedures for closing such offices.

A representative or liaison office can help a foreign company with developing business interests in Hong Kong to investigate the local business climate firsthand with an eye on upgrading its presence by forming a branch office or company. Representatives should make sure that the office does not exceed its authorized functions. If its activities change and the change places it outside the accepted roles assigned to representative and liaison offices, it must move to upgrade its status within one month or face heavy penalties.

Agent Relationships

Agents are individuals or firms that provide local sales representation for a foreign business in the buying of local goods or the selling of the foreign firm's goods in Hong Kong. Foreign entities interested in doing business in Hong Kong are not required to use local agents, and agent relationships are regulated only by the civil codes governing contractual relationships.

Because Hong Kong is small, a single local agent can usually handle all the business of a foreign firm unless the firm is involved in a wide range of industries requiring a variety of specialized expertise. A wide variety of middlemen with such expertise operate in Hong Kong. Trading companies handle nearly 50 percent of goods going in and out of Hong Kong, usually on a deal-by-deal basis. Foreign companies that expect to do substantial and continuous business in Hong Kong can retain an agent. The agent can in effect serve as a local office for the foreign business, but he will be concerned with day-to-day operations, not with business management or planning. Many such agents require that client firms do a minimum volume of business with them.

Information on sales, purchases, and middlemen in Hong Kong can be obtained from the Hong Kong Trade Development Council (HKTDC) and from the Hong Kong General Chamber of Commerce.

Licensing and Technical Assistance Agreements

Licensing and technical assistance agreements are contractual agreements by foreign nationals or firms to license or sell specific technologies to Hong Kong firms or individuals. In exchange, the local entity agrees to pay fees or royalties.

Prior approval is not required for such transfers and payments and there is no review for the terms and conditions in such agreements. Licensing and technical assistance agreements do not need to be registered with an official agency, and there is no restriction on repatriation of the proceeds from such agreements. Standard provisions of the civil code governing contracts provide the only regulatory framework for such arrangements.

Partnerships

A partnership is almost any unincorporated profit-making business in which contributions and assets are jointly agreed upon and held by two or more partners. Partnerships are registered and regulated under the Business Registration Ordinance. Limited partnerships register under special provisions of the Companies Ordinance.

Foreign individuals and companies are allowed to form partnerships, and this form can be advantageous for specific foreign investment activities, usually those in which the number of participants is limited. Although partnerships have no standing as separate legal persons and they are therefore open to a substantial degree of potential liability, this type of entity is familiar to members of the local business community, and it is generally viewed as a serious business format for certain types of operations.

Partnership Structure and Operation Partnerships can be general or limited. In a general partnership, all partners bear unlimited liability for the debts and obligations incurred by the partnership. A limited partnership requires at least one partner to have unlimited liability, while the liability of one or more partners is limited to the amount of their capital contribution. Failure of a limited partnership to register as such requires it to be declared a general partnership with unlimited liability for all partners. General partnerships are relatively common in Hong Kong, but limited partnerships are rare.

Partnerships are not required to execute and file a formal partnership agreement, although most do. There are no legal minimum capital requirements for the establishment of a partnership. Profits are taxable at the standard corporate rate, but under some circumstances they may be taxed at a lower rate. All capital and earnings are eligible for repatriation. A partnership is not required to file an annual financial statement, although an outside audit is usually required to satisfy tax authorities. Any change in ownership or in partners must be registered with the authorities, and at least one partner must continue for the partnership to remain in effect.

Partnerships are limited to 20 individuals. However, professional practices organized as partnerships in such areas as law, accounting, and stock brokerage that are regulated by other agencies may have more partners. Partners may be either foreign or domestic individuals or corporations. Foreign investors can form new partnerships or join existing partnerships. Partnerships can be composed of local and foreign members or exclusively of foreign members, who may be of different nationalities.

Disputes among partners and between the partnership and third parties are generally handled under civil and criminal codes as though the claimants were individuals. A partnership can dissolve at will as long as the partners agree unanimously to do so and the dissolution is not designed to avoid obligations. There are no specific requirements for closing out a partnership.

Sole Proprietorships

Proprietorships, also known locally as sole traders, consist of a single individual engaged in a profit-seeking enterprise. No prior approvals are required to form a proprietorship, but it must register under the Business Registration Ordinance. A proprietorship has no separate legal status, and the proprietor's liability is therefore unlimited. Both foreigners and Hong Kong residents may form sole proprietorships.

There are no minimum capital requirements. Earnings are subject to taxation at the standard corporate rate, and they can be repatriated. There are no official filing requirements, but the proprietor has to satisfy the tax authorities, who often require an outside audit. A sole proprietorship can dissolve at will, but the proprietor's personal liability is continuing.

Joint Ventures

As in much of the rest of Asia, a joint venture in Hong Kong is a vague description that refers to a wide range of mutual agreements between contracting parties, often—but not always—of different nationalities. It is not a specific type of business structure or independent entity with legal standing, as it is in much of Western law. Hong Kong recognizes joint ventures on a practical level, and it is quite familiar with them, because it handles much of the business of adjacent China, which recognizes joint ventures as separate legal entities, but there is no specific legal authorization for joint ventures in the colony. In practice, joint ventures in Hong Kong are usually formed to complete a specific project rather than establish an ongoing business relationship.

A joint venture can be established as a partnership or as an incorporated company, and it is governed accordingly. Joint ventures can be made up of individual or corporate members, and they can consist entirely of foreigners or a mix of foreigners and locals.

REGISTERING A BUSINESS

Hong Kong generally does not require foreign businesses to obtain prior approval before investing or operating in the colony. However, all entities conducting business in Hong Kong must register with the appropriate authorities. This section outlines the procedures and documentation required to register a business in Hong Kong. Entities are formed under the Business Registration Ordinance or the Companies Ordinance, administered by the Registrar of Companies.

A foreign company is not considered to have a place of business in Hong Kong—and it is therefore not required to establish or register as a local business entity—if it does not create an obligation for its sponsoring entity. Most foreign companies can conduct a wide range of businesses, including those that generate income payable in Hong Kong—as long as the income does not originate from activities contracted in Hong Kong—and still maintain independent status. (*See* Offshore Servicing sidebar.) Foreign investors should seek professional advice and official confirmation that their specific operation is not considered to constitute local business activity that requires registration.

Although business formation and registration procedures in Hong Kong are relatively straightforward, simple, and transparent compared with those found in some other countries, they are also some of the more technically complex and sophisticated. Therefore, those interested in setting up in Hong Kong should seek professional assistance. Moreover, only licensed accountants and lawyers are as a rule authorized to complete the formation and registration procedures for entities covered by the Companies Ordinance, which means most foreign businesses.

Unincorporated businesses—proprietorships and partnerships that register under the Business Registration Ordinance—can technically register themselves without outside help, but professional assistance is still recommended for such operations. The complex nature of the regulations governing formation and registration procedures makes it highly advisable that, besides conferring with government

Hong Kong as an Offshore Servicing Center

Hong Kong is becoming a center for companies that are registered in other jurisdictions but that for various reasons prefer to conduct certain operations—usually record keeping, communications, or financial operations—in other venues. Qualifying business activities can be conducted in Hong Kong without registering with authorities, being subject to company law, or being liable for taxes on earnings. Because of its excellent communications and its sophisticated financial and business community, Hong Kong would be a prime location for such functional operations even if it did not also have the added attraction of minimal regulation.

Operations involving servicing activities do not constitute having a place of business in Hong Kong under Section 341 of the Companies Ordinance as long as they do not create a legal obligation for the company. As long as a company stays within these guidelines, it can operate extralegally and carry out a variety of functions in Hong Kong without having to register as a business, submit to regulation, or abide by local corporate laws. Nor does it pay taxes based on its activities, even if it receives income from operations, as long as it does not directly originate the income-producing transaction from Hong Kong.

Hong Kong in turn cements its position as a regional operating center, achieves economies of scale and added revenues in such operations, and accrues the indirect benefits of collateral spending by such firms, even if it does not receive tax revenues directly from their activities.

A company interested in such operations should seek legal advice to ascertain that its projected activities are within the guidelines for unregulated status.

authorities, individuals or firms wishing to do business in Hong Kong obtain legal and accounting assistance early on in the decision process, no matter what level of presence they are contemplating. Such assistance will ensure that their individual or corporate enterprise complies with regulatory requirements and procedures and help to prevent potential problems. (Refer to "Important Addresses" chapter for a partial listing of government agencies, legal offices, and accounting firms.)

Licensing Entities doing business in Hong Kong are required to register with the Registrar of Companies. Incorporated companies require a certificate of incorporation, and unincorporated businesses require a certificate of registration. Some entities— usually those involved in finance or professional practice—also need a license from the separate authorities that regulate these activities.

Special Registration for Businesses Some areas of business require special authorization or licensing. Such businesses are allowed to register only after they have obtained the requisite authorizations. For financial industries, such as insurance, banking, securities brokerage and trading, and related financial services, approval is obtained through the Commissioner of Banking, which requires certain capital levels, debt-to-equity ratios, and other specifications that vary with the category of registration sought. Special approval and licenses are required for items that Hong Kong has defined as strategic commodities. These include computers, peripherals, integrated circuits, disk drives, arms and ammunition, meat, radioactive substances, pharmaceuticals, and pesticides. There are excise taxes on alcoholic beverages, tobacco, soft drinks, cosmetics, methyl alcohol, some hydrocarbon products, and automobiles, whether they have been imported for sale or as inputs in operations. Because of quotas, licenses are required for the import or export of textiles and garments. Permits for garment quotas are strictly controlled. Local authorities should be consulted for specifics regarding these areas and the requirements necessary to obtain special licenses for use of these items in business.

Restrictions The only areas not open to foreign participation are the media and public utilities that are operated as official franchise monopolies. The government is considering schemes to open up power generation, water supply, communications, and transportation to outside investment, but it has as yet made no concrete proposals.

Fees and Expenses A company's registration fee is figured on a sliding scale based on its authorized capital. The minimum registration fee is HK$1,000 (about US$130) plus HK$6 (about US$0.78) per every HK$1,000 of authorized capital. There is also an annual registration maintenance fee of HK$1,150 (about US$150). Registration fees for branch offices are the same as those for incorporated companies. Registration fees for unincorporated entities can be characterized as nominal processing fees.

Establishing a company requires professional assistance from certified public accountants and attorneys. Professional fees and associated costs for establishing any form of company are about HK$10,000 (about US$1,300). It should be possible to register a small, simple company for less. However, total costs can rise rapidly and substantially for larger, more complex businesses.

Basic Authorizations Needed and Applications Procedures

Hong Kong has specific provisions for the formation and registration of each type of entity. However, every entity must complete the following basic steps: First, it must obtain clearance for the use of a specific business name. Second, it must receive certification of incorporation by submitting details of its organization, proposed operations, and its parent, if it has one, to the Registrar of Companies. Third, it must register to receive a business license. Because business registration is through the Inland Revenue Service, there is no need to register separately with tax authorities. Tax authorities use registration information to find the taxable entity. Foreign companies do not need prior investment approval. A certified English-language translation of all documents in a foreign language must be submitted in all registration procedures.

Summary of Registration Procedures by Type of Entity

Companies A company must file for name clearance. It must then submit its memorandum of association and supplementary information to the Registrar of Companies. Once it has received name clearance, had the documents approved, and paid its fee, it receives a certificate of incorporation. It must then register and pay additional fees to receive a business registration certificate. A public company must file a prospectus if it is going to sell shares to the public. If it does not intend to sell shares before beginning business, it files a statement in lieu of prospectus. Any subsequent public offering requires a prospectus. A private company does not need to issue a prospectus.

Branch Offices A branch office must submit data on its proposed operations and its parent firm. Once it has received approval and paid its fees, it receives a certificate allowing it to operate.

Representative and Liaison Offices Representative and liaison offices are not required to register. However, most file for a business registration certificate.

Hong Kong as Gateway to China, Hong Kong as Alternative to China

Hong Kong's strategic location makes it the gateway to China. At least 45 percent of China's exports and 28 percent of its imports pass through Hong Kong, and it earns between 30 and 40 percent of its foreign exchange through the colony. Some 70 percent of all foreign investment in China passes through Hong Kong as well.

The costs of doing business in China are substantial, and many foreign investors prefer to deal with China through an office in Hong Kong. Access to China is easy from Hong Kong—most foreigners desiring to do business in China enter via Hong Kong anyway—and access to Hong Kong itself is even easier. In fact, it is often easier to arrange travel, even in outlying areas of China, from Hong Kong than it is from Beijing. And Hong Kong is geographically adjacent to Guangdong and Fujian Provinces, the centers of foreign business interests in China.

Despite the fact that nominal costs in China are a fraction of what they are elsewhere, the actual costs of maintaining a foreign business there can be astronomical—as high as anywhere else in the world. As expensive as it is, Hong Kong may actually compare favorably in terms of cost, and a Hong Kong location is likely to improve the morale of expatriate staff.

All major Chinese governmental agencies and organizations maintain offices in Hong Kong, and they are often more accessible there than they are in their home venues. The fact that these different entities are in competition gives the foreign operator a chance to shop projects among various Chinese units in order to obtain the best deal. Some of these offices lack the authority to close deals, but the main ones can handle all aspects of negotiations and some can even sign contracts.

Foreign businesses looking to use a Hong Kong office in place of one in China must remember that home offices in China generally have veto power over arrangements made by their representatives. Businesspeople must also remember that such representatives can get carried away and make promises on which they cannot deliver. This can occur due to the representative's desire to close the deal, to inexperience, or even to outright incompetence or fraud. And simply being on-site in no way guarantees that a business will get the best deal.

Hong Kong also supports hundreds of firms that act as agents, middlemen, and facilitators for foreign entities interested in doing business in China. The foreign business can sometimes obtain most of the benefits that it is seeking from China through such an agent without having to set foot in China, figuratively or literally. There are limits on what such agents can accomplish, and they do take a significant cut of the profits, but they may allow a firm with a less than total commitment to doing business in China or a relatively short-term need to gain certain benefits while minimizing its liabilities.

The buyer must beware of Hong Kong-based China business agents. Many are experienced and highly ethical, and some are even miracle workers, but others lack experience, ability, and perhaps even integrity. It is important to investigate the credentials and claims of these people.

For firms uncertain about whether to go to China or stay in Hong Kong, there remains the possibility of having it both ways. An office established in Hong Kong now will automatically become a Chinese office in 1997.

Partnerships and Sole Proprietorships Partnerships and sole proprietorships, which are unincorporated entities, must register in order to obtain a business registration certificate.

Agency Agreements No approval, review, or registration is required for agency agreements.

Licensing and Technical Assistance Agreements No approval, review, or registration is required for licensing or technical assistance agreements.

Joint Ventures A joint venture requires no advance approval. Most joint ventures will be set up as a separate entity, that must be registered either as a company or as a partnership, following the procedure just outlined.

Basic Procedures

Company Incorporation Requirements Every company must submit an application for name approval to the Registrar of Companies. The registrar must confirm that the proposed business name is allowed and available for use. The applicant's advisers will already have checked the index of companies to determine whether there are potential conflicts. Applicants are advised to list several names in order of preference in case one or more is rejected. If there is no conflict, the applicant can reserve the name chosen for a period of three months from the date of the initial application. If the business has not been registered at the end of that time, the name becomes available for use by another business. The registrar reserves the right to require a company to change its name within 12 months of incorporation.

The company must then submit the following materials to the Registrar of Companies:

- Memorandum of association—the equivalent of articles of incorporation—that must include the company's name, objectives for which it is being formed, its authorized share capital, and such other similar information as the relevant portions of the Companies Ordinance require.
- Articles of association, or bylaws, that stipulate the procedures for governing the entity; if none are submitted or if those submitted do not cover all areas, the Companies Ordinance position is used as the default.
- Notarized certificate of identity listing the officers and subscribers, a statutory declaration of compliance with legal requirements made by the accountant or lawyer handling the incorporation, and a statutory authorization for the directors and secretary to act in governing the company and acceptance by the directors and secretary of this authorization.
- Fees based on authorized capital.

When all these items have been received and approved, the registrar issues a certificate of incorporation. When the company receives this certificate, it can legally begin operations. This part of the procedure usually takes about four weeks, but it can take longer.

Additional Company Requirements Although a company can technically begin to operate as soon as it receives its certificate of incorporation, there are additional steps that it must take to become legal. A public company must file a prospectus if it intends to issue shares to the public as part of its initial capitalization or a statement in lieu of prospectus if it does not intend to issue public shares at that time. A private company does not need to file a prospectus or statement.

Within 14 days of its incorporation, a company must file particulars about its directors with the Registrar of Companies. Within 28 days, it must file official notice of the location of its office. A company must also arrange to hold its initial statutory shareholder meeting no sooner than one month and no later than three months after it is entitled to begin operations. A report of this meeting must be filed with the Registrar of Companies.

Business Registration Procedures Within one month after receiving its certificate of incorporation, a company must register with the Business Registration Office of the Inland Revenue Department to obtain a business registration certificate. No additional documentation is usually required for this step, but the company must be prepared to pay its registration certificate fee. Registration must be renewed annually. Unincorporated entities also register with this office.

Branch Office Requirements Foreign companies that desire to open a branch office in Hong Kong must provide the following information to the Registrar of Companies within one month of establishing a place of business:

- Certified copy of the parent's certificate of incorporation or the equivalent document from its place of origin;
- Certified copy of its home country memorandum and articles of association or equivalent documents;
- Roster of the parent company's directors with full particulars;
- Power of attorney executed by the parent company appointing its local representatives and full particulars on these official resident representatives;
- Notice of the location of local offices and home offices;
- Statutory declaration made by the agents of the company regarding compliance with relevant procedures;
- Certified copies of the parent's financial statements, unless the parent is a private company or otherwise exempt; and
- Fees for registration.

If the branch claims an exemption from having to provide data on its parent because that parent is a private entity, it must reapply annually to retain the exemption. Otherwise, it must file an updated financial statement annually along with a statement from an authorized representative stating that there has been no change in the information on file and pay a registration fee to maintain registration. Any changes necessitate reregistration.

Because a branch is by definition part of an entity that has already been incorporated in another jurisdiction, it does not have to go through the initial incorporation procedures. Therefore, it does not directly apply to use a name. However, the registrar can refuse to let it use its chosen name if that name is found to conflict with names already on file in Hong Kong.

Partnership and Sole Proprietorship Requirements Partnerships and sole proprietorships must apply for a business registration certificate. Partnerships are not required to submit copies of their partnership agreements, but many do. These entities must renew their registration annually. Limited partnerships must also register with the Registrar of Companies.

Representative and Liaison Office Procedures Registration is optional for representative and liaison offices. If an office wishes to register, it can file an application for a business registration certificate stating the proposed functions of the office and supply copies of documentation concerning the parent company. Offices must have a resident representative manager who signs the application. Such offices are not defined as constituting a place of business in Hong Kong. However, if their status changes, they must re-register either as a branch office or seek incorporation as a company within one month of the change.

TEN REMINDERS, RECOMMENDATIONS, AND RULES

1. Sole proprietorships and partnerships are registered under the terms of the Business Registration Ordinance. Incorporated companies and foreign companies, including their branches, are registered under the terms of the Companies Ordinance.
2. Businesses involving banking, insurance, securities, and other financial services are regulated under separate statutes administered by the Commissioner of Banking.
3. A company limited by shares is the most common vehicle for doing business in Hong Kong. A branch office is the next most common format. Partnerships are also relatively common in Hong Kong, especially among professional groups and among partners uniting to undertake a project of limited duration.
4. No prior approvals are required for foreign investment in Hong Kong. However, specific projects can require special licenses or permission if they are in restricted areas.
5. In general, there are no restrictions on foreign ownership in any recognized type of entity. There are some restrictions on foreign participation in specific activities and sectors of the economy.
6. Only an entity incorporated in Hong Kong is allowed to hold quotas to export garments from Hong Kong. A firm without access to quotas cannot export apparel items from Hong Kong or import them into most major markets around the world. Foreign firms operating in this major sector of the Hong Kong economy usually set up their local buying offices as an incorporated company limited by shares. Organizations authorized to issue the necessary certificates of origin to obtain such quotas include the Hong Kong Trade Department and the Hong Kong General Chamber of Commerce.
7. Foreign investors considering establishing a business in Hong Kong can contact the One-Stop Unit of the Department of Industry, the Hong Kong Trade Development Council, or the Hong Kong General Chamber of Commerce for information.
8. No restrictions are imposed on the movement of capital into or out of Hong Kong, including the repatriation of profits derived from foreign investments, and as a result foreign businesses do not have to register their flows of funds in order to obtain foreign exchange. They do have to account for such flows for tax purposes.
9. When commissions and other costs of using a Hong Kong agent approach the cost of establishing a local entity, firms should consider opening a Hong Kong office. The considerations involve more than just a financial break-even analysis. In particular, the firm should assess its commitment to the Hong Kong and Asian markets; the projected growth of its local and regional operations; the size and functions of the presence that it contemplates, that is, whether it is intended to function solely as a purchasing office or as a full-service operations center.
10. Company names must be approved for use in Hong Kong by the Registrar of Companies. Even established trade names can be pre-empted from use if the same or similar names are already in use by existing Hong Kong firms. In addition, names including such words as Royal, Imperial, Municipal, Chartered, British, Savings, Trust, or other similar words that in the opinion of the Registrar of Companies imply official connections or guarantees, cannot be used without the express prior permission from the governor's office.

USEFUL ADDRESSES

In addition to the government agencies listed here, individuals or firms should contact chambers of commerce, embassies, banks and financial service centers, local consultants, lawyers, and resident foreign businesses for assistance and information. (Refer to "Important Addresses" chapter for a more complete listing.)

Business Registration Office
Inland Revenue Department
Wanchai Tower
5 Gloucester Road
Wanchai, Hong Kong
Tel: [852] 5490888

Commissioner of Banking
9/F., Queensway Government Offices
66 Queensway
Wanchai, Hong Kong
Tel: [852] 8672671 Fax: [852] 8690462

Hong Kong General Chamber of Commerce
22/F., United Square
95 Queensway
Wanchai, Hong Kong
Tel: [852] 5299299 Fax: [852] 5279843
Tlx: 83535 TRIND

Hong Kong Trade Development Council
38/F., Convention Plaza
1 Harbour Road
Wanchai, Hong Kong
Tel: [852] 8334333 Fax: [852] 8240249
Tlx: 73595 CONHK

One-Stop Unit
Department of Industry
14/F., Ocean Centre, Canton Road
Kowloon, Hong Kong
Tel: [852] 7372573 Fax: [852] 7304633
Tlx: 50151 INDHK

Registrar of Companies
Companies Registry
13/F., Queensway Government Offices
66 Queensway
Wanchai, Hong Kong
Tel: [852] 8672600 Fax: [852] 8690423

FURTHER READING

The preceding discussion is provided as a basic guide for individuals interested in doing business in Hong Kong. The resources described in this section provide further information on company law, investment, taxation and accounting procedures, and procedural requirements.

Doing Business in Hong Kong, Ernst & Young. New York: Ernst & Young International, 1990. Available in the United States from Ernst & Young, 787 Seventh Avenue, New York, NY; Tel: (212) 773-3000. Available in Hong Kong from Ernst & Young, Hutchison House, 15th Floor, 10 Harcourt Road, Central, Hong Kong; Tel: [852] 8469888, 5265371. Provides an overview of the investment environment in Hong Kong together with information about taxation, business organizational structures, business practices, and accounting requirements.

Doing Business in Hong Kong, Price Waterhouse. Los Angeles: Price Waterhouse World Firm Limited, 1992. Available in the United States from Price Waterhouse, 400 South Hope Street, Los Angeles, CA 90071-2889; Tel: (213) 236-3000. Available in Hong Kong from Price Waterhouse, Prince's Building, 22nd Floor, Hong Kong; Tel: [852] 8262111. Covers the investment and business environment in

Hong Kong as well as audit, accounting and taxation requirements.

Hong Kong International Tax and Business Guide, DRT International. New York: DRT International, 1990. Available in the United States from DRT International, 1633 Broadway, New York, NY 10019-6754; Tel: (212) 489-1600. Available in Hong Kong from Deloitte Ross Tohmatsu, Wing On Centre, 26th Floor, 111 Connaught Road, Central, Hong Kong; Tel: [852] 5450303. Provides an overview of the business environment in Hong Kong with special reference to tax and accounting requirements.

Labor

THE LABOR ECONOMY

Hong Kong has experienced rapid growth in the last two decades, with per capita gross domestic product (GDP) at constant prices more than doubling between 1979 and 1992. It ranked after Japan among major Asian economies in terms of per capita GDP in 1992. Much of Hong Kong's economic success can be attributed to its hardworking and productive labor force that coexists in surprising harmony with business. Low labor costs, an efficient system for the resolution of labor disputes, and the minimal influence of organized labor help make Hong Kong one of the most attractive commercial centers in Asia.

The approaching transfer of sovereignty over Hong Kong from the United Kingdom to the People's Republic of China (PRC) in 1997 has created an atmosphere of increasing uncertainty. Despite repeated assurances from PRC officials that Hong Kong's social, economic, and judicial institutions will remain unchanged, growing numbers of educated professionals and middle managers are emigrating abroad. Their plans to return only after they have obtained a foreign passport as a hedge against a Communist crackdown. The resulting brain drain has caused a shortage of skilled labor and prompted demands from employers to import more workers.

Population

In 1992 Hong Kong had a total population of 5,754,800, a figure that was increasing at an annual rate of 0.8 percent. With a land area of 1,074 square kms (about 413 square miles), Hong Kong is one of the most densely populated places in the world. Life expectancy at birth is 77 years for males and 84 years for females. Ethnic Chinese make up 98 percent of the population.

Labor Force and Distribution by Sector

The civilian labor force in 1992 was approximately 3 million. Males comprised 64 percent of the labor force and females 36 percent. In 1991 some 38 percent were engaged in industry, 59.3 percent in services, and 2.7 percent in agriculture. Manufacturing employed the largest share, 28.5 percent of the total labor force; wholesale and retail, trade, restaurants, and hotels together employ another 27.9 percent.

Labor Availability

The shortages of skilled and even unskilled labor result from a combination of factors. First, Hong Kong enjoyed an impressive average annual growth rate of 7.8 percent during the 1980s; the result is that demand for labor is high. This has kept unemployment at around 2 percent and always below 3 percent for at least 15 years. Second, as already noted, uncertainty over the transfer of sovereignty over Hong Kong to the PRC in 1997 has led many professionals and managers to leave the islands at least long enough to obtain a foreign passport. Third, foreign businesses are both establishing and enlarging existing operations in Hong Kong to take advantage of emerging opportunities on the Chinese mainland and elsewhere in Asia, resulting in a shortage of qualified personnel.

Under pressure from employers to ease the labor shortage by relaxing Hong Kong's immigration laws, the government introduced a labor importation scheme in 1991. Under the scheme, which has angered unions and other groups whose members fear that their livelihoods will be threatened, employers are allowed to hire foreign workers on two-year contracts that can be renewed twice for a total stay in Hong Kong of six years. Not limited to skilled workers, the labor importation scheme includes semi-skilled and unskilled workers.

Foreign Workers

As just indicated, the number of holders of foreign passports in Hong Kong is growing not only for political reasons related to the transfer of sovereignty but also due to the increasing number of foreign companies that have established or expanded their operations there. The largest foreign community is Filipino, with a population of roughly 69,000. The American, British, Indian, Thai, Vietnamese, Canadian, Australian, and Japanese communities in Hong Kong are sizable.

While there are no restrictions on the number of foreign employees that a company in Hong Kong may recruit, foreign personnel must obtain an employment visa issued by the Immigration Department before they arrive in Hong Kong. Applications for visas may also be made through any British embassy or consulate, at least until 1997. In practice, employment visas are usually issued only to professionals and managers.

Hong Kong's unique blend of the Anglo and Chinese heritages, combined with its attractiveness as a commercial center, has drawn people from numerous backgrounds together to form one of the most dynamic and culturally mixed populations in Southeast Asia.

Hong Kong Immigration Department
2/F., Wanchai Tower II
7 Gloucester Road
Wanchai, Hong Kong
Tel: [852] 8293456 Fax: [852] 8241133 Tlx: 69996

Unemployment Trends

By world standards unemployment in Hong Kong has been astonishingly low for well over a decade. Nevertheless, after declining steadily during the 1980s from a high of about 3 percent in 1985 to a low of 1.3 percent at the end of 1990, the rate jumped to 2.1 percent in April 1991, the same rate recorded in the first quarter of 1993.

In the early 1990s business leaders blamed the persistent labor shortage for an upsurge in the annual inflation rate to 12 percent for consumer prices. Labor was also made to bear much of the cost of fighting inflation. The government refused to allow civil servants' pay to keep pace with inflation, and a large public company laid off hundreds of its workers at one time, which had never before occurred in Hong Kong.

Despite these developments and the accompanying protests by organized labor for improved government safeguards against rising living costs and for employment security, unemployment is not expected to be a problem in Hong Kong in the near future. Indeed, continuing labor shortages are apt to pose more problems for government and business. It remains to be seen what the 1997 transition will mean for Hong Kong's labor market.

HUMAN RESOURCES

Hong Kong offers a disciplined and well-educated work force. The government has focused in recent years on expanding opportunities for higher education. A variety of private schools are available for English-speaking children and the members of almost all major ethnic groups.

The small size of most companies in Hong Kong and the fact that the government does not normally provide funding for training have limited the number of worker training programs. A proposed retraining program would be financed by a levy imposed on businesses that employ foreign workers.

Education

Hong Kong's youths are generally better educated than the members of preceding generations. Of those over 15 years of age who have attended school, the literacy rate for males is 90 percent and 64 percent for females. The government has focused increasingly on developing a formal educational system as a way

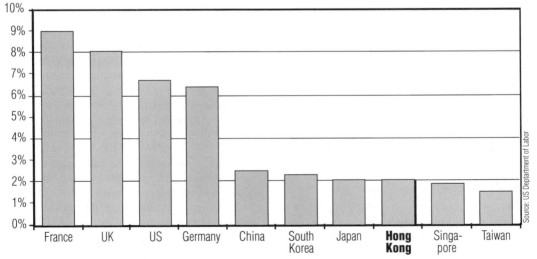

Comparative Unemployment 1990-1991

Source: US Department of Labor

of improving Hong Kong's competitiveness. While education and hard work are as highly valued in Hong Kong as they are in other Asian societies, institutionalized education is a relatively recent phenomenon. Traditionally, families were the primary provider of education to succeeding generations.

About one-quarter of Hong Kong's population is enrolled in a school, colleges, or other educational institution. Children receive nine years of free and compulsory education, spending six years in a primary school and three years in a secondary school. At the end of their last year, the so-called Form III year, students must qualify on the basis of examinations for subsidized places in senior secondary classes.

The government has plans to offer a subsidized place at the senior secondary level to about 85 percent of all 15-year-olds. At present, there are places for only 14 percent of those in this group, but the government intends to increase this figure to 60 percent by 1994.

Hong Kong has seven degree-granting institutions, and competition for admission is intense. Hong Kong's third university began admitting students in 1991. College-level education is not free, but it is heavily subsidized by the government. Most degrees awarded by Hong Kong's universities, colleges, and polytechnical institutes are recognized internationally.

Elementary and secondary education for English-speaking children is provided by a number of private schools and by the English Schools Foundation, which runs schools structured according to the British educational system. Other private schools are available for children of US, Canadian, Japanese, French, and German expatriates; the curricula follow those of the respective countries. Tuition fees for these private schools vary widely. Some companies subsidize the schooling of children of expatriate employees.

Training

Some employers provide employee training, which usually it takes the form of on-the-job training. Because the vast majority of employers in Hong Kong have fewer than 10 employees, it is generally not feasible for them to offer structured training programs. The companies that do offer training programs typically have many employees, and they tend to be multinational or foreign-owned corporations.

The government of Hong Kong does not fund training programs. Nevertheless, in an attempt to calm local labor groups, the government has proposed a worker retraining program that is to be funded by a HK$400 (about US$52) monthly levy that an employer must pay for each foreign worker that he or she brings into Hong Kong. Unionists maintain that such funding will cover only one-tenth of the workers in need of retraining. Moreover, the program

is not likely to benefit older workers, who are often the first to lose their jobs to foreign labor. The proposed retraining program has angered business leaders, who view it as aimed at discouraging them from importing foreign labor. It is unclear whether the government will proceed with the program.

Women in the Work Force There are no equal opportunity regulations in Hong Kong. The government has conducted a study of discrimination against women in the workplace, but the results were not available at the time of this writing. In general, the mixture of Western and Chinese business practices in Hong Kong means that it is not uncommon to find women in positions of power in business. Nor is it frequent.

CONDITIONS OF EMPLOYMENT

The Commissioner for Labour advises the government on most labor matters. The Department of Labour issues labor legislation and ensures that Hong Kong's obligations under international labor conventions are observed. The Employment Ordinance, which is generally applicable to all employees in Hong Kong, covers the following areas: compensation for injury arising out of or in the course of employment; child labor; paid allowances for illness and maternity leave; payments for long service and at termination; holiday pay and annual leave; hours and conditions of work in industry; antiunion discrimination by an employer; and standards of industrial health, safety, and welfare.

Department of Labour
16/F., Harbour Building
38 Pier Road
Central, Hong Kong
Tel: [852] 8524118 Fax: [852] 5443271

Working Hours, Overtime, and Vacations

Employees are entitled to one day of rest during each seven-day period in addition to regular holidays. The customary workweek is 48 hours, although it can vary by industry. There are no legal restrictions on the number of hours that men can work per week. The Women and Young Persons Regulations stipulate that women and people between 15 and 17 years of age employed in industry may work a maximum of eight hours per day and six days per week. No child under the age of 15 may be employed in industry. Finally, women may not work more than 200 hours of overtime per year, while young people are prohibited from working overtime.

Government personnel and those employed in trade and commerce typically work five and a half days per week. However, there is a trend toward a five day week, especially among larger companies with foreign affiliations.

All workers are entitled to 11 paid holidays each year. Paid holidays include two floating holidays. An employer should designate them at the start of the new year and post them in a conspicuous place. If the employer does not designate dates for one or both floating holidays, a worker may request ask to combine them with his or her paid annual leave. If an employee does not make such a request and an employer does not designate the dates of the two floating holidays, employees should be granted paid days off on the Monday immediately following the Queen's birthday (June 14) and on the last Monday in August.

All workers in Hong Kong are entitled to seven continuous days of paid annual leave after 12 months with the same employer. After three years of service with the same employer, the worker receives eight days of paid annual leave. A worker receives an additional day of annual leave for each subsequent year of service, up to a total of 14 days. Employees in the most service industries usually receive two weeks of paid annual leave in addition to the general holidays. Senior-level employees and executives generally receive four to six weeks of paid annual vacation time.

Sick Days

A worker is entitled to two days of paid sick leave per month during the first year of employment. For each month of service after one year, a worker is granted four days of paid sick leave. The daily rate of sickness allowance for four or more days off in one month is equal to two-thirds the worker's normal wage (excluding overtime pay). The sickness allowance is paid on the worker's usual payday.

A worker may draw on his sickness allowance

for as many as 36 days a year if he provides certificate issued by a medical practitioner. For sick days in excess of 36, but not exceeding 120, the employer may request a medical certificate designating the worker as the outpatient or inpatient of a hospital. The certificate should describe the medical examination carried out and the treatment prescribed by the hospital doctor.

A worker is not entitled to paid sick leave if the worker fails to produce a medical certificate when required by the employer; the worker refuses medical treatment by a recognized company doctor or disregards the advice of a hospital doctor; the worker's unfitness for work is the result of willful misconduct; compensation is payable under the Employees' Compensation Ordinance; or the worker's sick day falls on a statutory holiday for which the worker would ordinarily receive full pay.

Maternity Leave

A woman who has worked for the same employer for at least 26 weeks is entitled to 10 weeks of unpaid maternity leave. A woman who has worked for the same employer for 40 weeks or more and who has no more than two surviving children is entitled to four weeks of maternity leave at full pay and to an additional six weeks at two-thirds pay after the child is born.

If a female employee has fulfilled all the conditions specified in the Employment Ordinance and she is not otherwise liable for dismissal, her employer may not terminate her contract of employment between the date on which she gives notice of her intention to take maternity leave and the date on which she returns to work.

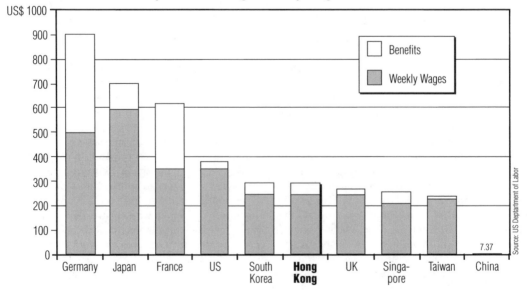

Comparative Average Weekly Wages - 1991

Source: US Department of Labor

Termination of Employment

Employers in Hong Kong may dismiss an employee at any time and for any reason unless the employee is a pregnant woman who has requested maternity leave. Even so, unless the employer can justify otherwise, workers are entitled to one month's advance notice prior to dismissal or to one month's salary in lieu of such notice.

A worker who has been with the same employer for at least 24 months immediately prior to dismissal by reason of redundancy or layoff is entitled to severance pay of two-thirds of a month's pay or two-thirds of HK$15,000 (about US$1,935)—whichever is less—for each year of service. A piece rate worker receives 18 days' wages or two-thirds of HK$15,000, whichever is less. The maximum severance payment is not to exceed total wages earned during the 12 month period immediately prior to dismissal or HK$180,000 (about US$23,225), whichever is less.

When an employee is entitled both to severance pay and to a contractual gratuity or retirement payment, the latter is reduced by the amount of the severance pay. Any retirement payment not made as result of such reduction and that is under outside trusteeship is returned to the employer.

WAGES AND BENEFITS

Total labor costs in Hong Kong compare favorably to those in other major industrial centers in the region. Wages are low by Western standards, while professionals and upper managers typically receive pay equal to that prevailing in other major cities of the world. Fringe benefits, such as annual bonuses and subsidized meals, are expected by most employees.

There is no contributory social security system in Hong Kong for the provision of health care or retirement pensions. The government provides such benefits in limited amounts. Increasingly, workers are looking to the private sector for individual retirement plans and health insurance, but those receiving them represent a very small percentage of the labor force. Public assistance for unemployed very-low-income earners serves as a type of unemployment compensation. Employers are required to pay workmen's compensation insurance, although the expense is minimal. An employer can establish an optional retirement plan for the workers in the company.

Information on the average cost of benefits as a percentage of total labor costs is not available. However, an employer who pays for workmen's compensation coverage, various fringe benefits, and a retirement plan can expect to the benefits package to be at least 15 to 20 percent of payroll.

Wages and Salaries

Unskilled workers in Hong Kong's manufacturing industries are normally paid at a piece rate, although daily wages are also common. Skilled industrial workers, technicians, supervisors, and clerical and administrative workers in the nonmanufacturing sectors receive monthly salaries. On the whole, wages of the industrial work force are low by Western standards.

Average Monthly Salary Rates of Managerial and Professional Employees in the Manufacturing and Utilities Sectors, 1990

Occupation	$HK	$US
Financial Manager	22,900	2,936
Production Manager	17,200	2,205
Marketing/Sales Manager	18,600	2,385
Plant/Mills Manager	16,500	2,115
Personnel Manager	16,400	2,103
Accountant	25,900	3,321
Electrical Engineer	27,400	3,513
Mechanical Engineer	22,900	2,936

Source: Census and Statistics Department, Hong Kong

The salary rate includes basic wages (including paid holidays and leave), cost-of-living allowance, guaranteed year-end bonus, commission and tips, and other regular and guaranteed bonuses and allowances.

To get an idea of current wage and salary levels and of the demand for particular jobs, consult employment and temporary agencies, and check *The Hong Kong Standard* newspaper on Fridays and the *South China Morning Post* on Saturdays; they have the largest selection of job announcements.

Professional and executive pay scales vary considerably. In general, salaries are comparable to those in other world-class cities.

Fringe Benefits

In addition to their regular wage or salary, workers typically receive fringe benefits. These can include subsidized meals or food allowances, bonuses for high attendance, free medical treatment, transportation allowances, and a Chinese New Year's bonus equal to at least one months' pay.

Fringe benefits for top-level personnel can represent a significant expense in Hong Kong. Senior local managers often receive free or subsidized accommodation (expensive in Hong Kong), an annual bonus, and a subsidy toward a child's education. In addition to these benefits, expatriate executives usually receive free round trip airfare for annual home leave.

Minimum Wage

There is no minimum wage in Hong Kong.

Health Care

Government hospitals offer inexpensive treatment to all patients, and some clinics provide free medical services. As noted, many employers provide subsidized or free medical care for their employees. Female workers receive maternity leave. The worker pays her own maternity expenses unless she qualifies for public assistance or has private health insurance.

Workmen's Compensation

Since 1984 the Employees Compensation Ordinance has required all employers to pay workmen's compensation insurance. Premiums amount to approximately 1 percent of payroll. If a worker suffers injury due to an accident arising out of and in the course of employment, the employer is responsible for paying compensation. In many instances, the employer pays whether or not the worker's accident was a result of the worker's own negligence.

Unemployment Insurance

While there is no formal system of unemployment insurance, public assistance is available for the poorest members of Hong Kong's population. Families and individuals whose income falls below a prescribed level receive a cash allowance. Since an individual or family must be registered with the Local Employment Service to be eligible for public assistance, these cash payments serve essentially as an unemployment benefit.

Retirement Plan

In recent years increasing numbers of employers have started retirement or provident funds to provide their employees with long-term security. Such funds are entirely voluntary, and only about 20 percent of the work force has access to this benefit. An employer may define the terms of the provident fund and administer it either in-house or through an outside private company. Employer contributions can be as much as 10 percent of payroll. To receive a tax concession for contributions to the provident fund, the employer must have the fund approved by the Inland Revenue Department.

LABOR RELATIONS

Serious labor disputes in Hong Kong are rare, and business operations are seldom interrupted. The number of worker days lost to industrial disputes in 1990 was 3,495. In 1991 that number dropped to an astonishingly low 202. While each worker has the right to join a union and he or she is protected by law against discrimination for being a member, participation is not obligatory. Only 18 percent of the labor force was unionized in 1992.

Unions and the Labor Movement

Hong Kong's existing unions are not militant. Instead, they function as self-help groups, passing on important information to members and addressing issues of concern. Registering with the Registrar of Trade Unions under the Trade Unions Ordinance gives a union in Hong Kong the legal status of a corporate body. Such status gives a union immunity from certain civil law suits.

As noted, only 18 percent of the three million people in Hong Kong's labor force in 1992 belonged to one of Hong Kong's 511 registered trade unions— 469 employees' unions, 28 employers' associations, and 14 organizations mixing employees and employers. Approximately one-third of Hong Kong's unions are affiliated with one of the two principal trade federations: the pro-Beijing Hong Kong Federation of Trade Unions (FTU), and the pro-Taiwan Hong Kong and Kowloon Trade Union Council (TUC). The FTU, with 84 affiliated unions, draws the bulk of its support from shipyards, textile mills, public transport, and public utilities. The TUC, with 69 affiliated unions, is strongest in the catering and building trades.

However, the Hong Kong Confederation of Trade Unions (CFU), with 316 affiliated unions, is the largest union group. Although quite modest by international standards, the CFU has demonstrated its ability to mobilize in support of labor issues.

Collective Bargaining

Unions and employers do not enter into binding contracts or settlements as they do in most other industrialized countries, and no sanctions can be brought against unions. Therefore, regular negotiations or collective bargaining sessions do not normally take place in Hong Kong. Instead, employers negotiate working conditions and employment contracts with individual workers or with the entire personnel. Actual conditions of employment and work contracts vary widely. Of course, they must meet the terms stipulated by the Employment Ordinance and government regulations.

The government's labor importation program of 1991 created a rare unified labor front, with the pro-Beijing, pro-Taiwan, and independent trade unions all united against the government and business. Even so, the action failed to block implementation of the labor importation scheme discussed earlier. This unprecedented cooperation among Hong Kong's major labor groups demonstrated the potential of increased political consciousness within organized labor.

Managing to Keep Employees in Hong Kong

With a negligible unemployment rate, especially among skilled and technical personnel, many foreign businesspeople find that they can experience 100 percent staff turnover within months of beginning operations in Hong Kong. If employers have to keep bringing new people up to speed at the same time they are trying to bring themselves up to speed in new ventures in a new, fast-paced, cutthroat business environment, the prospects for success are significantly diminished. And even experienced businesspeople find they often have a lot to learn about the Hong Kong labor market.

Although it may strain your budget and even go against the grain, you must be willing to spare no expense in hiring the best personnel available. This goes double for a local manager. Hong Kong is highly westernized but it is still Chinese, and local knowledge is critical in dealing with local conditions and staff. A strong local manager can handle labor issues before they become labor problems; sensitize you to local customs, norms, and procedures; and help you through special situations that are outside your previous range of experience.

To be effective such a manager must be given adequate information. This includes being in on all aspects of the venture, not just on a functional or need-to-know basis. Managers can't help as much as they might if they don't know the whole story. This means trust, which in turn means that the chemistry must be right. You are hiring a partner, not a servant. Your manager must also have adequate authority to act. Yes, you remain in charge, but give your manager enough independent power to do the job. That includes the power to negotiate on money and other critical issues.

Always remember that money is more important than virtually anything to Hong Kong workers. You cannot expect to attract good people on the cheap or often even at prevailing wages. Paying premium is dangerous, the main danger being that it leads to bidding wars and an insidious upward cost spiral. However, a unilateral decision on your part not to participate won't do you any good, and you can be sure that others will be offering such inducements. It is a fact of business life that Hong Kong personnel job-hop shamelessly, often for what seem like capricious reasons and insignificant incremental sums. If you can't compete with upfront money, try offering performance and profit-sharing incentives. Make sure that such incentives vest early and often—employees should be able to cash in every six months or so or they may lose interest. Offer the best benefits package you can, but remember that the focus of the work force is on actual cash received and their time horizon is usually a short one.

Even though they are mercenary, Hong Kong workers are also Confucian in orientation. They would like to be loyal if at all possible. Make it easy for them by maintaining the best working conditions and atmosphere you can. Take a paternalistic interest and share the wealth. Give banquets, take them on annual outings to Macao or to some of the sites on the outer islands. You might consider sponsoring a karaoke night out. Remember birthdays with a birthday cake or a luncheon for the staff (because many firms offer subsidized meals, this should be something different and special and include everyone in the unit involved). These sorts of things may seem hokey to some hard-nosed Western managers, but they help build the ties that bind.

This area can also represent a cross-cultural minefield. The Confucian ethic requires that the superior take responsibility for the subordinate, often in ways that would be intrusive in Western cultures, but also in an appropriate fashion. You can make any number of faux pas even when operating with the best of intentions. Being inappropriate can be offensive. And overdoing it in an inappropriate manner can also be interpreted as a sign of insincerity. There is often a fine line between what is acceptable and what is not, and it is often further obscured by cultural differences. Here again a good local manager can help in setting up the kind of program that will achieve the desired results while avoiding potential pitfalls.

Don't cause an employee to lose face by criticizing him or her directly. Not even in private, but most especially never in public or in the presence of colleagues.

(continued next page)

Managing to Keep Employees (cont'd.)

The Confucian system is extremely hierarchical, but it does not allow for such face-destroying direct confrontations, even among equals. Westerners with their "straight talk," not to mention the cathartic habit of flying off the handle, can blow things all out of proportion and ruin otherwise salvageable situations by failing to remember this. The result can be not only the loss of an employee, but also the creation of an enemy. Impatience and losing your temper are cardinal sins in the Confucian system. Remember to retreat to your office or bite your tongue if necessary. If there is some doubt as to whether you can get the message across obliquely, let the manager relay it. If you must deal with it yourself, the best way to do so is to couch the reprimand in terms of needing the employee's help to rectify a situation of mutual concern.

Finally, expand your search to include people who may have been left out of the mainstream. Consider women and younger people. Although women have an easier time of it in the Hong Kong business world than elsewhere in Asia, they usually have been relegated to lower level jobs in what is still a patriarchal system. Younger workers are also often left out in a system that values age and contacts that are built up over time. Don't try to change the world, but do look for talent in places where it is often overlooked. You may be able to find some great employees, and by giving these people a chance and responsibility, you earn loyalty.

Business Law

INTRODUCTION

Hong Kong is reforming its business laws, particularly as they relate to the activities of foreign businesses. Changes are frequent, and the trend is to improve the climate for foreign investment. In addition, many rules and regulations that significantly affect foreign businesses are in unpublished government advisories and internal policy statements, rather than in the statutes. You should investigate the status of the legal requirements that may affect your particular business activities. The information in this chapter is intended to emphasize the important issues in commercial law, but it should not replace legal advice or council. You should be certain to review your business activities with an attorney familiar with international transactions, the laws of Hong Kong, and the laws of your own country. Refer to "Important Addresses" chapter for a list of attorneys in Hong Kong.

BASIS OF HONG KONG'S LEGAL SYSTEM

Hong Kong is a common law country, which means that its courts rely on judicial precedent, as set by court decisions in earlier cases, in determining disputes currently under litigation.

China ceded Hong Kong to Britain after the Opium War in 1842, at which time the Colony was placed under the British legal system. Over time, however, the law has been adapted to Chinese traditions, producing a unique hybrid. Hong Kong's law is expected to change in 1997, when China regains control of Hong Kong. However, Chinese authorities have indicated that Chinese law will be implemented in Hong Kong in such a way as to retain Hong Kong's business structure. The specifics of how this is to be accomplished remain unclear.

STRUCTURE OF HONG KONG'S GOVERNMENT AND LAWS

Hong Kong's government is organized in traditional British colonial fashion under its Letters Patent and Royal Instructions. A governor who represents Britain holds veto power over all legislation passed by Hong Kong's Legislative Council. A third branch, the Executive Council, exercises executive functions. The court system is independent of the other government branches, and the highest court, the Privy Council, sits in London.

In 1997 a 50-year interim period of Basic Law will begin in Hong Kong under the doctrine of "one country, two systems." Basic Law provides for the establishment of a local political and judicial structure headed by an appointed Chief Executive, the continuation of capitalism, and the exercise of substantial autonomy in internal affairs. Laws in effect in Hong Kong prior to 1997 will remain in force, except for those that are contrary to Basic Law.

Until 1997 Hong Kong will continue to operate under its Letters Patent and Royal Instructions, not under a constitution. British common law and statutory law retain control, except when in conflict with a special Hong Kong ordinance. Treaties ratified by Britain may be extended to Hong Kong, but the dependency cannot enter independently into treaties, except when given separate recognition by a particular community, such as the Asian Development Bank. (*See* Treaties.)

LAWS GOVERNING BUSINESS IN HONG KONG

Business transactions in Hong Kong are primarily regulated by British law. (*See* Contracts.) Foreign firms doing business in Hong Kong must register to operate in the colony. (*See* Commercial Regis-

---

Introduction based on interviews with Frankie Leung, of Lewis, D'Amato, Brisbois & Bisgaard, in Los Angeles, California; and John Lo, of Lewis, D'Amato, Brisbois & Bisgaard, in San Francisco, California.

BUSINESS LAW
TABLE OF CONTENTS

Foreign Corrupt Practices Act 177
Legal Glossary 178
International Sales
   Contract Provisions 180
Law Digest 183
   Absentees 183
   Acknowledgments 183
   Actions 183
   Affidavits and Statutory
     Declarations 183
   Agency 184
   Aliens 184
   Assignments 184
   Assignments for Benefit
     Exhibits of Creditors 185
   Associations 185
   Attachment 185
   Bankruptcy 185
   Bills and Notes 186
   Bills of Sale 187
   Collatoral Security 187
   Commercial Register 187
   Contracts 187
   Copyright and Registered Designs .. 188
   Corporations 190
   Customs 191
   Deeds 191
   Exchange Control 191
   Executions 191
   Foreign Corporations 193
   Foreign Exchange 193
   Foreign Investment 193
   Frauds, Statute of 193
   Fraudulent Preference 193
   Fraudulent Trading 193
   Garnishment 193
   Immigration 193
   Industrial Property Rights 194
   Insolvency 194
   Interest 195
   Judgments 195
   Labor Relations 196
   Liens 196
   Limitation of Actions 197
   Limited Partnerships 197
   Negotiable Instruments 197
   Notories Public 197
   Partnerships 197
   Patents 197
   Pledges 198
   Power of Attorney 198
   Principal and Agent 198
   Receivers 198
   Sales 198
   Shipping 198
   Statute of Frauds 199
   Statutory Declarations 199
   Trade Descriptions 199
   Trademarks 199
   Treaties 200

ter.) A few special laws regulate particular aspects of business, such as the Crown Proceedings Ordinance on government contracts, the Control of Exemption Clauses Ordinance on unfair contract terms, the Misrepresentation Ordinance on false representations, the Companies Ordinance on fraudulent trading and transactions, and the Protection of Investors Ordinance on the securities brokerage industry. (*See* Contracts; Fraudulent Preference; and Fraudulent Trading.) In addition, contracts for sales of goods are subject to the Sale of Goods Ordinance. (*See* Sales.) Negotiable instruments, such as bills of exchange, promissory notes, and checks, must meet the requirements of Hong Kong's Bills of Exchange Ordinance. (*See* Bills and Notes.)

Companies formed in Hong Kong must comply with the Companies Ordinance. (*See* Corporations.) Partnerships may be formed under either the Partnership Ordinance or Limited Partnerships Ordinance. (*See* Partnerships.)

Intellectual property and trademark rights are protected under British law, Hong Kong ordinances, and international treaties. (*See* Copyright and Registered Designs; and Patents.) The Trade Marks Ordinance closely follows British law. (*See* Trademarks.) Labor relations are primarily governed by the Employment Ordinance. (*See* Labor Relations.)

GEOGRAPHICAL SCOPE
OF HONG KONG LAWS

Laws digested in this section are in force throughout the territory of Hong Kong.

PRACTICAL APPLICATION OF
HONG KONG LAWS

Contracts Hong Kong firms tend to use contracts with terms that resemble those in British agreements, but these contracts usually provide only general guidelines for continuing relationships. Despite the indefiniteness of contract terms, Hong Kong business owners respect contract obligations. If they sign a contract, they intend to perform and are aware of the consequences of breach although specifics may be in dispute.

Dispute Resolution Hong Kong business owners prefer to negotiate informally to resolve contract or other disagreements. If negotiations fail, firms will usually mediate before resorting to litigation. Practical solutions that will work for all parties are preferred to strict interpretations of contract rights and damage awards for breach.

Role of Attorneys A foreign business owner may retain a foreign attorney in Hong Kong, but foreign firms are permitted to practice only foreign law; a local attorney must be employed for legal advice

Foreign Corrupts Practices Act

United States business owners are subject to the Foreign Corrupt Practices Act (FCPA). The FCPA makes it unlawful for any United States citizen or firm (or any person who acts on behalf of a US citizen or firm) to use a means of US interstate commerce (examples: mail, telephone, telegram, or electronic mail) to offer, pay, transfer, promise to pay or transfer, or authorize a payment, transfer, or promise of money or anything of value to any foreign appointed or elected government official, foreign political party, or candidate for a foreign political office for a corrupt purpose (that is, to influence a discretionary act or decision of the official) and for the purpose of obtaining or retaining business.

It is also unlawful for a US business owner to make such an offer, promise, payment, or transfer to any person if the US business owner knows, or has reason to know, that the person will offer, give, or promise directly or indirectly all or any part of the payment to a foreign government official, political party, or candidate. For purposes of the FCPA, the term *knowledge* means *actual knowledge*—the business owner in fact knew that the offer, payment, or transfer was included in the transaction—and *implied knowledge*—the business owner should have known from the facts and circumstances of a transaction that the agent paid a bribe but failed to carry out a reasonable investigation into the transaction. A business owner should make a reasonable investigation into a transaction if, for example, the sales representative requests a higher commission on a particular sale for no apparent reason, the buyer is a foreign government, the product has a military use, or the buyer's country is one in which bribes are considered customary in business relationships.

The FCPA also contains provisions applicable to US publicly held companies concerning financial record keeping and internal accounting controls.

Legal Payments

The provisions of the FCPA do not prohibit payments made to *facilitate* a routine government action. A facilitating payment is one made in connection with an action that a foreign official must perform as part of the job. In comparison, a corrupt payment is made to influence an official's discretionary decision. For example, payments are not generally considered corrupt if made to cover an official's overtime required to expedite the processing of export documentation for a legal shipment of merchandise or to cover the expense of additional crew to handle a shipment.

A person charged with violating FCPA provisions may assert as a defense that the payment was lawful under the written laws and regulations of the foreign country and therefore was not for a corrupt purpose. Alternatively, a person may contend that the payment was associated with demonstrating a product or performing a preexisting contractual obligation and therefore was not for obtaining or retaining business.

Enforcing Agencies and Penalties

Criminal Proceedings The Department of Justice prosecutes criminal proceedings for FCPA violations. Firms are subject to a fine of up to US$2 million. Officers, directors, employees, agents, and stockholders are subject to fines of up to US$100,000, imprisonment for up to five years, or both.

A US business owner may also be charged under other federal criminal laws, and on conviction may be liable for fines of up to US$250,000 or up to twice the amount of the gross gain or gross loss, provided the defendant derived pecuniary gain from the offense or caused pecuniary loss to another person.

Civil Proceedings Two agencies are responsible for enforcing civil provisions of the FCPA: The Department of Justice handles actions against domestic concerns, and the Securities and Exchange Commission (SEC) files actions against issuers. Civil fines of up to US$100,000 may be imposed on a firm; any officer, director, employee, or agent of a firm; or any stockholder acting for a firm. In addition, the appropriate government agency may seek an injunction against a person or firm that has violated or is about to violate FCPA provisions.

Conduct that constitutes a violation of FCPA provisions may also give rise to a cause of action under the federal Racketeer-Influenced and Corrupt Organizations Act (RICO), as well as under a similar state statute if enacted in the state with jurisdiction over the US business owner.

Administrative Penalties A person or firm that is held to have violated any FCPA provisions may be barred from doing business with the US government. Indictment alone may result in suspension of the right to do business with the government.

Department of Justice Opinion Procedure

Any person may request the Department of Justice to issue a statement of opinion on whether specific proposed business conduct would be considered a violation of the FCPA. The opinion procedure is detailed in 28 C.F.R. Part 77. If the Department of Justice issues an opinion stating that certain conduct conforms with current enforcement policy, conduct in accordance with that opinion is presumed to comply with FCPA provisions.

Legal Glossary

Ad valorem tax A property tax calculated based on the value of the property.

Agent A person authorized to act on behalf of another person (the principal). Example: A sales representative is an agent of the seller.

Attachment The legal process for seizing property before a judgment to secure payment of damages if awarded. This process is also referred to as sequestration. Example: A party who claims damages for breach of contract may request a court to issue an order freezing funds in a bank account belonging to the breaching party pending resolution of the dispute.

Authentication The act of conferring legal authenticity on a written document, typically made by a notary public who attests and certifies that the document is in proper legal form and that it is executed by a person identified as having authority to do so.

Bill of exchange A written instrument signed by a person (the drawer) and addressed to another person (the drawee), typically a bank, ordering the drawee to pay unconditionally a stated sum of money to yet another person (the payee) on demand or at a future time.

Bona fide In or with good faith, honesty, and sincerity. Example: A bona fide purchaser is one who buys goods for value and without knowledge of fraud or unfair dealing in the transaction. Knowledge of fraud or unfair dealing may be implied if the facts are such that the purchaser should have reasonably known that the transaction involved deceit, such as when goods that are susceptible to piracy are provided without documentation of their origin.

Chose in action See Thing in action.

Composition with creditors An agreement between an insolvent debtor and one or more creditors under which the creditors consent to accept less than the total amount of their claims so as to secure immediate payment.

Equitable assignment An assignment that does not meet statutory requirements but that the courts will nevertheless recognize and enforce in equity, that is, to do justice between the parties.

Execution The legal process for enforcing a judgment for damages, usually by seizure and sale of the debtor's personal property. Example: If a court awards damages in a breach of contract action and the breaching party has failed to remit the sum due, the party awarded damages may request the court to order seizure and sale of the breaching party's inventory to the extent necessary to satisfy the award.

Ex parte By one party or side only. Example: An application ex parte is a request that is made by only one of the parties involved in an action.

Fieri facias writ A court writ to "cause to be done," which orders an officer of the law or another authorized person to satisfy a judgment by seizing and selling a debtor's property.

Interlocutory Temporary or interim. Example: An interlocutory injunction can be granted before a trial is held as a temporary restraint against one of the parties.

Jurat A certificate, affidavit or verification added to a document stating when, where and before whom it was made.

Negotiable instrument A written document that can be transferred merely by endorsement or delivery. Example: A check or bill of exchange is a negotiable instrument.

Nexus A party's connection with, or presence in, a place that is sufficient to subject in fairness that party to the jurisdiction of the court or government located there.

Pari passu On an equal basis without preference. Example: Creditors who receive payment pari passu are paid in proportion to their interests without regard to whether the claims of some would have taken priority over others.

Power of attorney A written document by which one person (the principal) authorizes another person (the agent) to perform stated acts on the principal's behalf. Example: A principal may execute a special power

Legal Glossary (cont'd.)

of attorney authorizing an agent to sign a specific contract or a general power of attorney authorizing the agent to sign all contracts for the principal.

Prima facie Presumption of fact as true unless contradicted by other evidence. Example: In the absence of contrary evidence, a party to a bill of exchange is prima facie deemed to be a holder in due course, that is, a party who took the bill in good faith and for value and who may thus enforce payment of the bill.

Principal A person who authorizes another party (the agent) to act on the principal's behalf.

Rescind A contracting party's right to cancel the contract. Example: A contract may give one party a right to rescind if the other party fails to perform within a reasonable time.

Rescission See Rescind.

Sequestration See Attachment.

Sight draft An instrument payable on demand. Example: A bill of exchange may be made payable at sight (that is, payable on demand) or after sight (that is, payable within a particular period after demand has been made).

Statute of Frauds A law that requires designated documents to be in writing in order to be enforced by a court. Example: Contracting parties may agree orally to convey land, but a court may not enforce that contract, and may not award damages for breach, unless the contract was written.

Thing in action A right to bring an action to recover personal property, money, damages, or a debt. Example: A seller who has a right to recover payment for goods and who is not in possession of the buyer's payment has a thing in action, that is, a right to procure payment by lawsuit.

and transactions involving Hong Kong law. Many large US and British law firms have opened offices in Hong Kong.

Intellectual Property and Trademark Rights Some piracy of intellectual property rights, particularly of computer software, exists in Hong Kong, but the enforcement system is stricter than in most other Asian countries. Hong Kong has adopted British copyright and patent law and its own trademark law, providing sophisticated legal protection for intellectual property and trademark rights.

Monopolies and Unfair Trade Restraints There is no antimonopoly law; companies are free to dominate the Hong Kong market and, in certain industries, government-authorized franchises are given. However, monopolies are few because of fierce competition.

RELATED SECTIONS

Refer to "Personal Taxation" and "Corporate Taxation" chapters for a discussion of tax issues, and *see* the Immigration section for details on immigration and visa requirements.

International Sales Contract Provisions

When dealing internationally, you must consider the business practices and legal requirements of the country where the buyer or seller is located. For a small, one-time sale, an invoice may be commonly accepted. For a more involved business transaction, a formal written contract may be preferable to define clearly the rights, responsibilities, and remedies of all parties. The laws of your country or the foreign country may require a written contract and may even specify all or some of the contract terms. Refer to Contracts and to Sales for specific laws on contracts and the sale of goods.

Parties generally have freedom to agree to any contract terms that they desire. Whether a contract term is valid in a particular country is of concern only if you have to seek enforcement. Thus, you have fairly broad flexibility in negotiating contract terms. However, you should always be certain to come to a definite understanding on four issues: the goods (quantity, type, and quality), the time of delivery, the price, and the time of payment.

You need to consider the following clauses when you negotiate an international sales contract.

Contract date

State the date when the contract is signed. This date is particularly important if payment or delivery times are fixed in reference to it—for example, "shipment within 30 days of the contract date."

Identification of parties

Designate the names of the parties, and describe their relation to each other.

Goods

Description Describe the type and quality of the goods. You may simply indicate a model number, or you may have to attach detailed lists, plans, or drawings. This clause should be clear enough that both parties fully understand the specifications and have no discretion in interpreting them.

Quantity Specify the number of units, or other measure of quantity, of the goods. If the goods are measured by weight, you should specify net weight, dry weight, or drained weight. If the goods are prepack-

aged and are subject to weight restrictions in the end market, you may want to provide that the seller will ensure that the goods delivered will comply with those restrictions.

Price Indicate the price per unit or other measure, such as per pound or ton, and the extended price.

Packaging arrangements

Set forth packaging specifications, especially for goods that can be damaged in transit. At a minimum, this provision should require the seller to package the goods in such a way as to withstand transportation. If special packaging requirements are necessary to meet consumer and product liability standards in the end market, you should specify them also.

Transportation arrangements

Carrier Name a preferred carrier for transporting the goods. You should designate a particular carrier if, for example, a carrier offers you special pricing or is better able than others to transport the product.

Storage Specify any particular requirements for storage of the goods before or during shipment, such as security arrangements, special climate demands, and weather protection needs.

Notice provisions Require the seller to notify the buyer when the goods are ready for delivery or pickup, particularly if the goods are perishable or fluctuate in value. If your transaction is time-sensitive, you could even provide for several notices to allow the buyer to track the goods and take steps to minimize damages if delivery is delayed.

Shipping time State the exact date for shipping or provide for shipment within a reasonable time from the contract date. If this clause is included and the seller fails to ship on time, the buyer may claim a right to cancel the contract, even if the goods have been shipped, provided that the buyer has not yet accepted delivery.

Costs and charges

Specify which party is to pay the additional costs and charges related to the sale.

Duties and taxes Designate the party that will be responsible for import, export, and other fees and taxes and for obtaining all required licenses. For example, a party may be made responsible for paying the duties, taxes, and charges imposed by that party's own country, since that party is best situated to know the legal requirements of that country.

Insurance costs Identify the party that will pay costs of insuring the goods in transit. This is a critical provision because the party responsible bears the risk if the goods are lost during transit. A seller is typically responsible for insurance until title to the goods passes to the buyer, at which time the buyer becomes responsible for insurance or becomes the named beneficiary under the seller's insurance policy.

Handling and transport Specify the party that will pay shipping, handling, packaging, security, and any other costs related to transportation, which should be specified.

Terms defined Explain the meaning of all abbreviations—for example, FAS (free alongside ship), FOB (free on board), CIF (cost, insurance, and freight)—used in your contract to assign responsibility and costs for goods, transportation, and insurance. If you define your own terms, you can make the definitions specific to your own circumstances and needs. As an alternative, you may agree to adopt a particular standard, such as the Revised American Foreign Trade Definitions or Incoterms 1990. In either case, this clause should be clear enough that both parties understand when each is responsible for insuring the goods.

Insurance or risk of loss protection

Specify the insurance required, the beneficiary of the policy, the party who will obtain the insurance, and the date by which it will have been obtained.

Payment provisions

Provisions for payment vary with such factors as the length of the relationship between the contracting parties, the extent of trust between them, and the availability of certain forms of payment within a particular country. A seller will typically seek the most secure form of payment before committing to shipment, while a buyer wants the goods cleared through customs and delivered in satisfactory condition before remitting full payment.

Method of payment State the means by which payment will be tendered—for example, prepayment in cash, traveler's checks, or bank check; delivery of a documentary letter of credit or documents against payment; credit card, credit on open account, or credit for a specified number of days.

Medium of exchange Designate the currency to be used—for example, US currency, currency of the country of origin, or currency of a third country.

Exchange rate Specify a fixed exchange rate for the price stated in the contract. You may use this clause to lock in a specific price and ensure against fluctuating currency values.

Import documentation

Require that the seller be responsible for presenting to customs all required documentation for the shipment.

Inspection rights

Provide that the buyer has a right to inspect goods before taking delivery to determine whether the goods meet the contract specifications. This clause should specify the person who will do the inspection—for example, the buyer, a third party, a licensed inspector; the location where the inspection will occur—for example at the seller's plant, the buyer's warehouse, a receiving dock; the time at which the inspection will occur; the need for a certified document of inspection; and any requirements related to the return of nonconforming goods, such as payment of return freight by the seller.

Warranty provisions

Limit or extend any implied warranties, and define any express warranties on property fitness and quality. The contract may, for example, state that the seller warrants that the goods are of merchantable quality, are fit for any purpose for which they would ordinarily be used,

International Sales Contract Provisions (cont'd.)

or are fit for a particular purpose requested by the buyer. The seller may also warrant that the goods will be of the same quality as any sample or model that the seller has furnished as representative of the goods. Finally, the seller may warrant that the goods will be packaged in a specific way or in a way that will adequately preserve and protect the goods.

Indemnity

Agree that one party will hold the other harmless from damages that arise from specific causes, such as the design or manufacture of a product.

Enforcement and Remedies

Time is of the essence Specify that timely performance of the contract is essential. The inclusion of this clause allows a party to claim breach merely because the other party fails to perform within the time prescribed in the contract. Common in United States contracts, a clause of this type is considered less important in other countries.

Modification Require the parties to make all changes to the contract in advance and in a signed written modification.

Cancellation State the reasons for which either party may cancel the contract and the notice required for cancellation.

Contingencies Specify any events that must occur before a party is obligated to perform the contract. For example, you may agree that the seller has no duty to ship goods until the buyer forwards documents that secure the payment for the goods.

Governing law Choose the law of a specific jurisdiction to control any interpretation of the contract terms. The law that you choose will usually affect where you can sue or enforce a judgment and what rules and procedures will be applied.

Choice of forum Identify the place where a dispute may be settled—for example, the country of origin of the goods, the country of destination, a third country that is convenient to both parties.

Arbitration provisions Agree to arbitration as an alternative to litigation for the resolution of any disputes that arise. You should agree to arbitrate only if you seriously intend to settle disputes in this way. If you agree to arbitrate but later file suit, the court is likely to uphold the arbitration clause and force you to settle your dispute as you agreed under the contract.

An arbitration clause should specify whether arbitration is binding or nonbinding on the parties; the place where arbitration will be conducted (which should be a country that has adopted a convention for enforcing arbitration awards, such as the United Nations Convention on Recognition and Enforcement of Foreign Awards); the procedure by which an arbitration award may be enforced; the rules governing the arbitration, such as the United Nations Commission on International Trade Law Model Rules; the institute that will administer the arbitration, such as the International Chamber of Commerce (Paris), the American Arbitration Association (New York), the Japan Commercial Arbitration Association, the United Nations Economic and Social Commission for Asia and the Pacific, the London Court of Arbitration, or the United Nations Commission International Trade Law; the law that will govern procedural issues or the merits of the dispute; any limitations on the selection of arbitrators (for example, a national of a disputing party may be excluded from being an arbitrator); the qualifications or expertise of the arbitrators; the language in which the arbitration will be conducted; and the availability of translations and translators if needed.

Severability Provide that individual clauses can be removed from the contract without affecting the validity of the contract as a whole. This clause is important because it provides that, if one clause is declared invalid and unenforceable for any reason, the rest of the contract remains in force.

LAW DIGEST

References to "Cap." mean the Chapter of the Laws of Hong Kong. [Note: Italicized portions of the text are appended from the England Law Digest.]

ABSENTEES

In absence abroad, person may generally delegate authority to any person of full capacity, usually by power of attorney. It is not necessary to file powers of attorney with any governmental or judicial authority. Power may be limited or unlimited as donor wishes.

As long as permitted by and in accordance with company's constitution, its directors may empower any person either generally or in respect of specified matters as company's attorney to execute deeds on its behalf outside Hong Kong. Deed executed by such attorney binds company as if under its seal.

ACKNOWLEDGMENTS

For form see Affidavits, sub head Form, Jurat.

ACTIONS

Generally, any person may sue or be sued in Hong Kong courts subject to applicable procedural rules.

Action on foreign contract or course of dealings can be brought in Hong Kong if any party to action is in Hong Kong, if contract was made or was to be performed in Hong Kong, if there is sufficient connection with Hong Kong or if Court is of view that Hong Kong is appropriate jurisdiction for case to be tried more suitably in interests of parties and for end of justice.

Unsuccessful party to action will pay costs of successful party. Plaintiff not resident in jurisdiction may be required to lodge in Court or otherwise give security for amount equivalent to defendant's costs. In practice usually only proportion of costs will be recoverable.

Limitation *See* Limitation of Actions.

Service of foreign process can be effected in accordance with rules applicable to service of Hong Kong process, for example, by postal or personal service.

Alternatively, service of process issued in country which is party to civil procedure convention, including Hague Convention, can be effected by written request from Consulate or other authority from that country to Chief Secretary of Hong Kong requesting that service be effected through Supreme Court.

Proof of Foreign Law Where foreign law is pleaded in any action, particulars must be given.

There is presumption that foreign law is same as Hong Kong law unless contrary is proved by party who asserts it is different. Foreign law can be proved by expert giving oral evidence at trial. Finding or decision on question of foreign law can be adduced in evidence on appropriate notice.

AFFIDAVITS AND STATUTORY DECLARATIONS

Affidavits must be expressed in first person and unless directed otherwise by Court state deponent's place of residence, occupation and description. If deponent is employee of party to cause or matter in which affidavit is sworn, he must state that fact. If deponent is deposing as professional or in business or other occupational capacity, he may state his address as being his place of work, identifying position held and name of his firm or employer, if any.

Every affidavit must be signed by deponent and jurat completed and signed by person before whom it is sworn. Affidavits must be sworn by deponent personally attending before Hong Kong solicitor, notary public or other officer duly authorized to administer oaths.

Affidavits may be sworn in any part of Commonwealth outside Hong Kong before judge, officer or other person duly authorized, or any commissioner authorized by Court. In any other foreign country, affidavit may be sworn before judge or magistrate, being authenticated by his relevant official seal, or before notary public or British Consular Officer.

Deponent can affirm his statement in alternative to swearing oath. (Oaths and Declarations Ordinance [Cap. 11]).

Form, content and jurat of affidavits and affirmations similar to that included for England Law Digest.

*[**Jurat** An affidavit is formally concluded by the jurat a memorandum of the place, time and person before whom it is sworn.*

Full address sufficient for identification must be given and jurat should follow immediately after end of text. It must not be written on page upon which no part of statements in affidavit appears.

The deponent must sign his usual signature or make his mark at the right of the jurat, not beneath it, and the signature and full official character and description of the person before whom the affidavit is sworn, his official seal of office attached, must follow imme-

---

diately after the jurat, in the form indicated (See Form of Jurat sidebar)

On the front page of affidavit and on backsheet one must state: (i) Party on whose behalf it is filed, (ii) initials and surname of deponent, (iii) number of affidavit in relation to deponent and (iv) date when sworn e.g. Defendant: J Smith: 1st: 6.6.1986.]

Statutory declarations may be taken and received by justice, notary, commissioner or other person authorized by law to administer oaths. Declaration shall be made in the form indicated. (See Form of Statuatory Declaration sidebar.)

Affidavit, affirmation or declaration of person who is unfamiliar with English language should contain declaration or oath by interpreter to effect that contents of statement have been interpreted to deponent.

AGENCY

See Principal and Agent.

ALIENS

See Immigration.

ASSIGNMENTS

Assignments of debts and other legal things in action and equitable assignments of both legal and equitable things in action, similar to law of England.

See England Law Digest.

[Assignments of legal choses in action are governed by Law of Property Act, 1925. Any absolute assignment by writing under the hand of the assignor (not purporting to be by way of charge only) of any debt or other legal thing in action of which express notice in writing has been given to the debtor, trustee or other person from whom assignor would have been entitled to claim such debt or thing in action, is effectual in law (subject to equities having priority over right of assignee) to pass and transfer from date of such notice: (a) The legal right to such debt or thing in action; (b) all legal and other remedies for the same and (c) power to give a good discharge for the same without concurrence of assignor. Provided that if debtor, trustee or other person liable in respect of such debt or thing in action has notice (a) that assignment is disputed by assignor or any person claiming under him or (b) of any other opposing or conflicting claims to such debt, or thing in action, he may either call on persons making claim thereto to interplead concerning the same or pay the

---

Form of Jurat

Sworn by the deponent . . . . (Name) . . . . at . . . .
in the County of . . . . State of . . . . United States
of America on the . . . . day of . . . . 19 . ., Before
me, ...   (Signature of Deponent)
                          (Signature of Officer)
(Seal)   . . . . (Title of Officer)

Sworn at . . . . this . . . . . day of . . . .
Before me,   (Signature of Deponent)

(Signature of Solicitor/Commissioner for Oaths)
Solicitor/Commissioner for Oaths

Form of Statutory Declaration

Declaration
I, ... [name], of . . . ., solemnly and sincerely declare [Insert facts].
And I make this solemn declaration conscientiously believing the same to be true and
by virtue of the Oaths and Declarations Ordinance.
Declared at . . . .
this . . . . day of . . . . 19 . . .
Before me
[Signature and designation] . . . .

debt or other thing in action into court. (§136).

This section enables legal assignments of legal things in action to be made so that assignee can sue in his own name without joining assignor as a party. Assignments of this kind need not be for valuable consideration but must be of the whole debt and not of a part thereof and written notice to debtor or trustee of the fund is essential. The assignment is subject to prior equities.

Equitable assignments both of legal and equitable things in action are recognized as valid. In such assignments the formalities of the statute need not be complied with, but must be complete so that the assignee can demand payment from the debtor. The equitable assignee cannot sue in his own name but must use assignor's name. Notice in writing to debtor is essential, as priority of assignee's rights depends on date of such notice and he is entitled to be paid out of the fund in the order in which he gives notice to the debtor or other person by whom the fund is distributable.

ASSIGNMENTS FOR BENEFIT EXHIBITS OF CREDITORS

By the Deeds of Arrangement Act, 1914, under which any instrument whether, under seal or not, made by, for or in respect of the affairs of a debtor (a) for the benefit of his creditors generally or (b) where debtor was insolvent at date of execution of instrument, for benefit of any three or more of his creditors, otherwise than in pursuance of the law relating to bankruptcy, is deemed to be a deed of arrangement and subject to the provisions of the Act. The following classes of instruments in particular are included: (a) Assignments of property; (b) deeds of, or agreements for, composition; (c) in cases where creditors of the debtor obtain control over his property or business, a deed of inspectorship for the purpose of carrying on or winding up a business; (d) a letter of license authorizing the debtor or any other person to manage, carry on, realize or dispose of a business with a view to payment of debts and (e) any agreement entered into for the purpose of carrying on or winding up the debtor's business or authorizing the debtor or any other person to manage, carry on, realize, or dispose of debtor's business, with a view to payment of his debts.

A deed of arrangement is void unless it bears ad valorem duty stamp and is registered with Registrar of Bills of Sale within seven clear days after its execution, if executed in England, or if executed abroad, within seven clear days after time at which it would in ordinary course of post, arrive in England if posted within one week after execution thereof.

A deed for benefit of creditors generally is void unless before or within 21 days of registration it receives the assent in writing of a majority in number and value of creditors. A trustee under a deed must file a statutory declaration that the requisite majority of creditors have assented at time of registration or if deed is assented to after registration within 28 days thereof. He must also give security unless a majority of creditors dispense with it.

A debtor is at liberty to make a private arrangement with his creditors upon any terms to which he can get them to agree, but no creditor is bound to join in such a deed unless he thinks proper.

Sees Bankruptcy and Insolvency for additional arrangements available.]

ASSOCIATIONS

See Partnerships.

ATTACHMENT

Any sum standing to credit of person in deposit account with recognized financial institution can be attached.

No attachment of wages of judgment debtor except in favor of Crown in respect of civil debt due to it.

See Executions.

BANKRUPTCY

Law is contained in Bankruptcy Ordinance. (Cap. 6).

Debtor commits act of bankruptcy if (a) in Hong Kong or elsewhere he makes conveyance or assignment of his property to trustee for benefit of his creditors generally, (b) in Hong Kong or elsewhere he makes fraudulent conveyance, gift, delivery or transfer of his property, (c) in Hong Kong or elsewhere he makes deposit of any part of his property or creates any charge which would be void as fraudulent preference if he were adjudged bankrupt (fraudulent preference is made when debtor is insolvent and he transfers or mortgages property to creditor with intention of preferring that creditor over others if adjudged bankrupt on petition presented within six months of transfer—it is not necessary to demonstrate fraud), (d) with intention to defeat or delay his creditors he departs from Hong Kong or departs from his dwelling-house or usual place of business or removes his property or any part of his property out of jurisdiction of Hong Kong courts, (e) there has been execution against him and goods have been either sold or held by bailiff for more than 21 days, (f) he files in Court declaration of his inability to pay his debts or presents bankruptcy petition against himself, (g) creditor files and serves bankruptcy notice and debtor has not complied with notice within prescribed time or is unable to resist notice (bankruptcy notice may be issued by Court to judgment creditor who has obtained final order; notice must be in prescribed form and will state that debtor should pay judgment debt or amount due or secure or compound it to satisfaction of Court), (h) he gives notice to any of his creditors that he has suspended or that he is about to suspend payment of his debts.

Hong Kong courts have jurisdiction in bankruptcy proceedings if at time of act of bankruptcy debtor (a) was present in Hong Kong, (b) was ordinarily resident in Hong Kong or had place of residence in Hong Kong, (c) was carrying on business in Hong Kong personally or by means of agent or manager or (d) was member of firm or partnership which carried on business in Hong Kong. This nexus must be demonstrated when petition is presented.

Creditor shall not be entitled to present bankruptcy petition against debtor unless (a) debt owed by debtor to petitioning creditor or to two or more petitioning creditors is in aggregate at least HK$5,000, (b) debt is liquidated sum payable immediately or at some certain time in future, (c) act of bankruptcy relied on must have occurred within three months before presentation of petition, (d) debtor has requisite nexus with Hong Kong.

On Court making receiving order, Official Receiver is constituted receiver of assets of debtor and will take control of them. Assets do not vest until adjudication. Official Receiver may appoint special manager if satisfied that nature of debtor's business requires such appointment. General meeting of creditors must be held for purpose of considering whether proposal for composition and scheme of arrangement is to be accepted, to adjudicate debtor bankrupt, to appoint trustee and decide whether there should be committee of inspection. Trustee's function is to realize bankrupt's assets. Official Receiver or any other person may be appointed trustee.

Bankruptcy relates back to time of act of bankruptcy on which receiving order is based. All property will be available for distribution to creditors except (a) property held by bankrupt on trust for another person and (b) tools of trade of bankrupt, necessary clothing and bedding and that of his family not exceeding HK$3,000.

As general rule bankruptcy does not affect rights of secured creditors.

Claims are paid in following order or priority (a) preferential creditors (including employees claiming under Protection of Wages on Insolvency Fund and Crown), (b) ordinary creditors (dealt with pari passu), (c) creditors who have claims for interest in excess of 8%, (d) deferred claims (where married woman has been adjudicated bankrupt, her husband will not be entitled to any dividend until claims of other creditors have been met).

Bankrupt may at any time apply to court for discharge from bankruptcy. Application cannot be heard until after public examination. Trustee may make application for discharge. Trustee will make report

on bankrupt's affairs and conduct.

Official Receiver is permanent official appointed by Government with powers and duties defined by Ordinance.

See also Insolvency.

BILLS AND NOTES

Bills of Exchange Ordinance (Cap. 19) is substantially reproduction of English Bills of Exchange Act 1882 and Cheques Act 1957. As in England, rules of common law, save insofar as inconsistent with express provisions of Ordinance, continue to apply to bills of exchange, promissory notes and checks. Conflict of law rules substantially same as English rules.

[Bills of exchange (including checks) and promissory notes are regulated by Bills of Exchange Act, 1882, and Cheques Act 1957.

A bill is not invalid because it (a) is not dated, (b) does not specify the value given or that any value has been given therefor or (c) does not specify place where drawn or where payable.

Cheques *Bill of exchange drawn on a banker and payable on demand. However (a) checks are not accepted and therefore holder cannot sue banker on whom a check is drawn and (b) drawer is not discharged by holder's failure to present in due time unless he suffers damage and (c) under Acts a banker is protected in certain cases where wrong payment is made or an endorsement is unauthorized or forged and (d) drawer is under a duty of reasonable care towards banker in drawing check and (e) rules as to crossing only apply to checks.*

Days of Grace *Three days of grace no longer added to time of payment where bill not payable on demand (matter now governed by Banking and Financial Dealings Act 1971). Bill is due and payable on last day of time for payment, as fixed by bill unless it is a nonbusiness day when it is then due on succeeding business day. Nonbusiness day is (a) Sun., Sat., Good Friday, Christmas Day; (b) Bank holiday under Act; (c) day proclaimed by Crown as a public fast or thanksgiving; and (d) any day declared by order under Act as a nonbusiness day.*

Holder in Due Course *A person who takes a bill complete and regular on its face before it was overdue, without notice of previous dishonor, in good faith and for value and without notice of defect in title of person who negotiated it, is a holder in due course and holds the bill free of defects of title of prior parties and may enforce payment against all parties liable on the bill. One who derives title from a holder in due course and is not himself a party to any fraud or illegality affecting the bill has all the rights of holder in due course, although he may have notice of the prior defect. This does not apply to checks marked "not negotiable," to which the holder cannot give better title* than the person from whom he took it had. *Every party to a bill is deemed to have become a party thereto for value and each holder is prima facie deemed to be a holder in due course.*

***Presentment for acceptance** is necessary where bill (1) is payable after sight, (2) expressly stipulates it shall be presented for acceptance or (3) is payable elsewhere than at residence or place of business of drawee. If on presentment for acceptance it is not accepted within customary time (stated to be 24 hours) the presenter must treat it as dishonored by nonacceptance. These provisions do not apply to checks and notes.*

***Presentment for payment** must be made in case of bill not payable on demand on day it falls due and in case of bill payable on demand within reasonable time after issue or indorsement. Where bill is dishonored by nonacceptance, presentment for payment is not necessary.*

***Notice of dishonor** must be given, in case of dishonor by nonacceptance or nonpayment, to the drawer and each indorser. Any drawer or indorser to whom notice is not given is discharged unless notice is waived or otherwise dispensed with in accordance with the Act. Dishonored foreign bills must be noted and protested. There is no need to note and protest a foreign note as distinguished from a foreign bill.*

***Conflict of Laws** Where a bill drawn in one country is negotiated, accepted or payable in another, the rights, duties and liabilities of the parties are determined as follows: (1) Validity of the bill as regards requisites of form is determined by the law of the place of issue; validity of a supervening contract (e.g., acceptance, indorsement, etc.) is determined by the law of the place where such contract was made. (2) Interpretation of the drawing, indorsement or acceptance is determined by the law where the contract was made, provided that where an inland bill is indorsed in a foreign country the indorsement must, as regards the payer, be interpreted according to the law of the United Kingdom.]*

BILLS OF SALE

Bills of Sale Ordinance (Cap. 20) is substantially reproduction of English Bills of Sale Acts, 1878 to 1891. Bill of sale must be for sum of not less than HK$150, be duly attested and registered within seven days or, if executed out of Hong Kong, within seven days after time at which it would in course of post arrive in Hong Kong. Further, bill of sale will be void unless made in accordance with form specified in Ordinance. Registration must be renewed at least once every five years.

COLLATERAL SECURITY

See Pledges.

COMMERCIAL REGISTER

There is a requirement to register businesses and overseas corporations with a place of business in Hong Kong.

See also Corporations; Patents; Trademarks.

CONTRACTS

Hong Kong law of contract essentially follows that of England and in many respects English common law and equity applies.

See also Sales.

[Gratuitous promise even though made in writing is not enforceable unless it is made in deed under seal. Otherwise there must be agreement between parties intending to create legal relationship based upon offer and acceptance with consideration moving from promisee to promisor. Adequacy of consideration immaterial but there must be some benefit accruing to promisor.]

Applicable Law Same as under English law.

*[**Applicable Law** Interpretation and effect and rights and obligations of parties are governed (with certain exceptions) by law which parties agree or intend shall govern it or which they are presumed to have intended, known as the proper law of the contract. Law expressly stipulated will be proper law of contract provided selection is bona fide and there is no objection on grounds of public policy even where law has no real connection with contract. Where parties make no stipulation courts decide by considering contract as a whole and are guided by certain presumptions.]*

Excuses for Nonperformance Same as under English law.

*[**Excuses for Nonperformance** A contract which is not capable of performance when made is in general void. Doctrine of frustration operates to excuse further performance where (i) it appears from nature of contract and surrounding circumstances that parties have contracted on the basis that some fundamental thing or state of things will continue to exist or that some particular person will continue to be available or that some future event which forms the foundation of the contract will take place, and (ii) before breach performance becomes impossible or only possible in a very different way to that contemplated without default of either party or owing to a fundamental change of circumstances beyond control and original contemplation of parties. To excuse nonperformance impossibility must be in nature of a physical or legal one and not merely a relative impossibility, i.e., referable solely to the ability or circumstances of the promisor.*

Act of God or Queen's enemies may also excuse performance. Act of God is generally an extraordinary occurrence or circumstance which could not have been foreseen or which could not have been guarded against.

A statute may also render performance impossible,

which is sufficient excuse.]

Exemption Clauses See subhead Unfair Terms, infra.

Under Motor Vehicle Insurance (Third Party Risks) Ordinance (Cap. 272) and Employees Compensation Ordinance (Cap. 282) any condition in policy of insurance providing that liability shall be denied by reference to act or omission happening after event giving rise to claim shall be of no effect upon that claim.

Government Contracts Proceedings can be taken and enforced against Crown. Such proceedings are governed by Crown Proceedings Ordinance. (Cap. 300).

Infants Contracts Infancy is defense in respect to debts, damages or demand where jurisdiction for such claims falls within High Court or Small Claims Tribunal (jurisdiction in respect to claims not exceeding HK$15,000) save and except for (a) necessary goods and services for which infant must pay reasonable price (Sale of Goods Ordinance); (b) benefits of permanent nature other than for necessary goods and services unless avoided upon reaching majority or within reasonable time thereafter.

However, in District Court there is no exemption for infant from liability in respect to action for any debt, damages or demand for claim up to HK$60,000.

Privity Same as under English law. *See also* Assignments.

*[**Privity** Person not a party to contract cannot sue upon it even if it is for his benefit unless it is insurance policy of vendor of property and he is purchaser, or he is a principal suing on contract made for him by agent or contract constitutes a trust and person seeking to sue is beneficiary thereunder.*

***No action may be brought** in following cases, unless agreement or promise, or some note or memorandum thereof, be in writing and signed by party to be charged or someone by him lawfully authorized: (1) Whereby to charge a defendant on any special promise to answer for debt, default or miscarriage of another; (2) or on any contract for sale of lands or of any interest therein or concerning them or for any lease thereof for more than three years. (Statute of Frauds, 1677, §4; Law of Property Act 1925, §40).]*

Rescission Essentially same as under English law. See England Law Digest.

*[**Rescission** Contract may be rescinded at instance of party induced to enter it by a misrepresentation of facts made by other party. This is so, even if contract performed. Damages may be ordered by court in lieu of rescission and are also available in addition to rescission (or damages in lieu) where this representation is negligent or fraudulent.]*

Unfair Terms Pursuant to Control of Exemption Clauses Ordinance 1989 (Cap. 71), similar to English law except that limits and reasonableness of unfair terms provisions do not apply to international sup-ply contracts. Also, such provisions do not apply if Hong Kong law is law of contract only by choice of parties but will apply if contract term applies or purports to apply law of another territory in order to evade operation of Ordinance or if one party to contract dealt as consumer and was then habitually resident, and contract was essentially made, in Hong Kong.

Misrepresentation Ordinance (Cap. 284) deals with misrepresentations, whether fraudulent or innocent.

*[**Unfair Terms** Liability for death or personal injury through negligence cannot be restricted by contract. Liability for other damage through negligence can only be restricted by contract if reasonable. Consumer protected against unreasonable exclusion of liability clauses in written standard terms of business; consumer also protected against unreasonable indemnity clauses. Unfair terms provisions do not apply to international supply contracts unless one party consumer resident in England and essential steps necessary for contract were taken in England. Special provisions apply to international passengers. (Unfair Contract Terms Act 1977).]*

COPYRIGHT AND REGISTERED DESIGNS

Statute Copyright Act 1956 as amended by Design Copyright Act 1968 extends to HK by Copyright (Hong Kong) Orders 1972 and 1979.

Treaties Through UK, Berne Convention and Universal Copyright Convention extend to HK, hence convention countries enjoy copyright protection in HK.

Protection Law protects artistic, dramatic, musical and literary works, sound recordings, cinematograph films, television and sound broadcasts and published editions of works. No registration is required.

For artistic, dramatic, musical and literary works, copyright extends to reproducing, publishing, performing, broadcasting, retransmitting or adapting work. Monopoly shall subsist for 50 years from death of author or 50 years after first publication.

For films, copyright extends to copying, broadcasting or showing in public. Soundtrack associated with film is sound recording which is entitled to separate protection. Monopoly shall subsist for 50 years from first publication.

For television or sound broadcasts, copyright extends to copying or rebroadcasting. Monopoly shall subsist for 50 years from first publication.

For typographical arrangement, copyright extends to making reproduction of typographical arrangement by any photographic or similar process. Monopoly shall subsist for 50 years from first publication.

By 1987 Order in Council, UK Copyright (Computer Software) Amendment Act 1985 (merged into

UK Copyright, Designs and Patents Act 1988) was extended to HK. Under this Act, computer programs are protected as literary works.

Assignment must be in writing signed by or on behalf of assignor.

License granted by owner of copyright shall be binding upon every successor in title to his interest in copyright, except purchaser in good faith for valuable consideration and without notice (actual or constructive) of license or person deriving title from such purchaser.

Infringement Affidavit purporting to have been made by copyright owner before notary public and stating that (i) at time specified therein copyright subsisted in work or other subject matter; (ii) person named therein is owner of copyright in work or other subject matter; and (iii) copy of work or other subject matter exhibited to affidavit is true copy of work or other subject matter, shall be admitted without further proof in any proceedings under Ordinance.

Civil remedies including injunctions, seizure of goods, recovery of damages (including, where appropriate, damages on conversion basis), taking of accounts and discovery are available.

Criminal remedies are available under Copyright Ordinance by which any person who possesses, for purposes of trade or business, infringing copy of work or other subject matter in which copyright subsists is guilty of offense.

Enforcement of provisions under Copyright Ordinance is through Customs and Excise Department. Penalties shall be by way of fine as well as imprisonment.

Registered Designs

Statute United Kingdom Designs (Protection) Ordinance 1964.

Procedure No independent registration in HK is necessary as Ordinance extends like privileges and rights as though certificate of registration in UK had been issued with extension to HK.

Protection lasts for as long as UK registered design is in force.

Registered proprietor of design shall not be entitled to recover any damages in respect of any infringement of copyright in design from defendant who proves that at date of infringement he was not aware, nor had any reasonable means of making him aware, of existence of registration of design.

For design which has been industrially applied by manufacture of three-dimensional products in accordance therewith, term of copyright protection shall be for 15 years only from first publication or marketing.

Infringement In determining question of infringement, only shapes and configuration will be considered and not functions. Matter must be judged by eyes of inexpert customers. Not only articles may be put side-by-side for comparison but test of imperfect recollection also applies.

Civil remedies such as injunction, seizure of goods, damages and discovery are available.

[Registered Designs and Design Rights Where design of article comprises simply work of art, e.g. painting of vase, such works are protected by copyright for 50 years and even prevents three dimensional reproductions of it. If design is inventive, product may be patentable and therefore protected for 20 years.

Under Registered Designs Act 1949, as amended by Copyright, Designs and Patents Act 1988, new design may be registered affording 25 years protection (extended from 15 years). Design means "the features of shape, configuration, pattern or ornament applied to an article by any industrial process, being features which in the finished article appeal to and are judged by the eye, but does not include a method or principle of construction or features of shape or configuration of an article which are dictated solely by function which the article has to perform or are dependent upon the appearance of another article of which the article is intended by the author of the design to form an integral part." Design is not registerable if appearance of article is not material to whether or not someone buys it. There are special provisions where applications have been lodged for existing designs which would have been registerable before 1988 Act, but are no longer so as they are now under definition of unregistered design right.

Under above methods, protection was therefore not given to designs of purely functional nonartistic works. New design right introduced by Act now subsists in original (not common place) design of "any aspect of the shape or configuration (internal or external) of the whole or part of an article." As there is no reference to eye appeal, right applies to functional and aesthetic designs. Design right does not subsist in method of principle of construction (which may be patentable), features of shape or configuration of article which enable article to be connected to or placed in, around or against another article so that either article may perform its function or are dependent upon appearance of another article of which article is intended by designer to form integral part or surface decoration. However, design rights may subsist in such articles if they include special original design features.

Designer is first owner of design rights unless it is created by employee in course of his employment or commissioned, in which case right belongs respectively to employer or commissioner.

Design rights expire 15 years from year in which design was first recorded in design document or article was first made from design, whichever is first. However, if article is exploited commercially in first five years of that period, duration is ten years from first commercial exploitation.

Owner has exclusive right to reproduce design for commercial purposes. Owner's rights are infringed if someone copies designs or article, or knowingly deals with designs or articles which are in infringement.

Licenses of right are to be available to anyone to manufacture protected article during final five years of term.

Design right and copyright may subsist concurrently but if copyright protection is available, this method of protection must be used first. Design rights can subsist concurrently with registered design.

Design rights only apply to designs recorded or articles made after 1st Aug. 1988.]

CORPORATIONS

Companies Ordinance (Cap. 32) which regulates corporations is substantially based on UK Companies Act of 1948.

Any two or more persons (including bodies corporate) may form limited company. Apart from issuance of at least two shares, there is no prescribed minimum amount for issued or authorized share capital although normal minimum authorized share capital for private companies is HK$10,000.

Private company means company which by its Articles of Association restricts right to transfer its shares, limits number of shareholders to 50 and prohibits any invitation to public to subscribe for its shares or debentures. Company which does not impose such restrictions is public company. Public company may invite public to subscribe for its shares, usually by issue of prospectus. Name of limited company must end with word "limited" or its abbreviation "ltd."

Companies may be formed as limited company (liability of member limited by shares or guarantee) or unlimited company (liability of members unlimited). Unlimited company can be reregistered as limited company, but not vice versa.

Public company may choose to become listed company, defined in Companies Ordinance as company which has any shares listed on Hong Kong Stock Exchange. Stricter requirements are imposed on listed companies or companies which are member of groups of which listed company is member.

Listed company is also regulated by Listing Rules of Stock Exchange and by legislation such as Securities (Stock Exchange Listing) Rules and Securities (Disclosure of Interests) Ordinance. (Cap. 396). See subhead Registers, infra.

Securities (Insider Dealing) Ordinance 1990 prohibits insider dealing although it has not been made criminal offense.

Significant number of listed companies have, in recent years, re-domiciled in offshore jurisdictions. Listing Rules apply with modifications to these and other overseas issuers as they do to Hong Kong issuers.

Companies must register Memorandum of Association setting out name, address, registered office, objects, statement of liability of members and amount of company's authorized share capital with number and value of shares into which such capital is divided.

Objects of company are set out in Memorandum which is company's charter. Acts which do not come within scope of "objects clause" (or ancillary powers) are ultra vires. Powers of company formed on or after 31st Aug. 1984 shall include, unless excluded or modified, those set forth in Ordinance.

Companies almost invariably file Articles of Association which are rules governing internal regulation, duties of directors, rights of voting, etc. If articles not filed, statutory regulations known as "Table A" govern internal management. Applications for registrations of companies are made to Registrar of Companies to whom proposed Memorandum and Articles are submitted.

Prospectus Public company issuing prospectus (or if applicable, statement in lieu of prospectus) must set out particulars specified in ordinance and if applicable must comply with Stock Exchange and Securities and Futures Commission requirements. Copy of every such prospectus (or statement) signed by every named director or proposed director or by his agent authorized in writing must be duly delivered to Registrar as required by Ordinance. No prospectus may be issued (or shares or debentures allotted) until this has been done. Every prospectus must be in English language and contain Chinese translation. Registrar takes no responsibility as to contents of prospectus.

Reports Every year companies must file with Registrar annual return in requisite form signed by director and company secretary containing specified information such as names of members, details of directors, etc. If company has share capital, return must give particulars of its share capital including extent to which it is paid up. Public companies are required to file accounts. Overseas corporations which have place of business in Hong Kong need to deliver to Registrar for registration return of any alteration in prescribed particulars and, for public company equivalent corporations, accounts.

In addition to foregoing, company is required to register with Registrar changes in share capital, special resolutions, changes in directors, secretary, registered office etc.

Directors Bodies corporate can act as directors of another company provided latter is private company which is not member of group which includes listed company.

Secretary of company must, if individual, ordinarily reside in Hong Kong or, if body corporate, have registered office or place of business in Hong Kong.

Registers Company must maintain various registers (available for inspection) including registers of members, directors, debenture holders and charges.

Under Securities (Disclosure of Interests) Ordinance (Cap. 396) listed company must maintain register of substantial shareholders' interests in its shares (where interest including related parties exceeds 10% of share capital carrying voting rights) and of directors' interests including related parties in its shares and debentures and in those of associated companies. Such information is also to be supplied to Stock Exchange.

Registration of Mortgages Mortgages and charges falling within categories specified in Companies Ordinance shall, so far as any security is conferred thereby, be void against liquidator and any creditor of company unless prescribed particulars and relevant instrument are delivered to Registrar within five weeks after date of creation. Time is slightly extended for charges created out of Hong Kong comprising property situate outside Hong Kong.

Categories include charges to secure any issue of debentures; charges on land or any interest therein; charges on book debts; floating charges on company's undertaking or property; charges on ship or any share in ship; and charges on goodwill, on patent, or license under patent, on trademark or on copyright or license under copyright.

Control of company is generally vested in its directors. Ordinance obtains provisions on liability of directors.

Companies Ordinance and, where applicable, Listing Rules make provision for protection of minority shareholders including protection against oppression of minorities shareholders, maintenance of capital, restriction on distribution of profits and assets and disclosure of notifiable transactions.

Winding up *See* Insolvency.

Foreign corporations establishing place of business in Hong Kong are required to register under Ordinance.

Companies (Amendment) Ordinance 1991 introduced major changes based on 1985 UK Act regarding financial assistance by company for acquisition of its own shares and purchase of such shares and also restrictions on distributions. Listing Rules are relevant for listed companies.

See also Fraudulent Preference; Fraudulent Trading.

CUSTOMS

Hong Kong is generally perceived as free port although customs duties are levied on some imports. Rates applicable to relevant categories of goods are governed by Dutiable Commodities Ordinance. (Cap. 109).

DEEDS

In case of individuals, every deed must be signed, sealed and delivered by party to be bound or by his attorney and attested by at least one witness who must add to his signature his address and occupation or description. In case of companies, common seal must be used and attestation must be in accordance with company's Articles of Association.

Conveyancing and Property Ordinance (Cap. 279) states that any deed signed by individual shall be presumed to be sealed as such provided that document describes itself as deed or states that it has been sealed or bears any mark, impression or addition intended to be or to represent seal or position of seal. Further, where deed is executed by corporation in favor of person dealing with it, it will be deemed to have been duly executed if it purports to bear company seal affixed in presence of and attested by its secretary or other permanent officer of company and member of its board of directors or by two members of that board.

Person authorized by power of attorney to execute deed on behalf of corporation may execute deed by signing his own name or name of corporation and affixing his seal.

EXCHANGE CONTROL

There are no exchange control restrictions on transfer of funds into or out of Hong Kong.

EXECUTIONS

Judgment or order of Court, including judgments or awards of foreign courts or arbitrators enforceable in Hong Kong, may be enforced as follows:

1. Writs of Execution: (i) Writ of fieri facias—order to Court appointed officers to take possession of judgment debtor's goods and chattels of value to satisfy judgment and sell such goods at public auction and pay proceeds after deduction of costs of execution to judgment creditor. Property of company liable to seizure includes debentures; (ii) writ of possession—to enforce judgment or order giving possession of land; (iii) writ of delivery—to enforce judgment or order giving delivery of any goods; (iv) writ of sequestration—rarely used process of contempt in cases of disobedience of order or judgment by judgment debtor permitting property to be seized until judgment debtor has purged his contempt and complied with original order.

Execution can be issued to enforce payment of any money or costs by Crown, any government department or officer of Crown.

2. Garnishment Judgment creditor who has obtained judgment or order for at least HK$1,000 against judgment debtor who is owed any debt or some other sum by third party (garnishee) may seek order that such sum be paid directly to creditor in full or partial satisfaction of judgment or order.

Application is made ex parte by affidavit. Garnishee is required to attend before Court to show cause why such sum should not be paid to judgment creditor. If garnishee does not dispute debt, Court will make order absolute which can be enforced in same manner as any other order for payment of money. If liability is disputed, Court will determine issue summarily or order that any question necessary for determining liability of garnishee be tried.

See Attachment.

3. Examination of judgment debtor Court may on application of judgment creditor order judgment debtor to attend before Court and be orally examined on oath as to (1) what debts he may have owing to him (2) what means he has of satisfying judgment or order.

If judgment debtor is body corporate, director or other officer can be ordered to attend and be asked same questions.

Court may order judgment debtor to produce any relevant books or documents.

Failure to comply with order to attend court, refusal to make full disclosure or willful disposal of assets to avoid satisfying judgment amount is contempt punishable by committal to prison or prohibition from leaving Hong Kong until debt is satisfied.

4. Charging Order Judgment creditor may apply ex parte on notice for order imposing charge over any property of judgment debtor or property in respect of which judgment debtor has interest to secure payment.

Interest includes interest held by debtor beneficially or under trust.

Property includes: (1) land; (2) securities including (a) government stock, (b) stock of any body incorporated in Hong Kong or outside Hong Kong being stock registered in register kept in Hong Kong, (c) units of any unit trust in respect of which register of unit holders is kept in Hong Kong; (3) funds in Court.

Charge may be extended to cover dividends, interest, other distributions or bonus issues.

Court will take into account personal circumstances of debtor and whether any other creditor of debtor will be unduly prejudiced by such order.

Court will, if satisfied that sums are owned to judgment creditor, make order to show cause why charging order should not be granted. On further consideration of matter, Court will either make order absolute, with or without modification, or discharge it.

Court has power to order enforcement of charging order by sale of property charged.

5. Stop Notice Order obtainable by person claiming to be beneficially entitled to interest in any securities in respect of which Charging Order can be obtained may seek order prohibiting judgment debtor from disposing of or dealing with securities without notice to judgment creditor of proposed transfer or payment. Similarly Court may make order prohibiting transfer of or dealing with securities or payment out of funds in Court.

6. Appointment of Receiver Court has power to appoint receiver by way of equitable execution which shall operate in relation to all legal estates and interests in land of judgment debtor.

7. Injunctions High Court may grant Interlocutory or final injunction during course of proceedings or following judgment to restrain party to proceedings whether or not domiciled, resident or present in jurisdiction, from removing from jurisdiction of High Court or otherwise prohibiting removal of assets within jurisdiction.

Court is also empowered to grant injunction to prevent any threatened or apprehended waste or trespass.

Court has power to order delivery up of goods and restrain disposal of goods, property and assets of debtor or judgment debtor.

8. Committal Court has power to punish contempt by committal to imprisonment.

9. Bankruptcy; Winding-up of Company *See* Insolvency.

10. Prohibition Order Court, if satisfied that person owing money or subject to monetary judgment or order will leave Hong Kong thereby obstructing or delaying satisfaction of judgment, may make order prohibiting that person from leaving Hong Kong. Order renewable after one month for total of three months. Order is served on Director of Immigration and Commissioner for Police. Judgment debtor is liable to arrest and to be brought before Court in event he seeks to leave Hong Kong. Court can, on application, discharge order or impose such terms as it considers fit including ordering debtor to pay amount into Court.

11. Exemptions from Execution Tools and equipment necessary for debtor's employment, clothing, bedding, furniture and household equipment necessary for basic needs of debtor and his family may not be seized.

Chattels in which judgment debtor has equitable interest cannot be seized. Property owned by co-owners cannot be seized on behalf of third party unless two persons have separate and different interests in chattel in which case judgment debtor's interest only can be sold. Property on hire cannot be seized.

Person who claims ownership or interest in property seized on execution can intervene and apply to Court to determine any question relating to ownership.

FOREIGN CORPORATIONS

See Corporations.

FOREIGN EXCHANGE

No restrictions on foreign exchange. Local dollar is pegged to US dollar.

FOREIGN INVESTMENT

Generally no restrictions on foreign investment.

FRAUDS, STATUTE OF

In Hong Kong all that remains of UK Statute of Frauds Act is provision relating to formalities for contracts for sale of land. This provision is found in § 3 of Conveyancing and Property Ordinance. (Cap. 219).

Conveyance of property to any person other than bona fide purchaser for value without notice made with intent to defraud creditors is voidable at instance of any person thereby prejudiced.

Voluntary disposition of land made with intent to defraud subsequent purchaser is voidable at instance of such purchaser.

Voluntary settlements, although not fraudulent, are voidable under certain circumstances. (Bankruptcy Ordinance Cap. 6).

FRAUDULENT PREFERENCE

By Companies Ordinance any conveyance, mortgage, delivery of goods, payment, execution or other act relating to property made or done by company within six months before commencement of its winding up which for individual would be fraudulent preference shall, if company is wound up, be deemed fraudulent preference of its creditors and be invalid accordingly. Any conveyance or assignment by company of all its property to trustees for benefit of all its creditors shall be void. Where anything made or done is void as fraudulent preference of person interested in property mortgaged or charged to secure company's debt, person so preferred shall be subject to same liabilities, and have same rights, as if he had undertaken to be personally liable as surety for debt to extent of charge in property or value of his interest, whichever is less.

FRAUDULENT TRADING

Companies Ordinance provides that if in course of winding up company it appears that any business of company has been carried on with intent to defraud creditors or for any fraudulent purpose, Court may declare that any person knowingly party shall be personally responsible without limitation of liability for all debts or other liabilities of company as Court may direct.

GARNISHMENT

See Executions.

IMMIGRATION

Law relating to immigration and deportation is set out in Immigration Ordinance. (Cap. 115). Hong Kong permanent resident enjoys right of abode in Hong Kong, that is to say he has right (a) to land in Hong Kong; (b) not to have condition of stay imposed upon him; (c) not to have deportation order made against him; (d) not to have removal order made against him.

Immigrant is person not Hong Kong permanent resident. Hong Kong permanent resident is: (1) Any person wholly or partly of Chinese race who has at any time been ordinarily resident in Hong Kong for continuous period of not less than seven years. (2)(A) Any person who is British Dependent Territories citizen and who has connection with Hong Kong (there are detailed provisions on whether person has connection with Hong Kong); (B) Any person who is British Dependent Territories citizen who has at any time been married to person specified in subparagraph (A). (3) Any person who is Commonwealth citizen and who immediately before 1st Jan. 1983 had right to land in Hong Kong by virtue of §8(1)(a) of Ordinance as then in force.

Resident British Citizen—British citizen who has at any time been ordinarily resident in Hong Kong for continuous period of not less than seven years.

Resident UK belonger—UK belonger who was at any time before 1st Jan. 1983 ordinarily resident in Hong Kong for continuous period of not less than seven years.

Rights enjoyed by Resident British Citizen and Resident UK belonger are similar to those enjoyed by permanent resident except that deportation orders may be imposed against them.

Under new visa regulations introduced in mid-Sept. 1992, persons from many parts of world are allowed to visit Hong Kong for up to three months without visa.

Persons having right of abode or right to land in Hong Kong do not require visa to work in Hong Kong. Similarly, British citizens do not require such visa.

Persons having no right of abode or right to land in Hong Kong and who are not British citizens must obtain visa to come to Hong Kong for employment or investment.

INDUSTRIAL PROPERTY RIGHTS

See Copyright; Trademarks; Patents.

INSOLVENCY

Insolvency law is contained in Companies Ordinance, Companies (Winding Up) Rules and Bankruptcy Ordinance. Companies Ordinance provides for application of bankruptcy law in winding up companies. Companies incorporated in Hong Kong can be placed in either voluntary liquidation or compulsory liquidation by order of Court. Voluntary liquidation can be either members voluntary liquidation or creditors voluntary liquidation.

Voluntary liquidation may be commenced by resolution of directors supported by statutory declaration that company cannot by reason of its liabilities continue its business.

Basis on which company can be placed in voluntary liquidation is same for both members voluntary and creditors voluntary winding up. Company may be placed in voluntary liquidation if (a) Memorandum and Articles of Association provide for company to exist for specified duration and that has expired, (b) shareholders resolve by special resolution (75 percentof those who attend personally or by proxy) to wind up company, (c) shareholders resolve by special resolution that company cannot by reason of its liabilities continue its business and it is advisable to wind it up.

In members voluntary liquidation declaration of solvency must be made and special resolution is required. Liquidator must be appointed at same time as special resolution is passed.

Liquidator will realize assets of company and complete administration and pay dividend. Assets do not vest in liquidator; they remain assets of company. Liquidator acts as agent of company and is in fiduciary position to company and in compulsory liquidation is officer of Court.

Compulsory liquidation is commenced when petition is filed. Court will hear petition and make winding up order if appropriate. Official Receiver will be appointed as Provisional Liquidator and convene first meeting of creditors and contributories (contributory has been held to be member holding partially or fully paid shares). First meeting of creditors and contributories will vote on appointment of liquidator and whether or not to appoint committee of inspection.

Company may be placed into compulsory liquidation if (a) shareholders resolve by special resolution to wind company up, (b) company suspends its business within one year of incorporation or suspends its business for one year, (c) number of shareholders is reduced below two, (d) company is unable to pay its debts, (e) Memorandum and Articles of Association of company provide that company be wound up on certain event occurring and that event occurs, (f) it is just and equitable for company to be wound up. Registrar of Companies may petition for winding up if (a) company is being carried on for unlawful purpose or for any lawful purpose but which it cannot carry out, (b) in last six months company has not had two directors or secretary (c) company has persistently failed to pay statutory fees or been in breach of Companies Ordinance.

At any time after petition has been presented, Court may make order staying legal proceedings commenced against company.

After winding up order is made Official Receiver as Provisional Liquidator takes possession and control of company's property. After winding up order has been made, statement of affairs must be made by director of company. Statement of affairs will include (a) particulars of assets and liability, (b) list of secured and nonsecured creditors, (c) particulars of securities.

Any transfer or mortgage of property to creditor made within six months prior to commencement of winding up which if done by individual would be fraudulent preference will be invalid as fraudulent preference. *See* Fraudulent Preference.

If in course of liquidation it appears that any business of company has been carried on with intent to defraud creditors of company or creditors of any other person or for any fraudulent purpose, persons who were knowingly parties can be held responsible for all or any of company's debts without limitation. *See* Fraudulent Trading.

Where company is being wound up, floating charge on undertaking or property of company created within 12 months of commencement of winding up shall, unless proved that company was solvent immediately after charge created, be invalid except to cash amount paid to company at or after creation of and in consideration for charge together with prescribed interest.

Preferential claims of unsecured creditors are paid before ordinary creditors. Preferential claims include certain employees' claims and Crown claims which have become due and payable within 12 months before commencement of winding up. Ordinary creditors' claims are dealt with pari passu. *See* Bankruptcy.

If debt did not specifically provide for rate of interest, interest may be recovered at rate of 8% per annum from time debt was repayable up to date of winding up order.

Company incorporated outside Hong Kong whether or not registered as foreign corporation and whether or not carrying on business in Hong Kong may be wound up in Hong Kong if (a) company has been dissolved or ceased to carry on business, (b) it is unable to pay its debts, (c) it is just and equitable that it be wound up.

Most provisions relating to winding up of companies in Hong Kong apply to foreign companies wound up in Hong Kong.

See also Bankruptcy.

INTEREST

Interest can be charged only if agreed between parties.

Claim for interest can be made in any action at such rate and for such period as may have been agreed. In absence of any contractual entitlement for interest, interest is recoverable generally from date of issue of proceedings at rates fixed by Court from time to time.

It is offense to lend or offer to lend money at effective rate of interest which exceeds 60 percent per annum. No agreement for repayment of loan or interest where rate exceeds 60 percent per annum is enforceable. Court may reopen loan transactions if interest is extortionate. Loan transaction is presumed to be extortionate if effective rate of interest exceeds 48 percent.

JUDGMENTS

Monetary judgments, awards and orders of Court can be enforced in prescribed manner—*See* Executions.

Judgment can be entered if defendant fails to acknowledge service, file defense or comply with Court Order.

Summary judgment may be granted if Court is satisfied upon hearing affidavit evidence that there is no defense or no issue which should be tried at trial with oral evidence.

Enforcement of Foreign Judgments Judgments of some reciprocating Commonwealth and foreign countries can be registered and enforced in Hong Kong as if judgments of Hong Kong Courts if: (1) judgment is final and conclusive and not interlocutory or default judgment and no appeal lies against it or is still pending; (2) judgment is for sum of money not being sum payable in respect of taxes or like charges or fine or penalty; (3) bringing of proceedings in overseas court was not contrary to agreement under which any dispute would be settled otherwise than by proceedings in that foreign court; (4) party against whom judgment was given, brought or

agreed to bringing of proceedings in overseas court and counterclaimed or otherwise submitted to jurisdiction of overseas court.

Party will not be regarded as having submitted to jurisdiction of overseas court if he appeared only to (1) contest jurisdiction of court; (2) seek dismissal or stay of proceedings on grounds that dispute should be submitted to arbitration or determination of courts in another country; (3) protect or obtain release of property seized or threatened to be seized in proceedings.

No proceedings may be brought by party in Hong Kong on cause of action in respect of which judgment has been given in his favor in proceedings between same parties in court of overseas country unless that judgment is not enforceable or entitled to recognition in Hong Kong.

Application to register judgment is made ex parte on affidavit within six years of date of judgment or, if appeal, last judgment. Judgment, if registered, is enforceable in same manner as judgment of Hong Kong Court.

Registration of judgment may be set aside if Court is satisfied (1) judgment is not judgment to which provisions apply, (2) courts of country of original court had no jurisdiction, (3) judgment debtor did not receive notice of proceedings in sufficient time to enable him to defend action and did not appear, (4) judgment was obtained by fraud, (5) enforcement of judgment is contrary to public policy in Hong Kong, (6) rights of judgment are not vested in person by whom application for registration is made, (7) subject matter of proceedings was immovable property outside country of original court, (8) judgment debtor was person entitled to immunity in country of original court and did not submit to jurisdiction of that court.

Reciprocal Enforcement of Maintenance Orders Maintenance Orders made in some reciprocating Commonwealth countries may be registered in Hong Kong if it appears that person to make payment under Order was residing in Hong Kong; Order may be enforced as judgment made in District Court of Hong Kong subject to Court's entitlement to refuse to confirm Order if payer establishes any defense he may have raised in proceedings in which Order was made, or confirm Order or made such alterations as it thinks reasonable.

Registered Order is enforceable as civil debt. Court has power to vary registered Order.

Judgments of nonreciprocating jurisdictions cannot be registered but if final can be sued upon and may be relied upon in such proceedings.

LABOR RELATIONS

Individual rights principally governed by Employment Ordinance. (Cap. 57). Any term in contract of employment purporting to reduce employee's benefit under ordinance is void.

Following Employment (Amendment) Ordinance 1990, Employment Ordinance now applies to all employees but there are limits on amounts payable.

Labor Tribunal deals with disputes.

In absence of contractual provision, contract of employment is deemed to be contract for one month renewable from month to month determinable on one month's notice or payment of money in lieu.

Employer entitled to dismiss summarily if employee willfully disobeys lawful or reasonable order; misconducts himself, such conduct being inconsistent with due and faithful discharge of his duty; guilty of fraud or dishonesty; or habitually neglectful of duties; or for any other common law ground entitling determination without notice.

Damages for wrongful termination of contract of such sum as is equal to amount of wages that would have accrued during period of notice.

Employee may terminate without notice on grounds including fear of physical danger by violence or disease not contemplated by employment; being permanently unfit; subjected to ill-treatment by employer.

Female employees employed for 26 weeks are entitled to maternity leave of four weeks before and six weeks after confinement and if employed for more than 40 weeks, paid maternity leave. Employer is not permitted to pay money in lieu of maternity leave.

Employment of pregnant woman employed for period of 12 weeks or more cannot be terminated unless she fails to give requisite notice of pregnancy.

Employee is entitled to be member of union. Employers are prohibited from preventing exercise of union activities, discriminating against union member when offering employment and terminating employment because of union membership.

Wages are to be paid directly to employee in legal tender.

Employees employed under continuous contract of employment are entitled to: (1) end of year payment equal to one month's salary or proportionate to period of year worked, if such payment is term of contract of employment; (2) sickness allowance, if employed for one month or more, accruing at rate of two days for each completed month of employment in first 12 months and thereafter four paid days each month to cumulative total of 120 days; (3) paid leave for public holidays, at least one rest day per week and not less than seven days holidays.

Subject as provided, there is entitlement to severance pay if employee employed for continuous period of not less than 24 months, if laid off or dismissed by reason of redundancy, i.e. employer has ceased to carry on business for which employee was employed or requirement of business for employees to carry out work of particular kind has ceased or diminished. Long service payment provisions may be applicable if no liability for severance payment.

Employer is liable to pay compensation for: (a) personal injury by accident or contraction of occupational disease resulting in total or partial incapacity or (b) death arising out of or in course of employment.

Employer not entitled to employ employee unless there is in force in relation to such employee policy of insurance issued by insurer for full amount of liability of employer for any injury to such employee by accident arising out of or in course of his employment.

LIENS

Lien is legal right entitling person in possession of chattels to retain them until all claims and accounts of person in possession against owner of chattels for services rendered or monies spent or work carried out on property of other has been satisfied.

Lien can be (1) general, i.e. common law right arising from general usage or by express agreement entitling person in possession to retain goods until all claims and accounts of person in possession against owner are satisfied (e.g. solicitor's entitlement to retain client's papers until discharge of all sums due); (2) particular, i.e. right at common law to retain goods in respect of which charges have been incurred until those charges are paid (e.g. carrier's right to retain goods in respect of which freight remains unpaid).

Lien is unassignable personal right which lasts for as long as possession of goods persists. It is defense not right of action. There is no entitlement of sale unless provided for by statute.

Lien is lost by (1) tender of payment, (2) abandonment, (3) taking alternative security, (4) loss of possession and (5) in cases of liquidation, receivership and bankruptcy where lien had not fully taken effect at relevant time.

Express entitlement in Sale of Goods Ordinance for unpaid seller, i.e. one to whom full price has not been paid or tendered, including seller's agent to whom bill of lading has been endorsed, to exercise lien until payment notwithstanding that title may have passed to buyer. There is limited right or resale where property has not passed from unpaid seller. *See* Sales.

Lien is terminated when (a) unpaid seller delivers goods to carrier or other bailee for purpose of transmission to buyer without reserving right of disposal, (b) buyer or agent lawfully obtains possession of goods, (c) by waiver.

LIMITATION OF ACTIONS

Governed by Limitation Ordinance. (Cap. 347).

Actions in contract or tort or to enforce award must be brought within six years from date on which cause of action accrued.

Claims for or in respect of land including claims to secure land or money secured by mortgage must be brought within 12 years. Crown is entitled to bring any action in respect of land at any time prior to expiration of 60 years from date on which right of action accrued.

Claims based on fraud or relief from mistake or in circumstances of concealment by defendant of any fact relevant to plaintiff's right of action must be brought within six year of discovery of fraud, mistake or concealment or time when such fraud, mistake or concealment could with reasonable diligence have been discovered. However, no action can be brought to recover property or set aside any transaction where innocent third party has acquired property for valuable consideration since fraud, concealment or transaction took place.

Limitation period in respect of right of action accruing to person under disability is extended to six years from date when person ceased to be under disability or died whichever event first occurred.

LIMITED PARTNERSHIPS

See Partnerships.

NEGOTIABLE INSTRUMENTS

See Bills and Notes.

NOTARIES PUBLIC

Notaries exercise functions in Hong Kong and are governed by Legal Practitioners Ordinance (Cap. 159) which has same regulations as under English law.

[Applications for appointment as notary public for this country must be made at the Court of Faculties: The Sanctuary, Westminster. Notarial Faculties for . . . are granted: (1) After service with a notary for five years; (2) to solicitors, where the applicant can show, by memorial to the Master of the Faculties, the need for the appointment.]

PARTNERSHIPS

There are either ordinary partnerships (Partnership Ordinance—Cap. 38) or limited ones (Limited Partnerships Ordinance—Cap. 37). Partnership Ordinance is based on UK Partnership Act of 1890 and Limited Partnership Ordinance is based on UK Limited Partnership Act of 1907. Law is almost identical to English law.

In ordinary partnership each partner impliedly confers upon his co-partners authority to incur debts on behalf of partnership to bind all partners. Limited partnerships are very rare; limited partner's liability is restricted to amount of his capital.

Partnership firm has no legal personality distinct from members composing it but partners can sue and are liable to be sued in their firm name.

Under Companies Ordinance, permitted number of partners shall be not more than 20 but with no restriction for solicitors, accountants and stockbrokers partnerships.

PATENTS

Statute Registration of United Kingdom Patents Ordinance 1979.

Treaties Paris Convention (International Union) 1883-1967 (effective for Hong Kong as from 16th Nov., 1977), Patent Cooperation Treat 1970 (effective for Hong Kong as from 15th Apr., 1981). There is no independent patent granting system in Hong Kong.

Procedure To acquire protection under Registration of Patents Ordinance, once British patent or European patent designating UK has been obtained, grantee must apply for its reregistration in HK within five years of grant. Application must be accompanied by (1) certificate from British Controller—General of Patents, Design and Trade Marks giving full particulars of grant, (2) certified copy of specification together with drawings (if any) relating to patent, (3) statutory declaration setting out interest and title of applicant, (4) Authorization of Agent, (5) in case of patent specification not in English, certified copy of English translation.

Upon payment of prescribed fees and after application is advertised in Hong Kong Government Gazette, Certificate of Registration will be granted.

Protection Reregistration in HK conveys same protection as for UK or European patentees and remains in force for so long as patent shall be maintained.

Assignment/license of patent or patent application should be recorded in order to be effective against third parties.

Infringement Patent is infringed if anyone without consent of proprietor makes, disposes of, offers to dispose of, uses or imports any items including items embodying patent process and keeps any such items whether for disposal or otherwise as well as uses invention process.

Usual remedies available are injunction, damages, seizure of goods and discovery.

PLEDGES

Same as under England Law Digest.

[A pledge of personal chattels is the transfer by delivery of immediate possession thereof by way of security for an advance, whether past or present, the pledger remaining the owner of the chattel but the pledgee acquiring a right to sell (but not to foreclose) if the advance be not repaid on the due date.]

POWER OF ATTORNEY

See Absentees.

PRINCIPAL AND AGENT

Common law rules apply. In general principal is responsible for acts of his duly authorized agent. Agent acting for undisclosed principal is personally liable. Agent acting outside his authority is liable on action for breach of warrant of authority.

RECEIVERS

See Executions; Bankruptcy; Insolvency.

SALES

Sale of Goods Ordinance (Cap. 26) substantially reproduces UK 1893 Act. Ordinance is codification of law on subject and deals with formalities of contract, ascertainment of price, implied undertakings, sale by sample, rights of unpaid sellers, actions for breach of contract and so on.

Contract of sale may be made in writing or by word of mouth, or partly in writing and partly by word of mouth, or may be implied from conduct of parties. Contract for sales of goods is defined as contract whereby seller transfers or agrees to transfer property in goods to buyer for money consideration called price. Contract may be absolute or conditional.

Unless expressly stipulated, time of payment is not deemed to be of essence. Whether any other stipulation as to time is of essence or not depends on terms of contract.

Implied terms include: (1) seller has right to sell goods, (2) in sales by description, goods will correspond with description, (3) for goods sold in course of business, goods are of merchantable quality but not for defects specifically drawn to buyer's attention or if buyer examines goods prior to making contract, as regards defects inspection ought to have revealed, (4) if buyer makes known purpose for which goods bought, goods are reasonable fit for that purpose except where buyer does not or it is unreasonable for him to rely on seller's skill and judgment, (5) in sale of sample, bulk will correspond with sample in quality; buyer shall have reasonable op-portunity to compare bulk with sample and goods are free from defects rendering them unmerchantable which would not be apparent on reasonable examination of sample, (6) goods are free from any charge or encumbrance not disclosed or known to buyer before contract made and buyer will have quiet enjoyment subject to any charge which seller has disclosed.

Unpaid seller entitled to withhold delivery and exercise lien if property has not passed to buyer. *See* Liens.

Remedies If title has passed and buyer has not paid, seller entitled to bring actions for price.

If buyer does not accept and pay for goods, seller can claim estimated loss directly resulting from refusal to accept. Measure of damages is usually difference between contract price and market or current price at time goods ought to have been accepted or if no time for acceptance stipulated, at time of neglect or refusal to accept.

Buyer entitled to bring action for damages for nondelivery. Measure of damages is difference between contract and market or current price at time of delivery.

Court can order specific performance of contract.

Seller may be liable for rescission and/or damages in event of misrepresentation. *See* Contracts, subhead Misrepresentation Ordinance.

Provisions seeking to exclude liability for breach of contract or negligence not prohibited by statute or contained in international supply contract will only be upheld to extent that they are reasonable. (Control of Exemption Clauses Ordinance 1989). *See* contract, subhead Unfair Terms.

See also Contract; Trade Descriptions.

SHIPPING

Admiralty jurisdiction is exercised by High Court.

Navigation Main statutes governing shipping and navigation are English Merchant Shipping Acts as applied to Hong Kong and Hong Kong Merchant Shipping Ordinance and Merchant Shipping (Safety) Ordinance and subsidiary legislation. Regulations made under Merchant Shipping (Safety) Ordinance and subsidiary legislation. Regulations made under Merchant Shipping (Safety) Ordinance implement International Convention for Safety of Life at Sea 1974 and International Convention on Load Lines 1966. These Ordinances deal with seaworthiness, safety, lifesaving appliances, fire appliances and protection, signals of distress and prevention of collision, load lines, certification, discipline and welfare of master, officer and crew, accidents, marine courts, tonnage measurement, construction, survey and safety certificates, etc.

Registration By coming into force of Merchant

Shipping (Registration) Ordinance in Dec. 1990, independent Hong Kong Shipping Registry was established. Ordinance makes provision for registration of ships and mortgages in Hong Kong. Previously ship and mortgage registrations in Hong Kong were governed by English Merchant Shipping Acts as applied to Hong Kong. Under and subject to provisions of Merchant Shipping (Registration) Ordinance, ship is registrable if (i) majority interest is owned by one or more qualified person or persons, or (ii) it is operated under demise charter by body corporate being qualified person. "Qualified person" means any of (i) Hong Kong resident, (ii) Hong Kong incorporated company, and (iii) overseas company registered under Part XI of Companies Ordinance. Demise charter registration has been introduced. When survey cannot be carried out in time, provisional certificate of registry can be obtained pending completion of survey and issuance of certificate of registry. With provisional registration, ship can commence trading immediately and mortgages can be registered. Ships on Hong Kong register will be British ships and can continue to enjoy those right and privileges until 30th June 1997.

Crew Previous nationality restrictions for ranks of master, chief mate and chief engineer have been removed. There are no nationality or residence requirements for master and crew serving on Hong Kong registered foreign-going ships. Manning scale and certificate requirement in respect of officers serving on various categories of ships are governed by Merchant Shipping (Certification of Officers) Regulations 1990.

Merchant Shipping (Recruitment of Seamen) Ordinance makes provisions for control of recruiting, engagement and supply of seamen for service on foreign-going ships. Except with permission of Superintendent of Seamen's Recruiting Office, recruitment of such seamen must be at or through Seamen's Recruiting Office or, subject to Ordinance, by licensed company or Royal Fleet Auxiliary recruiting officer.

Pilotage Pilotage Ordinance stipulates for compulsory pilotage by licensed pilots except certain exempted ships, e.g. government ships, vessels engaging in salvage operation, passenger ferries between Hong Kong, Macao and China within river trade limits and other vessels exempted by Pilotage Authority.

Port Control Control of vessels, port facilities, dues and clearance, etc. are governed by Shipping and Port Control Ordinance.

Pollution English Prevention of Oil Pollution Act 1971 and Dumping at Sea Act 1974 have been extended to apply to Hong Kong. Under Shipping and Port Control Ordinance, it is offense for vessel to discharge oil or mixture containing oil in Hong Kong waters unless falling within defense under Ordinance (i) securing safety of vessel, (ii) preventing damage to vessel or its cargo, or (iii) saving life. Emission of smoke in such quantity as to be nuisance by vessels in Hong Kong waters is offense.

Carriage of Goods by Sea English Carriage of Goods by Sea Act 1971 has been extended to apply in Hong Kong.

Liens Maritime liens recognized under English law are applicable in Hong Kong.

STATUTE OF FRAUDS

See Frauds, Statute of.

STATUTORY DECLARATIONS

See Affidavits and Statutory Declarations.

TRADE DESCRIPTIONS

Trade Descriptions Ordinance (Cap. 362) prohibits false trade descriptions, false marks and misstatements in respect of goods provided in course of trade; confers power to require information or instructions relating to goods to be marked on or to accompany goods or to be included in advertisements; restates law relating to forgery of trademarks.

Enforcement of provisions under Ordinance is through Customs and Excise Department.

Remedy shall be by way of criminal prosecution by Crown. Complainants may institute separate civil proceedings.

TRADEMARKS

Statutes Trade Marks Ordinance (Cap. 43) and Rules follow UK counterparts closely. Enactment of Trade Marks (Amendment) Ordinance 1991, which came into operation in Mar. 1992, expanded existing systems of registration to provide for registration of trademarks for services in addition to those for goods.

Treaties Hong Kong, though UK, has acceded to Paris Convention. Convention priority may be claimed for applications filed within six months from first convention application.

Trademark is mark used or proposed to be used in relation to goods or services for purpose of indicating, or so as to indicate, connection in course of trade between goods or services and some person having right either as proprietor or as registered user to use mark, whether with or without indication of identity of that person. Trademark may be device, name, signature, word, letter, numeral or any combination thereof.

As in UK, register is divided into two parts, viz. A and B. Trademark can only be registered if it is adapted to distinguish or is capable of distinguishing goods or services of owner from those of another person.

To be registrable in Part A, mark must contain or consist of at least one of following particulars (1) name of company, individual or firm represented in special or particular manner; (2) signature (except in Chinese characters) of applicant; (3) invented word or words; (4) word or words not descriptive of goods or services for which mark is used and not geographical name or surname; (5) any other distinctive mark.

In some cases mark which does not appear, on face of it, to be inherently distinctive can nevertheless be registered in Part B. In determining whether trademark is capable of distinguishing goods or services as aforesaid, Registrar may have regard to extent to which (a) trademark is inherently capable of distinguishing goods or services and/or (b) by reasons of use of trademark or of any other circumstances, trademark is in fact capable of distinguishing as aforesaid.

Trademark may be registered in Part B notwithstanding any registration in Part A or vice versa (subject of course to compliance with respective registrability requirements as stated above) in name of same proprietor of same trade mark or any part of parts thereof.

Protection Trademark when registered is initially valid for seven years and can thereafter by renewed indefinitely for successive periods of 14 years each.

Assignment of trademark may be with or without goodwill of business concerned. In case of assignment without goodwill, it must be recorded with Trade Marks Registry within six months from date of assignment.

Associated marks must always be assigned as whole and not separately.

Under new Trade Marks Rules, assignee of pending application is to be treated as applicant for registration where assignor also assigns registered mark or marks, one of more of which relates to (i) same goods or (ii) same description of goods, or (iii) services or description of services associated with goods or goods of that description.

Infringement Civil remedies of damages, injunction, seizure of goods and discovery apply. As regards action in respect of marks registered under: (1) Part A of register: plaintiff has only to prove (a) his mark is registered and (b) defendant uses mark identical or so nearly resembling it as to be likely to deceive or cause confusion. (2) Part B of register: no injunction or other relief shall be granted to plaintiff if defendant establishes that use of which plaintiff complains is not likely to deceive or cause confusion.

Common Law Rights Common law tortious action of passing-off is available if trademark owner (whether registered or not) can prove (1) trade reputation; (2) infringer has used substantially confusing similar mark; (3) confusion and/or deception has been caused as result of such use and (4) damage is likely or has occurred.

TREATIES

Being dependent territory of UK, Hong Kong lacks full international personality to enter into treaties. Normally international treaty is entered into by government of UK and, if desired, extended to Hong Kong. Examples of treaties extended to Hong Kong include International Covenant on Civil and Political Rights, Berne Convention on copyright, Universal Copyright Convention and Geneva Convention on the Execution of Foreign Arbitral Awards.

As far as external commercial relations are concerned, Governor has been formally entrusted with executive authority to conclude and implement trade agreements with states, regions and international organizations. By way of example, Hong Kong is separate contracting party to General Agreement on Tariffs and Trade (GATT) and to Multi-Fiber Arrangement (MFA).

As from 1st July 1997, Hong Kong Special Administrative Region is empowered by Basic Law and using name "Hong Kong, China" to maintain and develop relations and conclude and implement agreements with foreign states and regions and relevant international organizations in areas such as economic, trade, financial and monetary, sports and communications fields.

Financial Institutions

As the financial backbone of Chinese East Asia and a world-class international financial center, Hong Kong boasts banks and other financial institutions that are among the most sophisticated and highly developed in the world. The colony's success in this arena can be attributed to its fortuitous geographic location, exceptional communications and other business infrastructure, free-market principles that reduce government interference and limit taxes, and its basic political neutrality. Hong Kong is the major conduit for trade to and from the People's Republic of China (PRC). The premier financial center in Southeast Asia, it offers international financial services to operators throughout the region regardless of country of origin.

Hong Kong ranks between third and fifth as a world financial center. It consistently ranks behind New York and London. Some observers put it substantially ahead of the larger but more heavily regulated Tokyo financial market; others put it slightly behind both Tokyo and up-and-coming Singapore, although most concede that Hong Kong still retains its edge over Singapore as well as the more established and staid European markets.

From its founding as a British outpost, Hong Kong has been a free trade port, and the colonial government has maintained a laissez-faire approach to the business conducted through it. As a truly international city Hong Kong encourages participation by foreign firms in virtually all activities on all levels. No protectionist policies discriminate against foreign interests.

In short Hong Kong is probably the most purely capitalist entity on earth. The structure of Hong Kong's financial industries demonstrates this status. Hong Kong lacks a central bank—central bank functions are delegated to major local banks subject to government consultation—and generally maintains a policy of self-regulation, except for registration, capitalization, and a few other requirements. It has no deposit insurance system.

Because of Hong Kong's focus on international trade, trade financing, arrangements and related instruments are well understood and widely available. Accounts can be held for any purpose in any major international currency, although local transactions usually must be in local currency. Complete confidentiality and secrecy exist; no public disclosures with regard to accounts held are required. Operations are subject to British common law, which provides a comprehensive legal framework for what otherwise might be a somewhat chaotic situation.

In recent years banks in Hong Kong have made tremendous profits from local real estate activity and the financing of investments and provision of services related to the economic development of China's neighboring Guangdong Province. In addition, because the rapidly increasing trade between Taiwan and the PRC remains illegal in Taiwan, Hong Kong institutions typically serve as the intermediaries in these exchanges, providing the financial services that facilitate trade and investment. As a result of these factors and a widening of the spreads between borrowing and lending rates, many Hong Kong banks have reported annual profit growth of 50 to 100 percent in recent years. The Hong Kong stock exchange has been the best-performing equities market in the world since 1982.

The thundercloud on the horizon in this sunny scenario is the impending takeover of Hong Kong by the PRC in 1997. Under the Basic Law negotiated between China and Hong Kong's colonial master, Great Britain, Hong Kong will retain its economic autonomy for a period of 50 years following the transfer of political control. This autonomy includes local sovereignty extending to the capitalist system and guarantees of free flow of capital, freedom from foreign exchange controls, and continued convertibility of the Hong Kong dollar (HK$). The Chinese profess to want an undamaged Hong Kong—which provides them with the bulk of their foreign exchange and investment funds—and the agreement is designed to reassure residents and foreign investors that things will, in fact, continue as they have in the past. However, fears remain as to whether the control-oriented Chinese will be able to keep their hands off this goose that lays such golden eggs.

THE BANKING SYSTEM

Although Hong Kong has a full range of developed financial institutions, its banks, which are known as authorized institutions and allowed to operate in virtually all areas of financial services, dominate the dynamic scene.

In 1993 there were 366 authorized institutions of all categories, operating 1,410 local branch offices. Foreign banks from 27 countries operated Hong Kong authorized institutions, and 147 overseas banks from 35 countries operated separate representative offices in Hong Kong. As of mid-1992 four-fifths of interbank transactions, which equaled 40 percent of all assets in the Hong Kong banking system, were with affiliated or correspondent banks located overseas, an indication of Hong Kong's international orientation

At the end of 1992 total bank assets in Hong Kong stood at nearly US$740 billion. In 1992 assets increased by 2 percent, deposits rose by 9.3 percent, and total lending grew by 10.1 percent. Demand for loans is beginning to outstrip growth in deposits and other funding sources. In November 1993 Hongkong and Shanghai Bank announced that it would sell HK$3 billion (about US$390 million) in 10-year floating-rate bonds to build up reserves for local lending. Estimated annual real growth from 1992 through 1995 is expected to average 10 percent.

Central Bank Functions

Because Hong Kong has no central bank most of the functions normally associated with a central bank have been performed by various government offices under the Monetary Affairs Branch of the Government Secretariat or delegated to selected commercial banks. The Hong Kong Monetary Authority was formed in mid-1993 to further formalize this arrangement and assume more of the functions of a central bank. As such it manages the exchange fund, which is used to stabilize foreign exchange and underwrite the issue of currency by private banks; operates a discount window and serves as lender of last resort; and advises the government on fiscal and monetary policy. The Monetary Authority and most activity in the banking industry is dominated by Hongkong and Shanghai Banking Corporation (HSBC), the Standard Chartered Bank, and, increasingly, the Bank of China.

The Commercial Banking System

Hong Kong has had a three-tiered banking system since 1981. These tiers are known collectively as authorized institutions. Following a partial reclassification of financial institutions under an amendment to the Banking Ordinance passed in 1990, Hong Kong now recognizes licensed banks, restricted license banks, and deposit-taking companies. There were few substantive changes under the new regulations beyond an increase in required capital for domestically incorporated institutions and an easing of restrictions on their use of the term "bank" in the institution's name and in its advertising. The changes were also designed to allow foreign banks that were not large enough to obtain full banking licenses to participate as upgraded restricted license banks. Although each category has specific requirements, limits, and target clientele, all are diversifying into a wide range of financial services, including funds management, investment advice, securities operations, leasing, and insurance.

Licensed Banks

In 1993 there were 164 licensed banks with 1,404 branches operating in Hong Kong; 30 of these were domestically incorporated institutions, while the remaining 134 were foreign institutions, reflecting Hong Kong's role as an international banking mecca. Domestic licensed banks operated 181 overseas branches and 27 overseas representative offices. Licensed banks are authorized by the governor's office.

Only licensed banks may offer retail consumer checking and savings accounts. They are allowed to accept demand deposits of any size and maturity; however, interest rates paid to depositors on Hong Kong dollar deposits up to HK$500,000 (about US$64,500) with a maximum maturity of 15 months are governed by the rules of the Hong Kong Association of Banks. All licensed banks must be members of this statutory trade organization, which sets limits on the interest that can be paid and the fees that can be charged for certain services. Almost all rates paid exceed the minimums set by the association, which has fixed floor and ceiling rates that do not unduly hamper free competition among its members. Licensed banks are allowed to use the word "bank" in a generally unrestricted manner.

Licensed banks must have minimum capital of HK$150 million (about US$19.4 million), up from the HK$100 million (US$13 million) that was required before 1990. Local candidates must hold public deposits of at least HK$3 billion (about US$390 million), have total assets of at least HK$4 billion (about US$520 million), and have been in the lending and deposit-taking business in the colony for ten years.

Restricted License Banks

In 1993 there were 58 restricted license banks with 12 branch offices operating in Hong Kong. The domestic restricted license banks operated three overseas branches and eight overseas representative offices. Restricted license banks are authorized by the colony's financial secretary.

These banks are primarily engaged in merchant banking and capital market activities, two of the core elements of Hong Kong's wholesale financial business. They cannot offer retail consumer banking services, although they are not prohibited from accepting large individual accounts. Restricted license banks may take minimum deposits of HK$500,000 (US$64,500) or more with any maturity. These banks are allowed to accept deposits that do not meet this size qualification provided that the deposits are originated by another financial institution licensed in Hong Kong, are from a foreign financial institution operating outside Hong Kong, an employee, or are accepted strictly for remittance abroad as a service to a customer. These banks are allowed to use the word "bank" in their advertisements and may describe themselves as merchant banks but not as retail or commercial banks.

Domestically incorporated restricted license banks must have capital of HK$100 million (about US$13 million), up from the HK$75 million (US$9.75 million) that was required before 1990. They must also meet standards of acceptability of ownership, quality of management, and adequacy of supervision, as determined by the commissioner of banking. Foreign institutions wishing to register as restricted license banks must meet the same requirements.

Deposit-Taking Companies

In 1993 there were 144 deposit-taking companies with 66 branches in Hong Kong. Domestic companies operated five overseas branch offices and three representative offices. Deposit-taking companies are authorized by the commissioner of banking.

Deposit-taking companies can accept minimum deposits of HK$100,000 (about US$13,000) or more with maturities of less than three months. They cannot offer savings accounts. They can accept smaller deposits that are originated by another Hong Kong financial institution or a financial institution outside Hong Kong, are from an employee, or are accepted for remittance outside Hong Kong as a service to a customer. Deposit-taking companies are prohibited from using the term "bank" in their name or advertising.

The 1990 banking amendment raised the minimum capital requirement for deposit-taking companies to HK$25 million (about US$3.25 million) from HK$10 million (US$1.3 million). At least 50 percent of equity must be owned by a licensed financial institution. Many deposit-taking companies are relatively small institutions, and most are wholly owned by overseas or domestic banks.

Foreign Banks

The majority of the world's 100 largest banks are represented in Hong Kong, operating as authorized institutions or as representative offices. Foreign banks in Hong Kong hold more than half of all deposits, with Chinese banks accounting for the largest share (21 percent of total deposits), followed by European banks (15 percent), Japanese banks (10 percent), and US banks (8 percent).

Foreign financial institutions seeking to operate as authorized institutions can apply as either separate incorporated wholly owned subsidiaries or as branches of the parent entity. Subsidiaries must bring in dedicated capital to meet Hong Kong's requirements. Branches can count the parent firm's capital toward the satisfaction of the minimum capital requirement and need only have adequate working capital in the colony.

Foreign banks must meet all the requirements set for the specific type of authorized institution. In addition, they must be licensed at a comparable level in their home countries, and home regulatory standards must meet those established by the Basle Committee on Banking Supervision. Banks need home country regulatory authorization to open an operation in Hong Kong, and some form of acceptable reciprocal authorization must be available for Hong Kong-based banks to operate in the foreign bank's home jurisdiction. Foreign parent banking institutions must have minimum total capital of US$16 billion.

The only real restriction on foreign banks that does not apply equally to domestic banks is the limitation on establishing branch offices. Foreign banks licensed before 1978 are free to operate offices throughout the colony, but later registrants are limited to a single office. A foreign bank desiring to have branch offices may purchase the right to open branches by buying an existing bank that has such rights, but otherwise it has no recourse. However, automated teller machines (ATMs) are not considered branches, and these have proliferated as foreign banks seek an enhanced presence and domestic banks respond in order not to be outdone.

Western bankers generally find Hong Kong regulations and requirements to be well within acceptable parameters for banking supervision, often in fact much looser than those to which they are accustomed in their home jurisdictions. The rules are applied evenly and do not discriminate between local and international institutions. Although the responsibility for administering many regulations and operations is delegated to large local banks, foreign bankers have found that neither requirements nor their implementation unfairly favor the banks that monitor the system.

Offshore Banking

Hong Kong's international focus and ambiance works both ways. Its domestic banks operate overseas branches and representative offices to cover virtually all Asian and most major world markets. At the end of 1992 the ubiquitous HSBC ranked sixteenth in the world on an asset basis. It operates large full-service subsidiaries in the United States, Britain, Canada, Australia, and the Middle East, as well as in Hong Kong itself, where it also runs the local Hang Seng Bank. When Hong Kong-based banks don't operate overseas directly through subsidiaries, branches, or representative offices, they maintain a complex web of international correspondent relations.

Hong Kong also serves as a major world offshore banking center itself. Offshore income is not taxable in the colony, and minimal disclosure is required with regard to such activities. The lack of exchange controls and Hong Kong's geographic location, central to Asian markets and intermediate between North America and Europe, recommend it as a center for financial transactions.

The Commissioner of Banking

The office of the commissioner has broad supervisory powers involving audit, conference, and sanction authority over all authorized institutions. It also has authority to delegate certain official operations to private banks, and much day-to-day administration of the banking system is handled by large local banks, particularly Hongkong and Shanghai Bank.

Regulators endorse international standards, primarily those established by the Bank for International Settlements (BIS) and the Basle Committee on Banking Supervision. They also rely on reciprocal arrangements with home country regulators of foreign banks. Hong Kong regulators operate two standing advisory committees, the Banking Advisory Committee and the Deposit-Taking Companies Committee, to deal with issues arising over banking practice and policy.

The commissioner requires that authorized institutions maintain certain standards of liquidity and capital adequacy ratios. Loans to any single customer and to officers, directors, employees, and other affiliated persons or firms are restricted, and limits apply to holdings of shares in other firms and in real property not directly involved in bank operations.

Authorized banks must make periodic filings with the commissioner of banking, detailing their assets and liabilities, profit and loss accounts, capital adequacy and liquidity ratios, and other financial information designed to allow the commissioner to monitor their financial soundness.

The Commissioner of Banking is empowered to issue guidelines on principles and practices that must be followed by regulated institutions. Code of conduct guidelines, issued in 1986, govern ethics and business practice; loan guidelines, issued in 1987, specify the principles and documentation required for lending. The commissioner has recently issued

guidelines dealing the with the loan loss reserves required for sovereign lending, capitalization levels, and foreign exchange operations. The commission set the capital adequacy position at 8 percent but retains the option to boost it as high as 12 percent for licensed banks and 16 percent for restricted license banks and deposit-taking companies on a case-by-case basis. Open foreign exchange positions for domestic institutions are limited to a maximum range of between 5 and 15 percent of capital. Foreign institutions in Hong Kong operate with no specific limits, this area of supervision being delegated to home country authorities.

The commissioner's approval is required for the appointment of directors, senior management, and controllers by licensed institutions. This approval process can be used to veto the appointment of individuals who for some reason are considered to be detrimental to the reputation and prudent operations of Hong Kong's otherwise freewheeling but impeccable banking system. This veto power has been exercised sparingly and has not been used to promote the appointment of locals or to interfere with business prerogatives.

Limitations on Bank Activities

In an effort to prevent very large banks from acquiring too much influence and blurring the lines among sectors, Hong Kong has placed significant limitations on bank involvement in nonbank businesses and real estate. Authorized institutions cannot own more than 25 percent of the equity of a nonbank company, unless such equity is held as collateral or taken in lieu of payment of debt owed to the institution. Authorized institutions cannot hold businesses acquired through such foreclosures for longer than 18 months unless specifically authorized by the Commissioner of Banking.

Banks in Hong Kong have long been involved in the lucrative local real estate market. In recent years, the price of land has skyrocketed, contributing significantly to bank profits and assets, especially during the early 1990s. Although Hong Kong law places limitations on the degree to which a bank is allowed to become directly involved in real estate, no restrictions are imposed on lending to the real estate sector other than general limits on loans to a single borrower. A bank may not hold or acquire interest in land valued at greater than 25 percent of its own capital plus reserves, with improvements—specifically buildings—being included in the definition of land (virtually all land in Hong Kong is owned by the government, so long-term building leases serve as a proxy for real estate). Real property specifically used to conduct bank business is exempt, as is land dedicated to the provision of employee benefits. Real estate acquired through securing or satisfying a debt is exempted from the total allowable amount, but it may not be held for more than 18 months without specific approval from the Commissioner of Banking.

Clearing House Activities

All authorized financial institutions must be members of Hong Kong's clearing houses. Checks—an average of more than 400,000 per day—are handled through the Paper Clearing System. The Electronic Clearing System and the Clearing House Automated Transfer System (CHATS) handle electronic book transfers. The 10 settlement banks are overseen by the Hongkong and Shanghai Bank, which maintains reserve deposits to cover daily activity. Average daily clearing volume is HK$84 million (about US$11 million).

Specialized Banks

Specialized institutions such as agricultural and fisheries cooperatives and similar institutions designed to service specific clienteles do not play a role in Hong Kong's finance industry. The types of general financial institutions already noted are usually able to cover financing needs for any viable project no matter what the sector. Few regulations serve to authorize or regulate such specialized institutions.

Banking Services

Authorized institutions in Hong Kong operate comprehensive banking facilities that include large wholesale operations, foreign exchange facilities, project financing operations, and a complete network of local branches that focus primarily on retail trade.

Banks offer a variety of checking and savings accounts for both personal and business use, denominated in HK$, US$, or any of a number of other currencies. They also assure confidentiality of these accounts.

Short-term loans and bank overdrafts or lines of credit are available from local and overseas banks. Medium- and long-term credit is available from large banks and other financial firms. All banks in Hong Kong maintain liberal lending policies, and sound projects can readily find financing in the colony. All licensed banks are authorized to provide loans to residents and nonresidents in the currency of the borrower's choice. Because so many institutions operate in the market, most fees are highly competitive. Interest rates are determined by market conditions, project risk, and customer creditworthiness. Consumer real estate financing alone is conservative. Banks have a self-imposed 30 percent equity requirement for residential housing lending. However, some observers consider this limit largely irrelevant, citing the degree of bank exposure to Hong Kong's inflated commercial real estate market.

Unlike many other less developed Asian financial institutions, Hong Kong banks view long-term lending as something with a horizon greater than 12 months. As in the West, term loans are designed to help a customer make capital investments or provide permanent working capital. Term loans, such as mortgages, equipment loans, and some leasing arrangements, are usually repaid on an installment basis and can be either fixed- or floating-rate loans. Credit lines are usually used up to an agreed-upon limit and replenished as necessary. They are used for short-term working capital, to complete specific transactions, and as bridge loans to even out receipts and expenditures. Most credit lines require a commitment fee and bear a floating rate on amounts drawn down. Because of the competitiveness of the market many Hong Kong banks may waive collateral on lending, although, depending on the project, they may not only require collateral but also specify levels greater than the amount of the loan.

Because of its trade focus, Hong Kong offers a variety of trade financing options. Letters of credit, documentary collections, open accounts, and other standard forms of international remittances are readily available. Other common trade financing services include preshipment financing, advances against collections, discounting of bills, and trust receipts. A form of factoring that serves primarily as a means of financing trade is offered by many Hong Kong banks that discount invoices, postdated checks, and drawings against uncollected items.

Recent Trends

Since 1991 the Hong Kong financial community has experienced a contraction in the number of authorized financial institutions from 405 to 375. This decline reflects a continuing process of consolidation, particularly among the smaller deposit-taking companies. Some of these institutions simply gave up their authorizations because they were little used. This contraction does not appear to be due to concerns over Hong Kong's future as a financial center after its return to Chinese control. On the contrary, the China trade has made Hong Kong even more attractive to those banks that wish to enter Chinese markets while at the same time functioning in an established business environment.

In 1991 and 1992 five authorizations were granted to overseas banks to establish Hong Kong licensed banks. Nine licenses were revoked at the holders' request. Three banks closed operations as a consequence of mergers overseas, and six banks withdrew because of cutbacks in their operations. The number of licensed banks stood at 164 at the beginning of 1993, with 152 of these representing overseas banks.

During 1991 nine new authorizations were granted for restricted license banks. One was granted

Hong Kong Banking Services for Foreign Businesses

Foreign businesspeople operating in Hong Kong are able to take advantage of a wide range of financial services to assist them in their dealings. Although Hong Kong banks offer virtually every personal and commercial banking service, they focus on high-volume, trade-related international transactions. Because of this focus and the volume of business they do in these areas, their personnel are world-class experts at handling international financing, payments, and financial trading. Commonly offered special services include the facilitation of international transactions using letters of credit (L/Cs), intermediary services for transactions between China and a business' home country, the maintenance of local currency accounts, the provision of local and regional business loans, the handling of foreign exchange (forex) transactions, and brokerage services for investing and trading in stocks, bonds, futures, and precious metals on Hong Kong exchanges.

International Payments Hong Kong banks specialize in handling international payments to and from Asia. Local bankers are far more experienced with this type of activity than are many of their Western counterparts, and they can provide expert counsel in choosing and executing the most suitable form of payment for a particular business or type of transaction. Various types of letters of credit and other payment formats can be handled through Hong Kong banks.

Purchasers of goods from Hong Kong need to be able to transfer funds from a home country bank account to the supplier's Hong Kong account. Opening a home account at an international bank with major representation in Hong Kong may be the best way to keep transfer fees to a minimum. Because payment is usually the riskiest part of a business deal and local experience is invaluable, the use of reputable international banks with extensive experience in Hong Kong is highly recommended. (Refer to "Important Addresses" chapter for a listing of major international banks with Hong Kong offices.)

Intermediary Services Foreigners operating in China's Special Economic Zones (SEZs) and other areas often transact their financial business through accounts established in Hong Kong. There are many reasons for using Hong Kong as a finance center for trade conducted with China. Hong Kong has a well-developed banking system that meets high international standards, as opposed to China's rather backward, undeveloped, and idiosyncratic system. Transactions in various international currencies are unrestricted in Hong Kong, while international currency transactions in China are tightly controlled and subject to the policies of a government with little understanding of financial markets or business needs and a chronic shortage of hard currency. Hong Kong's economy is also far more stable than China's, and capital holdings in Hong Kong can be quickly repatriated in the event of social or economic turmoil.

The disadvantage of using Hong Kong as a financial intermediary is that involving a third party increases costs. However, most businesses involved in China trade view the added cost as not only as relatively minor but also as a small price to pay for the security that it provides. Usually banks include a cable charge of about HK$100 (about US$13) for wiring money from Hong Kong to China, plus a transfer commission of perhaps HK$30 (about US$4).

Hong Kong Bank Accounts International businesspeople may wish to open accounts in Hong Kong for a number of reasons in addition to the transfer accounts mentioned above. Banks can set their own terms for specific accounts, but several common types of accounts are of interest to business customers. The standard local business account is a Hong Kong dollar checking account. There are few or no fees, but no interest is paid on balances, and the bank sets the minimum initial deposit. Most banks also offer HK$ and US$ savings accounts, HK$ time deposit accounts, international offshore deposit accounts (usually offered in all major currencies for terms of up to 12 months), and foreign currency onshore accounts denominated in a variety of major world currencies for fixed terms. Interest earned is not taxable in Hong Kong. Banks usually accept written instructions or authenticated telexes for deposit and withdrawal transactions. Remittances can be made through branch or correspondent banks.

Commercial deposit account minimums are common. Some basic accounts can be opened for as little as HK$1,000 (about US$130), but most require larger deposits and balances. For instance, Citibank Hong Kong has required a minimum deposit of HK$50,000 (about US$6,450) or equivalent amounts in another currency to open a commercial account, charging HK$100 (about US$13) for each month in which the average daily balance falls below that minimum.

Individual accounts are usually easy to open. The account generally must be opened on site, although most subsequent transactions can be handled from elsewhere. Banks generally require extensive documentation to open a business account. For a corporation, the paperwork includes an application form, authorized signature card, mandate from company officials, an initial deposit that must be made at the time the account is opened, copies of corporate documents such as the memorandum of association (charter), articles of association (bylaws) plus any amendments, to either a Hong Kong certificate of incorporation, a Hong Kong business registration certificate, Form X (particulars of directors), and acceptance and appointment documents. For sole proprietorships and partnerships banks generally require certified copies of business registrations from the Inland Revenue Department. If a business is not registered in Hong Kong, it must produce similar documentation from its country of origin. All business accounts require an introduction from a recognized bank, domestic or foreign, or from a known existing customer who has had an account with the bank for at least one year.

Accounts held in Hong Kong can also be used to fund business expenses in Asia or to finance expanded operations. Such funds allow a businessperson to pay for bank guarantees or other financing expenses from the Hong Kong bank. Keeping such an account further enables foreigners to gain easy access to a variety of foreign currencies because no exchange restrictions exist in Hong Kong. Such accounts are often used to pay commissions to local intermediaries. Funds from a Hong Kong account can also provide cash for up-front payments to a supplier in order to undervalue a letter of credit and thereby lower customs duties at the destination. Such arrangements are common, but businesspeople must depend on the supplier to make good on the agreement and realize that customs frowns on such behavior and that banks may not choose to cooperate.

Buyer commission accounts are common. Such accounts are set up expressly for commissions earned by buyers from the supplier. For example, a garment buyer may require that a supplier wire 2 percent of a purchase amount into a special account that has been set up in Hong Kong. This is essentially a kickback, which is illegal in many countries. However, it is a common practice in Hong Kong, and because of strict confidentiality requirements regarding accounts maintained in the colony, foreign nationals are unlikely to be found in violation of home country laws. Banks may choose not to allow such an account and the accounts are subject to taxation in Hong Kong.

The greatest danger of maintaining an account in Hong Kong is the lack of deposit insurance. An investor could lose assets if the bank were to become insolvent, as was the case with BCCI in 1991. Foreigners should thoroughly investigate a bank's soundness, especially its investment portfolio, before opening an account and be particularly wary of a bank's overcommitment to the volatile local real estate market. Recognized large multinational banks are generally more secure, as their investments are more diverse and their backing broader.

Business Loans Many banks and other financial institutions in Hong Kong provide loans and other financing for business endeavors in the colony, in China, and elsewhere in Asia. Foreigners wishing to procure financing in Hong Kong must have either substantial assets in Hong Kong to serve as collateral, a Hong Kong-based associate with a long-term relationship with a Hong Kong lender, or a close relationship with a home bank that operates in Hong Kong or has a close correspondent relationship with a Hong Kong bank. Interest rates charged depend on the nature of the project, the size of the loan, and the reputation of the borrower.

Foreign Currency Exchange Operations Hong Kong is one of the largest foreign exchange centers in the world, trading about US$60 billion on an average day. Because there are no official restrictions on amounts or currencies that can be traded and the volume and level of expertise are high, Hong Kong banks provide some of the smoothest and least expensive forex services in the world during hours when other major world financial centers such as New York and London are closed.

Brokerage Services Brokers assist foreign and local individual investors in the buying and selling of stocks, bonds, futures, and precious metals. Most major banks provide these services, and 174 overseas specialized securities and futures firms also operate in Hong Kong. Securities trading is conducted in Hong Kong dollars, so foreign funds destined for the local exchanges must be converted into local currency, although the depth and breadth of the foreign exchange market makes this a relatively easy and inexpensive added step. Locally earned revenues from securities operations or other business sources can be easily reinvested in securities markets because the funds do not need to be converted and there is no local capital gains tax.

Hong Kong's return to Chinese control in 1997 is a major source of concern for investors in its booming financial markets. Many are wary of China's promises to leave the financial system intact for 50 years, and some have reincorporated themselves in other Commonwealth locations. While retaining their listings on the Hong Kong exchange, these corporations have also been seeking listings on other international exchanges as insurance against nationalization by China. However, the main danger remains not the viability of the trading firms themselves but the safety of the fixed local assets of the firms whose securities are traded on the exchanges.

to a locally incorporated deposit-taking company that had applied to upgrade its status, while the rest were granted to foreign banks, most from Asia. Two restricted licenses were revoked at the holders' request. At the end of the year there were 53 restricted license banks, compared with 46 at the end of 1990.

In 1991 the number of deposit-taking companies fell to 159, 32 fewer than in the previous year. Six new companies—all subsidiaries of Japanese banks—were granted deposit-taking status. All told, 38 deposit-taking companies voluntarily gave up their registrations. However, in two of these cases the voluntary surrender came as the result of a bank examination that showed significant weaknesses in the credit and management control systems of the institutions.

The number of representative offices fell by three, to a total of 152. A new development was the registration for the first time of representative offices of Taiwanese banks with three established in 1992.

The Real Estate Bubble

Regardless of the official limitations on involvement in real estate, bank assets are heavily weighted in the sector. Due to scarcity of land and an excess of liquidity, real property prices in Hong Kong have been growing far beyond rational expectations, and many observers now wonder when—not if—the real estate market will crash, as it has in the United States and Japan. According to many observers, this crash is the greatest current threat to Hong Kong's financial stability, even among authorized institutions that have kept their own exposure to real estate at seemingly manageable levels. If the real estate bubble were to burst today, many banks would become insolvent. Judging a financial institution solely on its gross assets can be misleading, and foreign businesses are advised to avoid large transactions with institutions that have large exposure to the local real estate market.

Arguing for More Regulation

Some analysts have argued that the lack of regulation that makes Hong Kong so attractive could ultimately backfire on it. For example, the lack of deposit insurance causes depositors to have limited faith in the banking system, and runs on banks are not uncommon. Runs on local banks were spurred by the failure of the Bank of Credit and Commerce International (BCCI). Individual depositors and holders of letters of credit and other bank obligations lost billions of dollars in the unbuffered collapse of this large and apparently solid institution.

In recent years rumors of instability at Citibank and Standard Chartered—two of the sounder international financial institutions—resulted in long lines outside their doors. Both banks weathered the storm, and one local banking official indicated that

95 percent of the deposits withdrawn were returned to the institutions within two weeks. Such volatility is disquieting at best. Nevertheless, local banks have continued to lobby against the added expense that the imposition of any form of insurance would entail. In spite of the problems, the savings to banks and customers of not providing costly insurance has so far outweighed any security considerations of the customers.

NONBANK FINANCIAL INSTITUTIONS

Because authorized institutions have such freedom to operate in a variety of businesses and effectively serve the full range of clients, Hong Kong has little need for the ancillary nonbank financial institutions found in many other markets in Asia and around the world.

Loan agencies that are regulated by the Money Lenders Ordinance generally deal in domestic consumer installment loans, usually those used to purchase real estate or cars, but they also provide some business financing. They are prohibited from offering checking and savings accounts and may not accept deposits for terms of less than 90 days.

Venture capital firms are numerous, and Hong Kong is second in Asia only to Japan in this area of endeavor. Hong Kong venture capital institutions committed about US$1.5 billion to projects in 1991, the majority of which were in China. Capital gains in Hong Kong are generally tax-free, which gives an added impetus to venture capital investment. However, the lack of an over-the-counter market for unlisted shares may make it somewhat difficult to cash out of such investments.

Insurance Companies

Insurance is generally unappreciated in Asia because the savings and indemnification functions of insurance have traditionally been assumed in good Confucian fashion by a group, usually the extended family. Nevertheless, the concept of insurance both as a set of products and services and as a business is taking hold in Asia.

Hong Kong is home to a variety of insurance, reinsurance, and brokering businesses. At the end of 1992 there were 233 firms registered as insurance underwriters. Of these, 106 were domestic firms. The remaining foreign firms represented 29 countries. Some 40 firms were classed as life companies, 20 were composite life and property and casualty firms, and 173 were property and casualty or reinsurance firms.

These firms are regulated by the Insurance Ordinance of 1983, which specifies licensing, capital, asset, and personnel requirements. The Office of the Commissioner of Insurance was established in 1990, and the Hong Kong Federation of Insurers instituted agent registration and disciplinary and dispute arbitration procedures in 1993. Insurance regulation is still relatively loose, although observers expect it to become tighter in the near future.

Composite—full-line life and property and casualty—companies must have minimum capital of HK$10 million (about US$1.3 million). Life insurance companies must have minimum solvency margins—assets over liabilities—of HK$2 billion (about US$260 million). Property and casualty companies must maintain solvency margins based on their premium income level. Insurers are required to file detailed monthly reports and annual audited financial statements with the authorities. The ordinance also sets requirements for directors and controllers.

Hong Kong life insurers commonly manage private retirement plans. Government regulations are pending that would mandate additional pension coverage. This could result in the creation of 20,000 to 50,000 additional retirement plans and the accumulation of substantial funds requiring management and investment.

Hong Kong insurers have few restrictions on how they invest their funds, although most maintain fairly conservative investment policies involving short-term instruments, investment-grade listed securities, and overseas placements. However, given the growth in the insurance market and the increased flow of funds insurers are receiving, more are beginning to look into local private placements and venture capital operations run out of Hong Kong.

The Hong Kong Export Credit Insurance Company, a government-owned firm founded in 1966, offers specialty insurance coverage to exporters and reexporters to cover business risks of nonpayment by the buyer and country risks in the buyer's jurisdiction. The Export Credit company offers coverage for up to 90 percent of the value of the export to any firm registered in Hong Kong regardless of country of origin.

Underground Financial Operations

Because there is no shortage of credit or aboveground legal service sources for all but the smallest and riskiest activities, no developed underground market for financial services exists. However, cosmopolitan Hong Kong is recognized as supporting a variety of local and international illicit activities that require financing and produce cash flows that require laundering and placement. Local loan sharking operations, mostly run by the criminal societies known as *triads,* exist in profusion, and Hong Kong is an international hub for smuggling, vice, the drug trade, and money laundering. Awareness of the economic aspect of these illicit activities is codified in Hong Kong's 1989 Drug Trafficking Ordinance

which requires authorized institutions to establish procedures to detect money laundering from such illicit activities and provides for the seizure of illegal funds. Foreign businesses are not likely to run into such illicit operations and should be careful to give them a wide berth.

FINANCIAL MARKETS

The Securities Industry

The Stock Exchange The Hong Kong Stock Exchange (HKSE), the largest and most active in Asia outside Japan, was formed in 1986 through the merger of four competing local exchanges. It is the most important capital-raising mechanism for domestic Hong Kong firms and, indirectly, for Chinese firms as well. Foreign firms incorporated in Hong Kong are eligible to list shares on the exchange, although few have done so.

Because the HKSE offers easy access to Asian equities, it has attracted considerable interest among international traders looking to diversify their portfolios. The exchange operates with one of the most advanced high-tech trading systems in the world, one that it is constantly updating. The system is so efficient that settlement of trades usually takes place the next business day, although foreign transactions can be allowed an extra day in which to settle. Securities trading is conducted in local currency, so foreign funds destined for securities investment must first be converted. This is a simple and inexpensive chore because no foreign exchange restrictions exist and the foreign exchange markets are highly developed and competitive. As with all other financial operations in the colony, there are no restrictions on foreign participation, and capital and profits can be freely remitted overseas. Nor is there any local capital gains or withholding tax on market earnings.

Although the HKSE still represents an insignificant percentage of total world equity markets, it is growing explosively. And it is the best place to gain access to Asian markets and acquire experience in them. The HKSE provides one of the few ways, and probably the best way, to invest in securities in the developing Chinese market.

The HKSE market capitalization has more than tripled in the last five years and doubled in the last two. Total market capitalization at the end of 1992 was HK$1,332.2 billion (about US$170.8 billion) and average daily trading volume was HK$2.7 billion (about US$346 million). During 1992 total turnover on the HKSE more than doubled to more than HK$700 billion (about US$90 billion), and companies raised HK$9.2 billion (about US$1.2 billion) in new capital on the exchange.

In early 1993 there were 423 companies listed on

the stock exchange, 66 more than a year earlier. Unit trusts (closed-end funds), warrants, and debt instruments are also listed on the exchange, although these account for a relatively small fraction of trading volume. Issues of and trading in warrants are both increasing. At the end of 1992 there were 270 listed warrants, double the number a year earlier, and total volume of trading in warrants had increased 176 percent to HK$92 billion (about US$12 billion).

The Hang Seng Stock Index, named after the founding Hang Seng Bank, is modeled on the Dow-Jones Industrial Average. It consists of the daily market value of 33 major listed companies selected according to the size of their market capitalization. A competing Hong Kong Index including 45 stocks and an All Ordinaries (total market) index exist; however, the established Hang Seng Index remains the preferred indicator.

The Hang Seng Index provides a measure of both the performance and the volatility of the HKSE. It fell almost 29 percent from a high of 3,900 to 2,779 in one day during the crash of 1987 and dipped as low as 2,093 following the riots in China in 1989. The Hang Seng Index began to recover in 1991 and finished 1992 at 5,512, up 28.3 percent during that year, although it fell 23 percent in three weeks during the fall of that year when relations between China and Britain were especially chilly. The Hang Seng Index ended 1993 by reaching a new high of 11,888.39, up more than 115 percent for the year and topped 12,000 on the first trading day of 1994.

Between 1985 and mid-1993 the HKSE delivered total returns of 553 percent. During the same period the New York Stock Exchange rose 198 percent. Over the last ten years the HKSE has produced the highest returns in the world in US dollar terms. A significant amount of this recent rise can be attributed to flight capital from the PRC. Many observers suspect that the high-flying HKSE is overbought and due for a major setback.

The HKSE is not an unmitigated capitalist paradise. It was the only major world stock exchange to suspend trading during the crash of 1987. The float—the percentage of a company's stock available for public trading—is often small and virtually all Hong Kong-listed companies are effectively controlled by individuals, so liquidity is often limited and bid and ask spreads are often large. Despite controls, the possibility for manipulation exists. Real estate companies account for one-fourth of the market's capitalization and one-third of its turnover, which given the speculative expansion of property values tends to make the market frothy indeed.

Hong Kong is a relatively expensive market on which to do business, levying a host of transaction fees that are either lower or nonexistent in other major world markets. Because of such charges, the majority of trading in Hong Kong stocks that are listed on other exchanges occurs offshore. The HKSE is in a bind in that it must allow such overseas listings to make itself truly international, but it must also keep the high charges because they provide revenues for the government and funds to pay for advanced communications and automated trading systems.

Most major banks provide brokerage services either directly or through subsidiaries, and 174 overseas securities and futures companies operate in Hong Kong. As is the case with most major exchanges, only the 620 HKSE members are allowed to trade on the exchange. Although outside share ownership is promoted, access to the trading floor is somewhat restricted. The HKSE has approved expanding the number of trading seats to accommodate more outsiders from major worldwide trading firms, and the atmosphere of a club of insiders may eventually fade.

Regulation The HKSE and all other securities markets are governed by the Securities and Futures Commission (SFC), which was reorganized in 1989 to improve on the somewhat dismal performance of regulators in the crash of 1987. This body is responsible for regulating exchange activities; monitoring compliance; registering dealers, traders, investment advisors, and products; and enforcing regulations. A separate committee oversees listing of companies on the exchange, and the separate Registrar of Companies is responsible for seeing that prospectuses are issued that comply with stated requirements and accurately reflect available information.

A few years ago the SFC was notoriously lax in its operations, but following a series of embarrassments, regulators have tightened the reins, regularizing operations and cracking down on insider trading and market manipulation. Even with renewed attempts at regulation, Hong Kong's securities markets remain among the most wide-open in the world. For instance, new regulations prohibit insider trading but make no provision for penalties for the offense.

Many observers consider that regulators, in reaction to the HKSE's past sins and Wild West image, have gone too far in restricting activity on the exchange without getting at the underlying structural problems of what is still, however polished, essentially a Third World emerging market.

Listing and Operating Requirements In order to list on the HKSE, a company must first be a public company and commit to remaining public. The listing committee of the SFC, which has broad discretionary powers in approving listings, must subjectively find that there is sufficient public interest in the company to justify listing its shares. Companies must have an initial capitalization of at least HK$100 million (about US$13 million), and proposed new rules would raise this level to HK$150 million (about

US$19.4 million). The listing committee at its discretion can require higher or accept lower capitalizations. The capitalization of each separate class of securities to be listed must be at least HK$30 million (about US$3.9 million).

At least 25 percent of shares outstanding or shares valued at a minimum of HK$24.5 million (about US$3.2 million), whichever is greater, must be made available to the public, although the committee has broad discretion in setting the actual level of the initial public float. This proportion of public shares should be maintained during subsequent trading, and the committee can take steps to enforce provisions against firms that reduce the percentage of shares in public hands after the initial listing. Listing can be denied if an individual or corporation owns more than 35 percent of all shares, calling into question whether such concentrated ownership would present a de facto conflict of interest with smaller owners in certain circumstances.

Listed firms are expected to be seasoned, that is to have a track record of operations, usually for three years, prior to listing. In the case of foreign companies seeking to list on the HKSE, the committee can impose conditions more stringent than those normally required in order to match the level of regulation found in the company's home jurisdiction. This practice is designed to prevent foreign firms from conducting questionable trading practices on an exchange that is less tightly controlled than their accustomed home venue. Banks or, more commonly, merchant banks usually underwrite initial public offerings.

Listed companies must provide audited financial statements conforming to standards and particulars established by Hong Kong certified public accountants. An annual report must be provided to all shareholders at least 21 days before the company's annual meeting. Shareholders must also receive unaudited interim six-month reports. These documents become public record.

Hong Kong has provided for greater disclosure regarding listed companies, although it has been slow to put the provisions into effect. Sales and purchases amounting to more than 15 percent of a company's assets or net profits must be disclosed. Moves to acquire more than 50 percent of assets or net profits constitute a tender offer and require shareholder approval. The 1988 Securities Bill requires holders of more than 10 percent of the shares of a listed company to disclose this information to the company. The company is responsible for notifying the exchange and the SFC, which then makes this information public.

Other provisions require directors and officers and their families and other affiliated persons or firms to disclose any transactions in company stock and the level of their holdings. Companies can also require a shareholder of record to disclose the underlying beneficial owner if the shareholder is acting as a nominee. Shareholders collectively holding 10 percent of the stock in a listed company can require the company to institute such inquiries or petition the SFC to investigate.

There is no secondary or over-the-counter (OTC) market in Hong Kong. At present, smaller companies are unable to list equities and secondary trading of unlisted equities and debt issues is by private placement. Some have argued for reducing listing requirements to open up the HKSE to such enterprises and broaden its offerings, but there appears to be little demand and the trend is toward tightening rather than loosening listing requirements.

Chinese Stock Listings Over the long term, the HKSE can expect to expand listings to include many China-based corporations seeking overseas capitalization. Four Chinese companies had been listed on the HKSE as of mid-1993 and five others had been approved for listing by year's end with more scheduled for 1994. Many Hong Kong companies serve as proxies for investment in China because of their extensive holdings in Shenzhen, Guangzhou, and Shanghai, and money from China has boosted stock prices on the HKSE.

Some observers worry that this dependence on Chinese capital is dangerous, especially given the austerity measures instituted in China during mid-1993. If austerity had bitten hard enough to slow growth in China as significantly as it was supposed to, Chinese investors would have been expected to pull funds out of the HKSE to keep things going at home. Such an abrupt withdrawal of support could make the Hong Kong market more illiquid and send it into a tailspin. However, official China wants to see Hong Kong stock prices remain high. The PRC is counting on funds that come from the listing of Chinese firms on the HKSE to bail out those firms, and the market must stay high for the Chinese to get good prices on future offerings.

The current hope is that if the formal Chinese stock markets in Shenzhen and Shanghai settle down to become relatively stable, organized markets, they may be able to establish some form of cross-listing arrangement with the HKSE. Such a linkage, which would need to include some minimal listing and operational requirements, would enable overseas investors to have greater confidence in Chinese stocks as an investment.

Hong Kong's return to Chinese control in 1997 is a major source of concern for stock market investors. Many are wary of PRC promises to leave the financial system intact for 50 years, and as a result about 100 Hong Kong businesses have reincorporated themselves as holding companies in Bermuda and other Commonwealth venues. While retaining their listings on the HKSE, these groups are also seeking secondary or cross-listings on other international exchanges as insurance against nationalization by China.

Debt Markets Hong Kong has a domestic bond market consisting of private debt issues listed on the HKSE—mostly bank-issued certificates of deposit—and a money market consisting of dealer-managed trading primarily in short-term government paper—two-year government bonds and 91 day government exchange fund bills. There is no recognized issuance of tradable corporate commercial paper. The money market is managed by dealers appointed by the Monetary Authority.

Total debt listed on the Hong Kong exchange was HK$3.78 billion (about US$488 million) in 1992, equal to only about one-quarter of one percent of the total market value of the stock exchange. In mid-1991, total government bills outstanding amounted to HK$8 billion (about US$1 billion), up from HK$6 billion in 1990. Short-term government paper turns over quite rapidly through direct sales and repurchase agreements to manage the colony's foreign exchange position and interest rates and the reserves and financial positions of various financial institutions. Arbitrage traders are also extremely active, adding to turnover and liquidity.

There are no long government bonds, although the government guaranteed the 10 year bonds of the Mass Transit Railway Corporation and has considered issuing its own three-year notes. In general, corporations that wish to issue debt do so overseas, mostly in the Eurobond market or, increasingly, in the United States. In the past, Hong Kong companies were dissuaded from issuing debt because onshore interest income was taxable, although new rules have abolished withholding on interest, removing this as an obstacle. Most debt continues to be issued offshore and used to fund overseas operations. In practice banks have been accustomed to privately placing debt and made markets for secondary transactions in the small volume of debt that has been issued in Hong Kong. Until there is greater volume and competition, the banks will have a vested interest in keeping control of this niche-servicing position.

The development of bond markets has been slow throughout Asia and particularly so in Hong Kong, given its otherwise high level of financial sophistication. Asian investors and issuers have taken to stocks, which despite volatility have performed marvelously well over the period that they have been available. In addition to providing startling returns which attract investor interest, stocks have been cheap for companies to issue. Basically, private investor interest in bonds, which offer relatively puny returns and fewer opportunities for capital appreciation or trading profits, has been slight. This lack of interest has meant a lack of instruments, markets on which to trade them,

and individual and institutional clients to buy them. A further hurdle has been the lack of a rating system which means that interested issuers must often pay premiums both in added interest and in underwriting and guarantee fees.

The halting moves to establish a long bond market have been due mainly to issuance of so-called dragon bonds by international agencies such as the World Bank and the Asia Development Bank, as well as by some large foreign corporations such as General Electric Credit Corporation, that want to tap Asian sources of funds. It will take some time—and probably a prolonged reversal in stock market performance—for bonds to reach the threshold level necessary to sustain a functioning bond market. This period could be shortened significantly if Chinese entities begin issuing bonds though Hong Kong, as some analysts predict.

Other Securities Investment Opportunities Hong Kong allows a variety of financial instruments and ways to invest in them. In 1990 the government revised its code regarding unit trusts (closed-end funds) and mutual funds (known as trusts in British usage). The SFC now has jurisdiction over the registration of such instruments in Hong Kong. Unregistered funds can be sold and traded in the colony, but cannot be advertised or publicly offered. Local purchases of such funds have been low to date.

Pension funds have been a minor factor on the Hong Kong financial scene. As with insurance, the Chinese have generally avoided pension schemes because they have tended to rely on family and group support. Also, most employment in Hong Kong has not entailed or accrued pension benefits. Since 1992 companies have been required to fund provident arrangements—pensions—for workers who meet certain criteria, which will result in the accumulation of funds. Civil service pensions have also been mandated for some time, although they have not been funded. Government workers are lobbying for full funding to assure payments after 1997. Any funding for this sector would add to available investment funds. Overall, the tight labor market leading to generally higher wages should also provide a source of savings and investment funds to fuel increased demand for financial instruments and the intermediaries that provide them.

Even if it is not a net consumer of financial products itself, Hong Kong serves as an international center for fund and investment management far out of proportion to its small size. In March 1991 there were 920 registered managed investment funds, up 16.5 percent from just three months earlier. Because of Hong Kong's favorable regulatory climate, low taxes, location, and excellent communications infrastructure, this growth is expected to continue, despite the fact that the local market is relatively small and lacking in instruments. Most activity by these fund managers consists of offshore trading.

Futures Markets

The Hong Kong Futures Exchange was established in 1977 and reorganized in 1984. It is regulated by the Commodities Trading Ordinance and governed by the Securities and Futures Commission Ordinance. Contracts include Hang Seng Stock Index and sub-index futures, gold futures, sugar futures, a new stock index option, and HIBOR (Hong Kong interbank offering rate) interest rate futures. In 1992 little-used soybean and cotton futures contracts were discontinued, and the stock index option and sub-index futures were introduced in an attempt to bolster interest and volume, which had lagged following the stock market crash in 1987. Volume is still disappointing, and the exchange may drop gold futures because the more active gold exchange, although a spot market, often acts as a futures market for trading in this commodity. The highest volume is in contracts for Hang Seng Index futures, which traded 181,000 lots in December 1992.

Gold Exchanges

The Chinese Gold and Silver Exchange, operated by a private cooperative society, is the largest in Asia, ranking just behind similar markets in London and Zurich in size and influence. Volume is high and prices generally move in line with those of international precious metals markets. Actual turnover may be double the already high official figure due to off-the-books side deals made among traders. The Chinese have had a high regard for precious metals as a store of wealth, which fuels activity in this market. Far from being an idiosyncratic local phenomenon, the gold market attracts Chinese and non-Chinese traders from all over Asia.

Trading is in 99 percent fine gold measured in *taels*, a Chinese measure equal to about 1.2 troy ounces, the internationally recognized unit for gold. Quotes and settlement are in HK dollars. Only spot contracts are traded. However, because most contracts do not specify a delivery date, and margin facilities are available, the exchange functions as an unofficial quasi-futures market as well. Trading is virtually unregulated, and traders have been trying to form an association for self-regulation to give the operation more standing. Several banks have recently been licensed to operate on the exchange, adding to its depth and respectability.

Although the gold market is active and arbitrage keeps it in line with international markets, those markets deal in 99.95 percent fine gold measured in troy ounces and quoted and settled in US dollars, making the Hong Kong market somewhat inconvenient for institutional traders. In response, the so-called Loco-London Gold Market has grown up, offering standard gold contracts for delivery in London.

FURTHER READING

This discussion is provided as a basic guide to money, finances, financial institutions, and financial markets in Hong Kong. Those interested in current developments may wish to consult the *Far Eastern Economic Review* and *Asia Money*, both of which frequently cover economic and financial developments in Hong Kong.

Currency & Foreign Exchange

INTERNATIONAL PAYMENT INSTRUMENTS

The business of Hong Kong is business, especially international trade, and the colony's financial institutions are adept at all forms of payment arrangements. Hong Kong banks can arrange virtually any kind of payment tailored to individual needs, but the vast majority of business is conducted using three standard instruments: letters of credit (L/Cs), documents against payment (D/Ps), and documents against acceptance (D/As). Banks negotiate three-fourths of L/Cs, that is they reach agreements between the buyer and seller at the time of delivery over aspects of the actual shipment and documents that are not in compliance with the stated terms of the original L/C. Hong Kong also serves as a major reinvoicing center, accepting payments on contracts negotiated elsewhere. (Refer to "International Payments" chapter.)

CURRENCY

Unlike most other currencies, the Hong Kong dollar (HK$) is controlled by government agencies in conjunction with two private banks, the Hongkong and Shanghai Banking Corporation and the Standard Chartered Bank. These two banks issue bank notes used as currency in bills of HK$10, HK$20, HK$50, HK$100, HK$500, and HK$1,000. The exchange rate was HK$7.723 = US$1 as of the beginning of January 1994. The HK$50 bill is worth about US$6.50, with the largest bill, the HK$1,000 bill, being worth about US$130. The government issues coins of HK$0.10, HK$0.20, HK$0.50, HK$1, HK$2, and HK$5, and a paper note worth one Hong Kong cent, as well as special commemorative numismatic items that are legal tender but are not found in regular circulation. Beginning in 1994, a HK$10 coin will begin to replace the HK$10 bill. Plans are under way for the Bank of China to begin issuing currency in conjunction with the other issuing banks in preparation for China's assuming jurisdiction over Hong Kong in 1997.

The value of the currency is backed by the Hong Kong government's exchange fund, which provides the legal basis for the privately issued currency. All local currency must be backed by hard currency reserves consisting primarily of foreign exchange. The banks that issue local currency must deposit the US dollar equivalent of funds in the exchange fund at no interest to cover all bank notes issued.

REMITTANCE AND EXCHANGE CONTROLS

Hong Kong boasts the most liberal foreign exchange policies in the world. Most local transactions are in HK$, but this currency is fully convertible. There are no limitations on foreign exchange with regard to currencies or amounts, except for monitoring of large cash exchanges to control the laundering of suspected illicit funds such as drug proceeds. There are no foreign currency controls, no restrictions on ownership of foreign currency or foreign currency accounts—which are confidential—and no restrictions on transactions using foreign currency. There are no rules governing the inward or outward remittance of any currency. Approximately half of all private bank accounts are held in US dollars.

Because there are no exchange controls, there is no black market, although exchange rates do vary depending on the outlet where the transaction occurs and to some extent the size of the transaction. Businesses will almost always operate through a bank and may be able to negotiate wholesale rates, although the spread will be marginal. For smaller transactions, the airport generally has the least favorable exchange rate, while the banks generally offer the best rates. Rates vary even among banks, with some offering better rates and others negating favorable rates with minimum and sliding scale service fees. However, banks close for a seemingly inordinate number of holidays, both Western and Chinese, and changing funds over a long holiday weekend can be difficult.

Licensed money changers abound, especially in

tourist areas. Their posted rates are unfavorable, but they expect to bargain. Most hotels will also change money, usually at unfavorable rates. It is also important to remember the exchange rate when making retail purchases. Most retail outlets expect to bargain and will try to raise their profits by offering unfavorable exchange rates on purchases as an accommodation to users of currencies other than HK$ or credit cards.

FOREIGN EXCHANGE OPERATIONS

The business of trading money is huge in Hong Kong. Average daily foreign exchange turnover in mid-1992 averaged more than US$60 billion and was growing at a 10 to 15 percent annual rate. However, some observers argue that conditions are in place for Hong Kong's foreign exchange (forex) market to begin to contract at a 10 percent annual rate as more traders and businesses move offshore to Singapore because of sophisticated new competition there as well as concerns over long-term freedom of operation under the Chinese after 1997. These observers also note that the size of the average transaction in Hong Kong is shrinking.

Because of both the lack of limits and the volumes handled, Hong Kong banks provide some of the cheapest and most efficient service on foreign exchange transactions available anywhere in the world. Hong Kong's sophisticated forex markets also deal in forward contracts for both speculative and hedging purposes. In addition to standard 30-day, 60-day, 90-day, and 180-day contracts, Hong Kong forex traders have been known to write forward contracts as far out as five years.

Because of its geographic location Hong Kong's banks are open when other major financial centers such as New York and London are closed, giving currency traders the opportunity to operate 24 hours a day.

RATES OF EXCHANGE

Monetary policy focuses on maintaining exchange rate stability under the linked exchange rate system introduced in late 1983. The government sells foreign exchange to the currency-issuing banks at a fixed rate for new note issues. Other banks and the public have no access to this so-called linked rate. In theory this practice should lead to a two-tiered exchange rate between the fixed rate and the free-market rate based on supply and demand. In practice competition and arbitrage keep the rates essentially the same.

The HK$ has been pegged at 7.8 to the US$ and has fluctuated within 2 percent of the peg since the inception of the linked rate policy. As a consequence, local interest rates track overseas rates for the US dollar and relative trading competitiveness is affected by movements in the value of the US currency, which is the de facto medium of exchange. The government issues short-term bills, in which there is an active trading market, to manage the money supply and to fine-tune interest rates to maintain parity.

The government has shown no indication that it intends to modify this policy, and the exchange rate is expected to remain at roughly HK$7.8 to the US$ for the foreseeable future. Despite some concerns on the part of specific constituencies—if the US$ rises, Hong Kong imports are cheaper but its exports are more expensive and vice versa—most observers see the strong linkage with the US$ as necessary to maintain stability.

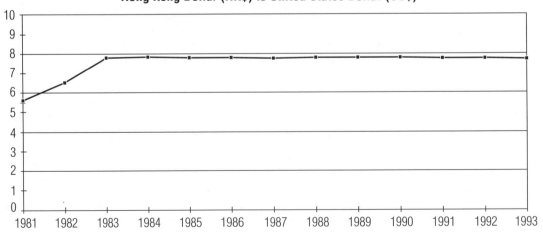

Hong Kong's Foreign Exchange Rates - Year End Actual
Hong Kong Dollar (HK$) to United States Dollar (US$)

January 1, 1994 US$1 = HK$7.72

Exchange Rates—HK$/US$

	Jan	Feb	Mar	Apr	May	Jun	Jul	Aug	Sep	Oct	Nov	Dec
1981	5.182	5.301	5.301	5.357	5.447	5.515	5.704	5.938	6.026	5.987	5.668	5.633
1982	5.796	5.886	5.833	5.827	5.755	5.867	5.902	6.060	6.125	6.604	6.672	6.542
1983	6.525	6.606	6.654	6.787	6.967	7.282	7.168	7.442	8.008	8.095	7.812	7.804
1984	7.797	7.788	7.794	7.807	7.816	7.813	7.852	7.839	7.843	7.824	7.823	7.829
1985	7.811	7.802	7.801	7.790	7.777	7.770	7.753	7.791	7.804	7.791	7.804	7.806
1986	7.808	7.804	7.812	7.796	7.808	7.811	7.812	7.800	7.803	7.800	7.797	7.793
1987	7.777	7.795	7.802	7.802	7.805	7.808	7.809	7.809	7.803	7.808	7.797	7.773
1988	7.787	7.798	7.803	7.816	7.816	7.807	7.813	7.805	7.811	7.813	7.809	7.806
1989	7.805	7.801	7.797	7.783	7.780	7.793	7.804	7.808	7.808	7.808	7.814	7.810
1990	7.812	7.810	7.813	7.797	7.788	7.785	7.770	7.771	7.765	7.772	7.795	7.803
1991	7.795	7.794	7.791	7.794	7.780	7.734	7.761	7.765	7.752	7.754	7.759	7.773
1992	7.761	7.758	7.746	7.740	7.742	7.734	7.734	7.732	7.730	7.730	7.735	7.744
1993	7.738	7.733	7.733	7.731	7.729	7.736	7.756	7.751	7.738	7.730	7.725	7.723

Source: US Federal Reserve System

FOREIGN RESERVES

At the end of 1991 Hong Kong's foreign reserves stood at US$28.9 billion, more than double the level of the more liberal estimates. The size of Hong Kong's foreign exchange reserves, which had been an official secret, was publicly revealed for the first and so far only time in 1992, when the government disclosed international reserves in an attempt to placate the Chinese over anticipated deficits due to massive infrastructure projects. Most observers suggest that despite a merchandise trade deficit, the reserve figure is growing steadily due to Hong Kong's burgeoning surplus in intangibles trade, derived from its service exports and revenues from its booming financial services sector. Reserves are invested in securities denominated in major foreign currencies.

As a dependent colony, Hong Kong has no independent international borrowing authority, and thus it has no official external debt. The government does have guarantor responsibility for bonds issued by the Mass Transit Railway Corporation. In 1990 it began issuing exchange fund short-term bills and began issuing two-year notes in 1991 to finance infrastructure projects. Some foreign intelligence sources place Hong Kong's actual external debt at around US$9.5 billion, a manageable 10 percent of GDP. Most observers expect Hong Kong to begin deficit financing to fund its ambitious infrastructure projects, which could eat into its foreign reserve position and affect exchange rate stability to some extent.

FURTHER READING

This discussion is provided as a basic guide to money and financial markets in Hong Kong. Those interested in current developments may wish to consult the *Far Eastern Economic Review* and *Asia Money,* both of which frequently cover economic and financial developments in Hong Kong.

International Payments

International transactions add an additional layer of risk for buyers and sellers that are familiar only with doing business domestically. Currency regulations, foreign exchange risk, political, economic, or social upheaval in the buyer's or seller's country, and different business customs may all contribute to uncertainty. Ultimately, however, the seller wants to make sure he gets paid and the buyer wants to get what he pays for. Choosing the right payment method can be the key to the transaction's feasibility and profitability.

There are four common methods of international payment, each providing the buyer and the seller with varying degrees of protection for getting paid and for guaranteeing shipment. Ranked in order of most security for the supplier to most security for the buyer, they are: Cash in Advance, Documentary Letters of Credit (L/C), Documentary Collections (D/P and D/A Terms), and Open Account (O/A).

Cash in Advance

In cash in advance terms the buyer simply prepays the supplier prior to shipment of goods. Cash in advance terms are generally used in new relationships where transactions are small and the buyer has no choice but to pre-pay. These terms give maximum security to the seller but leave the buyer at great risk. Since the buyer has no guarantee that the goods will be shipped, he must have a high degree of trust in the seller's ability and willingness to follow through. The buyer must also consider the economic, political and social stability of the seller's country, as these conditions may make it impossible for the seller to ship as promised.

Documentary Letters of Credit

A letter of credit is a bank's promise to pay a supplier on behalf of the buyer so long as the supplier meets the terms and conditions stated in the credit. Documents are the key issue in letter of credit transactions. Banks act as intermediaries, and have nothing to do with the goods themselves.

Letters of credit are the most common form of international payment because they provide a high degree of protection for both the seller and the buyer. The buyer specifies the documentation that he requires from the seller before the bank is to make payment, and the seller is given assurance that he will receive payment after shipping his goods so long as the documentation is in order.

Documentary Collections

A documentary collection is like an international cash on delivery (COD), but with a few twists. The exporter ships goods to the importer, but forwards shipping documents (including title document) to his bank for transmission to the buyer's bank. The buyer's bank is instructed not to transfer the documents to the buyer until payment is made (Documents against Payment, D/P) or upon guarantee that payment will be made within a specified period of time (Documents against Acceptance, D/A). Once the buyer has the documentation for the shipment he is able to take possession of the goods.

D/P and D/A terms are commonly used in ongoing business relationships and provide a measure of protection for both parties. The buyer and seller, however, both assume risk in the transaction, ranging from refusal on the part of the buyer to pay for the documents, to the seller's shipping of unacceptable goods.

Open Account

This is an agreement by the buyer to pay for goods within a designated time after their shipment, usually in 30, 60, or 90 days. Open account terms give maximum security to the buyer and greatest risk to the seller. This form of payment is used only when the seller has significant trust and faith in the buyer's ability and willingness to pay once the goods have been shipped. The seller must also consider the economic, political and social stability of the buyer's country as these conditions may make it impossible for the buyer to pay as promised.

DOCUMENTARY COLLECTIONS (D/P, D/A)

Documentary collections focus on the transfer of documents such as bills of lading for the transfer of ownership of goods rather than on the goods themselves. They are easier to use than letters of credit and bank service charges are generally lower.

This form of payment is excellent for buyers who wish to purchase goods without risking prepayment and without having to go through the more cumbersome letter of credit process.

Documentary collection procedures, however, entail risk for the supplier, because payment is not made until after goods are shipped. In addition, the supplier assumes the risk while the goods are in tran sit and storage until payment/acceptance take place. Banks involved in the transaction do not guarantee payments. A supplier should therefore only agree to a documentary collection procedure if the transaction includes the following characteristics:

- The supplier does not doubt the buyer's ability and willingness to pay for the goods;
- The buyer's country is politically, economically, and legally stable;
- There are no foreign exchange restrictions in the buyer's home country, or unless all necessary licenses for foreign exchange have already been obtained; and
- The goods to be shipped are easily marketable.

Types of Collections

The three types of documentary collections are:

1. Documents against Payment (D/P)
2. Documents against Acceptance (D/A)
3. Collection with Acceptance (Acceptance D/P)

All of these collection procedures follow the same general step-by-step process of exchanging documents proving title to goods for either cash or a contracted promise to pay at a later time. The documents are transferred from the supplier (called the remitter) to the buyer (called the drawee) via intermediary banks. When the supplier ships goods, he presents documents such as the bill of lading, invoices, and certificate of origin to his representative bank (the remitting bank), which then forwards them to the buyer's bank (the collecting bank). According to the type of documentary collection, the buyer may then do one of the following:

- With Documents against Payment (D/P), the buyer may only receive the title and other documents after paying for the goods;
- With Documents against Acceptance (D/A), the buyer may receive the title and other documents after signing a time draft promising to pay at a later date; or

- With Acceptance Documents against Payment, the buyer signs a time draft for payment at a latter date. However, he may only obtain the documents after the time draft reaches maturity. In essence, the goods remain in escrow until payment has been made.

In all cases the buyer may take possession of the goods only by presenting the bill of lading to customs or shipping authorities.

In the event that the prospective buyer cannot or will not pay for the goods shipped, they remain in legal possession of the supplier, but he may be stuck with them in an unfavorable situation. Also, the supplier has no legal basis to file claim against the prospective buyer. At this point the supplier may:

- Have the goods returned and sell them on his domestic market; or
- Sell the goods to another buyer near where the goods are currently held.

If the supplier takes no action the goods will be auctioned or otherwise disposed of by customs.

Documentary Collection Procedure

The documentary collection process has been standardized by a set of rules published by the International Chamber of Commerce (ICC). These rules are called the Uniform Rules for Collections (URC) and are contained in ICC Publication No. 322. (See the last page of this section for ICC addresses and list of available publications.)

The following is the basic set of steps used in a documentary collection. Refer to the illustration on the following page for a graphic representation of the procedure.

(1) The seller (remitter, exporter) ships the goods.

(2) and (3) The seller forwards the agreed upon documents to his bank, the remitting bank, which in turn forwards them to the collecting bank (buyer's bank).

(4) The collecting bank notifies the buyer (drawee, importer) and informs him of the conditions under which he can take possession of the documents.

(5) To take possession of the documents, the buyer makes payment or signs a time deposit.

(6) and (7) If the buyer draws the documents against payment, the collecting bank transfers payment to the remitting bank for credit to the supplier's account. If the buyer draws the documents against acceptance, the collecting bank sends the acceptance to the remitting bank or retains it up to maturity. On maturity, the collecting bank collects the bill and transfers it to the remitting bank for payment to the supplier.

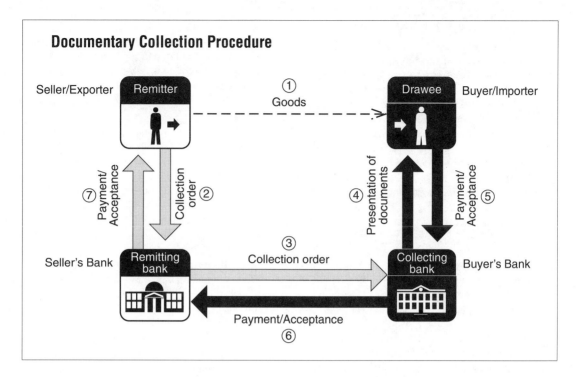

TIPS FOR BUYERS

1. The buyer is generally in a secure position because he does not assume ownership or responsibility for goods until he has paid for the documents or signed a time draft.
2. The buyer may not sample or inspect the goods before accepting and paying for the documents without authorization from the seller. However, the buyer may in advance specify a certificate of inspection as part of the required documentation package.
3. As a special favor, the collecting bank can allow the buyer to inspect the documents before payment. The collecting bank assumes responsibility for the documents until their redemption.
4. In the above case, the buyer should immediately return the entire set of documents to the collecting bank if he cannot meet the agreed payment procedure.
5. The buyer assumes no liability for goods if he refuses to take possession of the documents.
6. Partial payment in exchange for the documents is not allowed unless authorized in the collection order.
7. With documents against acceptance, the buyer may receive the goods and resell them for profit before the time draft matures, thereby using the proceeds of the sale to pay for the goods. The buyer remains responsible for payment, however, even if he cannot sell the goods.

TIPS FOR SUPPLIERS

1. The supplier assumes risk because he ships goods before receiving payment. The buyer is under no legal obligation to pay for or to accept the goods.
2. Before agreeing to a documentary collection, the supplier should check on the buyer's creditworthiness and business reputation.
3. The supplier should make sure the buyer's country is politically and financially stable.
4. The supplier should find out what documents are required for customs clearance in the buyer's country. Consulates may be of help.
5. The supplier should assemble the documents carefully and make sure they are in the required form and endorsed as necessary.
6. As a rule, the remitting bank will not review the documents before forwarding them to the collecting bank. This is the responsibility of the seller.
7. The goods travel and are stored at the risk of the supplier until payment or acceptance.
8. If the buyer refuses acceptance or payment for the documents, the supplier retains ownership. The supplier may have the goods shipped back or try to sell them to another buyer in the region.
9. If the buyer takes no action, customs authorities may seize the goods and auction them off or otherwise dispose of them.
10. Because goods may be refused, the supplier should only ship goods which are readily marketable to other sources.

LETTERS OF CREDIT (L/C)

A letter of credit is a document issued by a bank stating its commitment to pay someone (supplier/exporter/seller) a stated amount of money on behalf of a buyer (importer) so long as the seller meets very specific terms and conditions. Letters of credit are often called documentary letters of credit because the banks handling the transaction deal in documents as opposed to goods. Letters of credit are the most common method of making international payments, because the risks of the transaction are shared by both the buyer and the supplier.

STEPS IN USING AN L/C

The letter of credit process has been standardized by a set of rules published by the International Chamber of Commerce (ICC). These rules are called the Uniform Customs and Practice for Documentary Credits (UCP) and are contained in ICC Publication No. 400. (See the last page of this section for ICC addresses and list of available publications.) The following is the basic set of steps used in a letter of credit transaction. Specific letter of credit transactions follow somewhat different procedures.

- After the buyer and supplier agree on the terms of a sale, the buyer arranges for his bank to open a letter of credit in favor of the supplier.
- The buyer's bank (the issuing bank), prepares the letter of credit, including all of the buyer's instructions to the seller concerning shipment and required documentation.
- The buyer's bank sends the letter of credit to a correspondent bank (the advising bank), in the seller's country. The seller may request that a particular bank be the advising bank, or the domestic bank may select one of its correspondent banks in the seller's country.
- The advising bank forwards the letter of credit to the supplier.

- The supplier carefully reviews all conditions the buyer has stipulated in the letter of credit. If the supplier cannot comply with one or more of the provisions he immediately notifies the buyer and asks that an amendment be made to the letter of credit.
- After final terms are agreed upon, the supplier prepares the goods and arranges for their shipment to the appropriate port.
- The supplier ships the goods, and obtains a bill of lading and other documents as required by the buyer in the letter of credit. Some of these documents may need to be obtained prior to shipment.
- The supplier presents the required documents to the advising bank, indicating full compliance with the terms of the letter of credit. Required documents usually include a bill of lading, commercial invoice, certificate of origin, and possibly an inspection certificate if required by the buyer.
- The advising bank reviews the documents. If they are in order, the documents are forwarded to the issuing bank. If it is an irrevocable, confirmed letter of credit the supplier is guaranteed payment and may be paid immediately by the advising bank.
- Once the issuing bank receives the documents it notifies the buyer who then reviews the documents himself. If the documents are in order the buyer signs off, taking possession of the documents, including the bill of lading, which he uses to take possession of the shipment.
- The issuing bank initiates payment to the advising bank, which pays the supplier.

The transfer of funds from the buyer to his bank, from the buyer's bank to the supplier's bank, and from the supplier's bank to the supplier may be handled at the same time as the exchange of documents, or under terms agreed upon in advance.

Parties to a Letter of Credit Transaction

Buyer/Importer  Buyer's bank

Seller/Supplier/Exporter   Seller's bank

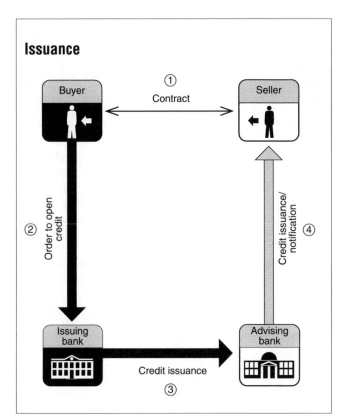

Issuance of a Letter of Credit

① Buyer and seller agree on purchase contract.
② Buyer applies for and opens a letter of credit with issuing ("buyer's") bank.
③ Issuing bank issues the letter of credit, forwarding it to advising ("seller's") bank.
④ Advising bank notifies seller of letter of credit.

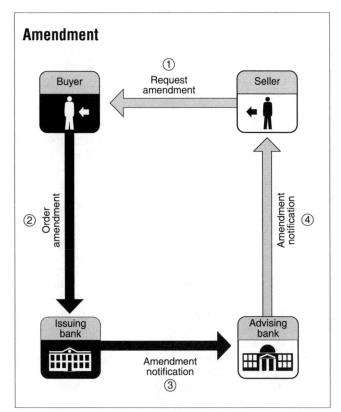

Amendment of a Letter of Credit

① Seller requests (of the buyer) a modification (amendment) of the terms of the letter of credit. Once the terms are agreed upon:
② Buyer issues order to issuing ("buyer's") bank to make an amendment to the terms of the letter of credit.
③ Issuing bank notifies advising ("seller's") bank of amendment.
④ Advising bank notifies seller of amendment.

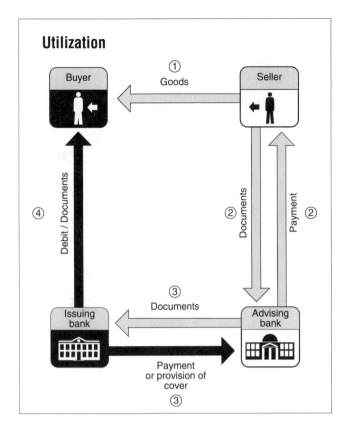

Utilization

Utilization of a Letter of Credit

(irrevocable, confirmed credit)

① Seller ships goods to buyer.
② Seller forwards all documents (as stipulated in the letter of credit) to advising bank. Once documents are reviewed and accepted, advising bank pays seller for the goods.
③ Advising bank forwards documents to issuing bank. Once documents are reviewed and accepted, issuing bank pays advising bank.
④ Issuing bank forwards documents to buyer. Seller's letter of credit, or account, is debited.

COMMON PROBLEMS IN LETTER OF CREDIT TRANSACTIONS

Most problems with letter of credit transactions have to do with the ability of the supplier to fulfill obligations the buyer establishes in the original letter of credit. The supplier may find the terms of the credit difficult or impossible to fulfill and either tries to do so and fails, or asks the buyer for an amendment to the letter of credit. Observers note that over half of all letters of credit involving parties in East Asia are amended or renegotiated entirely. Since most letters of credit are irrevocable, amendments to the original letter of credit can only be made after further negotiations and agreements between the buyer and the supplier. Suppliers may have one or more of the following problems:

- Shipment schedule stipulated in the letter of credit cannot be met.
- Stipulations concerning freight cost are deemed unacceptable.
- Price is insufficient due to changes in exchange rates.
- Quantity of product ordered is not the expected amount.
- Description of product to be shipped is either insufficient or too detailed.
- Documents stipulated in the letter of credit are difficult or impossible to obtain.

Even when suppliers accept the terms of a letter of credit, problems often arise at the stage where banks review, or negotiate, the documents provided by the supplier against the requirements specified in the letter of credit. If the documents are found not to be in accord with those specified in the letter of credit, the bank's commitment to pay is invalidated. In some cases the supplier can correct the documents and present them within the time specified in the letter of credit. Or, the advising bank may ask the issuing bank for authorization to accept the documents despite the discrepancies found.

Limits on Legal Obligations of Banks

It is important to note once again that banks *deal in documents and not in goods*. Only the wording of the credit is binding on the bank. Banks are not responsible for verifying the authenticity of the documents, nor for the quality or quantity of the goods being shipped. As long as the *documents* comply with the specified terms of the letter of credit, banks may accept them and initiate the payment process as stipulated in the letter of credit. Banks are free from liability for delays in sending messages caused by another party, consequences of Acts of God, or the acts of third parties whom they have instructed to carry out transactions.

TYPES OF LETTERS OF CREDIT

Basic Letters of Credit

There are two basic forms of letters of credit: the Revocable Credit and the Irrevocable Credit. There are also two types of irrevocable credit: the Irrevocable Credit not Confirmed, and the Irrevocable Confirmed Credit. Each type of credit has advantages and disadvantages for the buyer and for the seller. Also note that the more the banks assume risk by guaranteeing payment, the more they will charge for providing the service.

1. Revocable credit This credit can be changed or canceled by the buyer without prior notice to the supplier. Because it offers little security to the seller revocable credits are generally unacceptable to the seller and are rarely used.

2. Irrevocable credit The irrevocable credit is one which the issuing bank commits itself irrevocably to honor, provided the beneficiary complies with all stipulated conditions. This credit cannot be changed or canceled without the consent of both the buyer and the seller. As a result, this type of credit is the most widely used in international trade. Irrevocable credits are more expensive because of the issuing bank's added liability in guaranteeing the credit. There are two types of irrevocable credits:

a. The Irrevocable Credit not Confirmed by the Advising Bank (Unconfirmed Credit) This means that the buyer's bank which issues the credit is the only party responsible for payment to the supplier, and the supplier's bank is obliged to pay the supplier only after receiving payment from the buyer's bank. The supplier's bank merely acts on behalf of the issuing bank and therefore incurs no risk.

b. The Irrevocable, Confirmed Credit In a confirmed credit, the advising bank adds its guarantee to pay the supplier to that of the issuing bank. If the issuing bank fails to make payment the advising bank will pay. If a supplier is unfamiliar with the buyer's bank which issues the letter of credit, he may insist on an irrevocable confirmed credit. These credits may be used when trade is conducted in a high risk area where there are fears of outbreak of war or social, political, or financial instability. Confirmed credits may also be used by the supplier to enlist the aid of a local bank to extend financing to enable him to fill the order. A confirmed credit costs more because the bank has added liability.

Special Letters of Credit

There are numerous special letters of credit designed to meet specific needs of buyers, suppliers, and intermediaries. Special letters of credit usually involve increased participation by banks, so financing and service charges are higher than those for basic letters of credit. The following is a brief description of some special letters of credit.

1. Standby Letter of Credit This credit is primarily a payment or performance guarantee. It is used primarily in the United States because US banks are prevented by law from giving certain guarantees. Standby credits are often called non-performing letters of credit because they are only used as a backup payment method if the collection on a primary payment method is past due.

Standby letters of credit can be used, for example, to guarantee the following types of payment and performance:

- repayment of loans;
- fulfillment by subcontractors;
- securing the payment for goods delivered by third parties.

The beneficiary to a standby letter of credit can draw from it on demand, so the buyer assumes added risk.

2. Revolving Letter of Credit This credit is a commitment on the part of the issuing bank to restore the credit to the original amount after it has been used or drawn down. The number of times it can be utilized and the period of validity is stated in the credit. The credit can be cumulative or noncumulative. Cumulative means that unutilized sums can be added to the next installment whereas noncumulative means that partial amounts not utilized in time expire.

3. Deferred Payment Letter of Credit In this credit the buyer takes delivery of the shipped goods by accepting the documents and agreeing to pay his bank after a fixed period of time. This credit gives the buyer a grace period, and ensures that the seller gets payment on the due date.

4. Red Clause Letter of Credit This is used to provide the supplier with some funds prior to shipment to finance production of the goods. The credit may be advanced in part or in full, and the buyer's bank finances the advance payment. The buyer, in essence, extends financing to the seller and incurs ultimate risk for all advanced credits.

5. Transferable Letter of Credit This allows the supplier to transfer all or part of the proceeds of the letter of credit to a second beneficiary, usually the ultimate producer of the goods. This is a common financing tactic for middlemen and is used extensively in the Far East.

6. Back-to-Back Letter of Credit This is a new credit opened on the basis of an already existing, nontransferable credit. It is used by traders to make payment to the ultimate supplier. A trader receives a letter of credit from the buyer and then opens another letter of credit in favor of the supplier. The first letter of credit is used as collateral for the second credit. The second credit makes price adjustments from which come the trader's profit.

OPENING A LETTER OF CREDIT

The wording in a letter of credit should be simple but specific. The more detailed an L/C is, the more likely the supplier will reject it as too difficult to fulfill. At the same time, the buyer will wish to define in detail what he is paying for.

Although the L/C process is designed to ensure the satisfaction of all parties to the transaction, it cannot be considered a substitute for face-to-face agreements on doing business in good faith. It should therefore contain only those stipulations required from the banks involved in the documentary process.

L/Cs used in trade with East Asia are usually either irrevocable unconfirmed credits or irrevocable confirmed credits. In choosing the type of L/C to open in favor of the supplier, the buyer should take into consideration generally accepted payment processes in the supplier's country, the value and demand for the goods to be shipped, and the reputation of the supplier.

In specifying documents necessary from the supplier, it is very important to demand documents that are required for customs clearance and those that reflect the agreement reached between the buyer and the supplier. Required documents usually include the bill of lading, a commercial and/or consular invoice, the bill of exchange, the certificate of origin, and the insurance document. Other documents required may be copies of a cable sent to the buyer with shipping information, a confirmation from the shipping company of the state of its ship, and a confirmation from the forwarder that the goods are accompanied by a certificate of origin. Prices should be stated in the currency of the L/C, and documents should be supplied in the language of the L/C.

THE APPLICATION

The following information should be included on an application form for opening an L/C.

(1) **Beneficiary** The seller's company name and address should be written completely and correctly. Incomplete or incorrect information results in delays and unnecessary additional cost.

(2) **Amount** Is the figure a maximum amount or an approximate amount? If words like "circa," "ca.," "about," etc., are used in connection with the amount of the credit, it means that a difference as high as 10 percent upwards or downwards is permitted. In such a case, the same word should also be used in connection with the quantity.

(3) **Validity Period** The validity and period for presentation of the documents following shipment of the goods should be sufficiently long to allow the exporter time to prepare his documents and ship them to the bank. Under place of validity, state the domicile of either the advising bank or the issuing bank.

(4) **Beneficiary's Bank** If no bank is named, the issuing bank is free to select the correspondent bank.

(5) **Type of Payment Availability** Sight drafts, time drafts, or deferred payment may be used, as previously agreed to by the supplier and buyer.

(6) **Desired Documents** Here the buyer specifies precisely which documents he requires. To obtain effective protection against the supply of poor quality goods, for instance, he can demand the submission of analysis or quality certificates. These are generally issued by specialized inspection companies or laboratories.

(7) **Notify Address** An address is given for notification of the imminent arrival of goods at the port or airport of destination. Damage of goods in shipment is also cause for notification. An agent representing the buyer may be used.

(8) **Description of Goods** Here a short, precise description of the goods is given, along with quantity. If the credit amount carries the notation "ca.," the same notation should appear with the quantity.

(9) **Confirmation Order** It may happen that the foreign beneficiary insists on having the credit confirmed by the bank in his country.

Sample Letter of Credit Application

Sender American Import-Export Co., Inc. 123 Main Street San Francisco, California Our reference AB/02	**Instructions** **to open a Documentary Credit** San Francisco, 30th September 19.. Place / Date

Please open the following [X] irrevocable [ ] revocable documentary credit	**Domestic Bank Corporation** Documentary Credits P.O. Box 1040 San Francisco, California

Beneficiary ① Hong Kong Trading Corporation Parker House 72 Queens Road Central, Hong Kong	Beneficiary's bank (if known) ④ Hong Kong Commercial Bank Kowloon Main Office Kowloon, HONG KONG

Amount ② US$70,200.--	
Date and place of expiry ③ 25th November 19.. in San Francisco	Please advise this bank [ ] by letter [X] by letter, cabling main details in advance [ ] by telex / telegram with full text of credit

Partial shipments [X] allowed [ ] not allowed	Transhipment [ ] allowed [X] not allowed	Terms of shipment (FOB, C & F, CIF) CIF San Francisco

Despatch from / Taking in charge at For transportation to Hong Kong San Francisco	Latest date of shipment Documents must be presented not later than 10th Nov. 19.. ③ 15 days after date of despatch

Beneficiary may dispose of the credit amount as follows [X] at sight upon presentation of documents ⑤ [ ] after ....days, calculated from date of	[ ] by a draft due .... drawn on [ ] you [ ] your correspondents which you / your correspondents will please accept

against surrender of the following documents ⑥ [X] invoice (...3...copies) Shipping document [X] sea: bill of lading, to order, endorsed in blank [ ] rail: dublicate waybill [ ] air: air consignment note [ ]	[X] insurance policy, certificte (........... copies) covering the following risks: "all risks" including war up to [ ] Additional documents final destination in the USA [X] Confirmation of the carrier that the ship is not more than 15 years old [X] packing list (3 copies)

Notify address in bill of lading / goods addressed to American Import-Export Co., Inc. ⑦ 123 Main Street San Francisco, California	Goods insured by [ ] us [X] seller

Goods ⑧ 1'000 "Record players ANC 83 as per proforma invoice no. 74/1853 dd 10th September 19.." at US$70.20 per item	

Your correspondents to advise beneficiary [ ] adding their confirmation [X] without adding their confirmation ⑨

Payments to be debited to our U.S. Dollars............account no 10-32679150

NB. The applicable text is marked by [X]

American Import-Export Co., Inc.

E 6801 N 1/2 3.81 5000

Signature _

For mailing please see overleaf

This credit is subject to the «Uniform customs and practice for documentary credits» fixed by the International Chamber of Commerce. It is understood that you do not assume any responsibility neither for the correctness, validity or genuineness of the documents which will be remitted to you nor for the description, quality, quantity and weight of the goods hereby represented.

TIPS FOR PARTIES TO A LETTER OF CREDIT

Buyer

1. Before opening a letter of credit, the buyer should reach agreement with the supplier on all particulars of payment procedures, schedules of shipment, type of goods to be sent, and documents to be supplied by the supplier.
2. When choosing the type of L/C to be used, the buyer should take into account standard payment methods in the country with which he is doing business.
3. When opening a letter of credit, the buyer should keep the details of the purchase short and concise.
4. The buyer should be prepared to amend or renegotiate terms of the L/C with the supplier. This is a common procedure in international trade. On irrevocable L/Cs, the most common type, amendments may be made only if all parties involved in the L/C agree.
5. The buyer can eliminate exchange risk involved with import credits in foreign currencies by purchasing foreign exchange on the forward markets.
6. The buyer should use a bank experienced in foreign trade as the L/C issuing bank.
7. The validation time stated on the L/C should give the supplier ample time to produce the goods or to pull them out of stock.
8. The buyer should be aware that an L/C is not failsafe. Banks are only responsible for the documents exchanged and not the goods shipped. Documents in conformity with L/C specifications cannot be rejected on grounds that the goods were not delivered as specified in the contract. The goods shipped may not in fact be the goods ordered and paid for.
9. Purchase contracts and other agreements pertaining to the sale between the buyer and supplier are not the concern of the issuing bank. Only the terms of the L/C are binding on the bank.
10. Documents specified in the L/C should include those the buyer requires for customs clearance.

Supplier

1. Before signing a contract, the supplier should make inquiries about the buyer's creditworthiness and business practices. The supplier's bank will generally assist in this investigation.
2. The supplier should confirm the good standing of the buyer's bank if the credit is unconfirmed.
3. For confirmed credit, the supplier should determine that his local bank is willing to confirm credits from the buyer and his bank.
4. The supplier should carefully review the L/C to make sure he can meet the specified schedules of shipment, type of goods to be sent, packaging, and documentation. All aspects of the L/C must be in conformance with the terms agreed upon, including the supplier's address, the amount to be paid, and the prescribed transport route.
5. The supplier must comply with every detail of the L/C specifications, otherwise the security given by the credit is lost.
6. The supplier should ensure that the L/C is irrevocable.
7. If conditions of the credit have to be modified, the supplier should contact the buyer immediately so that he can instruct the issuing bank to make the necessary amendments.
8. The supplier should confirm with his insurance company that it can provide the coverage specified in the credit, and that insurance charges in the L/C are correct. Insurance coverage often is for CIF (cost, insurance, freight) value of the goods plus 10 percent.
9. The supplier must ensure that the details of goods being sent comply with the description in the L/C, and that the description on the invoice matches that on the L/C.
10. The supplier should be familiar with foreign exchange limitations in the buyer's country which may hinder payment procedures.

GLOSSARY OF DOCUMENTS IN INTERNATIONAL TRADE

The following is a list and description of some of the more common documents importers and exporters encounter in the course of international trade. For the importer/buyer this serves as a checklist of documents he may require of the seller/exporter in a letter of credit or documents against payment method.

Bill of Lading A document issued by a transportation company (such as a shipping line) to the shipper which serves as a receipt for goods shipped, a contract for delivery, and may serve as a title document. The major types are:

Straight (non-negotiable) Bill of Lading Indicates that the shipper will deliver the goods to the consignee. The document itself does not give title to the goods. The consignee need only identify himself to claim the goods. A straight bill of lading is often used when the goods have been paid for in advance.

Order (negotiable or "shippers order") Bill of Lading This is a title document which must be in the possession of the consignee (buyer/importer) in order for him to take possession of the shipped goods. Because this bill of lading is negotiable, it is usually made out "to the order of" the consignor (seller/exporter).

Air Waybill A bill of lading issued for air shipment of goods, which is always made out in straight non-negotiable form. It serves as a receipt for the shipper and needs to be made out to someone who can take possession of the goods upon arrival—without waiting for other documents to arrive.

Overland/Inland Bill of Lading Similar to an Air Waybill, except that it covers ground or water transport.

Certificate of Origin A document which certifies the country of origin of the goods. Because a certificate of origin is often required by customs for entry, a buyer will often stipulate in his letter of credit that a certificate of origin is a required document.

Certificate of Manufacture A document in which the producer of goods certifies that production has been completed and that the goods are at the disposal of the buyer.

Consular Invoice An invoice prepared on a special form supplied by the consul of an importing country, in the language of the importing country, and certified by a consular official of the foreign country.

Dock Receipt A document/receipt issued by an ocean carrier when the seller/exporter is not responsible for moving the goods to their final destination, but only to a dock in the exporting country. The document/receipt indicates that the goods were, in fact, delivered and received at the specified dock.

Export License A document, issued by a government agency, giving authorization to export certain commodities to specified countries.

Import License A document, issued by a government agency, giving authorization to import certain commodities.

Inspection Certificate An affidavit signed by the seller/exporter or an independent inspection firm (as required by the buyer/importer), confirming that merchandise meets certain specifications.

Insurance Document A document certifying that goods are insured for shipment.

Invoice/Commercial Invoice A document identifying the seller and buyer of goods or services, identifying numbers such as invoice number, date, shipping date, mode of transport, delivery and payment terms, and a complete listing and description of the goods or services being sold including prices, discounts, and quantities. The commercial invoice is usually used by customs to determine the true cost of goods when assessing duty.

Packing List A document listing the merchandise contained in a particular box, crate, or container, plus type, dimensions, and weight of the container.

Phytosanitary (plant health) Inspection Certificate A document certifying that an export shipment has been inspected and is free from pests and plant diseases considered harmful by the importing country.

Shipper's Export Declaration A form prepared by a shipper/exporter indicating the value, weight, destination, and other information about an export shipment.

GLOSSARY OF TERMS OF SALE

The following is a basic glossary of common terms of sale in international trade. Note that issues regarding responsibility for loss and insurance are complex and beyond the scope of this publication. The international standard of trade terms of sale are "Incoterms," published by the International Chamber of Commerce (ICC), 38, Cours Albert Ier, F-75008 Paris, France. Other offices of the ICC are British National Committee of the ICC, Centre Point, 103 New Oxford Street, London WC1A 1QB, England and US Council of the ICC, 1212 Avenue of the Americas, New York, NY 10010 USA.

C&F (Cost and Freight) Named Point of Destination The seller's price includes the cost of the goods and transportation up to a named port of destination, but does not cover insurance. Under these terms insurance is the responsibility of the buyer/importer.

CIF (Cost, Insurance, and Freight) Named Point of Destination The seller's price includes the cost of the goods, insurance, and transportation up to a named port of destination.

Ex Point of Origin ("Ex Works" "Ex Warehouse" etc.) The seller's price includes the cost of the goods and packing, but without any transport. The seller agrees to place the goods at the disposal of the buyer at a specified point of origin, on a specified date, and within a fixed period of time. The buyer is under obligation to take delivery of the goods at the agreed place and bear all costs of freight, transport and insurance.

FAS (Free Alongside Ship) The seller's price includes the cost of the goods and transportation up to the port of shipment alongside the vessel or on a designated dock. Insurance under these terms is usually the responsibility of the buyer.

FOB (Free On Board) The seller's price includes the cost of the goods , transportation to the port of shipment, and loading charges on a vessel. This might be on a ship, railway car, or truck at an inland point of departure. Loss or damage to the shipment is borne by the seller until loaded at the point named and by the buyer after loading at that point.

Ex Dock—Named Port of Importation The seller's price includes the cost of the goods, and all additional charges necessary to put them on the dock at the named port of importation with import duty paid. The seller is obligated to pay for insurance and freight charges.

GLOSSARY OF INTERNATIONAL PAYMENT TERMS

Advice The forwarding of a letter of credit or an amendment to a letter of credit to the seller, or beneficiary of the letter of credit, by the advising bank (seller's bank).

Advising bank The bank (usually the seller's bank) which receives a letter of credit from the issuing bank (the buyer's bank) and handles the transaction from the seller's side. This includes: validating the letter of credit, reviewing it for internal consistency, forwarding it to the seller, forwarding seller's documentation back to the issuing bank, and, in the case of a confirmed letter of credit, guaranteeing payment to the seller if his documents are in order and the terms of the credit are met.

Amendment A change in the terms and conditions of a letter of credit, usually to meet the needs of the seller. The seller requests an amendment of the buyer who, if he agrees, instructs his bank (the issuing bank) to issue the amendment. The issuing bank informs the seller's bank (the advising bank) who then notifies the seller of the amendment. In the case of irrevocable letters of credit, amendments may only be made with the agreement of all parties to the transaction.

Back-to-Back Letter of Credit A new letter of credit opened in favor of another beneficiary on the basis of an already existing, nontransferable letter of credit.

Beneficiary The entity to whom credits and payments are made, usually the seller/supplier of goods.

Bill of Exchange A written order from one person to another to pay a specified sum of money to a designated person. The following two versions are the most common:

Draft A financial/legal document where one individual (the drawer) instructs another individual (the drawee) to pay a certain amount of money to a named person, usually in payment for the transfer of goods or services. Sight Drafts are payable when presented. Time Drafts (also called usance drafts) are payable at a future fixed (specific) date or determinable (30, 60, 90 days etc.) date. Time drafts are used as a financing tool (as with Documents against Acceptance D/P terms) to give the buyer time to pay for his purchase.

Promissory Note A financial/legal document wherein one individual (the issuer) promises to pay another individual a certain amount.

Collecting Bank (also called the presenting bank) In a Documentary Collection, the bank (usually the buyer's bank) that collects payment or a time draft from the buyer to be forwarded to the remitting bank (usually the seller's bank) in exchange for shipping and other documents which enable the buyer to take possession of the goods.

Confirmed Letter of Credit A letter of credit which contains a guarantee on the part of both the issuing and advising bank of payment to the seller so long as the seller's documentation is in order and terms of the credit are met.

Deferred Payment Letter of Credit A letter of credit where the buyer takes possession of the title documents and the goods by agreeing to pay the issuing bank at a fixed time in the future.

Discrepancy The noncompliance with the terms and conditions of a letter of credit. A discrepancy may be as small as a misspelling, an inconsistency in dates or amounts, or a missing document. Some discrepancies can easily be fixed; others may lead to the eventual invalidation of the letter of credit.

D/A Abbreviation for "Documents against Acceptance."

D/P Abbreviation for "Documents against Payment."

Documents against Acceptance (D/A) *See* Documentary Collection

Documents against Payment (D/P) *See* Documentary Collection

Documentary Collection A method of effecting payment for goods whereby the seller/exporter instructs his bank to collect a certain sum from the buyer/importer in exchange for the transfer of shipping and other documentation enabling the buyer/importer to take possession of the goods. The two main types of Documentary Collection are:

Documents against Payment (D/P) Where the bank releases the documents to the buyer/importer only against a cash payment in a prescribed currency; and

Documents against Acceptance (D/A) Where the bank releases the documents to the buyer/importer against acceptance of a bill of exchange guaranteeing payment at a later date.

Draft *See* Bill of exchange.

Drawee The buyer in a documentary collection.

Forward Foreign Exchange An agreement to purchase foreign exchange (currency) at a future date at a predetermined rate of exchange. Forward foreign exchange contracts are often purchased by buyers of merchandise who wish to hedge against foreign exchange fluctuations between the time the contract is negotiated and the time payment is made.

Irrevocable Credit A letter of credit which cannot be revoked or amended without prior mutual consent of the supplier, the buyer, and all intermediaries.

Issuance The act of the issuing bank (buyer's bank) establishing a letter of credit based on the buyer's application.

Issuing Bank The buyer's bank which establishes a letter of credit in favor of the supplier, or beneficiary.

Letter of Credit A document stating commitment on the part of a bank to place an agreed upon sum of money at the disposal of a seller on behalf of a buyer under precisely defined conditions.

Negotiation In a letter of credit transaction, the examination of seller's documentation by the (negotiating) bank to determine if they comply with the terms and conditions of the letter of credit.

Open Account The shipping of goods by the supplier to the buyer prior to payment for the goods. The supplier will usually specify expected payment terms of 30, 60, or 90 days from date of shipment.

Red Clause Letter of Credit A letter of credit which makes funds available to the seller prior to shipment in order to provide him with funds for production of the goods.

Remitter In a documentary collection, an alternate name given to the seller who forwards documents to the buyer through banks.

Remitting Bank In a documentary collection, a bank which acts as an intermediary, forwarding the remitter's documents to, and payments from the collecting bank.

Sight Draft *See* Bill of Exchange.

Standby Letter of Credit A letter of credit used as a secondary payment method in the event that the primary payment method cannot be fulfilled.

Time Draft *See* Bill of Exchange.

Validity The time period for which a letter of credit is valid. After receiving notice of a letter of credit opened on his behalf, the seller/exporter must meet all the requirements of the letter of credit within the period of validity.

Revocable Letter of Credit A letter of credit which may be revoked or amended by the issuer (buyer) without prior notice to other parties in the letter of credit process. It is rarely used.

Revolving Letter of Credit A letter of credit which is automatically restored to its full amount after the completion of each documentary exchange. It is used when there are several shipments to be made over a specified period of time.

FURTHER READING

For more detailed information on international trade payments, refer to the following publications of the International Chamber of Commerce (ICC), Paris, France.

Uniform Rules for Collections This publication describes the conditions governing collections, including those for presentation, payment and acceptance terms. The Articles also specify the responsibility of the bank regarding protest, case of need and actions to protect the merchandise. An indispensable aid to everyday banking operations. (A revised, updated edition will be published in 1995.) ICC Publication No. 322.

Documentary Credits: UCP 500 and 400 Compared This publication was developed to train managers, supervisors, and practitioners of international trade in critical areas of the new UCP 500 Rules. It pays particular attention to those Articles that have been the source of litigation. ICC Publication No. 511.

The New ICC Standard Documentary Credit Forms Standard Documentary Credit Forms are a series of forms designed for bankers, attorneys, importers/exporters, and anyone involved in documentary credit transactions around the world. This comprehensive new edition, prepared by Charles del Busto, Chairman of the ICC Banking Commission, reflects the major changes instituted by the new "UCP 500." ICC Publication No. 516.

The New ICC Guide to Documentary Credit Operations This new Guide is a fully revised and expanded edition of the "Guide to Documentary Credits" (ICC publication No. 415, published in conjunction with the UCP No. 400). The new Guide uses a unique combination of graphs, charts, and sample documents to illustrate the Documentary Credit process. An indispensable tool for import/export traders, bankers, training services, and anyone involved in day-to-day Credit operations. ICC Publication No. 515.

Guide to Incoterms 1990 A companion to "Incoterms," the ICC "Guide to Incoterms 1990" gives detailed comments on the changes to the 1980 edition and indicates why it may be in the interest of a buyer or seller to use one or another trade term. This guide is indispensable for exporters/importers, bankers, insurers, and transporters. ICC Publication No. 461/90.

These and other relevant ICC publications may be obtained from the following sources:

ICC Publishing S.A.
International Chamber of Commerce
38, Cours Albert I[er]
75008 Paris, France
Tel: [33] (1) 49-53-28-28 Fax: [33] (1) 49-53-28-62
Telex: 650770

International Chamber of Commerce
Borsenstrasse 26
P.O. Box 4138
8022 Zurich, Switzerland

British National Committee of the ICC
Centre Point, New Oxford Street
London WC1A QB, UK

ICC Publishing, Inc.
US Council of the ICC
156 Fifth Avenue, Suite 820
New York, NY 10010, USA
Tel: [1] (212) 206-1150 Fax: [1] (212) 633-6025

Corporate Taxation

AT A GLANCE

Corporate Income Tax Rate (%)	17.5
Capital Gains Tax Rate (%)	0
Branch Tax Rate (%)	17.5
Withholding Tax (%)	
Dividends	0
Interest	0
Royalties from Patents, Know-how, etc.*	
Paid to Corporations	1.75
Paid to Individuals	1.5
Branch Remittance Tax	0
Net Operating Losses (Years)	
Carryback	0
Carryforward	Unlimited

Final tax applicable to persons not carrying on business in Hong Kong.

TAXES ON CORPORATE INCOME AND GAINS

Profits Tax

Companies carrying on business in Hong Kong will be subject to profits tax on profits arising in or derived from Hong Kong. However, a company not carrying on business in Hong Kong will not be subject to profits tax even on income from sources in Hong Kong. A Hong Kong business is not subject to profits tax on income sourced outside Hong Kong.

The basis of taxation in Hong Kong is territorial. The determination of the locality of the source of profits or income can be extremely complicated and often involves uncertainty. It requires case-by-case consideration.

Rates of Profits Tax

For the financial year commencing April 1,1992, the corporate rate of profits tax is 17.5 percent. When an accounting period does not coincide with a finan-

cial year, the profit for the accounting period is deemed to be the profit of the fiscal year in which the period ends. Special rules govern commencements and cessations of businesses, and deal with accounting periods of shorter or longer duration than 12 months.

Capital Gains

Capital gains are not taxed, nor are capital losses deductible for profits tax purposes.

Administration

Profits tax is paid in two provisional installments plus a final payment. The first installment of provisional tax is paid with the final payment for the previous year. The timing of payments is determined by assessment notices rather than by set dates. However, the 75 percent provisional tax is usually paid in January of the fiscal year and the 25 percent balance in the following May. The final installment is then usually due in January of the following fiscal year.

Dividends

Dividends from companies that have been subject to profits tax are specifically exempt from further tax in the hands of the recipient. There is neither a withholding tax nor a credit system on dividends in Hong Kong, all dividends being paid gross as declared and no taxes being payable upon declaration.

Foreign Tax Relief

An agreement with the United States concerning the taxation of shipping income is the only form of foreign tax relief that Hong Kong has negotiated with any other country. Except for limited relief due to certain Commonwealth countries (which is rarely seen in practice), no credit is given for foreign taxes. In certain circumstances, a deduction is given for foreign taxes.

Note: This section is courtesy of and © Ernst & Young from their Worldwide Corporate Tax Guide, 1993 Edition. This material should not be regarded as offering a complete explanation of the taxation matters referred to. Ernst & Young is a leading international professional services firm with offices in 100 countries, including Hong Kong. Refer to "Important Addresses" chapter for addresses and telephone numbers of Ernst & Young offices in Hong Kong.

DETERMINATION OF ASSESSABLE PROFITS

General

The assessment is based on accounts prepared on generally accepted accounting principles, subject to certain adjustments and provisos.

Expenses must be incurred in the production of chargeable profits. Certain specified expenses are not allowed, including domestic and private expenses, capital expenditures, the cost of improvements, sums recoverable under insurance and tax payments. The deductibility of interest is subject to detailed rules (*see* Miscellaneous Matters).

Inventories

Stock is normally valued at the lower of cost or net realizable value. Cost must be determined using FIFO or an average cost, standard cost or adjusted selling price basis. The LIFO method is not acceptable.

CAPITAL ALLOWANCES

Plant and Machinery An initial allowance is available in the year in which the expenditure is incurred. The rate is currently 60 percent. An annual allowance of 10 percent, 20 percent or 30 percent a year on a declining balance basis is available on the balance of the expenditure; it is also available in the same year as the initial allowance. Thus, the allowances in the first year can be 64 percent, 68 percent or 72 percent.

Industrial Buildings An initial allowance of 20 percent is granted on new buildings in the year in which the expenditure is incurred, and annual depreciation allowances are 4 percent of cost beginning in the year the building is first put into use. No initial allowance is granted on existing buildings, but annual depreciation allowances may be available. The definition of industrial building is broad, but it does not include commercial buildings such as hotels and office buildings.

Commercial Buildings Capital allowances (2 percent of cost each year) are available on commercial buildings such as offices and hotels.

Recapture Allowances are generally subject to recapture if the assets are sold for amounts in excess of their tax-depreciated value. However, allowances for commercial buildings are not recaptured.

Relief for Business Losses

A company's business losses may be used to relieve any other income of the company in the same year or may be carried forward without time limit for relief of any profits of the company, regardless of whether these are from the business or whether the same business is still being carried on. No carryback is possible. There are rules to prevent trafficking in loss companies.

Groups of Companies

Consolidated filing is not permitted.

MISCELLANEOUS MATTERS

Antiavoidance Legislation

Legislation permits the Inland Revenue to tax a foreign affiliate on profits derived from transactions not at an arm's length price. This legislation is, however, rarely invoked successfully.

Transactions that are generally artificial or fictitious may be wholly disregarded, and there are provisions designed to generally counteract blatant tax avoidance motivated transactions including cross-border "big ticket" leasing.

Foreign Exchange Controls

Hong Kong imposes no foreign exchange controls.

Interest Expenses

In an attempt to combat avoidance, heavy restrictions were placed on the deductibility of interest expense in 1984. The application of these extensive provisions together with the absence of a withholding tax on interest paid abroad, could result in unusual consequences including an effective debt-to-equity ratio of 0:1 and the effective reclassification of debt as equity.

TREATY WITHHOIDING TAX RATES

Hong Kong has not concluded tax treaties with any other jurisdiction in relation to withholding taxes.

Personal Taxation

AT A GLANCE—MAXIMUM RATES

Income Tax Rate (%)	25*
Capital Gains Rate (%)	0
Net Worth Tax Rate (%)	0
Estate Tax Rate (%)	18
Gift Tax Rate (%)	0

Most income is taxed at 15 percent. See Income Taxes—Employment—Income Tax Rates.

INCOME TAXES—EMPLOYMENT

Who Is Liable

Anyone earning income that arises in or is derived from a Hong Kong office or employment, or is in relation to services rendered in Hong Kong during visits to Hong Kong of more than 60 days in any fiscal year, is liable for salaries tax. Salaries tax is separately levied on employment income of each spouse and payable separately by each of them. A married couple not wishing to be separately assessed must make an election for joint assessment.

Taxable Income

Taxable income consists of all cash emoluments, including bonuses and gratuities but specifically excluding holiday warrants and passages and allowances to the extent disbursed for holiday warrant or passage. Benefits in kind are largely nontaxable, except when they are convertible into cash, are a contribution to the education of the employee's child or represent an employer's assumption of an employee's pecuniary obligation. The provision of accommodation creates a taxable benefit equal to 10 percent of other income subject to salaries tax.

Income Tax Rates

There are three separate income taxes in Hong Kong rather than a single unified income tax. The taxes and rates for the year ending March 31, 1993, are:

- profits tax (on business/trade income): flat rate of 15 percent;
- property tax (levied on rental income less a standard deduction of 20 percent): flat rate of 15 percent; and
- salaries tax: progressive rates of 2 percent to 25 percent, after deduction of allowances, or a flat rate of 15 percent on gross salary, whichever produces the lower tax liability.

The progressive rates are as follows:

Taxable Income Exceeding HK$	Taxable Income Not Exceeding HK$	Tax on Lower Amount HK$	Rate on Excess %
0	20,000	0	2
20,000	40,000	400	9
40,000	60,000	2,200	17
60,000	—	5,600	25

Deductible Expenses

Expenses must be incurred wholly, exclusively and necessarily in the production of assessable income to be deductible. In addition, deprecation allowances (that is, capital allowances) may be claimed on plant and machinery used for production of assessable income. Charitable donations are also deductible within certain limits.

Note: This section is courtesy of and © Ernst & Young from their Worldwide Personal Tax Guide, 1993 Edition. This material should not be regarded as offering a complete explanation of the taxation matters referred to. Ernst & Young is a leading international professional services firm with offices in 100 countries, including Hong Kong. Refer to the "Important Addresses" chapter for addresses and telephone numbers of Ernst & Young offices in Hong Kong.

Personal Deductions and Allowances

Personal allowances are deductible below the "break-even" point (that is, the point at which the standard rate of 15 percent applies). *See* Income Taxes—Employment—Income Tax Rates.

Personal Allowances	HK$
Prescribed allowances	
Single[1]	46,000
Married[2]	92,000
Child allowance	
1st child	15,500
2nd child	11,500
3rd child	3,000
4th to 6th child (each)	2,000
7th to 9th child (each)	1,000
Dependent parent allowance (each)	
Residing with taxpayer	15,000
Not residing with taxpayer	13,500
Single parent child allowance	23,500

[1] *Granted to a single person or a married person who has not elected joint assessment.*
[2] *Granted to a married person whose spouse does not have any assessable income or to a person who, together with his or her spouse, has elected to be jointly assessed.*

INCOME TAXES— SELF-EMPLOYMENT/ BUSINESS INCOME

Who Is Liable

Anyone carrying on a trade or business in Hong Kong is liable for profits tax on income from that trade or business arising in or derived from Hong Kong. A person not carrying on business in Hong Kong is not liable for profits tax, even on income derived from sources in Hong Kong. Certain provisions in the tax law, however, deem specified types of income to be derived in Hong Kong from a Hong Kong business. For example, royalties paid to a non-resident for the use of intellectual property rights in Hong Kong are subject to profits tax on a notional 10 percent net profit element, for an effective tax rate of 1.5 percent.

Taxable Income

Taxable income is determined in accordance with generally accepted accounting principles, as modified by the Inland Revenue Ordinance and principles derived from case law. For applicable rates, *see* Income Taxes—Employment—Income Tax Rates.

If individuals receive rental income but the rental activities do not constitute a business, the income is subject to property tax rather than profits tax. Property tax is charged on 80 percent of rent receivable from real estate situated in Hong Kong, for an effective rate of 12 percent.

If beneficial, individuals with business profits or property income may elect to use the allowances and progressive rates of the salaries tax.

Interest derived in Hong Kong from funds of a business carried on in Hong Kong is subject to profits tax.

Deductible Expenses

To be deductible, expenses must be incurred in the production of taxable profits. Certain specified expenses are not deductible, including domestic and private expenses, capital expenditures, the cost of improvements and tax. The deductibility of interest is subject to detailed rules.

Capital Allowances

Plant and machinery qualify for an initial allowance of 60 percent and then an annual allowance of 10 percent, 20 percent or 30 percent, calculated using the declining-balance method. Both initial and annual allowances may be claimed for the year of acquisition and use, for total allowances of 64 percent, 68 percent or 72 percent.

An initial allowance of 20 percent is granted on new buildings, and annual allowances are 4 percent of cost. No initial allowance is granted on buildings that have already been in use.

These allowances may be subject to recapture if the assets are sold for amounts in excess of their tax-depreciated value.

Commercial Buildings An annual allowance of 2 percent of cost is available on commercial buildings.

DIRECTORS' FEES

Directors' fees are subject to salaries tax (*see* Income Taxes—Employment) if the directorship is held with a company that has its central management and control in Hong Kong. Otherwise, directors' fees are not taxable, even if paid in relation to services rendered in Hong Kong.

INVESTMENT INCOME

Interest income not related to the funds of a business and all dividend income are exempt from taxation.

RELIEF FOR LOSSES

Losses are calculated in the same manner as profits and may be carried forward indefinitely against future income. They may also offset other sources of income. Losses may not be carried back.

CAPITAL GAINS AND LOSSES

There is no tax on capital gains in Hong Kong.

ESTATE AND GIFT TAXES

Estate duty is levied on the value of property situated in Hong Kong that is transferred on death. For the year ended March 31,1993, the duty is charged at flat rates of 6 percent (on an estate valued at HK$4 million to HK$4.5 million), 12 percent (on an estate valued at HK$4.5 million to HK$5 million) and 18 percent (on an estate valued at over HK$5 million). Because strict application of the rates would produce anomalies, marginal relief is available if the value of an estate is only slightly in excess of one of the limits.

There are extensive provisions designed to prevent avoidance of estate duty by holding Hong Kong assets in offshore companies.

No tax is levied on gifts.

SOCIAL SECURITY TAXES

There are no social security taxes in Hong Kong.

ADMINISTRATION

All taxpayers must file separate returns for income subject to profits tax, salaries tax or property tax. The tax year runs from April 1 to March 31. A married couple may elect to be jointly assessed on its salary incomes, if beneficial. There are penalties for breaches of time limits in filing returns.

There are no payroll or withholding tax requirements for salaries tax. Profits, property and salaries tax all operate under a system of prepaid tax known as provisional tax. The provisional assessment is an estimate, normally based on the previous year's assessment, and is payable in two installments: one of 75 percent, usually payable in the final quarter of the year of assessment, and the remaining 25 percent, payable three months later, usually just after the end of the year of assessment. When the actual income for a year is determined, a final tax assessment is issued giving credit for provisional tax already paid. The final tax assessment is combined with a provisional tax assessment for the following year. The final tax is payable at the same time as the 75 percent installment of provisional tax for the next year.

NONRESIDENTS

Hong Kong observes a territorial basis of taxation. This means that the concept of tax residency has no significance except in very limited circumstances. Accordingly, an employee will be subject to salaries tax if his or her employment is fundamentally sourced in Hong Kong, notwithstanding that he or she is not ordinarily resident in the territory. This is a common situation for recipients of directors' fees from Hong Kong companies. However, there is a specific statutory exemption if the employee renders all services outside Hong Kong, with a de minimis allowance for visits to the territory not exceeding 60 days in any year. Conversely, if a nonresident with non-Hong Kong employment renders services in Hong Kong during visits totaling more than 60 days, he or she will be taxed on a pro rata basis. Profits tax will be levied on the income of residents and nonresidents alike, if the statutory criteria are met.

No withholding taxes are levied on salaries, dividends, or interest. However, royalties paid overseas are subject to an effective 1.5 percent withholding tax (*see* Income Taxes—Self-Employment/Business Income—Who Is Liable), which is assessed on the payer as agent for the recipient.

DOUBLE TAX RELIEF/ DOUBLE TAX TREATIES

Except for limited relief in relation to certain Commonwealth countries (rarely seen in practice), no credit is given for foreign taxes, although in some circumstances they may be deductible for Hong Kong tax purposes.

An employee of a Hong Kong establishment is exempt from salaries tax on income derived from services performed outside Hong Kong if the income is subject to tax in that foreign jurisdiction and the tax has been paid.

Hong Kong has no tax treaties with other countries, with the exception of an arrangement with the US government concerning international shipping operations.

Ports & Airports

The late 1980s and early 1990s have seen a major increase in the amount of air and shipping traffic passing through East Asia. Planners saw this coming some years back, and have been scrambling to expand and improve facilities at ports and airports throughout the regions, many of which are currently at or over capacity.

Air cargo traffic has been growing faster in Asia than anywhere else in the world, and passenger traffic has increased by leaps and bounds. However, with all the new facilities opening in the near future, there are estimates that by 1997 airport capacity will actually exceed demand. This may mean that airlines and cargo carriers will schedule more frequent service with smaller aircraft, something which is not currently possible, largely because of the small number of slots available at airport terminals and the many major airports operating with only one runway.

Long a major center for shipping, Asia is fast becoming the leader in container port traffic. The largest increases in container traffic worldwide have been at the Asian hub ports, and four of the world's five leading countries in container traffic are located on the western side of the Pacific Rim: Japan, Singapore, Hong Kong, and Taiwan are ranked two through five, respectively. The number one ranked US handles traffic from across the Pacific.

AIRPORT

Hong Kong's international airport and its support facilities are literally bursting at the seams. Kai Tak hit its annual passenger capacity of 24 million in 1993 and exceeded its annual air cargo capacity of 720,000 metric tons by 40,000 tons in 1990. It currently holds the record for delayed takeoffs among Asia-Pacific airports, with one of every three flights departing late, largely due to limited parking space for aircraft, major gate constraints, and the lack of a second runway. A new airport to replace Kai Tak is currently under construction on Lantau Island, and is set to open in 1997.

The entire planning process has been a contentious one, marked by battles between Chinese and Hong Kong officials. Because the airport's 1997 opening date coincides with that of Hong Kong rule reverting to China, the Chinese government has had to approve most of the airport plans for this US$14.6 billion project. Hong Kong's airport is clearly being put into competition with the two-year-old Shenzhen airport, and it has even been suggested by Chinese officials that the plans for Chek Lap Kok be scrapped so that the money earmarked for it can be invested into upgrading Shenzhen. Nevertheless, it appears that Hong Kong will have a new airport at Lantau Island soon, although it is certainly possible that its opening will be delayed.

When Chek Lap Kok becomes operational, it will have, like Kai Tak, a single runway. The annual passenger capacity will be 35 million, the annual air cargo capacity 1.3 million metric tons, and 60 parking stands will be available. However, by the end of Phase One in 2010, a second runway and two more terminals will be in place, to increase annual capacities to 45 million passengers and 2.5 million metric tons of cargo. The construction plans also include a large amount of land reclamation to allow for this expansion, as well as business, hotel, residential, and transportation facilities. A mass transit system will link the airport to the Central District and new expressways are to be built, including bridges and, eventually, tunnels through Kowloon and across the harbor.

Terminal 2, a new air cargo handling terminal at Kai Tak, opened in October 1991, even though it will be abandoned in 1997. While some saw this US$167 million building as a luxury that can be ill afforded at this time, others argued successfully that it had to be afforded, given that Hong Kong air cargo growth is forecast at 8 percent a year. This new facility, together with Hong Kong's free-port status and small number of customs controls has made the new terminal one of the most efficient operations in the world, albeit one of the more expensive as well. Hongkong Air Cargo Terminals Ltd. (HACTL) plans to raise handling rates by about 30 percent a year for three years, beginning in 1992, in part to pay for the new terminal before 1997.

Hong Kong currently has 54 air cargo carriers serving its international airport. As Hong Kong's flagship airline, Cathay Pacific is the most important. Major carriers include British Airlines, Continental, Delta, Japan Airlines, KLM, Korea Air, Lufthansa, Northwest, Malaysia Airlines, Singapore Airlines, Swissair, and United, while some all-cargo carriers such as Federal Express, United Parcel Service, and Nippon Cargo also deserve note. Five Chinese airlines serve Hong Kong: Air China, China Northern, China Southern, China Eastern, and China Southwest. For address and telephone information, refer to the Transportation section of "Important Addresses" chapter.

The Hong Kong International Airports are administered by :

Civil Aviation Department
Queensway Government Offices
66 Queensway
Hong Kong
Tel: [852] 8674332 Fax: [852] 8690093

For more information on airport development, contact:

Provisional Airport Authority
25/F., Central Plaza
Wanchai, Hong Kong
Tel: [852] 8247111 Fax: [852] 8240717

New Airport Project Coordinating Office
Works Branch, Hong Kong Government
7/F., Shui On Centre
8 Harbour Road
Wanchai, Hong Kong
Tel: [852] 8023408, 8296774 Fax: [852] 8242008

PORT

Hong Kong is the second busiest port in the world after Singapore, and the world's biggest container port, with approximately 65 percent of the cargo passing through the port in containerized form. Most of this is handled at the main Kwai Chung Container Port. The annual handling capacity for containers is now 5 million TEU's (210-foot equivalent units), since the completion of Kwai Chung Container Terminal No. 7 in 1990. Terminal 8, under construction at Stonecutters Island, will have a capacity of an additional 1.8 million TEU's, and should be completed by 1995. Terminal 9 on Tsing Yi island will have four berths when it is finished; the first of these berths is expected to be in operation by late 1995. Turnaround times for modern container ships, often less than 12 hours, are among the fastest in the world. Despite this, the present capacity of the port does not meet

the demand, so that plans have been made to upgrade and expand facilities significantly. Construction will begin in late 1994 on two new berths on the Tsing Chau Tsai Peninsula on Lantau Island, also the planned site of a replacement airport to open in 1997.

The port is administered by:

Marine Department (Hong Kong Port Authority)
22/F. Harbour Bldg., 38 Pier Rd.,
Central GPO Box 4155, Hong Kong
Tel: [852] 8523001 Fax: [852] 5449241
Tlx: 64553 MARHG

For information on port development contact:

Port Development Board
5/F., Yu Yuet Lai Building
Central, Hong Kong
Tel: [852] 8015825 Fax: [852] 8770583

Port Facilities
Transportation Service—Truck and barge.
Cargo Storage—Ample covered and open storage is available; total capacity is approximately 1.4 million metric tons.
Special Cranes—Heavy lift capacity is 350 metric tons. Container, 14 with 40 metric ton capacity.
Air Cargo—Kai Tak Airport adjacent to port.
Cargo Handling—Containerized, bulk, and general cargo can all be adequately handled by existing port equipment. Hong Kong has extensive liquid and dry bulk and Ro-Ro equipment for specialized cargoes.
Weather—Temperatures range from 10°C to 31°C with annual rainfall at 222 cms. Heaviest rains occur from April through September.
Construction—New container terminals and additional storage are planned for the near future; the expansion is predicated on the port's continuing role as a transshipment port for Chinese goods.

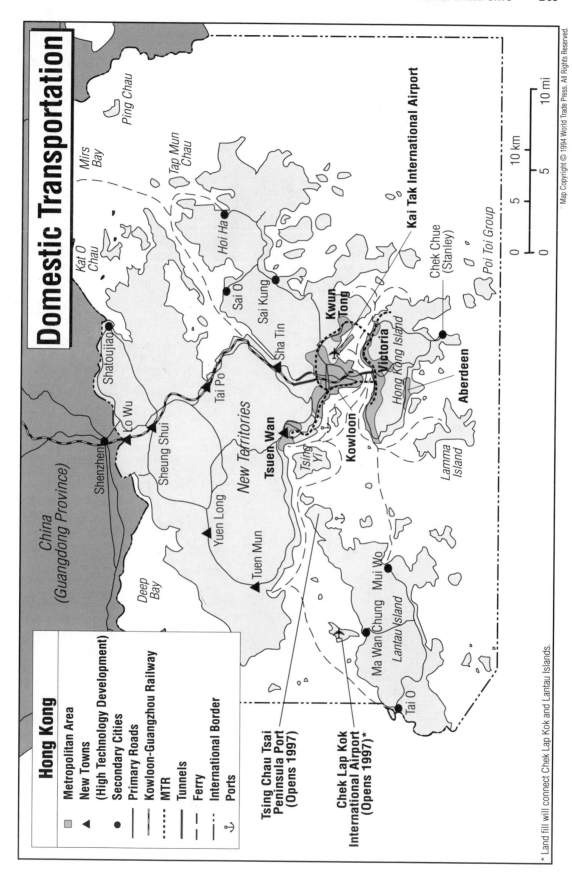

Domestic Transportation

Hong Kong

▦	Metropolitan Area
▲	New Towns (High Technology Development)
●	Secondary Cities
——	Primary Roads
┼┼	Kowloon-Guangzhou Railway
——	MTR
┆┆┆┆	Tunnels
——	Ferry
– –	International Border
⚓	Ports

China (Guangdong Province)

Shenzhen

Shatoujiao

Lo Wu

Sheung Shui

Deep Bay

Yuen Long

Tuen Mun

Tai Po

New Territories

Sha Tin

Sai O

Sai Kung

Hoi Ha

Kat O Chau

Mirs Bay

Tap Mun Chau

Ping Chau

Tsuen Wan

Tsing Yi

Kowloon

Victoria

Kwun Tong

Hong Kong Island

Aberdeen

Chek Chue (Stanley)

Lamma Island

Poi Toi Group

Kai Tak International Airport

Hong Kong Airport

Lantau Island

Ma Wan Chung

Mui Wo

Tai O

Tsing Chau Tsai Peninsula Port (Opens 1997)

Chek Lap Kok International Airport (Opens 1997)*

0   5   10 km

0   5   10 mi

* Map Copyright © 1994 World Trade Press. All Rights Reserved.

* Land fill will connect Chek Lap Kok and Lantau Islands.

Business Dictionary

CANTONESE PRONUNCIATION

Cantonese is the dialect of Guangdong Province, of which Hong Kong is geographically an important part. Because of its British links and the influence of Western culture, in Hong Kong you will often hear English words sprinkled liberally throughout a Cantonese conversation.

Most Hong Kong residents can understand English and many also understand a little Mandarin (Modern Standard Chinese) from pop songs and Kung Fu movies made in Taiwan.

Chinese as a written language is standard throughout China, although the characters will be pronounced differently depending on the local dialect.

Since Cantonese is a spoken dialect rather than a formal written language, many expressions for every-day things and activities are different in their spoken form than in written Chinese.

In the Cantonese version of this mini-dictionary you will find the standard Chinese characters for each expression a Cantonese would use when writing although the pronunciation guide may give the Cantonese spoken version.

In Cantonese there are a greater number of words with the same basic sound (homophones, such as the English worlds "bough" and "bow") than in Mandarin, the official language of China. Instead of the standard four tones of Mandarin, Cantonese has seven. Together with colloquialisms and slang (often very "earthy"), these differences can make learning the dialect very difficult both for Westerners and for Chinese from other parts of the country.

The pronunciation guide is an attempt to represent some of the very complex and unusual sounds of Cantonese in a manner easily understood by a native speaker of English. Because of the complexity of the Cantonese tone system, no attempt has been made to represent the tones for each syllable.

As with any spoken language, if possible it is best to listen to a native speaker and learn the correct pronunciation through your ears rather than from the printed page.

English	*Cantonese*	*Pronunciation*
GREETINGS AND POLITE EXPRESSIONS		
Hello.	您好嗎？	lay gay hoe (rhymes with toe) mah?
(in the evening)	晚安	joe-tao
Good-bye.	再見	bye-bye (dzoy geen)
Please.	請	ng (pronounced like ng in thing) goy
Pleased to meet (know) you.	很高興能見到（認識）您	hoe goe-hing nung gow (as in how) geen dow (ying-sik) lay
Please excuse me.	對不起	dui (rhymes with Looey) ng joo
Excuse me for a moment. (when leaving a meeting)	對不起，請稍等	dui ng joo, ng goy dung-dung
Congratulations.	恭喜您	gong-hay lay
Thank you (for a gift)	謝謝	daw jyeh
Thank you (for service)	謝謝	ng goy
Thank you very much.	非常感謝	jun-high hoe daw jyeh
Thank you for the gift.	謝謝您的禮物	daw jyeh lay-gay ligh-mut
I am sorry. I don't understand Chinese.	對不起，我不懂中文	dui ng joo, ngaw ng sik jong-mun
Do you speak English?	您會說英語嗎？	lay sik ng sik-gong ying-mun?
My name is...	我的名字叫...	ngaw gaw meng gyoo...
Is Mr/Ms Gong there? (on the telephone)	江先生/小姐在嗎？	Gong sang/Gong siu-jieh high-ng-high dow (rhymes with low)?
Can we meet (tomorrow)?	我們明天見好嗎？	ngaw-day ting-yut geen hoe mah?
Would you like to have dinner together?	我們一起吃晚飯好嗎？	ngaw-day yut-chy sik mahn fahn hoe mah?
Yes.	好的	hoe-geh
No.	不行	ng-tak

English	Cantonese	Pronunciation
English	*Cantonese*	*Pronunciation*

DAY/TIME OF DAY

English	Cantonese	Pronunciation
morning	早上	joe-sun
noon	中午	jong-ng
afternoon	下午	hah-joe
evening	晚上	mahn-sherng
night	夜晚	yeh-mahn
today	今天	gum-yut
yesterday	昨天	kum-yut
tomorrow	明天	ting-yut
Monday	星期一	sing-kay yut
Tuesday	星期二	sing-kay ee
Wednesday	星期三	sing-kay sahm
Thursday	星期四	sing-kay say
Friday	星期五	sing-kay ng
Saturday	星期六	sing-kay look
Sunday	星期日	sing-kay yut
holiday	假日	gah kay
New Year's Day	新年，元旦	sun neen, yune (rhymes with French lune) dahn
time	時間	see-gahn

NUMBERS

English	Cantonese	Pronunciation
one	一	yut
two	二	ee
three	三	sahm
four	四	say
five	五	ng
six	六	look
seven	七	chut
eight	八	bah
nine	九	gow (rhymes with how)
ten	十	sup
eleven	十一	sup-yut

English	Cantonese	Pronunciation
fifteen	十五	sup-ng
twenty	二十	ee-sup
twenty-one	二十一	ee-sup-yut
thirty	三十	sahm-sup
thirty-one	三十一	sahm-sup-yut
fifty	五十	ng-sup
one hundred	一百	yut-bahk
one hundred one	一百零一	yut-bahk ling yut
one thousand	一千	yut-cheen
one million	一百萬	yut-bahk mahn
first	第一	dye-yut
second	第二	dye-ee
third	第三	dye-sahm

GETTING AROUND TOWN

Where is...?	. . .在哪裡？	...hye been dow (rhymes with low)?
Does this train go to ...?	這輛火車去 . . .嗎？	nee-gah faw cheh hoy...ah?
Please take me to (location)	請送我到 . . .（地點）	ng goy how-ng-how yee-dye ngaw hoy...
Where am I?	這是哪裡？	ngaw hay been dow?
airplane	飛機	fay-gay
airport	飛機場	fay-gay-cherng
bus (public)	巴士	bah-see
taxi	的士	dik-see
train	火車	faw-cheh
train station	火車站	faw-cheh-jahm
ticket:	車票，車費	cheh pyew, cheh-fay
one-way (single) ticket	單程車費	dahn ching cheh-fay
round trip (return) ticket	雙程（來回）車費	serng ching (loy wuy) cheh-fay

English	Cantonese	Pronunciation
English	*Cantonese*	*Pronunciation*

PLACES

English	Cantonese	Pronunciation
airport	飛機場	fay-gay-cherng
bank	銀行	ngahn-hohng
barber shop	理髮店	fay faat pow (rhymes with low)
beauty parlor	美容院	may-yong-yune (rhymes with French lune)
business district	商業區	serng-yip koy
chamber of commerce	商會	serng-wuy
clothes store	服裝店	fook-johng deem
exhibition	展覽	jeen-lahm
factory	工廠	gong-chong
hotel	酒店	jow (rhymes with how)-deem
hospital	醫院	yee-yune
market	街市	guy-see
post office	郵局	yow (rhymes with how)-gook
restaurant	餐館	tsahn-goon
rest room/toilet (W.C.)	洗手間	sigh-sow-gahn
sea port	海港	hoy-gohng
train station	火車站	faw-cheh-jahm

At the bank

English	Cantonese	Pronunciation
What is the exchange rate?	兌換率是多少？	dway-wune-look gay daw?
I want to exchange...	我想兌換 . . .	ngaw serng dway-yune...
Australian dollar	澳元	oh-yune
British pound	英磅	ying bong
Chinese yuan (PRC)	人民幣	yun (as in sun)-mun bye
French franc	法郎	fah-long
German mark	德國馬克	duk-gok mah-huk
Hong Kong dollar	港幣	gong bye
Indonesia rupiah	印度尼西亞虜比	yun(as in sun)-nay jee
Japanese yen	日元	yut yune

English	Cantonese	Pronunciation
Korean won	韓國幣	hohn-gok jee
Malaysia ringgit	馬來西亞林吉特	mah-loy-sye-a jee
Philippines peso	菲律賓比索	fye-lok-bun pay-saw
Singapore dollar	新加坡幣	sun-gah-baw jee
New Taiwan dollar (ROC)	新台幣	sun toy bye
Thailand baht	泰幣	tye-bye
U.S. dollar	美元	may gum
Can you cash a personal check?	可以兌現個人支票嗎？	nay haw ng-haw yee-doy yin cherng see-yun jee-pyew ah?
Where should I sign?	我在哪裡里簽字？	ngaw high been-dow (rhymes with low) cheem meng?
Traveler's check	旅行支票	luy-hahng jee-pyew
Bank draft	銀行匯票	ngahn-hohng wuy-pyew

At the hotel

I have a reservation.	我已經預訂了房間	ngaw yee-ging deng-jaw gahm-fong
Could you give me a single/ double room?	能給我訂一個單人/雙人房間嗎？	nay haw ng-haw yee bay gahn dahn-yun-fong/serng-yun-fong?
Is there...?	有沒...？	yow (as in how) mo...?
air-conditioning	冷氣	lahng hay
heating	暖氣	nyuhn hay
private toilet	私人洗手間	see-yun sye-sow gahn
hot water	熱水	yit soy
May I see the room?	我能否看一看間房嗎？	ngaw haw ng-haw yee tye hah gahn fong?
Would you mail this for me please?	您能幫我郵寄這份東西嗎？	lay haw ng-haw yee bong ngaw-gay jaw kui?
Do you have any stamps?	您有郵票嗎？	lay yow mo-yow pyew ah?
May I have my bill?	請給我帳單	ng goy bay jerng dahn

English	Cantonese	Pronunciation
English	*Cantonese*	*Pronunciation*

At the store

Do you sell...?	這裡有沒有 . . . ?	lee-dough yow (as in how) mow (as in low)...?
Do you have anything less expensive?	有便宜些的嗎？	lee-dough yow mo peng-dee geh yeh ah?
I would like (quantity).	我想要（數量）	ngaw seung yoo (gay daw)
I'll take it.	我要這件	ngaw yoo lee-geen
I want this one.	我想要這個	ngaw seung yoo lee-gaw
When does it open/close?	什麼時候開／關門	gay-see hoy moon/sang moon

COUNTRIES

America (USA)	美國	may-gok
Australia	澳洲	oh-dzow (as in how)
China (PRC)	中華人民共和國	dai look
France	法國	faht-gok
Germany	德國	duk-gok
Hong Kong	香港	herng-gong
Indonesia	印度尼西亞	yun-nay
Japan	日本	yut-born
Korea	韓國	horn-gok
Malaysia	馬來西亞	mah-loy-sye-a
Philippines	菲律賓	fay-look-bahn
Singapore	新加坡	sing-gah-baw
Taiwan (ROC)	台灣	toy-wahn
Thailand	泰國	tye-gok
United Kingdom	英國	ying-gok

EXPRESSIONS IN BUSINESS

1) General business-related terms

accounting	會計	wuy-gigh
additional charge	附加費	foo gah figh
advertise	登廣告	dung gong-goe
advertisement	廣告	gong-goe

English	Cantonese	Pronunciation
bankrupt	破產	paw-chahn
brand name	商標名稱，牌子	pigh-jee meng
business	公司	sahng-yee (or gong-see)
buyer	買家	migh-gah
capital (money)	資金	jee-gum
cash	現金	yeen-gum
charge	記帳	gay-jerng
check	支票	jee-pyew
claim	賠償	poy-serng
collect	收帳	sow (as in cow) jerng
commission	傭金	yong-gum
company	公司	gong-see
copyright	版權	bahn-kune (rhymes with French lune)
corporation	集團	jahp-tune or kay-yip
cost (expense)	費用	fye-yong
currency	貨幣	faw-bye
customer	客戶	hahk-woo
D/A (documents against acceptance)	承兌交單	duy yeen jee how buy fahn jerng sow (as in how) guy (as in looey)
D/P (documents against payment)	付款交單	bay cheen gow dahn
deferred payment	延期付款	yeen kay foo-foon
deposit	存款	chune (rhymes with French lune)-foon
design	設計	cheek-gye
discount	折扣	cheek-kow
distribution	分配	fun-poy
dividends	紅利	hong-lay
documents	文件	mun-geen
due date	到期日	gow-kay
exhibit	証據	jing-guy
ex works	工廠交貨	gong-chong hay-faw
facsimile (fax)	傳眞	chune-jun
finance	財務，金融	choy-mow (as in low)
foreign businessman	外商家	oy serng gah

English	Cantonese	Pronunciation
foreign capital	外資	oy jee
foreign currency	外匯	oy wuy
foreign trade	對外貿易	duy oy mow (rhymes with how) yik
government	政府	jing foo
industry	工業	gong-yip
inspection	檢查	geem-chah
insurance	保險	bow (rhymes with low) heen
interest	利息	lay-sik
international	國際的	gok-jigh-sing
joint venture	合資	hup-jee
label	標簽	byew-cheem
letter of credit	信用證	son-yong-cheng
license	許可證	hoy-haw-jing
loan	貸款	tigh-foon
model (of a product)	產品模型	chahn-bahn-mow (as in low)-ying
monopoly	壟斷，專利	long-doon, june-lay
office	辦公室	bahn-gong-sup
patent	專利	june-lay
pay	支付	bay-cheen
payment for goods	貨款	foe-foon
payment by installment	分期付款	fun-kay foe-foon
permit	許可證	hoy-haw-jing
principal	本金	boon-gum or jee-boon
private (not government)	私營（非政府性）	see-ying (fay jing foo sing)
product	產品	chahn-bahn
profit margin	利潤幅度	lay-yon fook-doe
registration	註冊	joo-chah
report	報告	bo-go
research and development (R&D)	研究與發展	yeen-gow yu (French u) faat-dzeen
return (on investment)	投資利潤	tow (as in how)-jee lay-yon
sample	樣品	yerng-bahn

English	Cantonese	Pronunciation
seller	賣方	my-fahng
settle accounts	結帳	geet-jerng
service charge	服務費	fook-moe-figh
sight draft	即期匯票	jig-see wuy-pyew
tax	稅	soy
telephone	電話	deen-wah
telex	電傳	deen-chune
trademark	商標	serng-byew
visa:(credit card)	Visa信用卡	Visa son-yong kah

2) Labor

English	Cantonese	Pronunciation
compensation	薪金，薪水	sun-gum, sun-sui
employee	僱員	goo-yune
employer	僱主	goo-ju (French u)
fire/dismiss	解僱	gigh-goo
foreign worker	外籍勞工	oy-jik low-gong
hire	僱用	goo-yong
interview	面試	meen-see
laborer:	工人	gong-yun
skilled	熟練工（熟手）	souk(as in look)-sow (rhymes with how)
unskilled	非熟練工（生手）	serng-sow
labor force	勞動力	low (rhymes with show)-dong-lik
labor shortage	勞力短缺	low-gong dune-ku (both French u)
labor stoppage	停工	ting-gong
labor surplus	勞工過剩	low-gong gaw (rhymes with law)-seng
minimum wage	最低工資	dzoy-digh gong-jee
profession/occupation	職業	jik-yip
salary	薪金	sun-gum
strike	罷工	bah-gong
training	培訓，訓練	poy-fun, fun-lean
union	工會	gong-wuy
wage	工資，薪金	gong-jee, sun-gum

English	Cantonese	Pronunciation

3) Negotiations (Buying/Selling)

English	Cantonese	Pronunciation
agreement	協議	hip-yee
arbitrate	仲裁	jong-choy
brochure/pamphlet	手冊，小冊子	sow (as in how)-chah, syew chah-jee
buy	買	migh
confirm	確認	kok-ying
contract	合約	hahp-yer
cooperate	合作	hahp-jok
cost	價值	gah-jik
counteroffer	還價	wahn-gah
countersign	聯署	wuy-jeem or lune-chu (both with French u)
deadline	截止日期	jik-jee yut-kay
demand	要求	yew-kow (rhymes with how)
estimate	估計	goo-gigh
guarantee	保證	bow (rhymes with low)-jeng
label	標籤	byew-jeem
license	許可證	huy-haw (rhymes with law)-jing
market	市場	see-cherng
market price	市價	see-gah
minimum quantity	最低量	dzoy syew show-lyerng
negotiate	談判	tahm-poon
negotiate payment	付款談判	foo-foon tahm-poon
order	訂單	deng dahn
packaging	包裝	bow (as in how)-jong
place an order	發出定單	faat-chout (ou as in could) deng-dahn
price	價格	gah-gah
price list	價格表	gah-gah-byew
product features	產品特點	chahn-bun tak-deem
product line	產品系列	chahn-bun high-leet
quality	質量，品質	juck-lyerng, bun-juck

English	*Cantonese*	*Pronunciation*
quantity	數量	sow (as in low)-lyerng
quota	配額	poy-ngah
quote (offer)	報價	bow (as in low)-gah
sale	銷售，賣	syew-sow (as in how), my
sales confirmation	銷售確認書	syew-sow kok-ying shu (French u)
sell	銷售，賣	syew-sow, my
sign	簽署	cheem-chu (French u)
signature	簽字	cheem-meng
specifications	規格	kwigh-gah
standard (quality)	標準（質量）	byew-jun
superior (quality)	優質	yow (as in how)-juk
trade	貿易	mow (as in how)-yik
unit price	單價，每個價錢	dahn-gah, mui-gaw gah-chin
value	價值	gah-jik
value added	增值	jung jik
warranty (and services)	保證書（及服務）	bow (as in low)-jeng shu (French u)
The price is too high.	價錢太貴	gah-cheen tigh-gwigh
We need a faster delivery.	我們需要盡快交貨	ngaw-day soy-yew jon figh gow (as in how)-faw
We need it by...	我們需在...之前收到	ngaw-day soy-yew dzoy...jee cheen sow (as in how) dough
We need a better quality.	我們要比這個質量更好的	ngaw-day soy-yew gung how (as in low)-geh juk-lyerng
We need it to these specifications.	我們要符合這個規格的產品	ngaw-day yow foo-hap lee-gor jee-deng geh chahn-bun
I want to pay less.	我想要便宜些的	ngaw seung yew peng dee
I want the price to include	我希望這個價錢包括	ngaw seung lee-gor gah-cheem bow (as in how) kout

English	Cantonese	Pronunciation
Can you guarantee delivery?	您能保證交貨時間嗎?	lay nung ng nung gow (as in how) bow (as in low) jeng gow for yut kay?

4) Products/Industries

aluminum	鋁	loy
automobile	汽車	hay-cheh
automotive accessories	汽車零件	hay-cheh ling-geen
biotechnology	生物工藝學	sung-mut gong ngigh
camera	相機	serng-gay
carpets	地毯	day-jeen
cement	水泥	soy-nigh
ceramics	瓷器	chee-hay
chemicals	化學品	fah-hok bahn
clothing:	服裝	sahm
for women	女裝	noui (rhymes with Louey) johng
for men	男裝	nahm johng
for children	童裝	tong johng
coal	煤	moui (rhymes with Louey)
computer	電腦	deen-now (as in low)
computer hardware	電腦硬件	deen-now yerng-geen
computer software	電腦軟件	deen-now yune-geen
construction	建築	geen-jouk (ou as in would)
electrical equipment	電器設備	geen-hay jeek-bay
electronics	電子	deen-jee
engineering	工程	gong-ching
fireworks	炮竹	pow (as in how)-jouk (ou as in would), pow-cheung
fishery products	漁業產品	yu (French u)-yip chahn-bahn
food products	食品	sik-bahn
footwear	鞋類	high-loui (rhymes with French Louey)

English	Cantonese	Pronunciation
forestry products	木材產品	mouk (ou as in would)-choy chahn-bahn
fuel	燃料	yeen-lyou
furniture	家俱	gah-see
games	遊戲	yow (as in now)-hay
gas	氣體	hay-tigh
gemstone	寶石	bow-(as in how)sek
glass	玻璃	bow (as in low)-lay
gold	金子	gum
hardware	五金器件	ng-gum hay-geen
iron	鐵	teek
jewelry	珠寶	ju (French u)-bow (as in low)
lighting fixtures	燈飾	dung-sik
leather goods	皮具	pay-goy
machinery	機械	gay-high
minerals	礦物質	kong-mut-juk
musical instruments	樂器	ok-hay
paper	紙	jee
petroleum	石油	sek-yow(as in how)
pharmaceuticals	藥	yerk
plastics	塑膠	sow (as in low)-gow (as in how)
pottery	陶器	gong-ngah
rubber	橡膠	jerng-gow (as in how)
silk	絲綢	see
silver	銀器	ngahn-hay
spare parts	零件	ling-geen
sporting goods	體育用品	tigh-youk (ou as in would) yong-bahn
steel	鋼	gong
telecommunication equipment	電訊器材	deen-son hay-choy
television	電視	deen-see
textiles	紡織品	fong-jok-bahn
tobacco	煙草	yeen, (yeen-tsow)(as in low)

English	Cantonese	Pronunciation
tools:	工具	gong-goy
hand (powered)	手動	sow (as in low)-dong
power	電力	deen lik
tourism	旅遊	loui (as in French Louey)-yow (as in how)
toys	玩具	woon-goy
watches/clocks	手錶/鐘	sow (as in low)-byew/jong
wood	木材	mouk (ou as in would)-choy

5) Services

English	Cantonese	Pronunciation
accounting service	會計服務	oui (as in French Louey)-gigh fook-mow (as in low)
advertising agency	廣告代理商	gwong-gow (as in low) doy-lay-serng
agent	經紀，代理人	ging-gay, doy-lay-yun
customs broker	海關經紀人	high-goon ging-gay
distributor	經銷商	ging-syew-serng
employment agency	職業介紹所	jik-yip gigh-syew saw
exporter	出口商	chout (ou as in would)-how (as in now)-serng
freight forwarder	貨運代理人	faw-one doy-lay-yun
importer	入口商	yap-how(as in now) serng
manufacturer	製造商	jigh-joe (as in low) serng
packing service	包裝服務	bow (as in how)-jong fook-mow (as in low)
printing company	印刷公司	yun-chahk gong-see
retailer	零售商	ling-sow (as in how) serng
service(s)	服務	fook-mow (as in low)
supplier	供應商	gong-ying-serng
translation services	翻譯服務	fahn-yik fook-mow (as in low)
wholesaler	批發商	pigh-faat serng

English	Cantonese	Pronunciation
English	*Cantonese*	*Pronunciation*

6) Shipping/Transportation

English	Cantonese	Pronunciation
bill of lading	提貨單	tigh-faw-dahn
cost, insurance, freight (CIF)	成本、保險加運費價（到岸價）	seng-boon, bow (as in low) -heem gah one-figh-gah(dough ohn gah)
customs	海關	hoy-gwahn
customs duty	關稅	gwahn-soy
date of delivery	交貨日期	gow (as in how)-faw yat-kay
deliver (delivery)	交貨	gow (as in how)-faw
export	出口	chout (ou as in would)-how (as in now)
first class mail	快信	figh-shun (as in sun)
free on board (F.O.B.)	船上交貨價（離岸價）	sune (French u)-serng gow-faw-gah (lay -ohn-gah
freight	運費	one-figh
import	入口	yap-how (as in now)
in bulk	散裝	sahn-jong
mail (post)	郵寄	yow (as in how)-gay
country of origin	原產地	yune-chahn-day
packing	包裝	bow (as in how)-jong
packing list	裝箱單	jong-serng-dahn
port	港口	gong-how (as in now)
ship (to send):	運輸	one-shu (French u)
by air	空運	hong-one
by sea	海運	hoy-one
by train	火車運輸	faw (with a rising tone)- cheh-one-shu (French u)
by truck	貨車運輸	faw (with a falling tone)- cheh-one-shu (French u)

English	Cantonese	Pronunciation

WEIGHTS, MEASURES, AMOUNTS

English	Cantonese	Pronunciation
barrel	桶	tong
centimeter	厘米，公分	lay-my, gong fun
dozen	一打（十二個）	yat-dah, (sup-ee gaw)
foot	英尺	ying-chek
gallon	加侖	gah-lon
gram	克	hahk
gross (144 pieces)	羅（144 個）	law (yut-bahk say-sup-say gaw)
gross weight	總重量	jong-chong-lerng
hectare	公頃	gong-king
hundred (100)	一百	yut-bahk
inch	英寸	ying-chune (French u)
kilogram	公斤	gong-gun
kilometer	公里，千米	gong-lay, cheen my
meter	米，公尺	my, gong-chek
net weight	淨重	jing-chong
mile (English)	英里	ying-lay
liter	升	sing
ounce	盎司	on-see
pint	品脫	bahn-tut (French u)
pound (weight measure avoirdupois)	磅	bong
quart (avoirdupois)	夸脫	kwah-tut (French u)
square meter	平方米，平方公尺	ping-fong-my, ping-fong gong-chek
square yard	平方碼	ping-fong mah
size	尺寸	chek-chune
ton	噸	don
yard	碼	mah
jin (Chinese pound)	斤	gun
liang (Chinese ounce)	兩	lerng
cun (Chinese inch)	寸	chune (French u)
chi (Chinese foot)	尺	chek

English	*Cantonese*	*Pronunciation*
HONG KONG-SPECIFIC EXPRESSIONS AND TERMS		
You are welcome	不需要客氣	ng sigh hahk-hay
It doesn't matter	沒關係	mow (as in low) gwahn-high
Please do not smoke	請勿吸煙	ching mut cup-yin
Have a nice trip	旅途愉快	lui-tow (as in low) yu (French u)-figh
COMMON SIGNS		
Please do not disturb (sign to put on the door of hotel room)	請勿騷擾	ching mut sow (as in low)-yew
Enter	入口	yap-how (as in now)
Exit	出口	chout-how (as in now)
Men: (word for "restroom" usually not written on door)	男（男洗手間）	nahm sy-sau-gahn
Women: (word for "restroom" usually not written on door)	女（女洗手間）	nuy sy-sau-gahn
No smoking	禁止吸煙	gum-jee kahp-yin
Handle with care	小心輕放	syew-sum hing-fong

Important Addresses

IMPORTANT ADDRESSES TABLE OF CONTENTS

Government 261
  Government Agencies 261
  Overseas Diplomatic Missions of
    the United Kingdom 264
  Foreign Diplomatic Missions
    in Hong Kong 265
Trade Promotion Organizations 268
  World Trade Center 268
  General Trade Associations & Local
    Chambers of Commerce 268
  Foreign Chambers of Commerce &
    Business Organizations 268
  Hong Kong Trade Development Council
    (HKTDC) Offices in Hong Kong 269
  Hong Kong Trade Development Council
    (HKTDC) Offices Overseas 269
  Industry-Specific Trade Organizations ... 271
Financial Institutions 277
  Banks 277
  Insurance Companies 278
  Stock & Commodity Exchanges 278
Services 279
  Accounting Firms 279
  Advertising Agencies 279
  Law Firms 281
  Translators & Interpreters 281
Transportation 283
  Airlines 283
  Transportation & Customs
    Brokerage Firms 284
Publications, Media &
  Information Sources 287
  Directories & Yearbooks 287
  Newspapers 288
  General Business & Trade Periodicals ... 288
  Industry-Specific Periodicals 289
  Radio & Television 293
  Libraries 293

GOVERNMENT

GOVERNMENT AGENCIES

Agriculture & Fisheries Department
12/F., Canton Road Government Offices
393 Canton Road
Kowloon, Hong Kong
Tel: 7332235, 7332211 Fax: 3113731

Building & Lands Department
Mezzanine F., Murray Building
Garden Road
Hong Kong
Tel: 8482198 Fax: 8684707

Census & Statistics Department
20/F., Wanchai Tower I
12 Harbour Road
Wanchai, Hong Kong
Tel: 8235077, 8234807 Fax: 8652900

City and New Territories Administration
Southern Centre
130 Hennessy Road
Wanchai, Hong Kong
Tel: 8351444 Fax: 8347649

Civil Aviation Department
46/F., Queensway Government Offices
66 Queensway
Hong Kong
Tel: 8674332 Fax: 8690093 Tlx: 61361 CAD

Civil Engineering Services Department
9/F., Empire Centre
68 Mody Road
Kowloon, Hong Kong
Tel: 7212527, 8481111 Fax: 3110725

Companies Registry
13/F., Queensway Government Offices
66 Queensway
Wanchai, Hong Kong
Tel: 8672600 Fax: 8690423

Consumer Council
19/F., China HK City, Tower 6
3 Canton Road, Tsimshatsui
Kowloon, Hong Kong
Tel: 7365322

Customs & Excise Department
8/F., Harbour Building
38 Pier Road
Central, Hong Kong
Tel: 8521411, 8523324 Fax: 5423334

Department of Health
Sunning Plaza
4-13/F., 10 Hysan Avenue
Causeway Bay, Hong Kong
Tel: 8900770 Fax: 5765166

Economic Services Branch
Government Secretariat
2/F., Main and East Wings
Central Government Offices
Lower Albert Road
Hong Kong
Tel: 8102717 Fax: 8101530

Electrical & Mechanical Services Department
98 Caroline Hill Road
Hong Kong
Tel: 8958620 Fax: 8907493, 8685916

Environmental Protection Department
28/F., Southorn Centre
130 Hennessy Road
Wanchai, Hong Kong
Tel: 8351349 Fax: 5910636

Finance Branch
Government Secretariat
4/F., Main and East Wings
Central Government Offices
Lower Albert Road
Hong Kong
Tel: 8102717 Fax: 8101530

Government Land Transport Agency
25/F., Wanchai Tower I
12 Harbour Road
Hong Kong
Tel: 8235286 Fax: 8656780

Government Industry Department
One-Stop Unit
14/F., Ocean Centre
5 Canton Rd.
Kowloon, Hong Kong
Tel: 7372434 Fax: 7304633

Government Supplies Department
12 Oil Street
Hong Kong
Tel: 8026100, 8026104 Fax: 5107904, 8072764
Tlx: 61675 HKGSD

Intellectual Property Department
15/F., Ocean Centre Curved Block
5 Canton Road
Kowloon, Hong Kong
Tel: 7372633

Highways Department
10/F., Empire Centre
68 Mody Road
Kowloon, Hong Kong
Tel: 7210564

Hong Kong Export Credit Insurance Corporation
South Seas Centre, Tower I
75 Mody Road, 2/F.
Tsimshatsui East
Kowloon, Hong Kong
Tel: 7233883 Fax: 7226277

Hong Kong Productivity Council
World Commerce Centre, 12-13/F.
Harbour City, 11 Canton Road
Kowloon, Hong Kong
Tel: 7351656 Fax: 7357229

Hong Kong Securities and Futures Commission
(SEC)
Exchange Square, 38/F., Tower II
Hong Kong
Tel: 8409222 Fax: 8459553

Immigration Department
2/F., Wanchai Tower II
7 Gloucester Road
Wanchai, Hong Kong
Tel: 8293456, 8246111 Fax: 8241133 Tlx: 69996

Industry Department
14/F., Ocean Centre
5 Canton Road
Kowloon, Hong Kong
Tel: 7372573, 7372208 Fax: 7304633 Tlx: 50151
INDHK

Information Services Department
Beaconsfield House
4 Queen's Road Central
Hong Kong
Tel: 8428777

Information Technology Services Department
15/F., Wanchai Tower II
12 Harbour Road
Wanchai, Hong Kong
Tel: 8234520 Fax: 8656549

Inland Revenue Department
Windsor House
311 Gloucester Road
Hong Kong
Tel: 8945098 Fax: 5766359

Inland Revenue Department
Business Registration Office
Wanchai Tower
5 Gloucester Road
Wanchai, Hong Kong
Tel: 5490888

Judiciary Department
Supreme Court
38 Queensway
Hong Kong
Tel: 8690869

Labour Department
16/F., Harbour Building
38 Pier Road
Hong Kong
Tel: 8524118, 8155066 Fax: 5443271

Land Registry
Queensway Government Offices
66 Queensway
Wanchai, Hong Kong
Tel: 8672811 Fax: 5960281

Legal Department
1-8/F., Highblock
Queensway Government Offices
66 Queensway
Hong Kong
Tel: 8672123 Fax: 8690720

Marine Department (Hong Kong Port Authority)
22/F., Harbour Building
38 Pier Road
Central GPO Box 4155
Hong Kong
Tel: 8523001 Fax: 5449241 Tlx: 64553

Monetary Affairs Branch
Government Secretariat
Admiralty Centre, Tower II
Hong Kong
Tel: 5290003 Fax: 8656146

Monetary Authority
30/F., 3 Garden Road
Central, Hong Kong
Tel: 8788196

New Airport Project Coordinating Office
Works Branch, Hong Kong Government
7/F., Shui On Centre
8 Harbour Road
Wanchai, Hong Kong
Tel: [852] 8023408, 8296774 Fax: [852] 8242008

Office of the Commissioner of Banking
28/F., Queensway Government Office
66 Queensway
Central, Hong Kong
Tel: 8672671 Fax: 8690462 Tlx: 64282

Office of the Commissioner of Insurance
22/F., Queensway Government Office
66 Queensway
Central, Hong Kong
Tel: 8672565

Planning Department
17/F., Murray Building
Garden Road
Hong Kong
Tel: 8684497 Fax: 8770329

Planning, Environment and Lands Branch
Murray Building
Garden Road
Hong Kong
Tel: 8482111 Fax: 8453489

Port Development Board
5/F., Yu Yuet Lai Building
Central, Hong Kong
Tel: [852] 8015825 Fax: [852] 8770583

Post Office
2 Connaught Place
Hong Kong
Tel: 5231071 Fax: 8680094

Provisional Airport Authority
25/F., Central Plaza
Wanchai, Hong Kong
Tel: [852] 8247111 Fax: [852] 8240717

Radio Television Hong Kong
Broadcasting House
30 Broadcast Drive
Kowloon, Hong Kong
Tel: 3396441 Fax: 3380279

Recreation and Culture Branch
Government Secretariat
Harbour Centre, 25 Harbour Road
Wanchai, Hong Kong
Tel: 5741455 Fax: 8383646

Registrar General's Department
10-21/F., Queensway Government Offices
66 Queensway
Central, Hong Kong
Tel: 8672811

Registry of Trade Unions
11/F., Harbour Building
38 Pier Road
Hong Kong
Tel: 8523456

Television and Entertainment Licensing Authority
National Mutual Centre, 9/F.
151 Gloucester Road
Wanchai, Hong Kong
Tel: 5743130 Fax: 8382219

Territory Development Department
18/F., Murray Building
Garden Road
Hong Kong
Tel: 8482828, 8482846 Fax: 8684560

Trade and Industry Branch
Government Secretariat
2/F., East Wing, Central Government Offices
Lower Albert Road
Hong Kong
Tel: 8102717 Fax: 8401621

Trade Department
Trade Department Tower
700 Nathan Road
Kowloon, Hong Kong
Tel: 7897555 Fax: 7892491 Tlx: 45126 CNDI

Transport Department
2-6/F., East Wing, Central Government Offices
Lower Albert Road
Hong Kong
Tel: 8102717 Fax: 8684643

All addresses and telephone numbers are in Hong Kong unless otherwise noted. The country code for Hong Kong is [852].

Treasury Department
8/F., West Wing Central Government Offices
11 Ice House Street
Hong Kong
Tel: 8102402 Fax: 8684193

Urban Services Department
42-45/F., Queensway Government Office
66 Queensway
Central, Hong Kong
Tel: 8625578

Water Supplies Department
12/F., Leighton Centre
77 Leighton Road
Hong Kong
Tel: 8900333 Fax: 8952439

OVERSEAS DIPLOMATIC MISSIONS OF THE UNITED KINGDOM

As a British Crown Colony (until 1997), Hong Kong has no diplomatic missions of its own, but is represented by those of the United Kingdom. A selective list of these follow.

Australia
British Consulate General
CML Building
330 Collins Street
Melbourne, Vic. 3000, Australia
Tel: [61] (3) 67-5879 Fax: [61] (3) 600-0878

Austria
British Embassy
Juaresgasse 12
1030 Vienna, Austria
Tel: [43] (1) 7131575 Fax: [43] (1) 757824

Belgium
British Embassy
Britannia House
rue Joseph II, 28
1040 Brussels, Belgium
Tel: [32] (2) 179000 Fax: [32] (2) 2176763

Canada
British High Commission
80 Elgin Street
Ottawa, ON K1P 5K7, Canada
Tel: [1] (613) 237-1530
Fax: [1] (613) 217-7980

Denmark
British Embassy
36-40 Kastelsvej
DK-2100 Copenhagen, Denmark
Tel: [45] 31-26-46-00 Fax: [45] 31-43-14-00

Finland
British Embassy
16-20 Uudemaakatu
00120 Helsinki 12, Finland
Tel: [358] (0) 647922 Fax: [358] (0) 611747

France
British Embassy
35 rue du Faubourg St. Honoré
75383 Paris Cedex 08, France
Tel: [33] (1) 42-66-91-42
Fax: [33] (1) 42-66-95-90

Germany
British Consulate General
Amalienstrasse 62
8000 Munich 40, Germany
Tel: [49] (89) 394015 Fax: [49] (89) 331848

Italy
British Embassy
via XX Settembre, 80A
00187 Rome, Italy
Tel: [39] (6) 5441475 Fax: [39] (6) 4741836

Japan
British Embassy
1, Ichiban-cho, Chiyoda-ku
Tokyo 102
Tel: [81] (3) 3265-5511 Fax: [81] (3) 3265-5580

Korea
British Embassy
4, Chung-dong, Chung-ku
Seoul 100, Korea
Tel: [82] (2) 735-7341/3
Fax: [82] (2) 733-8368

Netherlands
British Embassy
Lange Voorhout 10
2514 ED The Hague, Netherlands
Tel: [31] (70) 645800

New Zealand
British High Commission
Reserve Bank of N.Z. Building, 9/F.
2 The Terrace
Wellington 1, New Zealand
Tel: [64] (4) 726-049 Fax: [64] (4) 711-794

Norway
British Embassy
Thomas Heftyesgate 8
Oslo 2, Norway
Tel: [47] (2) 552400 Fax: [47] (2) 551041

Singapore
British High Commission
Tanglin Road
Singapore 1024
Tel: 4739333 Fax: 4759706, 4752320

Spain
British Embassy
Calle de Fernando el Santo 16
Madrid 4, Spain
Tel: [34] (1) 419-0200 Fax: [34] (1) 419-0423

Sweden
British Embassy
Skarpogatan 6-8
11527 Stockholm, Sweden
Tel: [46] (8) 6670140 Fax: [46] (8) 629989

Switzerland
British Consulate General
Dufourstrasse 56
8008 Zurich, Switzerland
Tel: [41] (1) 4715-2026 Fax: [41] (1) 252-8351

United States of America
British Embassy
3100 Massachusetts Avenue NW
Washington, DC 20008, USA
Tel: [1] (202) 462-1340
Fax: [1] (202) 898-4255

FOREIGN DIPLOMATIC
MISSIONS IN HONG KONG

Australia
Counsulate General & Trade Commission
23/F., Harbour Centre
25 Harbour Road
Hong Kong
Consulate Gen. Tel: 5731881 Fax: 8345354
Trade Comm. Tel: 8331133 Fax: 8344145

Austria
Consulate General
2201 Wang Kee Building
36 Connaught Road Central
Hong Kong
Tel: 5239716 Fax: 5218773 Tlx: 86006

Trade Commission
14/F., Diamond Exchange Building
8 Duddell Street
Hong Kong
Tel: 5237555 Fax: 8106493 Tlx: 74004 AHST

Belgium
Consulate General &
Trade Commission
9/F., Street John's Building
33 Garden Road
Hong Kong
Tel: 5243111 Fax: 8685997 Tlx: 73185 CGBEL

Brazil
Consulate General
1504 Dina House
11 Duddell Street
Hong Kong
Tel: 5257002 Fax: 5218761 Tlx: 74742 BRAHK

Canada
Commission
12/F., One Exchange Square
Hong Kong
Tel: 8104321

Chile
General Consulate
1408 Great Eagle Centre
23 Harbour Road
Hong Kong
Tel: 8271826 Fax: 8271119 Tlx: 72842 CHILE

Consulate
1107 Melbourne Plaza
33 Queen's Road Central
Hong Kong
Tel: 8681122 Tlx: 72842 CHILE

Colombia
Consulate General
Unit A, 6/F., CMA Building
64 Connaught Road Central
Hong Kong
Tel: 5458547

Costa Rica
Consulate General
C-10 Hung On Building
3 Tin Hau Temple Road
Hong Kong
Tel: 5665181

Cyprus
Consulate
19/F., United Centre
95 Queensway
Hong Kong
Tel: 5292161 Fax: 8611150 Tlx: 73630 INTMA

Denmark
Consulate General
24/F., Great Eagle Centre
23 Harbour Road
Hong Kong
Tel: 8936265 Fax: 5723555 Tlx: 83671 GKLDK

Dominican Republic
Consulate General
602A Ocean Centre
7 Canton Road
Kowloon, Hong Kong
Tel: 7303306

Egypt
Consulate General
9/F., Woodland Garden
10 MacDonnel Road
Hong Kong
Tel: 5244174 Fax: 5212080 Tlx: 73030 ZAFAR

Commercial Representative Office
501 Yue Yuet Lai Building
43 Wyndham Street
Hong Kong
Tel: 5233947

Finland
Consulate & Trade Commission
1818 Hutchison House
10 Harcourt Road
Hong Kong
Tel: 5255385 Fax: 8101232 Tlx: 76531 FINLA

France
Consulate General
26/F., Admiralty Centre, Tower II
18 Harcourt Road
Hong Kong
Tel: 5294351 Fax: 8610019 Tlx: 83331 ECOFR

Trade Commission
25/F., Admiralty Centre, Tower II
18 Harcourt Road
Hong Kong
Tel: 5294316 Fax: 8610019 Tlx: 83331

All addresses and telephone numbers are in Hong Kong unless otherwise noted. The country code for Hong Kong is [852].

Germany
Consulate General & Trade Commission
21/F., United Centre
95 Queensway
Hong Kong
Tel: 5298855

Greece
Consulate General
914 Hunghom Commercial Centre
39 Ma Tau Wei Road
Kowloon, Hong Kong
Tel: 7741682

Honduras
Consulate
1303 Pacific House
20 Queen's Road Central
Hong Kong
Tel: 5226593

India
Commission and Trade Commission
15/F., United Centre
95 Queensway
Hong Kong
Commission Tel: 5284028
Trade Commission Tel: 5284475

Indonesia
Consulate General & Trade Commission
6 Keswick Street
Hong Kong
Tel: 8904421

Ireland
Consulate
801 Prince's Building
Chater Rd.
Hong Kong
Tel: 5226022

Israel
Consulate General & Trade Commission
701 Admiralty Centre, Tower II
18 Harcourt Road
Hong Kong
Tel: 5296091

Italy
Consulate General
810 Hutchison House
Harcourt Road
Hong Kong
Tel: 5220033

Trade Commission
701 Three Exchange Square
8 Connaught Pl.
Hong Kong
Tel: 8466500 Fax: 8684779 Tlx: 65939 INACE

Jamaica
Consulate
23/F., Shanghai Industrial Investment Bldg.
48 Hennessy Road
Hong Kong
Tel: 8238238

Japan
Consulate General
25/F., Bank of America Tower
Hong Kong
Tel: 5250796

Jordan
Consulate
911 World Shipping Centre
Harbour City
Kowloon, Hong Kong
Tel: 7356399

Korea (South)
Consulate General & Trade Commission
5/F., Far East Finance Centre
16 Harcourt Road
Hong Kong
Tel: 5294141 Fax: 8613699

Malaysia
Commission & Trade Commission
24/F., Malaysian Building
50 Gloucester Road
Hong Kong
Tel: 5270921 Fax: 8661148 Tlx: 60567

Mexico
Consulate General
1809 World Wide House
19 Des Voeux Road C.
Hong Kong
Tel: 5214365 Fax: 8453404 Tlx: 61866 MAYA

Netherlands
Consulate General
3/F., China Building
29 Queen's Road Central
Hong Kong
Tel: 5225127 Fax: 8685388 Tlx: 65588 NEERL

New Zealand
Commission
3414 Jardine House
Hong Kong
Tel: 5255044 Fax: 8452915 Tlx: 73932 KAKA

Nigeria
Commission
25/F., Tung Wai Commercial Building
109 Gloucester Road
Hong Kong
Tel: 8939444

Norway
Consulate General
1401 AIA Building
1 Stubbs Road
Hong Kong
Tel: 5748253

Peru
Consulate General
10/F., 10 Wyndham Street
Hong Kong
Tel: 8682622

Philippines
Consulate General & Trade Commission
22/F., Regent Centre
88 Queen's Road Central
Hong Kong
Consulate General Tel: 8100183
Trade Commission Tel: 8100770

Portugal
Consulate General
1001 Two Exchange Square
Hong Kong
Tel: 5225789

Singapore
Commission
901 Admiralty Centre, Tower I
18 Harcourt Road
Hong Kong
Tel: 5272212 Fax: 8613595 Tlx: 73194

South Africa
Consulate General
27/F., Sunning Plaza
10 Hysan Avenue
Hong Kong
Tel: 5773279 Fax: 5774532 Tlx: 83742 SACON

Spain
Consulate General
8/F., Printing House
18 Ice House Street
Hong Kong
Tel: 5253041

Trade Commission
2004 Bond Centre, East Tower
89 Queensway
Hong Kong
Tel: 5217433 Fax: 8453448 Tlx: 67573 OFCOM

Sweden
Consulate General
8/F., Hong Kong Club Building
3A Chater Road
Hong Kong
Tel: 5211212 Fax: 8105977 Tlx: 74374 SVENS

Switzerland
Consulate General
3703 Gloucester Tower, The Landmark
11 Pedder Street
Hong Kong
Tel: 5227147 Fax: 8452619

Thailand
Consulate General & Trade Commission
8/F., Fairmont House
8 Cotton Tree Drive
Hong Kong
Tel: 5216481 Fax: 5218629 Tlx: 83141

United Kingdom
Trade Commission
9/F., Bank of America Tower
12 Harcourt Road
Hong Kong
Tel: 5230176 Fax: 8452870 Tlx: 73031

United States of America
Consulate General
26 Garden Road
Hong Kong
Tel: 5211467 Fax: 8459800 Tlx: 63141 USDOC

Venezuela
Consulate General
805 Star House
3 Salisbury Rd.
Kowloon, Hong Kong
Tel: 3678099

All addresses and telephone numbers are in Hong Kong unless otherwise noted. The country code for Hong Kong is [852].

TRADE PROMOTION ORGANIZATIONS

WORLD TRADE CENTER

World Trade Centre Club Hong Kong
2-3/F., World Trade Centre
Causeway Bay, Hong Kong
Tel: 5779528 Fax: 8952692, 8818663 Tlx: 71729 WTCEN

GENERAL TRADE ASSOCIATIONS & LOCAL CHAMBERS OF COMMERCE

Chinese Manufacturers' Association
3-4/F., CMA Building
64-66 Connaught Road
Central, Hong Kong
Tel: 5456166 Fax: 5414541 Tlx: 63526 MAFTS

Federation of Hong Kong Industries
Hankow Centre, 4/F.
5-15 Hankow Road, Tsimshatsui
Kowloon, Hong Kong
Tel: 7230818 Fax: 7213494 Tlx: 30101 FHKI

Hong Kong Chinese Importers & Exporters
Association
7-8/F., Champion Building
287-291 Des Voeux Road Central
Central, Hong Kong
Tel: 5448474 Fax: 5444677

Hong Kong Exporters' Association
Rm. 825, Star House
3 Salisbury Road, Tsimshatsui
Kowloon, Hong Kong
Tel: 7309851 Fax: 7301869

Hong Kong General Chamber of Commerce
22/F., United Square
95 Queensway
Hong Kong
Tel: 5299229 Fax: 5279843 Tlx: 83535 TRIND

Hong Kong Junior Chamber of Commerce
1/F., 60 Bonham Strand East
Sheung Wan, Hong Kong
Tel: 5438913 Fax: 5436271

Kowloon Chamber of Commerce
3/F., KCC Building
2 Liberty Avenue
Kowloon, Hong Kong
Tel: 7600393 Fax: 7610166 Tlx: 32624

New Territories General Chamber of Commerce
25/F., 11 Nelson Street
Kowloon, Hong Kong
Tel: 3961845

Po Yick General Chinese & Foreign Goods Import &
Export Commercial Society of Hong Kong
2/F., 17-19 Hillier Street
Hong Kong
Tel: 5439524, 5457490

Wah On Exporters & Importers Association
1/F., 46 Bonham Strand East
Sheung Wan, Hong Kong
Tel: 5433111

FOREIGN CHAMBERS OF COMMERCE & BUSINESS ORGANIZATIONS

American Chamber of Commerce
1030 Swire House
6 Chater Road
Hong Kong
Tel: 5260165 Fax: 8101289 Tlx: 83664 AMCC

Australian Chamber of Commerce
701A Euro Trade Centre
13 Connaught Road Central
Hong Kong
Tel: 5225054 Fax: 8770860

British Chamber of Commerce
1712 Shui On Centre
8 Harbour Road
Hong Kong
Tel: 8242211 Fax: 8241333 Tlx: 82759 BRIT

Canadian Chamber of Commerce
13/F., One Exchange Square
Hong Kong
Tel: 5263207 Fax: 8451654

Chinese Chamber of Commerce, Kowloon
2/F., 8 Nga Tsin Long Road
Kowloon, Hong Kong
Tel: 3822309

Chinese General Chamber of Commerce
24 Connaught Road C, 7/F.
Hong Kong
Tel: 5256385 Fax: 8452610 Tlx: 89854 CGCC

Dutch Business Association
104 Hollywood Commercial House
3-5 Old Bailey Street
Central, Hong Kong
Tel: 5257906 Fax: 5218777

French Business Association
Rm. 401, Far East Exchange Building
8 Wyndham Street
Central, Hong Kong
Tel: 5236818 Fax: 5241428

German Business Association of Hong Kong
701 Euro Trade Centre
13 Connaught Road Central
Hong Kong
Tel: 5265481 Fax: 8106093 Tlx: 60128 VDKHK

Hong Kong Japanese Chamber of Commerce &
Industry
38/F., Hennessy Centre
500 Hennessy Road
Hong Kong
Tel: 5776129 Fax: 5770525

Hong Kong Taiwan Chamber of Commerce
10/F., Chevalier House
45 Chatham Road
Kowloon, Hong Kong
Tel: 7217636 Fax: 7213470

Hong Kong/Japan Business Co-operation
Committee
38/F., Convention Plaza
1 Harbour Road
Wanchai, Hong Kong
Tel: 8334333 Fax: 5730249 Tlx: 73595 CONHK

Indian Chamber of Commerce
2/F., Hoseinee House
69 Wyndham Street
Hong Kong
Tel: 5233877 Fax: 8450300 Tlx: 64993 INCHA

Korean Foreign Trade Association
400 Korea Centre Building
119 Connaught Road Central
Hong Kong
Tel: 5432234 Fax: 8540006

Korean Society of Commerce in Hong Kong
5/F., Korea Centre Building
119 Connaught Road Central
Hong Kong
Tel: 5447602

New Zealand Trade Development Board
3414 Jardine House
Hong Kong
Tel: 5255044 Fax: 8770739

New Zealand-Hong Kong Business Association
c/o Bayleys Asia Ltd.
504 Central Building
Hong Kong
Tel: 5216465

Swedish Chamber of Commerce in Hong Kong
7B Shung Ho Tower
24-30 Ice House Street
Central, Hong Kong
Tel: 5250349 Fax: 8685344 Tlx: 68350

Swiss Business Council in Hong Kong
GPO Box 9501
Hong Kong
Tel: 5240590 Fax: 8772504 Tlx: 60360 CSKHB

Taiwan Trade Centre
80 Gloucester Road, 2/F.
Hong Kong
Tel: 8655372 Fax: 8562423

HONG KONG TRADE DEVELOPMENT COUNCIL (HKTDC) OFFICES IN HONG KONG

Head Office
38/F., Convention Plaza
1 Harbour Road
Wanchai, Hong Kong
Tel: 5844333 Fax: 8240249 Tlx: 73595 CONHK

Advertising Department
Rm. 1303, Block A
13/F., Sea View Estate
2 Watson Road
North Point, Hong Kong
Tel: 5667292 Fax: 8876490

Datashop Central
General Post Office, Ground F.
2 Connaught Place
Central, Hong Kong
Tel: 8771787

Datashop Kwun Tong
Ground F., Chung Nam Centre
414 Kwun Tong Road, Kwun Tong
Kowloon, Hong Kong
Tel: 3412314

Datashop Mongkok
Trade Department Tower, Ground F.
700 Nathan Road, Mongkok
Kowloon, Hong Kong
Tel: 3900276

HONG KONG TRADE DEVELOPMENT COUNCIL (HKTDC) OFFICES OVERSEAS

Argentina
c/o International Marketing Service
Reconquista 513, Piso 3
1003 Buenos Aires, Rep. of Argentina
Tel: [54] (1) 3931636 Fax: [54] (1) 3268304

Australia
71 York Street
Sydney, NSW 2000, Australia
Postal address: GPO Box 3877
Sydney, NSW 2001, Australia
Tel: [61] (2) 299-8343 Fax: [61] (2) 290-1889

Austria
Rotenturnmstrasse 1-3/8/24
A-1010 Vienna, Austria
Tel: [43] (1) 533-3156 Fax: [43] (1) 535-3156
Tlx: 11509 HKTDC A

Canada
Suite 1100, National Building
347 Bay Street
Toronto, ON M5H 2R7 Canada
Tel: [1] (416) 366-3594 Fax: [1] (416) 366-1569

Suite 700, 1550 Alberni Street
Vancouver, BC V6G 1A3, Canada
Tel: [1] (604) 685-0883, 669-4444
Fax: [1] (604) 681-0093

China
Rm. 901, CITIC Building
19 Jian Guo Men Wai Dajie
Beijing 100004, PRC
Tel: [86] (1) 5128661 Fax: [86] (1) 5003285

Unit A, 26/F.
Guangdong International Bldg., Annex A
339 Huanshi Dong Lu
Guangzhou, PRC
Tel: [86] (20) 3312889 Fax: [86] (20) 3311081

Rm. 1004, Shanghai Union Building
100 Yanan Dong Lu
Shanghai 200002, PRC
Tel: [86] (21) 3264196, 3265935
Fax: [86] (21) 3287478 Tlx: 30175 TDCSH CN

All addresses and telephone numbers are in Hong Kong unless otherwise noted. The country code for Hong Kong is [852].

France
18, rue d'Aguesseau
75008 Paris, France
Tel: [33] (1) 47-42-41-50 Fax: [33] (1) 47-42-77-44

Germany
Kreuzerhol 5-7
W-6000 Frankfurt/Main 50, Germany
Postal address: PO Box 500551
W-6000 Frankfurt/Main 50, Germany
Tel: [49] (69) 586001 Fax: [49] (69) 5890752

Greece
48, Aegialias Street
Paradissos
GR 151 25 Amaroussion, Greece
Tel: [30] (1) 685-0830 Fax: [30] (1) 685-0832

Hungary
Dorottya utca 8
H-1051 Budapest, Hungary
Tel: [36] (1) 266-1988 Fax: [36] (1) 266-1944

Italy
2 Piazzetta Pattari
20122 Milan, Italy
Tel: [39] (2) 865405, 865715 Fax: [39] (2) 860304

Japan
Sakae-Machi Building, 4/F.
3-23-31 Nishiki, Naka-ku
Nagoya 460, Japan
Tel: [81] (52) 971-3626 Fax: [81] (52) 962-0613

Osaka Ekimae Dai-San Building
6/F., 1-1-13 Umeda, Kita-ku
Osaka 530, Japan
Tel: [81] (6) 344-5211 Fax: [81] (6) 347-0791

Toho Twin Tower Building
4/F., 1-5-2 Yurakucho, Chiyoda-ku
Tokyo 100, Japan
Tel: [81] (3) 3502-3251/5 Fax: [81] (3) 3591-6484

Korea
720-721 KFSB Building
16-2 Yoido-dong, Youngdeungpo-ku
Seoul, Korea
Tel: [82] (2) 782-6115/7 Fax: [82] (2) 782-6118

Mexico
Manuel E. Isaguirre #13, 3er piso
Ciudad Satellite
Mexico City 53310, Mexico
Tel: [52] (5) 572-4113, 572-4131
Fax: [52] (5) 393-5940

Netherlands
Prinsengracht 771, G/F.
1017 JZ Amsterdam, The Netherlands
Tel: [31] (20) 627-7101 Fax: [31] (20) 622-8529

Panama
Condominio Plaza Internacional
Premer Alto, Oficina No. 27
Edificio del Banco Nac. de Panama
Via Espana y Calle 55
Panama City, Rep. of Panama
Tel: [507] 69-5894, 69-5611, 69-5109
Fax: [507] 69-6183

Singapore
20 Kallang Avenue
2/F., Pico Creative Centre
Singapore 1233
Tel: [65] 293-7977 Fax: [65] 292-7577

Spain
Balmes, 184, Atico 3
08006 Barcelona, Spain
Tel: [34] (3) 415-8382, 415-6628, 415-9458
Fax: [34] (3) 416-0148

Sweden
Kunsgatan 6
S-111 43 Stockholm, Sweden
Postal address: PO Box 7505
S-103 92 Stockholm, Sweden
Tel: [46] (8) 100677, 115690
Fax: [46] (8) 7231630

Switzerland
Seestrasse 135
PO Box
CH-8027 Zurich, Switzerland
Tel: [41] (1) 281-3155 Fax: [41] (1) 281-3191

Taiwan
7/F., 315 Sung Chiang Road
Taipei, Taiwan
Tel: [886] (2) 516-6085 Fax: [886] (2) 502-2115

Thailand
20/F., TST Tower
21 Vibhavadi Rangsit Road
Bangkok 10900, Thailand
Tel: [66] (2) 273-8800 Fax: [66] (2) 273-8880

Turkey
Piyalepasa Bulvari
Kastel Is Merkezi
D. Blok Kat: 5
80370 Piyalepasa
Istanbul, Turkey
Tel: [90] (1) 237-0225 Fax: [90] (1) 254-9867

United Arab Emirates
New Juma al-Majid Building
Dubai Sharjah Road
Dubai, United Arab Emirates
Postal address: PO Box 7434
Dubai, United Arab Emirates
Tel: [971] (4) 625255 Fax: [971] (4) 663764
Tlx: 46361 MARKET EM

United Kingdom
Swire House, G/F.
59 Buckingham Gate
London SW1E 6AJ, UK
Tel: [44] (71) 828-1661
Fax: [44] (71) 828-9976
Trade inquiries in the UK: (800) 282-980

United States of America
333 N. Michigan Ave., Suite 2028
Chicago, IL 60601, USA
Tel: [1] (312) 726-4515 Fax: [1] (312) 726-2441

World Trade Center, Suite 120
2050 Stemmons Freeway
Dallas, TX 75207 USA
Postal address: PO Box 58329
Dallas, TX 75258, USA
Tel: [1] (214) 748-8162 Fax: [1] (214) 742-6701

Los Angeles World Trade Centre
350 S. Figueroa Street, Suite 282
Los Angeles, CA 90071-1386, USA
Tel: [1] (213) 622-3194 Fax: [1] (213) 613-1490

Courvoisier Centre, Suite 402
501 Brickell Key Drive
Miami, FL 33131, USA
Tel: [1] (305) 577-0414 Fax: [1] (305) 372-9142

219 East 46th Street
New York, NY 10017, USA
Tel: [1] (212) 838-8688 Fax: [1] (212) 838-8941

c/o HK Economic & Trade Office
222 Kearny Street, Suite 402
San Francisco, CA 94108, USA
Tel: [1] (415) 677-9038 Fax: [1] (415) 421-0646

INDUSTRY-SPECIFIC
TRADE ORGANIZATIONS

Accountants, Hong Kong Branch [Association of
International]
GPO Box 6778
Hong Kong
Tel: 5292021 Fax: 5297436

Accountants, Hong Kong Branch [Chartered
Association of Certified]
Rm. 602, Wilson House
19 Wyndham Street
Central, Hong Kong
Tel: 5244988 Fax: 8684909

Accountants [Hong Kong Society of]
17/F., Belgian House
77-79 Gloucester Road
Wanchai, Hong Kong
Tel: 5299271 Fax: 8656603

Advertisers Association [Hong Kong]
Rm. 1002, Cameron Commercial Centre
458-468 Hennessy Road
Causeway Bay, Hong Kong
Tel: 8329321 Fax: 8381595

Advertising Agents of Hong Kong [Association of
Accredited]
504-505 Dominion Centre
43-59 Queen's Road East
Wanchai, Hong Kong
Tel: 5299656 Fax: 8610375

Air Conditioning & Refrigeration Association, Hong
Kong
GPO Box 10158, Hong Kong
Tel: 6945359 Fax: 6919113

Aluminum Manufacturers' Association [Hong
Kong]
11/F., Front Portion, 550 Nathan Road
Kowloon, Hong Kong
Tel: 8506288, 3852874 Fax: 8506112

Art Carved Furniture & Camphor-Wood Chests
Merchants Association [Hong Kong & Kowloon]
Flat A, 13/F., Lee Wah Building
740 Nathan Road
Kowloon, Hong Kong
Tel: 3949162

Artcraft Merchants Association Ltd.
Flat E, 16/F., Alpha House
27-33 Nathan Road
Kowloon, Hong Kong
Tel: 3684462, 3682347 Fax: 7393470

Article Numbering Association [Hong Kong]
Rm. 2002, United Centre
95 Queensway
Hong Kong
Tel: 8612819 Fax: 8612423

Bamboo Goods Merchants Association [Hong Kong
& Kowloon]
2/F., 128 Yee Kuk Street
Kowloon, Hong Kong
Tel: 3869917

Banks Association Ltd. [Chinese]
5/F., South China Building
1-3 Wyndham Street
Central, Hong Kong
Tel: 5266086

Banks [Hong Kong Association of]
Rm. 525, Prince's Building
Chater Road
Central, Hong Kong
Tel: 5211169 Fax: 8685053

Bar Association [Hong Kong]
LG3, Supreme Court
38 Queensway
Hong Kong
Tel: 8690210 Fax: 8690189

Beverage Manufacturers Association of Hong Kong
c/o Byrne Corporate Services Ltd.
40F, Bond Centre, East Tower
89 Queensway
Hong Kong
Tel: 8401188 Fax: 8400789

Builders Hong Kong [Society of]
Rm. 801/2, On Lok Yuen Building
25 Des Voeux Road
Central, Hong Kong
Tel: 5232081/2 Fax: 8454749

Cargo-Vessel Traders' Association Ltd. [Hong
Kong]
2/F., Man Wai Building
21-23 Man Cheong Street, Ferry Point
Kowloon, Hong Kong
Tel: 3847102, 3855221 Fax: 7820342

Chinese Patent Medicine Manufacturers
Association Ltd. [Hong Kong]
17/F., Hang Lung House
184 Queen's Road
Central, Hong Kong
Tel: 5451331, 5455810

All addresses and telephone numbers are in Hong Kong unless otherwise noted. The country code for Hong Kong is [852].

Computer Society [Hong Kong]
14/F., Evernew House
485 Lockhart Road
Causeway Bay, Hong Kong
Tel: 8342228 Fax: 8343003

Contractors' Association [Hong Kong E&M]
Quarry Bay Reclamation Area
Hoi Tai Street
Quarry Bay, Hong Kong
Tel: 5655411

Corrugated Paper Manufacturers Association Ltd.
[Hong Kong]
15/F., Kiu Kin Building
568 Nathan Road
Kowloon, Hong Kong
Tel: 3856894 Fax: 7704727

Cosmetic & Perfumery Association of Hong Kong
Ltd.
Rm. 308, 3/F., Winning Commercial Bldg.
46-48 Hillwood Road, Tsimshatsui
Kowloon, Hong Kong
Tel: 3668801 Fax: 3120348

Cotton Made Up Goods Manufacturers Association
Ltd. [Hong Kong]
12/F., Flat D, 739 Nathan Road
Kowloon, Hong Kong
Tel: 3944546 Fax: 3418582

Cotton Weavers [Federation of Hong Kong]
Flat B, 14/F., Astoria Building
23-34 Ashley Road
Kowloon, Hong Kong
Tel: 3672383 Fax: 7213233

Courier Association [Hong Kong International]
c/o DHL International Ltd.
13 Mok Cheong Street, Tokwawan
Kowloon, Hong Kong
Tel: 7747298 Fax: 3339668

Design Council of Hong Kong
Rm. 407, Hankow Centre
5-15 Hankow Road, Tsimshatsui
Kowloon, Hong Kong
Tel: 7230818 Fax: 7213494

Designers Association [Hong Kong]
Rm. 407-411, Hankow Centre
5-15 Hankow Road, Tsimshatsui
Kowloon, Hong Kong
Tel: 7230818 Fax: 7213494

Diamond Importers Association Ltd.
Rm. 1102, Parker House
72 Queen's Road
Central, Hong Kong
Tel: 5235497, 5260561 Fax: 8459649

Edible Oil Importers and Exporters Ltd. [Hong
Kong General Association of]
4/F., Hang Seng Bank Building
77 Des Voeux Road
Central, Hong Kong
Tel: 8468347 Fax: 8450222

Electric Trade Association [Hong Kong & Kowloon]
6/F., 350-354 Hennessy Road
Wanchai, Hong Kong
Tel: 5737007, 5737005 Fax: 8345885

Electrical Appliances Merchants Association Ltd.
[Hong Kong & Kowloon]
4/F., 732 Nathan Road, Mongkok
Kowloon, Hong Kong
Tel: 3949991, 3942135 Fax: 3980147

Electronics Association [Hong Kong]
Rm. 1806-8, Beverly House
93-107 Lockhart Road
Wanchai, Hong Kong
Tel: 8662669 Fax: 8656843

Engineering Employers Association Ltd. [Hong
Kong & Kowloon]
2/F., 43 Bute Street
Kowloon, Hong Kong
Tel: 3948360, 3398446

Fish Culture Association [Hong Kong New
Territories]
1/F., 51 Fau Tsoi Street, Yuen Long
New Territories, Hong Kong
Tel: 4782828

Flour Merchants Association [Hong Kong]
5/F., 155 Des Voeux Road West
Hong Kong
Tel: 8580723

Food Trades Association Ltd. [Hong Kong]
1/F., C.M.A. Building
64-66 Connaught Road
Central, Hong Kong
Tel: 5428600 Fax: 5414541

Freight Forwarding Agents Ltd. [Hong Kong
Association of]
M/F., AHAFA Cargo Centre
12 Kai Shun Road
Kowloon, Hong Kong
Tel: 7963121 Fax: 7963719

Fresh Fruits Importers Association Ltd. [Hong
Kong]
Rm. 401-3, Prosperous Building
48 Des Voeux Road Central
Central, Hong Kong
Tel: 5211228 Fax: 8684402

Fur Manufacturers & Dealers (Hong Kong) Ltd.
[Federation of]
Rm. 603, Chevalier House
45-51 Chatham Road South, Tsimshatsui
Kowloon, Hong Kong
Tel: 3674646 Fax: 7390799

Furniture & Shop Fittings Merchants Association
[Hong Kong & Kowloon]
Flat A, 13/F., Lee Wah Building
740 Nathan Road
Kowloon, Hong Kong
Tel: 3949162

Furniture Dealers & Decorators General
Association Ltd. [Hong Kong]
10/F., Kwong Ah Building
114 Thomson Road
Wanchai, Hong Kong
Tel: 5752755 Fax: 8344643

Furniture Manufacturers [Federation of Hong
Kong]
13/F., Flat A, 740 Nathan Road
Kowloon, Hong Kong
Tel: 3949162

Garment Manufacturers Association [Hong Kong]
Rm. 708, Universal Commercial Bldg.
69 Peking Road
Kowloon, Hong Kong
Tel: 3673392 Fax: 7217537

Garment Manufacturers [Federation of Hong Kong]
4/F., 25 Kimberley Road
Kowloon, Hong Kong
Tel: 7211383

Gloves Manufacturers Ltd. [Association of Hong
Kong]
c/o Action Secretarial Ltd.
Rm. D, 10/F., Harvard House
111 Thompson Road
Wanchai, Hong Kong
Tel: 5728224 Fax: 8382229

Gold & Silver Exchange Society [Chinese]
1/F., 12-18 Mercer Street
Hong Kong
Tel: 5441945 Fax: 8540869

Hide & Leather Traders Association Ltd. [Hong
Kong]
1/F., 33 Portland Street
Kowloon, Hong Kong
Tel: 3887644 Fax: 7830804

Information Technology Federation [Hong Kong]
1/F., Centre Point
181 Gloucester Road
Wanchai, Hong Kong
Tel: 8363356 Fax: 5910975

Insurance Association of Hong Kong [Chinese]
Rm. 2413, Sincere Building
173 Des Voeux Road Central
Central, Hong Kong
Tel: 8157700 Fax: 5410615

Insurance Brokers Association [Hong Kong]
15/F., Fleet House
38 Gloucester Road
Wanchai, Hong Kong
Tel: 8616561 Fax: 8656736

Insurers [Hong Kong Federation of]
Rm. 1205, National Mutual Centre
151 Gloucester Road
Wanchai, Hong Kong
Tel: 8343832 Fax: 8346169

Ivory Manufacturers Association Ltd.
[Hong Kong & Kowloon]
B1, 3/F., Mirador Mansion
58 Nathan Road
Kowloon, Hong Kong
Tel: 3675336

Jade & Stone Manufacturers Association
[Hong Kong]
16/F., Hang Lung House
184-192 Queen's Road
Central, Hong Kong
Tel: 5430543 Fax: 8150164

Jewellers & Goldsmiths Association Ltd.
[Hong Kong]
13/4, Hong Kong Jewellery Building
178-180 Queen's Road
Central, Hong Kong
Tel: 5439633 Fax: 8507361

Jewellery Manufacturers Association [Hong Kong]
Unit 5, 1/F., Hunghom Square
37 Ma Tau Wai Road, Hunghom
Kowloon, Hong Kong
Tel: 7663002 Fax: 3623647

Knitted Fabrics Dyeing & Finishing Manufacturers'
Association Ltd. [Hong Kong]
20/F., Wah Kit Commercial Centre
300 Des Voeux Road Central
Central, Hong Kong
Tel: 5453222 Fax: 5433622

Knitwear Exporters & Manufacturers Association
Ltd. [Hong Kong]
Hang Pont Commercial Building
12/F., 31 Tonkin Street
Kowloon, Hong Kong
Tel: 7290111

Law Society of Hong Kong
Rm. 910, Swire House
Chater Road
Hong Kong
Tel: 8640500 Fax: 8690189

Leather Goods Manufacturers Trade Association
Ltd. [Hong Kong]
Unit 1-2, 4/F., Kai Fuk Industrial Centre
1 Wang Tung Road, Kowloon Bay
Kowloon, Hong Kong
Tel: 7953883 Fax: 7998745

Leather Shoe Merchants Association Ltd.
[Hong Kong]
Flat E, 5/F., 88 Argyle Street
Kowloon, Hong Kong
Tel: 3955302 Fax: 3966020

Liquor & Provision Importers Association
GPO Box 8689
Hong Kong
Tel: 5986833 Fax: 5987300

Liquor Dealers & Distillers [Hong Kong and Kowloon General Association of]
7/F., Block A, New Lucky House
300 Nathan Road
Kowloon, Hong Kong
Tel: 3851257

Machinery & Instrument Merchants Association Ltd. [Hong Kong & Kowloon]
3/F., 85-91 Lai Chi Kok Road
Kowloon, Hong Kong
Tel: 3934384

Maize & Feed Importers Association Ltd. [Hong Kong]
1/F., 79-81 Connaught Road West
Hong Kong
Tel: 5473623, 5463025 Fax: 5598265

Marine Products Merchants Association Ltd. [Hong Kong & Kowloon]
2/F., 17A Cadogan Street
Hong Kong
Tel: 8187764

Metal Merchants Association [Hong Kong]
Rm. 6A, Hankow Apartment
43-49 Hankow Road
Kowloon, Hong Kong
Tel: 7227485 Fax: 7392402

Mineral Products Merchants Association Ltd. [Hong Kong & Kowloon]
3/F., 21 Lee Yuen Street West
Central, Hong Kong
Tel: 5264437

Motor Traders Association of Hong Kong
40/F., Bond Centre East Tower
Queensway
Hong Kong
Tel: 8401188 Fax: 8400789

Native Products & Raw Material Merchants Association Ltd. [Hong Kong]
Rm. 305 Ha Lung Building
25-29 Ko Shing Street
Sheung Wan, Hong Kong
Tel: 5491091

Office Equipment Association Ltd. [Hong Kong]
c/o Kodak (Far East) Ltd.
Kodak House, 321 Java Road
North Point, Hong Kong
Tel: 5649333 Fax: 5657474

Oil Merchants Association Ltd. [Hong Kong]
Block J, 11/F., Sun On Building
492 Queen's Road West
Hong Kong
Tel: 5474334

Optical Manufacturers Association Ltd. [Hong Kong]
2/F., 11 Fa Yuen Street, Mongkok
Kowloon, Hong Kong
Tel: 3326505 Fax: 7705786

Paper Merchants Association Hong Kong [South China]
Rm. 901, Hong Kong House
17-19 Wellington Street
Central, Hong Kong
Tel: 5244604

Paper Merchants Association [Chinese]
4/F., 132-136 Des Voeux Road West
Hong Kong
Tel: 5481969

Pearls, Precious Stones, Jade, Gold & Silver Ornament Merchants Association [Kowloon]
6/F., Front Section, 506-508 Nathan Road
Kowloon, Hong Kong
Tel: 3843105, 3846863

Pharmaceutical Manufacturers Association Ltd. [Hong Kong]
c/o Neochem Pharmaceutical Laboratories
5B Cheung Wah Industrial Building
10-12 Shipyard Lane
Quarry Bay, Hong Kong
Tel: 5626255 Fax: 5634018

Pharmaceutical Trade Federation Ltd.
Rm. 401-3, Cornyun Centre
3 Jupiter Street, North Point
Hong Kong
Tel: 8063112

Photographic Equipment Importers Ltd. [Association of Hong Kong]
Causeway Bay PO Box 31373
Hong Kong
Tel: 5468228 Fax: 8581578

Photographic Merchants Association Ltd. [Hong Kong & Kowloon]
Rm. 304, Beverley Commercial Centre
87-105 Chatham Road
Kowloon, Hong Kong
Tel: 3669997 Fax: 7218107

Plastic Material Suppliers Association Ltd. [Hong Kong]
1/F., 11 Lai Yip Street, Kwun Tong
Kowloon, Hong Kong
Tel: 7579331 Fax: 7968885

Plastic Products Merchants United Association Ltd. [Hong Kong & Kowloon]
13/F., 491 Nathan Road
Kowloon, Hong Kong
Tel: 3840171 Fax: 7810107

Plastics Manufacturers Association Ltd. [Hong Kong]
Rm. 302, Red A Central Building
37 Wellington Street
Central, Hong Kong
Tel: 5232229 Fax: 8400704

Polyethylene Tubing Manufacturers' Association [Hong Kong]
10/F., Lee Fat Building
40 Bute Street, Mongkok
Kowloon, Hong Kong
Tel: 3945912 Fax: 3990152

Printers & Dyers Association Ltd. [Hong Kong]
11/F., Wing Wong Building
557-559 Nathan Road
Kowloon, Hong Kong
Tel: 3882372 Fax: 3857184

Printers Association [Hong Kong]
1/F., 48-50 Johnston Road
Wanchai, Hong Kong
Tel: 5271859, 5275050 Fax: 8610463

Provisions, Wine & Spirit Dealers' Association
[Hong Kong & Kowloon]
Flat B, 2/F., Fu Lok Building
131-133 Wing Lok Street
Sheung Wan, Hong Kong
Tel: 8542514, 8542544 Fax: 8543816

Rattan Merchants Association [Hong Kong]
1/F., 314 Des Voeux Road West
Hong Kong
Tel: 5472900

Rice Importers & Exporters Association
[Hong Kong]
Rm. 301, Chiu Chow Association Building
81-85 Des Voeux Road West
Hong Kong
Tel: 5477323

Rice Merchants' Association of Hong Kong Ltd.
3/F., Rice Merchants Building
77-78 Connaught Road West
Hong Kong
Tel: 5483630

Rubber & Footwear Manufacturers Association
Ltd. [Hong Kong]
Block A, 2/F., 185 Prince Edward Road
Kowloon, Hong Kong
Tel: 3822297 Fax: 3976927

Salt Merchants Association [Hong Kong &
Kowloon]
Flat B, 3/F., 123 Des Voeux Road West
Hong Kong
Tel: 5486935 Fax: 5471772

Shipbreaking & Steel Rolling Industries Association
[Hong Kong]
Rm. 1706, President Commercial Centre
608 Nathan Road
Kowloon, Hong Kong
Tel: 3847181 Fax: 7701271

Shipowners Association Ltd. [Hong Kong]
12/F., Queen's Centre
58 Queen's Road East
Wanchai, Hong Kong
Tel: 5200206 Fax: 5298246

Shippers' Council [Hong Kong]
Rm. 2707A, Convention Plaza
1 Harbour Road
Wanchai, Hong Kong
Tel: 8241228 Fax: 8240394

Shipping Association [Hong Kong Liner]
2111 Wing On Centre
111 Connaught Road Central
Central, Hong Kong
Tel: 5445077 Fax: 8151350

Shipping Industry Institute [Hong Kong]
1002 Great Eagle Centre
23 Harbour Road
Wanchai, Hong Kong
Tel: 8933485 Fax: 8345172

Silk Piece-Goods Merchants Association [Hong
Kong]
Flat 5D, Wing Cheong Commercial Building
19-25 Jervois Street
Hong Kong
Tel: 3845570, 5441143

Steel & Metal Importers & Exporters Association
Ltd. [Hong Kong & Kowloon]
10/F., Champion Building
287-291 Des Voeux Road
Central, Hong Kong
Tel: 5436626, 5452356

Sugar Merchants' Association
2/F., 135 Bonham Strand East
Sheung Wan, Hong Kong
Tel: 5440298

Tea Trade Merchants Association [Hong Kong &
Kowloon]
1/F., 234-242 Des Voeux Road West
Hong Kong
Tel: 5401321 Fax: 8583063

Telecom Association [Hong Kong]
GPO Box 13461
Hong Kong
Tel: 8770781 Fax: 8779115

Textile Bleachers, Dyers, Printers & Finishers Ltd.
[Hong Kong Association of]
3/F., C.M.A. Building
64 Connaught Road Central
Central, Hong Kong
Tel: 5428600 Fax: 5414541

Textile Council of Hong Kong Ltd.
Rm. 744, Star House
3 Salisbury Road, Tsimshatsui
Kowloon, Hong Kong
Tel: 7357793 Fax: 7357795

Timber Merchants Association
[Hong Kong & Kowloon]
1/F., 50 Portland Street
Kowloon, Hong Kong
Tel: 3850465

Tobacco Institute of Hong Kong Ltd.
Rm. 1807, Harbour Centre
25 Harbour Road
Wanchai, Hong Kong
Tel: 8277383 Fax: 8274799

Tourist Association [Hong Kong]
35/F., Jardine House
1 Connaught Place
Central, Hong Kong
Tel: 8017111 Fax: 8104877

Toys Council [Hong Kong]
4/F., Hankow Centre
5-15 Hankow Road, Tsimshatsui
Kowloon, Hong Kong
Tel: 7230818 Fax: 7213494

Translation Society Ltd. [Hong Kong]
Kowloon Central PO Box 70335
Kowloon, Hong Kong
Tel: 6952632 Fax: 8363334

Umbrella Dealers Association of Hong Kong &
Kowloon
Flat A, 3/F., 39-43 Gage Street
Central, Hong Kong
Tel: 8158232, 5435500 Fax: 8541712

Vegetable Marketing Co-operative Societies Ltd.
[Federation of]
2/F., 757 Lai Chi Kok Road
Cheung Sha Wan
Kowloon, Hong Kong
Tel: 3874176 Fax: 7258624

Watch Importers Association [Hong Kong]
GPO Box 5311
Hong Kong
Tel: 7354248 Fax: 7304570

Watch Manufacturers Association Ltd. [Hong
Kong]
11/F., Yu Wing Building
64-66 Wellington Street
Central, Hong Kong
Tel: 5253902 Fax: 8106614

Watch Trades & Industries Ltd. [Federation of
Hong Kong]
Rm. 604, Peter Building
58-62 Queen's Road
Central, Hong Kong
Tel: 5233232 Fax: 8684485

Woollen & Synthetic Knitting Manufacturers
Association Ltd. [Hong Kong]
Rm. 506C, Harbor Crystal Centre
100 Granville Road, Tsimshatsui East
Kowloon, Hong Kong
Tel: 3682091 Fax: 3691720

FINANCIAL INSTITUTIONS

BANKS

Chinese Banks Association Ltd.
5/F., South China Building
1-3 Wyndham Street
Central, Hong Kong
Tel: 5266086

Hong Kong Association of Banks
Rm. 525, Prince's Building
Chater Road
Central, Hong Kong
Tel: 5211169 Fax: 8685053

Office of the Commissioner of Banking
Queensway Government Offices, 28/F.
66 Queensway
Central, Hong Kong
Tel: 8672671 Fax: 8690462 Tlx: 64282

Banks of Issue

Hongkong and Shanghai Banking Corporation Ltd.
1 Queen's Road
Central, Hong Kong
Tel: 8221111 Fax: 8101112 Tlx: 73201

Standard Chartered Bank
Standard Chartered Bank Building
4-4A Des Voeux Road
Central, Hong Kong
Tel: 8203333 Fax: 8100651

Commercial Banks

Banks of East Asia Ltd.
10 Des Voeux Road
Central, Hong Kong
Tel: 8423200 Fax: 8459333 Tlx: 73017

Commercial Bank of Hong Kong, Ltd.
120-122 Des Voeux Road
Central, Hong Kong
Tel: 5419222 Fax: 5410009 Tlx: 73085

Dao Heng Bank Ltd.
7-19 Bonham Strand
Hong Kong
Tel: 5447141 Fax: 8152042 Tlx: 73345

Hang Seng Bank Ltd.
83 Des Voeux Road
Central, Hong Kong
Tel: 8255111 Fax: 8459301 Tlx: 733111

Nanyang Commercial Bank Ltd.
151 Des Voeux Road
Central, Hong Kong
Tel: 8520888 Fax: 8153333 Tlx: 73412

Overseas Trust Bank Ltd.
OTB Building
160 Gloucester Road
Hong Kong
Tel: 5756657 Fax: 5727535 Tlx: 74545

Shanghai Commercial Bank Ltd.
12 Queen's Road
Central, Hong Kong
Tel: 8415415 Fax: 8104623 Tlx: 73390

Foreign Banks

Bank of America NT and SA (USA)
12 Harcourt Road
Central, Hong Kong
Tel: 8475333 Tlx: 63372

Bank of China (PRC)
1 Garden Road
Central, Hong Kong
Tel: 8266888 Fax: 8105963 Tlx: 73772

Bank of Communications (PRC)
20 Pedder St.,
Central, Hong Kong
Tel: 8419611 Fax: 8106993

Bank of Tokyo Ltd.
Far East Finance Centre, 1/F.
16 Harcourt Road
Central, Hong Kong
Tel: 8627888 Fax: 8652006 Tlx: 73252

Banque Nationale de Paris
Central Building
23 Queen's Road
Central, Hong Kong
Tel: 5218218 Fax; 8106252 Tlx: 73442

Barclays Bank PLC (UK)
United Centre, 11/F.
95 Queensway, PO Box 9716
Hong Kong
Tel: 5201181 Fax: 8610851 Tlx: 74077

Citibank, NA (USA)
Citicorp Centre, 18 Whitfield Road
Causeway Bay, Hong Kong
Tel: 8078211 Fax: 8078322 Tlx: 73243

Deutsche Bank AG (Germany)
New World Tower, 16-18 Queen's Road
Central, Hong Kong
Tel: 8430400 Fax: 8459056 Tlx: 73498

Korea Exchange Bank
Far East Finance Centre, 32/F.
16 Harcourt Road
Hong Kong
Tel: 5201221 Fax: 8612379 Tlx: 73459

National Westminster Bank PLC (UK)
One Exchange Square, 23/F.
8 Connaught Place
Central, Hong Kong
Tel: 5247071 Fax: 8459025 Tlx: 61672

Oversea-Chinese Banking Corporation Ltd.
(Singapore)
Suite 602-604, Edinburgh Tower
The Landmark, 15 Queen's Road
Central, Hong Kong
Tel: 8682086 Fax: 8453439 Tlx: 73417

Royal Bank of Canada
Gloucester Tower, 18/F.
11 Pedder Street
Central, Hong Kong
Tel: 8430888 Fax: 8685802 Tlx: 60884

INSURANCE COMPANIES

Chinese Insurance Association of Hong Kong
Rm. 2413, Sincere Building
173 Des Voeux Road Central
Central, Hong Kong
Tel: 8157700 Fax: 5410615

Hong Kong Export Credit Insurance Corporation
2/F., South Sea Centre, Tower 1
75 Mody Road
Tsim Sha Tsui East
Kowloon, Hong Kong
Tel: 7233883

Hong Kong Federation of Insurers
Rm. 1205, National Mutual Centre
151 Gloucester Road
Wanchai, Hong Kong
Tel: 8343832 Fax: 8346169

Hong Kong Insurance Brokers Association
15/F., Fleet House
38 Gloucester Road
Wanchai, Hong Kong
Tel: 8616561 Fax: 8656736

Asia Insurance Co. Ltd.
World-Wide House, 16/F.
19 Des Voeux Road
Central, Hong Kong
Tel: 5266202 Fax: 8100218 Tlx: 74542

Lombard General Insurance Ltd.
14/F., Convention Plaza
1 Harbour Road
Wanchai, Hong Kong
Tel: 8299399 Fax: 8240198 Tlx: 69795

Mercantile and General Reinsurance Co. PLC
19/F., Finance Tower
57-59 Connaught Road
Central, Hong Kong
Tel: 5456330 Fax: 5454039 Tlx: 74062

Ming An Insurance Co. (HK) Ltd.
International Building, 14-11/F.
141 Des Voeux Road
Central, Hong Kong
Tel: 8151551 Fax: 5416567 Tlx: 74172

Prudential Assurance Co. Ltd.
Bank of East Asia Building, 18/F.
10 Des Voeux Road
Central, Hong Kong
Tel: 5252367 Fax: 8104903 Tlx: 65399

South British Insurance Co. Ltd.
36/F., World Trade Centre
Causeway Bay, Hong Kong
Tel: 8940666 Fax: 8950426 Tlx: 75609

Summit Insurance (Asia) Ltd.
Shanghai Industrial Investment Bldg.
22-24/F., 48-62 Hennessy Road
Tel: 8238238 Fax: 8652395 Tlx: 65188

Sun Alliance and London Insurance PLC
Dina House, 3/F.
11 Duddell Street
Hong Kong
Tel: 8107383 Fax: 8450389 Tlx: 80139

Taikoo Royal Insurance Co. Ltd.
Swire House, 3/F.
Chater Road
Central, Hong Kong
Tel: 5262361 Fax: 8101007

Willis Faber (Far East) Ltd.
Dina House, 18/F.
11 Duddell Street
Central, Hong Kong
Tel: 8680366 Fax: 8106071 Tlx: 85240

STOCK & COMMODITY EXCHANGES

Hong Kong Securities and Futures Commission (SEC)
Exchange Square, 38/F., Tower II
Hong Kong
Tel: 8409222 Fax: 8459553

Chinese Gold & Silver Exchange Society
Gold & Silver Commercial Building
1/F., 12-18 Mercer Street
Hong Kong
Tel: 5441945 Fax: 8540869

The Hong Kong Commodity Exchange Ltd.
2/F., Hutchison House
Harcourt Road
Hong Kong
Tlx: 65326 HKCE

Hong Kong Diamond Bourse Ltd.
5/F., Hong Kong Diamond Exchange Building
8-10 Duddell Street
Central, Hong Kong
Tel: 5245081 Fax: 8681647

Hong Kong Futures Exchange Ltd. (HKFE)
Rm. 911, New World Tower
16-18 Queen's Road
Hong Kong
Tel: 5251005 Fax: 8105089

Hong Kong Stock Exchange (HKSE)
Exchange Square, Towers I & II
Hong Kong
Tel: 5221122 Fax: 8104475

SERVICES

ACCOUNTING FIRMS

Association of International Accountants, Hong Kong Branch
GPO Box 6778
Hong Kong
Tel: 5292021 Fax: 5297436

Chartered Association of Certified Accountants, Hong Kong Branch
Rm. 602, Wilson House
19 Wyndham Street
Central, Hong Kong
Tel: 5244988 Fax: 8684909

Hong Kong Society of Accountants
17/F., Belgian House
77-79 Gloucester Road
Wanchai, Hong Kong
Tel: 5299271 Fax: 8656603

Arthur Andersen & Co.
Wing On Centre, 25/F.
111 Connaught Road Central
Hong Kong
Tel: 8520222 Fax: 8150548, 5412893

Coopers & Lybrand
Sunning Plaza
10 Hysan Avenue
Hong Kong
Tel: 8394321 Fax: 5765356 Tlx: 74378

Deloitte Ross Tohmatsu
Wing On Centre, 26/F.
111 Connaught Road
Central, Hong Kong
Tel: 5450303 Fax: 5411911

Ernst & Young
15/F., Hutchinson House
10 Harcourt Road
Central, Hong Kong
Tel: 8459888 Fax: 8459208 Tlx: 76449

Ernst & Young
26/F., Great Eagle Centre
23 Harbour Road
Wanchai, Hong Kong
Tel: 8278938 Fax: 8275223 Tlx: 74301

Ernst & Young
6/F., World Commerce Centre
Harbour City II, 11 Canton Road
Kowloon, Hong Kong
Tel: 7304188, 7377200 Fax: 7304677

Horwath & Co.
5/F., On Lan Centre
11 On Lan Street
Hong Kong
Tel: 5262191 Fax: 8100502 Tlx: 65590 SKCO

KMPG Peat Marwick
8/F., Prince's Building
10 Chater Road
Hong Kong
Postal address: GPO Box 50, Hong Kong
Tel: 5226022 Fax: 8452588 Tlx: 74391 PMMHK

Moores Rowland
501 China Building
29 Queen's Road
Central, Hong Kong
Tel: 8104311 Fax: 8100032

Price Waterhouse Hong Kong
Prince's Building, 22/F.
10 Chater Road
Hong Kong
Postal address: GPO Box 690, Hong Kong
Tel: 8262111, 5222111 Fax: 8109888

ADVERTISING AGENCIES

Association of Accredited Advertising Agents of Hong Kong
504-505 Dominion Centre
43-59 Queen's Road East
Wanchai, Hong Kong
Tel: 5299656 Fax: 8610375

Hong Kong Advertisers Association
Rm. 1002, Cameron Commercial Centre
458-468 Hennessy Road
Causeway Bay, Hong Kong
Tel: 8329321 Fax: 8381595

Asatsu International (HK), Ltd.
1 9/F., 11 I Leighton Road
Causeway Bay, Hong Kong
Tel: 8952805 Fax: 5764762

Backer Spielvogel Bates
10/F., Malaysia Building
50 Gloucester Road
Hong Kong
Tel: 8230111 Fax: 8613935 Tlx: 65321 BATES

Ball Partnership
12/F., Vicwood Plaza
199 Des Voeux Road
Central, Hong Kong
Tel: 5443800 Fax: 8455411 Tlx: 62517 BALL

BBDO
30/F., Bank of China Tower
1 Garden Road
Central, Hong Kong
Tel: 8201888 Fax: 8772164 Tlx: 66806 BBDO

Bozell
1101 Citicorp Centre
18 Whitfield Road
Causeway Bay, Hong Kong
Tel: 8075678 Fax: 8073503, 8063846
Tlx: 74383

BSB Graffix Limited
1201 Lam Chung Building
52-54 Jaffee Road
Wanchai, Hong Kong
Tel: 5272766 Fax: 8611216

BSB Hong Kong
2/F., Asian House
1 Hennessy Road
Hong Kong
Tel: 8230111 Fax: 8613935 Tlx: 65321 BATES

CCAA International Ltd. Alliance
10/F., OTB Building
259-265 Des Voeux Road
Central, Hong Kong
Tel: 5412091 Fax: 5430445

Chuo Senko Advertising (HK) ltd.
Rm. 503, Silvercord, Tower 1
30 Canton Road
Kowloon, Hong Kong
Tel: 7211194 Fax: 7210574 Tlx: 45615 CSAD

Daiko Communications Asia Co., Ltd.
Rm. 513-516, Sun Hung Kai Centre
30 Harbour Road
Hong Kong
Tel: 8919688 Fax: 8384896

D'Arcy Masius Benton & Bowles (DMB&B)
10/F., East Wing, Hennessy Centre
500 Hennessy Road
Causeway Bay, Hong Kong
Tel: 8905340, 8903923 Fax: 5766480
Tlx: 65160 DMBB

DDB Needham Worldwide DIK Ltd.
Sun Hung Kai Centre, 33/F.
30 Harbour Road
Wanchai, Hong Kong
Tel: 8280328 Fax: 8272700 Tlx: 66445 DDBNW

Dentsu Inc. Hong Kong
Rm. 3603, EIE Tower, Bond Centre
89 Queensway
Central, Hong Kong
Tel: 8683118 Fax: 8685496

Dentsu, Young & Rubicam/Hong Kong
418 Mount Parker House
1111 King's Road
Hong Kong
Tel: 8846668 Fax: 8853208, 8860989

FCB International
605 Mount Parker House
1111 Kings Road
Quarry Bay, Hong Kong
Tel: 8860933 Fax: 5685080 Tlx: 68375 FCBI

Grey Advertising Hong Kong
Unit B., 33-34/F., Manulife Tower
169 Electric Road
North Point, Hong Kong
Tel: 5106888 Fax: 5107541
Grey Pacific Tel: 5107402

HDM, Ltd.
418 Mount Parker House
1111 King's Road
Hong Kong
Tel: 8846668 Fax: 9960999 Tlx: 86012 DYRHK

J. Walter Thompson
3/F., Shui On Centre
6-8 Harbour Road
Wanchai, Hong Kong
JWT China Tel: 8644739 Fax: 8240522
JWT Co. Ltd. Tel: 8644668 Fax: 8240823
JWT Int'l Tel: 8241772 Fax: 8241391
JWT Direct Tel: 8644668 Fax: 8241807

Lee Davis Ayer
8/F., C.C. Wu Building
302-308 Hennessy Road
Hong Kong
Tel: 8332033 Fax: 8345877

Leo Burnett International
City Plaza 3, 6/F.
14 Taikoo Wan Road
Quarry Bay, Hong Kong
Tel: 5674333 Fax: 8853209

Lintas Hong Kong
25/F., 108 Gloucester Road
Wanchai, Hong Kong
Tel: 5078222 Fax: 5985143 Tlx: 63811 hklin

McCann-Erickson (H.K.) Ltd.
1/F., Sunning Plaza
10 Hysan Avenue
Hong Kong
Tel: 8827333 Fax: 5760136

Ogilvy & Mather Asia/Pacific
Mount Parker House, 7-8/F.
Taikoo Shing, Hong Kong
Ogilvy & Mather China
Tel: 5680161 Fax: 8853510, 3215, 5674917
Ogilvy & Mather Direct
Tel: 5691177 Fax: 8858195
Ogilvy & Mather Public Relations
Tel: 5674461 Fax: 8853227

Oriental Source
2/F., Mount Parker House
1111 King's Road
Hong Kong
Tel: 8865184 Fax: 8865468

Saatchi & Saatchi Advertising
22/F., Shui On Centre
6-8 Harbour Road
Wanchai, Hong Kong
Tel: 8643333 Fax: 8651213, 8652602
Tlx: 60625 COMAD

Triangle Pacific
2/F., Mount Parker House
1111 King's Road
Hong Kong
Tel: 8865128 Fax: 8865470

Wunderman
4/F., Mount Parker House
1111 King's Road
Hong Kong
Tel: 8846668 Fax: 5675701 Tlx: 78086012

LAW FIRMS

Hong Kong Bar Association
LG3, Supreme Court
38 Queensway
Hong Kong
Tel: 8690210 Fax: 8690189

Law Society of Hong Kong
Rm. 910, Swire House
Chater Road
Hong Kong
Tel: 8640500 Fax: 8690189

Baker & McKenzie
14/F., Hutchinson House
Harcourt Road
Hong Kong
Tel: 8461888 Fax: 8450476, 8450490
Tlx: 76416

Bull, Housser & Tupper (Canada)
3304 Gloucester Tower
11 Pedder Street
Hong Kong
Tel: 2105478 Fax: 8684545

Buxbaum and Choy (USA)
2013 Hutchison House
Harcourt Road
Hong Kong
Tel: 5237001 Fax: 8450947 Tlx: 61667 LUSHI

Clyde & Co. (UK)
Admiralty Centre Tower II, 19/F.
Harcourt Road
Hong Kong
Tel: 5290017 Fax: 8654259 Tlx: 61972 CLYDE

Coudert Brothers (USA)
31/F., Alexandra House
20 Chater Road
Hong Kong
Tel: 5265951, 8104111 Fax: 8681417, 8459021,
8459241

Deacons (in assoc. w/ Graham & James)
Alexandra House, 3-6/F.
Hong Kong
Tel: 8259211 Fax: 8100431 Tlx: 73475 OTERY

Fairbairn, Catley, Low & Kong
11-12/F., Wheelock House
20 Pedder Street
Central, Hong Kong
Tel: 5222041 Fax: 8452928, 8459282
Tlx: 69219 EFKAT

Johnson, Stokes & Master
17/F., Prince's Building
10 Chater Road
Hong Kong
Tel: 8432211 Fax: 8451735, 8459121

Kennedys
8/F., Wing Lung Bank Building
45 Des Voeux Road
Central, Hong Kong
Tel: 5228147 Fax: 8100950

Mallesons, Stephen, Jaques
Two Exchange Square
Connaught Road
Central, Hong Kong
Tel: 8484678 Fax: 8685878

McKenna & Co.
36/F., Gloucester Tower
11 Pedder Street
Central, Hong Kong
Tel: 8469100 Fax: 8453575 Tlx: 61515

Norton Rose
18/F., Prince's Building
10 Chater Road
Hong Kong
Tel: 8432211 Fax: 8459121 Tlx: NOHON 75107

Simmons & Simmons
2408 Jardine House
One Connaught Place
Central, Hong Kong
Tel: 8681131 Fax: 8105040 Tlx: 75888 SANDS

Sinclair Roche
42/F., Bank of China Tower
1 Garden Road
Hong Kong
Tel: 8200200 Fax: 8459244 Tlx: 63646 SNCLR

Thelan, Marrin, Johnson & Bridges (USA)
9/F., Three Exchange Square
8 Connaught Place
Central, Hong Kong
Tel: 8401303 Fax: 8400645 Tlx: 68940 TMJEB

Vincent T.K. Cheung, Yap & Company
17/F., Worldwide House
19 Des Voeux Road
Central, Hong Kong
Tel: 5235011 Fax: 8612944

Walker & Corsa
1603 The Centre Mark
287 Queen's Road
Central, Hong Kong
Tel: 8541718 Fax: 5416189 Tlx: 65117 NAIAD

Wilkinson & Grist
Prince's Building, 6/F.
10 Chater Road
Hong Kong
Tel: 5246011 Fax: 5279041 Tlx: 75603 WILGR

TRANSLATORS & INTERPRETERS

Hong Kong Translation Society Ltd.
Kowloon Central PO Box 70335
Kowloon, Hong Kong
Tel: 6952632 Fax: 8363334

Abraham, Wong, Hoffman & Associates
167-169 Hennessy Road, 16/F.
Wanchai, Hong Kong
Tel: 5738836 Fax: 8345604

All addresses and telephone numbers are in Hong Kong unless otherwise noted. The country code for Hong Kong is [852].

Ace Language & Translation Centre
Rm. 1003, Sincere Insurance Building
4 Hennessy Road
Hong Kong
Tel: 5299552 Fax: 8652136

Central Language Services, Ltd.
Rm. 1202, Kam Chang Building
54 Jaffe Road
Hong Kong
Tel: 8610801 Fax: 5270743

Chiang Jiang Translanguage Centre
3/F., Wai Hing Commercial Building
17 Wing On Street
Hong Kong
Tel: 8153145, 5433493 Fax: 8541620

China Communication Translation Services
1701 Chit Lee Commercial Building
30-36 Shau Kei Wan Road
Hong Kong
Tel: 5683813, 5683924 Fax: 5680827

Interlingua Language Services Ltd.
Rm. 201-2, The Centre Mark
287-299 Queen's Road
Hong Kong
Tel: 5430188 Fax: 5412468

International Information Service Ltd.
103 Wing On Plaza
62 Mody Road
Kowloon, Hong Kong
Tel: 7391818 Fax: 7213692

KCL Language Consultancy
20/F., United Building
447 Hennessy Road
Causeway Bay, Hong Kong
Tel: 8388281 Fax: 8385269

Linguaphone
Rm. 2013, C.C. Wu Building
302-308 Hennessy Road
Hong Kong
Tel: 5737112 Fax: 5721998

Polyglot Translations
1702 Chinese Bank Building
61 Des Voeux Road
Central, Hong Kong
Tel: 5215689 Fax: 8450533, 7604467

Persona Personnel Services
Rm. 3702, Far East Finance Centre
16 Harcourt Road
Hong Kong
Tel: 5202628 Fax: 5297153

Translanguage-IRH Ltd.
Rm. 1604, Tung Wah Mansion
199 Hennessy Road
Hong Kong
Tel: 5732728 Fax: 8345146

TRANSPORTATION

AIRLINES

Aeroflot
96A New Henry House
Ice House Street
Hong Kong
Tel: 8454232

Air China
Tel: 8610322

Air France
2104 Alexandra House
Hong Kong
Tel: 5248145, 5248210 Fax: 86804546

Air India
1002 Gloucester Tower
11 Pedder Street
Hong Kong
Tel: 5211176, 5221178

Airlanka
52, 2/F., Admiralty Centre Tower II
18 Harcourt Road
Hong Kong
Tel: 5299708, 5299906 Fax: 5276984

Air Mauritius
1512 Melbourne Plaza
33 Queen's Road Central
Hong Kong
Tel: 5231114

Air New Zealand
902 Three Exchange Square
Hong Kong
Tel: 5249041 Fax: 8455366

Air Niugini
705 Century Square
1 d'Aguilar Street
Hong Kong
Tel: 5242151 Fax: 5267291

Alitalia
2101 Hutchison House
10 Harcourt Road
Hong Kong
Tel: 5237047 Fax: 8685398

All Nippon
902 Fairmont House
8 Cotton Tree Drive
Hong Kong
Tel: 8107100, 8104433 Fax: 8459111

Asiana Airlines
Tel: 5238585

British Airways
3404 Gloucester Tower
11 Pedder Street
Hong Kong
Tel: 8680303, 5233031 Fax: 8681408

Canadian Airlines Int'l.
1702 Swire House
Chater Road
Hong Kong
Tel: 8683123, 5248161

Cathay Pacific
G/F., Swire House
Chater Road
Hong Kong
Tel: 7471888, 7475522 Fax: 8680176

China Airlines
6/F., Street George's Building
2 Ice House Street
Hong Kong
Tel: 8682299, 8439800 Fax: 8450155

China Eastern
Tel: 8610288

China Southern
Tel: 8652576

Continental
Tel: 5237065

Delta
18/F., Euro Trade Centre
13 Connaught Road Central
Hong Kong
Tel: 5265875 Fax: 8452120

Dragonair
12/F., Ching Hong Kong City Tower 6
33 Canton Road
Kowloon, Hong Kong
Tel: 7360202, 7393388

Emirates
Tel: 5267171

Garuda Indonesia
2/A Sing Po Centre
8 Queen's Road Central
Hong Kong
Tel: 8400000

Gulf Air
1305 Shui On Centre
8 Harbour Road
Hong Kong
Tel: 8027883, 8651031 Fax: 8651145

Japan Airlines
Gloucester Tower, The Landmark
11 Pedder Street
Hong Kong
Tel: 5230081

Japan Asia
20/F., Gloucester Tower, The Landmark
11 Pedder Street
Hong Kong
Tel: 5218102 Fax: 8680179

All addresses and telephone numbers are in Hong Kong unless otherwise noted. The country code for Hong Kong is [852].

KLM
701 Jardine House
Hong Kong
Tel: 8228118 Fax: 8685985

Korean Air
11 South Seas Centre Tower 2
Kowloon, Hong Kong
Tel: 3686221

Lauda Air
1007 Entertainment Building
30 Queen's Road Central
Hong Kong
Tel: 5246178, 5255221

Lufthansa
6/F., Landmark East
12 Ice House Street
Hong Kong
Tel: 8682313, 8466388 Fax: 5211916

Malaysia Airlines
1306 Prince's Building
10 Chater Road
Hong Kong
Tel: 5218181, 5252321 Fax: 8684080

Myanma
Tel: 8272244

Northwest
2908 Alexandra House
16 Chater Road
Hong Kong
Tel: 8104288, 5249261 Fax: 8684148

Philippine Airlines
305 East Ocean Centre
98 Granville Road
Kowloon, Hong Kong
Tel: 3694521, 3688988 Fax: 3688408

Qantas
1422 Swire House
Chater Road
Hong Kong
Tel: 5242101, 8421441 Fax: 8680135

Royal Brunei
1406 Central Building
3 Pedder Street
Hong Kong
Tel: 7471888, 5223799

Royal Nepal Airlines
704 Sun Plaza
28 Canton Road
Kowloon, Hong Kong
Tel: 7212180 Fax: 3117069

SAS
2/F., Wilson House
19 Wyndham Street
Hong Kong
Tel: 5265978

Singapore Airlines
17/F., United Square
95 Queensway
Hong Kong
Tel: 5202233, 5201313 Fax: 8611423

South African Airways
702 New World Office Building, West
18 Salisbury Road
Kowloon, Hong Kong
Tel: 7225768 Fax: 3111174

Swissair
8/F., Admiralty Centre Tower II
18 Harcourt Road
Hong Kong
Tel: 5293670, 5292193

Thai Airways
24/F., United Centre
Queensway
Hong Kong
Tel: 5295601, 5295681 Fax: 8654121

United
29/F., Gloucester Tower
11 Pedder Street
Hong Kong
Tel: 8104888 Fax: 8100877

TRANSPORTATION & CUSTOMS BROKERAGE FIRMS

Companies may offer more services in addition to those listed here. Service information is provided as a guideline and is not intended to be comprehensive.

Hong Kong Association of Freight Forwarding Agents Ltd.
M/F., AHAFA Cargo Centre
12 Kai Shun Road
Kowloon, Hong Kong
Tel: 7963121 Fax: 7963719

Hong Kong International Courier Association
c/o DHL International Ltd.
13 Mok Cheong Street, Tokwawan
Kowloon, Hong Kong
Tel: 7747298 Fax: 3339668

Hong Kong Liner Shipping Association
2111 Wing On Centre
111 Connaught Road Central
Central, Hong Kong
Tel: 5445077 Fax: 8151350

Hong Kong Shippers' Council
Rm. 2707A, Convention Plaza
1 Harbour Road
Wanchai, Hong Kong
Tel: 8241228 Fax: 8240394

Hong Kong Shipping Industry Institute
1002 Great Eagle Centre
23 Harbour Road
Wanchai, Hong Kong
Tel: 8933485 Fax: 8345172

Air Sea Worldwide Logistics Ltd.
1102 Kan Chung Building
52 Jaffe Road
Hong Kong
Tel: 8656868 Fax: 5296928 Tlx: 67851
Shipping, international freight forwarding

American President Lines Ltd.
16/F., World Shipping Centre
7 Canton Road
Kowloon, Hong Kong
Tel: 7353630 Fax: 7225870 Tlx: 54953
Shipping

Barwil Agencies Ltd.
10/F., Stanhope House
738 King's Road
Hong Kong
Tel: 8801688 Fax: 8805048
Shipping

China Resources Transportation & Godown Co.
Ltd.
19/F., China Resources Building
26 Harbour Road
Hong Kong
Tel: 8283668 Fax: 8345584 Tlx: 73333
Shipping agency, air/sea/land freight forwarding,
warehousing

Crown Pacific Ltd.
Crown Pacific Building
9 Yuen On Street
Siu Lek Yuen, Hong Kong
Tel: 6368388 Fax: 6371677 Tlx: 33894

Danzas Freight (HK) Ltd.
P-05 Hunghom Commercial Centre
Tower A
37 Ma Tau Wai Road
Kowloon, Hong Kong
Tel: 3330211 Fax: 7656379
International freight forwarder

DHL International Ltd.
DHL House
13 Mok Cheong Street
Kowloon, Hong Kong
Tel: 7644888 Fax: 7640641
Air cargo, freight forwarding, courier

Dong Woo Shipping Co.
912 Wing On Centre
111 Connaught Road Central
Hong Kong
Tel: 5444126 Tlx: 83408
Shipping

East Asiatic Co (HK) Ltd.
11/F., Great Eagle Centre
23 Harbour Road
Hong Kong
Tel: 8326888 Fax: 8343829
Shipping agency

Everett Steamship Corp.
2109 Sincere Building
173 Des Voeux Road Central
Hong Kong
Tel: 5453911 Tlx: 73281

Federal Express Hong Kong Ltd.
Shop Adm.-09, MTR Station
Admiralty, Hong Kong
Tel: 8653302
Air cargo, courier

Federal Express Hong Kong Ltd.
UG/F., HOP Shi Factory Building
22-24 Cheung Lee Street
Chaiwan, Hong Kong
Tel: 8890329
Air cargo, courier

Federal Express Hong Kong Ltd.
Shop G09B3, Cheung Sha Wan Plaza
Phase 2, 833 Cheung Sha Wan Road
Cheung Sha Wan, Hong Kong
Tel: 3071061
Air cargo, courier

Federal Express Hong Kong Ltd.
100 Sung Wong Toi Road, Tokwawan
Kowloon, Hong Kong
Tel: 7303333 Fax: 7657055 Tlx: 40182
Air cargo, courier

Federal Express Hong Kong Ltd.
Shop 127 B, 1/F., Shopping Arcade
New Mandarin Plaza, Tsimshatsui East
Kowloon, Hong Kong
Tel: 3661889
Air cargo, courier

Federal Express Hong Kong Ltd.
Unit B, 1/F., CDW Building
388 Castle Peak Road, Tsuen Wan
New Territories, Hong Kong
Tel: 4174163
Air cargo, courier

Flynt International Forwarders Ltd.
1 Newport Centre, Phase 2
116 Ma Tau Kok Road
Kowloon, Hong Kong
Tel: 3341313 Fax: 7640664
International freight forwarder

Freight Express International Ltd.
306 Kowloon Airfrieght Agents Terminal
70 Sung Wong Toi Road
Kowloon, Hong Kong
Tel: 3632133 Fax: 7642331 Tlx: 44834
Air cargo, freight forwarding

Freight-Trans International Co. Ltd.
918 Jardine House
Central, Hong Kong
Tel: 8449198 Fax: 8459166
Brokerage, chartering, container leasing, insurance,
project cargo, shipping agency, transportation,
warehousing

Guangdong Transport Ltd.
21/F., Yardley Commercial Building
1 Connaught Road West
Hong Kong
Tel: 8153398 Tlx: 89580
Cargo transportation, China trade, shipping services

Hapag Lloyd
1003 Vicwood Plaza
199 Des Voeux Road Central
Hong Kong
Tel: 8539696 Fax: 8539600
Shipping

All addresses and telephone numbers are in Hong Kong unless otherwise noted. The country code for Hong Kong is [852].

Hyundai Merchant Marine Co. Ltd.
3/F., Swire House
Chater Road
Hong Kong
Tel: 8408633 Fax: 8452596
Shipping, fixed-schedule container service to USA

Kawasaki (HK) Ltd.
33/F., United Centre
95 Queensway
Hong Kong
Tel: 8615511 Tlx: 73776
Shipping

Kintetsu World Express (HK) Ltd.
506 AHAFA Cargo Centre
12 Kai Shun Road
Kowloon, Hong Kong
Tel: 7963225 Fax: 7956706 Tlx: 43597
Air and sea freight forwarding, courier

Maersk Hong Kong Ltd.
19/F., Sunning Plaza
10 Hysan Avenue
Hong Kong
Tel: 8372222 Fax: 5778909 Tlx: 73756
Shipping, transportation

Mitsubishi Warehouse & Transportation Co. Ltd.
1612 Hang Lung Centre
2 Paterson Street
Hong Kong
Tel: 8950762 Fax: 5774050
Warehouse and transportation services

Nedlloyd (HK) Ltd.
22/F., Sincere Building
173 Des Voeux Road Central
Hong Kong
Tel: 5455633 Tlx: 73608
Shipping Agents

Neptune Orient Lines Ltd.
28/F., Bank of America Tower
12 Harcourt Road
Hong Kong
Tel: 8464888 Tlx: 74570
Shipping

Nippon Express (HK) Co. Ltd.
601 Mandarin Plaza, Tower A
14 Science Museum Road
Kowloon, Hong Kong
Tel: 7232272 Fax: 7398770 Tlx: 43115
Air cargo, freight forwarding

NYK Line (HK) Ltd.
31/F., Admiralty Centre, Tower I
18 Harcourt Road
Hong Kong
Tel: 8645100 Fax: 8651401
Shipping

Orient Overseas Container Line (OOCL)
Harbour Centre
31/F., 25 Harbour Road
Wanchai, Hong Kong
Tel: 8333888 Fax: 8389779
Hong Kong flagship shipping line and container transport organziation

Orient Trucking Ltd.
Berth 3, Kwai Chung Container Terminal
Kwai Chung, Hong Kong
Tel: 4894733 Fax: 4202238
Container transportation services

Pacific International Lines (HK) Ltd.
19/F., Belgian House
77 Gloucester Road
Hong Kong
Tel: 5293283 Fax: 8669497
Shipping

Pan Pacific Services Ltd.
1 Au Pui Wan Street, 2/F.
Fo Tan, Shatin
Hong Kong
Tel: 6015015 Fax: 6923546
Domestic and international shipping and forwarding

Santa Fe Transport International Ltd.
18/F., C.C. Wu Building
302 Hennessy Road
Hong Kong
Tel: 8335083 Fax: 8345479
Packing, forwarding, warehousing

Sea-Land Orient Ltd.
Berth 3, Kwai Chung Container Terminal
Kwai Chung, Hong Kong
Tel: 4235231 Fax: 4898100
Shipping

Thyssen Haniel Logistics (HK) Ltd.
11/F., Chi Wo Commercial Building
20 Saigon Street
Kowloon, Hong Kong
Tel: 3321481 Fax: 7211198 Tlx: 44450
Air cargo, Freight forwarding

TNT Express Worldwide (HK) Ltd.
6/F., Chung Nam Centre
414 Kwun Tong Road, Kwun Tong
Kowloon, Hong Kong
Tel: 3895279, 3895288, 3898292/8
Fax: 3432714, 3425276 Tlx: 38811 SKYHK
Air cargo, Courier

UPS Parcel Delivery Service Ltd.
Suite 602, N Tower, World Finance Ctr.
Harbour City, Tsimshatsui
Kowloon, Hong Kong
Tel: 7353535 Fax: 7385073
Air cargo, Courier

Wallem & Co. Ltd.
48/F., Hopewell Centre
Hong Kong
Tel: 5283911 Fax: 8613557
Ship managers, agents, brokers

Yick Fung Shipping & Enterprises Co. Ltd.
7/F., Ocean Building
167 Connaught Road West
Hong Kong
Tel: 8591133 Tlx: 73723
Shipping

PUBLICATIONS, MEDIA & INFORMATION SOURCES

All publications are in English unless otherwise noted.

DIRECTORIES & YEARBOOKS

Asia Pacific Leather Directory
(Annual)
Asia Pacific Leather Yearbook
(Annual)
Asia Pacific Directories, Ltd.
6/F., Wah Hen Commercial Centre
381 Hennessy Road
Hong Kong
Tel: 8936377 Fax: 8935752

Asia Yearbook
(Annual)
PO Box 160
Hong Kong
Tel: 8328300 Tlx: 66452 REVCD

Asian Computer Directory
(Monthly)
Washington Plaza
1/F., 230 Wanchai Road
Wanchai, Hong Kong
Tel: 8327123 Fax: 8329208

Asian Printing Directory
(Annual; English, Chinese)
Travel & Trade Publishing (Asia)
16/F., Capitol Centre
5-19 Jardines Bazaar
Causeway Bay, Hong Kong
Tel: 8903067 Fax: 8952378

Bankers Handbook For Asia
(Annual)
Asian Finance Publications
Suite 9D, Hyde Centre
223 Gloucester Road
Hong Kong

Computer-Asia Software Guide
(Annual)
Syme Media Enterprises
6-12 Wing Kut Street
Central, Hong Kong

Contractor's Plant & Equipment
(Annual)
Far East Trade Press Ltd.
2/F., Kai Tak Commercial Building
317 Des Voeux Road
Central, Hong Kong
Tel: 5453028 Fax: 5446979

Directory of Hong Kong Industries
(Annual)
Hong Kong Productivity Council
HKPC Building
78 Tat Chee Avenue, Yau Yat Chuen
Kowloon, Hong Kong
Tel: 7885964 Fax: 7885900

Government Publications Directory
(Annual; English, Chinese)
HK Information Services Department
Beaconsfield House
4 Queen's Road Central
Hong Kong
Tel: 8428777

Hong Kong Annual Digest of Statistics
(Annual)
HK Information Services Department
Beaconsfield House
4 Queen's Road Central
Hong Kong
Tel: 8428777

Hong Kong Builder Directory
(Annual)
Far East Trade Press Ltd.
2/F., Kai Tak Commercial Building
317 Des Voeux Road
Central, Hong Kong
Tel: 5453028 Fax: 5446979

Hong Kong Review of Overseas Trade
(Annual)
HK Information Services Department
Beaconsfield House
4 Queen's Road Central
Hong Kong
Tel: 8428777

International Tax and Duty Free Buyers Index
(Annual)
Pearl & Dean Publishing, Ltd.
9/F., Chung Nam Building
1 Lockhart Road
Hong Kong
Tel: 8660395 Fax: 2999810

Textile Asia Index
(Annual)
Business Press Ltd
Tak Yan Commercial Building
11/F.30-32 d'Aguilar Street
GPO Box 185
Central Hong Kong
Tel: 5247441 Tlx: 60275 TEXIA

World Jewelogue
(Annual)
Headway International Publications Co.
907 Great Eagle Centre
23 Harbour Road
Hong Kong
Tel: 8275121 Fax: 8277064

NEWSPAPERS

Asian Wall Street Journal
Dow Jones Publishing Co. (Asia)
2/F., AIA Building
1 Stubbs Road
GPO Box 9825
Hong Kong
Tel: 5737121 Fax: 8345291

Hong Kong Standard
Sing Tao Building, 4/F.
1 Wang Kwong Road
Kowloon Bay, Hong Kong
Tel: 7982798 Fax: 7957330

International Herald Tribune
7/F., Malaysia Building
50 Gloucester Road
Wanchai, Hong Kong
Tel: 8610616 Fax: 8613073

Oriental Daily News
(Chinese)
Oriental Press Centre
Wang Tai Road
Kowloon Bay, Hong Kong
Tel: 7953333 Fax: 7953322

Sing Pao Daily News
(Chinese)
Sing Pao Building
101 King's Road
North Point, Hong Kong
Tel: 5702201 Fax: 8072013

South China Morning Post
Tong Chong Street, PO Box 47
Hong Kong
Tel: 5652222 Fax: 8111278

Wah Kiu Yat Po (Overseas Chinese Daily News)
(Chinese)
106-116 Hollywood Road, PO Box 30
Hong Kong
Tel: 5491181 Fax: 5594238

GENERAL BUSINESS & TRADE PERIODICALS

Asia Labour Monitor
(Bimonthly)
Asia Monitor Resource Centre
444-446 Nathan Road, 8/F., Flat B
Kowloon, Hong Kong
Tel: 3321346

Asian Business
(Monthly)
Far East Trade Press, Ltd.
2/F., Kai Tak Commercial Building
317 Des Voeux Road
Central, Hong Kong
Tel: 5457200 Fax: 5446979

Asian Finance
(Monthly)
3/F., Hollywood Centre
233 Hollywood Road
Tel: 8155221 Fax: 8504437

Asian Monetary Monitor
(Bimonthly)
Asian Monetary Monitor
GPO Box 12964
Hong Kong
Tel: 8427200

Asiaweek
(Weekly)
Asiaweek Ltd.
199 Des Voeux Road
Central, Hong Kong
Tel: 8155662 Fax: 8155903

Business Week, Asia Edition
(Weekly)
2405 Dominion Centre
43-59 Queen's Road East
Hong Kong
Tel: 3361160 Fax: 5294046

The Economist, Asia Edition
(Weekly)
The Economist Newspaper, Ltd.
1329 Chater Road
Hong Kong
Tel: 8681425

The Executive
(Monthly)
Asian Finance Publications
Suite 9D, Hyde Centre
223 Gloucester Road
Hong Kong
Tel: 7244221 Tlx: 83013

Export International
Pearl Publications
PO Box 33749
Southwest, Hong Kong

Far Eastern Economic Review
(Weekly)
Review Publishing Company Ltd.
6-7/F., 181-185 Gloucester Road
Hong Kong
Tel: 8328381 Fax: 8345571

Hong Kong Enterprise
(Monthly)
HKTDC
38/F., Convention Plaza
1 Harbour Road
Wanchai, Hong Kong
Tel: 8334333 Fax: 8240249 Tlx: 73595 CONHK

Hong Kong Trader
Hong Kong Trade Development Council
38/F., Convention Plaza
1 Harbour Road
Wanchai, Hong Kong
Tel: 5844333 Fax: 8240249 Tlx: 73595 CONHK

Hong Kong Trade Statistics
(Monthly)
Census and Statistics Department
Beaconsfield House, 6/F.
Queen's Road
Central Victoria, Hong Kong
Tel: 8428801/4 Tlx: 61190 HKGIS

All publications are in English unless otherwise noted.

Newsweek International, Asia Edition
(Weekly)
Newsweek, Inc.
47/F., Bank of China Tower
1 Garden Road
Central, Hong Kong
Tel: 8104555

Quarterly Business Survey Report
(Quarterly)
Director of Information Services
Information Services Department
Beaconsfield House
4 Queen's Road Central
Hong Kong
Te: 8428777

Time, Asia Edition
(Weekly)
Time, Inc.
31/F., East Tower, Bond Centre
89 Queensway
Hong Kong
Tel: 8446660 Fax: 5108799

World Executives Digest
(Monthly)
3/F., Garden Square Building
Greenbelt Drive Cor.
Legaspi Makati
Metro Manila, Philippines
Tel: [63] (2) 8179126

INDUSTRY-SPECIFIC PERIODICALS

Asia 2000
(Bimonthly)
10/F., 146 Prince Edward Road West
Kowloon, Hong Kong

Asia Computer Weekly
(Bimonthly)
Asian Business Press Pte., Ltd.
100 Beach Road, #26-00 Shaw Towers
Singapore 0718
Tel: [65] 2943366 Fax: [65] 2985534

Asiamac Journal: The Machine-Building and Metal
Working Journal for the Asia Pacific Region
(Quarterly; English, Chinese)
Adsale Publishing Company
21/F., Tung Wai Commercial Building
109-111 Gloucester Road
Hong Kong
Tel: 8920511 Fax: 8384119, 8345014
Tlx: 63109 ADSAP

Asian Architect And Contractor
(Monthly)
Thompson Press Hong Kong Ltd
Tai Sang Commercial Building, 19/F.
24-34 Hennessy Road
Hong Kong

Asian Aviation
(Monthly)
Asian Aviation Publications
2 Leng Kee Road, #04-01 Thye Hong Centre
Singapore 0315
Tel: [65] 4747088 Fax: [65] 4796668

Asian Computer Monthly
(Monthly)
Computer Publications Ltd.
Washington Plaza, 1/F.
230 Wanchai Road
Wanchai, Hong Kong
Tel: 9327123 Fax: 8329208

Asian Defence Journal
(Monthly)
Syed Hussain Publications (Sdn)
61 A&B Jelan Dato, Haji Eusoff
Damai Complex
PO Box 10836
50726 Kuala Lumpur, Malaysia
Tel: [60] (3) 4420852 Fax: [60] (3) 4427840

Asian Electricity
(11 per year)
Reed Business Publishing Ltd.
5001 Beach Road #06-12
Golden Mile Complex
Singapore 0719
Tel: [65] 2913188 Fax: [65] 2913180

Asian Electronics Engineer
(Monthly)
Trade Media Ltd.
29 Wong Chuck Hang Road
Hong Kong
Tel: 5554777 Fax: 8700816

Asian Hospital
(Quarterly)
Techni-Press Asia Ltd
Hennessy Road PO Box 20494
Hong Kong
Tel: 5278682 Fax: 5278399

Asian Hotel & Catering Times
(Bimonthly)
Thomson Press (HK)
19/F., Tai Sang Commercial Building
23-34 Hennessy Road
Hong Kong
Tel: 5283351 Fax: 8650825

Asian Manufacturing
Far East Trade Press Ltd.
2/F., Kai Tak Commercial Building
317 Des Voeux Road
Central, Hong Kong
Tel: 5453028 Fax: 5446979

Asian Medical News
(Bimonthly)
MediMedia Pacific Ltd.
Unit 1216, Seaview Estate
2-8 Watson Road
North Point, Hong Kong
Tel: 5700708 Fax: 5705076

Asian Meetings & Incentives
(Monthly)
Travel & Trade Publishing (Asia)
16/F., Capitol Centre
5-19 Jardines Bazaar
Causeway Bay, Hong Kong
Tel: 8903067 Fax: 8952378

Asian Oil & Gas
(Monthly)
Intercontinental Marketing Corp.
PO Box 5056
Tokyo 100-31, Japan
Fax: [81] (3) 3667-9646

Asian Plastic News
(Quarterly)
Reed Asian Publishing Pte., Ltd.
5001 Beach Road #06-12
Golden Mile Complex
Singapore 0719
Tel: [65] 2913188 Fax: [65] 2913180

Asian Printing: The Magazine for the Graphic Arts
Industry
(Monthly; English, Chinese)
Travel & Trade Publishing (Asia)
16/F., Capitol Centre
5-19 Jardines Bazaar
Causeway Bay, Hong Kong
Tel: 8903067 Fax: 8952378

Asian Security & Safety Journal
(Bimonthly)
Elgin Consultants, Ltd.
Tungnam Building
Suite 5D, 475 Hennessy Road
Causeway Bay, Hong Kong
Tel: 5724427 Fax: 5725731

Asian Shipping
(Monthly)
Asia Trade Journals Ltd.
7/F., Sincere Insurance Building
4 Hennessy Road
Wanchai, Hong Kong
Tel: 5278532 Fax: 5278753

Asian Sources: Computer Products
Asian Sources: Electronic Components
Asian Sources: Gifts & Home Products
Asian Sources: Hardware
Asian Sources: Timepieces
(Monthly)
Asian Sources Media Group
22/F., Vita Tower
29 Wong Chuk Hang Road
Wong Chuk Hang, Hong Kong
Tel: 5554777 Fax: 8730488

Asian Water & Sewage
(Quarterly)
Techni-Press Asia, Ltd.
Hennessy Road PO Box 20494
Hong Kong
Fax: 5278399

Asia Pacific Broadcasting & Telecommunications
(Monthly)
Asian Business Press Pte., Ltd.
100 Beach Road
#26-00 Shaw Towers
Singapore 0718
Tel: [65] 2943366 Fax: [65] 2985534

Asia-Pacific Dental News
(Quarterly)
Adrienne Yo Publishing Ltd.
4/F., Vogue Building
67 Wyndham Street
Central, Hong Kong
Tel: 5253133 Fax: 8106512

Asia Pacific Food Industry
(Monthly)
Asia Pacific Food Industry Publications
24 Peck Sea Street, #03-00 Nehsons Bldg.
Singapore 0207
Tel: [65] 2223422 Fax: [65] 2225587

Asia Pacific Food Industry Business Report
(Monthly)
Asia Pacific Food Industry Publications
24 Peck Sea Street, #03-00 Nehsons Bldg.
Singapore 0207
Tel: [65] 2223422 Fax: [65] 2225587

Asiatechnology
(Monthly)
Review Publishing Company Ltd
6-7/F., 181-185 Gloucester Road
GPO Box 160
Hong Kong
Tel: 8328381 Fax: 8345571

Asia Travel Guide
(Monthly)
Interasia Publications, Ltd.
190 Middle Road, #11-01 Fortune Centre
Singapore 0718
Tel: [65] 3397622 Fax: [65] 3398521

ATA Journal: Journal for Asia on Textile & Apparel
(Bimonthly)
Adsale Publishing Company
Tung Wai Commercial Building, 21/F.
109-111 Gloucester Road
Wanchai, Hong Kong
Subscriptions: Hennessy Road PO Box 20032, Hong
Kong
Tel: 8920511 Fax: 8384119

Building & Construction News
(Weekly)
Al Hilal Publishing (FE) Ltd.
50 Jalan Sultan #20-06
Jalan Sultan Centre
Singapore 0719
Tel: [65] 2939233 Fax: [65] 2970862

Building Journal
(Monthly)
Trend Publishing (HK) Ltd.
19/F., Washington Plaza
230 Wanchai Road
Wanchai, Hong Kong
Tel: 8329298 Fax: 8329667

Business Traveller Asia-Pacific
(Monthly)
Interasia Publications
200 Lockhart Road, 13/F.
Wanchai, Hong Kong
Tel: 5749317 Fax: 5726846

Cargo Clan
(Quarterly)
Emphasis (HK), Ltd.
10/F., Wilson House
19-27 Wyndam Street
Central, Hong Kong
Tel: 5215392 Fax: 8106738

Cargonews Asia
(Bimonthly)
Far East Trade Press, Ltd.
2/F., Kai Tak Commercial Building
317 Des Voeux Road
Central, Hong Kong
Tel: 5453028 Fax: 5446979

Catering & Hotel News, International
(Biweekly)
Al Hilal Publishing (FE) Ltd.
50 Jalan Sultan #20-26
Jalan Sultan Centre
Singapore 0719
Tel: 2939233 Fax: 2970862

Computerworld Hong Kong
(Weekly)
Asia Computerworld Communications, Ltd.
701-4 Kam Chung Building
54 Jaffe Road
Wanchai, Hong Kong
Tel: 86132258 Fax: 8610953

Construction & Contract News
(Bimonthly)
Trend Publishing (HK) Ltd.
19/F., Washington Plaza
230 Wanchai Road
Wanchai, Hong Kong
Tel: 8329298 Fax: 8329667

Electronic Business Asia
(Monthly)
Cahners Publishing Company
249 West 17th Street
New York, NY 10011-5301, USA
Subscription Address: PO Box 173306, Denver, CO
80217-3306, USA

Electronic Product News-Asia
(7 issues per year)
Pan Asian Publishing Co.
c/o Elsevier Librico N.V.
Taman Warna, PO Box 0092
Singapore 9127

Electronics Bulletin
(Monthly)
Information Services Division
Hong Kong Productivity Council
HKPC Building
78 Tat Chee Avenue, Yau Yat Chuen
Kowloon, Hong Kong
Tel: 7885964 Fax: 7885900

Energy Asia
(Monthly)
Petroleum News Southeast Asia, Ltd.
6/F., 146 Prince Edward Road West
Kowloon, Hong Kong
Tel: 3805294 Fax: 3970959

Far East Health
(10 per year)
Update-Siebert Publications
Reed Asian Publishing Pte
5001 Beach Road #06-12
Golden Mile Complex
Singapore 0719
Tel: [65] 2913188 Fax: [65] 2913180

Fashion Accessories
(Monthly)
Asian Sources Media Group
22/F., Vita Tower
29 Wong Chuk Hang Road
Wong Chuk Hang, Hong Kong
Tel: 5554777 Fax: 8730488

Green Productivity: Pollution Control Engineering
(Quarterly)
Hong Kong Productivity Council
HKPC Building
78 Tat Chee Avenue, Yau Yat Chuen
Kowloon, Hong Kong
Tel: 7885678 Fax: 7885959

Hong Kong Electronics
(Quarterly)
Hong Kong Trade Development Council
38/F., Convention Plaza
1 Harbour Road
Wanchai, Hong Kong
Tel: 5844333 Fax: 8240249 Tlx: 73595 CONHK

Hong Kong Gifts & Premiums
(Biennial)
Hong Kong Trade Development Council
38/F., Convention Plaza
1 Harbour Road
Wanchai, Hong Kong
Tel: 5844333 Fax: 8240249 Tlx: 73595 CONHK

Hong Kong Household
Hong Kong Trade Development Council
38/F., Convention Plaza
1 Harbour Road
Wanchai, Hong Kong
Tel: 5844333 Fax: 8240249 Tlx: 73595 CONHK

Hong Kong Industrialist
Federation of Hong Kong Industries
Hankow Centre, 4/F.
5-15 Hankow Road, Tsimshatsui
Kowloon, Hong Kong
Tel: 7230818 Fax: 7213494 Tlx: 30101 FHKI

Hong Kong Jewellery
(Quarterly)
Ridgeville Ltd.
Flat A, 12/F., Kaiser Estate Phase 1
41 Man Yue Street
Hunghom, Kowloon, Hong Kong
Tel: 3344311 Fax: 7641956

Hong Kong Law Journal
(Irregular)
Hong Kong Law Journal
1030 Prince's Building
10 Chater Road
Hong Kong

All addresses and telephone numbers are in Hong Kong unless otherwise noted. The country code for Hong Kong is [852].

Hong Kong Monthly Digest of Statistics
(Monthly)
HK Information Services Department
Beaconsfield House
4 Queen's Road Central
Hong Kong
Tel: 8428777

Hong Kong Watches & Clocks
(Semiannual)
Hong Kong Trade Development Council
38/F., Convention Plaza
1 Harbour Road
Wanchai, Hong Kong
Tel: 8334333 Fax: 8240249 Tlx: 73595 CONHK

International Construction
(Monthly)
Reed Business Publishing, Ltd.
Reed Asian Publishing Pte
5001 Beach Road #06-12
Golden Mile Complex
Singapore 0719
Tel: [65] 2913188 Fax: [65] 2913180

Jewellery News Asia
(Monthly)
Jewellery News Asia Ltd.
Rm. 601-603, Guardian House
32 Oi Kwan Road
Wanchai, Hong Kong
Tel: 8322011 Fax: 8329208

Jewellery Review
(Bimonthly)
Brilliant-Art Publishing Ltd.
1101 Tung Wai Commercial Building
111 Gloucester Road
Wanchai, Hong Kong
Tel: 5116077 Fax: 5075855

Lloyd's Maritime Asia
(Monthly)
Lloyd's of London Press (FE)
Rm. 1101 Hollywood Centre
233 Hollywood Road
Hong Kong
Tel: 8543222 Fax: 8541538

Media: Asia's Media and Marketing Newspaper
(Biweekly)
Media & Marketing Ltd.
1002 McDonald's Building
46-54 Yee Wo Street
Causeway Bay, Hong Kong
Tel: 5772628 Fax: 5769171

Medicine Digest Asia
(Monthly)
Rm. 1903, Tung Sun Commercial Centre
194-200 Lockhart Road
Wanchai, Hong Kong
Tel: 8939303 Fax: 8912591

Oil & Gas News
(Weekly)
Al Hilal Publishing (FE) Ltd.
50 Jalan Sultan #20-06
Jalan Sultan Centre
Singapore 0719
Tel: [65] 2939233 Fax: [65] 2970862

PATA Travel News
(Monthly)
Asian Business Press (HK) Ltd.
1302 East Point Centre
555 Hennessy Road
Causeway Bay, Hong Kong
Tel: 8335022 Fax: 8345132

Petroleum News, Asia's Energy Journal
(Monthly)
Petroleum News Southeast Asia, Ltd.
6/F., 146 Prince Edward Road West
Kowloon, Hong Kong
Tel: 3805294 Fax: 3970959

Shipping & Transport News
(Monthly)
Al Hilal Publishing (FE) Ltd.
50 Jalan Sultan #20-06
Jalan Sultan Centre
Singapore 0719
Tel: [65] 2939233 Fax: [65] 2970862

Southeast Asia Building Magazine
(Monthly)
Safan Publishing Pte.
510 Thomson Road
Block A, #08-01 SLF Complex
Singapore 1129
Tel: [65] 2586988 Fax: [65] 2589945

Telecom Asia
(Bimonthly)
CCI Asia-Pacific (HK)
Suite 905, Guardian House
32 Oi Kwan Road
Wanchai, Hong Kong
Tel: 8332181 Fax: 8345620

Textile Asia: The Asian Textile and Apparel
Monthly
(Monthly)
Business Press Ltd.
11/F., California Tower
30-32 d'Aguilar Street
Central, Hong Kong
Tel: 5247467 Fax: 8106966

Travel News Asia
(Bimonthly)
Far East Trade Press, Ltd.
2/F., Kai Tak Commercial Building
317 Des Voeux Road
Central, Hong Kong
Tel: 5453028 Fax: 5446979

Travel Trade Gazette Asia
(Weekly)
Asian Business Press Pte., Ltd.
100 Beach Road #26-00
Shaw Towers
Singapore 0718
Tel: [65] 2943366 Fax: [65] 2985534

What's New in Computing
(Monthly)
Asian Business Press Pte., Ltd.
100 Beach Road #26-00
Shaw Towers
Singapore 0718
Tel: [65] 2943366 Fax: [65] 2985534

RADIO & TELEVISION

Asia Television Ltd.
81 Broadcast Drive
Kowloon, Hong Kong
Tel: 3387123 Fax: 3384347
*Operates two commercial television stations, one
broadcasting in English and one in Cantonese.*

Hong Kong Commercial Broadcasting Co.
GPO Box 30
Hong Kong
Tel: 3365111
*Broadcasts in English on one radio station and
Chinese on two stations.*

Radio Television Hong Kong
Broadcasting House
30 Broadcast Drive
Kowloon, Hong Kong
Tel: 3396441 Fax: 3380279
*Government-run; operates several English and
Chinese radio stations; produces public affairs
television programs broadcast on the commercial
stations.*

Television and Entertainment Licensing Authority
National Mutual Centre, 9/F.
151 Gloucester Road
Wanchai, Hong Kong
Tel: 5743130 Fax: 8382219

Television Broadcasts Ltd.
TV City, Clearwater Bay Road
Kowloon, Hong Kong
Tel: 7194828 Fax: 3581337
*Operates two commercial television stations, one
broadcasting in English and one in Cantonese.*

LIBRARIES

British Council Library
Easey Commercial Building, 1/F.
255 Hennessy Road
Hong Kong
Tel: 8315145 Fax: 8345731 Tlx: 74141 BCOUN

Electronics Library
Ground F., Chung Nam Centre
414 Kwun Tong Road
Kowloon, Hong Kong
Tel: 3412314 Fax: 3432545

Fashion Library
Block B, Rm. 1304
Sea View Estate, Watson Road
North Point, Hong Kong
Tel: 5701756 Fax: 5107263

Hong Kong Trade Development Council
Reference Library, China Trade Library
38/F., Convention Plaza
1 Harbour Road
Wanchai, Hong Kong
Tel: 8334333 Fax: 8240249

Labour Department Library
15/F., Harbour Building
38 Pier Road
Central, Hong Kong
Tel: 8524022

United States Cultural Centre Library
United Centre, 1/F.
95 Queensway
Hong Kong
Tel: 5299661 Fax: 8656114

University of Hong Kong Libraries
Pokfulam Road
Hong Kong
Tel: 8592200

Urban Council Public Libraries
City Hall
Edinburgh Place
Tel: 5233688

Index

A

absentees
  legal discussion of, 183
accounting firms
  addresses, 279
actions
  legal discussion of, 183
ad valorem tax
  definition of, 178
addresses and telephone numbers, 261–293
administrative service companies, 158
advantages to doing business in Hong Kong,
  45–46, 145
advertising, 147–150
advertising agencies, 149
  addresses, 279–281
advertising samples
  importation of, 60
advice
  definition of, 230
advising bank
  definition of, 230
affidavits
  legal discussion of, 183–184
agents, 152–153, 159–160
  advantages/disadvantages of hiring, 146
  definition of, 178
  tips for helping, 151
  tips on getting best from, 147
agriculture, 10
air conditioning equipment industry
  market, 33
air travel
  time to Hong Kong, 115
Airbus, 116
airlines, 115
  addresses, 283–284
airports, 14, 19, 239–240. See also Port and
  Airport Development Strategy;
  transportation: domestic: map of
  air cargo facilities at, 14, 239–240
  Chek Lap Kok
    construction of, 239–240
    cost of construction, 39
    public procurement opportunities, 40

Kai Tak, 115, 239–240
  ground transport to/from, 116
Akers-Jones, Sir David, 24
amendment
  definition of, 230
American Chamber of Commerce in Hong Kong,
  45, 49
apparel industry, 11, 29–30, 78–80
  trade fairs, 108–110
appliance industry, 73. See also housewares
  industry
Asia Pacific Economic Cooperation, 57
Asian Development Bank, 57
Asian Productivity Organization, 57
assignments
  legal discussion of, 184–185
ATA carnets, 60
attachment
  definition of, 178
  legal discussion of, 185
attorneys. See also law firms
  role of, 176–179
authentication
  definition of, 178
automated teller machines (ATMs)
  presence of, 203
automobile industry
  trade fairs, 88
automobiles
  hiring with driver, 121
avionics equipment industry
  market, 33

B

back-to-back letter of credit. See letter of credit
Bank for International Settlements (BIS), 204
Bank of China, 18, 202, 215
Bank of Credit and Commerce International (BCCI)
  failure of, 208
Banking Advisory Committee, 204
banking industry, 13–14, 202–208. See also banks
  brokerage services, 207
  commissioner of banking, 204

banking industry (cont.)
   foreign investment in, 37
   limitations on, 204–205
   regulation of, 208
   services for foreign businesses, 206–207
   trends in, 205–208
bankruptcy. *See also* insolvency
   legal discussion of, 185–186
banks. *See also* banking industry
   addresses, 279–280
   deposit-taking companies, 203
   foreign, 203
   lack of deposit insurance, 207
   licensed, 202
   number of, 205–208
   offshore, 203–204
   opening accounts in, 206–207
   performing central bank functions, 202
   restricted license, 202–203
   services provided by, 205
   specialized, 205
banquets, 120
   etiquette at, 135–137
Basic Law, 19, 21–22, 24, 46. *See also* sovereignty:
   1997 transfer of
   impact on economic autonomy, 201
   impact on legal and government structure, 175
Basle Committee on Banking Supervision, 204
BCCI. *See* Bank of Credit and Commerce International
beneficiary
   definition of, 230
big business, 6–7
bill of exchange
   definition of, 178, 230
bill of lading
   definition of, 229
   for exports, 65
   for imports, 62
bill of sale
   legal discussion of, 187
bills and notes
   legal discussion of, 186–187
birth rate, 142
BIS. *See* Bank for International Settlements
body language, 133–134
bona fide
   definition of, 178
bond market, 212
bribery. *See* corruption
business cards
   exchange of, 120, 132
business centers, 124
business culture and etiquette, 120, 127–140
business directories
   addresses, 287
business entities and formation, 155–166
   further reading, 166
   reminders and recommendations, 165
   selected useful addresses, 165–166
business environment, 131–137

business hours, 121, 131
business licenses, 162
business negotiations, 137–140
   etiquette, 138
   tactics, 138–139
   tips for foreigners, 139
business organizations
   forms of, 155–161
   laws governing, 175–176
business registration, 46, 161–165
   basic authorizations and procedures, 162
   fees and expenses, 162
   restrictions on, 162
Business Registration Office, 46, 47
   definition of, 156
Business Registration Ordinance, 155
   regulation of business entities, 161
business services industries, 13
   trade fairs, 102–105
business transactions
   laws governing, 175
business travel, 113–125
business yearbooks
   addresses, 287
buyer commission accounts, 207

C

C&F (cost and freight)
   definition of, 230
Cable & Wireless (telecommunications company), 122
CAD/CAM/CAE systems industry
   market, 34
Cantonese dialect, 134, 243. *See also* dictionary (Cantonese/English)
cargo handling equipment industry
   market, 36
carnets. *See* ATA carnets
cash. *See also* currency
   personal customs allowances, 115
cash in advance
   terms of, 219
certificates of manufacture
   definition of, 229
certificates of origin
   definition of, 229
   for exports, 65
   for imports, 62
CFU. *See* Hong Kong Confederation of Trade Unions
chambers of commerce addresses, 268–269. *See also* Hong Kong General Chamber of Commerce
child mortality rate, 142
China. *See also* Guangdong Province
   Hong Kong as trade intermediary for, 4, 163, 206
   importance of Hong Kong to, 5
   Open Door policy of, 127–128
   relations with, 4
   response to democracy movement, 24

Chinese Gold and Silver Exchange, 213
Chinese products
    trade fairs, 88–90
chopsticks
    etiquette of use, 135–136
CIF (cost, insurance, and freight) terms
    definition of, 230
Clearing House Automated Transfer System, 205
clearing houses, 205
climate, 114
clothing
    appropriate for business, 114, 131
collecting bank
    definition of, 231
commercial and industrial land
    leasing of, 48–49
commercial invoices
    definition of, 229
    for exports, 64
    for imports, 61
Commercial Radio, 150
commercial register
    legal discussion of, 187
Commissioner of Banking, 204
commodity exchanges, 213
    addresses, 278
companies, 155–157
    capital requirements for establishing, 156–157
    dissolution of, 157
    governance of, 157
    incorporation requirements, 163–164
    laws governing, 176
    legal discussion of, 190–191
    limited by guarantee, 155
    limited by shares, 155
    listing requirements for stock exchange, 210–211
    public vs. private, 155–156
    registration procedures for, 162, 164
    unlimited, 155
Companies Ordinance, 49, 155
    regulation of business entities, 161
Companies Registry, 46, 48
composition with creditors
    definition of, 178
computer industry, 67–69
    market, 33–34
    trade fairs, 90–92
computer software industry, 68
Conference on Trade and Development, 57
Confucianism, 120, 128–129
construction industry, 12
    public procurement opportunities, 39–40
    trade fairs, 92–93
consular invoice
    definition of, 229
consumer prices
    consumer price index (CPI)
        (1982-1992), 7, 143
    index by category, 143
contracts, 176. *See also* sales
    attitudes toward, 140

international sales provisions, 180–182
    laws governing, 176
    legal discussion of, 187–188
conversation etiquette, 133
copyright, 8, 147
    legal discussion of, 188–190
corporations
    legal discussion of, 190–191
corruption, 7–8
cosmetics industry
    market, 36
countertrade, 60, 63
courier services, 123–124
credit. *See also* letter of credit; loans
    availability for foreign investors, 48
credit cards, 115, 216
crime, 124
Cultural Revolution, 127
culture. *See also* business culture and etiquette
    history of, 127–128
    keys to understanding, 128–131
currency, 13, 115, 215
current issues, 21–28
customs
    brokers
        addresses, 284–286
    classification, 59
    clearance
        for imports, 61
        personal, 114–115, 125
    declaration
        for exports, 63
        for imports, 61
    duties, 59
    invoices
        for exports, 65
    legal discussion of, 191
    valuation, 60
Customs and Excise Department, 61, 63
Customs Cooperation Council, 57

D

death rate, 142
debt markets, 212
deeds
    legal discussion of, 191
democracy movement, 24–25
demographics, 141–144
Department of Labour, 169
Deposit-Taking Companies Committee, 204
Dialcom, 123
dictionary (Cantonese/English), 243–260
diplomatic and trade relations, 4
    between China and the UK, 19, 24
diplomatic mission addresses
    foreign in Hong Kong, 265–267
    of the United Kingdom, 264–265
direct mail advertising, 150
direct marketing
    advantages/disadvantages of, 146

discrepancy
    definition of, 231
distribution, 12
distributors, 152–153
    advantages/disadvantages of hiring, 146
distributorship
    advantages/disadvantages of opening, 146
divorce rate, 142
dock receipt
    definition of, 229
document against acceptance (D/A), 215, 219, 220
    definition of, 231
document against payment (D/P), 215, 219, 220
    definition of, 231
documentary collection, 219, 220
    definition of, 231
    procedures, 220
    tips for buyers and suppliers, 221
    types of, 220
documentation
    for exports, 64–66
    for imports, 61–62
dollar (Hong Kong). *See* currency
draft
    definition of, 230
dragon bonds, 212
drinking etiquette, 136–137
Drug Trafficking Ordinance, 209

E

Economic and Social Commission for Asia and the
        Pacific, 57
economy, 3–19
    British influence on, 5–6
    context of, 5–7
    government control of, 5–6
    government development strategy, 19
    history of, 3–4
    labor, 167–168
    link between Hong Kong and China, 4, 27–28
    political outlook, 19
    sectors of, 10
    size of, 4–5
    structure of, 9
    underground, 7–8
educational system, 168–169
    government subsidization of, 6
electric current standard, 61
Electronic Clearing System, 205
electronic data services, 123
electronics industry, 11, 30, 69–70
    market, 34
    relocation of assembly plants to China, 30
    trade fairs, 93–94
emergency information, 124–125
emigration, 8, 22–23
    to the United Kingdom, 23
employees
    tips on retaining, 173–174

employment
    benefits, 9–10, 171–172
    conditions of, 169–171, 196
    termination of, 171, 196
Employment Ordinance, 169
English language, 134
equitable assignment
    definition of, 178
ex dock
    definition of, 230
ex parte
    definition of, 178
ex point of origin
    definition of, 230
excise duties, 59
executions
    definition of, 178
    legal discussion of, 191–193
Executive Council, 24, 175
exhibits of creditors
    legal discussion of, 185
expenses (typical household), 143
export licenses, 63–64
    application for, 64
    definition of, 229
export marketing
    five rules for, 150–151
export policy, 63
export procedures, 63–64
exporters
    leading, 17, 57
exporting, 15
    opportunities, 33–36
    regulatory authority for, 63
    to China, 28
exports, 16, 54–55. *See also* reexports
    domestic
        leading, 52
    leading, 16
    total, 14
        leading, 52
external debt, 10, 217

F

face (concept), 129
factory space, 48
family
    importance of, 129–130
FAS (free alongside ship) terms
    definition of, 230
fax service, 123
FCPA. *See* Foreign Corrupt Practices Act
ferry travel, 120
fertility rate, 142
fieri facias writ
    definition of, 178
financial institutions, 201–213
    further reading, 213
financial markets, 209–213

financial service industries, 13
  foreign investment in, 37
  trade fairs, 102–105
  underground, 209
FOB (free on board) terms
  definition of, 230
food industry
  trade fairs, 94–95
footwear industry, 31–32, 71
  trade fairs, 106
Foreign Corrupt Practices Act (FCPA), 177
foreign exchange, 115, 215–217
  controls, 191, 215–216, 234
  further reading, 217
  involvement of banks in, 207
  legal discussion of, 193
  market, 216
  operations, 216
  rates, 13, 115, 215, 216
    detailed (1981-1993), 217
    year-end (1981-1993), 216
foreign investment, 17–18, 45–49
  assistance, 49
  bilateral agreements, 49
  by Asian neighbors, 47
  by China, 18, 47
  by Hong Kong
    in China, 27
    in Guangdong Province, 28
  by Japan, 18, 47
  by the United Kingdom, 18, 47
  by the United States, 18, 47
  by Western Europe, 47
  climate and trends, 45–46
  incentives, 47
  legal discussion of, 193
  opportunities, 37–38
  policy, 46–47
  regulation of, 46, 47
  restrictions, 18
  scope of, 18
foreign investors
  leading, 47
foreign ownership of businesses, 46
foreign reserves, 217
foreign trade, 12, 14–15, 51–57. *See also*
    exports; imports; reexports
  balance of, 15
  China/Taiwan intermediary role, 15, 53–54
  deficit, 55–56
  importance of China to, 15, 51–53
  opening to, 127
  partners, 17, 56–57
    leading, 56
  total, 14
    reexports as a portion of, 54
  with Canada, 17, 56–57
  with China, 17, 27–28, 56–57
  with Germany, 17, 56–57
  with Japan, 17, 56
  with Singapore, 17, 56–57

  with South Korea, 17, 56–57
  with Taiwan, 17, 56–57, 201
  with the Netherlands, 17, 56–57
  with the United Kingdom, 17, 56–57
  with the United States, 17, 56–57
forward foreign future
  definition of, 231
franchising
  foreign investment in, 38
fraudulent preference, 193
fraudulent training, 193
FTU. *See* Hong Kong Federation of Trade Unions
furniture industry, 72–73
  trade fairs, 96
futures markets, 213
  address, 278

G

General Agreement on Tariffs and Trade (GATT),
    19, 42, 57, 200
  Customs Valuation Agreement, 60
General System of Preferences, 57
geography, 3
gifts
  etiquette of giving and receiving, 132–133
giftware industry
  trade fairs, 96–99
gold exchange, 213
  address, 278
government agencies
  addresses, 261–264
government services, 14
government structure, 175
Government Supplies Department, 42
graphic arts equipment industry
  market, 35
greeting etiquette, 132
gross domestic product (GDP), 4–5
  effect of Chinese economy on, 53
  per capita, 5, 143, 149, 167
gross national product (GNP)
    (1982-1992), 5
Guangdong Province (China). *See also* China
  growth rate of, 45
  labor force, 27, 28
  links to, 127–128, 201
  proximity to, 3
  refugees, 127
  textile manufacturing in, 29
  trains to, 121
guidebooks on Hong Kong, 125

H

handshaking etiquette, 132
Hang Seng Bank, 210
Hang Seng Stock Index, 210, 213
Harmonized Commodity Description and Coding
    System, 57, 59

health care
   benefits, 9, 172
   expenditures, 144
health care industry
   foreign investment in, 38
health precautions for travelers, 124
HIBOR (Hong Kong interbank offering rate), 213
history
   of culture, 127–128
   of economy, 3–4
HKSE. *See* Hong Kong Stock Exchange
HKTA. *See* Hong Kong Tourist Association
HKTDC. *See* Hong Kong Trade Development
      Council
holidays, 9, 38, 121, 170
   list of, 122
Hong Kong and Kowloon Trade Union Council
      (TUC), 23, 172
Hong Kong Association of Banks, 202
Hong Kong Confederation of Trade Unions (CFU),
      23, 172
Hong Kong Export Credit Insurance Company, 209
Hong Kong Federation of Insurers, 209
Hong Kong Federation of Trade Unions (FTU),
      23, 172
Hong Kong Futures Exchange, 213
Hong Kong General Chamber of Commerce,
      60, 160, 165
Hong Kong Stock Exchange (HKSE), 209–210. *See*
      also stock exchange
   bond market, 212
   listing and operating requirements, 210–211
   listing of Chinese companies on, 211–212
   regulation of, 210
Hong Kong Telecom (telecommunications com-
      pany), 122, 123
Hong Kong Tourist Association (HKTA)
   worldwide office addresses, 113–114
Hong Kong Trade Development Council (HKTDC),
      57, 83–85, 160, 165
   definition of, 156
   libraries, 123
   office addresses, 269–271
Hongkong and Shanghai Banking Corporation
      (HSBC), 202, 204, 205, 215
hongs, 7, 12. *See also* trading companies
hospitals, 125
hotels, 116–119
housewares industry, 73
   trade fairs, 96
HSBC. *See* Hongkong and Shanghai Banking
      Corporation
human resources, 46, 168–169

I

ICC. *See* International Chamber of Commerce
immigration. *See also* visa requirements
   legal discussion of, 193–194
immunization requirements, 114

import licenses, 61
   definition of, 229
import policy, 59–61
import procedures, 59, 61
import restrictions, 59–60
importers
   leading, 57
importing, 15
   opportunities, 29–32
   regulatory authority for, 59
imports, 16–17, 55–56
   leading, 17, 55
   total, 14
income
   distribution of, 143
   household, 143
   per capita, 55. *See also* gross domestic product
      (GDP): per capita
Independent Commission Against Corruption, 7
industrial estates, 48
industrial materials industry
   trade fairs, 101–102
industrial process control (IPC) equipment
      industry
   market, 34–35
industries
   reviews of, 67–81
industry
   as sector of economy, 10–12
   light, 12
   medium and heavy, 12
Industry Department, 49
inflation, 8
   (1982-1992), 6
   average annual (1975-1992), 143
Infonet, 123
infrastructure, 45
   development plans, 57
insolvency. *See also* bankruptcy
   legal discussion of, 194–195
inspection
   certificates
      definition of, 229
   of exports, 66
   of imports, 61
instrument industry
   trade fairs, 107–108
insurance
   documents
      definition of, 229
   unemployment, 172
   workmen's compensation, 9, 171, 172
insurance certificates
   for imports, 62
insurance companies
   addresses, 278
insurance industry, 13, 208–209
   foreign investment in, 37
   Office of the Commissioner of Insurance, 208
intellectual property rights, 8, 49, 179
   laws governing, 176

interest
   legal discussion of, 195
   rates, 205
interlocutory
   definition of, 178
International Chamber of Commerce (ICC),
   220, 222, 230, 232
International Database Access Service, 123
International High-Speed Document Transfer
   Service, 123
international organization membership, 19, 57
international payments, 205, 206, 215, 219–232
   further reading, 232
   glossary, 230
   overview, 219
international trade documents
   glossary, 229
investment promotion and protection agreements
   (IPPAs), 49
investment rates, 10
invoice certification
   for exports, 65
IPPAs. *See* investment promotion and protection
   agreements
irrevocable confirmed credit. *See* letter of credit
irrevocable credit. *See* letter of credit
issuance
   definition of, 231
issuing bank
   definition of, 231

J

jewelry industry, 31, 74–75
   trade fairs, 96–99
job training, 169
Joint Declaration, 19, 21–22, 24, 46–47
   effect on foreign investment, 49
Joint Liaison Group, 21
joint ventures, 160–161
   advantages/disadvantages, 146–147
   registration procedures for, 163
judgements
   legal discussion of, 195
judicial branch
   future structure of, 22
jurat
   form of, 184
   legal discussion of, 183–184

K

karaoke, 137–138
Korean War, 4
Kowloon-Canton Railway, 41, 121
Kuomintang, 4

L

labeling
   of imports, 60–61
labor, 8–10, 167–174
   availability, 167
   costs, 9–10. *See also* wages
   foreign, 8
   shortage, 8
labor force
   children in, 169
   composition of, 167
   distribution by sector, 167
   foreign, 167–168
   women in, 169
labor relations, 172
   legal discussion of, 196
labor unions, 9, 23, 172, 196
Land Offices, 48
Land Registry, 48
languages in use, 134
   for advertising, 149
law, 175–200
   digest, 183–200
   geographical scope of, 176
   practical application of, 176–179
law firms
   addresses, 281
leather goods industry
   trade fairs, 106
leaves of absence, 9, 170
legal disputes
   resolution of, 176
legal glossary, 178–179
legal system
   basis of, 175
LEGCO. *See* Legislative Council
Legislative Council (LEGCO), 6, 19, 22, 24, 175
   possible dissolution of, 25
letter of credit (L/C), 215, 219, 222, 231
   amendment of, 223
   application, 226, 227
   back-to-back, 225, 230
   common problems, 224
   confirmed, 231
   deferred payment, 225, 231
   irrevocable, 231
   irrevocable confirmed credit, 225
   irrevocable credit, 225
   issuance of, 223
   legal obligations of banks toward, 224
   opening, 226
   parties to, 222
   red clause, 225
   revocable, 225, 231
   revolving, 225, 231
   special, 225
   standby, 225, 231
   steps in using, 222
   tips for buyers and sellers, 228
   transferable, 225

letter of credit (cont.)
  types of, 225
  unconfirmed, 225
  utilization of, 224
letters of introduction, 132
Li Peng, 24
libraries, 123
  addresses, 293
licensing
  agreements, 160
  of imports and exports, 18
liens
  legal discussion of, 196
life expectancy, 142, 167
limitation of actions, 197
little dragons, 28
loan agencies, 208
loans, 205
  availability of, 48, 205, 207
  regulation of, 204
location
  favorability of, 45

M

Macao
  proximity to, 3
machine industry
  trade fairs, 107–108
magazines. *See also* periodicals
  English-language, 123
Mandarin dialect, 134
manufacturing
  areas of specialization, 11
  as sector of economy, 10–12
  relocation of plants to China, 32
marketing, 145–153
marking
  of imports, 60–61
marriage rate, 142
Mass Transit Railway (MTR), 41, 120–121
matchmakers
  choosing, 130
maternity leave, 170, 196
media
  English-language, 123
medical equipment industry
  market, 35
metal industry
  trade fairs, 101–102
Metro Broadcast, 150
MFA. *See* Multi-Fiber Arrangement
MFN status. *See* Most Favored Nation status
Monetary Affairs Branch, 202
Monetary Authority, 202, 212
money changers, 115, 215–216
Money Lenders Ordinance, 208
monopolies, 179
Most Favored Nation (MFN) status
  effect of China's status on Hong Kong, 5,
    25–27, 53

MTR. *See* Mass Transit Railway
Multi-Fiber Arrangement (MFA),
    19, 53, 57, 64, 200
mutual funds, 212

N

names in Hong Kong, 134
negotiable instruments
  definition of, 178
  laws governing, 176
negotiation. *See also* business negotiations
  definition of, 231
New Territories, 3, 48, 127
  agricultural plots in, 10
  industrial parks in, 11
newspapers, 144
  addresses, 288
  English-language, 123
nexus
  definition of, 178
notaries public
  legal discussion of, 197
nutrition, 144

O

office space, 48–49
offices
  branch, 157–159
    operating requirements, 159
    registration procedures for, 162, 164
  instant, 158
  liaison, 159
    registration procedures, 165
    registration procedures for, 162
  representative, 159
    advantages/disadvantages, 146
    business registration procedures for, 165
    registration procedures for, 162
offshore servicing centers, 161
One-Stop Unit, 18, 165
open account (O/A) terms, 219
  definition of, 231
open market policy, 43
Opium Wars, 3, 21, 127
Organization for Economic Cooperation and
    Development, 57
outdoor advertising, 150
overseas relationships
  tips for building, 152–153

P

Pacific Economic Cooperation Conference, 57
packaging industry
  trade fairs, 108
packing list
  definition of, 229
  for imports, 62

PADS. *See* Port and Airport Development Strategy
Paper Clearing System, 205
paper industry
    market, 35
pari passu
    definition of, 178
partnerships, 160
    basic registration procedures for, 163
    business registration procedures for, 164–165
    laws governing, 176
    legal discussion of, 197
    structure and operation, 160
patents
    legal discussion of, 197
Patten, Chris (Governor), 22
    push for democracy, 24–25
    support of MFN status for China, 26
pension funds, 212
People's Republic of China. *See* China
periodicals
    general business and trade
        addresses, 288–289
    industry-specific
        addresses, 289–293
personal connections
    cultivation of, 130–131
    value of, 129–130
personal service industries, 14
plastic goods industry, 75–76
plastics industry
    market, 35
pledges
    legal discussion of, 198
political developments. *See also* current issues
    outlook for future, 19
population, 3, 141, 167
    (1986-2025), 141
    age structure, 141
    by age and sex, 142
    density, 3
    growth rates, 141
    growth since 19th century, 3
    of principal areas, 142
    urban, 141
Port and Airport Development Strategy (PADS), 39
port facilities, 14, 239, 240. *See also* Port and
    Airport Development Strategy;
        transportation: domestic: map of
    construction of, 40
postal service, 123
power of attorney
    definition of, 178
prima facie
    definition of, 179
principal
    definition of, 179
    legal discussion of, 198
print media advertising, 150
printing industry, 31
    trade fairs, 108
Privy Council, 175

promissory note. *See also* bills and notes
    definition of, 230
Provisional Airport Authority, 40
public procurement
    advantages/disadvantages to entering bids on,
        147
    opportunities, 39–42
    process, 42
public works projects, 19, 39–42
publishing industry
    trade fairs, 99

R

radio
    addresses, 293
    English-language, 123
    sets in use, 144
radio advertising, 150
Radio Television Hong Kong (RTHK), 123
railway. *See also* Kowloon-Canton Railway
    development of, 41
real estate
    foreign investment in, 37
    involvement of banking industry in, 204–
        205, 208
red clause letter of credit. *See* letter of credit
reexports, 15, 45, 53–54. *See also* exports
    Chinese, 28, 29, 53
        leading, 54
    countries of destination of, 53
    countries of origin of, 53
    leading, 52
    Taiwanese, 53–54
Registrar of Companies, 156, 161
    definition of, 156
    filing of annual reports with, 157
remittance controls, 215–216
remitter
    definition of, 231
remitting bank
    definition of, 231
rescind
    definition of, 179
restaurants, 119–120
retail industry, 12
    foreign investment in, 37–38
retail stores
    advantages/disadvantages of opening, 146
retirement benefits, 9, 172, 209
revocable credit. *See* letter of credit
RTHK. *See* Radio Television Hong Kong

S

safety industry, 76–77
salaries. *See* wages
sales
    glossary of terms, 230
    legal discussion of, 198
    seven rules for, 148–149

SAR. *See* Special Administrative Region of China
Satellite Television Asia Region (STAR), 149
savings rates, 10
secretarial services, 124
Securities and Futures Commission (SFC), 48, 210
securities industry, 13–14, 209–213
    brokerage houses, 210
        laws governing, 176
security industry, 76–77
service industries
    as sector of economy, 12–14
severance pay, 9, 196
SEZs. *See* Special Economic Zones of China
SFC. *See* Securities and Futures Commission
shelf companies, 158
shipper's export declaration
    definition of, 229
shipping
    legal discussion of, 198–199
sick leave, 170
sight draft
    definition of, 179
Sino-British Joint Declaration. *See* Joint Declaration
small business, 6
smoking etiquette, 136
social security system, 6, 9, 171
social services
    government expenditures on, 6
sole proprietorships, 160
    registration procedures for, 163
sovereignty
    1997 transfer of, 4, 19, 21–23, 51. *See also* Basic Law; Joint Declaration
        effect on civil servants, 14
        effect on financial institutions, 201–202
        effect on financial markets, 207
        effect on foreign investment, 46–47
        effect on labor force, 8, 167
        effect on legal system, 175
        effect on manufacturing industries, 11
        effect on stock exchange, 211–212
        view by Hong Kong natives of, 25
Special Administrative Region (SAR) of China, 19, 21, 200
Special Economic Zones (SEZs) of China, 206
special trade zones, 43
sporting goods industry
    trade fairs, 100
Standard Chartered Bank, 202, 215
standby letter of credit. *See* letter of credit
STAR. *See* Satellite Television Asia Region
Star Ferry, 120
stationery industry
    trade fairs, 96–98
status
    importance of, 135
Statute of Frauds
    definition of, 179
    legal discussion of, 193

statutory declarations
    legal discussion of, 183–184
stock exchange, 46, 201, 209–210. *See also* Hong Kong Stock Exchange
    address, 278
    listing on, 156
subway travel, 120–121

T

table manners, 136
tariffs, 59
tax relief (foreign), 233
tax treaties, 234, 237
taxes
    ad valorem. *See* ad valorem tax: definition of
    capital gains, 233, 237
    corporate, 10, 45, 47, 233–234
    estate, 237
    excise. *See* excise duties
    gift, 237
    motor vehicle registration, 59
    personal, 10, 45, 47
    personal, 235–237
    profit, 233
    property, 45, 47
    social security, 237
taxis, 116, 121
TDC-link, 85
technical assistance agreements, 160
telecommunications equipment industry, 30, 77–78
telecommunications industry
    foreign investment in, 37
telecommunications system, 45, 122–123, 144
telephone service, 122–123
    English-language directories, 123
    international dialing codes, 123
television
    English-language, 123
    sets in use, 144
television advertising, 149
telex service, 123
textile industry, 11, 29–30, 78–80
    trade fairs, 108–110
Textiles Export Control System, 64. *See also* Multi-Fiber Arrangement (MFA)
thing in action
    definition of, 179
time zones, 115–116
timepiece industry, 30, 74–75
    trade fairs, 96–99
tipping, 115
tobacco consumption, 144
toiletries industry
    market, 36
    trade fairs, 99
tool industry
    trade fairs, 110

tourism industry, 13
   foreign investment in, 38
   trade fairs, 99–100
toy industry, 31, 80–81
   trade fairs, 99–100
trade and commerce
   as sector of economy, 12
trade association addresses
   foreign, 268–269
   general, 268
   industry-specific, 271–276
trade delegations, 134–135
Trade Department, 49, 57, 59
   determination of import tax refund, 59
   endorsement of commercial invoices, 65
   issuance of import licenses, 61
   regulation of exporting by, 63
trade descriptions
   legal discussion of, 199
trade fairs, 83–111
   advantages/disadvantages of exhibiting at, 146
   tips for attending, 85–87
trademark rights, 179
   laws governing, 176
   legal discussion of, 199–200
trading companies, 159–160. *See also* hongs
train travel, 121
tram travel, 121
translators and interpreters, 124
   addresses, 281–282
transportation
   construction of new links, 40–41
   domestic, 120–121
      map of, 241
   facilities, 14
transportation firms
   addresses, 284–286
travel. *See* business travel
Travel Industry Council of Hong Kong, 38
traveler's checks, 115
treaties
   legal discussion of, 200
triads, 7, 209
TUC. *See* Hong Kong and Kowloon Trade Union
      Council

U

unconfirmed credit. *See* letter of credit
unemployment, 9
   comparative, 168
   trends, 168
Uniform Customs and Practices (UCP), 222
Uniform Rules for Collections (URC), 220
unit trusts, 212
United Kingdom
   ceding of Hong Kong to China, 22. *See also*
      sovereignty: 1997 transfer of
   colonization of Hong Kong, 3–4, 127
United Nations, 57

V

vacation benefits, 9, 38, 170
validity
   definition of, 231
venture capital firms, 208
videoconferencing services, 123
visa requirements, 114
   legal discussion of, 193
vocational training, 169

W

wages, 171–172
   average monthly managerial, 171
   average weekly
      comparative, 170
   average weekly manufacturing, 9
   daily manufacturing, 142
   minimum, 172
warehousing, 61
waste management
   public projects, 42
Waste Management Policy Group, 42
water supply
   expansion projects, 41–42
weights and measures, 61
women. *See also* labor force: women in
   in business and society, 131, 135
Women and Young Persons Regulations, 169
workweek, 10, 169–170
World Trade Center
   address, 268

Z

Zhu Rongji, 24